A WORLD OF baby names

Anemone Aneurin Angel Angela Angelica Angelina Arline Armada Armada Armando Arthur Artie Arturia Arturo Artus Aru Arub Aruis
Ubrey Aubrianne Auburn Auburn Audrey Audric Audwin August Augusta Auguste Augustin Augusto Augustus Aukai Aymon Ayo Azc
ilbo Bamburr Bambur Banabi Banan Banan Bancroft Bandi Baretto Bari Barika Barinda Baringa Baringa Baris Barkala Barkala Barker
gard Beaver Bebe Beca Beccalynn Beck Becket Becko Becky Beda Bede Bedelia Bedelie Bedriska Beetunkara Beetunkara Begoni
etsy Betty Betulah Beulah Bevan Beverley Bevliah Beyhan Bhagwandas Bharani Bharat Bharati Bhas Bhavna Bhavta Biajito Bianca Bi
air Blair Blaise Blake Blakelea Blanche Blanco Bland Blanda Blane Blaze Blaze Bledig Blenda Bleniki Bliss Blodwen Blossom Blue Blyth
Bree Breeze Brenda Brendan Bret Brett Brewster Bri Brian Briand Brianna Bridget Bridie Brier Brigette Brigham Brigida Brinley Brinsley B
Bruce Brunhilda Bruno Brutus Bryan Bryant Bryce Brychan Brydie Brymer Bryn Brynmor Bryony Bureiku Burenda Burendan Burenna Bu
Cadman Cadmus Cadoc Cadogan Cadwallen Cadyn Caeden Caesar Cagney Caiden Caillin Caimile Cain Cairbre Cairenn C
Calli Callidor Calliope Callis Calluella Candan Candida Canning Cantara Cantara Canterbury Canute Canwindra Canwindra
Carlotta Carmen Carmichael Carmina Carna Carney Carol Carolan Carolina Caroline Caron Carpenter Carr Carreen Carribie Co
Casper Cassandra Cassia Cassidy Cassidy Cassie Cassie Cassius Casta Castor Casuarina Catalina Catalonia Catava Catava Co
o Celie Celine Celosia Cemal Cemal Cerae Ceres Cerise Cervantes Cerwyn Cesar Chacha Chad Chadwick Chaika Chaim Ch
a Chandler Charlotta Charlotte Charlton Charma Charmain Charmaine Charmian Charro Chase Chashiti Chaska Chastity Chat
Cherokee Cherry Cherub Cherubino Chesmu Chester Chevalier Chevy Cheyenne Chiaga Chiamaka Chiara Chiesa Chifley C
here Clayborne Clayton Cleary Cleaver Cleaver Cledwyn Clem Clematis Clement Cleo Cleon Cleopatra Cleva Cleve Cleveland
Coby Coccino Cocheta Coco Cody Cody Coel Coen Cola Colbert Colby Cole Coleman Coleridge Colette Colin Colina Collee
a Cort Corwin Cosima Cosmo Costa Coty Cougar Coulter Courtenay Courtland Courtney Courtney Crosley Crystal Csaba Cseke
D D Da Da'ud Da'ud Dabi Dabina Dacey Dacey Dacey Dacio Dae Daelan Daffodil Dafne Dafydd Dafydd Dag Dag Dagan De
Daku Dalal Dalbert Dale Dalia Dallas Dallen Dallin Dalton Daly Dalziel Dalziel Darnara Damaris DamenDamian Damiano Damiano
arton Daru Darwin Darya Dasha Dave Davey David Davide Davidson Davin Davina Davine Davis Dawa Da-wa Dawn Dawson Day
n Deiondre Deiphobus Deirdre Deiri Deja Delaney Delanna Delano Delbert Delfine Dell Della Delma Delmar Delmore Delphine
Derron Derry Derward Derwent Derwood Derya Desdemona Desiderio Desirata Desiree Desmond Destinee Destry Dev Devaki De
hitori Dimitri Dimity Din Dina Dinah Dine Dinesh Dino Dinsdale Diomedes Dione Dirk Divya Dixie Dixon Diya Djalyup Djanjarak Djardal
Domenico Domingo Dominic Dominica Dominique Don Dona Donahue Donalbain Donald Donaldina Donatien Donato Dooley
Douglas Douran Dov Dover Dow Doyle Dragan Drake Draper Draper Dreama Drew Drew Drik-Drik Driscoll Drisia Dromio Drostan Dr
Durwin Durwood Dusan Dustin Dutch Dutch Dwaine Dwayne Dyer Dylan Dyllis Dymphna Dyna Dynami Dynand Dynasty Dynawd D
d Eberhardstrong Ebert Eberta Ebi Eboni Ebony Edan Edana Edbert Edda Eddan Eddie Eddy Ede Edeline Eden Eder Edeva Edgar E
na Edwin Edwina Eerlana Effie Efia Efrain Efrat Efrem Egan Egil Egypt Eiddwen Eildon Eileen Eilidh Eiluned Einar Elnin Eitan Eithne Ek
su Elsworth Elton Elu Elvan Elvern Elvern Elvin Elvina Elvio Elvira Elvis Elvy Elwin Elwold Elwood Elys Elysia Elyssa Erna Emalia Emaline Eor
bre Etu Euchunga Eucla Euard Eudora Eugene Eugenia Eunice Euph Euphony Euphrasia Eusebius Eustace Eva Evaline Evan Eva
ilda Eymer Eyota Ezar Ezara Eze Ezechiele Ezekiel Ezra Ezrela Ezura Fabia Fabian Fabiano Fabiola Fabricious Fabricius Fabrizio Fa
Farquhar Farr Fath Fay Fayanne Faye Ferguson Feride Ferishia Fern Fernanda Fernando Ferran Ferris Festus Fidel Fidelia Fielding Fir
ranz Floreat Florence Florencia Florian Florida Flower Floyd Flynn Fola Folan Fontaine Forbes Ford Fordon Forest Forester Fortuna F
ius Galahad Galatea Galen Galen Galeus Gali Galiana Galiena Gamal Gamaliel Garvey Garvin Gary Gaspar Gaston Gasu G
Gi Gia Giacinto Giacoma Giacomo Gian-Carlo Gianina Gian-Luca Gianni Giano Gianpaolo Gib Gibor Gibson Gideon Gie Giffc
izella Gladwin Gladys Glaginye Gleda Glen Glenda Glendon Glendora Glenna Gloria Glover Glyceria Glyn Glynis Gnernpa Godd
Grady Graeme Graham Grande Granger Grania Grant Grantland Granville Gray Grayson Grazia Greeley Greenwood Greer Greer
et Guruwa Gurvir Gus Gustave Gustavo Gustee Guthrie Gutierre Guy Guyapi Guyapi Habika Hacket Hadad Hadar Hadi Hadiya Had
al Hala Halah Halcyone Halden Hale Haley Haley Halford Halil Halim Halimah Halisea Hall Halla Hallam Hallan Hardy Hare Harel H
tford Hartman Hartwood Haru Harun Harvest Harvey Hasad Hasan Hasana Hasani Hashim Hasin Haskel Haslett Hasna Hassan Has
d Hazel He Healoha Heath Heathcliff Heather Heather Heaven Hebbe Hebe Heber Hector Hedda Heddwyn Hedley Hedwig He
son Henoch Henri Henrietta Henry Hepetipa Hephziba Hera Herb Herbert Hercules Heremon Heren Herman Hermes Hermione Herm
ieu Hilary Hilda Hildebrand Hildegard Hilel Hillel Hilliard Hilliary Hilton Hinto Hippocrates Hiram Hirari Hiroshi Hisham Hisoka Hiu Hope
habod Ida Iden Idette Idi Idonia Idwal Ierne Iestin Iggi Iggy Ignatia Ignatius Igor Ihilani Ihorangi Ihsan Iida Ilima Ike Ikram Ilan Ilana
olda Israel Issa Istas Ita Itamar Itzak Iukini Iulia Ivan Ivana Ivar Ivena Ivo Ivone Ivory Ivy Iwalani Iwone Ixia Iye Izabella Izabera Izak
na Jamaica Jamari Jambu Jamie Jamila Jan Jana Jancis Jane Janelle Janessa Janet Jebong Jei Jeia Jeido Jein Jelena Jemim
a Jiani Jianna Jianruka Jiao Jidangie Jie Jill Jillian Jimena Jin Jina Jingella Jini Jinni Jinty Jinx Jiri Jiru Jivanta Jo Joakima Joalah J
nta Juventia Jyotis Ka'ohe Ka'ohu Kacey Kachina Kadan Kadija Kae Kahlia Kahoku Kai Kai'mi Kaili Kainoa Kaipo Kairo Kaitlyn Kakal
Karandora Kareela Karei Kareilia Karen Kari Kariba Karida Karima Karina Karinya Karisa Karissa Karisuta Karka Karla Karma Karnka
rtmai Katorina Katrina Kau'i Kaula Kaulana Kaveri Kavindra Kawailani Kawen Kentigerna Keona Kepola Kerani Kerrajinga Kerri Kesc
iley Kiliwia Killa Kim Kimberley Kina Kinan Kineta Kini Kinta Kiona Kira Kiran Kirby Kiri Kiribati Kirisuti Kirrakee Kirsi Kirsten Kirsty Kisa Kis
Kyasarin Kyashi Kyasurin Kyeema Kyla Kylie Kyna Kynthia Kynthia Kyoko Kyra Laanecoorie Laikin Laine Lainee Lainet Lais Lajila Lakees
amie Lari Lariathe Larissa Lark Larraine Lass Lassie Lateefah Latika Latonia Latoya Laura Laurana Lauren Laurette Laveda Lavender
Leita Leiya Lela Lele Lelia Lemuela Letizia Letteria Levana Levanna Levina Lewanna Leya Lhamu Li Li Ming Li Qin Lia Liadan Lian Li
nette Linley Liona Lionelle Liria Lisa Lisbet Lisetta Lisha Lita Livana Livia Liz Liza Lo Lobelia Lodema Loinnir Lois Lokelani Lola Lolita Lo
n Luca Lucetta Luci Lucinda Lucretia Lucy Lud Ludelia Ludmilla Luella Luigia Luisa Luloah Lulu Luna Luneda Lunetta Lupe Lupine
Mablevi Mabs Mabyn Macalla Macaria Macayle Macey Mackay MacKenna MacKenzie MacKinley Macy Madalena Maddalena M
ka Makarim Makayla Makayla Makeeley Makeira Makkenji Mala Malak Malay Malaya Mali Malia Malika Malinda Malita Mallagane
ria Mariabella Mariam Mariamu Marian Marianna Marianne Marianu Maribel Marie Marie Matana Mateo Mathilda Mathuri Matilda
nah Mayotte Maysa Mayyadah Mayyali McKayla McKenna Meadow Meagan Meaghan Meara Meari Media Medina Mee Meedi
akoda Miami Micah Minerva Minette Ming Minna Minstrel Minuet Mioko Mira Mirabel Mirage Miralie Mirambeena Miranda Miri Mi
urphy Musetta Mushirah Music Musique Muslimah Mutsuko Myee Myfanwy Myiesha Mylene Myra Myrna Myrtle Na'ima Naama N
a Najah Najat Najibah Najiyah Najla Najwa Najya Nalani Nama Nami Namiko Nashida Nashwa Nasiha Nasira Nassa Nata Natal
Nazirah Nea Neala Neba Nebula Neda Neemuri Neena Nehama Neka Nella Nell Nellie Nellwyn Neola Neoma Nerida Nerida
Nola Nolana Nollaig Nomi Nona Noni Nora Nori Noriko Norma Norna Nouf Nova Noya Nozomi Nuala Nudar Nuhkeri Nuku Numa
e Odelia Odessa Odetta Odette Ofelia Ofelia Ofira Ofra Okelani Oksana Ola Olalla Olathe Oldina Oleander Olga Oliana Olind
Oprah Oralee Oralia Orana Orara Ordella Orela Orenda Oriana Oriel Orinthia Oriola Orlan Orlenda Orline Ormanda Orpah Orr
Paiton Paka Pakuna Pallas Palma Palmeda Palmer Paloma Pamela Pancha Pandora Pania Paniga Pansy Panthea Panyin Paola Paoli
Pavita Pavla Payge Payton Paz Pazia Peace Peach Peadaria Pearl Pebbles Pegeen Peggy Pelagia Pema Pemba Penda Penelope
nterry Piper Pipipa Pippi Pixie Placida Pleasance Poesy Poetry Polina Pollianna Polly Pomona Poni Poppy Pora Portia Porzia Posy Pre
adira Qamra Qi Qing Qitara Quaashie Quartas Queena Queenie Quella Quenby Quenisha Querida Quest Questa Quiana Quir
Rada Radella Radeyah Radha Radinka Radmilla Radwa Rae Raeanna Raegina Raelene Raelin Raena Raeven Rafa Rafaela R
amira Ramla Ramona Ramya Ran Rand Randi Rane Ranee Rangi Rani Raniate Raniyah Rapa Raphaela Raquel Rarissa Ra
zi Raziya Razu Rea Reagan Realtin Reba Rebecca Rebekah Rebel Redenta Reena Reese Rio Riona Riri Risa Risha Rishona Rita Rit
Romy Rona Ronaidh Ronalda Roneisha Rongo Roni Rora Roren Rori Rorita Ros Rosa Rosabel Rosabell Rosabelle Rosalba Rose
nd Rosetta Roshan Rosie Rosina Rosita Roslin Roslyn Rossanna Rowena Roxana Roxanna Roxy Royale Roz Rozalina Rozario Rozene
ah Ruza Rya Ryan Ryder Ryesen Rylee Saada Saarah Saba Saben Sabi Sabina Sabirah Sachi Sachiko Sada Sade Sadella Sadho
akari Saki Sakinah Sakti Sakujna Sakura Sal Sala Salali Salama Salena Salida Salihah Salimah Salina Sally ble Secilia Seema Sefika Sel
aedyn Shaelisa Shaella Shaelona Shafira Shah Shahar Shahina Shahla Shahnaz Shahrazad Shaila Shaima Shajauna Shakara Shan
Sharmila Sharnae Sharnie Sharo Sharona Shashi Shasmecka Shasta Shatara Shayonne Shawna Shawnay Shawnassy Shay

A WORLD OF
baby names

HB
Hinkler
Books

Author: Elsie Agnes Allen
Project editor: Karen Comer
Typesetter: Midland Typesetters
Cover design: Katy Wall
Prepress: Graphic Print Group

A World of Baby Names
First published in 2006 by Hinkler Books Pty Ltd
45–55 Fairchild Street
Heatherton VIC 3202 Australia
www.hinklerbooks.com

10 9 8 7 6 5 4 3
11 10 09 08 07

ISBN-13: 978 1 7415 7243 8
ISBN-10: 1 7415 7243 6
Printed in China

contents

introduction

How do you go about naming your precious new family member?

A name is the label that your baby will take through life. To a certain extent, it will determine how other people react to him or her. Consider it one of the most important things that you will do for your little one.

A name differentiates a child from others. Through their name, an individual becomes part of society, and, because of their name, their life will exist separately from the lives of others.

When we introduce ourselves we say, 'I am ...' We intuitively associate our identity with our name. The link between name and identity is so strong that we can get annoyed or even resent a person who does not pronounce our name correctly, or has the ignorance or presumptuousness to spell our name incorrectly.

To have one's name dragged through the mud or brought into disrepute is one of the worst things that can happen to a person and their family. Our good name is paramount.

The birth certificate parents receive when they register the child's birth becomes a kind of ticket to the services the society offers its members. Without a birth certificate we cannot obtain government benefits, marry, get a passport, or use the educational and medical services that society provides.

I was named after my father's beloved mother. She died when my father was only a little boy of ten. Unfortunately, her name was Elsie Agnes – not the most modern name for a young girl – and I have had to deal with that name and its implications all my life. I grew up in Australia in the '50s and '60s. In the groovy '60s, it was uncool to be different. The name 'Elsie' evoked images of old maiden aunts who liked to gossip a lot. I would tell people my name and they would laugh and say to me, 'You're having me on! You can't be serious'. It was not good for my self-esteem and ultimately I was reluctant to let people know that I was, indeed, Elsie.

As a result, I was very careful when naming my four children. They have all grown up loving the names that my husband and I gave them. However, I had been so scarred by my unfashionable name that we didn't give our children second names. The idea was that if they decided that the name they were given was unsuitable they had the option of adding a name of choice to their birth certificate. None of them did.

Perhaps that is why I have taken such an interest in names over the years. I realise through harsh experience what ramifications a bad name choice can have on a child. It has taken me 50 years to come to terms with my name, and I still never voluntarily disclose my second name. I now realise that Elsie is a pretty name and it belongs only to me. There are no other Elsies in my life, so I am a bit like Elvis or Madonna! I do not need a surname to be identified. I am Elsie.

How does it look?

When choosing a name, give some consideration to how a name looks when written down and also to how it sounds when spoken. The parents of young Anna Mouille didn't consider that when their daughter went to school she would become 'Animal'. The name looks good but it sounds terrible. Then there is the family Crapp who sentenced their son to a lifetime of teasing by calling him Hugh! The solution is to try each proposed name out by saying

it and the surname aloud, and by writing them down and looking closely at them.

Beware of words that when combined can mean something else, especially when a shortened version is used. For example, Robert Catte easily changes to Bob Catte, Eleanor Pell can become Elle Pell and Charles Buck can become Chuck Buck.

How does it sound?

A good way to check how a name sounds is to try the 'screech' test. Open the back door and shout the name as if you are calling your child. Have a neighbourhood child call the name several times, like it would be called in a playground. If it grates, don't use it!

What does it mean?

For some parents, the meaning of the name is just as important as the way it sounds and looks. For example, Cameron is a lovely-sounding name, can be used for girls and boys, is not too popular and yet is the name of a famous American actress. It means 'crooked nose'. Some parents may not mind what a name means, but other parents may not want to doom their child to a not-so-straight nose!

In the same vein, many parents will choose a name which means a special quality or attribute. Religious parents may name their daughter Gabrielle; 'devoted to God'. A son may be named Richard for the meaning 'powerful ruler'. A Hawaiian couple may choose Kalia, meaning 'beauty'.

Syllables

Often it is a good idea to vary the number of syllables in the given names and the family name. Select a single or double syllable first name to go with a multi-syllable surname, and vice versa. For example, Anne Robinson, Anita Brown and Alexander Jones.

Acronyms

Be careful about initials. You will be surprised at how quickly children cotton on to the 'naughty initial' and how unrelenting they can be in their exploitation of the joke. Be sure to steer away from initials like Arthur Richard Smith, Phoebe Ivy Somers or Barbara Una Mackie. Names like this will just make your child the butt of all the schoolyard jokes.

Shortened names

Be aware that many names will be shortened or lengthened whether you like it or not. Joseph often becomes Joe, Thomas becomes Tom or Tommy, Susanne becomes Sue and Christopher becomes Chris.

One friend named her son Thomas and then changed it to David six weeks later, after several friends insisted on calling him Tommy. Remember, if you don't like the abbreviation of the name, don't use it.

Connotations

No matter what you think, certain names do have certain connotations and the mere sound of that name can bring positive or negative thoughts to mind. Few parents call their son Adolf any more and Saddam is also pretty unpopular.

Audrey was popular name when Audrey Hepburn was at the height of her popularity, but now it is a name that conjures up thoughts of an older lady. Make sure to be careful and do your best for your child.

People you admire

If you know and dislike a person by a certain name, no matter how nice the name is, do not give it to your child. Conversely, try to think of names of people you like and admire, as you'll be more likely to be fond of those names.

Avoid the temptation to name your baby after an old boyfriend or girlfriend. Your partner will not like it!

Complementary names

If you have older children, try to use a name that is in keeping with the other children's names. A young couple chose an Australian Aboriginal name for their first child, and then decided to limit their search for their second child's name to Australian Aboriginal names. Fortunately, they came up with two names that work well together – Alkira (sky) and Iluka (close to the sea).

Cultural names

Many couples will look to their own culture for inspiration, as it is a very nice way of honouring their family background. Many names from an English-language background have cultural alternatives. For example, Mateo is the Spanish equivalent to Matthew.

Maybe you come from a cultural tradition where the name is determined for you. The name is predetermined and it is passed from generation to generation. The manner in which this is done varies, but is consistent within that social, family or cultural group. (For example, in some societies the first girl is named for the paternal grandmother, the second for the maternal grandmother and so forth.)

There is nothing wrong with this method of naming a baby. In fact, there are some advantages, as it takes a huge responsibility off the parents' shoulders. However, remember you need to be happy with your child's name.

Relatively speaking

Sometimes a young couple will, for one reason or another, hand over the naming of their child to a relative. It may be a tradition for the grandparents to name the baby, or it may be that due to unfortunate circumstances the parents could not do it.

My mother was named Kathleen by her Aunty Kate – who whisked her away and had the paperwork done when no-one was looking – as her mother was very sick after she was born and her father had other children to care for. This was not the name her parents wished for her, so she has spent her whole life being called Theresa, even though she is registered as Kathleen!

In some families, the mother names all the children. 'I went through the pregnancy and the birth so why shouldn't I?' she says. This is fine if the father agrees. In other families, the mother names the girls and the father the boys, while in others, one parent chooses the first name while the other parent chooses the second name. No way is the right way.

Family names

Consider looking a little further back in your family tree. The perfect baby name may be hidden among the branches. Keeping names in the family can be a wonderful way to keep a sense of continuity between the generations and can provide a source of identity and pride for your child. This can create a sense of continuity and heritage.

When naming our own children we used family names. However, we altered them slightly to make them more modern. Kathleen was adapted into Caitlin, Theresa resurfaced as Tessa, and Elsie became Eloise.

Referring to your family tree can provide you with many middle names and surnames which you may not otherwise have considered. You may choose a child's middle name to honour a family surname, and it is good way of including the mother's maiden name. Giving your child the middle name of an ancestor or the surname of a grandparent can also be a great way to maintain a family connection without saddling them with a name that may not follow current trends.

Some people name their child in honour of the Saint's day on which they were born. Others use the names of religious saints and important holy figures. In some religions, certain names are considered to bring blessings.

Standing out

Are you a person who likes to be different and stand out in the crowd? Perhaps you will choose a name that is a little bit different.

However, be wary and don't go overboard. Your child may not be like you. He or she may be like your more conservative sibling who doesn't like to stand out in a crowd. You could ruin their self-image by giving your child a name that is too 'out there'. He or she may end up choosing their own name later that realigns them with the average Joes.

Take no chances

When you are choosing names, make sure that you have both a boy's name and a girl's name handy. Ultrasounds and scans are not 100 per cent correct all the time. Some people like to have a group of names for either sex so that when they meet the new baby, they can give the baby a name that best suits him or her.

Trendy names

Are you a trendy name giver? The trendy name may be a new variation on an old name or a popular name. If you are the type of person who loves gossip magazines and enjoys reading about the lives of celebrities, then you may prefer names of current media, movie and sports stars and political personalities. You may look to the current roster of Hollywood stars, football heroes or Olympic medallists for inspiration.

Be aware that trendy names can date a person. Nearly all boys named Graeme and girls named Dianne were post-World War II babies. There were few before and even fewer since. Similarly, the Madisons and Keanus of today will be identifiable in future years.

Traditional names

The opposite of the trendy name is the traditional name. A traditionalist will name a child a name that has been around a long time and is used by every generation. The names that fall into this category are names like David, Peter, Paul, Michael, Elizabeth, Catherine, Margaret, Mary and Jennifer. They are names that you can never go wrong with; they are good, solid and reliable.

Monday's child

The Ashanti, an African tribe, sincerely believed that the day of the week on which a person was born had a lot to do with the kind of character traits and behaviour the person showed throughout life.

The Ashanti were keenly aware of the day of the week they were born on because one of their customs dictated that the day's name be included in the person's name.

They believed that a boy born on Monday would be calm and measured in his approach, while a child born on Wednesday would be a troublemaker all of his life. We have a similar stereotyping in our culture where redheaded children are often excused for temper tantrums and wild behaviour as it is considered that they are 'hot headed'.

Some people's interest in the astrological chart, and the characteristics that it attributes to people born at a certain time of the month – when the planets are in a certain alignment – is similar to the Ashanti way of naming children. We have all said, 'You must be a Virgo, as you are precise and take notes,' or 'Cancers are home loving and domesticated'.

We also have a nursery rhyme that describes the attributes of a baby depending upon the day on which it was born.

On which day were you born?

Monday's child is fair of face
Tuesday's child is full of grace
Wednesday's child is full of woe
Thursday's child has far to go
Friday's child is loving and giving

Saturday's child works hard for a
    living
But the child that is born on the
    Sabbath day
Is bonny and blithe and good
    and gay.

The importance of names

The sense of personal identity and uniqueness that a name gives us is at the heart of why names interest us, and why they are important to us as individuals and to our society as a whole.

It is also important to remember that no matter what name you give your child – traditional, trendy, cultural or familial – there will be those who love it and those who don't. You may need to decide whether you will tell family and friends your potential baby names and risk hearing their opinion, or whether you will keep the names to yourself and surprise your family and friends when the baby is born.

For every person who tells you that Abriella is unique and original, there will always be another person who will say, 'Oh, I don't like Abriella. I like names such as Susan!'

Of course, once the baby is a few weeks old, it will seem to you and everyone around you that your baby's name could only be Abriella – or Susan.

Just remember that it is your baby who has to wear the name you choose for the rest of their life. Be kind!

Elsie Agnes Allen

LISTS OF NAMES

Top 10 Names in Australia for 2005

South Australia

Boys	Girls
Jack	Emily
Joshua	Chloe
Thomas	Ella
Lachlan	Charlotte
Ethan	Olivia
William	Jessica
Ryan	Isabella
James	Mia
Liam	Lily
Cooper	Sophie

Western Australia

Boys	Girls
Jack	Ella
Joshua	Jessica
Lachlan	Emily
Thomas	Chloe
Ethan	Sophie
Benjamin	Olivia
James	Grace
Riley	Charlotte
Liam	Isabella
Luke	Lily

Queensland

Boys	Girls
Jack	Ella
Lachlan	Emily
Thomas	Olivia
Ethan	Chloe
William	Sophie
Joshua	Charlotte
Ryan	Jessica
Samuel	Lily
Matthew	Isabella
Benjamin	Hannah

Victoria

Boys	Girls
Jack	Olivia
Joshua	Chloe
Thomas	Ella
William	Emily
James	Charlotte
Lachlan	Jessica
Ethan	Isabella
Daniel	Mia
Benjamin	Sophie
Ryan	Sienna

New South Wales

Boys	Girls
Jack	Olivia
Lachlan	Charlotte
William	Emily
Joshua	Chloe
Thomas	Ella
James	Jessica
Ryan	Isabella
Daniel	Sophie
Matthew	Mia
Samuel	Emma

Northern Territory

Boys	Girls
Jack	Emily
James	Lily
Lachlan	Sophie
Benjamin	Chloe
Joshua	Grace
Ryan	Jessica
John	Charlotte
Patrick	Emma
Samuel	Georgia
William	Mia

Australian Capital Territory

Boys	Girls
Jack	Charlotte
Joshua	Jessica
Thomas	Olivia
Lachlan	Sophie
William	Emily
Benjamin	Ella
James	Grace
Nicholas	Chloe
Ryan	Georgia
Samuel	Zoe

Sources: New South Wales Registry of Births, Deaths and Marriages

Northern Territory Department of Justice

Victorian Registry of Births, Deaths and Marriages

South Australian Office of Consumer and Business Affairs

Western Australian Department of the Attorney General

ACT Registrar General's Office

Queensland Department of Justice and Attorney-General

Top 10 Names in the USA

Girls

1880	1890	1900	1910	1920
Mary	Mary	Mary	Mary	Mary
Anna	Anna	Helen	Helen	Dorothy
Elizabeth	Elizabeth	Anna	Margaret	Helen
Margaret	Emma	Margaret	Dorothy	Margaret
Minnie	Margaret	Ruth	Ruth	Ruth
Emma	Rose	Elizabeth	Anna	Virginia
Martha	Ethel	Marie	Mildred	Elizabeth
Alice	Florence	Rose	Elizabeth	Anna
Marie	Ida	Florence	Alice	Mildred
Annie/Sarah (equal)	Bertha/ Helen (equal)	Bertha	Ethel	Betty

1930	1940	1950	1960	1970
Mary	Mary	Linda	Mary	Jennifer
Betty	Barbara	Mary	Susan	Lisa
Dorothy	Patricia	Patricia	Maria	Kimberly
Helen	Carol	Barbara	Karen	Michelle
Barbara	Judith	Susan	Lisa	Angela
Margaret	Betty	Maria	Linda	Maria
Maria	Nancy	Sandra	Donna	Amy
Patricia	Maria	Nancy	Patricia	Melissa
Doris	Margaret	Deborah	Debra	Mary
Joan/Ruth (equal)	Linda	Kathleen	Deborah	Tracy

1980	1990	2000	2002
Jennifer	Jessica	Emily	Emily
Jessica	Ashley	Hannah	Madison
Amanda	Brittany	Madison	Hannah
Melissa	Amanda	Ashley	Emma
Sarah	Stephanie	Sarah	Alexis
Nicole	Jennifer	Alexis	Ashley
Heather	Samantha	Samantha	Abigail
Amy	Sarah	Jessica	Sarah
Michelle	Megan	Taylor	Samantha
Elizabeth	Lauren	Elizabeth	Olivia

2003	2004	2005
Emily	Emily	Emily
Emma	Emma	Emma
Madison	Madison	Madison
Hannah	Olivia	Abigail
Olivia	Hannah	Olivia
Abigail	Abigail	Isabella
Alexis	Isabella	Hannah
Ashley	Ashley	Samantha
Elizabeth	Samantha	Ava
Samantha	Elizabeth	Ashley

Source: US Social Security Administration

Top 10 Names in the USA

Boys

1880	1890	1900	1910	1920
John	John	John	John	John
William	William	William	William	William
Charles	James	James	James	James
George	George	George	Robert	Robert
James	Charles	Charles	Joseph	Joseph
Joseph	Joseph	Joseph	Charles/George (equal)	Charles
Frank	Frank	Frank		George
Henry	Harry	Henry	Edward	Edward
Thomas	Henry	Robert	Frank	Thomas
Harry	Edward	Harry	Henry	Frank

1930	1940	1950	1960	1970
Robert	James	John	David	Michael
James	Robert	James	Michael	David
John	John	Robert	John	John
William	William	William	James	James
Richard	Richard	Michael	Robert	Robert
Charles	Charles	David	Mark	Christopher
Donald	David	Richard	William	William
George	Thomas	Thomas	Richard	Mark
Joseph	Donald	Charles	Thomas	Richard
Edward	Ronald	Gary	Steven	Brian

1980	1990	2000	2002
Michael	Michael	Jacob	Jacob
Jason	Christopher	Michael	Michael
Christopher	Joshua	Matthew	Joshua
David	Matthew	Joshua	Matthew
James	David	Christopher	Ethan
Matthew	Daniel	Nicholas	Joseph
John	Andrew	Andrew	Andrew
Joshua	Joseph	Joseph	Christopher
Robert	Justin	Daniel	Daniel
Daniel	James	Tyler	Nicholas

2003	2004	2005
Jacob	Jacob	Jacob
Michael	Michael	Michael
Joshua	Joshua	Joshua
Matthew	Matthew	Matthew
Andrew	Ethan	Ethan
Joseph	Andrew	Andrew
Ethan	Daniel	Daniel
Daniel	William	Anthony
Christopher	Joseph	Christopher
Anthony	Christopher	Joseph

Source: US Social
Security Administration

Top Five Names in England and Wales

Girls

1904

Mary

Florence

Doris

Edith

Dorothy

1914

Mary

Margaret

Doris

Dorothy

Kathleen

1924

Margaret

Mary

Joan

Joyce

Dorothy

1934

Margaret

Jean

Mary

Joan

Patricia

1944

Margaret

Patricia,

Christine

Mary

Jean

1954

Susan

Linda

Christine

Margaret

Janet

1964

Susan

Julie

Karen

Jacqueline

Deborah

1974

Sarah

Claire

Nicola

Emma

Lisa

1984

Sarah

Laura

Gemma

Emma

Rebecca

1994

Rebecca

Lauren

Jessica

Charlotte

Hannah

2004

Emily

Ellie

Jessica

Sophie

Chloe

Source: The Office for
National Statistics

Top Five Names in England and Wales

Boys

1904

William

John

George

Thomas

Arthur

1914

John

William

George

Thomas

James

1924

John

William

George

James

Thomas

1934

John

Peter

William

Brian

David

1944

John

David

Michael

Peter

Robert

1954

David

John

Stephen

Michael

Peter

1964

David

Paul

Andrew

Mark

John

1974

Paul

Mark

David

Andrew

Richard

1984

Christopher

James

David

Daniel

Michael

1994

Thomas

James

Jack

Daniel

Matthew

2004

Jack

Joshua

Thomas

James

Daniel

Source: The Office for National Statistics

Top 20 Names in England and Wales 2005

Girls

1. Jessica
2. Emily
3. Sophie
4. Olivia
5. Chloe
6. Ellie
7. Grace
8. Lucy
9. Charlotte
10. Katie
11. Ella
12. Megan
13. Hannah
14. Amelia
15. Ruby
16. Lily
17. Amy
18. Mia
19. Abigail
20. Millie

Boys

1. Jack
2. Joshua
3. Thomas
4. James
5. Oliver
6. Daniel
7. Samuel
8. William
9. Harry
10. Joseph
11. Benjamin
12. Charlie
13. Luke
14. Matthew
15. Callum
16. Jake
17. Ethan
18. George
19. Lewis
20. Alexander

Source: The Office for National Statistics

Top 20 Names in Wales 2005

Girls

1. Megan
2. Chloë
3. Emily
4. Ellie
5. Ffion
6. Sophie
7. Jessica
8. Ella
9. Olivia
10. Katie
11. Caitlin
12. Seren
13. Cerys
14. Mia
15. Lucy
16. Amelia
17. Ruby
18. Molly
19. Carys
20. Charlotte

Boys

1. Joshua
2. Jack
3. Dylan
4. Thomas
5. Ethan
6. Rhys
7. Callum
8. Samuel
9. Daniel
10. Morgan
11. William
12. James
13. Luke
14. Oliver
15. Ryan
16. Benjamin
17. Joseph
18. Lewis
19. Matthew
20. Cameron

Source: The Office for National Statistics

Top 20 Names in Scotland 2005

Girls

1. Sophie
2. Emma
3. Ellie
4. Amy
5. Erin
6. Lucy
7. Katie
8. Chloë
9. Rebecca
10. Emily
11. Hannah
12. Olivia
13. Rachel
14. Leah
15. Megan
16. Aimee
17. Holly
18. Abbie
19. Jessica
20. Lauren

Boys

1. Lewis
2. Jack
3. Callum
4. James
5. Ryan
6. Cameron
7. Kyle
8. Jamie
9. Daniel
10. Matthew
11. Ben
12. Liam
13. Adam
14. Dylan
15. Connor
16. Andrew
17. Alexander
18. Aidan
19. Thomas
20. Aiden

Source: The General Register Office for Scotland

10 Most Popular Names in Northern Ireland 2005

Girls

1. Katie
2. Emma
3. Ellie
4. Sophie
5. Niamh
6. Hannah
7. Amy
8. Sarah
9. Anna
10. Leah

Boys

1. Jack
2. Matthew
3. James
4. Adam
5. Ryan
6. Daniel
7. Jamie
8. Joshua
9. Ben
10. Conor/Ethan

Source: The Northern Ireland Statistics and Research Agency

20 Most Popular Names in New Zealand

Girls

1999	2000	2001	2002	2003
Jessica	Jessica	Jessica	Jessica	Emma
Georgia	Olivia	Hannah	Olivia	Sophie
Emma	Hannah	Emma	Hannah	Ella
Olivia	Georgia	Olivia	Emma	Emily
Hannah	Grace	Grace	Sophie	Jessica
Grace	Sophie	Georgia	Grace	Hannah
Sarah	Emma	Sophie	Ella	Olivia
Sophie	Emily	Samantha	Emily	Grace
Samantha	Sarah	Sarah	Sarah	Charlotte
Emily	Samantha	Emily	Georgia	Georgia
Caitlin	Caitlin	Caitlin	Charlotte	Sarah
Ella	Ella	Ella	Caitlin	Paige
Tayla	Amy	Brooke	Samantha	Isabella
Brooke	Kate	Madison	Paige	Caitlin
Rebecca	Charlotte	Isabella	Lucy	Lucy
Shania	Rebecca	Charlotte	Isabella	Holly
Courtney	Courtney	Kate	Holly	Samantha
Kate	Holly	Amy	Madison	Brooke
Madison	Madison	Anna	Chloe	Kate
Charlotte	Paige	Jade	Ruby	Lily

Source: New Zealand Department of Internal Affairs

20 Most Popular Names in New Zealand

Boys

1999	2000	2001	2002	2003
Joshua	Joshua	Joshua	Joshua	Joshua
Liam	Jack	Jack	Jack	Jack
Samuel	Samuel	Samuel	Samuel	Benjamin
Matthew	James	Thomas	Benjamin	Samuel
Jack	Matthew	Benjamin	Ethan	Daniel
Benjamin	Liam	James	James	Jacob
Daniel	Daniel	Jacob	Liam	Ethan
James	Thomas	Liam	Daniel	James
Thomas	Jacob	Matthew	Jacob	Thomas
Jacob	Benjamin	Daniel	Thomas	Matthew
Connor	Cameron	Ethan	Matthew	Liam
Caleb	Ethan	William	William	William
Jordan	Caleb	Caleb	Caleb	Caleb
Dylan	Dylan	Dylan	Jayden	Luke
Cameron	William	Cameron	Ryan	Oliver
Michael	Michael	Connor	Oliver	Ryan
William	Jordan	Luke	Jordan	Jayden
Ethan	Ryan	Logan	Dylan	Cameron
Ryan	Luke	Ryan	Logan	Connor
Luke	Connor	Michael	Luke	Logan

Source: New Zealand Department of Internal Affairs

Baby Names that can be Shortened

Girls

Abigail – Abby, Abbie, Nabby, Gail

Agnes – Aggy, Inez, Nessa

Aileen – Allie, Lena

Alberta – Allie, Bert, Bertie

Alexandra – Alexis, Alex, Lexie

Alicia – Allie, Elsie, Lisa

Almeda – Mary

Almena – Allie, Mena

Amanda – Manda, Mandy

Amelia – Emily, Mel, Millie, Amy

Antoinette – Ann, Tony, Netta, Nettie

Arabella – Ara, Arry, Belle, Bella

Augusta – Aggy, Gatsy, Gussie

Barbara – Bab, Babs, Barby, Bobbie

Belinda – Belle, Linda

Bridget – Biddie, Biddy, Bridgie, Bridie

Camille – Cammie, Millie

Carol – Carrie

Catherine – Cathy, Kathy

Cecilia – Celia, Cissy, Sissie

Christine – Chris, Kris, Crissy, Christy, Kristy, Tina

Clarissa – Clara, Cissy

Cornelia – Nelle, Nelly, Nelia

Cynthia – Cindy, Cintha

Boys

Aaron – Ron, Ronnie

Abel – Abe, Eb, Ebbie

Abraham – Abe

Alan – Al

Albert – Al, Bert, Bertie

Alfred – Al, Fred

Alexander – Al, Alec, Alex, Eleck, Sandy

Alonzo – Al, Lon, Lonas, Lonzo

Anderson – Andy, Sonny, Ander

Andrew – Andy, Drew

Angus – Gus

Anthony – Tony, Tunis

Arnold – Arnie

Arthur – Artie

Augustine – August, Austin, Gus

Bartholomew – Bart, Bartel, Bat, Mees, Meus

Benjamin – Ben, Bennie, Benjy, Jamie

Bernard – Bern, Bernie, Berny

Broderick – Brady, Brody, Rod, Ricky

Buckley – Buck

Caleb – Cal, Cale

Cameron – Cam, Ronny, Ron

Carl – Charles, Charlie, Charley

Charles – Carl, Charlie, Chick, Chuck

Darlene – Lena, Darry

Deborah – Debby, Debbie, Deb

Dorothy – Dora, Dot, Dottie

Edith – Edie

Eleanor – Elaine, Ellen, Ellie, Lanna, Lenora, Nelly, Nora

Eldora – Dora

Elizabeth – Eliza, Bess, Bessie, Beth, Betsy, Betty, Lib, Libby, Liza, Lisa, Liz, Lizzie

Emeline – Emma, Emily, Emmy, Millie, Em

Emily – Emmy, Millie, Emma, Em

Estelle – Essy, Essie, Stella

Faith – Fay

Fredericka – Freda, Freddy, Ricka, Frieda

Gwendolyn – Gwen, Wendy

Frances – Frankie, Fanny, Fran, Cissy, Sis

Gabriella – Gabby, Ella

Hannah – Nan, Nanny, Anna

Harriet – Hattie

Helen – Ella, Ellen, Ellie, Lena

Isabel – Bella, Belle, Ib, Issy, Nib, Nibby, Tibbie

Isabella – Bella, Belle, Ib, Issy, Nib, Nibby, Tibbie

Isadora – Dora, Issy

Jane – Janie, Jean, Jennie, Jessie

Janet – Jessie, Jan

Jean – Jane, Jeannie

Jennifer – Jennie

Jessica – Jessie, Jess

Joanna – Joan, Jody, Hannah, Jo

Josephine – Jody, Jo, Joey, Josey, Fina

Christopher – Chris, Kit, Topher

Clement – Clem

Clifton – Cliff, Tony

Clinton – Clint

Conrad – Con, Conny, Connie

Courtney – Court, Curt

Cyrus – Cy, Si

Dalton – Dal

Daniel – Dan, Danny

David – Dave, Davey, Davy

Dennis – Den, Denny

Derrick – Eric, Rick, Ricky

Desmond – Des

Dominic – Dom

Donald – Don, Donny

Donavan – Don, Van

Edgar – Ed, Eddie

Edward – Ed, Eddie, Ned, Ted, Ward

Edwin – Ed, Eddie, Ned, Win

Elias – Eli, Lee, Lias

Elijah – Eli, Lige

Emmanual - Manny

Eric – Rick, Ricky, Derrick

Ernest – Ernie

Ezekiel – Ez, Zeke

Ferdinand – Ferd, Ferdy

Francis – Frank, Fran

Frederick – Fred, Freddy, Fritz

Gabriel – Gabe, Gabby

Geoffrey – Geoff

Gerard – Gerry, Jerry

Gilbert – Gil, Bert, Bertie

Gustav – Gus

Juanita – Nettie, Nita

Julia – Julie, Jill

Kathleen – Cathy, Kathy

Kristine – Chris, Kris, Crissy, Christy,
Kristy, Tina

Lavina – Ina, Vina, Viney

Lenora – Nora, Lee

Lillian – Lil, Lilly, Lolly

Linda – Lindy, Lynn, Melinda,
Philinda

Loretta – Etta, Lorrie, Retta, Lottie

Louise – Lou, Eliza, Lois, Loubelou

Lucille – Lu, Lou, Cille, Lucy

Luella – Ella, Lu, Lula

Lydia – Lyddy

Madeline – Lena, Maddy,
Madge, Magda, Maggie,
Maida, Maud

Margaret – Gretta, Madge,
Maggie, Margery, Marge,
Margie, Meg, Midge, Peg,
Peggy, Rita,

Margaretta – Greta, Madge,
Maggie, Margery, Marge,
Margie, Meg, Midge, Peg,
Peggy, Rita,

Mary – Molly, Polly, Mae, Mamie,
Mitzi

Matilda – Tilly, Matty, Maud

Maxine – Max

Melinda – Linda, Lindy, Mel,
Mindy

Melissa – Lisa, Lissa, Mel, Milly,
Missy

Michelle – Mickey, Shelly

Mildred – Milly

Millicent – Milly, Missy

Harold – Hal, Harry

Hiram – Hy

Isaac – Ike, Zeke

Jacob – Jake, Jay

James – Jamie, Jem, Jim, Jimmy

Jebediah – Jed

Jeremiah – Jeremy, Jerry

John – Jack, Jock, Johnny

Jonathan – Jon, John, Nathan

Joshua – Josh, Joe

Judson – Jud, Sonny

Kenneth – Ken, Kenny

Lafayette – Fate, Laffie

Lawrence – Larry, Lars, Lon,
Lonny, Lorne, Lorry, Lawry

Lincoln – Link

Lorenzo – Loren

Lucas – Luke

Lyndon – Lynn, Lindy

Malcolm – Mal

Marcus – Mark

Martin – Marty

Matthew – Matt, Thias, Thys

Maurice – Maurie, Morey

Michael – Mike, Micah, Mick,
Mickey

Mitchell – Mitch

Montgomery – Monty, Gum

Napoleon – Nap, Nappy, Leon

Nathan – Nate

Nathaniel – Nathan, Nate, Nat,
Natty, Than

Nicholas – Nick, Nickie, Claas,
Claes

Oliver – Ollie, Obbie, Obby

Miranda – Mandy, Mira, Randy

Miriam – Mimi, Mitzi

Nancy – Nan, Nannie

Natalie – Natty, Nettie, Tally

Olivia – Ol, Liv, Livvy

Parmelia – Amelia, Melia, Milly

Patricia – Pat, Patty, Patsy, Tricia

Paula – Polly, Lina

Penelope – Penny

Priscilla – Cissy, Cilla, Prissy

Rachel – Shelly

Rebecca – Reba, Becca, Becky, Beck

Roseann – Rose, Ann, Roz, Rosie

Roxanne – Ann, Rose, Roxie

Sabrina – Brina

Samantha – Sam

Sarah – Sally, Sadie

Selina – Lena

Serena – Rena

Silvana – Silvy

Susan – Sue, Susie

Tabitha – Tabby

Teresa – Terry, Tess, Tessie, Tessa, Thirza, Thursa, Tracy

Valerie – Val

Vanessa – Nessa, Essa, Vanna

Veronica – Franky, Frony, Ron, Ronnie, Ronna, Vonnie

Victoria – Vicky

Virginia – Ginger, Ginny, Jane, Jennie, Virgy, Virgie

Winifred – Winnie, Freddie, Winnet

Orlando – Orly, Lando

Patrick – Paddy, Pat, Patsy, Pate

Peter – Pete, Pate, Perry

Phillip – Phil

Prescott – Scott, Scotty, Pres

Randolph – Randy, Dolph

Reginald – Reg, Reggie, Naldo, Renny

Richard – Dick, Dickon, Rich, Rick, Ricky

Robert – Bob, Bobby, Rob, Robbie

Russell – Russ, Rusty

Samuel – Sam, Sammy

Shelton – Shelly, Shel, Tony

Sheridan – Dan, Danny, Sher

Sidney – Sid, Syd

Simon – Si, Sim, Sion

Solomon – Sal, Salmon, Saul, Sol, Solly, Zolly

Stanley – Stan

Stephen – Steve, Steph

Steven – Steve, Steph

Sullivan – Sully, Van

Terence – Terry

Theodore – Ted, Teddy, Theo

Thomas – Tom, Thom, Tommy

Timothy – Tim, Timmy

Vincent – Vince, Vin, Vinnie

William – Will, Willie, Bill, Billy

Zachariah – Zack

Names of Popes

Adrian	Lucius
Alexander	Marcellus
Anastasius	Mark
Benedict	Martin
Celestine	Nicholas
Clement	Pascale
Constantine	Paul
Cornelius	Peter
Eugene	Pius
Fabian	Sergius
Felix	Silvester
Gregory	Stephen
Honorius	Theodore
Innocent	Urban
John	Valentine
John Paul	Victor
Julius	Zachary
Leo	

Nature Inspired
Baby Names

Amethyst	Galaxy
Amber	Heather
Apple	Herb
Ash	Holly
Autumn	Iris
Azalea	Ivy
Basil	Jade
Berry	Jasmine
Birch	Jasper
Brooke	Jewel
Cherry	Lake
Coral	Lark
Dahlia	Laurel
Daisy	Lavender
Dale	Leaf
Dawn	Lily
Diamond	Marigold
Emerald	Oakes
Ember	Ocean
Fawn	Pear
Flint	Pebble
Forest	Poppy
Fox	Rain

Raven	Star
River	Steel
Robin	Storm
Rose	Summer
Ruby	Sunny
Saffron	Tiger
Sage	Violet
Savannah	Willow
Sky	Winter
Sienna	Wolf
Snow	Zephyr

Names from
Literature

Girls	Boys
Alice	Adrian
Anne	Arthur
Blanche	Asher
Bridget	Atticus
Charlotte	Bellamy
Dorothy	Bilbo
Elizabeth	Charlie
Emma	Dorian
Hedda	Edmund
Heidi	Fitzwilliam
Hermione	Frodo
Jane	Garth
Juliet	Harry
Katy	Heathcliff
Lolita	Hercule
Lucy	Huck
Matilda	James
Pippi	Peter
Pollyanna	Pip
Precious	Robinson
Scout	Romeo

Girls

Susan

Trixie

Vanessa

Wendy

Boys

Rupert

Sam

Sherlock

Winston

Golden Age
Movie Stars

Girls	Boys
Anne	Burt
Audrey	Carey
Ava	Charlie
Barbara	Clark
Bette	Dean
Betty	Errol
Deborah	Fred
Doris	Gary
Elizabeth	Gene
Ginger	Gregory
Grace	Henry
Greer	Humphrey
Greta	Jackie
Ingrid	James
Jane	Jerry
Jean	Jimmy
Joan	John
Judy	Laurence
Katherine	Mickey
Lana	Marlon
Marlene	Montgomery
Marilyn	Paul

Girls	Boys
Girls	**Boys**
Natalie	Rex
Olivia	Richard
Shelley	Rock
Shirley	Rudolf
Sophia	Spencer
Vivian	William

Modern Movie Stars

Girls	Boys
Alfre	Arnold
Angelina	Ben
Blythe	Brad
Cameron	Colin
Candice	David
Cate	Elijah
Catherine	Ewan
Charlize	Harrison
Courtney	Hayden
Gillian	Heath
Gwynneth	Hugh
Jennifer	Ian
Kate	Johnny
Katie	Keifer
Keira	Leonardo
Kyra	Liam
Lisa	Luke
Megan	Matthew
Naomi	Mel
Natalie	Orlando
Nicole	Owen

Girls	Boys
Sarah	Toby
Scarlett	Tom
Sigourney	Woody
Stockard	Zach

Names from the
Music World

Girls	Boys
Alanis	Axel
Aretha	Bob
Avril	Bon
Beyonce	Brian
Billie	Bruce
Brandee	Elton
Britney	Elvis
Carly	Eric
Celine	Frank
Christina	Garth
Cyndi	Gene
Deborah	George
Diana	Germaine
Dionne	Harry
Dolly	Jimi
Ella	John
Geri	Johnny
Gladys	Justin
Janis	Keith
Jessica	Kurt
Joni	Lionel

Girls

Karen

Kim

Kylie

Madonna

Mariah

Melissa

Patsy

Sade

Shania

Sheryl

Shirley

Suzie

Tiffany

Tina

Toni

Whitney

Boys

Louis

Luther

Marvin

Mich

Michael

Miles

Nat

Otis

Ozzie

Paul

Perry

Prince

Ray

Ringo

Waylon

Willie

Unique
Baby Names

Girls

Abianne

Abrianna

Acacia

Acanthus

Adelle

Admire

Ainsley

Akia

Alchemy

Aline

Alisanne

Amaryllis

Ambrosia

Anjelita

Aria

Atiyana

Axiom

Bay

Bailey

Berit

Bettina

Boys

Abel

Ackerley

Alcott

Alston

Ansel

Avery

Baylyn

Bellamy

Bennett

Blade

Blake

Blue

Booker

Boxer

Branson

Bridge

Brooks

Brown

Burr

Byrne

Cable

Girls	Boys
Bettine	Cameo
Beyonce	Carey
Brionne	Carlson
Cadence	Carter
Cairo	Cedric
Calliope	CeeJay
Camella	Cicero
Camryn	Connor
Cecille	Corbin
Coralee	Cranston
Cosette	Dakota
Courtlyn	Dalton
Danica	Damario
Denver	Darby
Diem	Daylon
Doneshia	Dennison
Eleven	Destin
Eliza	Dewayne
Eraman	Donnally
Ethereal	Dorsey
Fable	Drake
Fallon	Dunstan
Farin	Eadric
Freesia	Easton
Gabriell	Elliston

Girls	Boys
Girls	**Boys**
Glade	Esteban
Greta	Finch
Guardian	Flanagan
Gunilla	Fletcher
Gwen	Flint
Haley	Frost
Harmony	Forest
Hasana	Fox
Imagine	Gage
Indigo	Gerrell
Ireland	Glass
Isa	Grove
Jaden	Hayden
Jenibelle	Hoby
Jenna	Hurst
Kaelyn	Jaegar
Kalena	Jae'won
Karin	Jamari
Katilyn	Jaquelle
Kaylene	Joziah
Keilani	Kaden
Kennedy	Kellan
Kinsey	Keveen
Landry	Kingston
Lanie	Lamond

Girls	Boys
Lindsey	Laquan
Lisette	Lark
Loralei	Lawson
Lydia	Leaf
Mackenzie	Liam
Maddox	Mace
Madelynn	Madden
Maiti	Malik
Makayla	Manning
Maleaka	Marcoe
Marcelle	Nash
Marlaina	Nelson
Marlee	Neville
Maya	North
Meadow	Oak
Merilynn	Olin
Mica	Orson
Midori	Osment
Mikaela	Osmin
Mikki	Pace
Millicent	Padgett
Mimosa	Painter
Myeisha	Palmere
Nakeisha	Patton
Nannette	Pernell

Girls	Boys
Norabel	Phelan
Nuesha	Phoenix
Odessa	Pierson
Oksana	Pike
Ophelia	Powell
Orabelle	Quantiko
Parker	Racer
Pauline	Rain
Peyton	Ranger
Phoenix	Reshawn
Presley	River
Quianna	Rontae
Rachana	Ryland
Raven	Safari
Rosalyn	Shade
Sabina	Shaquan
Scout	Sheridan
Selene	Sibley
Shae	Simeon
Shadae	Sinclair
Shanae	Skylar
Shatrina	Slayton
Shiloh	Snow
Sibley	Sonnet
Sky	Stone

Girls	Boys
Storm	Tallon
Taheesha	Tanner
Tahlia	Tariq
Tamber	Terris
Tarragon	Thunder
Terryn	Tillman
Tierney	Tremaine
Tommie	Truman
Tory	Upton
Trinity	Vidal
Unity	Walcott
Vidette	Walten
Vivien	Wayman
Whitley	Wolf
Wren	Xander
Ximena	Yale
Yasmine	Yardley
Yolanda	York
Yvette	Zaccheus
Zoey	Zaine

Backward Names

It's becoming popular to create a unique name by turning a word around. Of course, some names like Noel and Leon exist in their own right, but more and more names are being created this way. Here's a small sampling of backwards names.

Evol (love)

Leon (Noel)

Neveah (Heaven)

Nivek (Kevin)

Noel (Leon)

Sacul (Lucas)

Semaj (James)

Senga (Agnes)

GIRLS' NAMES

Aasta (English, Norse, Teutonic) love.
Aastah, Asta, Astah

Aba (African) born on a Thursday.
Abah, Abba, Abbah

Abayoma/Abayomi (African) has come to bring joy.

Abbey (Hebrew) her father's joy, a form of Abigail.
Aabbee, Abbe, Abbea, Abbee, Abbeigh, Abbi, Abbie, Abby, Abea, Abee, Abeey, Abey, Abi, Abia, Abie, Aby

Abebi/Abeni (African) we asked or prayed for this baby and she came.
Abebea, Abebie, Abeby, Abeebe, Abeebee

Abeline/Abelina (American) combination of Abbey and Lina.
Abilana, Abilene

Abena (African) born on a Tuesday.
Abenah, Abeni, Abina, Abinah, Abyna, Abynah

Abeo (African) has come to bring happiness.

Abequa (Native American) home lover.
Abequah

Abey (Native American) leaf.

Abia (Arabic) great.
Abbia, Abbiah, Abiah, Abya

Abida (African, Arabic) worshipper.
Abedah, Abidah

Abigail (Hebrew) source of joy, father's joy, father rejoices.
Abagael, Abagail, Abagaile, Abagale, Abagil, Abagayle, Abaigael, Abbagael, Abbagail, Abbagale, Abbagayle, Abbegael, Abbegail, Abbegale, Abbegayle, Abbiegail, Abbiegayle, Abbigaeel, Abbigael, Abbigail, Abbigal, Abbigale, Abbigayl, Abbigayle, Abbrielle, Abbygael, Abbygail, Abbygale, Abbygayl, Abbygayle, Abegael, Abegail, Abegale, Abegayle, Abegeal, Abgail, Abgale, Abgayle, Abigaayil, Abigaayill, Abigaayille, Abigael, Abigaile, Abigaill, Abigaille, Abigal, Abigale, Abigayil, Abigayill, Abigayille, Abigayl, Abigayle, Abigel, Abigell, Abigelle, Abigial, Abigial, Abigialle, Abugail, Abugaill, Abugaille, Abygael, Abygail, Abygaile, Abygaille, Abygayl, Abygayle, Abygaylle, Avigail, Avigaill, Avigaille, Avygail, Avygayl, Avygayll, Avygaylle, Gail, Gayle

Abira (Hebrew) my strength, strong, heroic.
Abbiir, Abbiira, Abbiirah, Abbira, Abbirah, Abeer, Abeera, Abeerah, Abeir, Abeira, Abeirah, Aber, Abera, Aberah, Abiir, Abiira, Abiirah, Abir, Abirah, Abhira, Abyrah, Adira, Amiza

Abla (Arabic) perfectly formed, plump or full figured.
Aabblah, Aabblar, Aabblla, Aabla, Aablah, Aablar, Abbla, Abblah, Abblar, Ablah, Ablar, Ablla, Abllah, Abllar

Abra/Abrianna (Hebrew, Italian) mother of multitudes, mother of many nations, earth mother, feminine form of Abraham.

Abrah, Abranna, Abrannah, Abrea, Abreal, Abreana, Abreanna, Abreanne, Abree, Abreeana, Abreia, Abreona, Abreonia, Abri, Abria, Abriah, Abriana, Abrianah, Abriania, Abrianiah, Abriann, Abrianne, Abriannah, Abriea, Abrieana, Abriell, Abriella, Abrielle, Abrien, Abriena, Abrienah, Abrienna, Abriennah, Abrienne, Abrietta, Abrion, Abrionée, Abrionne, Abriunna, Abrya, Abryah, Abryan, Abryana, Abryanah, Abryane, Abryann, Abryanna, Abryannah, Abryanne, Abryona, Abryel, Abryela, Abryele, Abryell, Abryella, Abryelle, Abyan

Abrial/Abrielle (French) open, secure, protected.

Abrail, Abraille, Abreal, Abreale, Abreall, Abrealle, Abriale, Abriall, Abrialle, Abriel, Abriela, Abriell, Abriella, Abril, Abrilla, Abrille, Abryele, Abryell, Abryella, Abryelle

Abrienda (Spanish) opening.

Abrona (Latin) goddess of farewells.

Aabbrona, Aabbrone, Aabbroni, Aabrona, Aabrone, Aabroni, Abbron, Abbrona, Abbrone, Abrone, Abroni

Acacia (Greek) thorny, resurrection, the acacia tree is a symbol of immortality, according to myth.

Acaciah, Acacya, Acacyah, Acasha, Acassia, Acassiah, Acatia, Acatiah, Accassia, Accassiah, Acey, Acie, Akacia, Akaciah, Akacya, Akacyah, Akasha, Akassa, Akassia, Akassiah, Akatia, Akatiah, Akkassia, Akkassiah, Cacia, Caciah, Cacya, Cacyah, Casia, Casiah, Kacia, Kaciah, Kacya, Kacyah, Kasia, Kasiah

Achilla (Greek) without lips, brown, dark, feminine form of Achilles.

Achila, Achilah, Achillah, Achyla, Achylah, Achylla, Achyllah, Akila, Akilah

Acima (Illyrian) praised by God.

Acimah, Acma, Acmah, Acyma, Acymah

Acola (Teutonic) cool.

Ada (English, Teutonic) prosperous, joyous, happy; (Latin) noble; (Hebrew) ornament.

Adabelle, Adah, Adan, Adaya, Adayah, Adda, Addah, Addi, Addia, Addiah, Addie, Addy, Ade, Aida, Aud, Auda, Audah, Eda, Edah, Edna, Ednah

Adaeze (African) princess, king's daughter.

Adah (Hebrew) ornament.

Aadah, Addah

Adalia (Arabic) refuge of God; (German, Spanish) just, noble one; (English) kind, cheerful; (Spanish) a form of Adela.

Adal, Adala, Adalah, Adalea, Adaleah, Adalee, Adaleen, Adaleena, Adaleenah, Adalena, Adalenah, Adalene, Adali, Adaliah, Adalie, Adalin, Adalina, Adaline, Adalinn, Adall, Adalla, Adalle, Adallia, Adalliah, Adallya, Adallyah, Adaly, Adalya, Adalyah, Adalyn, Adalynn, Adalynna, Adalynne, Addala, Addalah, Addalene, Addalena, Addalenah, Addaleen, Addaleena, Addaleenah, Addaleene, Addaly, Addalya, Addalyah, Addalyn, Addalynn

Adama (Hebrew) earth; (Phoenician) woman, humankind; (English) child of beauty, feminine form of Adam.

Adamah, Adamia, Adamiah, Adamin, Adamina, Adaminah, Adamine, Adamma, Adammah, Adamya, Adamyah, Adamyn, Adamyna, Adamynah, Adamyne

Adana (English) place name; (Spanish) a form of Adama.

Adanah, Adania, Adaniah, Adanna, Adannah, Adanya

Adanna (African) her father's daughter, feminine form of Aidan.

Adana, Adanah, Adania, Adaniah, Adannah, Adannia, Adanniah, Adannya, Adannyah, Adanya, Adanyah

Adar (Syrian) ruler; (Hebrew) noble, exalted.

Adair, Adaira, Adairah, Adaire, Adara, Adarah, Adare, Adayr, Adayra, Adayrah

Adara (Arabic) beauty, virgin, purity, chaste; (Greek) beautiful, virgin.

Adair, Adaira, Adairah, Adaire, Adaora, Adar, Adarah, Adare, Adaria, Adarra, Adasha, Adauré, Adayra, Adayrah

Adawna (Latin) beautiful sunrise.

Adawnah

Adela/Adele (French, Teutonic) noble; (English) a form of Adelaide.

Ada, Addeline, Addi, Addy, Adel, Adelae, Adelah, Adelia, Adelie, Adeline, Adelista, Adella, Adellah, Adelle, Adelya, Adelyah, Adile, Adlina, Adline, Alina, Aline, Deely, Deeley, Dela, Delah, Delaney, Dele, Delia, Deliah, Della, Dellah, Edeline, Lela

Adelaide (Teutonic) noble rank, serene.

Adakube, Adalade, Adalaid, Adalaide, Adalayd, Adalin, Adelade, Adelaid, Adelaida,

Adelaidah, Adelais, Adelayd, Adelayda, Adelaydah, Adalayde, Adelei, Adelheid, Adeliade, Adelka, Adelkah, Adella, Adellah, Aley, Alley, Edelaid, Edelaide, Laidey, Laidy

Adelina/Adeline (German) noble protector of good; (English) a form of Adeline.

Adalina, Adalinah, Adaline, Addleena, Addleenah, Addlenna, Addlennah, Adelaine, Adele, Adeleana, Adeleanah, Adeleine, Adelena, Adelenah, Adelenee, Adeliana, Adelianah, Adelin, Adelinah, Adelind, Adelita, Adelitah, Adeliya, Adeliyah, Adelyn, Adelyne, Adelynn, Adelynne, Adelle, Adellena, Adellenah, Adellyna, Adellynah, Adileen, Adileena, Adileenah, Adilen, Adilene, Adileni, Adilenne, Adlaine, Adlen, Adlena, Adlenah, Adleena, Adleenah, Adlene, Adlenn, Adlenne, Adlin, Adlina, Adlinah, Adline, Adlinna, Adlinnah, Adlyn, Adlyna, Adlynah, Adlynn, Adlynna, Adlynnah, Aline, Alina, Alinah, Alinna, Alinnah

Adelpha (Greek) sister.

Adelfa, Adelfah, Adelfe, Adelfia, Adelphah, Adelphe, Adelphia, Adelphya, Adelphyah

Ademia (Greek) without husband.

Ademe, Ademiah

Adena (Hebrew) noble, adorned.

Adeana, Adeanah, Adeane, Adeen, Adeena, Adeenah, Adeene, Aden, Adene, Adenia, Adeniah, Adenna, Adennah, Adina, Adinah, Adinna, Adinnah

Adero (African) giver of life.

Adesina (African) beginning of the family, one who encourages more babies to come

Adesinah, Adesyna, Adesynah

Adia (African) gift, kindness.
*Aaddia, Aaddiah, Aadea,
Aadeah, Aadiah, Addia, Addiah,
Adea, Adéa, Adeah, Adiah*

Adiel (Hebrew) ornament of God.
*Adiela, Adielah, Adiele, Adiell,
Adiella, Adielle, Adyel, Adyela,
Adyelah, Adyele, Adyell, Adyella,
Ayellah, Adyelle*

Adila (Arabic) equal.
*Aadeala, Aadeela, Aadela,
Aadelah, Aadeola, Aadila,
Aadilah, Aadileh, Aadilia, Aadiliah,
Aadyla, Aadylah, Adeala, Adeela,
Adela, Adelah, Adeola, Adilah,
Adileh, Adilia, Adiliah, Adilla,
Adilleh, Adillia, Adilliah, Adyla,
Adylah, Adylla, Adyllah*

Adin (Hebrew) slender, voluptuous;
(English) beautiful, slender and
delicate, a form of Adelaide.
*Adeana, Adeanah, Adeane,
Adeena, Adeenah, Adeene,
Adena, Adenah, Adenia, Adina,
Adinah, Adine, Adyna, Adynah,
Adyne*

Adina/Adine (Australian
Aboriginal) good.
*Adeana, Adeanah, Adeane,
Adeena, Adeenah, Adeene,
Adenah, Adenia, Adinah, Adyna,
Adynah, Adyne, Dea, Dee,
Dee-Dee, Dena, Denah, Din, Dina,
Dinah, Dine, Dinee, Diney, Dini,
Dinie, Diny, Dyn, Dyna, Dynah, Dyne,
Dynee, Dyney, Dyni, Dynie, Dyny*

Adione (Latin) Roman goddess.

Adira (Hebrew) strong.
*Ader, Adera, Aderah, Aderra,
Adirah, Adirana, Adiranah, Adhira,
Adhirah, Adyra, Adyrah*

Adison (English) daughter of
Adam, a form of Addison.
Aaddyson, Aadis, Aadisa,

*Aadisen, Aadisenne, Aadisyn,
Aadisynne, Aadysen, Aadysenne,
Aadyson, Addison, Addyson, Adis,
Adisa, Adisen, Adisenne, Adisyn,
Adisynne, Adysen, Adysenne,
Adyson*

Aditi (Hindu) goddess, mother of
the gods, creative power, freedom,
unfettered.
*Aadhita, Aadhitah, Aadhithi,
Aadhitti, Aadita, Aaditah, Aadithi,
Aaditti, Adhita, Adhitah, Adhithi,
Adhitti, Adita, Aditah, Aditee,
Adithi, Aditie, Aditti, Adity, Adytee,
Adytey, Adyti, Adytie, Adyty*

Adiva (Arabic) pleasant, gentle.
*Aaddeeva, Aaddeevah, Aaddiva,
Aaddivah, Aadeeva, Aadeevah,
Aadivah, Addeeva, Addeevah,
Addiva, Addivah, Adeeva,
Adeevah, Adivah*

Adjua (African) born on a Monday.
Aadjuah, Adjuah

Adleigh (Hebrew) my ornament.
*Adla, Adlah, Adlee, Adleni,
Adlenia, Adleniah*

Adlinga (Australian Aboriginal)
hunting place.
Aadlinga, Aadlingah, Adlingah

Adolpha (Teutonic) noble,
she-wolf.
*Adolfa, Adolfah, Adolfia, Adolfiah,
Adolfya, Adolfyah, Adolphah,
Adolphia, Adolphiah, Adolphie,
Adolphya, Adolphyah, Dolfa*

Adonia (Greek) beautiful woman;
(Spanish) beautiful.
*Aadonica, Aadonicah, Aadonis,
Aadonnica, Aadonnicah,
Aadonya, Aadonyah, Adoniah,
Adonica, Adonicah, Adonis,
Adonna, Adonnah, Adonnica,
Adonnicah, Adonya, Adonyah*

Adonica (Spanish) sweet.
Aadonca, Aadoncah, Aadonceea, Aadonceeah, Aadonciah, Adonca, Adoncah, Adonceea, Adonceeah, Adonciah

Adora (Latin, French) beloved one.
Aadorah, Adorah, Adore, Adoree, Adoreea, Adoreeha, Adoria, Adoriah, Adorya, Adoryah

Adorna (Latin) adorned with jewels.
Adornah, Adornia, Adorniah, Adornya, Adornyah

Adra (Arabic) virgin.
Aadara, Aadarah, Aadra, Aadrah, Adara, Adarah, Adrah

Adrana (Greek) girl from Ardrea.
Aadrana, Aadranah, Adranah

Adrienne (Latin) dark one; (Greek) rich, black, mysterious, feminine form of Adrian.
Addie, Addriann, Addrianna, Addrionna, Addriyanna, Adranne, Adrea, Adreah, Adrean, Adreana, Adreanah, Adreane, Adreann, Adreanna, Adreannah, Adreanne, Adreauna, Adreeanna, Adreeannah, Adreen, Adreena, Adreenah, Adreene, Adreeyana, Adreeyanah, Adreeyanna, Adreeyannah, Adreiana, Adreinna, Adrene, Adrena, Adrenah, Adrenea, Adreneah, Adreona, Adreonah, Adreonia, Adreoniah, Adreonnah, Adria, Adriah, Adrian, Adriana, Adrianah, Adriane, Adriannah, Adrianne, Adriannea, Adriannia, Adriayon, Adrien, Adriena, Adrienah, Adriene, Adrienn, Adrienna, Adriennah, Adrienneah, Adrina, Adrinah, Adrine, Adrion, Adrionna, Adryan, Adryana, Adryanah, Adryane, Adryann, Adryannah, Adryanne, Hardia

Adsila (Native American) flowering blossom.
Adsilah, Adsilla, Adsillah

Adya (Indian) born on Sunday.
Aaddya, Aaddyah, Aadyah, Addya, Addyah, Adia, Adyah

Aerona (Welsh) berry.
Aeronah, Aeronna, Aeronnah

Afaf (Arabic) chaste, virtuous, decent, pure.
Afaff, Afaffi, Afafi, Affaf, Affafi

Afi (African) born on a Friday.
Afee, Affee, Affi, Afia, Efi, Efia

Afra/Afina (Hebrew) young female deer.
Affery, Affrah, Affrey, Affrie, Afinah, Afraa, Afrah, Afria, Afriah, Afrya, Afryah, Afynah, Aphina, Aphinah, Aphyna, Aphynah

Afton (English, Celtic) river name, from Afton, England.
Afftan, Afftine, Afftinn, Afftyn, Afftynne, Aftan, Aftine, Aftinn, Aftona, Aftonah, Aftone, Aftonia, Aftoniah, Aftonie, Aftony, Aftonya, Aftonyah, Aftonye, Aftyn, Aftynne

Agada (Hindu) healthy.
Agadah, Agadda, Agaddah

Agate (English, French, Greek) precious stone.
Agata, Agatah

Agatha (Greek) good, kind.
Agace, Agacia, Agafa, Agafia, Agaisha, Agase, Agasha, Agata, Agatah, Agathe, Agathi, Agathia, Agathiah, Agathie, Agathy, Agathya, Agathyah, Agatka, Ageia, Agetha, Aggie, Agota, Agotha, Agothah, Agueda, Agytha, Aphte, Apka, Atka

Agave (Greek) noble.
Agava, Agavah, Agavva, Agavvah

Aglaia (Greek) beautiful.

Aglae, Aglaiah, Aglaya, Aglayah, Aglaye

Agnella (Greek) purity.
Agnel, Agnela, Agnelah, Agnele, Agnelia, Agneliah, Agnelie, Agnell, Agnellah, Agnelle, Agnellia, Agnelliah, Agnellie, Agnelly, Agnellya, Agnellyah

Agnes (Greek) pure.
Adneda, Aganathea, Aggi, Aggie, Agna, Agne, Agneis, Agnelia, Agnella, Agnelle, Agnesa, Agnesca, Agnese, Agnesina, Agness, Agnessa, Agnesse, Agnessija, Agneta, Agnete, Agnetha, Agneti, Agnetis, Agnetta, Agnette, Agnies, Agnieszka, Agniya, Agnizica, Agnizika, Agnizka, Agnola, Agnus, Agytha, Aigneis, Ameyce, Aneesa, Aneesah, Aneessa, Aneshka, Aneska, Anessah, Anice, Anis, Anisha, Anka, Ankah, Annais, Annes, Anneyce, Anneys, Anneyse, Annice, Annis, Annisha, Annot, Annys, Ina, Ines, Inesila, Inessa, Inez, Nancy, Nesa, Nesi, Ness, Nessi, Nessie, Nessy, Nesta, Neta, Netta, Neza, Neziko, Nyusha, Una, Ynez

Ahava (Hebrew) beloved.
Ahavah, Ahiva, Ahuda, Ahuva, Ahuvah

Ahimsa (Hindu) peaceful.
Ahimsaa, Ahimsaah, Ahimsah, Ahimsia, Ahimsiah

Ahlam (Arabic) witty, one who has pleasant dreams, imaginative.
Ahlama, Ahlamah, Ahlami, Ahlamia, Ahlamiah

Ahulani (Hawaiian) heavenly shrine.
Ahulanee, Ahulaney, Ahulania, Ahulaniah, Ahulanie, Ahulanya, Ahulanyah

Ai (Japanese, Vietnamese) love.

Aida (French, Latin) helpful, a form of Ada.
Aidah, Aidan, Aidana, Aidanah, Aidane, Aidann, Aidanna, Aidannah, Aidanne, Aide, Aidee, Ayda, Aydah, Aydan, Aydana, Aydanae, Aydanah, Aydann, Aydanna, Aydannah, Aydanne, Iraida, Iraidah

Aiesha (Arabic) woman; (Swahili) life.
Aeisha, Aeshia, Aieshah, Aieshia, Aiiesha

Aiko (Japanese) beloved.

Ailani (Hawaiian) chieftan.
Aeilani, Aelani, Ailana, Ailanah

Aileen (Greek, Irish) shining light, a form of Helen.
Aila, Ailean, Aileana, Aileanah, Aileane, Ailee, Ailena, Ailenah, Ailene, Ailey, Alean, Aleana, Aleanah, Aleane, Aleen, Aleena, Aleenah, Aleene, Alena, Alene, Alina, Aline, Eilean, Eileana, Eileane, Eileen, Eileena, Eileene, Eilidh, Eilleen, Eleana, Eleanah, Eleane, Elena, Elenah, Elene, Ileana, Ileane, Ilina, Ilinah, Iline, Illean, Illeana, Illeanah, Illeane, Illian, Illiana, Illianah, Illiane, Illianna, Illiannah, Illianne, Leana, Leanah, Leane, Lena, Liana, Lianah, Lyan, Lyana, Lyann, Lyanna, Lyannah, Lyanne, Lynah

Aili/Ailie (Finnish, Irish) a form of Helen; (Scottish) a form of Alice.
Aila, Ailee, Ailey, Aily

Ailise (Irish) noble.
Ailis, Ailesh, Ailish, Ailyse, Eilis, Eylis

Ailsa (Scottish) Alfsigr's island, modern Scottish place name.
Ailsha, Aylsa, Aylsah, Aylsha, Aylshah

Aimee/Amy (French) loved; (Latin) loved, beloved.
Aime, Aimée, Aimey, Aimi, Aimia, Aimiah, Aimie, Aimy, Aimya, Aimyah, Amata, Amatah, Ame, Amee, Amei, Amey, Ami, Amia, Amiah, Amice, Amie, Amii, Amina, Aminah, Amine, Amity, Amorett, Amoretta, Amorette, Amorita, Amoritah, Amoritta, Amorittah, Amoritte, Amoryt, Amoryta, Amorytah, Amoryte, Amorytt, Amorytta, Amoryttah, Amorytte

Ain (Arabic) precious.

Aina (Scandinavian) always, until the end.

Aine (Irish) joy, fire.
Ain, Aithne, Ayn, Ayne, Eithne

Aingeal (Irish) angel.

Ainsley (Scottish) my meadow, my own place, my field, from the clearing, a unisex name.
Ainslea, Ainsleah, Ainslee, Ainslei, Ainsleigh, Ainslie, Ainsly, Anslee, Ansley, Anslie, Ansy, Aynsleah, Aynslee, Aynslei, Aynsleigh, Aynsley, Aynsli, Aynslie, Aynsly

Airleas (Irish) promise.
Airlea, Airleah, Airlee, Airlei, Airleigh, Airley, Airli, Airlie, Airly, Ayrlea, Ayrleas, Ayrlee, Ayrlei, Ayrleigh, Ayrley, Ayrli, Ayrlie, Ayrly

Airlia (Greek) of the air, ethereal.

Aisha (Arabic) alive; name of the prosperous, youngest wife of the prophet Muhammad; (African) life.
Aeisha, Aesha, Aeshah, Aeshia, Aheesha, Ahia, Aiasha, Aiesha, Aieysha, Aiiesha, Aisa, Aischa, Aish, Aishah, Aisheh, Aisia, Aiyesha, Aiysha, Asha, Ause, Ayeisha, Ayesha, Ayisha, Ayishah, Aysha, Ayshia, Aysa, Aytza

Aisling/Aislinn (Irish) dream, vision.
Aishellyn, Aishlinn, Aislee, Aisley, Aislin, Aislyn, Aislynn, Aislynne, Aissa, Aissah, Ayslin, Ayslinn, Ayslinne, Ayslyn, Ayslynn, Ayssa, Ayssah

Aissa (African) grateful to God.

Aithne (Celtic) little fire.
Aythne, Eithne, Ethne

Aiyana (Native American) eternal bloom, forever flowering.
Aiyanah, Aiyhana, Aiyona, Aiyonia

Akaisha (Irish) the akaisha flower.

Akala (Australian Aboriginal) parrot.

Akela (Hawaiian) noble.
Ahkayla, Ahkeelah, Akeia, Akeiah, Akelah, Akelia, Akeliah, Akeya, Akeyah

Aki (Japanese) born in autumn.
Akee, Akeeye, Akei, Akey, Akie, Aky

Akiko (Japanese) bright light.
Akyko

Akilah (Arabic) intelligent, logical, one who reasons.
Aikiela, Aikilah, Akeela, Akeelah, Akeila, Akeilah, Akeiyla, Akiela, Akielah, Akil, Akilaih, Akilia, Akilka, Akilkah, Akillah, Akkila, Akyla, Akylah

Akili (African) wisdom.
Akilea, Akileah, Akilee, Akilei, Akileigh, Akiliah, Akilie, Akily, Akylee, Akyli, Akylie

Akina (Japanese) bright spring flower, bright leaves.

Akira (Japanese, Scottish) anchor; (Japanese) bright, intelligent, a unisex name.

Alaba (African) second child.

Alaia (Greek) war goddess.

Alaini/Alani (Hawaiian) orange tree.

Alainie, Alana, Alanah, Alanea, Alanee, Alaney, Alani, Alania, Alaniah, Alanie, Alannie, Alany, Alanya, Alanyah, Allana, Allanah, Allona, Allonah, Allyn, Allyna, Allynah

Alamea (Hawaiian) ripe, precious.

Alameah, Alameya, Alameyah, Alamia, Alamiah, Almya, Almyah

Alameda (Spanish) a poplar tree.

Alamedah

Alana (Celtic) fair, distant place, beautiful, attractive, peaceful; (English) harmony, the feminine form of Alan; (Hawaiian) beautiful offering.

Alaana, Alaanah, Alain, Alaina, Alainah, Alaine, Alainna, Alainnah, Alanae, Alanah, Alanai, Alandra, Alandrah, Alandria, Alandriah, Alane, Alanea, Alania, Alaniah, Alanis, Alanna, Alannah, Alarna, Alarnah, Alawna, Alayna, Alaynah, Alaynna, Alaynnah, Allana, Allanah, Allanna, Allannah, Allarna, Allarnah, Allena, Allenah, Allene, Allyna, Allynah, Allyne, Allynee, Lana, Lanah, Larna, Larnah

Alanis (Irish) beautiful, bright.

Alanisa, Alanisah, Alanise, Alaniss, Alanissa, Alanissah, Alanisse, Alannis, Alannisa, Alannisah, Alannise, Alannys, Alannysa, Alannyse, Alanys, Alanysa, Alanysah, Alanyse, Alanyss, Alanyssa, Alanyssah, Alanysse

Alanza (Spanish) eager, noble.

Alaqua (Native American) sweet-gum tree.

Alaquah

Alastrina (Scottish) defender of humankind.

Alastriana, Alastrianah, Alastriane, Alastrianna, Alastriannah, Alastrianne, Alastrinah, Alastrine, Alastryan, Alastryana, Alastryanah, Alastryane, Alastryann, Alastryanna, Alastryannah, Alastryanne, Alastryn, Alastryna, Alastrynah, Alastryne, Alastrynia, Alastryniah, Alastrynya, Alastrynyah

Alatea/Alathea (Greek, Spanish) truth.

Aletta

Alaula (Hawaiian) dawn, light of early dawn.

Alaulah

Alba (Latin) white; (Australian Aboriginal) sand hill.

Albah, Albana, Albani, Albania, Albanie, Albany, Albeni, Albina, Albinah, Albine, Albinia, Albinka, Albyna, Albynah, Albyne, Aubina, Aubinah, Aubine, Aubyna, Aubynah, Aubyne, Elba

Alberta (Teutonic) noble, bright; (French) noble and bright, feminine form of Albert.

Albee, Albertina, Albertinah, Albertine, Albertyna, Albertyne, Albie, Albirta, Albirtina, Albirtine, Albirtyna, Albretina, Albrette, Albretyne, Alburta, Alburtah, Alburtina, Alburtinah, Alburtine, Alburtyna, Alburtynah, Alburtyne, Alby, Albyrta, Albyrtah, Albyrtine, Albyrtna, Albyrtnah, Albyrtyna, Alverta, Alvertah, Alvertina, Alvertinah, Alvertine, Berta, Bertha, Bertie, Berty

Albina/Albine (Latin) white, golden-haired, white-skinned.

Ala, Alba, Albinia, Albinka, Alva, Alvina, Alvinia, Alwine

Alcina (Greek) strong minded.

Alceena, Alcie, Alcinah, Alcine,

Alcinia, Alciniah, Alcyna, Alcynah, Alcyne, Alseena, Alsina, Alsinah, Alsine, Alsinia, Alsyn, Alsyna, Alsynah, Alsyne, Alzina, Alzinah, Alzine, Alzyna, Alzynah, Alzne

Alda (Teutonic) wise and rich, old.
Aldah, Aldina, Aldine

Alden (English) old, wise protector.
Aldan, Aldon, Aldyn

Aldercy (English) a chief.

Aldonza (Spanish) sweet.

Aldora (English) noble, superior.
Aldorah, Aldorra, Aldorrah

Alea (Arabic) high, exalted; (Persian) God's being.
Aalaya, Aalayah, Aalayaha, Aalea, Aaleah, Aaleaha, Aaleeyah, Aaleyah, Aaleyia, Aaleyiah, Aaliya, Aaliyah, Aalyya, Aalyyah, Ailea, Aileah, Aleah, Aleea, Aleeah, Alia, Aliah, Aliya, Aliyah, Allea, Alleah, Alleea, Alleeah, Allia, Alliah, Alyia, Alyiah, Alyya, Alyyah

Aleela (African) she cries.
Aleala, Alealah, Aleelah, Aleighla, Aleighlah, Aleila, Aleilah, Aleyla, Aleylah, Alila, Alilah, Alile, Alyla, Alylah

Alejandria (Spanish) the defender or helper of mankind, feminine form of Alejandro, a form of Alexandra.
Aleiandra, Alejandr, Alejandra, Alejandrea, Alejandria, Alejandrina, Alejandrine, Alejandro

Aleka (Hawaiian) noble, kind, a form of Alice.
Aleaka, Aleakah, Aleeka, Aleekah, Aleika, Aleikah, Alekah, Aleyka, Aleykah

Alena (Greek, Russian) pretty, shining light, a form of Helen.
Aleana, Aleanah, Aleane, Aleena, Aleenah, Aleighna, Aleighnah, Aleina, Aleinah, Alenah, Alene, Alenea, Aleneah, Aleni, Alenia, Alenka, Alenna, Alennah, Alenya, Aliena, Aliene, Alina, Alinah, Alyna, Alynah

Aleria (Latin) eagle.
Alearia, Aleariah, Alearya, Alearyah, Aleriah, Alerya, Aleryah

Aleshanee (Native American) she plays all the time.

Aleta (Greek, Latin) winged.
Aleata, Aleatah, Aleeta, Aleetah, Aleighta, Aleightah, Aleita, Aleitah, Aletah, Aletta, Alettah, Aleyta, Aleytah, Alita, Alitah, Alouetta, Alouette, Alyta, Alytah

Alethia/Alethea (Greek) truthful one.
Alata, Alatah, Alathea, Alatheah, Alathia, Alathiah, Aleathia, Aleathiah, Aleathya, Aleathyah, Aleethea, Aleetheah, Aleethia, Aleethiah, Aleethya, Aleethyah, Aleightha, Aleightheah, Aleighthia, Aleighthiah, Aleithea, Aleitheah, Aleithia, Aleithiah, Aleithya, Aleithyah, Aletah, Aletheah, Alethiah, Aletta, Alettah, Alithea, Alitheah, Alithiah, Allathea, Allatheah, Allathia, Allathiah, Allethea, Alletheah, Allethia, Allethiah, Allethya, Allethyah, Allythea, Allytheah, Allythia, Allythiah, Allythya, Allythyah, Alythea, Alytheah, Alythia, Alythiah, Alythya, Alythyah, Oletha

Alexandra (Greek) mother of mankind, helper or defender of humankind, feminine form of Alexander.
Alecsandra, Alecsandria, Alecsandrina, Alecsis, Alecxandra, Alejandra, Alejandrina,

*Alejandrine, Alejandryn, Aleksia,
Aleksiah, Aleksis, Aleksya,
Aleksyah, Alessandra, Alessandria,
Alessandriah, Alessandrie, Alex,
Alexa, Alexah, Alexandria,
Alexandriah, Alexandrina,
Alexandrine, Alexandrovna, Alexia,
Alexiah, Alexina, Alexinah, Alexine,
Alexis, Alexxandra, Alexxandrah,
Alexxandria, Alexyna, Alexynah,
Alexyne, Alis, Alisandra, Alix,
Alixandra, Alixandrah, Alixandria,
Olexa, Sacha, Sandra, Sandrine,
Sasha*

Alfonsa (Greek, Spanish) ready
for noble deeds, noble and eager,
feminine form of Alfonso.

*Alfonse, Alfonsia, Alfonsina,
Alfonsine, Alfonsyna, Alfonsyne,
Alonza, Alonzah*

Alfreda (English, Teutonic) wise
counsellor, elf.

*Alfi, Alfie, Alfredah, Alfredda,
Alfredia, Alfreeda, Alfrena,
Alfrene, Alfrida, Alfridah, Alfrieda,
Alfryda, Alfrydah, Alfrydda,
Alfryddah, Alfy, Elfrid, Elfrida,
Elfridah, Elfridia, Elfried, Elfrieda,
Elfrina, Elfrine, Freda, Fredah,
Fredda, Freddah, Freida, Freidah,
Freyda, Freydah, Fryda, Frydah,
Frydda, Fryddah*

Algoma (Native American) valley
of flowers.

Algom, Algomah, Algome

Alhena (Arabic) a ring, a star in
the constellation Gemini.

Ali (Arabic) God, the highest.

Aliah (Arabic) exalted, noble,
highest social standing.

Alice (Greek) truthful; (Teutonic)
noble.

*Aalisha, Addala, Adelice,
Adelicia, Ailis, Aleece, Aleese,
Aletta, Ali, Aliceie, Alicia, Alicija,*

*Alina, Aline, Alisa, Alisan, Alise,
Alisen, Alisha, Alisin, Alison, Alissa,
Alisun, Alisyn, Aliza, Allie, Allisan,
Allisen, Allisin, Allison, Allisun,
Allisyn, Ally, Allyce, Allyse, Alodia,
Alse, Alyce, Alys, Alyse, Alyssa,
Alyssia, Elice, Elisan, Elise, Elisen,
Elisin, Elsje, Elison, Elisun, Elisyn,
Ilyssa*

Alicia (Greek) truthful, noble.

*Aalisha, Aaleasha, Aaliayah,
Aleacia, Aleaciah, Aleecia,
Aleeciah, Aleicia, Aleiciah,
Aleighcia, Aleighciah, Aleighsia,
Aleighsiah, Aleighsya, Aleighsyah,
Aleisia, Aleisiah, Aleisya, Aleisyah,
Aliciah, Alisha, Alycia, Alyciah,
Alycya, Alycyah, Alysia, Alysiah,
Alysya, Alysyah*

Alida (Latin) small and winged;
(Spanish) noble; (Greek) beautiful
small winged one; (English, French,
Greek) beautifully dressed.

*Adelita, Aledah, Aleida, Alidah,
Alidia, Alidiah, Alita, Alitah, Alleda,
Alledah, Allida, Allidah, Alyda, Alydia,
Elida, Elidia*

Alika (Hawaiian) truthful; (African)
one who outshines all others in
beauty, most beautiful.

*Alikah, Aliqua, Aliquah, Alique,
Alyka, Alykah, Alyqua, Alyquah,
Alyque, Aleka, Alica, Alikah, Alike,
Alikee, Aliki*

Alima (Arabic) sea maiden,
musical mermaid, dancer.

Alimah, Alyma, Alymah

Alina (Scottish) bright, fair-haired
and beautiful; (Slavic) bright; (Latin)
straight line.

*Aleana, Aleanah, Aleen, Aleena,
Aleenah, Aleina, Aleinah, Aleyna,
Aleynah, Alinah, Alinda, Alindah,
Aline, Alyna, Alynah, Alynda,
Alyndah, Alyne*

Alinga (Australian Aboriginal) child of the sun.

Alingah, Alynga, Alyngah

Alisa (Hebrew) joyful.

Alisah, Alissa, Alissah, Alysa, Alysah, Alyssa, Alyssah, Allisa, Allissah, Allysa, Allysah, Allyssa, Allyssah, Aliza

Alison (English) noble birth, Alice's son, a unisex name; (Scottish) diminutive of Alice.

Aleason, Aleeson, Aleighson, Aleison, Alis, Alisan, Alisana, Alisanah, Alisen, Alisena, Alisenah, Alisin, Alisina, Alisinah, Alissa, Alissah, Alisson, Alissun, Alissyn, Alisun, Alisyn, Alisyna, Alisynah, Alisyne, Allisa, Allisah, Allisan, Allisana, Allisanah, Allisen, Allisena, Allisenah, Allisin, Allisina, Allisinah, Allisine, Allison, Allisona, Allisonah, Allisone, Alliss, Allissa, Allisah, Allisun, Allisuna, Allisyn, Allysna, Allysyne, Alson, Alsona, Alsonah, Alsone, Alysan, Alysen, Alysena, Alysenah, Alysene, Alysin, Alysina, Alysinah, Alysine, Alyson, Alysona, Alysonah, Alysone, Alyssa, Alyssah, Alysse, Alysun, Alysyn, Alysyna, Alysynah, Alysyn, Alysyne, Alyzan, Alyzana, Alyzane, Alyzen, Alyzena, Alyzene, Alyzin, Alyzina, Alyzine, Alyzyn, Alyzyna, Alyzyne

Aliya/Ailya (Hebrew) ascender.

Aeliya, Aeliyah, Alea, Aleah, Alee, Aleea, Aleia, Aleya, Alia, Aliah, Alieya, Alieyah, Aliyah, Aliyia, Aliyiah, Alliyha, Alliyia, Alliyiah, Aly

Aliza/Alize (Hebrew) joyful.

Aleeza, Alieza, Aliezah, Alitza, Aliz, Alizah, Alizee

Alka (Hindu) girl with long hair.

Alkira (Australian Aboriginal) sky.

Allegra (Latin) brisk, lively; (Spanish) cheerful, joyous; (Italian) jaunty, cheerful, lively.

Alegra, Alegrah, Alegria, Allegrah, Allegria, Legra

Allita (Greek) little winged creature.

Adelim, Adelita, Aleda, Aledah, Aleta, Aletah, Aletta, Alettah, Alette, Allitah, Allitta, Allittah, Allyta, Allytah, Alyta, Alytah

Alma (Latin) soul, nourishing; (Italian, Spanish) soul, spirit.

Almah, Almar, Almara, Almarah, Almaria, Almariah, Almarya, Almaryah

Almas (Arabic) diamond.

Almeda (Arabic) ambitious; (Latin) goal-orientated.

Allmeda, Allmedha, Allmeta, Allmetta, Allmettah, Almea, Almedah, Almeta, Almetah, Almetta, Almettah, Almida, Almidah, Almyda, Almydah

Almira (Arabic) princess.

Allmera, Allmerah, Allmeria, Allmira, Allmirah, Allysha, Almeera, Almeeria, Almeira, Almera, Almerah, Almeria, Almeriah, Almina, Alminah, Almine, Almirah, Almire, Almyra, Almyrah, Elmera, Elmerah, Elmira, Elmirah, Elmyra, Elmyrah

Almita (Latin) kind.

Allmita, Almitah, Almyta, Almytah

Alodie (English) wealthy, prosperous, rich.

Alodea, Alodee, Alodey, Alodi, Alodia, Alodiah, Alody, Alodya, Alodyah, Alodye, Elodee, Elodey, Elodi, Elodie, Elody

Aloha (Hawaiian) greetings, friendship and farewell.

Alohah, Alohalanee, Alohalaney, Alohalani, Alohalania, Alohalaniah, Alohalanie, Alohalany, Alohalanya, Alohi, Alohilanee, Alohilaney, Alohilani, Alohilania, Alohilaniah, Alohilany, Alohilanya, Alohilanyah

Alohi (Hawaiian) shining, brilliant.

Alohilani (Hawaiian) bright sky.

Alona (Hebrew, Native American) oak tree.

Al, Ally, Alonah, Loni

Althea (Greek) healer, healthy, wholesome.

Altha, Altheah, Altheda, Althedah, Altheya, Althia, Althiah, Althya, Althyah, Elthea, Eltheya, Elthia

Aludra (Arabic, Greek) virgin.

Alodra, Alodrah, Aludrah

Alva (Latin) white, fair complexion.

Alvah, Alvana, Alvanna, Alvannah, Alvara

Alvera (Latin) truthful, honest.

Alverah, Alveria, Alveriah, Alveryah, Alvira, Alvirah, Alvyra, Alvyrah, Elvera, Elverah, Elvira, Elvirah, Elvyra, Elvyrah

Alvina (English) friend to all, noble friend.

Alveana, Alveanah, Alveane, Alveanea, Alveen, Alveena, Alveenah, Alveene, Alveenia, Alvena, Alvenah, Alvenea, Alvie, Alvinae, Alvinah, Alvincia, Alvine, Alvinea, Alvinesha, Alvinia, Alvinna, Alvinnah, Alvita, Alvona, Alvyna, Alvynah, Alvyne, Alwin, Alwina, Alwyn, Elveana, Elveanah, Elvena, Elvenah, Elvina, Elvinah, Elvine, Elvyna, Elvynah

Alysa (Greek) princess.

Alysia (Greek) captivating.

Alyssa/Alyssum (Greek) logical, rational, flower.

Ahlyssa, Ailisa, Ailisah, Alisa, Alisah, Alissa, Alissah, Allissa, Allissah, Allyssa, Allyssah, Alyesa,

Alyessa, Alyissa, Alysa, Alysah, Alyssah, Alysumm, Alysun, Ilisa, Ilisah, Ilissa, Ilissah, Illissa, Illissah, Illysah, Illyssa, Ilysa, Ilysah, Ilyssa, Lisa, Lisah, Lissa, Lissah, Lysa, Lysah, Lyssa, Lyssah

Alzena (Arabic) woman.

Alsena, Alsenah, Alsina, Alsinah, Alxena, Alxenah, Alxina, Alxinah, Alxyna, Alxynah, Alzenah, Alzina, Alzinah, Alzyna, Alzynah

Alzubra (Arabic) a star in the constellation Leo.

Am (Vietnamese) lunar, female.

Amm, Amme

Ama (African) born on a Saturday.

Amah

Amabel (Latin) lovable.

Amabela, Amabelah, Amabele, Amabell, Amabella, Amabellah, Amabelle, Ambele, Ambell, Ambella, Ambellah, Amebelle, Amibel, Amibela, Amibelah, Amibele, Amibell, Amibella, Amibellah, Amibelle, Amybel, Amybell, Amybella, Amybelle, Anabel, Anabell, Anabella, Annabelle, Mabel

Amada (Spanish) beloved.

Amadea, Amadeah, Amadee, Amadey, Amadi, Amadia, Amadiah, Amadie, Amadita, Amadite, Amady, Amadya, Amadyah, Amata

Amadea (Italian) who loves God.

Amadeah, Amadee, Amadey, Amadeya, Amadeyah, Amadi, Amadia, Amadiah, Amadie, Amady, Amadya, Amadyah

Amal (Arabic) hopes, hopeful, aspirations; (Hebrew) worker.

A'mal, Amala, Amalah, Amalla, Amallah

Amanda (Latin) worthy of love, loveable.

Amandah, Amande, Amandea, Amandee, Amandey, Amandi, Amandia, Amandiah, Amandie, Amandina, Amandinah, Amandine, Amandy, Amandya, Amandyah, Amaranth, Amarantha, Amaranthe, Amata, Manda, Mandah, Mandea, Mandee, Mandey, Mandi, Mandie, Mandy

Amani (Arabic) wishes, aspirations.

Aamani, Ahmani, Amanee, Amaney

Amara (Greek) eternally beautiful.

Amaira, Amar, Amarah, Amargo, Amari, Amaria, Amariah, Amarie, Amarta, Amartah, Amary, Amarya, Amaryah

Amaranta (Greek, Spanish) a flower that never fades.

Amaranth, Amarantha, Amaranthe

Amarina (Australian Aboriginal) rain.

Amarin, Amarinah, Amarine, Amaryn, Amarynah, Amaryne

Amaris (Hebrew) promised by God, promise of God.

Amariah, Amarisa, Amarisah, Amariss, Amarissa, Amarissah, Amartissa, Amarys, Amarysa, Amarysah, Amaryss, Amaryssa, Amaryssah, Maris

Amaryllis (Greek) refreshing stream, fresh, flower.

Amarilis, Amarillis, Amaryl, Amaryla, Amarylah, Amarylis, Amarylla, Amaryllah

Amata (Spanish) beloved, a form of Amy.

Amaui (Hawaiian) a thrush.

Amaya (Japanese) night rain, raining at night.

Amaia, Amaiah, Amayah

Amba (Indian) a mother goddess.

Ambar (Hindu) sky.

Amber (Arabic) jewel, honey-coloured.

Aamber, Ambar, Ambarlea, Ambarlee, Ambarlei, Ambarleigh, Ambarley, Ambarli, Ambarlie, Ambarlina, Ambarline, Ambarly, Amberlea, Amberlee, Amberlei, Amberleigh, Amberley, Amberli, Amberlia, Amberliah, Amberlie, Amberlina, Amberline, Amberly, Amberlyah, Ambur, Amburlea, Amburlee, Amberlei, Amburleigh, Amburley, Amburli, Amburlia, Amburliah, Amburlie, Amburlina, Amburline, Amburly, Amburlya

Ambika (Hindu) name for Sakti, goddess mother of the universe, goddess of power and destruction.

Ambrosia (Latin) an immortal.

Ambrosa, Ambrosah, Ambrosiah, Ambrosina, Ambrosine, Ambrosyn, Ambrosyna, Ambrosyne, Ambrozin, Ambrozina, Ambrozinah, Ambrozine, Ambrozyn, Ambrozyna, Ambrozyne

Amelia (Latin) works for the Lord; (Teutonic) industrious.

Amala, Amalah, Amalea, Amaleah, Amalee, Amaleigh, Amaleta, Amali, Amalia, Amalie, Amaline, Amalita, Amalitah, Amelie, Amelija, Amelina, Amelinda, Amelindah, Ameline, Amelita, Amelitah, Amelynda, Amelyndah, Ami, Amie, Amilia, Amiliah, Amilina, Amilinda, Amiline, Amilita, Amilitah, Ammilina, Ammileine, Amylaya, Amylia, Amyliah, Amylyah, Em, Emelin, Emelina, Emeline, Emelita,

*Emelitah, Emilia, Emily, Emmelina,
Emmeline, Emmilyn, Emmilyna,
Emmilyne, Melia, Milly*

Amethyst (Greek) purple
semi-precious stone. The amethyst
stone was thought to prevent
intoxication in ancient times.

*Amathist, Amathista, Amathiste,
Amathysta, Amathyste, Amethist,
Amethista, Amethiste, Amethistia,
Amethysta, Amethyste, Amethystia,
Amethystya, Amethystyah*

Amina (Arabic) trustworthy,
faithful, sure, believable, right,
reliable, dependable.

*Aamena, Aamina, Ameena,
Ameenah, Aminah, Aminda,
Amindah, Aminta, Amintah*

Amineh (Arabic) faithful.

Aminta (Greek) protector.

*Aminte, Amintee, Amintey, Aminti,
Amintie, Aminty, Aminyah, Amynta,
Amyntah, Amynti, Amyntie, Amynthy,
Minta, Mintah, Mynta, Myntee,
Myntey, Mynti, Myntie, Mynty*

Amira (Hebrew) speech, (Arabic)
princess.

*Ameera, Ameerah, Amyra,
Amyrah, Amirah*

Amissa (Hebrew) friend.

*Amisa, Amisah, Amise, Amisia,
Amisiah, Amissah, Amiza, Amizah,
Amysa, Amysah, Amysia, Amysiah,
Amysya, Amysyah, Amyza, Amyzah*

Amita (Hebrew) truth, truthful.

*Ameeta, Ameetah, Amitah,
Amitha, Amyta, Amytah*

Amitola (Native American) rainbow.

Amitolah

Amity (Latin) friendship, friendly.

*Amitee, Amitey, Amiti, Amitie, Amytee,
Amytey, Amyti, Amytie, Amyty*

Amma (Hindu) a mother goddess.

Amorette (Latin) beloved, loving.

*Amoreta, Amoretah, Amorete,
Amorett, Amoretta, Amorettah,
Amorit, Amorita, Amoritah, Amoritt,
Amoritta, Amoritte, Amoryt,
Amoryta, Amorytah, Amoryte,
Amorytt, Amorytta, Amoryttah,
Amorytte*

Amorina (Latin) love.

Amore, Amoreena

An (Chinese) peace, peaceful.

Ann

Ana (Hawaiian) graceful.

*Anah, Anci, Anezka, Ania, Aniah,
Annaka, Annalie, Anneka, Annika,
Anniki, Annikki, Annus, Annushka*

Anais (Hebrew) graceful; (Greek)
fruitful.

*Anaise, Anaïse, Anaiss, Anays,
Anayss*

Anala (Hindu) fine.

Analah

Analise/Annalise (English,
German) combination of Anna
and Lisa.

*Analice, Analiese, Analis, Analisa,
Analissa, Anetta, Annaliesa,
Annaliese, Annalisa, Annalissa,
Annalisse, Annalyca, Annalyce,
Annalys, Annalysa, Annalyse,
Anneliese, Anneliesel, Annelisa,
Annelise, Annelys, Annelysa, Annelyse*

Anan (Arabic, Hebrew) clouds, a
unisex name.

Ananda (Hindu) bliss.

Anandah

Anapul (Scottish) lovable.

Anastasia (Greek) resurrection,
springtime birth.

Anastacia, Anastaciah, Anastacya, Anastacyah, Anastas, Anastase, Anastasee, Anastasie, Anastassia, Anastatia, Anastazia, Anastazya, Anastiacia, Anastiaciah, Anastzia, Anastziah, Annestas, Annestasia, Annestassia, Anstace, Ansteece, Ansteese, Anstes, Anstey, Anstice, Anstis, Nastasia, Natassia, Natassja, Nastasya, Nastenka, Nastia, Nastya, Nastyenka, Natasha, Naztasia, Naztasiah, Nitasse, Stacee, Stacey, Staci, Stacie, Stassee, Stassey, Stassi, Stassie, Stassy, Tas, Tasa, Tasi, Tasia, Tasie, Tasy

Anatola (Greek) woman of the east, sunrise.
Anatolah, Anatolia, Anatoliah, Anatolya, Anatolyah, Annatola, Annatolah, Annatolia, Annatoliah, Annatolya, Annatolyah

Andra (English) breath of fresh air.
Andrah

Andrea (Latin) womanly; (Greek) strong, courageous, ideal woman.
Aindrea, Andera, Anderea, Andie, Andra, Andraia, Andraya, Andre, Andréa, Andreah, Andreaka, Adreana, Andrée, Andreea, Andreja, Andreka, Andrel, Andrell, Andrelle, Andreo, Andressa, Andrette, Andria, Andrie, Andriea, Andrieka, Andrienne, Andrietta, Adrina, Andris, Androulla, Andrya, Andryah, Andy, Dreena, Drena, Drina, Ondrea, Rena, Rina

Andreana (Greek) man's woman.
Andreanah, Andreanna, Andreannah, Andreeana, Andreeanah, Andrena, Andreyana, Andreyonna, Andriana, Andrianna

Andria (Greek) strong, brave, courageous, feminine form of Andrew.
Aindrea, Anderea, Andra, Andrah, Andreana, Andreanah,

Andreane, Andreann, Andreanna, Andreannah, Andreanne, Andree, Andreean, Andreeana, Andreeanah, Andreeane, Andrel, Andrela, Andrelah, Andrell, Andrella, Andrellah, Andrelle, Andrena, Andrenah, Andretta, Andrette, Andriah, Andrian, Andriana, Andriann, Andrianna, Andriannah, Andrianne, Andrina, Adrinah, Andrinna, Andrinnah, Andrya, Andryah, Andryan, Andryana, Andryanah, Andryane, Andryann, Andryanna, Andryannah, Andryanne

Andromeda (Greek) ruler of men, rescued.

Aneko (Japanese) oldest sister.

Anemone (Greek) windflower.
Annemone

Angel (Greek, Latin) heavenly messenger, a unisex name.
Angell, Anjel

Angela (Greek) heavenly messenger of God.
Agnola, Ancela, Angel, Angele, Angelia, Angelica, Angelika, Angelin, Angelina, Angelinah, Angeline, Angelita, Angeliqua, Angeliquah, Angelique, Angella, Angellah, Angelle, Angelo, Angi, Angiola, Aniela, Anja, Anjah, Anjal, Anjala, Anjalah, Anjel, Anjela, Anjelah, Anjella, Anjellah, Anjelle, Engel, Engela, Engelah, Engelchen, Engelica, Engelika, Engell, Engella, Engellah, Engelle, Engelyca, Engelycka, Engelyka, Engeliqua, Engeliquah, Engelique, Enjel, Enjela, Enjelah, Enjele, Enjell, Enjella, Enjellah, Enjelle, Enjelliqua, Enjelliquah, Enjellique, Enjellyca, Enjellycah, Enjellycka, Enjellyka, Enjellyqua, Enjellyquah, Enjellyque

Angelica (Latin) angelic, messenger.
Angel, Angie

Angelina (Italian, Russian) little angel, sent from heaven.

Angeni (Native American) spirit, angel.

Ange, Angee, Angeenee, Angeeni, Angeenie, Angeeny, Angenia, Angey, Anjee, Anjeenee, Anjeeney, Anjeeni, Anjeenia, Anjeeniah, Anjeenie, Anjeeny, Anjeenya, Anjeenyah, Anjena, Anjenah, Anjenee, Anjeney, Anjeni, Anjenie, Anjeny

Angharad (Welsh) much loved.

Anchoret, Anchorett, Anchoretta, Anchorette, Ancret, Ancreta, Ancrett, Ancretta, Ankerita, Ingaret, Ingarett, Ingaretta, Ingarette

Anh (Vietnamese) intelligent, bright.

Ani (Hawaiian) beautiful.

Aany, Aanye, Anee, Aney, Aneya, Aneyah, Ania, Aniah, Anie, Any, Anya, Anyah

Anika (Scandinavian, Hebrew) graceful, gracious, a form of Ann.

Aanika, Anaka, Aneeky, Aneka, Anekah, Anica, Anicah, Anicka, Anikah, Anikka, Anikki, Aniko, Aniqua, Aniquah, Annaka, Annakka, Anniki, Annikki, Annikko, Anyca, Anycah, Anyka, Anykah, Anyqua, Anyquah

Anila (Hindu) wind god.

Anilah, Anilla, Anillah, Anyla, Anylah, Anylla, Anyllah

Anisa (Arabic) friendly.

Anisah, Annisa, Annisah, Annissa, Annissah, Annysa, Annysah, Anysa, Anysah, Anyssa, Anyssah

Anise (English) flower or spice, from the name of the herb.

Agnes, Annisa

Anita (Spanish) graceful and little, a form of Ann; (Hebrew) graceful, favoured.

Aneeta, Aneetah, Aneethah, Anetha, Anitha, Anithah, Anitia, Anitta, Anittah, Anitte, Annita, Annitah, Annite, Annitt, Annitta, Annittah, Annitte, Annyta, Annytah, Annytta, Annyttah, Annytte, Anyta, Anytah, Nita

Ann (Hebrew) graceful.

An, Ana, Anah, Anais, Anaisa, Anca, Anci, Ancika, Andula, Andulka, Ane, Anee, Aneta, Anetta, Anette, Aney, Anezka, Ani, Ania, Aniah, Anica, Anicka, Anita, Anitra, Anje, Anjuska, Anka, Anna, Annchen, Anne, Anneke, Anneli, Annette, Anni, Annie, Anny, Anouk, Anya, Hanna, Hannah, Hanne, Nan, Nana, Nancy, Nani, Nanna, Nina, Ninon, Nita, Noula

Anna (German) gracious.

Ahnna, Ana, Anah, Anica, Aniela, Annice, Annina, Annora, Anona, Anya, Anyu, Aska

Annabelle (Scottish) lovable; (Hawaiian) graceful or beautiful; (French) beautiful woman.

Anabel, Anabela, Anabele, Anabell, Anabelle, Annabell, Anna-Bell, Annabella, Annahbell, Annahbelle, Annebell, Annebelle, Annibell, Annibelle, Annybell, Annybelle

Anna Maria (Italian) combination of Anne and Mary.

Annapurna (Indian) shining one.

Anneke (Dutch, Scandanavian) little Ann, a form of Ann.

Annetta/Annette (Italian, French) little graceful one, a form of Anne.

Anet, Aneta, Anetah, Anete, Anetra, Anetrah, Anett, Anetta,

Anne, Annet, Anneta, Annettah, Annie, Nancy

Annice (English, Greek) pure, chaste, a form of Agnes.

Annina (Greek, Hebrew) graceful and sweet; (Italian) little graceful one.
Anina, Aninah, Annie, Anninah, Annyna, Annynah, Anyna, Anynah,

Annona (Roman) goddess of crops.
Annonah, Annonia, Annoniah, Annonya, Annonyah, Anona, Anonah, Anonia, Anoniah, Anonya, Anonyah

Annora (Latin) honour; (Greek) shining light.
Annorah, Annore, Annoria, Annoriah, Annorya, Annoryah, Anora, Anorah, Anoria, Anoriah, Anorya, Anoryah

Annunciata (Italian) honorific name, derived from Annunciation to Mary; (Latin) bearer of news.
Anunciata

Anona (English) pineapple; (Latin) annual crops.
Annona, Annonah, Annonia, Annoniah, Annonya, Annonyah Anonah, Anonia, Anoniah, Anonya, Anonyah

Anouk (Dutch) gracious, a form of Anna.

Anselma (Norse) protected by God; (German) divine protector.
Anselmah, Anzelma, Anzelmah, Selma, Selmah, Xelma, Xelmah, Zelma, Zelmah

Anthea (Greek) like a flower, flowery.
Antha, Anthe, Antheah, Anthia, Anthiah, Anthya, Anthyah, Thia

Antionetta/Antionette (French, Italian) priceless, praiseworthy, a form of Antonia.

Antje (Dutch, German) grace.

Antonia (Greek) precious and priceless, flourishing; (Latin) priceless, praiseworthy, feminine form of Anthony.
Antonee, Antoney, Antonett, Antonetta, Antonette, Antoni, Antonia, Antoniah, Antonias, Antonica, Antonicah, Antonie, Antonietta, Antoninas, Antonnia, Antonniah, Antonya, Antonyah, Toinetta, Toinette, Toynetta, Toynette, Tuanetta, Tueanette, Antoineta, Antoinette, Antointetta, Anna, Ant, Nina, Netta, Netti, Toinetta, Toinette, Toni, Tonia, Toney, Tony

Anuhea (Hawaiian) cool, soft, fragrance.

Anusha (Hindu) beautiful morning, a star.

Anwen (Welsh) very beautiful.

Anya (Russian) graceful.
Annya, Annyah, Anyah

Anzu (Japanese) apricot.

Aoife (Celtic) radiant, beauty.

Aolani (Hawaiian) heavenly cloud.
Aolanee, Aolaney, Aolania, Aolaniah, Aolanie, Aolany, Aolanya, Aolanyah

Aphra (Arabic) dust; (Hebrew) young doe.
Afra, Afrah, Aphrah, Ayfara, Ayfarah

Aphrodite (Greek) goddess of love and beauty.
Afrodita, Afrodite, Aphrodita, Aphroditah, Aphrodyta, Aphrodytah, Aphrodyte

Aponi (Native American) butterfly.
Aponee, Aponey, Aponie, Apony

Apria (Latin) from the apricot.

April (Latin) born in the month of April, open to the sun.
Aprel, Aprela, Aprelah, Aprella, Aprelle, Aprila, Aprilah, Aprilett, Apriletta, Aprilette, Aprill, Aprilla, Aprillah, Aprille, Apryl, Apryla, Aprylah, Apryll, Aprylla, Aprylle, Avril, Avrilett, Avriletta, Avrilette, Avryl, Avryla, Avrylah, Avryle, Avryletta, Avryll, Avrylla, Avryllah, Avrylle, Avryllettah, Avryllette

Aquene (Native American) peace, peaceful.
Aqueen, Aqueena, Aqueene

Ara (Arabic) opinions, opinionated, rainmaker.
Ahraya, Aira, Arae, Arah

Arabella (Scottish) yielding to prayer; (Teutonic) beautiful eagle; (Latin) beautiful altar.
Arabe, Arabel, Arabela, Arabelah, Arabele, Arabell, Arabellah, Arabelle, Araminta, Aramintah, Bel, Bella, Belle

Araru (Australian Aboriginal) mythical mother of Adjamatana tribe.

Ardella (Latin) warm, enthusiastic.
Ardeen, Ardeena, Ardeene, Ardel, Ardela, Ardelah, Ardele, Ardelia, Ardeliah, Ardelis, Ardelisa, Ardelise, Ardell, Ardellah, Ardelle, Ardena, Ardenah, Ardene, Ardin, Ardina, Ardinah, Ardine, Ardis, Ardra, Adrah

Arden (Latin) fiery; (English) dwelling place, ardent and sincere, valley of the eagles, a unisex name.
Ardan, Ardana, Ardane, Ardean, Adeana, Ardeane, Ardeen, Ardeena, Ardeenah, Ardeene, Ardena, Ardenah, Ardene, Ardenia, Ardin, Ardina, Ardinah, Ardine, Ardun, Ardyn, Ardyna, Ardynah, Ardyne

Ardith (Hebrew) flowering field, field of flowers.
Ardath, Ardis, Ardisa, Ardise, Ardiss, Ardissa, Ardisse, Ardyce, Ardys, Ardysa, Ardyse, Ardyth, Ardytha, Ardythe, Aridatha, Arydatha

Arella (Hebrew) angel, messenger.
Arela, Arelah, Arellah, Arelle, Ariel, Ariela, Arielah, Ariella, Ariellah, Arielle, Arien, Ariena, Arienah, Ariene, Arienna, Arienne, Aryel, Aryela, Aryelah, Aryell, Aryella, Aryellah, Aryelle, Orelia, Orelie, Orella, Orellah, Orelle, Orelliah, Orellya, Orellyah

Areta/Aretha (Greek) the finest, virtue, the best.
Areata, Areatah, Areatha, Areathah, Areathia, Areathiah, Areeta, Areetah, Areetha, Areethah, Areethia, Areethiah, Aretah, Arethia, Arethiah, Arethina, Aretta, Arettah, Arette, Arita, Aritha, Arithah, Arytha, Arythah, Arythia, Arythiah, Arythya, Arythyah, Retha, Rethah

Aria (Italian) melody.
Ari, Ariah, Ariann, Arianna, Ariannah, Arianne, Arya, Aryah, Aryan, Aryana, Aryanah, Aryane, Aryann, Aryanna, Aryannah, Aryanne

Ariadne (Greek) holy one.
Adriadna, Ariadnah, Ariana, Arianah, Ariane, Arianna, Ariannah, Arianne, Aryadna, Aryana, Aryanah, Aryane, Aryann, Aryanna, Aryannah, Aryanne

Ariana (Greek, Latin) holy; (Welsh) like silver.
Aeriana, Aerianna, Aerionna,

Ahreanna, Ahriana, Ahrianna, Airiana, Ariadna, Ariadnah, Ariadne, Arianah, Arianna, Ariannah, Ariane, Arianne, Arieana, Arihana, Arihanah, Arihanna, Arihannah, Ariona, Arionna, Aryan, Aryana, Aryanah, Aryane, Aryann, Aryanna, Aryannah, Aryanne, Aryonna

Ariel (Hebrew) lioness of God.
Aerial, Aeriale, Aeriel, Aeriela, Aerielah, Aeriele, Aeriell, Aeriella, Aeriellah, Aerielle, Aeril, Aerile, Aeryal, Aeryall, Aeryalla, Aeryallah, Ari, Ariela, Arielah, Ariell, Ariella, Ariellah, Arielle, Aryel, Aryela, Aryelah, Aryele, Aryell, Aryella, Aryellah, Aryelle

Arietta (Italian) melody.
Ariet, Arieta, Arietah, Ariete, Ariett, Ariettah, Ariette, Aryet, Aryeta, Aryetah, Aryete, Aryett, Aryetta, Aryettah, Aryette

Arica (Scandinavian) ruler, a form of Erica.
Aerica, Aericka, Aeryka, Aricah, Aricca, Ariccah, Aricka, Arickah, Arika, Arikah, Arike, Arikka, Arikkah, Ariqua, Aryca, Arycah, Arycca, Aryccah, Arycka, Aryckah, Aryka, Arykah, Arykka, Arykkah, Aryqua

Arika (Australian Aboriginal) waterlily.
Arica, Aricah, Aricka, Arickah, Arikah, Ariqua, Ariquah, Aryca, Arycah, Arycka, Aryckah, Aryka, Arykah, Aryqua, Aryquah

Arin (Hebrew) enlightened.
Arien, Aaren, Arein, Aieron, Arinn, Aryn

Arista (Greek) best, excellent.
Aris, Aristana, Aristen

Arline/Arlene (Celtic) pledge.
Airlen, Arlana, Arlanah, Arlea, Arleah, Arlee, Arleen, Arleena,

Arleene, Arleigh, Arlein, Arleina, Arleine, Arlen, Arlena, Arlenah, Arlenis, Arleta, Arletah, Arlete, Arletta, Arlettah, Arlette, Arleyna, Arleynah, Arleyne, Arlien, Arliena, Arlienah, Arliene, Arlin, Arlina, Arlinah, Arlind, Arlinda, Arlindah, Arlis, Arluena, Arluenah, Arluene, Arlyn, Arlynna, Arlynne

Armada (Spanish) the armed one.

Armina (Latin) noble warrior, feminine form of Herman.
Armeda, Armedah, Armedia, Armediah, Armida, Armidah, Armidia, Armidiah, Armin, Arminah, Arminda, Armindah, Armine, Arminee, Arminel, Arminella, Arminelle, Arminey, Armini, Arminie, Armyn, Armyna, Armynah, Armyne, Ermina, Erminah, Ermine, Ermyn, Ermyna, Ermynah, Ermyne

Arnelle (German) strong, like an eagle.
Arnel, Arnela, Arnelah, Arnele, Arnell, Arnella, Arnellah

Aroha (Maori) love.

Artemis (Greek) the goddess of the hunt and the moon.
Artema, Artemah, Artemisa, Artemise, Artemisia, Artemys, Artemysia, Artemysya

Aruna (Hindu) dawn.
Arunah

Arwen (Welsh) muse.

Asa (Japanese) born in the morning; (Hebrew) doctor, healer.
Asah

Asha (Persian) truth.
Ashah

Ashanti (African) life, from a tribe in Africa.
Achante, Achanti, Asante,

Ashaintae, Ashanta, Ashantae, Ashantah, Ashantee, Ashantey, Ashantia, Ashantie, Ashaunta, Ashauntee, Ashaunti, Ashauntia, Ashauntiah, Ashaunty, Ashauntya, Ashuntae, Ashunti, Ashuntie

Ashia (Arabic) life.
Asha, Ashah, Ayshia, Ayshiah, Ayshya, Ayshyah

Ashira (Hebrew) rich, wealthy.
Ashirah, Ashyra, Ashyrah

Ashleigh/Ashley (English) from the meadow, from the grove of ash trees, a unisex name.
Ashia, Ashiah, Ashla, Ashlana, Ashlanah, Ashlane, Ashlaney, Ashlea, Ashleah, Ashlee, Ashlei, Ashlen, Ashlena, Ashlenah, Ashlene, Ashli, Ashlia, Ashliah, Ashlie, Ashlin, Ashlina, Ashlinah, Ashline, Ashly, Ashlya, Ashlyn

Ashlyn (Irish) dream, vision, a form of Aislinn.

Asia (Greek) resurrection, eastern sunrise, place name.
Ahsia, Aisia, Aisian, Asian, Asianae, Ayzia, Esia, Esiah, Esya, Esyah

Asiya (Arabic) one who tends to the weak, one who heals.
Asiyah, Assiya, Assiyah

Asma (Arabic) excellent, precious.
Asmah

Aspasia (Greek) welcomed.
Aspasiah, Aspasya, Aspasyah

Aspen (English) flower from Brittany, aspen tree, a unisex name.
Aspin, Aspina, Aspine, Aspyn, Aspyna, Aspyne

Assunta (Italian) honorific name derived from Assumption of Mary.

Astra (Latin) star; (Greek) like a star.
Astrah, Astrea, Astreah, Astree, Astrey, Astria, Astriah, Astrya, Astryah

Astrid (Greek, Norse) divine strength.
Astra, Astrad, Astread, Astreada, Astreed, Astreeda, Astrod, Astrud, Astryd

Atalanta (Greek) unswaying, mighty huntress.
Atalantah, Atalaya, Atlanta, Atlee

Atara (Hebrew) crown.
Atarah, Ataree, Ataria, Atariah, Atarya, Ataryah, Atearea, Atearah, Atera, Aterah, Ateret

Athalia (Hebrew) the Lord is mighty, God is praised.
Atali, Atalie, Athalea, Athaleah, Athalee, Athalei, Athaleigh, Athaley, Athali, Athaliah, Athalie, Athaly, Athalya, Athalyah

Athela (English, Teutonic) noble.
Athelah

Athena (Greek) goddess of wisdom and war.
Atheana, Atheanah, Athenah, Athenais, Athene, Atherlea, Atherleah, Atherlee, Atherlei, Atherleigh, Atherley, Atherli, Atherlia, Atherliah, Atherlie, Atherly, Atherlya, Atherlyah

Atifa (Arabic, Islamic) affection.
Atifah, Atyfa, Atyfah

Atira (Hebrew) prayer.
Atirah, Atyra, Atyrah

Atiya (Arabic) gift.
Atiyah

Aubrey (German) noble, bright; (English, French) elf ruler, a unisex name.

Aubary, Aubery, Aubray, Aubrea, Aubreah, Aubrette, Aubrya, Aubryah, Aubury

Aubrianne (German, Hebrew) graceful, wise leader, one with auburn hair.

Aubrian, Aubriana, Aubrianah, Aubriane, Aubriann, Aubrianna, Aubriannah, Aubryan, Aubryana, Aubryanah, Aubryane, Aubryann, Aubryanna, Aubryannah, Aubryanne

Auburn (Latin) reddish brown.

Abern, Aberne, Abirn, Abirne, Aburn, Aburne, Abyrn, Abyrne, Aubern, Auberne, Aubin, Aubirn, Aubirne, Aubun, Auburne, Aubyrn, Aubyrne

Audrey (English) strong and noble, regal, strength, a character in Shakespeare's *As You Like It*.

Aude, Audey, Audi, Audie, Audra, Audrah, Audray, Audre, Audrea, Audree, Audreen, Audrei, Audri, Audria, Audriah, Audrianne, Audrie, Audrienne, Audrin, Audriya, Audry, Audrya, Audryah, Audrye

Augusta (Latin) sacred, venerable, majestic, feminine form of Augustus.

Agostina, Agostine, Agostinha, Agostyna, Agostyne, Agusta, August, Augustah, Auguste, Augusteen, Augusteena, Augusteene, Augustia, Augustina, Augustinah, Augustine, Augustus, Augustyna, Augustyne, Austin, Austina, Awsta

Aukai (Hawaiian) seafarer.

Aulani (Hawaiian) royal messenger.

Aulanee, Aulaney, Aulania, Aulaniah, Aulanie, Aulany, Aulanya, Aulanyah

Aulii (Hawaiian) delicious.

Aura (Greek) soft breeze.

Aurah, Aurea, Aureah, Auri, Auria, Auriah, Aurya, Auryah

Aurelia (Latin) golden.

Auralea, Auraleah, Auralia, Aurea, Aureah, Aureal, Aurel, Aurela, Aurelah, Aurele, Aurelea, Aureliana, Aurella, Aurellah, Auria, Auriah, Aurie, Aurilia, Auriola, Auriolah, Auriolla, Auriollah, Aurita

Aurora (Latin) goddess of the dawn, golden dawn.

Aurorah, Aurore, Aurure, Ora, Orah

Autumn (Latin) fall season.

Autom, Autum

Ava (French) song of joy; (Latin) bird.

Avada, Avae, Avah, Ave, Aveen, Aveh

Avalon (Latin) little island.

Avalona, Avalonah, Avaloni, Avalonia, Avaloniah, Avalonie, Avalony, Avalonya, Avalonyah

Avasa (Hindu) independent.

Avelina/Aveline (Teutonic) hazelnut.

Avalean, Avaleana, Avaleanah, Avaleane, Avaleen, Avaleenah, Avaleene, Avalina, Avaline, Avalyn, Avalyna, Avalynah, Avalyne, Avelanah, Avelean, Aveleana, Aveleane, Aveleen, Aveleena, Aveleenah, Aveleene, Avelin, Avelyn, Avelyna, Avelynah, Avelyne

Averil (English) slayer of the boar, boar-like, a unisex name.

Avaril, Avarila, Avarile, Avarilla, Avarille, Averila, Averilah, Averill, Averilla, Averille, Avery, Averyl, Averyla, Averyle, Averyll, Averylla, Averylle, Avril, Avrile, Avrille

Avis (Teutonic) refuge in war.
Avais, Aveis, Aves, Avi, Avia, Aviance, Avice, Avicia, Avise, Avyce, Avys, Avyse

Aviva (Hebrew) springtime.
Aviv, Avivah, Avivi, Avivice, Avivie, Avivit, Avni, Avnit, Avri, Avrit, Avy, Avyva, Avyvah

Avoca (Gaelic) sweet vale.
Avocah, Avocka, Avockah, Avoka, Avokah

Avril (English) born in April; (French) born in the month of April, open to the sun, a form of April.
Avaril, Avarila, Avarile, Avarill, Avarilla, Avarille, Averil, Averila, Averilah, Averill, Averilla, Averille, Averyl, Averyla, Averyle, Averyll, Averylla, Averylle, Avra, Avri, Avriletta, Avrilette, Avrilia, Avrill, Avrille, Avrillett, Avrilletta, Avrillette, Avrillia, Avryl, Avryla, Avrylah, Avryle, Avryll, Avrylla, Avryllah, Avrylle, Avryllett, Avrylletta, Avryllette, Avy

Aya (Hebrew) colourful bird, fly swiftly.
Aia, Aiah, Aiya, Aiyah, Ayaah

Ayanna (African) beautiful flower.
Ahyana, Ahyanna, Ayana, Ayania, Ayaniah, Ayannah, Ayannica, Ayna

Ayasha (African) life.
Aasha, Aiasha, Ayesha

Ayiana (Native American) eternal bloom.

Ayita (Native American) worker, first in the dance, first to dance.
Aita, Aitah, Ayitah

Ayla (Hebrew) oak tree.
Aylah, Aylana, Aylanah, Aylanna, Aylannah, Aylea, Aylee, Ayleena, Aylena, Aylene

Azalea (Greek) dry; (English) flower.
Azaleah, Azalee, Azalei, Azaleigh, Azaley, Azali, Azalia, Azaliah, Azalie, Azaly, Azalya, Azalyah

Azaria (Hebrew) God is my help.
Azariah, Azarya, Azaryah

Aziza (Arabic) esteemed, precious, cherished, beloved
Azeeza, Azizah

Azura (Latin, Persian) blue semiprecious stone.
Azora, Azorah, Azurah, Azure, Azurina, Azurine, Azuryn, Azuryna, Azurynah, Azuryne, Azzura

B

Baako (African) first born, a unisex name.

Baba (African) born on Thursday.
Aba, Abah, Babah

Babe (Latin) stranger, foreigner, a form of Barbara.
Babby, Bebe

Babette (French) stranger, foreigner, a form of Barbara.
Babet, Babeta, Babetah, Babett, Babetta, Babettah, Babita, Babitah, Babitta, Babittah, Babitte, Barbetta, Barbette, Bette, Betty

Baby (American) a baby.
Babby, Babe, Bebe

Badr (Arabic) full moon, a unisex name.

Badu (African) tenth born.

Bahija (Arabic) happy.

Bahiya (Arabic) beautiful, radiant.
Bahiyya

Bailey (English, Old French) bailiff, one who keeps guard, a unisex name.
Bailee, Baileigh, Bailie, Baily, Baylee, Bayley, Baylie

Bairbre (Irish) stranger, a form of Barbara.

Baka (Hindu) crane.
Bakah

Bakana (Australian Aboriginal) lookout, guardian.
Bakanah, Bakanna, Bakannah

Bakula (Hindu) flower, a mythological plant.
Bakulah

Bambi (Italian) child; (Japanese) small deer.
Bambea, Bambee, Bambia, Bambiah, Bambie, Bamby

Bambra (Australian Aboriginal) mushroom.
Bambrah

Banan (Arabic) delicate finger tips.

Baptista (Greek, Latin) baptised.
Baptiste, Batista, Battista

Bara (Australian Aboriginal) dawn, sunrise; (Hebrew) chosen.
Barah, Barra, Barrah

Baraka (Arabic) white one.

Barbara (Greek, Latin) stranger, foreigner, exotic, mysterious.
Babet, Babett, Babetta, Babette, Babita, Babitta, Babitte, Babrishcha, Babs, Barba, Barbarina, Barbary, Barbe, Barbea, Barbee, Barbel, Barbet, Barbett, Barbetta, Barbette, Barbey, Barbi, Barbica, Barbie, Barbita, Barbola, Barbora, Barbra, Barbraa, Barbro, Barbule, Barbutte, Barica, Barka, Varvara, Vavina, Vavinah, Vavyna, Vavynah, Vavyne

Barika (African) bloom, be successful.

Barran (Irish) little hill top.
Baran, Barana, Baranah, Barean, Bareana, Bareane, Bareen, Bareena, Bareenah, Bareene,

Bareyn, Bareyna, Bareynah,
Bareyne, Barin, Barina, Barinah,
Barine, Barreen, Barreena,
Barreenah, Barreene, Barrin,
Barrina, Barrinah, Barrine

Basia (Hebrew) daughter of God.

Bashiah, Bashya, Bashyah, Basiah,
Basya, Basyah, Bathia, Batia, Batya,
Bithia, Bitya

Basillia (Greek, Latin) like a queen,
royal.

Basila, Basilah, Basile, Basilla,
Basillah, Basilie, Basyla, Basylah,
Basyle, Basyll, Basylla, Basyllah,
Basylle, Bazila, Bazilah, Bazile, Bazill,
Bazilla, Bazillah, Bazille

Basima (Arabic) smiling.

Baseema, Baseemah, Basimah,
Basyma, Basymah

Bathsheba (Hebrew) daughter of
an oath, promise.

Bathsheva, Bathshevah, Bathshua,
Batsheva, Batshevah, Bethsabee,
Bethsheba, Sheba, Shebah

Batini (African) inner thoughts.

Batul (Arabic) palm tree shoot

Batool, Batula, Batulah

Beatrice (Latin) bringer of joy.

Bea, Beatrica, Béatrice, Beatricia,
Beatriks, Beatris, Beatrisa, Beatrise,
Beatriss, Beatrissa, Beatrix, Beatriz,
Beatryx, Beatryz, Beattie, Bee, Bei,
Beitris, Bey, Trice, Trixie

Beca (Hebrew) bound, faithful,
one who is emotionally tied for life,
a short form of Rebecca.

Becah, Becca, Beccah, Becka,
Beckah, Beka, Bekah, Bekka, Bekkah

Becky (Hebrew) bound, faithful,
one who is emotionally tied for life,
a short form of Rebecca.

Beckey, Becki, Beckie, Beki, Bekie,
Beky

Beda (Anglo-Saxon) warrior
maiden.

Bedah

Bedelia (French) possesses
strength; (Irish) strength, a form of
Bridget.

Bedeelia, Bedeliah, Bedelya,
Bedelyah, Biddy, Bidelia

Bedriska (Bohemian) ruler of
peace, feminine form of Frederick.

Bedriskah, Bedryska, Bedryskah

Bel (Hindu) sacred wood of apple
trees; (French) beautiful; a short
form of names starting with 'Bel',
e.g. Belinda, Belle.

Bell, Bella, Belle

Bela (Czech) she of porcelain
skin, white and bright; (Hungarian)
bright.

Bel, Belah, Belau, Belia, Beliah, Bell,
Bella, Bellah, Belle

Belicia (Spanish) dedicated to
God.

Beli, Belica, Beliciah, Belicya,
Belicyah, Belysia, Belysiah

Belinda (Spanish) beautiful
woman, pretty, bringer of wisdom;
(Teutonic) bringer of wisdom.

Balina, Balinah, Balind, Balinda,
Balindah, Balinde, Baline, Ballind,
Ballinda, Ballindah, Ballinde,
Belina, Belinah, Belindah, Belinde,
Bellind, Bellinda, Bellindah, Bellynd,
Bellynda, Bellynde, Belva, Belynda,
Beneta, Benita, Benyta, Benytah,
Benyte, Linda, Lindy

Belita (Spanish) the beautiful one.

Bella/Belle (French, Latin, Italian)
beautiful, a short form of Isabella,
Annabelle.

Bela, Belah, Belau, Belia, Beliah,

Belita, Belitah, Belite, Bellau, Belva,
Belvia, Belviah, Belvya, Belvyah

Belladonna (Italian) beautiful
woman.

Bellanca (Latin) beautiful and fair-
haired.

Belanca, Belancah, Belancka,
Belanckah, Belanka, Belankah,
Bellancah, Bellancka, Bellanckah,
Bellanka, Bellankah, Byanca,
Byancah, Byancka, Byanckah,
Byanka, Byankah

Belphoebe (Greek, Latin)
beautiful and bright.

Belaphoebe, Belphoebea,
Belphoebee, Belaphoeve,
Belphoevea

Beltana (Australian Aboriginal)
running water.

Belltan, Belltana, Belltanah,
Belltane, Beltan, Beltane, Beltania,
Beltanja, Beltanya

Belva (Latin) beautiful view.

Belvah, Belvia, Belviah, Belvya,
Belvyah

Bena (Native American)
pheasant.

Benah, Benea, Beneta, Benna,
Bennah

Benedicta (Latin) blessed.

Bendite, Benea, Benedetta,
Benedettah, Benedictina,
Benedikta, Bengta, Benicia, Benita,
Benna, Benni, Bennicia, Benoîte,
Betta, Bette, Bettina, Binney

Benita (Spanish) blessed, a form of
Benedicta.

Beneta, Benetta, Benite, Benitta,
Bennita, Benyta, Benytah, Benyte,
Neeta, Nita

Benquasha (Native American)
daughter of Ben.

Berdine (German) glorious, light.

Berdina, Berdinah, Berdyn,
Berdyna, Berdynah, Berdyne

Berenice (Greek) bringer of
victory, strong as a bear.

Bernece, Berneece, Berneese,
Bernese, Berneta, Bernetah,
Bernete, Bernetta, Bernettah,
Bernette, Bernica, Bernicah,
Bernice, Bernyc, Bernyce, Bernyse,
Berrice, Berry

Bernadette (French) strong and
brave, little bear.

Bernadeen, Bernadeena,
Bernadeenah, Bernadeene,
Bernaden, Bernadena,
Bernadenah, Bernadene,
Bernadet, Bernadeta, Bernadetah,
Bernadete, Bernadett, Bernadetta,
Bernadettah, Bernadine,
Bernadina, Bernadinah, Bernadine,
Bernadit, Bernadita, Bernadyta,
Bernadytah, Bernadyte, Bernadyn,
Bernadyna, Bernadynah,
Bernadyne, Bernit, Bernita,
Bernitah, Bernite, Bernyt, Bernyta,
Bernytah, Berynyte

Bernardine (German) brave as a
bear.

Bernadene, Bernadetta,
Bernadette, Bernadin, Bernadina,
Bernardina, Bernardine, Berni

Bernia (Latin) warrior.

Berniah, Bernya, Bernyah

Bernice (Greek) bringer of victory,
strong and brave, like a bear,
feminine form of Bernard.

Berenice, Bernece, Berneece,
Berneese, Bernese, Berneta,
Bernetah, Bernetta, Bernettah,
Bernette, Bernica, Bernicah,
Bernicka, Bernickah, Bernika,
Bernikah, Bernyc, Bernyce, Bernyse,
Vernice, Vernise, Veronica, Veronik,
Veronika, Veronique

Berry (English) fruit or berry, also a form of Berenice and Bernadette; (Australian Aboriginal) white box tree.

Beree, Berey, Beri, Berie, Berree, Berrey, Berri, Berrie, Bery

Bertha (German) bright, shining, a form of Alberta, feminine form of Albert.

Berta, Berte, Berth, Berthah, Berthe, Berthel, Bertilla, Bertille, Bertina, Bertle, Bertolda, Birtha, Birthe, Byrth, Byrtha, Byrthah, Holda, Holla, Huldr

Berthilda (Anglo-Saxon) bright, shining, illustrious, gleaming.

Berthildah, Berthilde, Berthylda, Berthyldah, Berthylde, Bertilda, Bertildah, Bertilde, Bertylda, Bertyldah, Bertylde

Bertina (English) bright, shining.

Bertine

Beryl (Greek) dazzling jewel, sea-green jewel.

Beral, Beril, Berila, Berile, Berill, Berille, Beryle, Berylee, Berylla, Rylla

Bessie (Hebrew) holy and sacred to God, a form of Elizabeth.

Besey, Besi, Besie, Bess, Bessee, Bessey, Bessi, Bessy, Besy

Beth (Hebrew, Aramaic) from the house of God, holy and sacred to God, a form of Elizabeth, a form of names starting with or containing 'Beth'.

Bethal, Bethany, Bethel, Bethil, Bethol, Bethyl

Bethany (Aramaic) house of poverty, house of figs.

Bethan, Bethana, Bethanah, Bathane, Bethanee, Bethaney, Bethani, Bethania, Bethaniah, Bethanie, Bethann, Bethanna,

Bethannah, Bethanny, Bethena, Bethenee, Betheney, Bethina, Bethinah, Bethine, Bethyn, Bethyna, Bethynah, Bethyne

Bethel (Hebrew) from the house of God.

Bethal, Bethall, Bethell, Bethil, Bethill, Bethyl, Bethyll

Bethesda (Hebrew) from the house of mercy.

Bethesdah

Bethia (Hebrew) daughter; (Gaelic) life.

Bethiah, Bethya, Bethyah

Bethshaya (English) combination of Beth and Shaya.

Betsy (American, Hebrew) holy and sacred to God, a shortened form of Elizabeth.

Betsee, Betsey, Betsi, Betsia, Betsiah, Betsie, Betsya, Betsyah, Betsye

Betty (Hebrew) from the house of God, holy and sacred to God, a shortened form of Bethel and Elizabeth.

Bet, Beta, Betah, Bete, Betea, Betee, Betey, Beti, Betia, Betie, Betha, Betje, Betka, Bett, Betta, Bettah, Bette, Bettee, Bettey, Bettja, Bettje, Bettys, Betuska, Bety

Betulah (Hebrew) woman.

Betula, Betulla, Betullah

Beulah (Hebrew) married one.

Beula, Beulla, Beullah

Beverley (English) from the stream of the beaver, near the meadow of beavers, a unisex name originally derived from a surname.

Bev, Beverie, Beverlea, Beverleah, Beverlee, Beverlei, Beverleigh,

*Beverlie, Beverly, Bevlea, Bevlee,
Bevlei, Bevleigh, Bevley, Bevli,
Bevlia, Bevliah, Bevly*

Bharati (Hindu) goddess.

Bhavna (Hindu) sentiments, wish,
feelings.

Bian (Vietnamese) hidden, secret.

Bianca (Latin, Italian) white.
*Biancha, Bianka, Biankah, Biannca,
Biannka, Biannqua, Biannquah,
Bianqua, Bianquah, Blanca,
Blannca, Blannka, Byanca,
Byancah, Byanka, Byankah,
Byanqua, Byanquah*

Bianka (Italian) white, a form of
Bianca.

Bibi (Arabic) lady.
Bebe, Beebee

Bibianna (Latin) lively.
*Bibi, Bibian, Bibiana, Bibianah,
Bibiane, Bibiann, Bibbiannah,
Bibianne, Bibyan, Bibyana,
Bibyanah, Bibyann, Bibyanna,
Bibyannah, Bibyanne, Bybian,
Bybiana, Bybianah, Bybiane,
Bybiann, Bybianna, Bybiannah,
Bybianne*

Billie (English) wilful, strong-willed,
feminine form of Billy, William.
*Bilea, Bileah, Bilee, Bilei, Bileigh,
Biley, Bili, Bilie, Billea, Billee, Billena,
Billeenah, Billey, Billi, Billy, Billyana,
Billyanna, Billyannah, Bily, Bilyana,
Bilyanah, Bilyanna, Bilyannah,
Bylea, Byleah, Bylee, Bylei, Byleigh,
Byley, Byli, Bylie, Byll, Byllea, Bylleah,
Byllee, Byllei, Bylleigh, Bylli, Byllie,
Bylly, Byly*

Bilqis (Arabic) name of the Queen
of Sheba.

Bimbimbie (Australian Aboriginal)
place of many birds.

Bina (Hebrew) wise; (African)
dancer.
*Binah, Binney, Binta, Bintah, Byna,
Bynah*

Birdie (English) bird.
Bird, Birdee, Birdey, Birdi, Birdy

Bjorg (Scandinavian) salvation.
Bjorga, Bjorgah

Blaine (Irish) thin.
Blain, Blane, Blayne

Blair (Scottish) field, battlefield;
(Irish) field or plain dweller, a unisex
name.
Blaire, Blayr, Blayre

Blake (English) dark, a unisex name.
*Blaik, Blaike, Blaiklea, Blaikleah,
Blaiklee, Blaikley, Blaikli, Blaiklie,
Blaikly, Blakelea, Blakeleah,
Blakelee, Blaque, Blayk, Blayke*

Blanche (French) white,
fair-haired.
*Blanch, Blanchardina, Blanchardine,
Blanka, Blinnie, Branca, Branka*

Blanda (Hebrew) giver of
compliments.
*Blandah, Blandia, Blandiah,
Blandya, Blandyah*

Blaze (English) flame, a unisex name.

Blenda (Teutonic) bright white,
dazzling.

Bleniki (Hawaiian) white.
Blanikee, Blanikey, Blanikie, Blaniky

Bliss (Anglo-Saxon) joy, blissful, a
unisex name.
*Blis, Blisa, Blissa, Blisse, Blys, Blysa,
Blyss, Blyssa*

Blodwen (Welsh) white flower.
Blodwin, Blodwina, Blodwinah,

Blodwine, Blodwyna, Blodwynah, Blodwyne, Blodwynn, Blodwynna, Blodwynnah, Blodwynne

Blondelle (French) blond, fair.
Blondell, Blondie

Blossom (Anglo-Saxon) blooming like a flower.
Blossoma

Blum (Hebrew) flower.
Bluma, Blumah

Bly (Native American) high, tall.

Blythe (English) happy, cheerful, gentle, a unisex name.
Blith, Blithe, Blyth

Bo (Chinese) precious, a unisex name.

Bona (Latin) good.
Bonah, Bonna, Bonnah

Bonita (Spanish) pretty, beautiful.
Bonitah, Bonitta, Bonittah, Bonnita, Bonnitah, Bonnitta, Bonnittah, Bonnyta, Bonyta, Bonytta

Bonne (French) good.

Bonnie (Scottish, Irish) fine, pretty, beautiful, a form of Bonita.
Bonea, Bonee, Boney, Boni, Bonia, Boniah, Bonie, Bonney, Bonni

Branda (Hebrew) blessing.
Brandah

Brandy (Dutch, Anglo-Saxon) burnt wine, a unisex name.
Brandee, Brandey, Brandi, Brandie

Breanna (English) strong and graceful.
Breana, Breanah, Breane, Breannah, Breanne, Breeana, Breeanah, Breeane, Breeann, Breeanna, Breeannah, Breeanne, Briana,

Brianah, Briane, Brianna, Briannah, Brianne, Brienna, Briennah, Brienne, Bryana, Bryanah, Bryanna, Bryannah, Bryanne

Breck (Irish) freckled.
Brec, Breca, Brecah, Breckah, Brek, Breka, Brekah

Bree (Irish) strong.
Brea, Breah, Breea, Breeah, Brei, Breigh

Breena (Irish) fairy palace.
Breina, Brena, Brina

Breeze (English) cool, refreshing, windy, carefree.
Brease, Breaz, Breaza, Breazah, Breaze, Brees, Breese

Brenda (English) fiery, flaming sword, on fire; (Irish) raven.
Branda, Brandah, Brendah, Brennda, Brenndah

Brenna (Irish) fiery, forceful, spirited.

Brianna (Irish) strong, virtuous, graceful victory, feminine form of Brian.
Brana, Breana, Breanah, Breanna, Breannah, Breanne, Breeana, Breeanah, Breeann, Breeanna, Breeannah, Breeanne, Breeannie, Breian, Breiana, Breianah, Breiane, Breiann, Breianna, Breiannah, Breianne, Briana, Brianah, Briane, Briannah, Brianne, Briel, Briela, Brielah, Briele, Briell, Briella, Briellah, Brielle, Brina, Brinah, Brinna, Brinnah, Bryana, Bryanna, Bryannah, Bryanne, Bryel, Bryela, Bryele, Bryell, Bryella, Bryelle

Briar (French) heather; (English) thorny rose, a unisex name.
Brear, Brier, Bryar

Bridget (Celtic) strength.
Berget, Birgitte, Bride, Bridey, Bridger,

Bridgete, Bridgett, Bridgette, Bridgid, Bridgit, Bridgitt, Bridgitta, Bridgitte, Bridgot, Brietta, Brigada, Brigid, Brigida, Brigitte, Briget, Brita

Bridie (English) strong woman, a form of Bridgette.

Bridee, Brideh, Brydee, Brydeh, Brydie

Brigette (French) strong.

Bridget, Briget, Brigid, Brigitte

Brigida (Spanish) strong spirited, a form of Bridget.

Briony/Bryony (Anglo-Saxon) hill, vine.

Brionee, Brioney, Bryonee, Bryoney, Bryoni, Bryonie

Brisa (Spanish) beloved.

Brisha, Brishia, Brissa, Bryssa

Brittany (English) from Britain.

Brita, Britah, Britan, Britana, Britanah, Britane, Britanee, Britaney, Britani, Britanie, Britann, Britanna, Britannah, Britanne, Britenee, Briteney, Britenie, Briteny, Britnee, Britney, Britni, Britnie, Britny, Britt, Britta, Brittainnee, Brittainney, Brittainni, Brittainnie, Brittainny, Brittan, Brittana, Brittanah, Brittanee, Brittaney, Brittani, Brittanie, Brittenee, Britteney, Britteni, Brittenie, Britteny, Brytanee, Brytaney, Brytani, Brytania, Brytanie, Brytany, Bryttanee, Bryttaney, Bryttani, Bryttanie, Bryttany

Bronte (Greek) thunder; (English) the surname of the Brontë sisters, novelists Charlotte, Emily and Anne; a unisex name.

Brontee, Brontey, Brontie

Bronwyn (Welsh) white skin.

Broney, Bronia, Broniah, Bronie, Bronnee, Bronnie, Bronwen,

Bronwin, Bronwina, Bronwinah, Bronwine, Bronwyna, Bronwynah, Bronwyne, Bronwynn, Bronwynna, Bronwynnah, Bronwynne

Brooke (English) stream, a unisex name.

Brook, Brookee, Brookel, Brookela, Brookele, Brookelina, Brookeline, Brookelle, Brookellin, Brookellina, Brookelline, Brookellyn, Brookellyna, Brookellyne, Brookelyn, Brookelyna, Brookelyne, Brookey, Brookia, Brookiah, Brookie, Brooklin, Brooklina, Brookline, Brooklyn, Brooklyna, Brooklyne

Brooklyn (American) place name, combination of Brooke and Lyn.

Brunhilda (Teutonic) heroine, armoured warrior.

Brinhilda, Brihilde, Bruna, Brunhilde, Brynhild, Brynhilda, Brynhilde, Hilda

Buena (Spanish) good.

Buffy (American) shortened version of buffalo.

Buffee, Buffey, Buffie, Buffye

Bunny (English) little rabbit, from Bernice.

Bunee, Buney, Buni, Bunie, Bunnee, Bunney, Bunni, Bunnie, Buny

Bunty (English) originally used as a pet name perhaps meaning a lamb.

Burdette (Anglo-Saxon) little bird.

Burgundy (French) place name, a red-brown colour.

Burgandi, Burgandy, Burgunde, Burgundi, Burgundie

Bushra (Arabic) good omen.

Butterfly (American) beautiful, like a butterfly.

Cachet (French) prestigious, desirous.
Cachae, Cache, Cachea, Cachee

Cadence (Latin) rhythm.
Cadena, Cadenah, Cadenza, Cadenzah, Cady, Kadena, Kadenah, Kadenza, Kadenzah

Cai (Vietnamese) feminine, womanly.
Cae, Cay, Caye

Cailida (Spanish) adoring.
Caelida, Caelidah, Cailidah, Cailidora, Cailidorah, Callidora, Callidorah, Caylida, Caylidah, Kailida, Kailidah, Kaylida, Kaylidah

Caimile (African) from a proverb.

Caitlin (Celtic) pure, a form of Catherine.
Caetlan, Caetlana, Caetlane, Caetlen, Caetlena, Caetlene, Caetlin, Caetlina, Caetline, Caetlyn, Caetlyna, Caetlyne, Caitlan, Caitlana, Caitlane, Caitlen, Caitlena, Caitlene, Caitlina, Caitline, Caitlyn, Caitlyna, Caitlyne, Kaitlan, Kaitlana, Kaitlane, Kaitlena, Kaitlene, Kaitlin, Kaitlina, Kaitline, Kaitlyn, Kaitlyna, Kaitlyne, Katlen, Katlena, Katlena, Katlin, Katlina, Katline, Katelyn, Katlyna, Katlyne

Cala (Arabic) castle.
Calah, Calia, Caliah, Calla, Callah

Calandra (Greek) lark.
Calandre, Calandrea, Calandria, Calandriah, Calendra, Calendrah, Calendre, Kalandra, Kalandria

Calantha (Greek) like a lovely blossom.
Calanthah, Calanthia, Calanthiah

Caledonia (Latin) from Scotland.

Calida (Spanish) ardent, warm.
Calina, Calinda, Calindah, Callida, Callidah, Callinda, Callindah, Calyda, Calydah, Callyda, Callydah, Calyda, Calydah

Calista (Greek) most beautiful.
Calesta, Callie, Callista, Calixte, Calysta, Kalesta, Kallie, Kalista, Kalixte, Kallista, Kalysta

Calla (Greek) beauty, beautiful.
Callah, Kalla, Kallah

Callan (Teutonic) talkative.
Callen, Callin

Callidora (Greek) a gift of beauty.
Callidor

Calliope (Greek) musical and poetic, lovely voice.
Calliopee, Calliopy

Callula (Greek) beauty, beautiful light.
Calluella, Callulah, Calula, Calulah, Kallula, Kallulah, Kalula, Kalulah

Calumina (Gaelic) dove.
Caluminah, Calumyna, Calumynah

Calvina (Latin) bald, a feminine form of Calvin.
Calveanah, Calveanah, Calveane, Calveania, Calveaniah, Calveane, Calveena, Calveenah, Calveenia, Calveeniah, Calvinah, Calvine

Calypso (Greek) hidden, concealed.
Calipso, Caly

Cam (Vietnamese) orange fruit, sweet citrus fruit.

Cambria (Latin) from Wales.
Cambrea, Cambree, Cambreia, Cambrie, Cambry, Cambrya, Cambryna, Cami, Kambrea, Kambree, Kambreia, Kambrie, Kambry, Kambrya, Kambryna, Kami

Camellia (Italian) a shrub with fragrant flowers.
Camala, Camalia, Camallia, Camela, Camelia, Camelita, Camellita, Cami, Kamelia, Kamellia, Kamellita

Cameo (Latin) gem or shell with a portrait on it.
Camio, Camyo, Kameo, Kamio, Kamyo

Cameron (Scottish) crooked nose, a unisex name.
Cameran, Camerin

Camilla (Italian) young attendant at ceremony.
Camia, Camila, Camilia, Camillia, Camilya, Cammilla, Chamelea, Chamelia, Chamika, Chamila, Chamilia, Chamilla, Chamillia, Chammilla, Kamilla, Milla

Camille (French) young ceremonial attendant.
Cam, Cami, Camiel, Camielle, Camil, Camila, Camile, Camilla, Cammillie, Cammilyn, Cammyl, Cammyll, Camylle, Chamelle, Chamille, Kamille

Camira (Australian Aboriginal) of the wind.

Candace/Candice (Greek) brilliant white, clarity, pure.

Canace, Cace, Canda, Candas, Candece, Candelle, Candes, Candiace, Candiss, Candus, Candy, Candyce, Kandace, Kandice, Kandyce

Candida (Latin) bright white.
Candeea

Candy (American) sweet one, a form of Candace.
Candee, Candie, Kandee, Kandie

Cantara (Arabic) small bridge, crossing.

Cantrelle (French) song.
Cantrel, Cantrela, Cantrelah, Cantrele, Cantrell, Cantrella, Cantrellah

Caprice (Italian) fanciful, unpredictable.
Cappi, Caprece, Caprecia, Capricia, Capris, Caprise

Cara (Celtic) friend; (Latin) dear one.
Carah, Carra, Carrah

Caress (French) tender touch.
Carass, Carassa, Caressa, Caresse, Caris, Carisa, Carisah, Carise, Cariss, Carissa, Carissah, Carisse, Karesse

Carey (Anglo-Saxon) carer, caring.

Cari (Turkish) flows like water, gentle stream.
Caree, Carey, Carie, Cary

Carina (Australian Aboriginal) bride.

Carissa (Greek) beloved.
Caress, Caressa, Caresse, Caris, Carisa, Carisah, Carise, Cariss, Carissah, Carisse, Caryss, Caryssa, Caryssah, Carysse, Karisa, Karisah, Karissa, Karissah, Karysa, Karysah, Karyssa, Karyssah

Carla (German) farmer; (English) strong.

Carleta, Carila, Carilla, Carlkia, Carliqua, Carlonda, Carlotta, Carlyle, Carlysle, Charlotte, Karla, Karlaeta, Karila, Karilla, Karlotta

Carlin (Irish) little champion, a unisex name.

Carlan, Carlana, Carline, Carlyn

Carlotta (Italian) little woman, a form of Charlotte.

Carleta, Carletah, Carlete, Carletta, Carlettah, Carlette

Carly (English) little woman, a form of Charlotte.

Carlea, Carleah, Carlee, Carlei, Carleigh, Carley, Carli, Carlie, Carlya, Carlyah

Carma (Hindu) destiny.

Carmah, Carmal, Carmala, Carmalah, Carmalina, Carmalinah, Carmaline, Karma, Karmah, Karmal, Karmala, Karmale

Carmel/Carmela (Hebrew) vineyard of the Lord, honorific name from Our Lady of Mount Carmel.

Carma, Carmalla, Carmeli, Carmelia, Carmelina, Carmelit, Carmella, Carmelle, Carmellia, Carmellina, Carmelo, Carmesa, Carmesha, Carmie, Carmiel, Carmil, Carmila, Carmile, Carmilla, Carmille, Carmisha, Leeta, Lita, Millie

Carmelita (Hebrew) a garden or orchard, a form of Carmel.

Carmen (Latin) to sing, a song.

Carma, Carmain, Carmaina, Carmaine, Carmana, Carmanah, Carmane, Carmena, Carmenah, Carmene, Carmi, Carmia, Carmin, Carmine, Carmita, Karmen, Karmin, Karmine

Carmine (Latin) song, crimson, a unisex name.

Carmina, Carminah, Carmyn, Carmyne

Carnelian (Latin) clear reddish-yellow stone.

Carnelia, Carneliah, Carnelyan

Carol (French) joyous song; (German) farmer.

Caral, Carall, Carel, Carele, Carell, Carelle, Caro, Carola, Carolenia, Carolinda, Caroll, Carral, Carrall, Carrel, Carrell, Carrelle, Caril, Carill, Carrol, Carroll

Carolina (Italian) strong, little, womanly, a form of Caroline; (American) place name.

Caroleana, Caroleanah, Caroleena, Carolena, Carolinah, Carroleena, Carroleenah, Carrolena, Carrolina, Carrolinah

Caroline/Carolyn (French) strong, little, womanly.

Caralyn, Carelyn, Carilyn, Carilynn, Carilynne, Caro, Carolean, Caroleane, Caroleen, Carolin, Carroleen, Carroleene, Carrolene, Carrolin, Carroline, Carolynn, Carolynne, Karoline, Karolyn, Karolynn, Karolynne

Caron (Welsh) kind-hearted, loving.

Caaron, Caren, Carin, Caronne, Caryn, Kaaron, Karen, Karin, Karon, Karyn

Carreen (American) character in Margaret Mitchell's *Gone With the Wind*.

Carrie (French, English) strong, little, womanly, a form of Caroline.

Carey, Cari, Carie, Carree, Carrey, Carri, Carry, Cary, Karrie, Karree

Carrington (English) town where goods are loaded, rocky town, town of the marsh, a unisex name.

Carter (English) cart maker, cart driver, a unisex name.
Carta, Cartia, Karter

Carys (Welsh) love.
Caris, Caryse, Caryss, Carysse

Casey (Celtic) brave, Irish surname, a unisex name.
Cacey, Caci, Cacie, Cacy, Caisee, Caisey, Caisi, Caisie, Caisy, Casee, Casi, Casia, Casie, Cassee, Cassey, Cassi, Cassie, Casy, Kacey, Kaci, Kacie, Kacy, Kasee, Kasey

Cassandra (Greek) helper of men, a prophetess who was ignored.
Casandera, Casandra, Casandre, Casandria, Casandrina, Casandrine, Cass, Cassander, Cassandera, Cassandre, Cassandri, Cassandry, Cassaundra, Cassie, Cassondra, Kass, Kassandra, Kassie, Sandra

Cassia (Greek) spicy cinnamon flower, a spice.
Casia, Casiah, Cassiah, Cazia, Caziah, Cazya, Cazyah, Cazzia, Cazziah, Kassia

Cassidy (Celtic) clever, curly-haired, a unisex name.
Carridee, Carridie, Cassidee, Cassidie, Cassie, Cassy, Kassidy, Kassidee, Kassie, Kassy

Cassie (Greek) helper of men, prophet, a form of Cassandra.
Cassy, Kassie, Kassy

Catalina (Spanish) pure, a form of Catherine, from Catalonia, a region of Spain.
Cataleen, Catalena, Catalene, Catalin, Catalinah, Cataline,

Catalyn, Catalyna

Catava (African) name from a proverb.

Cate (English) pure, a form of Catherine.
Cait, Caite, Caitie, Caity, Cat, Catee, Catey, Catie, Caty, Kait, Kaitee, Kaitey, Kaitie, Kaity, Kat, Kate, Katee, Katey, Katie, Katy

Caterina (Italian) pure, a form of Catherine.
Catereana, Catereanah, Catereane, Catereena, Catereenah, Catereene, Caterin, Caterinah, Caterine

Catherine (Greek) pure.
Cat, Cate, Catheren, Catherene, Catheria, Catherin, Catherina, Catherinah, Catheryn, Catheryne, Cathleen, Cathryn, Cathy, Catie, Kat, Kate, Katherine, Katheryn, Katheryne, Kathleen, Kathryn, Kathy, Katie

Catrina (Slavic, Greek) pure, a form of Katherine.
Caitreana, Caitreanah, Caitreena, Caitreenah, Caitriana, Caitrina, Caitrinah, Caitrona, Caitryna, Caitrynah, Catreena, Catren, Catrena, Catrenah, Catrene, Catrenia, Catrin, Catrinah, Catrine, Catrinia, Catryna, Catrynah, Katreen, Katreenah, Katrene, Katrin, Katrina, Katrine

Catriona (Celtic) pure, a form of Catherine.
Catrionah

Ceana (Celtic) God is gracious.

Cecania (German) free, freedom.
Cecanie, Cecaniah, Cecanya, Cecanyah

Cecile/Cecilia (Latin) blind, feminine form of Cecil.

Ceceli, Cecelia, Cecelie, Cecely,
Cecil, Cecila, Cecilea, Cecilee,
Ceciley, Ceciliah, Cecilie, Cecilla,
Cecille, Cecillia, Cecillie, Cecily,
Cecilya, Ceclia, Cecylia, Cee,
Ceila, Celia, Celya

Cedrica (English) battle chief,
feminine form of Cedric.

Cedricah, Cedryca, Cedrycah

Celandia/Celandine (Greek)
swallow, plant with yellow flowers.

Celandina, Celandinah,
Celandrina, Celandrinah

Celeste (Latin) from the sky,
heavenly, celestial, feminine form
of Celestine.

Cele, Celeeste, Celense, Celes,
Celesia, Celesly, Celest, Celesta,
Celestia, Celestial, Celestin,
Celestina, Celestine, Celestinia,
Celestyn, Celestyna, Cellest,
Ceslleste, Selestina

Celie (French) celestial, heavenly.

Celea, Celeah, Celee, Celie,
Celeigh, Celey, Celi

Celine (Greek) moon.

Celeane, Celeene, Celin, Celina,
Celyn, Celyne

Celosia (Greek) aflame, burning.

Celosiah, Celosya, Celosyah

Cerella (Latin) spring time.

Cerela, Cerelah, Cerele, Cerellah,
Cerelle

Ceres (Latin) Roman goddess of
agriculture.

Cerese, Ceress

Ceridwen (Welsh) goddess of poetry.

Ceridwyn, Cerydwen, Cerydwin,
Cerydwyn

Cerise (French) colour of russet,
cherry red.

Carise, Carisse, Cerice, Cericia,
Cerissa, Cerisse

Chablis (French) dry white wine.

Chablea, Chableah, Chablee,
Chabley, Chabli, Chablie, Chabliss,
Chablys, Chablyss

Chaitra (Hindu) lunar month
corresponding to Aries.

Chalice (French) goblet.

Chalace, Chalcia, Chalcie, Chalece,
Chalisa, Chalise, Chaliss, Chalissa,
Chalisse, Challa, Challis, Challisa,
Challise, Challiss, Challissa, Challisse,
Chalyce, Chalysa, Chalyse

Chan (Cambodian) tree with
sweet smell.

Chana (Hebrew) God is gracious,
a form of Hannah.

Chanae, Chanah, Chanai,
Chanay, Channa, Channah

Chanda (Hindu) fierce, a name
for goddess Sakti.

Chandah, Chandea, Chandee,
Chandi, Chandia, Chandiah,
Chandie, Chandy

Chandani (Hindu) moonlight.

Chandanee, Chandaney,
Chandania, Chandaniah,
Chandanya, Chandanyah

Chandelle (French) candle.

Chandal, Chandala, Chandalah,
Chandale, Chandel, Chandela,
Chandelah, Chandele, Chandell,
Chandella, Chandellah

Chandi (Hindu) threatening, a
name for goddess Sakti.

Chandler (Old English) candle
maker, a unisex name.

Chandra (Hindu) moon or moon
goddess.

Chanel (English) canal, channel, strait.

Chanal, Chanala, Chanall, Chanalla, Chanalle, Chanela, Chanele, Chanell, Chanella, Chanelle, Channel, Channell, Channella, Channelle

Channa (Hindu) chickpea.

Chantal/Chantel (French) singer, song, feminine form of Chante

Chante, Chantala, Chantalah, Chantale, Chantela, Chantelah, Chantele, Chantell, Chantella, Chantellah, Chantelle

Chantilly (French) fine lace.

Chantilee, Chantilei, Chantileigh, Chantili, Chantilia, Chantilie, Chantilla, Chantillea, Chantilleah, Chantillee, Chantillei, Chantilley, Chantilli, Chantillie, Chantily

Charis (Greek) grace, beauty, kindness.

Chareece, Chareeze, Charece, Charese, Chari, Charice, Charie, Charise, Charish, Charissa, Charisse, Charrys, Charryse, Charryss, Charrysse, Charys, Charyse, Charyss, Charysse

Charisma (Greek) leadership, attraction.

Charese, Charesse, Charise, Charrise, Charrisse, Charryse, Charrysma, Charrysse, Charyse, Charysma, Charysse

Charity (Latin) benevolent, kind, charitable.

Charista, Charita, Charitah, Charitas, Charitea, Charitee, Charitey, Chariti, Charitia, Charitiah, Charitie, Charytia, Charytiah

Charlene (French) little and womanly, strong, a form of Caroline.

Charlean, Charleana, Charleane, Charleen, Charlein, Charleina, Charleine, Charlena, Charlenah, Charlyn, Charlyna, Charlyne, Charlynn, Charlynne

Charlie (English) little and womanly, strong, feminine form of Charles.

Charlee, Charli, Charlia, Charliah, Charlize, Charly

Charlotte (French) petite and feminine, womanly.

Carlotta, Carly, Chara, Charil, Charl, Charla, Charlet, Charlett, Charletta, Charlette, Charlie, Charlisa, Charlita, Charlot, Charlott, Charlotta, Charolet, Charolette, Charolot, Charolotte, Lottie

Charmaine (French) joyful song.

Charma, Charmae, Charmain, Charmaina, Charmainah, Charma, Charmara, Charmayane, Charmayn, Charmayna, Charmaynah, Charmayne, Charmain, Charmin, Charmine, Charmyn, Charmyne, Charmynn, Charmynne

Charmian (Greek) small joy.

Charmiana

Chastity (Latin) pure.

Chasta, Chastidy, Chastitea, Chastitee, Chastitey, Chastiti, Chastitie

Chava (Hebrew) bird.

Chavah, Chavala, Chavalah, Chave, Chaveli, Chavelia, Chavelie

Chavi (Gypsy) girl.

Chavee, Chavela, Chavelah, Chavele, Chavell, Chavella, Chavellah

Chaya (Hebrew) life.

Chaia, Chaiah

Chelsea (English) port of ships, place name.
Chelcea, Chelcee, Chelcey, Chelci, Chelcia, Chelciah, Chelcie, Chelcy, Chelsee, Chelsey, Chelsi, Chelsie, Chelsy

Chemarin (Hebrew) girl wearing black.
Chemarina, Chemarine, Chermaryn, Chermaryna, Chermaryne

Chenetta (French) oak tree.
Chenet, Cheneta, Chenetah, Chenete, Chenett, Chenettah, Chenette

Chenoa (Native American) white dove.
Chenoah

Cher (French) beloved.
Chere, Cheree, Cherey, Cherida, Cherise, Cherita, Cherree, Cherrey, Cherri, Cherrie, Cherry, Cherrye, Chery, Cherye, Cheryl

Cherie (French) beloved.
Cheree, Cherey, Cheri, Chery, Cherree, Cherrey, Cherri, Cherrie, Cherry, Chery, Sheree, Sherey, Sheri, Sherie, Sherree, Sherrey, Sherri, Sherrie, Sherry, Shery

Cherilyn (English, French) combination of Cher or Cheryl and Lyn.
Cherilyna, Cherilynah, Cherilyne, Cherylyn, Cherylyna, Cherylynah, Cherylyne, Sherilyn, Sherilyna, Sherilynah, Sherilyne, Sherylyn, Sherylyna, Sherylynah, Sherylyne

Cherise (French) cherished, precious.
Charisa, Charisah, Charise, Charys, Charysa, Charysah, Charyse, Cheresa, Cheresah, Cherese, Cherys, Cherysa, Cherysah, Cheryse

Cherry (French) beloved; (English) red cherry.
Chere, Cheree, Cherey, Cheri, Cherie, Cherise, Cherree, Cherrey, Cherri, Cherrie, Chery

Cheryl (French) beloved.
Cheral, Cherel, Cherell, Cherella, Cherelle, Cheril, Cherila, Cherille, Cherril, Cherrila, Cherrile, Sheril, Sherill, Sherille, Sheryl, Sheryll, Sherylle

Chesna/Chezna (Slavic) peace, peaceful.
Chesnah, Chessna, Chessnah, Cheznah, Cheznia, Chezniah, Cheznya, Cheznyah

Cheyenne (Native American) tribal name.
Cheyan, Cheyana, Cheyane, Cheyann, Cheyanna, Cheyanne, Cheyena, Cheyene, Cheyenn, Cheyenna, Chyen, Chyena, Chyene, Chyenn, Chyenna, Chyenne

Chiara (Italian) clear, bright.
Cheara, Chyara

Chika (Japanese) near and dear one.
Chikah, Chyka, Chykah

Chiku (African) talkative.

Chilali (Native American) snowbird.
Chilalea, Chilaleah, Chilalee, Chilalei, Chilalie, Chilaly

Chimalis (Native American) bluebird.

China (Chinese) quality porcelain, place name.
Chinah, Chinasa, Chine, Chinea, Chinesia, Chinna

Chinira (African) God receives.
Chinara, Chinarah, Chinirah

Chinue (African) God's blessing.

Chiquita (Spanish) the little one.
Chica, Chikata, Chikita, Chiqueta, Chiquila, Chiquite, Chiquitha, Chiquitia, Chiquitta

Chiyo (Japanese) eternal.

Chloe (Greek) blooming, fresh like a young green shoot.
Chloé, Chlöe, Chloea, Chloee, Chloey, Cloe, Kloe

Chloris (Greek) pale.
Chlorise, Chlorys, Chloryse, Cloris, Clorise, Clorys, Cloryse

Cho (Korean) beautiful.

Cholena (Native American) bird.
Choleana, Choleanah, Choleane, Choleena, Choleenah, Choleene, Choleyna, Choleynah, Choleyne, Cholenah, Cholene, Cholyna, Cholynah, Cholyne

Chrissie/Chrissy (English) Christ-bearer, Christian, a form of Christine.
Chrisi, Chrisie, Chrissee, Chrissey, Chrissi, Christiana, Christie, Christina, Christine, Chrisy, Chryssie, Crissie, Khrissie, Khrissy, Krissie, Krissy, Kristie, Kristina, Kristine

Christabel (Latin, French) combination of Christina and Belle.
Christabela, Christabelah, Christabele, Christabell, Christabella, Christabellah, Christabelle, Christable, Christobel, Christobell, Christobella, Christobelle, Chrystabel, Chrystabela, Chrystabelah, Chrystabele, Chrystabell, Chrystabella, Chrystabellah, Chrystabelle, Chrystobel, Chrystobela, Chrystobelah, Chrystobele, Chrystobell, Chrystobella, Chrystobellah, Chrystobelle, Cristabel, Cristabela,

Cristabelah, Cristabele, Cristabell, Cristabella, Cristabellah, Cristabelle

Christina (French, Greek) carrier of Christ, anointed, follows Christ, feminine form of Christopher.
Chris, Chrissy, Christeana, Christeanah, Christeena, Christeenah, Christeina, Christeinah, Christiana, Christie, Christinah, Christine, Christinia, Christinna, Christinnah, Christna, Christyna, Christynah, Christynna, Chrystina, Chrystinah, Chrystyna, Chrystynah, Kris, Kristina, Kristine, Tina

Christine (French, Greek, English) Christ-bearer, follower of Christ, feminine form of Christopher.
Chris, Chrissy, Christea, Christeane, Christeen, Christeene, Christiana, Christina, Kristie, Kristina, Kristine

Christmas (English) born at Christmas time.

Chumani (Native American) dew drop.

Ciannait (Irish) ancient.

Ciara (Irish) black, feminine form of Ciarán.
Cianait

Cindy (Greek) moon, a form of Cynthia.
Cindea, Cindeah, Cindee, Cindey, Cindi, Cindie, Cyndea, Cyndeah, Cyndee, Cyndey, Cyndi, Cyndie, Cyndy

Cinnia (Latin) curly-haired.
Cinia, Ciniah, Cinniah

Cipriana (Italian) from the island of Cyprus.
Cipriane, Cipriann, Ciprianna, Ciprianne, Cyprian, Cypriana, Cypriane, Cyprienne

Circe (Greek) goddess who fell in love with Odysseus.

Claire/Clare (French) clear, bright.
Clair, Claira, Clairah, Claret, Clareta, Claretah, Clarete, Clarett, Claretta, Clarettah, Clarette, Clarina, Clarinah, Clarinda, Clarine, Clarita, Claritah

Clancy (Irish) surname, red warrior, a unisex name.
Clancee, Clancey, Clancie, Clansee, Clansey, Clansi, Clansie, Clansy

Clara (Italian) clear, bright, a form of Claire.
Claire, Clar, Clarah, Clare

Clarice (French) clear, bright, a form of Clara.
Claris, Clarise, Clariss

Clarinda (Latin) bright, wise.
Clairinda, Clairynda, Clarindah, Clarynda, Claryndah

Clarissa (Greek) shining one, bright, brilliant.
Claris, Clarisa, Clarisah, Clarise, Clariss, Clarissah, Clarisse, Clarys, Clarysa, Clarysah, Claryse, Claryss, Claryssa, Claryssah, Clarysse, Klarissa, Klarisah, Klarise, Klarissa, Klarissah, Klarisse, Klarysa, Klarysah, Klaryse, Klaryss, Klaryssa, Klaryssah, Klarysse

Claudia (Latin) lame, fragile one, feminine form of Claude.
Claud, Clauda, Claudah, Claude, Claudea, Claudee, Claudet, Claudeta, Claudete, Claudett, Claudetta, Claudettah, Claudette, Claudiah, Claudin, Claudina, Claudinah, Claudine, Claudyn, Claudyna, Claudynah, Claudyne, Klaudia, Klaudiah, Klaudja, Klaudya, Klaudyah

Clematis (Greek) a creeping vine with bright flowers.
Clematisa, Clematise, Clematiss, Clematissa, Clematisse, Clematys, Clematysa, Clematyse

Clementine (Latin) merciful.
Clemence, Clemencia, Clemencie, Clemency, Clemente, Clementia, Clementiah, Clementina, Clemenza

Cleo (English) father's glory, a form of Cleopatra.
Clio, Kleo, Klio

Cleone (Greek) famous.
Cleaona, Cleaonee, Cleoney, Cleoni, Cleonie, Cleony

Cleopatra (Greek) her father's glory.

Cleva (English) from the cliff, feminine form of Clive.

Clio (Greek) muse of history.

Cliona (Irish) shapely, name of a long-ago Irish princess.

Clodagh (Irish) name of a river in Tipperary.

Cloe (Italian) blooming, a form of Chloe.
Clo, Cloea, Cloee, Cloei, Cloey, Cloi, Cloie

Clothilda (Teutonic) heroine in loud battle.
Chlothilda, Chlothilde, Chlotilda, Chlotilde, Clothilde, Clotilda, Clotilde

Clover (English) lucky, a flower name.

Cocheta (Native American) unknown, foreigner.

Coco (Spanish) coconut, place name.

Cody (English) cushion, pillow, a unisex name.
Codea, Codee, Codey, Codi, Codie, Kodea, Kodee, Kodey, Kodi, Kodie, Kody

Colette (French, Greek) victory of the people, a form of Nicole.
Coe, Coetta, Coletta, Collett, Colletta, Collette, Koe, Koetta, Koletta, Kolette, Kollett, Kolletta, Kollette

Colleen (Irish) girl.
Coel, Coelen, Cole, Coleen, Colena, Colina, Colinda, Coline, Collen, Colleene, Collene, Collie, Collina, Colline, Colly

Columba/Columbia (Latin) dove.
Colombe, Columbina, Columbinah, Columbine, Colyumbyna, Columbynah, Columbyne

Concepcion (Spanish) relates to the Virgin Mary's immaculate conception.
Concepción, Conception

Concetta (Italian) pure.
Conceta, Concetina, Concettina, Concheta, Conchetina, Conchetta, Conchettina, Connie

Concha (Spanish) seashell.
Conchah

Concordia (Latin) harmony.
Concordiah, Koncordia, Koncordiah

Cong (Chinese) intelligent, clever, a unisex name.

Constance (Latin) constant, steady, firm.
Conni, Connie, Constancia, Constancy, Constanta, Constantia, Constantina, Constantine, Constanza, Constynse, Konni, Konnie, Konstance, Konstancia, Konstancy, Konstanta, Konstantia, Konstantina, Konstantine, Konstanza, Konstynse

Consuela/Consuelo (Latin) consolation.
Consolata, Consuella, Consula, Conzuello, Conzuelo, Conzula, Konsolata, Konsuela, Konsuella, Konsuelo, Konsula, Konzuelo, Konzuello, Konzula

Cooinda (Australian Aboriginal) happy place.

Cooper (English) barrel maker, a unisex name.
Coop, Couper

Coorah (Australian Aboriginal) woman.

Cora (Greek) girl, maiden.
Corah, Coralee, Coretta, Corey, Corissa, Corra, Kora, Korah, Koralee, Koretta, Korey, Korissa, Korra

Coral (Latin) coral; (Greek) from the sea.
Coraal, Coraale, Coralea, Coraleah, Coralee, Coralei, Coraleigh, Coralia, Coraliah, Coralie, Corel, Corela, Corelah, Corele, Corell, Corella, Corellah, Corelle, Corral, Koraal, Koraale, Koral, Korral

Corazon (Spanish) of the heart, often used in the Philippines.
Corazone, Corazonn, Corrazone, Corrazonne, Korazon, Korazone, Korazonn, Korrazone, Korrazonne

Cordelia (Celtic) jewel of the sea; (Latin) warm-hearted.
Cordae, Cordelie, Cordellia, Cordellie, Cordet, Cordett, Cordette, Cordi, Cordilia, Cordilla, Cordula, Cordy, Kordae, Kordelia, Kordelie, Kordellia, Kordellie,

Kordet, Kordett, Kordette, Kordi,
Kordilia, Kordilla, Kordula, Kordy

Coreen (Australian Aboriginal)
end of the hills.

Corina (Greek) maiden, girl.

Coreena, Coren, Corena, Coriana,
Corianna, Corin, Corinda, Corine,
Corinee, Corinna, Correna,
Corrina, Corrinna, Coryna, Corynn,
Corynne, Koreena, Koren, Korena,
Koriana, Korianna, Korin, Korina,
Korinda, Korine, Korinee, Korinna,
Korrena, Korrina, Korrinna, Koryna,
Korynn, Korynne

Corliss (English) cheerful one.

Corlisa, Corlise, Corlissa, Corly,
Korlisa, Korlise, Korliss, Korlissa, Korly

Cornelia (Latin) horn-coloured.

Carna, Carniella, Coirnie,
Corneillia, Cornela, Cornelie,
Cornella, Cornelle, Cornellia,
Cornileea, Cornisha, Corny,
Karna, Karniella, Koirnie, Korneillia,
Kornela, Kornelia, Kornelie,
Kornella, Kornelle, Kornellia,
Kornileea, Kornisha, Korny

Corona (Greek) a crown.

Coronah, Korona, Koronah

Corra (Gaelic) mountain glen.

Cora, Corah, Corrah, Kora, Korah,
Korra, Korrah

Cosima (Greek) universe, harmony.

Cosimah, Cosimo, Kosima,
Kosimah, Kosimo

Courtenay/Courtney (French)
short nose; (English) from the court,
a unisex name.

Cortney, Cortny, Courteen, Courtene,
Courteny, Courtnae, Courtnay,
Courtnea, Courtnee, Courtny,
Courtonie, Kortney, Kourteen,
Kourtenay, Kourtene, Kourtnae,
Kourtnay, Kourtnea, Kourtnee,
Kourtney, Kourtny, Kourtonie

Cressida (Greek) gold.

Cressidah, Kressida, Kressidah

Crispina (Latin) curly-headed.

Crispin, Crispine, Crispyn, Crispyne

Crystal (Latin) brilliant, clear glass.

Cristal, Cristala, Cristale, Cristalle,
Crystala, Crystale, Crystall,
Crystalle, Crystl, Crystle, Kristal,
Kristall, Kristalle, Krystal, Krystall,
Krystalle

Cuthberta (English) brilliant.

Cuthbertina, Cuthburta,
Curthburtina, Cuthbyrta,
Cuthbyrtina

Cyan (English) blue colour, a
unisex name.

Cybil (Greek) soothsayer, a form
of Sybil.

Cebel, Cebela, Cebele, Cibel,
Cibela, Cibele, Cibell, Cibella,
Cibelle, Cybel, Cybela, Cybele,
Cybell, Cybella, Cybelle, Cybyl,
Cybyla, Cybyle, Cybyll, Cybylla,
Cybylle

Cynara (Greek) thistle.

Cinara, Cinarah, Cynarah

Cynthia (Greek) moon, moon
goddess.

Cinthea, Cinthia, Cinthiah, Cinthya,
Cinthyah, Cynthea, Cynthiah,
Cynthya, Cynthyah, Sinthea,
Sinthia, Sinthiah, Sinthya, Sinthyah,
Synthea, Synthia, Synthiah,
Synthya, Synthyah

Cyra (Persian) sun.

Cyrilla (Latin) lordly; (Greek)
noble.

Cerelia, Cerella, Cerellah, Cira,
Cirah, Cirilla, Cirillah, Cyrella,
Cyrellah, Cyrila, Cyrilah, Cyrillah,
Cyrille

D

Dacey (Irish) southerner, from Candace, a unisex name.
Dacee, Dacei, Daci, Dacia, Daciah, Dacie, Dacy, Dacya, Dacyah, Daicee, Daici, Daicie, Daicy, Daycee, Daycie

Dae (English) day.
Dai, Daia, Daiah, Daya, Dayah

Daffodil (French) flower name.

Dafny (Italian) flower, a form of Daphne.
Dafany, Daffany, Daffie, Daffy, Dafne, Dafney, Dafnie

Dagmar (German) glorious.
Dagmara, Dagmarah, Dagmarayah, Dagmarya

Dagna (Teutonic) bright as the day.

Dagny (Scandinavian) day.
Dagna, Dagnah, Dagnana, Dagnanna, Dagne, Dagnee, Dagney, Dagnie

Dahlia (Scandinavian) valley; (English) flower, named for Swedish botanist Anders Dahl.
Dahl, Dahliah, Dahlya, Dahlyah

Dai (Japanese) great.
Dae, Day, Daye

Daina (English) from Denmark.
Dayna, Dana, Dainah, Daynah

Daisy (English) daisy flower, day's eye, pet name from Margaret.
Daisee, Daisey, Daisi, Daisia, Daisie, Dasee, Dasey, Dasi, Dasie, Dasy, Daysee, Daysey, Daysi, Daysia, Daysie, Daysy

Daiya (Polish) present, gift.
Daia, Daiah, Daiyah, Daya, Dayah

Dakini (Hindu) sky traveller.

Dakota (Native American) friend, tribal place name, a unisex name.
Dakotah, Dakotha, Dekoda, Dekodah, Dekota, Dekotah, Dekotha, Takota, Takotah

Dalal (Arabic) coquette.

Dalany (Irish) Descendant of the challenger, a form of Delaney.
Dalania, Dalena, Dalene, Daleney, Delainee, Delainey, Delana, Delanee, Delaney, Delani, Delanie, Dellanee, Dellaney, Dellani, Dellanie, Dellay

Dale (English) valley, dale, a unisex name.
Dael, Daela, Dahli, Dahlia, Dahlie, Dail, Daila, Daile, Dal, Dalelean, Daleleana, Dalena, Dalenah, Dalene, Daley, Dalina, Dalinah, Daline, Daly, Dalyn, Dalyna, Dalyne, Dayl, Dayla, Dayle

Dalia (Hebrew) a branch.
Daleia, Daliah, Dalya, Dalyah

Dallas (Irish) wise; (Scottish) valley of the water; a city in Texas; a unisex name.
Dalas, Dalishia, Dalishya, Dalisia, Daliss, Dalissa, Dalissia, Dalissiah, Dallis, Dalliss, Dallys, Dallyss, Dallyssa, Dallysse, Dalyce, Dalys, Dalyss, Dalyssa, Dalysse

Damara/Damaris (Greek) gentle girl.

Dama, Damar, Damarylis, Damarys, Damarysa, Damaryss, Damaryssa, Damarysse, Dameress, Dameressa, Dameris, Damiris, Demara, Demaras, Demaris, Demariss, Demarissa, Demarys, Demarysa, Demarysah, Demaryse, Demaryss, Demaryssa, Demaryssah, Demarysse

Damica (French) friendly.

Dameeca, Dameecah, Dameeka, Dameka, Damekah, Damicah, Damicka, Damika, Damikah, Demeeca, Demeecah, Demeeka, Demica, Demicah, Demicka, Demika, Demikah

Damita (Spanish) the little noble lady.

Dameeta, Dameetah, Dametia, Dametiah, Damitah, Damyta, Damytah

Damosel (Anglo-Saxon) young, unmarried woman.

Dana (English) from Denmark, bright as day, a unisex name.

Daena, Daenah, Daina, Dainah, Danae, Danah, Danala, Danale, Danalee, Danarra, Danean, Daneana, Dania, Daniah, Danja, Danjah, Danna, Dayna, Daynah

Dani (Hebrew) God is my judge, a form of Danielle.

Danie, Dany, Danne, Dannee, Danney, Danni, Dannie, Dannii, Danny, Dany

Danica/Danika (Slavic) morning star.

Daneeca, Daneecah, Daneeka, Daneekah, Danikah, Danikia, Danikiah, Daniqua, Daniquah, Danique, Danyca, Danycah, Danycka, Danyka, Danykah, Danyqua, Danyquah, Danyque

Danice (American) combination of Danielle and Janice.

Danis, Danisa, Danisah, Danise, Daniss, Danissa, Danissah, Danisse

Daniella (English, Italian) as God is my judge.

Daniela, Danniella

Danielle (Hebrew, French) God is my judge, feminine form of Daniel.

Danae, Danal, Daneen, Daneena, Daneil, Daneille, Danial, Danialla, Danialle, Danica, Danielan, Daniele, Danielka, Daniell, Daniella, Daniellah, Danika, Danikah, Danille, Danit, Dannee, Dannie, Danniele, Danniella, Dannielle, Danny, Danyela, Danyele, Danyella, Danyelle, Doniel, Doniela, Doniele, Doniell, Doniella, Donielle, Donniel, Donniela, Donniele, Donniell, Donniella, Donnielle, Donnyel, Donnyela, Donnyele, Donnyell, Donnnyella, Donnyelle, Donyel, Donyela, Donyela, Donyelah, Donyele, Donyell, Donyella, Donyellah, Donyelle,

Dante (Italian) lasting, enduring, a form of Durante, named after the poet and philosopher, a unisex name.

Dantae

Daphne (Greek) laurel tree with bell-shaped flowers.

Dafnee, Dafney, Dafni, Dafnie, Dafny, Daphnee, Daphney, Daphni, Daphnie, Daphny

Dara (Hebrew) compassionate.

Dahra, Dahrah, Daira, Dairah, Darah, Daralea, Daralee, Daraleigh, Daraley, Daralie, Daravie, Darda, Dardah, Darice, Darilyn, Darilyna, Darisa, Darissa, Darja, Darka, Darra, Darrah

Daralis (English) beloved.
*Daralisa, Daralisah, Daralise,
Daralysa, Daralyse*

Darby (Irish) free; (Scandinavian)
a deer estate, a unisex name.
*Darb, Darbe, Darbee, Darbey, Darbi,
Darbie, Darbra, D'Arby, Darbye*

Darci (French) fortress, from the
stronghold; (Irish) dark.
*D'Arcy, D'arcy, Darcea, Darcee,
Darcel, Darcey, Darcia, Darciah,
Darcie, Darcy, Darsea, Darsee,
Darsey, Darsi, Darsie, Darsy*

Daria (Greek) wealthy ruler,
feminine form of Darius.
*Dariah, Darian, Dariana, Dariane,
Dariann, Darianna, Darianne,
Darria, Darriah, Darrya, Darryah,
Darya, Daryah*

Darice (Persian) queen.
*Dareece, Darees, Daricia,
Dariciah, Daryca, Darycah,
Darycia, Darys, Darysa, Darysah,
Darysia, Darysiah, Darysya,
Darysyah*

Darlene (French) little darling.
*Darelyn, Darelyne, Darelynne,
Darilynn, Darla, Darlean, Darleen,
Darleene, Darlein, Darleina,
Darlena, Darlenna, Darlenne,
Darletha, Darlin, Darline, Darling,
Darlinn, Darlinne, Darlynn,
Darlynne*

Darrell/Daryl (English, French)
beloved darling, from the grove of
oak trees, a unisex name.
*Daralle, Darele, Darelle, Darielle,
Daril, Darile, Darill, Darille, Darilynn,
Darrel, Darryl, Darryll, Darrylle,
Daryle, Daryll, Darylle*

Darri (Australian Aboriginal) track.

Daru (Hindu) pine or cedar tree.
Darua, Darue

Darya (Russian, Persian) river, sea.

Dashawna (American)
combination of prefix Da and
Shawna.
*Dashaughna, Dashaughnah,
Dashauna, Dashaunah,
Dashawnah, Dashawnna*

Dashiki (African) African shirt.
*Dashika, Dashka, Desheka,
Deshiki*

Davalinda (American)
combination of Davida and Linda.
*Davalindah, Davalinde, Davelinda,
Davilinda, Davilynda, Davylinda,
Davylindah*

Davida (Hebrew) beloved,
feminine form of David.
*Daveda, Davedah, Davene,
Davina, Davinah, Davine, Davinna,
Davita, Devina, Devinna*

Davina (Scottish) beloved,
feminine form of David.
*Dava, Davannah, Davean,
Daveen, Daveena, Davena,
Daveon, Davey, Davi, Daviana,
Davie, Davin, Davine, Davinder,
Davine, Davinee, Davinia,
Davinna, Davira, Davonna,
Devean, Deveen, Devene, Devina,
Devine*

Dawn (English) born at daybreak,
the dawn, sunrise.
*Dawana, Dawandrea, Dawanna,
Dawin, Dawna, Dawnah, Dawne,
Dawnee, Dawnetta, Dawnisha,
Dawnlynn, Dawnna, Dawnnya,
Dawnrae, Dayna*

Dayna (English) bright day.
*Daena, Daenah, Daina, Dainah,
Dana, Danah, Daynah*

Dea (Latin) goddess.
Deah

Deana/Deanna/Deanne (English) of the valley; (Latin) divine, a form of Diana/Diane.

Deahana, Deahanne, Deandra, Deandre, Deane, Deann, Déanna, Déanne, Deannia, Deeann, Dee-Ann, Deeanna, Deeanne, Deena

Deandra (American) combination of Dee and Andrea.

Dandrea, Deandre, Deandrea, Deandree, Deandreia, Deandria, Deanndra, Deaundra, Deaundria, Deeandra, Deondra, Diandra, Diandre, Diandrea, Diondria, Dyandra, Dyandrea, Dyandria

Deborah (Hebrew) the bee, prophetess in the Bible.

Deb, Debbee, Debbey, Debbi, Debbie, Debbora, Debborah, Debby, Debee, Deberah, Debi, Debie, Debor, Debora, Deboran, Deborrah, Debra, Debrah, Debrena, Debrina, Debroah, Devora, Dobra

Decima (Latin) tenth.

Decimah, Decimma, Decimmah

Dee (Welsh) dark.

De, Dea, Deah, Dee-Dee, Dede, Dedie, Deea, Didi

Deianeira (Greek) wife of Hercules.

Daeianeira, Daeianeirah, Daenaira, Daenairah, Daianaira, Daianairah, Dayanaira, Dayanairah

Deiondre (French) valley, a unisex name.

Deirdre (Irish) sorrowful wanderer.

Deerdra, Deerdre, Deidra, Deidrah, Deidrea, Deidree, Deidrie, Deirdree, Deirdra, Deirdrah, Deirdrea, Deirdrie, Derda, Didi, Diedra, Diedre, Diérdre, Dierdrie

Déja (French) before.

Daeja, Daija, Daisia, Daja, Dasha, Deejai, Deja, Dejanel, Dejanela, Dejanelah, Dejanele, Dejanell, Dejanella, Dejanellah, Dejanelle, Dejay, Dejaya, Dejon

Deka (African) pleasing.

Dekah

Delana (German) noble protector.

Dalana, Dalanah, Dalaina, Dalainah, Dalaine, Dalanna, Dalannah, Dalayna, Dalaynah, Daleena, Dalena, Dalenah, Dalenna, Dalennah, Dalina, Dalinah, Dalinda, Dalinna, Delanah, Delanna, Delannah

Delaney (Irish) descendant of the challenger; (Latin) of the elder tree grove, a unisex name.

Dalanee, Dalaney, Dalani, Dalania, Dalanie, Dalany, Dalene, Daleney, Daline, Dallanee, Dallaney, Dallani, Dallania, Dallanie, Dallany, Dallene, Dalleney, Dalline, Del, Delainey, Delan, Delane, Delanee, Delani, Delania, Delanie, Delayne, Delayney, Delaynie, Deleaney, Deleani, Deleanie, Deleany, Deline, Dell, Della, Dellainey, Dellane, Dellanee, Dellaney, Dellani, Dellania, Dellanie, Dellany, Dellayne, Dellayney, Dellaynie, Delleaney, Delleani, Delleanie, Delleany, Delline

Deleena (French) small, dear, darling.

Deleana, Deleanah, Deleane, Deleenah, Deleene, Deleina, Deleinah, Deleine, Deleyna, Deleynah, Deleyne, Delina, Delinah, Deline

Delfina (Spanish) dolphin.

Delfeena, Delfi, Delfie, Delfin, Delfinah, Delfine, Delfyn, Delfyna, Delfyne, Delfynia

Delia (Greek) visible, moon goddess; (English) a form of Cordelia.

Dehlia, Delea, Deli, Deliah, Deliana, Delianne, Delilla, Delillah, Delillia, Delinda, Dellia, Dellya, Delya, Delyia, Delylah, Delylla, Delyllah

Delicia (English) delightful, a form of Lisa.

Delesha, Delica, Delice, Delight, Delighta, Delisa, Delisah, Delise, Delisia, Delisiah, Deliz, Deliza, Delizah, Delize, Delizia, Dellisha, Delya, Delys, Delyse, Delysia, Delysya, Delysyah, Leesa, Leesah, Lisa, Lisah

Delilah (Hebrew) brooding, beautiful temptress, lover of Samson.

Dalialah, Dalila, Dalilah, Daliliah, Delila, Delilia, Delilla, Delillah, Delillia, Delyla, Delylah, Delylla, Delyllah

Della (English) noble, a form of Adele and Adelaide.

Del, Dela, Delah, Dell, Dellah, Delle, Delli, Dellie, Dells, Dels

Delma (Spanish) of the sea.

Delmah, Delmar, Delmara, Delmarah, Delmare, Delmaria, Delmariah

Delphine (Greek) from Delphi.

Delfeena, Delfina, Delfine, Delpha, Delphe, Delphi, Delphia, Delphiah, Delphie, Delphina, Delphinah, Delphinia, Delphiniah, Delphinie, Delphy, Delphyna, Delphynah, Delphyne, Delvina, Delvinah, Delvine, Delvinia, Delviniah

Delta (Greek) fourth.

Deltah, Deltar, Deltare, Deltaria, Deltarya, Deltaryah, Delte, Deltora, Deltoria, Deltra

Delwyn (Welsh) friend from the valley, a unisex name.

Delwen, Delwin

Demetria (Greek) goddess of harvest, fertile cover of the earth.

Deitra, Demeta, Demeteria,

Demetra, Demetriana, Demetrianna, Demetrias, Demetrice, Demetriona, Demetris, Demetrish, Demetrius, Demi, Demia, Demitra, Demitria, Dymeta, Dymeteria, Dymetra, Dymetria, Dymetriana, Dymetrianna, Dymetrias, Dymetrice, Dymetriona, Dymetris, Dymetrish, Dymetrius, Dymi, Dymia, Dymitra, Dymitria

Demi (French) half, small.

Demia, Demiah, Demii, Demmi, Demmie, Demy

Dena (Native American) valley; (Anglo-Saxon) from the valley, feminine form of Dean.

Deane, Deanne, Deena, Deenah, Deeyn, Denae, Denaé, Denah, Denay, Dene, Denea, Denee, Deneé, Deney, Denna, Deonna, Dina, Dinah

Deni (French) follower of Dionysus, the god of wine, a form of Denise.

Deney, Denie, Denni, Dennie, Denny, Dinnie, Dinny

Denise (French) follower of Dionysus, the god of wine.

Danese, Danice, Danise, Denese, Denice, Denicy, Deniece, Denisha, Denisse, Denize, Dennise, Dennys, Denys, Denyse

Derika (German) ruler of the people.

Dereka, Derekah, Derekia, Derekiah, Derekya, Derekyah, Derica, Dericah, Dericka, Derikah, Deriqua, Deriquah, Derique, Derrica, Derricah, Derricka, Derrika, Derrikah

Derry (Irish) red-haired one.

Deree, Derey, Deri, Derie, Derree, Derrey, Derri, Derrie, Dery

Derwina (Anglo-Saxon) friend.

Derwen, Derwena, Derwin, Derwyn, Derwyna

Derya (Hawaiian) ocean.

Deryn (Welsh) bird.

Deran, Derana, Deranah, Derane, Deren, Derena, Derenah, Derene, Derin, Derina, Derinah, Derine, Deron, Derona, Deronah, Derone, Derran, Derrana, Derranah, Derrane, Derrin, Derrina, Derrinah, Derrine, Deryna, Derynah, Deryne

Desdemona (Greek) ill-fated one, unlucky.

Desdemonah, Desdimona, Desdimonah, Desdymona, Desdymonah, Desi, Desie, Desy, Mona, Monah

Desiree (French) desired, longed for.

Desara, Desarah, Desarae, Desarai, Desaral, Desaray, Desare, Desarea, Desaree, Desarey, Desaria, Desarie, Desary, Deserae, Deserah, Deserai, Deseraia, Deseraie, Desere, Deseree, Deserey, Deseri, Deseria, Deserie, Deserra, Deserrae, Deserray, Desery, Desira, Desirae, Desirah, Desirai, Desirata, Desire, Desirea, Desired, Desirey, Desiri, Desirie, Desiry, Desra, Desrai, Desray, Desserrai, Dessira, Dessirae, Dessire, Dessiree, Desyrae, Desyrai, Desyray, Dezarae, Dezerai, Dezeray, Dezere, Dezerea, Dezeree, Dezerie, Dezirae, Deziree, Dezorae, Dezorai, Dezoray, Dezrae, Dezrai, Dezray, Dezzirae, Dezzrae, Dezzrai, Dezzray

Dessa (Greek) wanderer.

Desa, Desah, Dessah

Destinee/Destiny (French) destiny, one's fate.

Desta, Destanee, Destaney, Destani, Destanie, Destanni, Destannie, Destany, Destenee, Desteni, Destenie, Desteny, Destiana, Destin, Destine, Destinee, Destiney, Destini, Destinie, Destonee, Destoney, Destoni, Destonie, Desty, Destyn, Destyne, Destynee, Destyni, Destynie

Deva (Hindu) divine.

Deeva, Deevah, Devah, Diva, Divah

Devaki (Hindu) dark.

Devi (Hindu) goddess of destruction.

Devin (Irish) poet, a unisex name.

Deavin, Dev, Devan, Deven, Devena, Devenje, Deveny, Devinn, Devinne, Devyn, Devynn

Devon (English) poet, from Devonshire, a unisex name.

Devin, Devina, Devinah, Devinn, Devinna, Devinnah, Devona, Devonah, Devonn, Devonna, Devonnah, Divon, Divona, Divonah, Divonn, Divonna, Divonnah, Dyvon, Dyvona, Dyvonah, Dyvonn, Dyvonna, Dyvonnah

Devona (English) from the county of Devon.

Davona, Davonda, Davondra, Davonna, Devona, Devonda, Devondra, Devonia, Devonna

Dextra (Latin) skilful, dexterous.

Dextrah, Dextria

Dhara (Hindu) earth.

Dharah

Diamante (Spanish) like a diamond, a form of Diamond, a unisex name.

Diamonte

Diamond (Latin) precious gem, shining protector, a unisex name.

Diamand, Diamanda, Diamande, Diamandia, Diamonda, Diamonde, Diamonia, Diamonique, Dimantina, Diamonte, Diamontina, Dyamanta, Dyamantina, Dyamond, Dyamonda, Dyamonde, Dyamonia, Dyamonique, Dyamonte, Dyamontina, Dymantina

Diana (Latin) divine, goddess of the hunt, the moon and fertility.

Daiana, Daianna, Daina, Dainah,
Dayana, Dayanah, Dayanna,
Dayannah, Di, Dia, Dianah,
Dianalyn, Dianarose, Dianatris,
Dianca, Diandra, Dianielle, Dianita,
Dianna, Diannah, Dianys, Diasnia,
Dyana, Dyanah, Dyanna, Dyannah

Diane (Latin) divine, goddess of
the hunt, the moon and fertility, a
version of Diana.

Deana, Deane, Deanna, Deanne,
Deeana, Deeane, Deeanna,
Deeanne, Diahann, Dian, Diani,
Dianie, Diann, Dianna, Dianne

Dianthe (Greek) divine flower.

Diantha, Dianthah, Dianthia,
Dianthiah, Dianthya, Dianthyah,
Dyantha, Dyanthah, Dyanthe,
Dyanthia, Dyanthiah, Dyanthya,
Dyanthyah

Diela (Latin) worshipper of God.

Diella

Dillian (Latin) worshipped,
devoted on, loved.

Dilliana, Dillianah, Dilliane, Dilliann,
Dillianna, Dilliannah, Dillianne,
Dylian, Dyliana, Dylianah, Dyliane,
Dyliann, Dylianna, Dyliannah,
Dylianne, Dyllian, Dylliana,
Dyllianah, Dyllianna, Dylliannah,
Dylyan, Dylyana, Dylyanah,
Dylyane, Dylyann, Dylyanna,
Dylyannah, Dylyanne

Dilys (Welsh) perfect, true.

Dilis, Dilisa, Dilisah, Dilise, Dillis,
Dillisa, Dillisah, Dillise, Dillys, Dilysa,
Dilysah, Dilyse

Dina/Dinah (Hebrew) God has
judged, vindicated.

Dinna, Dinnah, Dyna, Dynah,
Dynna, Dynnah

Dinka (African) people.

Dinkah, Dynka, Dynkah

Dionne (Greek) divine queen.

Deona, Deonda, Deondra, Deone,

Deonia, Deonna, Deonne, Deonya,
Dion, Diona, Dionda, Diondra,
Diondrea, Dione, Dionee, Dionis,
Dionna, Dionte

Dior (French) golden.

Diora, Diorah, Diore, Diorra, Diorrah,
Diorre, Dyor, Dyora, Dyorah, Dyore,
Dyorr, Dyorra, Dyorrah, Dyorre

Divinia (Latin) divine.

Divina, Divinah, Divine, Diviniah

Divya (Latin/Hindu) divine,
heavenly.

Divia, Diviah, Dyvia, Dyviah, Divyah

Dixie (French) tenth; (English) wall.

Dix, Dixee, Dixey, Dixi, Dixy

Diza (Hebrew) joy, joyful.

Deza, Dezah, Deeza, Deezah, Ditza,
Ditzah, Dizah, Dyza, Dyzah

Docila (Latin) gentle, docile.

Docilah, Docile, Docilla, Docillah,
Docille, Docyl, Docyla, Docylah,
Docyle, Docyll, Docylla, Docyllah,
Docylle

Dodie (Hebrew) beloved, a form
of Dorothy.

Doda, Dodah, Dode, Dodea,
Dodee, Dodey, Dodi, Dodia,
Dodiah, Dody

Dolly (English) doll-like, beautiful;
(American) sorrowful or lady of
sorrows, a form of Dolores.

Dolea, Doleah, Dolee, Dolei, Doley,
Doli, Dolie, Dollee, Dollei, Dolley,
Dolli, Dollie

Dolores (Spanish) sorrowful or lady
of sorrows.

Delorcitas, Delorea, Delores,
Deloria, Delorita, Deloritas,
Dolorcitas, Dolorea, Doloria,
Dolorita, Doloritas

Dominica (Latin) belonging to the
Lord, feminine form of Dominic.

Domenica, Domenika, Domineca,

Dominecea, Domineka, Dominga, Domini, Dominick, Dominicka, Dominika, Dominixe, Domino, Dominyca, Dominyka, Domka, Domnica, Domnicka, Domnika, Domonica, Domonice, Domonika

Dominique (French) belonging to the Lord, a form of Dominica.

Domanique, Domenique, Domenque, Domineque, Dominiqua, Domino, Dominoque, Dominque, Dominuque, Domique, Domminique, Domoniqua, Domonique

Dona (English) world leader, proud ruler.

Donail, Donaill, Donaille, Donalea, Donalisa, Doni, Donia, Donise, Donitrae

Donalda (Celtic) ruler of the world, proud leader, mighty, feminine form of Donald.

Donaldina

Donata (Latin) gift from God.

Donatha, Donathia, Donathiah, Donato, Donatta, Donetha, Donetia, Donetta, Donette, Donita, Donitha, Donitia, Donnette, Donnita, Donnitha, Donnitia

Donelle (Celtic) mighty, world leader.

Donell, Donella, Donnell, Donnella, Donnelle

Donna (Italian) lady.

Dona, Dondi, Donnae, Donnah, Donnalee, Donnalen, Donnay, Donne, Donni, Donnie, Donnise, Dontia, Donya

Dooriya (English, Irish) the sea, the deep.

Dora (Greek) gift, a form of Adora.

Dorah, Doralee, Doraley, Dorali, Doralia, Doraliee, Doralisa, Doraliy, Doralynn, Doran, Dorana, Dorchen,

Dore, Dorece, Doree, Doreece, Dorela, Dorelee, Doreley, Doreli, Dorelia, Dorella, Dorelle, Doressa, Doretta, Dori, Dorie, Dorielle, Dorika, Dorilee, Doriley, Dorilis, Dorina, Dorion, Dorita, Doro, Dooresha, Dory

Dorabella (English) combination of Dora and Bella.

Dorabel, Dorabela, Dorabelah, Dorabele, Dorabell, Dorabellah, Dorabelle

Dorcas (Greek) graceful, gazelle.

Doreen (French) golden; (Gaelic) moody.

Doreena, Doreenah, Dorena, Dorenah, Dorene, Dorina, Dorinah, Dorine

Doris (Greek) woman of the sea.

Dori, Dorice, Dorise, Dorris, Dorrise, Dorrys, Dorryse, Dory, Dorys, Doryse

Dorothy (Greek) gift of God.

Do, Doa, Doe, Dolly, Dorathy, Dordei, Dordi, Doretta, Dori, Dorika, Doritha, Dorka, Dorle, Dorlisa, Doro, Dorolica, Dorosia, Dorota, Dorotea, Doroteya, Doroteyah, Dorotha, Dorothea, Dorotheah, Dorothee, Dorothey, Dorothi, Dorothie, Dorotiha, Dorotthea, Dorottya, Dorte, Dortha, Dorthea, Dorthey, Dorthia, Dorthy, Dory, Dosi, Dossie, Dosya, Dot, Dotee, Dotie, Dottee, Dottie, Dotty

Dorrit (Greek) dwelling; (Hebrew) generation.

Doria, Doriah, Dorit, Doritt, Dorritt

Dreama (English) dreamer.

Dreamah, Dreamar, Dreamara, Dreamarah, Dreema, Dreemah, Dreemar, Dreemara, Dreemarah

Drew (Greek) wise, courageous, strong, a unisex name.

Drewe, Dru, Drue

Drina (Spanish) helper of the people, a form of Alexandrine.

Drinah, Dryna, Drynah

Drisia/Drisiana (Hindu) daughter of the sun.

Drisianah, Drisianna, Drisiannah, Drisianne, Drysia, Drysiana, Drysianah, Drysianna, Drysiannah, Drysianne

Drusilla (Latin) strong.

Drewsila, Drewsilah, Drucee, Drucell, Drucella, Drucellah, Drucey, Druci, Drucie, Drucill, Drucilla, Drucillah, Drucy, Druscee, Druscilla, Druscillah, Druscille, Drusee, Drusey, Drusi, Drusie, Drusillah, Drusy

Duana (Irish) poem or song, dark.

Duanah, Duanna, Duannah, Dwana, Dwanah, Dwanna, Dwannah

Duena (Spanish) a chaperone.

Dueena, Dueenah, Duenah, Duenna, Duennah

Duha (Arabic) forenoon, morning, a unisex name.

Dhuha

Dulcie (Latin) sweet or charming.

Delcina, Delcine, Delcinia, Delcy, Douce, Doucey, Doucie, Doucy, Dulce, Dulcea, Dulci, Dulcia, Dulciana, Dulcibel, Dulcibella, Dulcibelle, Dulcine, Dulcinea, Dulcinia, Dulcy, Dulse, Dulsea

Durene (Latin) enduring steadfast, feminine form of Durant.

Durean, Dureana, Dureanah, Dureane, Dureen, Dureena, Dureenah, Dureene, Duren, Durena, Durenah, Durin, Durina, Durinah, Durine, Duryn, Duryna, Durynah, Duryne

Durva (Hindu) grass.

Dustine (German) valiant fighter, dark stone, feminine form of Dustin.

Dustean, Dusteana, Dusteanah, Dusteane, Dusteena, Dusteenah, Dusteene, Dustina, Dustinah, Dustyna, Dustynah, Dustyne

Dyani (Native American) deer.

Dyan, Dyana, Dyane, Dyane, Dyann, Dyanna, Dyannah, Dyanne,

Dylan (Welsh) from the sea, a unisex name.

Dylaan, Dylaina, Dylana, Dylanah, Dylane, Dylanee, Dylaney, Dylanie, Dylann, Dylanna, Dylannah, Dylanne, Dylannee, Dylen, Dylena, Dylenah, Dylin, Dylina, Dylinah, Dyllan, Dyllana, Dyllanah, Dylon, Dylona, Dylonah, Dylyn, Dylyna, Dylynah

Dyllis (Welsh) sincere.

Dillis, Dilys, Dilyss, Dylis, Dyliss, Dylisse, Dylliss, Dyllisse, Dylys, Dylyse, Dylyss, Dylysse

Dymphna (Celtic) fawn, eligible, suitable.

Dimfna, Dimphna, Dymfna

Dyna (Greek) power, powerful.

Dynasty (Latin) strong leader.

Dynastee, Dynastey, Dynasti, Dynastie

Dyshawna (American) combination of prefix Dy and Shawna.

Dyshanta, Dyshantah, Dyshaun, Dyshauna, Dyshawn, Dyshawnah, Dyshona, Dyshonah, Dyshonda, Dyshondah, Dyshonna, Dyshonnah

Eadda (English) prosperous, wealthy.
Eada, Eadah, Eaddah

Earlene (English) of high rank, noble; (Irish) pledge, promise, a feminine version of Earl.
Earleen, Earleena, Earlena, Earlenah, Earlina, Earlinah, Earline

Eartha (English) of the earth.
Earthah, Earthia, Earthiah, Earthya, Earthyah, Ertha, Erthah, Erthia, Erthiah, Erthya, Erthyah

Easter (English) born at Easter.
Eastera, Easterina, Easterine, Easteryn, Easteryna, Easteryne

Eavan (Irish) fair.
Eavana, Eavanah, Eavane

Ebba (English) flowing back on the tide.
Eba, Ebah, Ebbah

Ebere (African) mercy.

Eberta (Teutonic) bright.
Ebertah, Eberte, Ebirt, Ebirta, Ebirte

Ebony (Greek) dark beauty, black, a hard wood.
Eban, Ebanee, Ebaney, Ebani, Ebanie, Ebany, Ebbony, Ebone, Ebonee, Eboney, Eboni, Ebonie, Ebonique, Ebonisha, Ebonye, Ebonyi

Echo (Greek) repeated sound, a nymph who pined away for the love of Narcissus until nothing was left but her voice.
Echoe, Ecko, Eckoe, Ekko, Ekkoe

Eda (English) rich, prosperous, a form of Edana, Edda and Edith.
Edah

Edana (Irish) little fiery one, Edana's fortress, Irish saint who came to Scotland – its capital, Edinburgh, was originally called Dun.
Adana, Adanah, Edan, Edanah, Edanna, Edannah, Edna, Ednah

Edda (English) rich; (German) battler, a form of Hedda; (Old Norse) poetry.
Eda, Edah, Eddah, Etta, Ettah, Ettie

Edeline (English) high-born, noble, kind.
Edelin, Edelina, Edelinah, Edelyn, Edelyna, Edelynah, Edelyne

Eden (Hebrew) paradise, delightful, enchanting, a unisex name; (Babylonian) a plain.
Eaden, Edan, Edana, Edane, Edania, Ede, Edena, Edene, Edenia, Edin, Edina, Edinah, Edine, Edinia, Edon, Edona, Edonah, Edone, Edonia, Edyn, Edyna, Edynah, Edyne, Edynia

Edeva (English) rich gift.
Eddeva, Eddevah, Eddeve, Edevah, Edeve

Edian (Hebrew) God's decoration.
Edia, Ediah, Edya, Edyah

Edina (English) prosperous, fort.
Edeen, Edeena, Edeenah, Edeene, Edena, Edenah, Edinah, Edine, Edyna, Edynah, Edyne

Edith (Anglo-Saxon) prosperous, happy, rich gift.

Eadith, Eda, Ede, Edetta, Edette, Edgith, Edgyth, Edi, Edie, Edit, Edita, Editha, Edithe, Editta, Ediva, Edy, Edye, Edyta, Edyth, Edytha, Edythe, Edyva, Eyde, Eydie

Edlyn (English) rich woman, noble.
Edlin, Edlina, Edline, Edlyna, Edlyne

Edmunda (Anglo-Saxon) rich, happy, prosperous protector, feminine form of Edmund.
Edmanda, Edmandah, Edmonda, Edmondah, Edmundah

Edna (Hebrew) delight, rejuvenation.
Adna, Adnah, Adnisha, Adnishah, Ednah, Edneisha, Edneishah, Edneshia, Edneshiah, Ednisha, Ednishah, Ednita, Ednitah, Edona, Edonah

Edolie (English) noble.
Edolee, Edoley, Edoli, Edoly

Edrea (English) prosperous, powerful.
Edra, Edrah, Edreah, Edria, Edriah, Edrya, Edryah

Edrice/Edris (English) prosperous ruler, wealthy owner, feminine form of Edric.
Edrea, Edree, Edren, Edrena, Edrene, Edrey, Edrica, Edricah, Edricia, Edriciah, Edrina, Edrinah, Edrine, Edriss, Edrissa, Edrisse, Edryca, Edrycah, Edrycia, Edryciah, Edrycya, Edrycyah, Edrys, Edryss, Edryssa, Edrysse

Eduarda/Eduardo (Spanish) prosperous guardian.

Edwardina (English) prosperous guardian, feminine form of Edward.
Edwardinah, Edwardine, Edwardinia, Edwardyna, Edwardynah, Edwardyne, Edwardynia

Edwina (English) prosperous friend, feminine form of Edwin.
Eaddy, Eadi, Eadina, Eadween, Eadweena, Eadweenah, Eadweene, Eadwina, Eadwinah, Eadwine, Eadwinna, Eadwinnah, Eadwinne, Eadwyna, Eadwynah, Eadwyne, Eadwynna, Eadwynnah, Eadwynne, Eddy, Edi, Edina, Edween, Edweena, Edweenah, Edweene, Edwinah, Edwine, Edwinna, Edwinnah, Edwinne, Edwyna, Edwynah, Edwyne, Edwynna, Edwynnah, Edwynne

Effie (Scots) pleasant, of good repute, spoken well of; (Greek) singer, from Euphemia.
Efea, Efee, Effea, Effee, Effi, Effia, Effy, Ephea, Ephee, Ephi, Ephia, Ephie

Efia (African) born on a Friday.
Efiah, Efya, Efyah

Efrata (Hebrew) honoured, respected.
Efratah, Ephrata, Ephratah

Efrona (Hebrew) singing bird.
Efronah, Efronna, Efronnah

Egberta (English) bright sword, feminine form of Egbert.
Egbertah, Egberte, Egbirt, Egbirta, Egbirtah, Egbirte, Egburt, Egburta, Egburtah, Egburte, Egbyrt, Egbyrta, Egbyrtah, Egbyrte

Egypt (Egyptian) from Egypt.

Eiddwen (Welsh) fond, faithful, fair.
Eddwin, Eddwina, Eddwinah, Eddwine, Eddwyn, Eddwyna, Eddwynah, Eddwyne, Edwina, Edwinah, Edwinah, Edwine, Edwyn, Edwyna, Edwynah, Edwyne, Eiddwena, Eiddwenah, Eiddwene, Eiddwin, Eiddwina, Eiddwine, Eiddwyn, Eiddwyna, Eiddwynah, Eiddwyne

Eileen (English, Greek, Irish) shining light, a form of Helen.

Ailean, Aileana, Aileen, Aileena, Ailein, Aileina, Aileyn, Aileyna, Aileynah, Ailin, Ailina, Ailyn, Ailyna, Aylean, Ayleana, Ayleen, Ayleena, Aylein, Ayleina, Ayleyn, Ayleyna, Aylin, Aylina, Aylyn, Aylyna, Eilean, Eileana, Eileena, Eileenah, Eileene, Eleen, Eleena, Eleenah, Eleene, Elin, Elina, Elinah, Eline, Elyn, Elyna, Elyne, Eylean, Eyleana, Eyleane, Eyleen, Eyleena, Eylein, Eyleina, Eyleyn, Eyleyna, Eylin, Eylina, Eylyn, Eylyna

Eiluned (Welsh) idol.

Eir (Old Norse) peaceful person, the Norse goddess of healing.
Eia, Eiah, Eira, Eirah, Eyr, Eyra, Eyrah

Eira (Welsh) snow.
Eir, Eirah, Eyr, Eyra, Eyrah

Eirwen (Welsh) white snow.
Eirwena, Eirwenah, Eirwene, Eyrwen, Eyrwena, Eyrwene, Irwen, Irwena, Irwenah, Irwene

Eithne (Celtic) fiery one.
Ethne

Ekateirna (Russian) pure, a form of Katherine.
Ekaterin, Ekaterina, Ekaterine, Ekaterini, Ekateirn, Ekateirni

Ela (Polish, German) noble, serene.
Elah, Ella, Ellah

Elaine (Greek) light.
Ealain, Ealaina, Ealaine, Ealaini, Ealainia, Eilain, Eilaina, Eilainah, Eilaine, Eilainia, Eilainiah, Eilan, Eilana, Eilane, Eilani, Eilania, Eilanie, Eilanit, Eilauna, Eilayn, Eilayna, Eilaynah, Eillain, Eillaina, Eillaine, Elain, Elaina, Elainah, Elainia, Elainiah, Elan, Elana, Elanah, Elane, Elani, Elanie, Elanit, Elauna, Elayn, Elayna, Elaynah, Elaynia, Ellaine,

Ellaina, Ellainah, Lainee, Lainey, Laini, Lainie, Lainy

Elana (Slavic) spirited; (Hebrew) oak tree.
Elanah, Elane, Elanna, Elannah, Elanne, Ellana, Ellanah, Ellann, Ellanna, Ellannah, Ellanne

Elanora (Australian Aboriginal) from the sea.
Elanorah, Elanore, Ellanora, Ellanorah, Ellanore, Ellanorra, Ellanorrah, Ellanorre

Elata (Latin) praised, elevated.
Elatah, Ellata, Ellatah

Elberta (Teutonic) noble, bright, a form of Alberta.
Elbertah, Elbertha, Elberthah, Elberthina, Elberthinah, Elberthine, Elbertina, Elbertinah, Elbertine

Eldora (Spanish) the golden one.
Eldorah, Eldorea, Eldoree, Eldorey, Eldori, Eldoria, Eldoriah, Eldorie, Eldory

Eleanor (Greek) light, a form of Helen.
Eladine, Elana, Elanah, Elanna, Elannor, Elannora, Elanor, Elanora, Elanore, Eleanora, Eleanore, Elena, Elenah, Eleni, Elenor, Elenora, Elianora, Elianore, Elinor, Elinora, Elinore, Elladine, Ellannor, Ellannore, Ellanor, Ellanora, Ellanore, Elleanora, Elleanore, Ellena, Elleni, Ellenor, Ellenora, Ellianore, Ellinor, Ellinora, Ellinore, Ellnor, Ellnora, Ellnore, Ellynora, Ellynore, Elna, Elnor, Elnore, Elynor, Elynora, Elynore

Electra (Greek) brilliant.
Eleckra, Eleckraa, Electraa, Electraah, Electrah, Elektra, Elektraa, Elektraah, Elektrah

Eleebana (Australian Aboriginal) beautiful.
Elebana, Elebanah, Elebanna,

*Elebannah, Eleebanah,
Eleebanna, Eleebannah, Ellebana,
Ellebanah*

Elena (Italian) light, a form of Helen.
*Eleana, Eleanah, Eleen, Eleena,
Eleenah, Elen, Elenah, Elene, Elenitsa,
Elenitsah, Elenka, Elenkah, Elenna,
Elennah, Elenoa, Elenoah, Elenola,
Elenolah, Elina, Elinah, Ellena, Ellenah,
Ellina, Ellinah, Lena, Lenah, Lenna,
Lennah, Lina, Linah*

Eleni (Greek) light, a form of
Eleanor.
Elenee, Eleney, Elenie, Eleny

Elenola (Hawaiian) light, bright, a
form of Eleanor.
Elenolah

Eleora (Hebrew) the Lord is my light.
Eleorah

Elese (German) noble; (Hawaiian)
noble, a form of Elsie.
*Eleese, Elesse, Elise, Elisse, Elleese,
Ellesse, Ellise, Ellisse*

Eletta (English) elf.
*Eleta, Eletah, Elete, Elett, Elettah,
Elette*

Elfreda (Anglo-Saxon) noble,
powerful elf.
*Elfrea, Elfreah, Elfredah, Elfredda,
Elfreddah, Elfreeda, Elfreedah,
Elfreyda, Elfreydah, Elfrida, Elfridah,
Elfryda, Elfrydah*

Elga (Scandinavian) holy.
Elgah, Elgar, Elgara

Eliana (Hebrew) God has
answered me.
*Elianah, Elianna, Eliannah, Elianne,
Elliana, Ellianah, Ellianna, Ellilannah,
Ellilanne, Ellyanna, Ellyannah,
Ellyanne, Elyana, Elyanah, Elyanna,
Elyannah, Elyanne*

Elina (Greek) light.
Elinah

Elisa (English, Spanish)
consecrated to God, holy and
sacred to God, a form of Elizabeth.
*Eleesa, Eleisa, Elesa, Elesia, Elise,
Elisia, Ellisa, Ellisia, Ellissa, Ellissia,
Ellsia, Ellysa, Ellysia, Elsa, Elysa,
Elysia, Elysiah, Elyssia, Elyssya, Elysya*

Elisabeth/Elizabeth (Hebrew)
consecrated to God, holy and
sacred to God.
*Belita, Bess, Bessie, Bessy, Beth,
Betina, Betine, Bette, Bettie,
Bettina, Betty, Eleece, Eleesa, Elice,
Elis, Elisa, Elisabet, Elisah, Elise,
Elissa, Elisse, Eliza, Elizaveta, Ellece,
Elleese, Elleeswa, Ellice, Ellisa, Ellise,
Ellyce, Ellysa, Ellyse, Elsa, Else, Elsie,
Elspeth, Elsy, Elyse, Lib, Libbie, Libby,
Lilbeth, Lisa, Lisette, Liz, Liza, Lizzie,
Lizzy, Ysebel*

Elisabetta (Italian) chosen child,
consecrated to God, holy and
sacred to God, a form of Elizabeth.
*Elisabet, Elisabeta, Elisabette,
Elizabet, Elizabeta, Elizabetta,
Elizabette*

Elise (English, French) consecrated
to God, holy and sacred to God, a
form of Elizabeth.
*Eleece, Eleesa, Elice, Elis, Elisa,
Elisah, Elissa, Elisse, Elleesa, Elleese,
Ellece, Ellice, Ellisa, Ellise, Ellyce,
Ellysa, Ellyse, Elsie, Elysa, Elyse*

Elishia (Greek,Hebrew)
consecrated to God, holy and
sacred to God, a form of Elizabeth.
*Eleacia, Eleecia, Eleesha, Eleeshia,
Eleesia, Elesha, Eleshia, Elishiah,
Elleccia, Ellecia, Elleeciah, Elleesa,
Elleesia, Ellesa, Ellesia, Ellisa,
Ellishah, Ellishia, Ellishiah, Ellisia,
Ellisiah, Ellysha, Ellyshah, Ellyshia,
Ellyshiah, Ellyshya, Ellyshyah*

GIRLS

Elissa (Greek/Hebrew) consecrated to God, holy and sacred to God, a form of Elizabeth.

Elisa, Elisah, Elissah, Eliza, Elizah, Elizza, Elizzah, Elysa, Elysah, Elyssa, Elyssah, Elyza, Elyzah

Elita (French) special one.

Eleata, Eleatah, Eleeta, Eleetah, Eleita, Eleitah, Elida, Elidah, Elitah, Elitia, Elitie, Ellita, Ellitah, Ellitia, Ellitie, Ellyta, Ellytah, Ellyte, Elyta, Elytah, Elyte, Elytia, Leeta, Leetah, Leita, Leitah, Lida, Lidah, Lita, Litah, Litia, Litiah, Lyta, Lytah, Lytia, Lytiah

Eliza (English) consecrated to God, holy and sacred to God, a form of Elizabeth.

Elisa, Elise, Elizah, Elize, Elizea, Elizeah, Elizza, Elizzah, Elliza, Ellizah, Ellizza, Ellizzah, Ellysa, Ellysah, Ellyza, Ellyzah, Elsa, Elspeth, Elsie, Elysa, Elysah, Elyssa, Elyssah, Elyza, Elyzah

Elke (German) noble.

Elkee, Elkey, Elki, Elkie, Elky

Ella (English) elfin, a fairy maiden, a form of Eleanor, Elizabeth, Ellen and Helen.

Ela, Elah, Elaine, Elani, Eleanor, Elin, Ellah, Ellen

Ellama (Hindu) mother goddess.

Elamma

Elle (French) she.

El, Ele, Ell

Ellen (English) light, a form of Eleanor and Helen.

Elaine, Elani, Eleanor, Elen, Elene, Elenee, Elenie, Elin, Eline, Ella, Ellan, Ellene, Ellin

Ellery (English) from the elder-tree island, a unisex name.

Elari, Elarie, Elery, Ellari, Ellarie, Ellary, Ellerey, Elleri, Ellerie

Ellice (English) noble, a form of Alice.

Elice, Elise, Ellise, Ellyce, Ellyse, Elyce, Elyse

Ellin (Australian Aboriginal) moving.

Elly (English) light, a form of Eleanor, Ella and Ellen.

El, Ele, Ell, Elle, Elli, Ellie

Elma (Turkish) sweet fruit.

Ellma, Ellmah, Ellmar, Elmah, Elmar

Elmira (Arabic, Spanish) princess.

Elmear, Elmearah, Elmeera, Elmeerah, Elmeira, Elmeirah, Elmera, Elmerah, Elmirah, Elmiria, Elmiriah, Elmyra, Elmyrah

Elodie (Greek, English) wealthy, rich.

Elodea, Elodee, Elodey, Elodi, Elodia, Elodiah, Elody, Elodya, Elodyah, Elodye

Eloisa/Eloise (Italian/Teutonic) battle maiden.

Elliose, Elouisa, Elouisah, Elouise, Heliose

Elouera (Australian Aboriginal) pleasant place.

Elrica (German) ruler.

Elsa (German) noble, holy and sacred to God, a form of Elizabeth.

Elcea, Elcee, Elcey, Ellcea, Ellcee, Ellcey, Ellci, Ellcia, Ellcie, Ellcy, Ellise, Ellsa, Ellsah, Ellsea, Ellsee, Ellsey, Ellsi, Ellsia, Ellsie, Ellsy, Elise, Elsa, Elsah, Elsea, Elsee, Elsey, Elsi, Elsia, Elsie, Elspeth, Elsy

Elsie (German) noble, holy and sacred to God, a form of Elizabeth.

Elcea, Elcee, Elcey, Elise, Ellcea, Ellcee, Ellcey, Ellci, Ellcia, Ellcie,

Ellcy, Ellise, Ellsa, Ellsah, Ellsea, Ellsee, Ellsey, Ellsi, Ellsia, Elsie, Ellsy, Elsa, Elsah, Elsea, Elsee, Elsey, Elsi, Elsia, Elsie, Elspeth, Elsy

Elspeth (English, Scottish) holy and sacred to God, a form of Elizabeth.
Elspet, Elspie

Elva (English) elf.
Elvah, Elvara, Elvarah, Elvena, Elvenah, Elvenea, Elvia, Elviah, Elvie, Elvina, Elvinah, Elvine, Elvinea, Elvinia, Elvinna, Elvinnia, Elvyna, Elvynah, Elvyne, Elvynia, Elvyniah, Elvynie, Elvyny, Elvynya, Elvynyah, Elvyne

Elvina (English) friend of the elves, little elf.
Elvinah, Elvinia, Elviniah, Elvyna, Elvynah, Elvyne

Elvira (Latin) white, blond; (Spanish) elf-like; (German) closed up.
Elva, Elvara, Elvarah, Elvie, Elvirah, Elvire, Elvyra, Elvyrah, Vera

Elysia (Latin) blissful sweetness.
Elisa, Elisah, Elise, Elisha, Elishia, Elishiah, Elysha, Elyshah, Elyshia, Elyshiah, Elysya, Elysyah, Ilisha, Ilishia, Ilysha, Ilysia

Elyssa (English) holy and sacred to God.
Elise, Elissa, Elisse, Elyse, Elysse, Elyssia

Ema (Spanish) like grandmother.

Emalia (Hawaiian) industrious, a form of Amelia, Emily.

Emanuela/Emmanuelle (Hebrew) God goes with you.
Emanual, Emanualla, Emanuel, Emanuelah, Emanuele, Emanuell, Emanuella, Emanuellah, Emanuelle, Emmanuel,

Emmanuela, Emmanuelah, Emmanuele, Emmanuell, Emmanuella, Emmanuellah

Ember (French) amber colour, a form of Amber; (English) remains of a fire.
Emberlee, Emberly

Eme (Hawaiian) beloved, a form of Amy.
Emee, Emey, Emy

Emerald (French) bright green gem.
Emelda, Emeldah, Emeralda, Emilda, Emildah, Esmeralda, Esmeraladah

Emilia (Italian) ambitious, industrious, a form of Amelie, Emily.
Emila, Emilea, Emileah, Emiliah, Emilya, Emilyah, Emmila, Emmilea, Emmileah, Emmilia, Emmiliah, Emmilya

Emily (German) industrious; (Latin) flatterer.
Eimile, Em, Emaily, Emalee, Emeli, Emelia, Emelie, Emelita, Emely, Emilee, Emiley, Emili, Emilia, Emilie, Emilis, Emilka, Emillie, Emilly, Emmaline, Emmaly, Emmélie, Emmi, Emmie, Emmily, Emmy, Emmye, Emylie, Emyle, Emyly

Emma (German) industrious, whole, universal; (Latin) flatterer.
Em, Ema, Emah, Emalin, Emalina, Emaline, Emalyn, Emalyna, Emalyne, Emelin, Emelina, Emeline, Emelyn, Emelyna, Emmah, Emmalin, Emmalina, Emmaline, Emmalyn, Emmalyna, Emmalyne, Emmelin, Emmelina, Emmeline, Emmelyn, Emmelyna, Emmelyne, Emmi, Emmie, Emmy

Ena (Gaelic) shining light, a form of Helen.
Enah

Enchantra (English) enchanting.
*Enchantrah, Enchantria,
Enchantriah, Enchantrya,
Enchantryah*

Endora (Hebrew) fountain.
Endorah, Endorra, Endorrah

Endota (Australian Aboriginal)
beautiful.
Endotah, Endotya, Endotyah

Engracia (Spanish) graceful.
*Engrace, Engracee, Engraciah,
Engracya, Engrasia, Engrasiah*

Enid (Welsh) spirit of life.
*Enida, Ennid, Ennida, Ennyd,
Ennyda, Enyd, Enyda, Enydah*

Enrica (Spanish) ruler of the home,
feminine form of Henry.
*Enricah, Enricka, Enrickah, Enrieta,
Enrietta, Enriette, Enrika, Enrikah,
Enrikka, Enrikkah, Enriqua, Enrique,
Enryca, Enrycah, Enryka, Enrykah*

Enrichetta (Italian) ruler of the
home, a form of Harriet, Henrietta.

Enrique (Spanish) ruler of the
home, a form of Harriet, Henrietta.

Enya (Scottish) jewel, blazing.
Enia, Eniah, Enyah

Epifania (Italian) honorific name
from the feast of the Epiphany on
January 6th.
*Ephana, Epifanee, Epifaney,
Epifani, Epifanie, Epiphanee,
Epiphaney, Epiphani, Epiphania,
Epiphanie*

Erasma (Greek) desired, loved.
Erasmah

Erica (Scandinavian, English)
honourable, brave ruler, feminine
form of Eric.

*Ericah, Ericca, Ericha, Erika, Erikah,
Eriqua, Erique, Errica, Errika*

Erin (Irish) peaceful, from Ireland.
*Eirann, Eirinn, Eran, Erana, Eranah,
Eren, Erena, Erenah, Erene, Ereni,
Erenia, Erian, Eriana, Eriane, Eriann,
Erianna, Erianne, Erina, Erinan,
Erine, Erineta, Erinete, Erinett,
Erinetta, Erinette, Erinia, Eriniah,
Erinn, Erinna, Erinnah, Erinne, Errin,
Errina, Errinn, Errinna, Eryn, Eryna,
Eryne, Erynna, Erynnah, Erynne*

Erline (Celtic) pledge, feminine
form of Earl.
*Erla, Erlana, Erlean, Erleana,
Erleanah, Erleane, Erleen, Erleena,
Erleene, Erlena, Erlene, Erlenna,
Erlenne, Erlin, Erlina, Erlinda, Erlyn,
Erlyna, Erlynah, Erlyne, Erlynn,
Erlynna, Erlynna, Erlynnah, Erlynne*

Ermine (Latin) noble, a form of
Hermina.
*Erma, Ermin, Ermina, Erminda,
Erminia, Erminie*

Ermintrude (Teutonic) whole.
Ermyntrude

Ernestine (English) sincere, earnest,
feminine form of Earnest.
*Erna, Ernaline, Ernesia, Ernesta,
Ernestia, Ernestina, Ernesztina,
Ernesztine*

Eryn (English) peaceful, a form of
Erin.
*Eirin, Eiryn, Erin, Errin, Erryn, Errynah,
Erryne, Errynna, Errynnah, Errynne,
Eryna, Eryne, Erynna, Erynnah,
Erynne*

Eshe (African) life.
Esha, Eshah

Esme (French, Greek, Spanish)
emerald jewel.
*Esma, Esmae, Esmah, Esmai, Esmay,
Esmé, Esmee, Esmée, Esmey*

Esmeralda (Spanish) emerald jewel.

Emelda, Emeldah, Emeldé, Esme, Esmeraldah, Esmerelda, Esmereldah, Esmerilda, Esmerildah, Esmiralda, Esmiraldah, Esmirelda, Esmireldah, Ezmerelda, Ezmereldah, Ezmirilda, Ezmirildah

Esperanza (Spanish) hopeful.

Esperanzah

Esta (Persian) star, a form of Esther.

Estah

Estebana (Spanish) crowned, a form of Stephanie.

Estebania

Estee (English) star, a form of Estelle.

Esta, Estah, Estey, Esti, Estie, Esty

Estefani (Spanish) crowned, a form of Stephanie.

Estefania, Estefaniah, Estifani, Estifania, Estifaniah

Estelle (French) star.

Essie, Estee, Estel, Estela, Estelah, Estele, Esteley, Estelina, Estelinah, Estelita, Estelitah, Estell, Estella, Estellah, Estellina, Estellinah, Estellita, Estellitah, Esthella, Esthellah

Ester (Persian) star.

Essie, Estee, Esthur, Eszter, Eszti

Estevanna (Spanish) crowned, a form of Stephanie.

Esther (Persian) star.

Esta, Estah, Estar, Ester, Estera, Esterre, Hersta, Herstar, Hestar, Hester, Hestera

Etenia (Native American) wealthy.

Eteniah, Etenya, Etenyah

Eternity (Latin) everlasting.

Ethana (Hebrew) reliable, firm, steadfast.

Ethanah, Ethena, Ethenah

Ethel (English) noble.

Ethelda, Etheldina, Etheldine, Ethelin, Etheline, Ethelinn, Ethelinne, Ethelle, Ethelyn, Ethelynn, Ethelynne, Ethil, Ethyl

Etienne (French) crowned, a form of Stephanie, a unisex name.

Estienne, Etian, Etiana, Etianna, Etianne, Etta, Ettian, Ettiana, Ettianna, Ettianne, Ettie, Ettienna

Etoile (French) star.

Etoila, Etoilah, Etoyla, Etoylah, Etoyle

Eudora (Greek) honoured gift.

Eudorah, Eudore

Eugenia (Greek) nobly born, a feminine form of Eugene.

Eugeena, Eugeenah, Eugeenee, Eugeeney, Eugeeni, Eugeenia, Eugeeniah, Eugeenie, Eugena, Eugenah, Eugenee, Eugeney, Eugeni, Eugeniah, Eugenie, Eugenina, Eugeninah, Eugina, Euginah, Eugine, Euginé, Euginée, Euginia, Euginie, Euginy, Eugyna, Eugynah, Eugynia, Eugynie, Eugyny, Evgenia, Evgeniah

Eulalia (Greek) well spoken.

Eula, Eulah, Eulalea, Eulalee, Eulalie, Eulalya, Eulalyah, Eulalyam, Eulia, Euliah, Eulya, Eulyah

Eun (Korean) silver.

Euna, Eunah

Eunice (Greek) happy.

Euna, Eunah, Eunique, Eunisa, Eunise, Euniss, Eunissa, Eunisse, Eunys, Eunysa, Eunysah, Eunyse

Euphemia (Greek) of good reputation.
Eufemia, Eufemiah, Euphan, Euphana, Euphania, Euphemie, Euphemy, Euphemya, Euphemyah

Eustacia (Greek) fruitful, productive; (Latin) calm, a feminine form of Eustace.
Eustaciah, Eustacya, Eustacyah, Eustasia, Eustasiah, Eustasya, Eustasyah

Eva (Hebrew) life.
Evà, Evah, Evalea, Evaleah, Evalee, Evalei, Evaleigh, Evaley, Evali, Evalia, Evalie, Evaly, Eve, Evelyn, Evette, Evita, Evva

Evaline (French/Hebrew) life, a form of Evelyn.
Evalean, Evaleana, Evaleanah, Evaleane, Evaleen, Evaleena, Evaleenah, Evaleene, Evalena, Evalenah, Evalene, Evalin, Evalina, Evalinah, Evalyn, Evalyna, Evalynah, Evalyne, Evalynn, Evalynna, Evalynnah, Evalynne

Evangaline/Evangeline (Greek) bringer of good news, angel, famous from Longfellow's poem of the same name.
Eva, Evangeleana, Evangeleanah, Evangeleane, Evangeleena, Evangeleenah, Evangeleene, Evangela, Evangelena, Evangelenah, Evangelene, Evangelia, Evangelica, Evangeliqua, Evangelique, Evangelista, Evangelyn, Evangelyna, Evangelynah, Evangelyne, Evangelynn, Evangelynna, Evangelynne, Eve, Vangie, Vangy

Evanthe (Greek) flower.
Evantha

Eve (Hebrew) life, first woman created by God.
Eva, Evalina, Evaline, Evelina, Eveline, Evelyn, Evette, Evita, Evlyn

Evelia (Hebrew) life, first woman created by God, a form of Eve.

Evelina (Italian) life, a form of Evelyn.

Evelyn (English) life, a unisex name.
Eva, Evaline, Evangelina, Evangelinah, Evelina, Eveline, Evelynn, Evelynne, Evette, Evita, Evlyn, Evlynn

Everilda (German) slayer of the boar.

Evette (French) archer, a form of Yvette.
Evet, Evete, Evett, Yvonne

Evgeniya (Russian) well-born.

Evita (Spanish) life, first woman created by God, a form of Eve.
Eva, Eve, Evelyn, Eveta, Evetah, Evetta, Evettah, Evette, Evitah, Evitta, Evyta, Evytta

Evonne (French) archer, a form of Yvonne.
Evanna, Evanne, Eveni, Evenie, Evenna, Evenne, Eveny, Evetta, Evon, Evona, Evonah, Evone, Evonn, Evonna, Evonny, Evony

Eyota (Native American) greatest.
Eyotah

Ezrela (Hebrew) reaffirming the belief in God.
Esrela, Esrelah, Esrele, Esrell, Esrella, Esrellah, Esrelle, Ezrelah, Ezrele, Ezrell, Ezrella, Ezrellah, Ezrelle

Ezri (Hebrew) helpful, a feminine form of Ezra.
Ezrah, Ezri, Ezria, Ezriah, Ezrya, Ezryah

Fabia (Latin) bean grower, a feminine form of Fabian.

Fabiana, Fabiann, Fabianna, Fabianne, Fabiena, Fabiene, Fabienna, Fabienne, Fabiola, Fabra, Fabreanne, Fabria, Fabrian, Fabriana, Fabrianna, Fabrianne

Fabiola (Latin) bean grower, a form of Fabia.

Fabiolah, Fabiole, Fabyola

Fabrice (French) works with the hands, a unisex name.

Fabriciana, Fabriziana

Fadila (Arabic) virtuous, superior, cultured, refined, purity.

Fadheela, Fadhila, Fadilah

Fae (French) fairy; (English) fairy or magical creature, a form of Faith.

Fai, Faie, Fay, Faye

Faiga (German) a bird.

Faina/Faine (English) happy, joyful.

Fainah, Fayin, Fayina, Fayinah, Fayine, Fayna, Faynah, Fayne, Feana, Feanah, Fenna, Fennah

Fairlee (English) from the yellow meadow.

Fairlea, Fairleah, Fairlei, Fairleigh, Fairley, Fairli, Fairlia, Fairliah, Fairlie, Fairly, Fairlya, Fayrlea, Fayrleah, Fayrlee, Fayrlei, Fayrleigh, Fayrley, Fayrli, Fayrlia, Fayrliah, Fayrlie, Fayrly, Fayrlya

Faith (Latin) trusting; (English) faithful, fidelity, trusting in God.

Fae, Faeth, Faethe, Faithe, Fay, Faye, Fayeth, Fayethe, Fayth, Faythe, Fidel, Fidela, Fidelah, Fidelaih, Fidele, Fidelia, Fidelitee, Fidelitey, Fideliti, Fidelitie, Fidelity, Fidella, Fidellah, Fidelle

Faiza (Arabic) victorious, winner.

Faizah, Fayza, Fayzah

Fala (Native American) crow.

Falah

Falda (Icelandic) folded wings.

Faida, Faidah, Faldah, Fayda, Faydah

Faline (Latin) catlike.

Falean, Faleana, Faleanah, Faleane, Faleen, Faleena, Faleenah, Faleene, Falena, Falenah, Falene, Falin, Falina, Falinah, Falinia, Faliniah, Fallin, Fallina, Fallinah, Falline, Faylina, Fayline, Faylyn, Faylyna, Faylyne, Faylynn, Faylynne, Felena, Felenia, Felina, Felinah, Feline, Felinia, Feliniah, Felyn, Felyna, Felynah, Felyne

Fanchon (French) free, freedom, a form of Frances.

Fanchona, Fanchonah, Fanchone

Fancy (French) betrothed; (English) decorative.

Fancee, Fanchette, Fanci, Fancia, Fancie

Fantasia (Greek) imagination.

Fantaisie, Fantaisy, Fantasi, Fantasie, Fantasy, Fantaysa, Fantaysia, Fantayza, Fantayzia, Fantazia, Fiantaisa, Fiantaisie, Fiantaisy, Fiantasa, Fiantasia, Fiantasy, Fiantaysa, Fiantaysia, Fiantayza, Fiantayzia, Fiantazia

Fantine (French) childlike.

Fanteen, Fantene

Farah (English) beautiful, delightful, pleasant; (Arabic) happy.

Fara, Farra, Farrah, Fayre

GIRLS

Farfalla (Italian) butterfly.

Farida (Arabic) unique, precious.
Faridah

Farley (Anglo-Saxon) from the far meadow, a unisex name.
Fairlea, Fairlee, Fairleigh, Fairley, Fairli, Fairlie, Fairly, Farlea, Farlee, Farleigh, Farli, Farlie, Farly

Fatima (Arabic) a daughter of the prophet, Muhammad.
Fatimah, Fatema, Fatemah, Fattim, Fattima, Fattimah, Fatime, Fatimeh, Fathma, Fathmah, Fatma, Fatmah, Fatme

Fatin (Arabic) charming, captivating, alluring, enchanting.
Fatina, Fatinah

Faustine (Anglo Saxon, Latin) auspicious, lucky, fortunate, a feminine version of Faust.
Fausta, Fauste, Faustina, Faustyna, Faustyne

Fawn (French) young deer.
Faun, Fauna, Faunah, Faune, Fauney, Faunia, Fauniah, Faunie, Faunna, Faunnah, Fauny, Faunya, Faunyah, Fawna, Fawnah, Fawne, Fawney, Fawnia, Fawniah, Fawnie, Fawnna, Fawnnah, Fawny, Fawnya, Fawnyah

Faxon (German) long-haired.
Faxan, Faxana, Faxanah, Faxane, Faxann, Faxanna, Faxannah, Faxane, Faxen, Faxena, Faxenah, Faxin, Faxina, Faxinah, Faxine, Faxyn, Faxyna, Faxynah, Faxyne

Fay/Faye (French) fairy; (English) fairy or magical creature; a form of Faith.
Fae, Fai, Faie, Fayann, Fayanna, Fayannah, Fayanne, Fayetta, Fayette, Fayina, Fey, Feye

Fayina, (Russian) free one.

Fayme (French) held in high esteem.
Faim, Faima, Faimah, Faime, Faimeé, Fama, Famah, Fame, Faym, Fayma, Fayme, Faymeé

Fayola (African) lucky.
Fayla, Faylah, Fayolah, Feyla, Feyola, Feyolah

Fayre (Anglo-Saxon) fair.
Fair, Faire, Fayr

Fazia (Arabic) successful, victorious.
Faziah, Fawzia, Fawziah, Fawziya, Fawziyah, Fawziyya, Fawziyyah

Fealty (French) faithful, true, trustworthy.
Fealtey, Fealti, Fealtie

Fedora (Greek) divine gift.
Fedorah, Fedorra, Fedorrah

Felicia (Latin) fortunate, happy, a form of Felicity; (Italian) green branch, a form of Phyllis.
Falecia, Faleshia, Falesia, Falicia, Felecia, Felesa, Feleshia, Felica, Feliciona, Felicya, Felisea, Felisha, Felisia, Felisiana, Felissya, Felita, Felixia, Felizia, Felka, Fellca, Fellcia, Felycia, Felysia, Felyssia, Fleasia, Fleishia, Flicha, Flichia

Feliciana (Italian) happy and joyful.
Felicianna, Felicianne, Felicijanna, Feliciona, Felicyanna, Felicyanne, Felisiana

Felicity (English) happy, fortunate, a form of Felicia.
Falicitee, Falicitey, Faliciti, Falicitia, Falicitie, Falicity, Felicita, Felicitas, Felicite, Felicité, Félicité, Felicitee, Felicitey, Feliciti, Felicitia, Felicitie,

Felicitti, Felycitee, Felycitey, Felycitie,
Felycity, Felycytee, Felycytey,
Felycyti, Felycytie, Felycyty

Felipa (Spanish) a lover of horses,
feminine form of Felipe.

Felipah, Felippa, Fellipa, Fellipah,
Fellippa

Femi (African) love me; (French)
woman.

Femey, Femia, Femiah, Femie,
Femmi, Femmie, Femy, Femya,
Femyah

Fenella (Gaelic) white-
shouldered, a form of Fionnghuala.

Fenel, Fenell, Fenellah, Fenelle,
Fennal, Fennall, Fennalla,
Fennallah, Fennela, Fennelle,
Finel, Finell, Finella, Finellah, Finelle,
Finnal, Finnala, Finnall, Finnalla,
Finnallah, Finnalle, Finnghala,
Finnoula, Finola, Finoulla, Fynela,
Fynelah, Fynele, Fynell, Fynella,
Fynelle, Fynnela, Fynnelah,
Fynnele, Fynnell, Fynnella,
Fynnellah, Fynnelle

Fern (English) from the plant name.

Ferna, Fernah, Ferne, Fernie,
Fernlee, Fernleigh, Fernly, Firn, Firne,
Furn, Furne, Fyrn, Fyrne

Fernanda (Spanish) adventurous,
courageous, a feminine form of
Ferdinand.

Ferdie, Ferdinanda, Ferdinandah,
Ferdinande, Fern, Fernande,
Fernandette, Fernandina,
Fernandinah, Nanda, Nandah

Fiala (Czech) violet flower.

Fialah, Fyala, Fyalah

Fidelia (Latin) faithful, a feminine
form of Fidel.

Fidea, Fideah, Fidel, Fidela, Fidelah,
Fidele, Fideliah, Fidelina, Fidelinah,
Fidelinna, Fidelinnah, Fidelita,
Fidelitah, Fidelity, Fidella, Fidellah,

Fidelle, Fydea, Fydeah, Fydel,
Fydela, Fydelah, Fydele, Fydelia,
Fydell, Fydella, Fydellah, Fydelle

Fifi (French) God shall add,
increase, a form of Josephine; fair,
white, a form of Fiona.

Fe, Fee, Feef, Feefe, Feefee, Fefe,
Fe-Fe, Fefi, Fefie, Fefy, Fi, Fi-Fi, Fefina,
Fefinah, Fifine

Filia (Greek) friend.

Filiah, Filya, Fylia, Fyliah, Fylya,
Fylyah

Filippa (Italian) horse lover, a form
of Philippa, feminine form of Phillip.

Felipa, Felipe, Felippa, Filipa, Filipe,
Filipina, Filippina, Flippa

Filma (German) veiled or misty.

Filmah, Filmar, Filmara, Filmaria,
Filmarya, Fylma, Fylmah, Fylmara,
Fylmaria, Fylmarya

Filomena (Italian, Greek) she
is loved, loved one, a form of
Philomena.

Fila, Filah, Filamena, Filemon,
Filemona, Filomen, Filomenah,
Filomene, Filomina, Filominah,
Filomyna, Filomyne, Fylomena,
Fylomenah, Fylomina, Fylomine,
Fylomyna, Fylomyne

Fiona (Celtic) fair, white.

Fee, Feeona, Feeonah, Feeoni,
Feeonia, Feeonie, Feeony, Feona,
Feonah, Feonia, Feoniah, Fifi, Finn,
Fionah, Fionan, Fionea, Fionia, Fionn,
Fionna, Fionnah, Fionni, Fionnia,
Fionniah, Fionne, Fionnea, Fionneah,
Fionnee, Fionnula, Fyona, Fyonah,
Fyoni, Fyonia, Fyoniah, Fyonie, Fyony,
Fyonya, Fyonyah, Phiona, Phionah,
Phyona, Phyonah

Fionnghuala (Gaelic) fair
shoulders.

Fenella, Fenellah, Fennela,
Fennelah, Fennella, Fenellah,

Finnoula, Finoulla, Fynella, Fynellah, Fynnela, Fynnelah, Fynnella, Fynnellah

Fioralba (Italian) dawn flower.

Fiorenza (Italian) flower, a form of Florence.

Fira (English) fiery.
Firah, Fyra, Fyrah

Flair (English) style.
Flaira, Flaire, Flare, Flayr, Flayra, Flayre

Flanna (Celtic) flame-coloured hair.
Flana, Flanah, Flann, Flannah, Flannea, Flannia

Flavia (Latin) yellow hair, a feminine form of Flavian.
Flaviah, Flavianna, Flavianne, Flavus, Flavya, Flavyah, Flawia, Flawiah, Flawya, Flawyah

Fleta (English) swift, fast.
Fleata, Fleatah, Fleeta, Fleetah, Fletah, Flita, Flitah, Flyta, Flytah

Fleur (French) flower.
Fleure, Fleuré, Fleuree, Fleurée

Fleurette (French) little flower.
Fleuret, Fleurett, Fleuretta, Fleurettah

Flora (Latin) flower.
Fiora, Fiorah, Fiore, Fiorenza, Fiorenzah, Flor, Florann, Floranna, Floranne, Florella, Florellah, Florelle, Floren, Florenna, Floria, Floriana, Florianna, Floriannah, Florianne, Florica, Floricah, Florimel

Florence (Latin) blooming; (Italian) place name.
Flo, Flora, Florance, Flore, Florencia, Florenciah, Florency, Florendra, Florendrah, Florentia, Florentiah, Florentina, Florentinah, Florentyna,

Florentynah, Florenza, Florenzah, Floretta, Florettah, Florette, Flori, Floria, Floriane, Florie, Florina, Florinah, Florine, Floris, Florisa, Florise, Florissa, Florisse, Florri, Florria, Florriah, Florrie, Florry, Flory, Flossie

Florida (Spanish) flourishing, blooming flowers, place name.
Floridah, Floridia, Floridiah, Florinda, Florindah, Florita, Floritah

Floris (English) a form of Florence.
Florisa, Florise, Floriss, Florissa, Florisse, Florris, Florrisa, Florrise, Florriss, Florrissa, Florrisse, Florys, Florysa, Floryse

Flossie (English) blooming, form of Florence.
Flos, Floss, Flossi, Flossy

Flower (English) blossom, flower.

Fola (African) honour, honourable.
Floa, Floah, Folah

Foluke (African) in God's care.
Foluc, Foluck, Foluk

Fontanna (French) from the fountain.
Fontain, Fontaina, Fontainah, Fontaine, Fontana, Fontanah, Fontane, Fontannah, Fontanne, Fontayn, Fontayna, Fontaynah, Fontayne

Forest (English) dweller in the forest, forester, guardian of the lord's forest, a unisex name.
Forrest, Forreste, Forrestt, Forrie

Fortuna (Latin) lucky, fortunate, a feminine form of Fortino.
Faustean, Fausteana, Fausteanah, Fausteane, Fausteen, Fausteena, Fausteenah, Fausteene, Faustina, Faustinah, Faustine, Faustyn, Faustyna, Faustynah, Faustyne, Fortinia, Fortiniah, Fortoona,

Fortoonah, Fortunah, Fortunata, Fortunatah, Fortunate, Fortune, Fortunia, Fortuniah, Fortunya, Fortunyah

Fosetta (French) dimpled.
Foset, Foseta, Fosetah, Fosete, Fosett, Fosettah, Fosette

Fotina (Greek) light.
Fotin, Fotinah, Fotine, Fotinia, Fotiniah, Fotinya, Fotinyah, Fotyna, Fotynah, Fotyne, Fotynia, Fotyniah, Fotynya, Fotynyah

Frances (Latin) free, from France, a feminine form of Francis.
Fanny, Fran, Franca, France, Francee, Francée, Francena, Francenah, Francesca, Francescah, Francess, Francesta, Francestah, Franceta, Francetah, Francetta, Francette, Francie, Francine, Francis, Francisca, Franciscah, Francisco, Franco, Francois, Francoise, Frankie, Frannie, Franny, Frencine

Francesca (Italian) a form of Frances.
Franceska, Franchesca, Francheska, Franchisca, Franchiska, Francisca, Franciska

Francine (French) free woman, a form of Frances.
Franceen, Franceine, Franceline, Francene, Francenia, Francin, Francina, Francyn, Francyna, Francyne, Fransin, Fransina, Fransinah, Fransine, Fransyn, Fransyna, Fransynah, Fransyne, Franzin, Franzina, Franzinah, Franzine, Franzyn, Franzyna, Franzynah, Franzyne

Freda (German) a shortened form of names ending in -fred.
Frea, Fredah, Fredda, Freia, Freida, Freidah, Freyda, Freydah, Frida, Fridah, Fridda, Friddah, Fryda, Frydah, Frydda, Fryddah

Frederica (German) peaceful ruler, feminine form of Frederick.
Farica, Faricah, Federica, Federicah, Freda, Fredah, Fredalena, Fredalenah, Fredalina, Fredaline, Freddi, Freddie, Frederickina, Frederickinah, Frederico, Frederika, Frederikah, Frederike, Frederina, Frederinah, Frederine, Fredi, Fredicia, Frediciah, Fredith, Fredora, Fredorah, Fredreca, Fredrecah, Fredrica, Fredricah, Freida, Freidah, Frida, Fridah, Frieda, Friedah, Fritzi, Fryderica, Frydericah

Frederique (French) a form of Frederica.
Frederiqua, Fredriqua, Fredrique, Frideriqua, Friderique, Fryderiqua, Fryderique

Freya (Scandinavian) goddess of love and fertility, noble woman.
Fraya, Frayah, Freyah, Freia, Freiah, Freja, Frejah

Fritzi (German) peaceful ruler, a form of Frederica.
Frietzi, Friezi, Fritze, Fritzie, Fritzin, Fritzina, Fritzinah, Fritzine, Fritzinn, Fritzinna, Fritzinnah, Fritzinne, Fritzlin, Fritzline, Fritzlinna, Fritzlinne, Fritzlyn, Fritzlyne, Fritzlynne, Fritzy

Fronde (French) a leafy branch.
Fronda, Frondah

Fronia (Greek) forehead.
Froniah, Fronya, Fronyah

Fulla (German) full.
Fula, Fulah, Fullah

Fulvia (Latin) tawny haired.
Fulvi, Fulviah, Fulvie, Fulvy, Fulvya, Fulvyah

Fynballa (Gaelic) fair-shouldered.
Finbala, Finbalah, Finballa, Finballah, Fynbala, Fynbalah, Fynballah

Gabby (English) devoted to God, God's messenger, a form of Gabrielle.
Gab, Gabbee, Gabbey, Gabbie, Gabe, Gabee, Gabey, Gabie, Gaby

Gabrielle (French) devoted to God, God's messenger, feminine form of Gabriel.
Gabbey, Gabbi, Gabbie, Gabbriella, Gabbrielle, Gabbryel, Gabby, Gabe, Gabey, Gabi, Gabie, Gabiella, Gabielle, Gabreal, Gabreale, Gabrealla, Gabrealle, Gabreil, Gabrial, Gabriala, Gabrialla, Gabrialle, Gabriana, Gabriel, Gabriela, Gabrielia, Gabriella, Gabrielle, Gabriellia, Gabrila, Gabrilla, Gabrille, Gabrina, Gabriylla, Gabriylle, Gabryel, Gabryella, Gabryelle, Gaby, Gavee, Gavi, Gavie, Gavriella, Gavrielle, Gavy

Gada (Hebrew) lucky.
Gadah

Gaea (Greek) goddess of the Earth, planet Earth.
Gaeah, Gaia, Gaiah, Gaiea, Gaya, Gayah

Gaetana (Italian) from Gaeta.
Gaeta, Gaetan, Gaetanah, Gaetane, Gaetanna, Gaetanne

Gagandeep (Hindu) sky's light.
Gagandip, Gagnadeep, Gagnadip, Gagndeep, Gagndip

Gage (French) pledge, promise, a unisex name.
Gaig, Gaige, Gayg, Gayge

Gail (Hebrew) father's joy, a form of Abigail.
Gael, Gaela, Gaell, Gaella, Gaelle, Gaila, Gaile, Gaill, Gailla, Gaille, Gale, Gayla, Gayle

Gaines (English) increase in wealth.
Gains, Gaynes, Gayns

Gala (Italian) finery; (Norwegian) singer.
Galah, Galla, Gallah

Galatea (Greek) milky-white, pale cream colour.
Galata, Galate, Galatee, Galatey, Galati, Galatia, Galatiah, Galatie, Galaty, Galatya, Galatyah

Galaxy (Latin) system of stars, universe.
Galaxee, Galaxey, Galaxi

Galen/Galena (Greek) healer, calm; (Irish) little, lively, a unisex name.
Gaelan, Gaelen, Gaelin, Gaellen, Gaellyn, Gaellynn, Gaelyn, Gaelynn, Gale, Galenah, Galyn, Gaylaine, Gayleen, Gaylen, Gaylene, Gayly

Gali (Hebrew) fountain or spring on a hill, a unisex name.
Gailee, Galea, Galeah, Galee, Galei, Galeigh, Galey, Galie, Gallee, Gallei, Galleigh, Galley, Galli, Gallie, Gally, Galy

Galiana/Galiena (Teutonic) lofty, supreme one.
Galian, Galianna, Galianne, Galien, Galienna, Galienne

Galina (Russian) light, a form of Helen.

Galaina, Galainah, Galaine, Galayna, Galaynah, Galayne, Galean, Galeana, Galeanah, Galeane, Galeen, Galeena, Galeenah, Galeene, Galena, Galenah, Galene, Galiana, Galianah, Galiane, Galinah, Galine

Galla (Celtic) stranger.

Gala, Galah, Gallah

Gamela (Scandinavian) elder.

Gamala, Gamalah, Gamale, Gamelah, Gamele

Gana (Hebrew) garden.

Ganah, Garna, Garnah

Ganesa (Hindu) fortunate, god of good luck and wisdom, a son of the god Shiva and goddess Pavarti, feminine form of Ganesh.

Ganesah, Ganessa, Ganessah

Ganya (Hebrew) garden of the Lord.

Gana, Gani, Gania, Ganiah, Ganyah

Garda (Teutonic) prepared, guarded, guardian.

Gardah

Gardenia (Latin) white flower.

Gardeen, Gardeena, Gardeene, Garden, Gardena, Gardene, Gardin, Gardina, Gardine, Gardinia

Garland (French) wreath of flowers, a unisex name.

Garlan, Garlana, Garlanah, Garlane, Garleen, Garleena, Garleenah, Garleene, Garlena, Garlenah, Garlene, Garlind, Garlinda, Garlindah, Garlinde

Garnet (Latin) dark red gem, a unisex name.

Garneta, Garnetah, Garnetta, Garnettah, Garnette

Garyn (English) spear carrier, feminine form of Gary.

Garan, Garana, Garane, Garen, Garena, Garin, Garina, Garine, Garra, Garran, Garrana, Garrane, Garrin, Garrina, Garrine, Garryn, Garryna, Garryne, Garyn, Garyna, Garyne, Garynn, Garynna, Garynne

Gasha (Russian) kind, good, a form of Agatha.

Gashah, Gashka

Gauri (Hindu) yellow or fair.

Gari, Gouri

Gay (French) light-hearted, gay.

Gae, Gai, Gaie, Gaye

Gaylia (English) a form of Gail.

Gaelia, Gaeliah, Gailia, Gailiah, Gayliah

Gayna (English) white wave, a form of Guinevere.

Gaena, Gaenah, Gaina, Gainah, Gaynah, Gayner, Gaynor

Gaynor (Irish) fair, child of the fair one, a unisex name.

Gainar, Gainer, Gainor, Gaynar, Gayner, Gaynnar, Gaynner, Gaynnor

Gedala (Australian Aboriginal) day.

Geela (Hebrew) joy.

Gela, Gelah, Gila, Gilah

Geetha (Hindu) song.

Geeta, Gita

Gelasia (Greek) predisposed to laughter, smiling.

Geltrude (Italian) warrior, from Gertrude.

Gemma (Latin) precious stone.
Gem, Gema, Gemah, Gemi, Gemia, Gemiah, Gemie, Gemmah, Gemmee, Gemmey, Gemmi, Gemmia, Gemmiah, Gemmie, Gemmy

Geneva (French) juniper berry, a city in Switzerland.
Geena, Gen, Gena, Geneive, Geneieve, Generva, Genieve, Gineve, Ginneva, Janeva, Jeaneva, Jeneva

Genevieve (French) white wave.
Genaveeve, Genaveve, Genavie, Genavieve, Genavive, Geneive, Geneveve, Genevievre, Genevive, Gennie, Genovieve, Genvieve, Ginette, Ginevieve, Ginevive, Ginevvev, Guinevieve, Guinivere, Guinvive, Gwenevieve, Gwenivive, Jen, Jenaveeve, Jenaveve, Jenavie, Jenavieve, Jenavive, Jeneive, Jeneveve, Jenevievre, Jenevive, Jennie, Jennifer, Jenny, Jenovieve, Jenvieve, Jinette, Jinevieve, Jinevive, Jinevvev, Nevie

Georgeanna (English) combination of Georgia and Anna.
Georgeana, Georgeanne, Georgiana, Georgianna

Georgette (French) farmer, feminine form of George.
Georget, Georgeta, Georgetta, Georjet, Georjett, Georjetta, Giorget, Giorgeta, Giorgetta, Giorgette

Georgia (Greek) farm girl, American state, feminine form of George.
Georgene, Georgette, Georgie, Giorgia

Georgie (English) farmer, a form of Georgina.
Georgee, Georgey, Georgi, Georgy

Georgina (English) farmer, feminine form of George.
Georgine, Gerogena, Gerogene, Giorgena, Giorgene, Giorgina, Giorgine, Jorgina, Jorgine

Geraldine (Teutonic) spear carrier, feminine form of Gerald.
Geraldeen, Geraldina, Geri, Gerie, Gerri, Gerrie, Gerry, Jeraldeen, Jeraldina, Jeraldine, Jeri, Jerie, Jerri, Jerrie, Jerry

Geranium (Latin) bright-red flower.

Gerarda (English) noble spear carrier, feminine form of Gerard.
Gerardina, Gerardine

Gerda (German, Norwegian) protector, warrior.
Garda, Gerdah, Gerdi

Geri (American, English) spear warrior, a form of Geraldine.
Gerie, Gerri, Gerrie, Gerry, Gery

Germaine (French) from Germany.
Gemaine, Germain, Germane, Germayn, Germayne

Gertrude (Teutonic) spear maiden, beloved warrior.
Gartred, Gartrud, Gartrude, Geertrud, Geertruda, Geertrude, Geertrudi, Geertrudie, Geertrudy, Geitruda, Geitrude, Gertina, Gertraud, Gertraude, Gertrud, Gertruda, Gertrudah, Gertrudia, Gertrudis, Gertruide, Gertruyd, Gertruyde, Trudi, Trudie, Trudy

Gervaise (French) skilled with a spear, a unisex name.
Gervayse, Gervis, Jedert, Jatrad

Geva (Hebrew) hill.
Gevah

Ghada (Arabic) young, tender graceful.
Gada, Gadah, Ghadah

Ghaliya (Arabic) precious.
Ghaliyah

Ghislaine (French) sweet pledge, loyal promise.
Ghislain, Gislain, Gislaine

Ghita (Italian) pearl.
Ghitah, Ghyta, Ghytah, Gita, Gyta, Gytah

Gia (Hebrew) God is gracious.
Giah, Gya, Gyah

Giacinta (Italian) hyacinth.
Giacintah, Jacinta, Jacintah, Jiacinta, Jiacintah

Giacobba (Hebrew) replacer, supplanter.
Giacoba, Giacobah, Giacobbah, Gyacoba, Gyacobah, Gyacobba, Gyacobbah

Gian/Giana (Italian) God is gracious, a form of Giovanna, feminine form of John.
Gean, Geana, Geane, Geann, Geanna, Geanne, Geean, Geeana, Geeane, Geeann, Geeanna, Geeanne, Gianah, Gianel, Gianela, Gianele, Gianell, Gianella, Gianelle, Gianet, Gianeta, Gianete, Gianett, Gianetta, Gianette, Gianina, Gianine, Gianinna, Gianna, Giannah, Gianne, Giannee, Gianni, Giannie, Giannina, Gianny, Gyan, Gyana, Gyanah, Gyann, Gyanna, Gyannah

Gidget (English) giddy.
Gidgett, Gydget

Gigi (French) brilliant, a form of Gilberta.
Geegee, Geygey, Gygy, Jeejee, Jeyjey, Jiji

Gilana (Hebrew) joyful.
Gila, Gilah, Gilanah, Gilane, Gilania, Gilanie, Gilena, Gilenia, Gylan, Gylana, Gylanah, Gylane

Gilberta (Teutonic) pledge, bright, brilliant, trustworthy, feminine form of Gilbert.
Gilberte, Gilbertia, Gilbertina, Gilbertine, Gilbertyna, Gilbertyne, Gilbirt, Gilbirta, Gilbirte, Gilbirtia, Gilbirtina, Gilbirtine, Gilburta, Gilburte, Gilburtia, Gilburtina, Gilburtine, Gilburtyna, Gilbyrta, Gilbyrte, Gilbyrtia, Gilbyrtina, Gilbyrtine, Gilbyrtyna, Gilbyrtyne

Gilda (Celtic) God's servant; (Anglo-Saxon) covered in gold.
Gildah, Gilded, Gylda, Gyldah, Gylded

Gillian (Latin) young with downy hair.
Gill, Gillane, Gilliana, Gilly, Gillyan, Gillyana, Gillyann, Gillyanna, Gillyanne, Giola, Giolla, Jill, Jillian, Lian

Gimbya (African) princess.

Gin (Japanese) silver.
Gina, Gyn, Gyna

Gina (Italian) a form of Regina, Angelina, Virginia.
Geena, Geenah, Ginah, Ginna, Gyna, Gynah, Jina, Jinah

Ginger (Latin) red-haired, ginger spice.
Ginata, Ginatah, Ginja, Ginjah, Ginjar, Ginjer, Gynger, Gynjer

Ginia (Latin) purity, a form of Virginia.

Ginata, Ginea, Gineah, Giniah, Ginya, Ginyah, Gynia, Gyniah, Gynya, Gynyah

Ginny (Latin) purity, a form of Virginia, Ginger.

Gin, Gini, Ginnee, Ginney, Ginni, Ginnie, Giny, Gynee, Gyni, Gynie, Gynnee, Gynni, Gynny, Jin, Jinni, Jinnie, Jinny, Jiny

Giolla (Italian) servant.

Giola

Giorgette (Italian) farmer, a form of Georgina.

Giorgetta

Giorgiana (English) farmer, a form of Georgina.

Giorgiane, Giorgina, Giorgine

Giorsala (Scottish) graceful.

Giorsal, Giorsalah, Gyorsal, Gyorsala, Gyorsalah

Giovanna (Italian) God is gracious, a form of Jane.

Giavana, Giavanah, Giavanna, Giavannah, Giovana, Giovanah, Giovannah, Giovannina, Giovona, Giovonah, Giovonna, Giovonnah, Jane, Joan, Johanna

Giralda (Teutonic) powerful contender, spear ruler.

Giraldah, Gyralda, Gyraldah

Girisa (Hindu) mountain lord, name for the god Shiva, feminine form of the name Girish.

Girisah, Girisha

Gisa (Hebrew) carved stone.

Gisah, Gysa, Gysah

Giselle (Teutonic) pledge, hostage.

Gisele, Gisella, Gisellea

Gita (Hindu) song.

Gitah, Gitta, Gittah, Gyta, Gytah

Gitana (Spanish) the gipsy.

Gitanna, Gytana, Gytanna

Githa (Greek) good.

Githah, Gytha, Gythah

Giuditta (Italian) praised, a form of Judith.

Giulia (Italian) soft-haired, youthful, a form of Julia.

Giulana, Giuletta, Giulette, Guila, Guiliana, Guilietta, Guiliette

Giuseppa (Italian) God shall add, increase, a form of Josephine.

Giuseppina, Giussepina, Giusseppa

Giustina (Italian) just, a form of Justina.

Giustinah, Giustine, Gustina, Gustinah, Gustine

Gizella (Czech) pledge, a form of Giselle.

Gizele, Gizelle, Gizellea

Gladys (Celtic) princess; (Latin) sword.

Glad, Gladdis, Gladdys, Gladis, Gladness, Glady, Gladyss, Gleddis, Gleddys

Gleda (Anglo-Saxon) happy, to make happy.

Glenda (Celtic) from the valley, feminine form of Glen.

Glanda, Glendah, Glennda, Glenndah

Glenna (Irish) from the valley, feminine form of Glen.
Glena, Glenetta, Glenina, Glenine, Glenn, Glenne, Glennia, Glennie, Gleny, Glyn, Glyna, Glynn, Glynna

Gloria (Latin) glory.
Glorea, Gloriah, Gloribel, Gloriela, Gloriella, Glorielle, Gloris, Glorisa, Glorisha, Glory, Glorya, Gloryah

Glynis (Welsh) from the valley, feminine form of Glyn.
Glenis, Glenise, Glennis, Glynise, Glynnis

Godiva (Anglo-Saxon) God's gift.

Golda (English) gold.
Goldah, Goldarina, Goldia, Goldiah, Goldie, Goldy, Goldya, Goldyah

Goldie (English) gold.
Golda, Goldee, Goldey, Goldy

Goma (African) dance of joy.
Gomah

Grace (Latin) graceful.
Graca, Gracelia, Gracella, Gracia, Gracie, Graciosa, Gracy, Graise, Grase, Gratia

Graciosa (Spanish) graceful.

Grady (Irish) illustrious, noble, a surname, a unisex name.
Gradee, Gradeigh, Gradey, Graidea, Graidey, Graidy

Gratiana (Hebrew) graceful.
Gratian, Gratiane, Gratiann, Gratianna, Gratianne, Gratyan, Gratyana, Gratane, Gratyann, Gratanna, Gratyanne

Grania (Celtic) love.
Granya

Grazia (Italian, Latin) grace.
Gratzia

Greer (Scottish) watchful, from a Gaelic form of Gregory, a unisex name.
Grear, Grier

Greta (German) pearl, a form of Margaret.
Grata, Gratah, Greata, Greatah, Greeta, Greetah, Gretah, Grete, Grett, Gretta, Grette, Grieta

Gretchen (German) pearl, a form of Margaret.
Gretchan, Gretchin, Gretchon, Gretchyn

Griselda (Teutonic) grey, battle maiden.
Grishelda, Grishilda, Grisilda

Guadalupe (Spanish) wolf valley; (Arabic) river of black stones, a unisex name.
Guadalup, Guadalop, Guadalope

Guda (Scandinavian) divine, good.
Gudah, Gudwin

Gudrun (Old Norse) divine, wisdom, battler.
Gudren, Gudrena, Gudrin, Gudrina, Gudrine, Gudrinn, Gudrinna, Gudrinne, Gudruna, Gudrunn, Gudrunna, Gudrunne

Guida (Italian) to guide.
Gaida, Guidah

Guinevere (Welsh, French) white wave, white phantom.
Guenevere, Guenna, Guinievre, Guinivere, Guinna, Gwen, Gwenevere, Gwenievre, Gwenivere

Gunhilda (Old Norse) brave, battle maid.
Gunhild

Guri (Hindu) goddess of abundance.

Gurit (Hebrew) innocent baby.
Gurita, Gurite, Guryt, Guryta, Guryte

Gurley (Australian Aboriginal) willow tree.
Gurlea, Gurleah, Gurlee, Gurlei, Gurleigh, Gurli, Gurlie, Gurly

Gustee (English) windy.
Gustea, Gustey, Gusti, Gustie, Gusty

Gwenda (Welsh) white, white wave, a form of Gwendolen.
Gwinda, Gwomda, Gwonda, Gwumda, Gwyna, Gwynna, Gwynda, Gwynedd

Gwendolen (Welsh) white wave, fair of face; (Celtic) fair of face, wife of Merlin the magician.
Gwen, Gwenda, Gwendolyn, Gwenna, Gwenney, Gwennie, Gwenny

Gwun (Native American) flute.
Gwuna

Gwyneth/Gwynneth (Celtic, Welsh) blessed, fair, blessed baby.
Gwen, Gwenda, Gwennedd, Gwenneth, Gwennie, Gwenny, Gwineth, Gwinneth, Gwynned, Guenna, Gyneth

Gypsy (English) wanderer.
Gipsea, Gipsee, Gipsey, Gipsi, Gipsie, Gipsy, Gypsea, Gypsee, Gypsey, Gypsi, Gypsie

Gytha (English) warlike.
Githa

Habiba (Arabic) beloved, sweetheart, darling.
Habeeba, Habeebah, Habibah, Habibeh

Habika (African) sweetheart.

Hachi (Native American) river.
Hachee, Hachie, Hachy

Hadara (Hebrew) adorned with beauty.
Hadarah, Hadaria, Hadariah

Hadiya (African) gift.
Hadaya, Hadia, Hadiyah, Hadya, Hadyah, Hadyea

Hadley (English) of the heath-covered meadow, a unisex name.
Haddley, Hadlea, Hadleah, Hadlee, Hadlei, Hadleigh, Hadley, Hadlie, Hadly, Lea, Lee, Leigh

Hafsah (Arabic) wife of the prophet Muhammad.

Hafthah (Arabic) preserved, protected.

Hafwen (Welsh) fair summer.
Hafwena, Hafwenah, Hafwene, Hafwin, Hafwina, Hafwinah, Hafwine

Hagar (Hebrew) forsaken, a unisex name.
Hagara, Hagarah, Hagarya, Hagaryah, Hager, Haggar, Hagir, Hagor, Hagyr

Haidee (Greek) modest.
Hadea, Hadie, Hady, Hadyee, Haide, Haidea, Haidey, Haidi, Haidia, Haidie, Haidy, Haydea, Haydee, Haydey, Haydie, Haydy

Haifa (Arabic) slender.
Haifah, Hayfa, Hayfah

Hailey/Haley/Hayley (English) from the meadow of hay; (Scandinavian) hero; (Irish) clever, ingenious, a unisex name.
Haile, Hailea, Hailee, Hailei, Haileigh, Haili, Hailie, Haily, Halle, Halley, Harley, Haylea, Haylee, Haylei, Hayleigh, Hayli, Haylie, Hayly

Haimi (Hawaiian) the seeker.

Hala (Latin) salty.
Halah

Halcyone (Greek) kingfisher, calm, peaceful.
Halcyon

Haldana (Norwegian) half Danish.
Hadanah, Haldania, Haldaniah, Haldanna, Haldannah, Haldanya, Haldanyah, Haldyanna, Haldyannah

Halia (Hawaiian) in loving memory of a relative.
Halea, Haleah, Haleea, Haleeah, Haleia, Haleiah, Haliah

Haliaka (Hawaiian) leader.
Haliakah, Halyaka, Halyakah

Halima (Arabic) gentle, patient.
Halimah, Haleema, Haleemah

Halimeda (Greek) loves, thinks of, the sea.
Halimedah, Halymeda, Halymedah

Halina (Hawaiian) resemblance, likeness.
Halinah, Haline, Halinka, Halyn, Halyna, Halynah, Halyne

Halla (African) unexpected gift.
Hallah, Hallia, Halliah

Helle (African) unexpected gift, a form of Halla.
Hallee, Halley, Hally

Hallie (Greek) thinking of the sea.
Hallea, Halleah, Hallee, Hallei, Halleigh, Halley, Halli, Hallia, Halliah, Hally

Halona (Native American) fortunate.
Hallona, Hallonah, Halonah

Hamida (Arabic) praiseworthy.
Hameeda, Hameedah, Hamidah

Hana/Hanah (Arabic) joy; (Japanese) flower.
Hanae

Hanako (Japanese) flower child.

Hanan (Arabic) mercy.

Hanele (Hebrew) merciful, compassionate, kind.
Hanal, Hanall, Hanalla, Hanalle, Hanel, Hanela, Hanelah, Hanell, Hanella, Hanelle, Hannel, Hannela, Hannele, Hannell, Hannella, Hannelle

Hanifa (Arabic) true believer.
Haneefa, Haneefah, Hanifah

Haniyyah (Arabic) pleasant, happy.
Haniya, Haniyah, Haniyya

Hanna/Hannah (Hebrew) grace of God.
Hana, Hanah

Hanya (Australian Aboriginal) stone.

Happy (English) happy, bright, cheerful.
Hap, Happ, Happee, Happey, Happi, Happie

Hara (Indian) seizer, name for Siva the destroyer, a unisex name.
Harah, Harra, Harrah

Haralda (English, Scandinavian) ruler of the army, feminine form of Harold.
Haraldah, Harralda, Harraldah

Harika (Turkish) wonderful.
Harikah, Harrika, Harrikah

Harlene (English) from the hare or stag meadow, feminine form of Harlan.
Harlan, Harlana, Harlanah, Harlane, Harlean, Harleana, Harleanah, Harleane, Harleen, Harleena, Harleenah, Harleene, Harleina, Harleinah, Harleine, Harlena, Harlenah, Harlin, Harlina, Harlinah, Harlyn, Harlyna, Harylnah, Harlyne

Harley (English) from the hare or stag meadow, a unisex name.
Harlea, Harleah, Harlee, Harleeah, Harleey, Harlei, Harleigh, Harli, Harlie, Harly

Harmony (Latin) harmony, concord.
Harmene, Harmenee, Harmeni, Harmenie, Harmeny, Harmon, Harmonee, Harmonei, Harmoney, Harmoni, Harmonia, Harmoniah, Harmonie

Harper (English) harp player or maker, a unisex name.
Harp, Harpa, Harpo

Harpreet (Punjabi) devoted to God, a unisex name.

Hardee, Hardeep, Harpee, Harpreete, Harprit, Harprite

Harriet (English) ruler of the household, feminine form of Harry.

Harri, Harrie, Harriett, Harrietta, Harriette, Harriot, Harriott, Hattie

Hasana (African) first-born girl, often used for the first-born female twin.

Hasanah, Hasanna, Hasannah, Hasna, Hasnah, Hassna, Hassnah, Hassona, Hassonah, Huseina

Hasia (Hebrew) protected by God.

Hasiah, Hasya, Hasyah

Hasina (African) good.

Hasinah, Hassina, Hassinah, Hasyn, Hasyna, Hasynah

Hasna (Arabic) beautiful.

Hasnah

Hateya (Native American) footprint in the sand, dust.

Hateia, Hateiah, Hateyah

Hathor (Egyptian) sky goddess.

Hathora, Hathorah

Hattie (English) ruler of the home, a form of Harriet, Henrietta.

Hatti, Hatty, Hetti, Hettie, Hetty

Haukea (Hawaiian) snow.

Haukeah, Haukia, Haukiah, Haukya, Haukyah

Hausu (Native American) yawning bear.

Haven (English) refuge, safe place, a unisex name.

Haeven, Haevin, Havin, Hayven, Hayvin

Hayat (Arabic) life.

Hazel (English) hazelnut tree, a light brown colour.

Hayzal, Hayzala, Hayzalah, Hayzale, Hayzall, Hayzalla, Hayzallah, Hayzalle, Hazal, Hazaline, Hazall, Hazalla, Hazallah, Hazalle, Haze, Hazela, Hazeline, Hazell, Hazella, Hazelle, Hazyl, Hazyle, Hazyll, Hazylle, Hazzal, Hazzel, Hazzell, Hazzella, Hazzellah, Hazzelle

Heather (English) flower, heather.

Heath, Heatherlee, Heatherley, Heathyr, Heathyre, Heathyree

Heaven (English) place of ultimate happiness.

Haven, Heavan, Heavenly, Heavin, Heavon, Heavyn, Heivan, Heiven, Heivin, Hevan, Hevean, Heven, Hevin

Hebe (Greek) young, youth.

Heba, Hebah, Hebee, Hebey, Hebi, Hebie, Heby

Hedda (Teutonic) struggler, she who battles on.

Heaida, Heaidah, Heda, Hedah, Hedaya, Hedayah, Heddah, Heddey, Heddi, Heddie, Heddy, Hede, Hedi, Hedia, Hediah, Hedvick, Hedvig, Hedvika, Hedvikah, Hedwig, Hedwiga, Hedy, Heid, Heidi, Hetta, Hettah, Hettie, Hetty

Hedwig (German) fighter, warrior, a unisex name.

Heddwig, Heddwyg, Hedvick, Hedvig, Hedvige, Hedvika, Hedvikah, Hedwiga, Hedwyg

Hedy (Greek) sweet and pleasant.

Heda, Hedda, Heddey, Heddi, Heddie, Heddy, Hede, Hedee, Hedey, Hedi, Hedie, Hedy

Heidi (German) noble, kind, a form of Adelaide.

Heida, Heide, Heidee, Heidie,

Heidy, Heydi, Heydy, Hidee, Hidi, Hidie, Hidy, Hiede, Hiedee, Hiedi, Hiedy, Hydea, Hydee, Hydi, Hydie, Hydy

Helen (Greek) light, shining.
Elana, Elane, Elena, Elene, Ena, Halina, Hela, Helaih, Hele, Helena, Helenea, Helin, Helina, Helle, Hellen, Helli, Hellin, Hellon, Hellone, Hellonne, Hellyn, Hellynn, Hellynne, Helon, Helone, Helonn, Helonne, Helyn

Helena (Greek) light, shining, a form of Helen.
Halana, Halania, Halena, Halina, Hallana, Hallanna, Helaina, Helana, Helayna, Heleana, Heleena, Helenia, Helenka, Helenna, Helina, Hellena, Hellenna, Helona, Helonna

Helene (French) light, shining, a form of Helen.
Helaine, Helanie, Helayne, Heleen, Heleine, Hèléne, Helenor, Heline, Hellenor

Helga (Norse) holy; (Teutonic) pious.
Elga, Helgah, Olga

Helice (Greek) spiral.
Helica, Helicia, Heliciah, Helise, Helisa, Helisia, Helyce, Helycia, Helyciah, Helycya, Helycyah, Helycye

Helki (Native American) to touch, touched.
Helke, Heklee, Helkey, Helkie, Helky

Heloise (French) battle maiden, famous warrior, a form of Eloise.
Eli, Elly, Eloise, Helois, Héloise, Helouise

Heltu (Native American) friendly bear reaching out.
Heltoo

Henrietta (English) ruler of the home, feminine form of Henry.
Henni, Hennrietta, Hennriette, Henny, Henretta, Henrette, Henrie, Henrieta, Henriette, Henrique, Henriquetta, Henriquette, Henriquieta, Henriquiette, Rieta, Rita

Hephziba (Hebrew) my joy is in her.
Hephzibaa, Hephzibaah, Hephzibah, Hepziba, Hepzibaa, Hepzibaah, Hepzibah

Hera (Greek) queen of heaven and wife of Zeus, according to myth.
Herah

Herberta (German) great warrior, feminine form of Herbert.
Herbertah, Herbertia, Herbertiah, Herbirta, Herbirtah, Herbirtia, Herbirtiah, Herburta, Herburtah, Herburtia, Herburtiah

Hermione (Greek) of the earth.
Hermalina, Hermalinah, Hermaline, Hermia, Hermiah, Hermina, Herminah, Hermine, Herminia, Herminiah, Hermiona, Hermionah

Hermosa (Spanish) beautiful.
Hermosah

Hernanda (Spanish) an adventurer or traveller, prepared for the journey.
Hernandia

Hertha (Teutonic) goddess of fertility, mother of the earth, child of the earth.
Heartha, Hearthah, Hearthea, Heartheah, Hearthia, Hearthiah, Herthah, Herthea, Hertheah, Herthia, Herthiah

Hester/Hesper (Greek) evening star.

*Hespa, Hespar, Hesta, Hestar,
Hestia, Hestiah*

Hestia (Greek) goddess of the
hearth; (Persian) star.
Hestea, Hesteah, Hestiah

Hialeah (Native American) lovely
meadow.
*Hialea, Hialee, Hialey, Hiali, Hialie,
Hialy, Hyalea, Hyaleah, Hyalee,
Hyaley, Hyali, Hyalie, Hyaly*

Hiawatha (Native American) river
creator, a unisex name.
Hiawathah, Hyawatha, Hyawathah

Hibah (Arabic) gift, a unisex name.
Hiba, Hibab, Hyba, Hybah

Hiberna (Latin) comes from Ireland.
*Hibberna, Hibbernah, Hibernah,
Hibernia, Hiberniah, Hibernna,
Hibernnah*

Hibiscus (Latin) tropical flower
with bright colours.

Hilary (Latin) cheerful, a unisex
name.
*Haillery, Hilairie, Hilairy, Hilann,
Hilaree, Hilari, Hilaria, Hilarie,
Hileary, Hileree, Hileri, Hilerie, Hilery,
Hilian, Hilianne, Hiliary, Hillann,
Hillaree, Hillari, Hillaria, Hillarie,
Hillary, Hilleary, Hilleree, Hilleri,
Hillery, Hillian, Hillianne, Hilliary*

Hilda (Teutonic) protector, warrior,
stronghold, a form of Brunhilda,
Hildegarde.
*Hildah, Hilde, Hildee, Hildey, Hildi,
Hildia, Hildie, Hildy, Hillda, Hilldah,
Hillde, Hilldee, Hilldey, Hilldi, Hilldia,
Hilldie, Hilldy*

Hildegard (Teutonic) warrior,
battle stronghold.
*Hella, Helle, Hellie, Hilda, Hildagard,
Hildagarde, Hilde, Hildegarde,*

*Hildey, Hildie, Hildur, Hildy,
Hillie, Hulda, Hylda, Hyldagard,
Hyldagarde*

Hilma (German) protected.
Hilmah, Hylma, Hylmah

Hinda (Hebrew) doe.
*Hindah, Hindi, Hindie, Hindy, Hynda,
Hyndah*

Hiriko (Japanese) generous.
Hiryko, Hyriko, Hyroko

Hisa (Japanese) long-lived.
Hisae, Hisah, Hisako, Hisayo

Hoa (Vietnamese) flower.
Hoah

Holda (German) gracious and
beloved.
Holdah, Holde

Holli/Hollie/Holly (English) holly
bush which blossoms at Christmas.
*Holeena, Holeigh, Holin, Holleah,
Hollee, Holleigh, Holley, Hollian,
Holliana, Holliann, Hollianna,
Hollianne, Hollie, Hollina, Hollinah,
Holline, Hollyan, Hollyana, Hollyann,
Hollyanna, Hollye, Hollyian,
Hollyiana, Hollyiann, Hollyianna,
Hollyianne, Hollyn, Hollyna, Hollynn,
Hollynna, Hollynne*

Hollis (English) holly tree, a unisex
name.
*Holice, Holisa, Holisah, Holise, Holiss,
Holissa, Holissah, Holisse, Hollyce,
Hollys, Hollysa, Hollysah, Hollyse,
Hollyss, Hollysse, Holyce, Holys,
Holysa, Holysah, Holyse, Holyss,
Holyssa, Holyssah, Holysse*

Honesta (Latin) honest.
*Honest, Honestah, Honnesta,
Honnestah*

Honey (English) sweet one.
Honee, Honnee, Honney, Honnie,

Honny, Hunalea, Hunaleah, Hunalee, Hunnalee, Hunnee, Hunney, Hunnie, Hunny

Honora (Latin) honourable.
Honner, Honnor, Honnora, Honnorah, Honnour, Honnoura, Honnourah, Honnoure, Honor, Honorah, Honorata, Honoratah, Honore, Honoree, Honoria, Honorina, Honorine, Honour, Honoura, Honoure

Hope (English) optimistic, hope.
Hopé, Hopey, Hopi, Hopie, Hoppe, Hoppé

Horatia (Latin) keeper of the clock, timekeeper, feminine form of Horace.
Horacia, Horaciah, Horacya, Horacyah, Horatiah, Oracia, Oraciah, Oracya, Oracyah, Oratia, Oratiah

Hortense (Latin) gardener, feminine form of Horton.
Hortence, Hortencia, Hortenciah, Hortensa, Hortensah, Hortensia, Hortensiah, Hortenze, Hortenzia, Hortenziah

Hoshi (Japanese) star.
Hoshee, Hoshey, Hoshie, Hoshiyo

Howi (Native American) dove.
Howee, Howey, Howie, Howy

Hua (Chinese) a flower, a unisex name
Huah

Huda (Arabic) right guidance, right path.
Hudah, Hooda, Hoodah

Hulda (German) gracious and beloved; (Hebrew) weasel.
Huldie, Huldy, Hullda, Hulldie, Hulldy

Humilia (Polish) humble.
Humiliah, Humillia, Humilliah

Hunter (English) the hunter, a unisex name.
Hunnta, Hunntah, Hunntar, Hunnter, Hunntta, Hunnttah, Hunta, Huntah, Huntar, Huntlea, Huntlee, Huntleigh, Huntley, Huntly, Huntta, Hunttah, Hunttar, Huntter

Huong (Vietnamese) flower.

Husniyah (Arabic) beautiful.
Husniya

Huyana (Native American) rain falling.

Hyacinth (Greek) colourful flower with fragrance.
Giacinta, Giacintha, Hyacintha, Hyacinthe, Hyacinthia, Hyacinthie, Hycynth, Hycynthe, Jacinta

Hydi (German) noble, kind, a form of Heidi.
Hyda, Hyde, Hydea, Hydee, Hydeia, Hydia, Hydiea, Hydie

Hye (Korean) graceful.

Hyptatia (Greek) highest superior.
Hiptatia, Hiptatiah, Hyptatiah

Ianira (Greek) enchantress.
Ianirah, Ianyra, Ianyrah

Ianthe (Greek) violet-coloured flower.
Ianna, Iannah, Iantha, Ianthah, Ianthia, Ianthiah, Ianthina, Ianthinah

Ibtihaj (Arabic) joy.

Ida (German) hardworking; (English) prosperous, happy.
Idah, Idaia, Idaiah, Idaleena, Idalena, Idalene, Idalia, Idaliah, Idalina, Idaline, Idalis, Idaly, Idamae, Idania, Idaniah, Idarina, Idarinah, Idarine, Idaya, Idayah, Ide, Ideh, Idella, Idelle, Idetta, Idette, Idys, Idyss, Idysse

Idalia (Greek) sun.
Idaliah, Idalya, Idalyah

Idelia (German) noble.
Ideliah, Idelya, Idelyah

Idette (German) serious worker.
Ideta, Idetah, Idete, Idetta, Idettah

Idris (Arabic) one of the prophets; (Welsh) fiery, eager, a unisex name.
Idreas, Idrease, Idrees, Idres, Idrisa, Idriss, Idrissa, Idryis, Idryisa, Idryiss, Idryissa, Idrys, Idrysa, Idryss, Idryssa

Ierne (Latin) girl from Ireland.

Iesha (African) life.
Iaisha, Ieachia, Ieachya, Ieaisha, Ieasha, Ieesha, Ieeshia, Ieisha, Ieishia, Ieshia, Ieysha, Ieyshah, Ieyshia

Ignacia (Latin) fiery, ardent.
Ignaciah, Ignacie, Ignasha, Ignashah, Ignashia, Ignashiah, Ignatia, Ignatiah, Ignatiza, Ignatizah, Ignatzia, Ignatziah

Iida (Finnish) hardworking, prosperous, happy, a form of Ida.

Ikia (Hebrew) God is my salvation.
Ikaisha, Ikea, Ikeasha, Ikeashia, Ikeesha, Ikeeshia, Ikeisha, Ikeishi, Ikeishia, Ikesha, Ikeshia, Ikiah, Ikya, Ikyah

Ikram (Arabic) honour.

Ila (Hungarian) shining light, a form of Helen.
Ilah, Illa, Illah

Ilana (Hebrew) great tree.
Ilaina, Ilainah, Ilanah, Ilane, Ilani, Ilania, Ilanit, Illaina, Illainah, Illana, Illanah, Illane, Illani, Illania, Illanit

Ilaria (Italian) cheerful, a form of Hilary.
Ilarya, Illaria, Illarya

Ileana (Greek) from the city of Troy, a name used by Greek royalty.
Ilea, Ileah, Ileanah, Ileanee, Ileaney, Ileani, Ileanie, Ileanna, Ileannah, Ileanne, Ileany, Illeana, Illeanah

Iliana (Greek) from Troy.
Ileana, Illeana, Illiana

Ilima (Hawaiian) name of a yellow flower, from Oahu.
Ilimah, Ilyma, Ilymah

Ilithyia (Greek) goddess of childbirth.
Ilythia

Ilka (Slavic) flattering, shining light, a form of Helen.
Elka, Elke, Elki, Elkie, Elky, Ilke, Ilki, Ilkie, Ilky

Ilona (Greek, Hungarian) light, a form of Helen.
Ilka, Ilkah, Illka, Illkah, Illona, Illonah, Illonia, Illoniah, Illonka, Illonkah, Illonya, Illonyah, Illyona, Illyonah Ilonah, Ilonia, Iloniah, Ilonka, Ilonkah, Ilonya, Ilonyah, Ilyona, Ilyonah

Ilse (German) holy and sacred to God, a form of Elizabeth.
Ilsa, Ilsey, Ilsie, Ilsy

Iluka (Australian Aboriginal) close to the sea.

Iluminada (Spanish) shining.
Illumina, Illuminada, Illuminah, Illumine, Illumyna, Illumynah, Illumyne, Ilumina, Iluminah, Ilumine, Ilumyna, Ilumynah, Ilumyne

Ilyssa (English, Scottish) holy and sacred to God, a form of Ilisa.
Illysa, Illysah, Illysia, Illyssa, Illyssah, Illysia, Ilysa, Ilysah, Ilysia, Ilyssah, Ilyssia

Imaculata (Latin) immaculate.
Imaculatah, Immaculata, Immaculatah

Imala (Native American) strong-minded.
Imalah

Iman (Arabic) believer.
Imana, Imanah, Imanee, Imani, Imania, Imaniah, Imanie, Imany

Imber (Polish) ginger.
Imbera, Imberah, Imbere

Imelda (German) warrior.
Imalda, Imaldah, Imeldah, Imhilde, Irmhilde, Melda, Meldah

Imena (African) dreamer.
Imee, Imenah, Imene

Imogene (Latin) image, in the image of her mother.
Emogeen, Emogen, Emogene, Emojean, Emojeana, Imagena, Imagene, Imagina, Imajean, Imogeen, Imogeene, Imogen, Imogenia, Imogina, Imogine, Imogyn, Imogyne, Imojean, Imojeen, Imojeene, Innogen, Innogenn, Innogenne

Imperia (Latin) imperial ruler.

Ina (Greek) pure.

Inam (Arabic) generous, benefaction.
In'am

Inari (Finnish) lake.
Inaree, Inarey, Inarie, Inary

Inas (Polynesian) wife of the moon.

India (Hindu) from India.
Indiah, Indiana, Indianah, Indianna, Indiannah

Indigo (English) dark blue, purple colour.
Indiga, Indygo

Indira (Hindu) splendid, great.
Indiara, Indirah, Indirra, Indirrah, Indra, Indrah, Indre, Indria, Indriah

Ines (Spanish) pure.
Inés, Inesa, Inésa, Inesah, Inésah, Inesita, Inésita, Inesitah, Inésitah, Inessa, Inéssa, Inessah, Inéssah, Inesta, Inestah, Inez, Innes, Innessa, Innesta, Innestah, Ynes, Ynez, Ynés, Ynnes

Infinity (English) endless, infinity.
Infinitee, Infinitey, Infiniti, Infinitie

Inga (Scandinavian) daughter of a hero, beautiful daughter, a form of Ingrid.
Ingaberg, Ingaborg, Inge, Ingeberg, Ingeborg, Ingela, Ingelah, Inger, Ingrid

Ingrid (Scandinavian) daughter of a hero, beautiful daughter.
Inger, Ingred, Ingrede, Ingride

Iniga (Latin) fiery, ardent one.
Ingata, Ingatia, Inigah, Inigata, Inigatia, Inyga, Ingyah

Innes (Celtic) island; (Scottish) strength, a unisex name.
Ines, Iness, Innes, Innis, Inniss

Inoa (Hawaiian) name or name chant.
Inoah

Inocenta (Latin) innocent.
Inocentah, Innocenta, Innocentah

Ioana (Hebrew) God is gracious, a form of Jane, Joan, Joanne.
Io'ana, Ioanah, Ioanna, Ioannah, Ioanne

Iola (Greek) dawn, violet-coloured.
Iolah, Iole, Iolee, Iolia, Ioliah

Iolana (Hawaiian) soaring like a hawk.
Iolanah, Iolane, Iolann, Iolanna, Iolannah, Iolanne

Iolanthe (Greek) violet flower, a form of Yolanda.
Iolanda, Iolandah, Iolanth, Iolantha, Yeolanda, Yeolandah, Yeolande, Yolanda, Yolandah, Yolande

Ione (Greek) purple jewel or stone.
Iona, Ionah, Ioney, Ioni, Ionia, Ioniah, Ionie, Iyona, Iyonah, Iyonna, Iyonnah

Iora (Latin) gold.
Iorah, Iore, Iorea, Ioréa, Ioree, Iorée, Ioria, Ioriah

Iphigenia (Greek) sacrifice.
Iphigena, Iphigenah, Iphigeniah, Iphigenya, Iphigenyah

Ipo (Hawaiian) sweetheart, darling.
Ipoe, Ipoeh, Ipoh

Ira (Hebrew) watchful, a unisex name.
Irah

Irene (Greek) peace, peaceful.
Ereen, Ereena, Ereene, Eireen, Eireena, Eiren, Eirena, Eirene, Ereen, Ereena, Erena, Irean, Ireana, Ireanah, Ireane, Ireen, Ireena, Ireenah, Irena, Irenah, Irenee, Irina, Irinah, Irine, Iryn, Iryna, Irynah, Iryne

Irina (Russian) peace, peaceful, a form of Irene.
Eirena, Erena, Ira, Irana, Iranda, Iranna, Iriana, Irin, Irinah, Irinia, Irona, Iryna, Irynah, Rina, Rinah

Iris (Greek) rainbow, iris flower.
Irisa, Irisha, Iriss, Irissa, Irisse, Irita, Irys, Irysa, Irysah, Iryse, Iryssa, Iryssah, Irysse

Irma (Latin) noble; (German) honourable.
Erma, Ermah, Ermina, Ermine, Irmah, Irmina, Irmine

Irmgaard (German) noble.
Irmgard, Irmguard

Irvette (English) friend from the sea.
Irvet, Irveta, Irvetah, Irvete, Irvett, Irvetta, Irvettah

Isa (Teutonic) iron-willed.
Isah, Issa, Issah

Isabel (Spanish) consecrated to God, a form of Elizabeth.
Isabal, Isabeal, Isabele, Isabeli, Isabelia, Isabelita, Isabella, Isabelle, Isbel, Ishbel, Issabel, Issie, Izabel, Izabele, Ysabel

Isabella (Italian) consecrated to God, a form of Isobelle.
Isabel, Issabella, Ysabella

Isabelle (French) consecrated to God.
Bel, Bela, Belica, Belita, Bell, Bella, Belle, Ezabel, Ezabell, Ezabella, Ezabelle, Isabeal, Isabeau, Isabel, Isabele, Isabelhina, Isabelita, Isabell, Isabella, Isbel, Isobel, Isobell, Isobella, Isobelle, Issabel, Issabell, Issabella, Issabelle, Izabel, Izabele, Izabell, Izabella, Izabelle, Ysabel, Ysabela, Ysabelah, Ysabele, Ysabell, Ysabella, Ysabellah, Ysabelle, Ysibel, Ysibela, Ysibelah, Ysibella, Ysibellah, Ysibelle, Ysybel, Ysybela, Ysybelah, Ysybele, Ysybell, Ysybella, Ysybelle

Isadora (Greek, Latin) gift of Isis.
Isadore, Isadoria, Isadoriah, Isadorra, Isadorya, Isadoryah, Isidora, Izadora, Izadorah, Izadore, Izadorra

Isibeal (Irish) consecrated to God, a form of Isabel.

Isis (Egyptian) goddess of fertility.
Iceea, Iceeah, Ices, Icesis, Icesses, Icey, Icia, Iciah, Icis, Icy

Isla (Scottish) island, a river in Scotland.
Islah

Isleen (Anglo-Saxon) shining light, a form of Eileen.

Ismaela (Hebrew) God listens, feminine form of Ishmael.
Ismaelah, Ismaila, Ismailah, Ismayla, Ismaylah

Ismena (Greek) wise.
Ismenah, Ismenia, Ismeniah, Ismenya, Ismenyah

Isobel (Spanish) consecrated to God, a form of Isabel.
Isobeau, Isobell, Isobella, Isobelle

Isoka (African) gift from God.
Isokah, Isoke, Soka

Isolde (Celtic) fair maiden.
Isault, Isolad, Isolada, Isold, Isolda, Isolt, isolte, Izolde, Izolt, Ysold, Ysolde

Istas (Native American) snow.

Ita (Gaelic) desire for truth.
Itah, Itar, Ite

Italia (Italian) from Italy.
Italea, Italeah, Italee, Italei, Italeigh, Itali, Italiah, Italie, Italy, Italya, Italyah

Iulia (Irish) soft-haired, youthful, a form of Julia.
Iulie

Ivana (Russian) God is gracious.
Iva, Ivanah, Ivania, Ivaniah, Ivanka, Ivanna, Ivannah, Ivannia, Ivanniah, Ivannka, Ivannya, Ivannyah, Ivanya, Ivanyah

Ivonne (French) archer, a form of Yvonne.
Ivone, Ivona, Ivonna

Ivory (African) white, ivory colour.
Ivoree, Ivorey, Ivori, Ivorie

Ivy (Anglo-Saxon) vine.
Iva, Ivee, Ivey, Ivi, Ivie

Iwalani (Hawaiian) heavenly girl.

Izabella (Spanish) consecrated to God, a form of Isabella.
Izabela, Izabell, Izabellah, Izabelle, Izobella

izdihar (Arabic) flourishing, blooming.

Izusa (Native American) white stone.
Izusah

J

Ja (Hawaiian) fiery.
Jah

Jaamini (Hindu) evening.
Jaaminee, Jaaminey, Jaaminie, Jaaminy

Jacinda (Greek) beautiful; (Spanish) colourful flower with fragrance, a form of Hyacinth.
Jacenda, Jacindah, Jacinde, Jacindea, Jacindee, Jacindey, Jacindi, Jacindia, Jacindie, Jacindy, Jacynda, Jacyndah, Jasinda, Jasindah, Jasinde, Jasindea

Jacinta (Greek) lovely, beautiful, colourful flower with fragrance, a form of Hyacinth.
Jacanta, Jacent, Jacenta, Jacentah, Jacente, Jacintah, Jacintia, Jacynta, Jacyntah, Jasinta, Jasintah, Jasinte, Jazinta, Jazintah, Jazynte

Jacinth (English) flower, the hyacinth.
Jacinthe

Jacki/Jackie/Jacky/Jacqui (American, French) substitute, supplanter, a form of Jacqueline.
Jackea, Jackee, Jackey, Jackia, Jackiah

Jaclyn (American) substitute, supplanter, a form of Jacqueline.
Jacklin, Jackline, Jacklyne, Jacklynn, Jacklynne, Jaclin,
Jacline, Jaclyne, Jaclynn, Jaclynne

Jacoba (Latin) the supplanter, feminine form of Jacob.
Jacobea, Jacobee, Jacobella, Jacobi, Jacobia, Jacobiah, Jacobie, Jacobina, Jacobinah, Jacobine, Jacoby, Jacobya, Jacobyah, Jacobye, Jacobyn, Jacobynna, Jakoba, Jakobah, Jakobi, Jakobia, Jakobiah, Jakobie, Jakoby, Jakobya

Jacqueline (French) substitute, supplanter.
Jacquel, Jacquelean, Jacqueleana, Jacqueleanah, Jacqueleane, Jacqueleen, Jacquelein, Jacqueleina, Jacqueleinah, Jacqueleine, Jacquelena, Jacquelene, Jacqueleyn, Jacqueleyna, Jacqueleynah, Jacqueleyne, Jacquelina, Jacquelinah, Jacquena, Jacquene

Jada (Hebrew) wise.
Jadah, Jaeda, Jaedah, Jaida, Jaidah, Jayda, Jaydah

Jade (Spanish) green gemstone, jade, a unisex name.
Jada, Jadah, Jadda, Jaddah, Jadea, Jadee, Jadeen, Jadeena, Jaden, Jadena, Jadene, Jadera, Jadielin, Jadieline, Jadielyn, Jadienna, Jadienne, Jaed, Jaeda, Jaedah, Jaeid, Jaeida, Jaeidah, Jaid, Jaida, Jaidah, Jaide, Jayd, Jayda, Jaydah, Jayde, Gada, Gadah, Gade, Gaid, Gaida, Gaidah, Gaide, Gayd, Gayda, Gaydah, Gayde

Jae (Latin) jaybird.
Jaea, Jai, Jaie, Jay, Jaya, Jaye

Jael (Hebrew) mountain goat, a unisex name.
Jaele, Jaelea, Jaeleah, Jaelee, Jaelei, Jaeleigh, Jaeley, Jaeli,

Jaeliah, Jaelie, Jaell, Jaelle, Jaelly, Jaely, Jailea, Jaileah, Jailee, Jailei, Jaileigh, Jailey, Jaili, Jailia, Jailiah, Jailie, Jaily

Jaha (African) dignified.
Jahaida, Jahaira, Jaharra, Jahayra, Jahida, Jahira, Jaia, Jaiah, Jaya, Jayah

Jaime (French) I love.
Jaimee, Jaimi, Jaimie, Jaimy, Jamee, Jamie

Jaira (Hebrew) God teaches.
Jahra, Jahrah, Jairah, Jayra, Jayrah

Jala (Arabic) clarity.
Jalah

Jalila (Arabic) great.
Jalilah, Jalile, Jallila, Jallilah, Jallile

Jalini (Hindu) lives by the ocean.
Jalinee, Jaliney, Jalinie, Jaliny

Jama (Hindu) daughter.
Jamah, Jamia, Jamiah, Jamya, Jamyah

Jamaica (Spanish) Caribbean island.
Jamaca, Jamacia, Jamica

Jamari (French) warrior.
Jamarie, Jemari, Jemarie

Jamie (English) the supplanter, feminine form of James.
Jaema, Jaemah, Jaemea, Jaemeah, Jaemee, Jaemey, Jaemi, Jaemia, Jaemie, Jaemy, Jaemya, Jaemyah, Jahmah, Jahmea, Jahmee, Jahmey, Jahmi, Jahmia, Jahmiah, Jahmie, Jahmy, Jahmia, Jaimea, Jaimeah, Jaimee, Jaimey, Jaimi, Jaimia, Jaimiah, Jaimie, Jaimmie, Jaimy, Jaimya, Jaimyah, Jama, Jamah, Jamea, Jameah, Jamee, Jamei, Jami, Jamia, Jamiah, Jamii, Jamiia

Jamila (Arabic) beautiful, graceful, lovely.
Jaimeala, Jaimealah, Jaimeale, Jaimila, Jaimilah, Jaimile, Jaimilla, Jaimillah, Jaimille, Jaimyla, Jaimylah, Jaimyle, Jaimylla, Jaimyllah, Jaimylle, Jameala, Jamealah, Jameale, Jameela, Jameela, Jameelah, Jameele, Jameelia, Jameeliah, Jamela, Jamelah, Jamelia, Jameliah, Jamell, Jamella, Jamellah, Jamelle, Jamilah, Jamilia, Jamiliah, Jamilla, Jamillah, Jamille, Jamillia, Jamilliah, Jamilya, Jamilyah

Jan (English) gracious, God is gracious, a unisex name.
Jaan, Jana, Janae, Jani, Jania, Janiah, Janice, Janina, Janine, Jann, Janne

Jana (Hebrew) gracious, God is gracious.
Jan, Janae, Janah, Jane, Jania, Janice, Janina, Janine, Janna, Jannah, Janne, Jannia, Janniah, Jannya, Jannyah, Janya, Janyah

Janaki (Hindu) mother.
Janakee, Janakey, Janakie, Janaky

Jancis (English) combination of Jane and Frances.

Jane (Hebrew) God is gracious.
Jain, Jaine, Jan, Jana, Janae, Janee, Janey, Jani, Jania, Janice, Janie, Janina, Janine, Janna, Jayn, Jayne

Janelle (Hebrew) God is gracious, a form of Jane.
Jaenel, Jaenela, Jaenelah, Jaenele, Jaenell, Jaenella, Jaenellah, Jaenelle, Janel, Janella, Janele, Janelah, Janell, Janella, Janellah, Jannell, Jannella, Jannelle, Jaynel, Jaynela, Jaynelah, Jaynele, Jaynell, Jaynella, Jaynelle

Janessa (American) combination of Jane and Vanessa.

Janesha, Janeska, Janiesa, Janiesha, Janish, Janissa, Janisse, Jannesa, Jannesha, Jannessa, Jannisa, Jannise, Jannissa, Jannisse, Jannys, Jannysa, Jannysah, Jannyse, Janys, Janysa, Janysah, Janyse, Janyss, Janyssa, Janyssah, Janysse, Jessana, Jessane

Janet (Hebrew) God is gracious, feminine form of John.

Jan, Janat, Janata, Janeta, Janete, Janett, Janetta, Janette, Janita, Jannet, Janneta, Jannetta, Jannette, Jannita, Jannitah, Jannite, Jannitta, Jannittah, Jannitte

Janette (French) God is gracious, feminine form of John.

Jan, Janae, Jane, Janett, Janetta, Jania, Janina, Janine, Jannet, Jannette

Janice (Hebrew) God is gracious, a form of Jane.

Janece, Janecia, Janeciah, Janese, Janesse, Janis, Janisa, Janisah, Janise, Janiss, Janissa, Janisse, Jannice, Jannis, Jannisa, Jannisah, Jannise, Janniss, Jannissa, Jannisse, Jannyce, Jannys, Jannysa, Jannysah, Jannyse, Jannyss, Jannyssa, Jannysse, Janyce, Janys, Janysa, Janysah, Janyse, Janyss, Janyssa, Janyssah, Janysse

Janine (French) God is gracious, a form of Jane.

Janean, Janeana, Janeane, Janeen, Janeena, Janeene, Janena, Janene, Janina, Janinah, Jannene, Jannina, Jannine, Jean, Jeanne

Janis (Latvian) God is gracious, a form of John, a unisex name.

Ansis, Jancis, Zanis, Zansis

Janna (Arabic) fruit harvest.

Jannae, Jannai, Jannia, Janniah, Jannya, Jannyah

Jannah (Hebrew) God is gracious, a form of Jane.

Jana, Janah, Janna

Jannali (Australian Aboriginal) moon.

Janali, Janalia, Janaliah, Janalie, Janaly, Janalya, Janalyah, Jannalia, Jannaliah, Jannalie, Jannaly, Jannalya, Jannalyah

Jarita (Hindu) legendary bird-mother; (Arabic) water jug.

Jareata, Jareatah, Jarietta, Jariette, Jaritta, Jaritte

Jarnila (Arabic) beautiful.

Jarnilah, Jarnile, Jarnill, Jarnilla, Jarnillah, Jarnille, Jarnyl, Jarnyla, Jarnylah, Jarnyll, Jarnylla, Jarnyllah

Jarvia (German) intelligent and sharp like a spear, clever with a spear.

Jarviah, Jarvya, Jaryvah

Jarvinia (Germanic) keen intelligence, like a spear.

Jarviniah, Jarvinya, Jarvinyah, Jarvynia, Jarvyniah, Jarvynya, Jarvynyah

Jasmine (Persian) a sweet perfumed flower that blossoms in spring.

Jasmain, Jasman, Jasme, Jasmen, Jasmene, Jasmin, Jasminne, Jasmyn, Jasmyne, Jesmin, Jesmine, Jesmyn, Jesmyne, Jessmin, Jessmine, Jessmyn, Jessmyne, Yasmin

Jasper (English) precious red, brown or golden stone, a unisex name.

Jaspa, Jaspah, Jaspar

Javiera (Spanish) owner of the bright new house, feminine form of Javier.

Javeera, Javeerah, Javierah

Jaya (Hindu) name of a god, victory, a unisex name.

Jaea, Jaia, Jaiah, Jayah

Jayda (Spanish) semi-precious green stone, a form of Jade.

Jaydah, Jayde

Jayme (English) the supplanter, a form of Jamie, feminine form of James.

Jayma, Jaymey, Jaymi, Jaymie, Jaymy, Jaymye

Jayne (Hindu) victorious; (English) God is gracious, a form of Jane.

Jayn, Jaynn, Jaynne

Jazmin (Persian) a sweet perfumed flower that blossoms in spring.

Jasmin, Jaz, Jazmen, Jazmine, Jazmyn, Jazmyne, Jazz, Jazzmin, Jazzmine, Jazzmyn, Jazzmyne

Jazz (American) improvised music of Afro-American roots, jazz music, a unisex name.

Jas, Jass, Jaz, Jazze, Jazzlea, Jazzlee, Jazzlei, Jazzy

Jean (Scottish/French) God is gracious, feminine form of John.

Jan, Jana, Janae, Jane, Jania, Janice, Janina, Janine, Jeana, Jeane, Jeanee, Jeaneen, Jeanetta, Jeanette, Jeaney, Jeani, Jeanie, Jeanina, Jeanine, Jeann, Jeanna, Jeannah, Jeanne, Jeannine, Jeany, Jeen, Jeena, Jeene, Jeenia, Jenela, Jenelah, Jenele, Jenell, Jenella, Jenellah, Jenelle

Jeanette (French) God is gracious.

Janeat, Janeata, Janeatah, Janeate, Janeatt, Janeatta, Janeattah, Janeatte, Janeet, Janeeta, Janeetah, Janeete, Janet, Janeta, Janetah, Janete, Janett, Janetta, Janettah, Janette, Jeanet, Jeaneta, Jeanetah, Jeanete, Jeanett, Jeanetta, Jeanettah

Jelena (Russian) shining light, a form of Helen.

Jalaina, Jalaine, Jalana, Jalane, Jalanna, Jalanne, Jalayna, Jalayne, Jalean, Jaleana, Jaleanah, Jaleane, Jaleen, Jaleena, Jaleenah, Jaleene, Jalenah, Jalene, Jalaina, Jalainah, Jalaine, Jalin, Jalina, Jalinah, Jaline, Jalyn, Jalyna, Jalynah, Jalyne

Jemima (Hebrew) dove, dove of peace.

Gemima, Gemimah, Gemma, Jemimah, Jemina, Jemma, Jemmah, Jemmia, Jemmiah, Jemyma, Jemymah, Mimi

Jemma (English) little gem, feminine form of James; (Hebrew) dove, a form of Jemima.

Gem, Gema, Gemah, Gemia, Gemiah, Gemma, Gemmah, Gemmia, Gemmiah, Gemmya, Gemmyah, Jem, Jema, Jemah, Jemia, Jemiah, Jemm, Jemmah, Jemmia, Jemmiah, Jemmya, Jemmyah

Jendaya (African) give thanks, thankful.

Jendaia, Jandaiah, Jendayah

Jenna (Arabic) small bird; (Welsh) white phantom, white wave, a form of Jennifer.

Jena, Jenah, Jennae, Jennah, Jennai, Jennay, Jennaya, Jennaye, Jhenna

Jennelle (American) combination of Jenny and Nell.
Jenelle

Jennessa (American) combination of Jennifer and Vanessa.
Jenessa

Jenni/Jennie/Jenny (Welsh) white phantom, white wave, a form of Jennifer.
Jen, Jeni, Jenie, Jenne, Jennee, Jenney

Jennifer (Welsh) white phantom, white wave.
Gen, Geni, Genni, Genny, Guinevere, Jen, Jenefar, Jenefer, Jenie, Jenifa, Jenifer, Jenn, Jenne, Jennee, Jennefar, Jennefer, Jenney, Jenni, Jennie, Jennifar, Jenniferanne, Jenniferlee, Jenny

Jeremia (Hebrew) God will exalt.
Jeramia, Jeramiah, Jeramya, Jeramyah, Jeremiah, Jeremya, Jeremyah

Jerri (German) spear carrier, a form of Geraldine.
Geri, Gerie, Gerri, Gerrie, Gerry, Jeri, Jerie, Jerrie, Jerry

Jerusha (Hebrew) married, inheritance.
Jerushah

Jess (Hebrew) wealthy, God beholds, a form of Jessica.
Jese, Jesey, Jesee, Jesi, Jesie, Jesse, Jessee, Jessey, Jessi, Jessie, Jessy, Jesy

Jessica (Hebrew) wealthy, God beholds.
Jess, Jessia, Jessiah, Jessicah, Jessicia, Jessicka, Jessie, Jessieca, Jessieka, Jezecah, Jezecka, Jezeka, Jezekah, Jezia, Jezicah, Jezicka, Jezika, Jezikah, Jezyca, Jezycah, Jezycka, Jezyka, Jisica, Jisicah, Jisicka, Jisika, Jisikah, Jisiqua, Jisiquah, Jysica, Jysicah, Jysicka, Jysika, Jyssica, Jyssicah, Jyssicka, Jyssika, Jyssikah, Jysyka, Jysykah

Jewel (French) precious gem.
Jewell, Jool, Jools

Jezabel (Hebrew) wicked, impure.
Jesabel, Jesabela, Jesabelah, Jesabele, Jesabell, Jesabella, Jesabellah, Jesabelle, Jessabel, Jessabela, Jessabelah, Jessabele, Jessabell, Jessabella, Jessabelle, Jezabela, Jezabelah, Jezabele, Jessabell, Jessabella, Jezabellah, Jezabelle, Jezebel, Jezebela, Jezebelah, Jezebele, Jezebell, Jezebella, Jezebellah, Jezebelle

Jianna (Italian) God is gracious, a form of Jane.
Jeana, Jeanah, Jeanna, Jeannah, Jiana, Jianah, Jiannah

Jibon (Hindu) life.
Jibona, Jibonah, Jibone

Jill (Latin/English) youthful, a form of Jillian.
Gill, Gillian, Jil, Jillana, Jillann, Jillanna, Jillanne, Jilliana, Jilliann, Jillianna, Jillianah, Jilly, Jillyana, Jillyanna, Jillyanne

Jillian (Latin) youthful.
Gilian, Giliana, Gilianah, Giliane, Gillian, Gilliana, Gillianah, Gilliane, Gillyan, Gillyana, Gillyanah, Gillyane, Gillyann, Gillyanna, Gillyannah, Gillyanne, Jil, Jilian, Jiliana, Jilianah, Jilane, Jilann, Jilanna, Jilanne, Jilianah, Jiliann, Jilianna, Jiliannah, Jilianne, Jill, Jilliana, Jilliane, Jilliann, Jillianna, Jilliannah, Jillianne, Jilly, Jillyann,

Jillyanna, Jillyannah, Jillyanne,
Julian, Juliana, Julianah, Juliane,
Juliann, Julianna, Juliannah,
Julianne

Jimena (Spanish) heard.
Jimenah, Jimenna, Jimennah,
Jymena, Jymenah

Jimi (Hebrew) replacer, supplanter,
feminine form of Jimmy.
Jimee, Jimey, Jimie, Jimmee,
Jimmey, Jimmi, Jimmie, Jimmy, Jimy

Jin (Japanese) tender.
Jyn

Jinx (Latin) under a spell, charmer.
Ginx, Gynx, Gynnx, Jynx, Jynnx

Jirakee (Australian Aboriginal)
waterfall, cascade of water.
Jirakei, Jirakey, Jiraki, Jirakie, Jiriky,
Jyrakee, Jyrakei, Jyrakey, Jyraki,
Jyrakie, Jyraky

Jivanta (Indian) to give life, create.
Jivantah, Jyvanta, Jyvantah

Jo (Hebrew, American) God
is gracious, a form of Joanna,
Josephine.
Joe, Joey, Jo Jo, Jo-Jo, Josie

Joakima (Hebrew) God will
build, establish, feminine form of
Joachim.
Joakimah

Joan (Hebrew) God is gracious.
Joani, Joanie, Joann, Joanna,
Joanne, Joen, Joenn, Johanna,
Johanne, Jonni

Joanne (English), God is gracious.
Joan, Joann, Joanna, Johann,
Johanna, Johanne

Jobina (Hebrew) one who has
suffered.

Jobeana, Jobeanah, Jobeena,
Jobeenah, Jobin, Jobinah, Jobine

Jocelyn (Latin) joyous, just.
Jocalin, Jocalina, Jocaline,
Jocalyn, Jocalynn, Jocalynne,
Jocelin, Joceline, Jocelynn,
Jocelynne, Joci, Jocia, Jocilyn,
Jocilynn, Jocilynne, Josilin, Josiline,
Josilyn, Josilynn, Josilynne, Jossalin,
Jossaline, Jossalyn, Jossalynn,
Jossalynne

Jocosa (Latin) brings laughter to
her home, jubiliant.
Jocose

Jodie (Hebrew, American) praised,
a form of Judith.
Jode, Jodea, Jodee, Jodey, Jodi,
Jodia, Jodiee, Jody, Joedea,
Joedee, Joedey, Joedi, Joedie,
Joedy, Johdea, Johdee, Johdey,
Johdi, Johdie, Johdy

Joelle (Hebrew) God is willing.,
feminine form of Joel
Joela, Joelah, Joele, Joelee,
Joeley, Joeli, Joelia, Joelie, Joell,
Joella, Joellah, Joellee, Joelley,
Joelli, Joellia, Joelly, Joely

Johanna (German) God is
gracious.
Joan, Joann, Joanna, Joanne,
Johan, Johana, Johanah, Johann,
Johonna

Joi (English) joy.
Joie, Joy, Joye

Jolan (Hungarian) violet flower,
violet colour.
Jola, Jolana, Jolanah, Jolane,
Jolanee, Jolaney, Jolani, Jolania,
Jolaniah, Jolanie, Jolany

Jolene (Hebrew) God increases.
Joelen, Joelena, Joelene, Joeleen,
Joeleena, Joeleene, Jolain,
Jolaina, Jolaine, Jolana, Jolane,

Jolanna, Jolanne, Jolean, Joleana, Joleane, Joleen, Joleena, Joleene, Jolena, Jolenna, Jolenne, Jolin, Jolina, Joline

Jolie (French) pretty, merry, a unisex name.

Jole, Jolea, Joleah, Jolee, Jolei, Joleigh, Joli, Jolle, Jollea, Jolleah, Jollee, Jollei, Jolleigh, Jolli, Jollie, Jolly, Jollye, Joly, Jolye

Jolisa (American) combination of Jo and Lisa.

Jolissa, Jolysa, Jolyssa

Jonina (Hebrew) dove.

Jona, Jonah, Jonae, Jonai, Joneen, Joneena, Joneene, Jonyna, Jonynah, Jonyne, Yoneena, Yoneene, Yonina, Yoninah, Yonine, Yonyna, Yonynah, Yonyne

Jonquil (Latin, English) perfumed yellow spring flower.

Jonquila, Jonquile, Jonquill, Jonquilla, Jonquille, Jonquyl, Jonquyla, Jonquylah, Jonquyle

Jora (Hebrew) autumn rain.

Jorah, Joree, Jorey, Jori, Joria, Joriah, Joriana, Jorianah, Joriane, Joriann, Jorianna, Joriannah, Jorianne, Jori, Jorie, Jory

Jordan (Hebrew) flowing down, descending, a unisex name.

Jorda, Jordah, Jordain, Jordaina, Jordaine, Jordana, Jordane, Jordann, Jordanna, Jordannah, Jordanne, Jordayn, Jordayna, Jordayne, Jorden, Jordena, Jordene, Jordenn, Jordenna, Jordenne, Jordin, Jordina, Jordine, Jordinn, Jordinna, Jordinne, Jordon, Jordona, Jordone, Jordonn, Jordonna, Jordonne, Jordyn, Jordyna, Jordyne, Jordynn, Jordynna, Jordynne, Joryn

Jorja (Greek) farmer, a form of Georgia.

Georga, Georgah, Georgan, Georgana, Georgane, Georgia, Georgina, Jorga, Jorgah, Jorgan, Jorgana, Jorgane, Jorgi, Jorgia, Jorjiah, Jorgie, Jorgina, Jorgine, Jorjah, Jorjan, Jorjana, Jorjanah, Jorjane, Jorjia, Jorjiah, Jorjina, Jorjya, Jorjyah

Jose (Spanish) God shall add, increase, feminine form of Joseph, a unisex name.

Josee, Josie

Josefina (Spanish), God shall add, increase, feminine form of Joseph.

Josefine, Josephina

Josephine (French) God shall add, increase, feminine form of Joseph.

Fifi, Fifine, Jo, Joette, Josee, Josefa, Josefina, Josefine, Josepha, Josephina, Josette, Josie, Josy, Pepita

Josi/Josie (Hebrew) God shall add, increase.

Josey, Jossey, Jossie, Josy

Jovita (Latin) joyful, jovial.

Jovet, Joveta, Jovetah, Jovete, Jovett, Jovetta, Jovette, Jovi, Jovit, Jovitah, Jovite, Jovitt, Jovitta, Jovittah, Jovitte, Jovyt, Jovyta, Jovytah, Jovyte, Jovytt, Jovytta, Jovyttah, Jovytte

Joy (Latin) joyful, a unisex name.

Joi, Joia, Joiah, Joie, Joya, Joyah, Joye

Joyce (Latin) joyful.

Joice, Joise, Joisy, Joycee, Joycey, Joycie, Joycy, Joyse

Joylyn (American) combination of Joy and Lyn.

Joilin, Joilina, Joilinah, Joiline,

Joilyn, Joilyna, Joilynah, Joilyne,
Joilynn, Joilynna, Joilynne, Joylin,
Joylina, Joylinah, Joyline, Joylyna,
Joylynah, Joylyne, Joylynn,
Joylynna, Joylynne

Juana (Spanish) God is gracious,
feminine form of Juan.

Juanah, Juanna, Juannah,
Juannia

Juanita (Spanish) God is gracious,
feminine form of Juan.

Juana, Juanah, Juandalin,
Juandalina, Juandaline,
Juandalyn, Juandalyna,
Juandalyne, Juaneice, Juanequa,
Juaneque, Juanesha, Juanica,
Juanice, Juanicia, Juaniqua,
Juanique, Juanisha, Juanishia,
Juanna

Judith (Hebrew) praised.

Jude, Judeth, Judey, Judi, Judian,
Judiana, Judiane, Judiann,
Judianna, Judiannah, Judianne,
Judie, Judy

Judi/Judy (Hebrew) a form of
Judith.

Jude, Judey, Judie

Julia/Julie (Latin) soft-haired,
youthful.

Giula, Giulia, Giuliana, Giulietta,
Giulette, Jules, Juley, Juliah, Julian,
Juliana, Julianah, Juliane, Juliann,
Julianna, Juliannah, Julianne,
Julienn, Julienna, Julienne, July

Juliet (French) youthful.

Guilietta, Juleata, Juleatah,
Juleate, Juleet, Juleeta,
Juleetah, Juleete, Julette,
Juliete, Juliett, Julietta, Juliettah,
Juliette

Jumana (Arabic) pearl.

Jumanah

Jun (Chinese) the truth, truthful, a
unisex name.

June (Latin) the month of June,
ruled by Jupiter.

Juin, Juine, Junell, Junella, Junelle,
Juni, Junia, Junie, Junill, Junilla,
Junille

Juno (Latin) queen of the Roman
gods.

Jurisa (Slavic) tempest, storm.

Jurisah, Jurissa, Jurissah, Jurysa,
Jurysah, Juryssa, Juryssah

Justine (Latin) just, feminine form
of Justin.

Juste, Justea, Justean, Justeana,
Justeanah, Justeane, Justeen,
Justeena, Justeenah, Justeene,
Justein, Justeina, Justeinah,
Justeine, Justena, Justene, Justeyn,
Justeyna, Justeynah, Justeyne,
Justyn, Justyna, Justynah, Justyne,

Juventia (Latin) youth.

Juventa, Juventah, Juventiah

Jyoti (Hindu) sun's light, a unisex
name.

Jioti, Jioty, Jyotis, Jyoty

K

Kacey (Irish) eagle-eyed, brave; (American) combination of the initials K.C., a unisex name.
Caisee, Caisey, Caisie, Caisy, Casee, Casey, Casie, Casy, Kacee, Kaci, Kacie, Kacy, Kaesi, Kaesie, Kaesy, Kaicee, Kaicey, Kaicie, Kaicy, Kaisee, Kaisey, Kaisie, Kaisy, Kasee

Kachina (Native American) sacred dancer.
Kachin, Kachinah, Kachine, Kachinee, Kachiney, Kachyn, Kachyna, Kachynah, Kachyne

Kadija (African) the prophet's gift, trustworthy.

Kagami (Japanese) mirror.
Kagamee

Kahoku (Hawaiian) the star.
Kahoko

Kai (Hawaiian) sea or sea water.
Kae, Kaie, Kay

Kailani (Hawaiian) sky, sea.
Kaelana, Kaelanah, Kaelanea, Kaelanee, Kaelaney, Kaelani, Kaelania, Kaelaniah, Kaelanie, Kaelany, Kaelanya, Kailana, Kailanah, Kailanea, Kailanee, Kailaney, Kailania, Kailaniah, Kailanie, Kailany, Kailanya

Kaili (Hawaiian) religious deity, a unisex name.
Kaeli, Kaely, Kailli

Kaimana (Hawaiian) diamond.

Kaemana, Kaemanah, Kaemane, Kaiman, Kaimanah, Kaimane, Kayman, Kaymana, Kaymanah, Kaymane

Kai'mi (Hawaiian) the seeker.
Kaimi

Kairos (Greek) a special or meaningful time, quality time.

Kaisa (Swedish) pure.
Kaisah, Kaysa, Kaysah

Kaitlyn (Irish) pure.
Caitlin, Caitlyn, Caytlin, Caytlyn, Kaitlin, Kaitlyne, Kaytline, Kaytlyn

Kakalina (Hawaiian) pure.
Kakalinah, Kakalyna, Kakalynah

Kala (Hawaiian) princess, a form of Sarah; (Hindu) black, name for god Siva, a unisex name.
Kalah

Kalama (Hawaiian) the flaming torch, a unisex name.

Kalani (Hawaiian) sky, heavenly chief, a unisex name.
Kalana, Kalanah, Kalanea, Kalanee, Kalaney, Kalania, Kalaniah, Kalanie, Kalany, Kalona, Kalonah, Kalonea, Kalonee, Kaloney, Kaloni, Kalonia, Kaloniah, Kalonie, Kalony

Kalauni (African) crown.
Kalaunea, Kalaunee, Kalauney, Kalaunia, Kalauniah, Kalaunie, Kalauny, Kalaunya

Kalea (Hawaiian) bright, clear, joyful, happy, a unisex name.
Kahlea, Kahleah, Kahlee, Kailea, Kaileah, Kaleah, Kalee, Kaleeia, Kalei, Kaleia, Kaleigh, Kaley, Kali, Kalie, Kallea, Kalleah, Kaly, Khalea, Khaleah

Kalei (Hawaiian) wreath of flowers.
Kahlei, Kailei, Kallei, Kaylei, Khalei

Kaleki (Hawaiian) graceful.

Kalena (Hawaiian) pure.
Kalenea, Kalenna

Kali (African) energetic black one.
Kaela, Kaelah, Kaelea, Kaeleah, Kaelee, Kaelei, Kaeleigh, Kaeley, Kaeli, Kaelia, Kaeliah, Kaelie, Kaely, Kaila, Kailah, Kailea, Kaileah, Kailee, Kailei, Kaileigh, Kailey, Kaili, Kailia, Kailiah, Kailie, Kaily, Kalea, Kaleah, Kalee, Kalei, Kaleigh, Kaley, Kalia, Kaliah, Kalie, Kaly, Kaylea, Kayleah, Kaylee, Kaylei, Kayleigh, Kayley, Kayli, Kaylia, Kayliah, Kaylie, Kayly, Kaylya

Kalia (Hawaiian) beauty.

Kalifa (African) holy, chaste.
Califa, Califah, Kalifah

Kalika/Kalyca (Greek) rosebud.
Kalica, Kalicah, Kalikah, Kaly, Kalycah, Kalyka, Kalykah

Kalila (Arabic) sweetheart, beloved.
Calila, Calilah, Kahlila, Kali, Kalih, Kalilah, Kaleela, Kalilla, Kallila, Kaylil, Kaylila

Kalina (Slavic) flower.
Kalinah, Kaline, Kalinna, Kalyna, Kalynah, Kalyne

Kalinda (Australian Aboriginal) lookout; (Hindu) sun.
Kalindah, Kalindi, Kalindie, Kalynda, Kalyndah

Kaliska (Native American) coyote-chasing deer.
Kaliskah, Kalyska, Kalyskah

Kalista (Greek) most beautiful one.
Calista, Calistah, Calistar, Calistarr, Callista, Callistah, Callistar, Callistarr, Kalistah, Kallista, Kallistah, Kallistar, Kallistara, Kallistarah, Kallistarr, Kallistarra, Kallistarrah

Kalola (Hawaiian) strong, a form of Carol.

Kaloni (African) perfume, fragrant.
Kalona, Kalonah, Kalonee, Kaloney, Kalonia, Kaloniah, Kalonie, Kalony, Kalonya, Kalonyah

Kama (Hindu) love.
Kamah, Kamma, Kammah

Kamala (Hindu) lotus.
Kamalah, Kamalla, Kammala

Kamballa (Australian Aboriginal) young woman.
Kambala, Kambalah, Kamballah

Kamea (Hawaiian) only one, precious child.
Camea, Cameah, Kameah, Kamee, Kameo, Kamia, Kamiah, Kammea, Kammeah, Kammia, Kammiah, Kamya, Kamyah

Kameko (Japanese) child of the turtle, child who lives long.
Kameeko, Kamiko, Kamyko

Kameli (Hawaiian) honey.
Kamely

Kamilah (Arabic) the perfect one.
Kameela, Kameelah, Kamila, Kamilla, Kamillah, Kammila, Kammilah, Kamyla, Kamylah, Kamylla, Kamyllah

Kamryn (English) crooked nose, feminine form of Cameron.
Kamrin, Kamrine, Kamryne

Kanani (Hawaiian) the beauty.
Kana, Kanae, Kanan, Kanana, Kananah, Kananea, Kananee,

Kanania, Kananiah, Kananie,
Kanany, Kananya, Kananyah

Kane (Japanese) two right hands.
Kanay, Kaneh

Kaneli (African) canary yellow.
Kanelea, Kaneleah, Kanelee,
Kanelei, Kaneleigh, Kanelia,
Kaneliah, Kanelie, Kanely, Kanelya

Kani (Hawaiian) sound.
Kanee, Kaney, Kanie, Kany

Kaniya (Native American) you are
my child.
Niya

Kannitha (Cambodian) angel.
Kanitha

Kanoa (Hawaiian) the free one.

Kantha (Hindu) wife.

Kanya (Hindu) the virgin, another
name for goddess.
Kanja, Kanjah, Kanyah, Kanyia

Kapua (Hawaiian) the blossom.
Kapuah

Kara (Australian Aboriginal)
possum; (Greek, Danish) pure.
Cara, Carah, Carra, Carrah,
Karah, Karalea, Karaleah, Karalee,
Karalei, Karaleigh, Karaley, Karali,
Karalia, Karaliah, Karalie, Karaly,
Karra, Karrah, Karralea, Karraleah,
Karralee, Karralei, Karraleigh,
Karraley, Karrali, Karralie, Karraly

Kareela (Australian Aboriginal)
south wind.
Kareala, Karealah, Karealla,
Kareallah, Karela, Karelah, Karella,
Karellah

Karen (Greek) pure, a form of
Catherine.

Caaran, Caran, Caren, Carian,
Carin, Carina, Caron, Carran,
Carren, Carrian, Carrin, Carrina,
Carrine, Carryn, Carryna,
Carrynah, Caryn, Caryna,
Carynah, Kaaran, Kaaren, Kaarin,
Kaaron, Kaaryn, Kara, Karah,
Karan, Karean, Kareana, Kareane,
Karreen, Kareena, Kareenah,
Kareene, Karena, Karenah, Karene,
Kari, Karia, Kariah, Karin, Karina,
Karinah, Karine, Karna, Karnah,
Karon, Karona, Karonah, Karone,
Karonia, Karoniah, Karonie, Karra,
Karrah, Karran, Karrana, Karranah,
Karrane, Karren, Karrena, Karrenah,
Karrin, Karrina, Karrinah, Karrine,
Karryn, Karryna, Karrynah, Karryne,
Karyn, Karyna, Karynah, Karyne

Karida (Arabic) untouched virgin.
Kareeda, Karidah, Karinda,
Karita, Karyda, Karydah, Karynda,
Karyndah

Karima (Arabic) generous, noble,
a unisex name.
Karimah, Kareema

Karina (Russian) pure, a form of
Karen.
Karinah

Karissa (Greek) love and grace,
favourite.
Karesa, Karesah, Karessa, Karessah,
Karisah, Karisha, Kariss, Karissah,
Karissimia, Karrissa, Kerisa

Karka (Hindu) the crab.

Karla (German) strong.
Carla, Carlah, Carlea, Carleah,
Carlee, Carlei, Carleigh, Carli,
Carlie, Carly, Karila, Karilla, Karlah,
Karle, Karlea, Karleah, Karlee,
Karlei, Karleigh, Karli, Karlie, Karlla,
Karlon, Karly

Karma (Hindu) action, destiny.
Carma, Carmah, Karmah

Karsten (Greek) blessed, anointed one, a unisex name.

Carsten, Karstan, Karstin

Kasa (Native American) fur-robe, dress.

Kasey (Celtic) brave and honourable, a form of Casey, a unisex name.

Casey, Caysee, Kaesee, Kaesesi, Kaesie, Kaesy, Kaisee, Kaisey, Kaisi, Kaisie, Kaisy, Kasci, Kascy, Kasee, Kasie, Kasy

Kasi (Hindu) one of seven holy Hindu cities.

Kasinda (African) earth closes up behind the last one, often used in a family with twins.

Kasmira (Slavonic) commands peace.

Kasmirah

Kassia (Greek) pure.

Casia, Casiah, Cassia, Cassiah, Cassya, Cassyah, Casya, Casyah, Kasia, Kasiah, Kassiah, Kassya, Kassyah, Kasya, Kasyah

Kassidy (Irish) clever.

Cassidy, Kasady, Kasidy, Kassady, Kassidee, Kassiddy, Kassidi, Kassity

Kate (Greek) pure, a form of Katherine.

Cait, Caite, Caitie, Cat, Cate, Catee, Catey, Caty, Kait, Kaitea, Kaitee, Kaitey, Kaitie, Kaity, Kat, Katee, Katey, Katie, Kaitlin, Katty, Katy, Katya

Katherine (Greek) pure.

Catharine, Catharyn, Catharyne, Catherine, Catheryn, Catheryne, Cathey, Cathi, Cathie, Cathlee, Cathy, Katarin, Katarina, Katarinah, Katarine, Kate, Katey, Katharin, Katharina, Katharinah, Katharine, Katherina, Katherinah, Kathi, Kathie, Kathrin, Kathryn, Kathy, Kati, Katie, Katrin, Katrine, Katy

Kathleen (Celtic) pure, a form of Katherine.

Cath, Cathie, Cathlean, Cathleen, Cathleena, Cathleenah, Cathleene, Cathlein, Cathleina, Cathleinah, Cathleine, Cathlena, Cathlene, Cathlina, Cathlinah, Cathline, Cathy, Kath, Katheleen, Kathelene, Kathi, Kathie, Kathlean, Kathleena, Kathleenah, Kathleene, Kathlein, Kathleina, Kathleinah, Kathleine, Kathlene, Kathlina, Kathlinah, Kathline, Kathy

Katriel (Hebrew) God is my crown, a unisex name.

Katrelle, Katri, Katrie, Katriela, Katrielah, Katriele, Katriell, Katriella, Katriellah, Katrielle, Katry, Katryel, Katryela, Katryelah, Katryele, Katryell, Katryella, Katryellah, Katryelle

Katrina (German) pure, a form of Katherine.

Catriona, Catrin, Catrina, Catriona, Katrien, Katriena, Katrienah, Katrin, Katrinah, Katrinia, Katrinna, Katrinnah, Katriona

Kaula (Hawaiian) prophet.

Kaulana (Hawaiian) fame.

Kahuna, Kaula, Kauna

Kaveri (Hindu) one of the seven sacred rivers of India.

Kavindra (Hindu) mighty poet.

Kawena (Hawaiian) the glow.

Kawana, Kawona

Kay (German) fort; (Greek) rejoice, a unisex name.

Kai, Kaie, Kaye

Kaya (Japanese) resting place.

Kayla (Hebrew) crown.
Cala, Calah, Calea, Caleah, Calee, Calei, Caleigh, Caley, Cali, Calia, Caliah, Calie, Caly, Cayla, Caylah, Caylea, Cayleah, Caylee, Caylei, Cayleigh, Cayley, Cayli, Caylia, Cayliah, Caylie, Cayly, Kala, Kalah, Kalea, Kaleah, Kalee, Kalei, Kaleigh, Kaley, Kali, Kalia, Kaliah, Kalie, Kaly, Kaylah, Kaylea, Kayleah, Kaylee, Kaylei, Kayleigh, Kayley, Kayli, Kaylia, Kayliah, Kaylie, Kayly

Kaylee (American) combination of Kay and Lee.
Caelee, Caelei, Caeleigh, Caeley, Caeli, Caelie, Caely, Cailee, Cailei, Caileigh, Cailey, Caili, Caily, Calee, Calei, Caleigh, Caley, Cali, Calie, Caly, Caylee, Caylei, Cayleigh, Cayley, Cayli, Cayly, Kaelee, Kaelei, Kaeleigh, Kaeley, Kaeli, Kaelie, Kaely, Kailee, Kailei, Kaileigh, Kailey, Kaili, Kailie, Kalee, Kalei, Kaleigh, Kaley, Kalie, Kaylei, Kayleigh, Kayley, Kayli, Kaylie, Kayly

Kazuko (Japanese) first, obedient daughter.

Keahi (Hawaiian) flames, the fire, a unisex name.

Keala (Hawaiian) path.
Kealah, Kealea, Kealeah, Kealee, Kealei, Kealeigh, Kealey, Keali, Kealia, Kealiah, Kealie, Kealy, Kealya

Keara (Irish) from a saint's name.

Keavy (Irish) loveliness, gentleness or grace.
Keava, Keeva, Keevy

Keegan (Irish) small, fiery one, a unisex name.
Kaegan, Kagan, Keagen, Keagin, Keagon, Keegen, Keeghan,

Keegin, Keegon, Keegun, Kegan, Kegen, Keigan, Keigen, Keygyn

Keeley/Keely (Gaelic) handsome, beautiful, a unisex name.
Kealea, Kealeah, Kealee, Kealei, Kealeigh, Kealey, Keali, Kealia, Kealiah, Kealie, Kealy, Kealya, Keelea, Keeleah, Keelee, Keelei, Keeleigh, Keeli, Keelia, Keeliah, Keelie, Keelya, Keighlea, Keighleah, Keighlee, Keighlei, Keighleigh, Keighley, Keighli, Keighlia, Keighliah, Keighlie, Keighly, Keilea, Keileah, Keilei, Keileigh, Keiley, Keili, Keilia, Keiliah, Keilie, Keily, Keilya, Kelea, Keleah, Kelee, Kelei, Keleigh, Keley, Keli, Kelia, Keliah, Kelie, Kely, Keylea, Keyleah, Keylee, Keylei, Keyleigh, Keyley, Keyli, Keylia, Keyliah, Keylie, Keyly

Keelin (Irish) fair and slender.
Kealin, Kealyn, Keelyn, Keilan, Keilin, Keilyn, Kielin, Kielyn

Keena (Irish) brave.
Keenah, Keenya, Keina, Keinah, Keinya, Keyna, Keynah, Kina, Kinah

Kefira (Hebrew) young lioness.
Kefirah, Kefire, Kefyra, Kefyrah, Kefyre

Kei (Japanese) reverent.

Keiki (Hawaiian) child.
Keikana, Keikann, Keikanna, Keikanne, Keyki, Kiki

Keiko (Japanese) happy, blessed daughter, pretty.
Keyko

Keilana (Hawaiian) gloriously calm.
Kealaina, Kealainah, Kealana, Kealanah, Kealanna, Kealannah, Keelaina, Keelainah, Keelana, Keelanah, Keelanna, Keelannah, Keelayna, Keelaynah, Keilaina,

*Keilainah, Keilana, Keilanah,
Keilanna, Keilannah, Keilayna,
Keilaynah, Keylaina, Keylainah,
Keylana, Keylanah, Keylayna,
Keylaynah*

Keilani (Hawaiian) glorious chief.

*Kealaine, Kealainee, Kealane,
Kealanee, Kealanne, Kealannee,
Keelane, Keelanee, Keelayn,
Keelayne, Keelaynee, Keilain,
Keilainee, Keilaine, Keilan, Keilane,
Keilanee, Keilanie, Keilanne,
Keilannee, Keilany, Keilayn,
Keilayne, Keilaynee, Kelana,
Kelanah, Kelane, Kelani, Kelanie,
Keylaine, Keylainee, Keylane,
Keylanee, Keylayn, Keylayne,
Keylaynee*

Keira (Irish) dark haired, black.

Ceira, Keera, Kira, Kirah, Kirra, Kirrah

Keisha (African) favourite.

*Keasha, Keashia, Keashya,
Keesha, Keeshia, Keeshiah, Keeshy,
Keeshya, Keeshyah, Keishah,
Keishia, Keishiah, Keishya, Keishyah,
Kesha, Keshah, Keshia, Keshiah,
Keshya, Keshyah, Keysha, Keyshah,
Keyshia, Keyshiah, Keyshya,
Keyshyah*

Kekona (Hawaiian) second-born
child.

Kelda (Scandinavian) bubbling
spring.

Keldah, Keldra, Keldrah

Kelila (Hebrew) crown, laurel.

Kelilah, Kelula, Kelulah

Kelly (Celtic) battle maiden of
the woods, brave warrior, a unisex
name.

Kellee, Kelli, Kellie, Kellye, Kely, Kelya

Kelsey (English) port of ships, a
form of Chelsea; (Scandinavian)
island of ships, a unisex name.

*Kelcea, Kelcee, Kelci, Kelcie,
Kelcy, Kellcea, Kellcee, Kellcey,
Kellci, Kellcia, Kellciah, Kellcie,
Kellcy, Kellsea, Kellsee, Kellsey,
Kellsi, Kellsia, Kellsiah, Kellsie, Kellsy,
Kelsea, Kelsee, Kelsi, Kelsie, Kelsy*

Kendra (Anglo-Saxon) knowing.

*Kendrah, Kendre, Kenndra, Kentra,
Kentrae, Kentrah*

Kenna (Scottish) fair one, feminine
form of Kenneth.

*Kena, Kenah, Kenina, Keninah,
Kennah*

Kennedy (Irish) helmeted chief, a
unisex name.

*Kenedy, Kenidee, Kenidi, Kenidie,
Kenidy, Kennady, Kennedee,
Kennedey, Kennidee, Kennidi,
Kennidy, Kynnedi*

Kentigerna (Celtic) ruler.

Kenti, Kentigern

Keona (Hawaiian) God's gracious
gift.

Keonah, Kiona, Kionah

Kerani (Indian) sacred bells.

*Kerana, Keranee, Keraney, Kerania,
Keraniah, Keranie, Kerany, Keranya,
Keranyah*

Kerry (Irish) dark-haired, a unisex
name.

*Keary, Keiry, Keree, Kerey, Keri, Kerie,
Kerree, Kerrey, Kerri, Kerrie, Kery*

Kesava (Hindu) having fine hair.

Keshet (Hebrew) rainbow.

*Kesetta, Kesettah, Kesette,
Kesheta, Keshetah, Keshete,
Keshett, Keshetta, Keshettah,
Keshette*

Kesia (African) favourite.

*Kesiah, Kessia, Kessiah, Kessya,
Kessyah*

Kestrel (English) falcon, a unisex name.
Kestrell

Ketifa (Arabic) flower, to pick a flower.
Ketifah, Kettifa, Kettifah, Kettyfa, Kettyfah, Ketyfa, Ketyfah

Ketina (Hebrew) girl.
Keteena, Keteenah, Ketinah, Ketyna, Ketynah

Ketura (Hebrew) perfume is in the air.
Keturah

Ketzia (Hebrew) scented bark, cinnamon.
Ketziah, Ketzya, Ketzyah

Keyna (Welsh) jewel.
Keynah

Kezia (Hebrew) cinnamon spice, from cassia tree.
Kazia, Kaziah, Ketzi, Ketzia, Ketziah, Ketzya, Ketzyah, Kezi, Kezya, Kezyah, Kezzia, Kezziah, Kizia, Kiziah, Kizzia, Kizziah, Kizzya, Kizzyah, Kyzia, Kyziah, Kyzzia, Kyzziah, Kyzzya, Kyzzyah

Khadijah (Arabic,) trustworthy, first wife of the prophet Muhammad.
Khadija, Khadeeja, Khadeejah

Khalidah (Arabic) immortal.
Khali, Khalia, Khalida, Khalita

Khayriyyah (Arabic) charitable, good.
Khairiya, Khairiyah, Khairiyya, Khayriya, Khayriyah, Khayriyya

Kia (African) born at the season's beginning.
Kiah, Kya, Kyah

Kiana (Hawaiian) moon goddess.
Kianah

Kiarah (Arabic) crowned princess.
Ciara, Ciarah, Ciera, Cierra, Kiara, Kiarra, Kiarrah, Kiera, Kierra, Kirra

Kiele (Hawaiian) gardenia, fragrant blossom, a unisex name.
Kiela, Kielah, Kielea, Kieleah, Kielee, Kielei, Kieleigh, Kieley, Kieli, Kielia, Kieliah, Kielie, Kielle, Kielli, Kielly, Kiely, Kyele, Kyelle

Kiki (Egyptian) castor plant.
Kikee, Kikie, Kiky

Kikilia (Hawaiian) a form of Cecilia, blind.

Kiku (Japanese) chrysanthemum.
Kiko

Kiley (Irish) attractive, good looking, one who returns, a unisex name.
Kielea, Kieleah, Kielee, Kielei, Kieleigh, Kieley, Kieli, Kielia, Kieliah, Kielie, Kiely, Kilea, Kileah, Kilee, Kilei, Kileigh, Kili, Kilia, Kiliah, Kilie, Killey, Killi, Killie, Killy, Kily, Kylea, Kyleah, Kylee, Kylei, Kyleigh, Kyley, Kyli, Kylia, Kyliah, Kylie, Kyly

Kilia (Hawaiian) heaven.
Kiliah, Killea, Killeah, Killia, Killiah, Kylia, Kyliah, Kylya, Kylyah

Kim (English) chief, a unisex name.
Kimi, Kimie, Kimm, Kimmie, Kimmy, Kym, Kyme, Kymi, Kymm, Kymy, Kymmi, Kymmie, Kymmy

Kimana (Native American) butterfly.
Kiman, Kimanah, Kimane, Kimann, Kimanna, Kimannah, Kimanne, Kyman, Kymana, Kymanah, Kymane, Kymann, Kymanna, Kymannah, Kymanne

Kimberley (Anglo-Saxon) warrior chief, from the royal meadow, a feminine form of Kimbal.

Kimbalee, Kimbaley, Kimbaly, Kimbely, Kimberely, Kimberlea, Kimberleah, Kimberlee, Kimberlei, Kimberleigh, Kimberli, Kimberlia, Kimberliah, Kimberlie, Kimberly, Kymberlea, Kymberleah, Kymberlee, Kymberlei, Kymberleigh, Kymberley, Kymberli, Kymberlia, Kymberliah, Kymberly

Kimiko (Japanese) righteous child.

Kimik, Kimika, Kimyko, Kymyko

Kina (Hawaiian) from China.

Kinah, Kyna, Kynah

Kineta (Greek) active one.

Kinet, Kinetah, Kinete, Kinett, Kinetta, Kinettah, Kinette, Kynet, Kyneta, Kynetah, Kynete, Kynett, Kynetta, Kynettah, Kynette

Kini (Hawaiian) God is gracious.

Kiona (Native American) brown hills.

Kionah, Kyona, Kyonah

Kira (Latin) light; (Persian) sun.

Kirah, Kiri, Kirra, Kirrah, Kyra, Kyrah, Kyri, Kyrra, Kyrrah

Kiran (Hindu) ray, beam of light, a unisex name.

Kearan, Kearen, Kearin, Kearon, Keeran, Keerana, Keeranah, Keerane, Keeren, Keerin, Keeron, Keiran, Keiren, Keirin, Keiron, Keiryn, Kirana, Kiranah, Kirane, Kiren, Kirin, Kiron, Kirran, Kirrana, Kirranah, Kirrane, Kiryn, Kiryne, Kyran, Kyrana, Kyranah, Kyrane, Kyren, Kyrin, Kyron, Kyryn

Kirby (English) church in the village or farm, a unisex name.

Kerbea, Kerbee, Kerbey, Kerbi, Kerbie, Kerby, Kirbea, Kirbea, Kirbey, Kirbi, Kirbie, Kyrbea, Kyrbee, Kyrbey, Kyrbi, Kyrbie, Kyrby

Kiri (Maori) tree bark.

Kirea, Kiree, Kirey, Kirie, Kiry

Kirrily (Australian Aboriginal) bark of a tree; (English) combination of the names Kiri or Kira and Lee.

Kiralea, Kiralee, Kiraley, Kiralie, Kiraly, Kirilea, Kirilee, Kiriley, Kirilie, Kirily, Kirralea, Kirralee, Kirraley, Kirralie, Kirraly, Kirrilea, Kirrilee, Kirriley, Kirrilie, Kyralea, Kyralee, Kyraley, Kyralie, Kyraly, Kyrilea, Kyrilee, Kyriley, Kyrilie, Kyrily

Kirsi (Hindu) amaranth.

Kirsten (Greek, Scandinavian, Scottish) annointed.

Kirstain, Kirstaine, Kirstan, Kirstane, Kirsteen, Kirstene, Kirsteni, Kirstien, Kirstiene, Kirstin, Kirstine, Kirston, Kirstone, Kirstyn, Kirstyne, Kirstynn, Kjersten, Kurstain, Kurstaine, Kurstean, Kursteane, Kursteen, Kursteene, Kursten, Kurstin, Kurstine, Kurstyn, Kurstyne

Kirsty (Scottish) annointed, from Kirsten.

Kerstea, Kerstee, Kerstey, Kersti, Kerstia, Kerstiah, Kerstie, Kersty, Kirstea, Kirstee, Kirstey, Kirsti, Kirstia, Kirstiah, Kirstie, Kirstya, Kirstye, Kjersti, Kurstea, Kurstee, Kurstey, Kursti, Kurstia, Kurstiah, Kurstie, Kursty, Kyrstea, Kyrstee, Kyrstey, Kyrsti, Kyrstia, Kyrstiah, Kyrstie, Kyrsty

Kisa (Russian) kitty.

Kisah, Kiska, Kysa, Kysah, Kyssa, Kyssah

Kishi (Japanese) long life with happiness.

Kiska (Russian) pure.

GIRLS

Kismet (Arabic) fate, destiny, fortune.

Kismeta, Kismetah, Kismete, Kismett, Kismetta, Kismettah, Kismette, Kissmet, Kissmeta, Kissmetah, Kissmete, Kissmett, Kissmetta, Kissmettah, Kissmette, Kysmet, Kysmeta, Kysmetah, Kysmete, Kysmett, Kysmetta, Kysmettah, Kysmette, Kyssmet, Kyssmeta, Kyssmetah, Kyssmete, Kyssmett, Kyssmetta, Kyssmettah, Kyssmette

Kissa (African) born after twins.

Kisa, Kisah, Kissah, Kysa, Kysah, Kyssa, Kyssah

Kitra (Hebrew) crowned.

Kitrah

Kitty (Greek) pure, from Katherine; (English) generic name for small cat.

Kit, Kittee, Kittey, Kitti, Kittie

Klesa (Hindu) pain given to ward off evil spirits.

Koko (Native American) night; (Japanese) stork.

Coco

Kolfinnia (Scandinavian) white.

Kolfina, Kolfinah, Kolfinia, Kolfiniah, Kolfinna, Kolfinnah, Kolfinniah

Kolika (Hawaiian) from the ocean.

Kolora (Australian Aboriginal) lake.

Kolorah, Kolori, Kolorie, Kolory

Kona (Hawaiian) lady.

Koni, Konia

Konane (Hawaiian) bright as moonlight.

Korena (Greek) maiden.

Koren, Korenah, Korene, Korin,

Korina, Korinah, Korine, Koryn, Koryna, Korynah, Koryne

Kris (Greek, Scandinavian) Christ-bearer, christian, a form of Kristine, Kristina.

Chris, Christian, Christin, Khris, Khriss, Khrista, Khristen, Khristin, Khristina, Khristine, Khrys, Khryss, Kriss, Krista, Kristen, Kristin, Kristina, Kristine, Krys, Kryss

Kristal/Krystal (Latin) clear.

Crystal, Crystale, Kristale, Kristall, Kristalle, Kristel, Kristele, Kristell, Kristella, Kristelle, Kristill, Kristl, Kristle, Krystale, Krystall, Krystalle, Krystel, Krystele, Krystell, Krystella, Krystelle, Krystil, Krystyl, Krystyle, Krystyll, Krystill, Krystylla, Krystylle

Kristina (Greek, Scandinavian) Christ-bearer, christian.

Khris, Khrista, Khristee, Khristen, Khristie, Khristin, Khristine, Khristiana, Khristianah, Khristianna, Khristiannah, Khristy, Khristyana, Khristyanah, Khristyanna, Khristyannah, Kris, Krista, Kristee, Kristen, Kristie, Kristin, Kristine, Kristiana, Kristianah, Kristianna, Kristiannah, Kristy, Kristyana, Kristyanah, Kristyanna, Kristyannah

Kuma (African) mouse.

Kumah

Kumari (Hindu) woman.

Kumaree, Kumarey, Kumaria, Kumariah, Kumarie, Kumary, Kumarya, Kumaryah

Kumberlin (Australian Aboriginal) sweet.

Cumberlin, Cumberlina, Cumberline, Cumberlyn, Cumberlyna, Cumberlyne, Kumberlina, Kumberline, Kumberlyn, Kumberlyna, Kumberlyne

Kumi (Japanese) braid.

Kumee, Kumie, Kumy

Kumuda (Hindu) lotus.

Kunani (Hawaiian) beautiful.
Kunanee, Kunaney, Kunanie, Kunany

Kura (Japanese) red treasure house.

Kusa (Hindu) sacred kusa grass.

Kwanita (Native American) God is gracious.

Kya (African) diamond.
Kia, Kiah, Kyah

Kyla (Irish) attractive, feminine form of Kyle; (Scottish) lovely; (Hebrew) crown.
Khyla, Kyela, Kyelah, Kyella, Kylah, Kylia

Kylie (Australian Aboriginal) boomerang.
Kilea, Kileah, Kilee, Kilei, Kileigh, Kiley, Kili, Kilia, Kiliah, Kilie, Killea, Killeah, Killee, Killei, Killeigh, Killey, Killi, Killia, Killiah, Killie, Killy, Kily, Kylea, Kyleah, Kylee, Kylei, Kyleigh, Kyley, Kyli, Kylia, Kyliah, Kyllea, Kylleah, Kyllee, Kyllei, Kylleigh, Kylley, Kylli, Kyllia, Kylliah, Kyllie, Kylly, Kyly, Kylya, Kylyah

Kyna (Gaelic) wisdom.
Kina, Kinah, Kynah

Kynthia (Greek) moon, moon goddess, a form of Cynthia, born under the sign of Cancer.
Cinthia, Kindi, Kinthia, Kinthiah, Kinthya, Kinthyah, Kyndi, Kynthiah, Kynthya, Kynthyah

Kyoko (Japanese) mirror.
Kyoka, Kyokah

Kyra (Greek) throne, ruler; (Perisan) sun.
Cyra, Kira, Kirah, Kyrah, Kyria, Kyriah, Kyrra, Kyrrah

Lacey (Greek) cheerful one.
Lace, Lacea, Lacee, Laci, Lacia, Laciah, Lacie, Lacy, Lacye, Laicea, Laicee, Laicey, Laici, Laicia, Laiciah, Laicie, Laicy, Larissa, Laysei, Laysi, Laysie, Laysy

Laine (French) light, a form of Elaine.
Laen, Laena, Laenah, Laene, Laenee, Laeney, Laeni, Laenia, Laeniah, Laenie, Laeny, Lain, Laina, Lainah, Lainee, Lainey, Laini, Lainia, Laniah, Lainie, Lainne, Lainy

Laione (African) lion.
Laeona, Laeonah, Laeone, Laiona, Laionah, Layona, Layonah, Layone

Lais (Greek) friendly.
Laeis, Laeise, Laeiss, Laeisse, Laise, Laiss, Laisse

Lajila (Hindu) shy, coy.
Jila, Laji, Lajilah, Lajilla, Lajillah

Laka (Hawaiian) attractive, seductive.
Lakah

Lakeisha (African) life; (Arabic) woman; (American) combination of La and Keisha.
Lakaiesha, Lakaisha, Lakasha, Lakecia, Lakeciah, Lakeesh, Lakeesha, Lakeishia, Lakeishiah, Lakeishya, Lakeishyah, Lakeisia, Lakeisiah, Lakeitia, Lakeitiah, Lakesha, Lakeshia, Lakeshiah, Lakeshya, Lakesia, Lakesiah, Laketia, Laketiah, Lakeysha, Lakeyshia

Lakia (Arabic) treasure.
Lakiah, Lakya, Lakyah

Lakkari (Australian Aboriginal) honeysuckle tree.
Lakaree, Lakarey, Lakari, Lakaria, Lakariah, Lakarie, Lakary, Lakkaree, Lakkarey, Lakkaria, Lakkariah, Lakkarie, Lakkary

Lakshmi (Hindu) mark, success, the goddess of good fortune.
Lakshmee, Lakshmey, Lakshmie, Lakshmy, Shami, Shamie

Lakya (Hindu) born on Thursday.
Lakia, Lakiah, Lakyah, Lakyia, Lakyiah

Lala (Slavic) tulip.
Laela, Laelah, Laella, Laellah, Laila, Lailah, Lailla, Laillah, Lalah, Lalla, Lallah, Layla, Laylah, Laylla, Layllah

Lalage (Greek) speaking freely.
Lal, Lallie, Lally, Laly

Lalasa (Hindu) love.
Lalassa, Lallasa, Lallassa

Lalita (Hindu) pleasing, charming, honest, one of the many names for the goddess Shakti.
Laleata, Laleatah, Laleate, Laleeta, Laleetah, Laleete, Laleita, Laleitah, Laleite, Lalitah, Lalite, Lalitt, Lalitta, Lalittah, Lalitte, Lalyta, Lalytah, Lalyte, Lalytta, Lalyttah, Lalytte

Lamani (African) lemon.
Lamanee, Lamaney, Lamania, Lamaniah, Lamanie, Lamany, Lamanya, Lamanyah

Lamis (Arabic) soft to the touch.
Laamees, Laamis, Lamees, Lamisa, Lamisah, Lamiss, Lamissa, Lamissah, Lamys, Lamysa, Lamysah, Lamyss, Lamyssa, Lamyssah

Lamya (Arabic) of dark lips.
Lamia, Lamiah, Lamyah

Lan (Vietnamese) orchid flower.
Lann, Lanne

Lana (Latin) wool, woolly; (Hawaiian) floating; (Irish) peaceful; (English) a form of of Alana, Helena, Svetlana.
Laina, Lainah, Laine, Laini, Lainna, Lainnah, Lainy, Lanah, Laney, Lanna, Lannah, Lanni, Lanny

Landra (German, Spanish) counsellor.
Landrada, Landrah, Landrea, Landreah, Landria, Landriah, Landrya, Landryah

Lane (English) narrow road, a unisex name.
Laen, Laena, Laene, Lain, Laina, Lainah, Laine, Lainee, Lainey, Laini, Lainia, Lainiah, Lainie, Lanee, Laney, Lannee, Lani, Lanie, Lanni, Lannia, Lanniah, Lannie, Lany, Layn, Layna, Laynah, Layne, Layni, Laynia, Layniah, Laynie

Lani (Hawaiian) heavenly sky, a unisex name.
Lanea, Lanee, Laney, Lania, Laniah, Lanie, Lannee, Lanney, Lanni, Lannia, Lanniah, Lannie, Lanny, Lannya, Lannyah, Lany, Lanya, Lanyah

Lara (Latin) shining, well-known, famous; (Greek) happy, cheerful.
Larah, Laretta, Larette, Laria, Lariah, Larra, Larrah, Larrya, Larryah, Larya, Laryah, Laura, Lauren, Lora, Loretta

La Reina (Spanish) queen.
Lareina, Lareine, La Reine, Lareena, Larena, Reina, Reine

Lari (Latin) holy, crowned with laurel.
Laree, Larie, Larri

Larissa (Greek) cheerful, happy one.
Larisa, Larisah, Larissah, Larisse

Lark (English) skylark, sings like a lark.
Larke, Larkee, Larkey

Larlene (Irish) promise.
Larlean, Larleana, Larleanah, Larleane, Larleen, Larleena, Larleenah, Larleene, Larlen, Larlena, Larlenah, Larlin, Larlina, Larlinah, Larline

Larmina (Persian) blue sky.
Larminah, Larmine, Larmyn, Larmyna, Larmynah, Larmyne

Lass/Lassie (Irish) young girl.
Lassi, Lassy

Lataree (Japanese) bent branch.
Latarea, Latarey, Latari, Latarie, Latary

Lateefah (Arabic) gentle, kind, pleasant friendly.
Lateefa, Lateifa, Lateifah, Lateyfa, Lateyfah, Latifa, Latifah, Leitifa, Leitifah

Latika (Hindu) a small creeper plant.
Latik, Latikah, Latyk, Latyka, Latykah

Latona (Latin) the mother of Apollo and Diana in Roman mythology.
Latonah, Latonia, Latoniah

Latoya (Spanish) victorious.
Latoia, Latoiah, Latoiya, Latoiyah, LaToya, Latoyah, Latoye, Latoyia, Latoyita, Latoyo

Laulani (Hawaiian) heavenly tree branch.

Laulanea, Laulanee, Laulaney, Laulania, Laulaniah, Laulanie, Laulany, Laulanya, Laulanyah

Laura (Latin) laurel-crowned.

Laudra, Launa, Laurah, Laurain, Lauraina, Laurainah, Lauraine, Laural, Lauralea, Lauraleah, Lauralee, Lauralei, Lauraleigh, Lauraley, Laurali, Lauralia, Lauraliah, Lauralie, Lauraly, Lauralya, Lora, Lorah, Loree, Loreen, Loreena, Lorel, Lorelea, Lorelee, Loreleigh, Lorell, Lorella, Lorelle, Lorna, Lory, Lorya, Loryah

Laurel (Latin) laurel leaves.

Laural, Laurala, Lauralah, Laurale, Laurela, Laurelah, Laurele, Laurell, Laurella, Laurellah, Laurelle

Lauren (English) laurel-crowned.

Laura, Lauran, Laurana, Lauranah, Laurane, Laurann, Lauranna, Laurannah, Lauranne, Laurena, Laurenah, Laurene, Laurenn, Laurenna, Larennah, Laurenne, Laurin, Laurina, Laurine, Loran, Lorana, Loranah, Loren, Lorena, Lorenah, Lorene, Lorin, Lorina, Lorine, Loryn, Loryna, Loryne

Lavani (African) necklace.

Lavane, Lavaneah, Lavanee, Lavaney, Lavania, Lavaniah, Lavany, Lavanya, Lavanyah

Laveda (Latin) purified one.

Lavedah, Laveta, Lavetah, Lavete, Lavett, Lavetta, Lavettah, Lavette

Lavender (English) sweetly scented flower.

Lavenda, Lavendah, Lavendar

Laverna/Laverne (French) from the alder grove; (Latin) spring-like.

Lavern, La Vern, Laverna, La Verna,

Lavernah, La Vernah, La Verne, Lavernia, Laverniah, Laveryna, Laverynah, Laveryne

Lavina/Lavinia (Latin) purity.

Lavania, Lavaniah, Laveni, Lavenia, Laveniah, Lavinah, Laviniah, Lavinie, Lavyna, Lavynah, Lavyne, Lavyni, Lavynia, Lavyniah, Lavyny, Lavynya, Lavynyah, Lyvina, Lyvinah, Lyvinia, Layviniah, Lyvynya, Lyvynyah

Lawan (Thai) pretty.

Lawana, Lawane

Layla (African) born at night, (Arabic) dark-haired.

Laela, Laelah, Laeli, Laelia, Laeliah, Laelie, Laely, Laila, Lailah, Laili, Lailia, Lailiah, Lailie, Laily, Laleh, Laylah, Layli, Laylia, Layliah, Laylie, Layly, Laylya, Laylyah, Leila, Leilah, Leyla, Leylah

Layna (Greek) light.

Laena, Laenah, Laina, Lainah, Laynah

Lazalea (Greek) ruling eagle.

Lazaleah, Lazalee, Lazalei, Lazaleigh, Lazaley, Lazali, Lazalia, Lazaliah, Lazalie, Lazaly, Lazalya

Le (Vietnamese) pearl.

Lea (Hebrew) weary; (English) meadow, a form of Leah.

Leah, Lee, Leia, Leigh, Lia, Liah

Leah (Hebrew) weary; (English) meadow.

Lea, Lee, Leia, Leigh, Lia, Liah

Leala (French) faithful and loyal.

Lealah, Lealia, Lealie, Leela, Leelah, Leiala, Leighla, Leighlah, Leila

Leandra (Latin) lion woman, feminine form of Leander.

Leanda, Leandrah, Leandre, Leandrea, Leandria, Leeanda, Leeandah, Leeandra, Leeandrah, Leianda, Leiandah, Leiandra, Leiandrah

Leanne (English) graceful meadow, combination of Lee and Anne; (French) to bind.

Lea-ann, Lea-anne, Leann, Leanna, Leannah, Leandra, Leandria, Leane, Leanka, Leeann, Leeanna, Leeanne, Leeona, Leeonah, Leiana, Leianah, Leiane, Leianna, Leiannah, Leianne, Leighana, Leighanah, Leighane, Leighann, Leighanna, Leighanne, Leyan, Leyana, Leyanah, Leyane, Leyann, Leyanna, Leyannah, Leyanne, Lian, Liana, Lianah, Liane, Liann, Lianna, Liannah, Lianne, Lyan, Lyana, Lyanah, Lyane, Lyann, Lyanna, Lyannah, Lyanne

Lecia (Latin) happy.

Leacia, Leaciah, Leacya, Leacyah, Leasia, Leasiah, Leasie, Leasy, Leasya, Leasyah, Leasye, Leecia, Leeciah, Leesha, Leeshia, Leeshiah, Leesia, Leesiah, Lesha, Leshah, Leshia, Leshiah, Lesia, Lesiah, Lesya, Lesyah

Leda (Greek) lady.

Leada, Leadah, Ledah, Ledda, Leddah, Lede, Ledel, Ledell, Leeda, Leedah, Leida, Leidah

Lee (English) meadow or clearing, a unisex name.

Lea, Leah, Leia, Leigh, Lia, Liah

Leena (Australian Aboriginal) possum or water.

Leenah

Lei (Hawaiian) flower, heavenly child.

Leah, Leaha, Lee, Leia, Leigh, Li, Lia, Liah, Ly, Lya, Lyah

Leigh (English) meadow or clearing, a unisex name.

Lea, Leah, Lee

Leiko (Japanese) arrogant.

Leako, Leeko, Leyko

Leilani (Hawaiian) heavenly child, heavenly flower.

Lani, Lealanea, Lealaneah, Lealanee, Lealaney, Lealani, Lealania, Lealaniah, Lealanie, Lealany, Leelanea, Leelaneah, Leelanee, Leelaney, Leelani, Lee-Lani, Leelania, Leelaniah, Leelanie, Leelany, Leigh-Lani, Leighlani, Leilanea, Leilanee, Leilaney, Leilania, Leilaniah, Leilanie, Leilany, Leylani, Leylania, Leylaniah, Leylanie, Leylany

Lela (Arabic) dark as the night, dark beauty.

Leela, Leelah, Leila, Leilah, Leilia, Leiliah, Lelah, Liela, Lielah, Lila, Lilah

Lelia (Greek) fair speech.

Leliah, Lelika, Lelita, Lellia, Lelliah

Lemana (Australian Aboriginal) oak tree.

Leaman, Leamanah, Leeman, Leemana, Leemanah, Leiman, Leimana, Leimanah, Lemanah, Leyman, Leymana, Leymanah

Lemuela (Hebrew) consecrated to God.

Leemewla, Lemuelah, Lemuella, Lemuellah

Lena (Latin) enchanting, temptress; (Greek) light, a form of Helen; (Norwegian) illustrious.

Lenah, Lenna, Lennah, Lina, Linah

Lenora/Lenore (Greek) light, a form of Helen.

Leanor, Leanora, Leanorah, Leanore, Lenor, Lenorah, Lenoree, Leonara, Leonarah, Leonora, Leonorah, Leonore

Leoda (German) woman of the people.

Leeoda, Leioda, Leodah, Leota, Leotah

Leola (Latin) lioness, feminine of Leo.

Leiola, Leolla

Leoma (English) light, bright.

Leioma, Lei-oma, Leiomma, Leomah

Leona (German) lion-like, brave like a lion.

Leeona, Leeonah, Lenora, Lenore, Leoina, Leoine, Leonae, Leonah, Leone, Leonel, Leonela, Leonelah, Leonella, Leonelle, Leonia, Leoniah, Liona, Lionia, Lioniah

Leonarda (German) as brave as a lion, feminine form of Leonard.

Leonardra, Leonardrea, Leonardria, Leonda, Leondra, Leondrea, Leondria

Leonie (German) brave as a lion.

Leona, Leonarda, Leonardra, Leonee, Leoney, Leonia, Leoniah, Leeona, Leoney, Leeonia, Leeoniah, Leeonie, Leeony

Leonora (Italian) shining light, a form of Helen.

Leonorah, Leeonora, Leeonorah

Leontine (Latin) like a lion.

Leonina, Leonine, Leonteen, Leontie, Leontina, Leonty, Leontyn, Leotyna, Leontyne, Lyontina, Lyontine, Lyontyna, Lyontyne

Leora (Hebrew) light.

Leeora, Leorah

Lepati (African) leopard.

Leapati, Leapatie, Leapaty, Leipati, Leipatie, Leipaty, Lepatie, Lepaty

Leslie/Lesley (Scottish) grey fortress, unisex name.

Lee, Leigh, Les, Leslea, Lesleah, Leslee, Leslei, Lesleigh, Lesli, Lesly, Leslye, Lesslie, Lessly, Lezley, Lezlie

Leta (Latin) happiness and joy.

Leahta, Leahtah, Leata, Leatah, Leeta, Leetah, Leita, Leitah, Leighta, Leightah, Letah, Letta, Lettah Leyta, Leytah, Lita, Litah, Lyta, Lytah

Letha (Greek) forgetful.

Lethia, Leitha, Leithia, Leta, Letia, Leytha, Leythia, Leythiah

Leticia (Latin) happiness, joy.

Laticia, Laticiah, Leisha, Leishah, Leshia, Leshiah, Let, Leta, Leteesha, Leteeshah, Letesa, Letesah, Letesha, Leteshah, Leteshia, Leteshiah, Letice, Leticiah, Letisa, Letisah, Letisha, Letishah, Letishia, Letishiah, Letisia, Letisiah, Letissa, Letissah, Letita, Letitah, Letitia, Letitiah, Letizia, Letiziah, Letha, Lethah, Lethia, Lethiah, Letteria, Letty, Letycia, Letyciah, Loutitia, Loutitiah, Teish, Tish

Letitia (Latin) happiness, joy.

Laticia, Laticiah, Leisha, Leishah, Leshia, Leshiah, Let, Leta, Leteesha, Leteeshah, Letesa, Letesah, Letesha, Leteshah, Leteshia, Leteshiah, Leticiah, Letice, Letisa, Letisah, Letisha, Letishah, Letishia, Letishiah, Letisia, Letisiah, Letissa, Letissah, Letita, Letitah, Letitia, Letizia, Letiziah, Letha, Lethah, Lethia, Lethiah, Letteria, Letty, Letycia, Letyciah, Loutitia, Loutitiah, Teish, Tish

Levana (Latin) morning sun; (Hebrew) white moon.

Levanah, Levanna, Levannah, Levena, Levenah, Levenna, Levennah

Levani (Fijian) anointed with oil.
Levanee, Levaney, Levania, Levaniah, Levanie, Levany, Levanya

Levina (Latin) lightning.
Levena, Levene, Levinah, Livina, Livinna

Levona (Hebrew) spice, incense.
Leavona, Leavonah, Leavonia, Leavoniah, Leavonna, Leavonnah, Leavonnia, Leevona, Leevonah, Leevonia, Leevoniah, Leevonna, Leevonnah, Leevonnia, Leevonniah, Leivona, Leivonah, Leivonia, Leivoniah, Leivonna, Leivonnah, Levonah, Levonia, Levoniah, Levonna, Levonnah, Levonnia, Levonniah, Leyvona, Leyvonah, Leyvonia, Leyvoniah, Leyvonna, Leyvonnah, Leyvonnia, Leyvonniah

Lewanna (Hebrew) a large white moon.
Leawana, Leawanah, Leawanna, Leawannah, Leewana, Leewanah, Leewanna, Leewannah, Lewana, Lewanah, Lewannah, Lewhana, Lewhanah, Lewhanna, Lewhannah, Louhana, Louhanah, Louhanna, Louhannah

Leya (Spanish) loyal to the law.
Lea, Leah, Leea, Leeah, Leia, Leiya, Leyah

Li (Chinese) strength, plum.

Lia (Hebrew/Dutch/Italian) dependent; (Greek) bringer of good news.
Liah, Lya, Lyah

Liadan (Irish) grey lady.

Lian (Chinese) graceful willow; (Irish) protector, a unisex name.
Lean, Leann, Liane, Liann, Lyan, Lyann

Liana (French) bound or wrapped up, covered with vines.
Lianah, Lianna, Liannah, Leeanna, Leeannah, Lyana, Lyanah, Lyanna, Lyannah

Liane (Chinese) graceful willow, a form of Lian.

Libby (Hebrew) consecrated to God, a form of Elizabeth.
Lib, Libba, Libbea, Libbee, Libbey, Libbi, Libbie, Libea, Libee, Libey, Libi, Libie, Liby, Lyb, Lybbi, Lybbie, Lybby

Liberty (Latin) free, freedom.
Libertee, Libertey, Liberti, Libertie, Libirtee, Libirtey, Libirti, Libirtie, Libirty, Liburtee, Liburtey, Liburti, Liburtie, Liburty, Lybertee, Lybertey, Lyberti, Lybertia, Lybertie, Lyberty, Lybertya, Lybirtee, Lybirtey, Lybirti, Lybirtie, Lybirty

Lide (Latin, Basque) life.
Lidee, Lyde, Lydee

Lidia (Greek) beautiful woman from Lydia, in Asia Minor.
Lidiah, Lidya, Lydia, Lydiah, Lydie, Lydya, Lydyah

Lien (Chinese) lotus.
Liena, Lienn, Lienna, Lienne, Leenne, Lyen, Lyena, Lyene, Lyenn, Lyenna, Lyenne

Lila (Arabic) night; (Hindu) unknown destiny according to God; (Persian) lilac.
Lilah, Lilla, Lillah, Lyla, Lylah, Lylla, Lyllah

Lilac (Hindu, Persian) purple flower.
Lia, Lilack, Lilah, Lilak, Lilia, Lylac, Lylack, Lylak

Lilia (Greek) the lily.
Lillia, Lillya, Lilya

Lilian/Lillian (Latin) lily.

Lili, Lilia, Liliana, Lilianah, Liliane, Lilliana, Lillianah, Lilliane, Lilliann, Lillianna, Lilliannah, Lillianne, Lilias, Lillis, Lyli, Lylia, Lyliah, Lylian, Lyliana, Lylianah, Lyliane, Lyliann, Lylianna, Lylianne

Lilith (Arabic) belonging to the night.

Lilis, Lillis, Lillith, Lillyth, Lilyth

Lily (Latin) lily flower.

Lilea, Lileah, Lilee, Lilei, Lileigh, Liley, Lili, Lilia, Liliah, Lilie, Lillea, Lilleah, Lillee, Lillei, Lilleigh, Lilley, Lilli, Lillia, Lilliah, Lillie, Lilly, Lylea, Lyleah, Lylee, Lylei, Lyleigh, Lyley, Lyli, Lylli, Lyllie, Lylie, Lylly, Lyly

Limber (African) joyfulness, happiness.

Limba, Limbah, Limbera, Limberah, Lymba, Lymbah

Li Mei (Chinese) beautiful plum blossom.

Li Ming (Chinese) beautiful and bright.

Lina (Arabic) tender; (Greek) light.

Linah, Linna, Linnah

Linda (Spanish) pretty one, a form of Belinda.

Lin, Lindah, Lindee, Lindey, Lindy, Linnda, Linndah, Lynda, Lyndah, Lynde, Lyndee, Lyndey, Lyndy, Lynnda, Lynndah

Linden (English) valley of the linden trees, protective shield, a unisex name.

Lin, Lindan, Lindin, Lindon, Lyndan, Lynden, Lyndin, Lyndon, Lyndyn

Lindley (English) from the meadow, a unisex name.

Lindly, Lyndly

Lindsay/Lindsey (Anglo-Saxon) linden trees by the water, a unisex name.

Lindsea, Lindsee, Lindsei, Lindsie, Lindsy, Linsay, Linsea, Linsee, Linsei, Linsey, Linsie, Linsy, Lyndsay, Lyndsea, Lyndsee, Lyndsey, Lyndsi, Lyndsie, Lyndsy, Lyndzee, Lyndzey, Lyndzi, Lyndzie, Lynndsie

Lindy (Spanish) pretty, a form of Belinda.

Linde, Lindee, Lindey, Lindi, Lindie

Linette (French) linnet bird; (Celtic) little, graceful.

Linet, Lineta, Linetah, Linete, Linett, Linetta, Linettah, Linnet, Linneta, Linnetah, Linnete, Linnett, Linnetta, Linnettah, Linnette, Lynet, Lyneta, Lynetah, Lynete, Lynett, Lynette

Linley (English) from the field of flax, flax meadow, a unisex name.

Linlea, Linleah, Linlee, Linlei, Linleigh, Linli, Linlia, Linliah, Linlie, Linly, Lynlea, Lynleah, Lynlee, Lynlei, Lynleigh, Lynley, Lynli, Lynlie, Lynly

Liona (German) lioness, feminine of Leo.

Leona, Leonah, Leonna, Leonnah, Lionah, Lione, Lionee, Lioney, Lioni, Lionia, Lioniah, Lionie, Liony, Lionna, Lionnah, Lona, Lyona, Lyonah, Lyone, Lyonee, Lyoney, Lyoni, Lyonia, Lyoniah, Lyonie, Lyony, Lyonya, Lyonyah

Lirissa (Greek) player of the lyre, harp.

Lirisa, Lirrisa, Lirrissa, Lyrisa, Lyrissa

Liron (Hebrew) my song.

Lirona, Lironah, Lirone, Lyron, Lyrona, Lyronah, Lyrone

Lisa (Hebrew, English) consecrated to God, a form of Elizabeth.

Leesa, Leetsa, Leetza, Leeza, Liesa,

Lietsa, Lietza, Lieza, Liisa, Liiza, Lise, Lisenka, Lisette, Liska, Litsa, Litza, Lysa, Lytsa, Lytza, Lyza

Lisbet (English) consecrated to God, a form of Elizabeth.
Lisabeta, Lisabete, Lisabeth, Lisabett, Lisabetta, Lisabette, Lisbeta, Lisbete, Lisbeth, Lisbett, Lisbetta, Lisbette, Lizbet, Lizbeta, Lizbeth, Lizbett, Lizbetta, Lizbette, Lysbet, Lysbeta, Lysbete, Lysbett, Lysbetta, Lysbette

Lisette (French) consecrated to God, a form of Lisa.
Liseta, Lisete, Lisett, Lisetta, Lisettina, Lissete, Lissett, Lissetta

Lisha (African) darkness before midnight.
Lishah, Lishe, Lysha, Lyshah, Lyshe

Lissa (Greek) honey bee, a form of Elissa, Melissa.
Lissah

Lita (English) a form of girls' names ending in -lita, such as Carmelita, Lolita, Melita.
Leata, Leatah, Leet, Leeta, Leetah, Litah, Litia, Litiah, Litta, Littah, Lyta, Lytah, Lytia, Lytiah, Lytya, Lytyah

Litonya (Native American) darting hummingbird.
Litania, Litaniah, Litanya, Litanyah, Litonia, Litoniah, Lytania, Lytaniah, Lytanya, Lytanyah, Lytonia, Lytoniah, Lytonya, Lytonyah

Livana (Hebrew) white like the moon.
Livanah, Livane, Livanna, Livannah, Livanne

Livia (Latin) olive tree, a form of Olivia.
Liviah, Liviya, Liviyah, Lyvia, Lyviah, Lyvya, Lyvyah, Olivia, Oliviah, Olivya, Olivyah

Liz (English) consecrated to God, a form of Elizabeth.
Lizz, Lyz, Lyzz

Liza (English, American) consecrated to God, a form of Elizabeth.
Lizah, Lizza, Lizzah, Lyza, Lyzah, Lyzza, Lyzzah

Llian (Welsh) linen.
Lian, Liana, Lianah, Liane, Lliana, Llianah, Lliane, Lliann, Llianna, Lliannah, Llianne, Llyan, Llyana, Llyanah, Llyane, Llylann, Llyanna, Llyannah, Llyanne

Lodema (English) guide.
Lodemah, Lodima, Lodimah, Lodyma, Lodymah

Loila (Australian Aboriginal) sky.
Loilah, Loyla, Loylah

Lois (German) strong and famous warrior in battle, a form of Louise.
Loisa, Loise, Loiss, Loissa, Loisse

Lokalia (Hawaiian) rose garland.
Lokaliah, Lokalya, Lokalyah

Lola (Spanish) sorrowful, strong woman.
Lolah, Lolita, Lolla, Lollah

Lolita (Spanish) sorrowful.
Loleata, Loleatah, Loleate, Loleeta, Loleetah, Loleete, Loleita, Loleitah, Loleta, Loletah, Lolete, Lolitah, Lolite, Lolyta, Lolytah, Lolyte

Lomasi (Native American) pretty flower.
Lomasee, Lomasey, Lomasie, Lomasy

Lona (English) alone, solitary.
Lonah, Lonee, Lonna, Lonnah, Lonnee, Loni

Lorelei (German) alluring, a siren of the river Rhine.

Lauralee, Loralea, Loraleah, Loralee, Loralei, Loraleigh, Loraley, Lorali, Loralie, Loraly, Lorilea, Lorileah, Lorilee, Lorilei, Lorileigh, Loriley, Lorilie, Lorily, Lorylea, Loryleah, Lorylee, Lorylei, Loryleigh, Loryley, Loryli, Lorylie, Loryly

Loren (English) laurel-crowned, a form of Lauren.

Lauran, Lauren, Laurene, Laurenn, Laurin, Laurine, Laurinn, Laurinne, Loran, Lorin, Lorine, Loryn, Loryne

Lorena (Latin) crown of laurel leaves.

Lauran, Laurana, Lauren, Laurena, Laurin, Laurina, Laurinah, Laurine, Lauryn, Lauryna, Laurynah, Lauryne, Loran, Lorana, Loranah, Loren, Lorenah, Lorene, Lorin, Lorina, Lorinah, Lorine, Loryn, Loryna, Lorynah, Loryne

Loreto (English) crown of laurel leaves, a form of Laura.

Loretto, Lorreto, Lorretto

Loretta (English) crown of laurel leaves, a form of Laura.

Lareta, Laretah, Laretta, Larettah, Larreta, Larretah, Larretta, Larrettah, Laureta, Lauretah, Lauretta, Laurettah, Laurreta, Laurretah, Laurretta, Laurrettah, Loreta, Loretah, Lorete, Lorettah, Lorette, Lorretta, Lorrettah, Lorrette, Lorita, Loritah

Loric (Latin) armour.

Lorick, Lorik, Loriq, Loriqu, Loriqua, Lorique, Loryc, Loryck, Loryk, Loryq, Loryqu, Loryqua, Loryque

Lorice (English) crown of laurel leaves.

Loreace, Lorease, Lorise, Loryce, Loryse

Lorikeet (Australian Aboriginal) brightly coloured bird.

Lorikeat, Lorikeata, Lorikeatah, Lorikeate, Lorikeeta, Lorikeetah, Loriket, Loriketa, Loriketah, Lorikete, Lorikett, Loriketta, Lorikette, Lorykeet

Lorna (English) crown of laurel leaves, used by R.D. Blackmore for the heroine of his 1860s novel *Lorna Doone* and possibly derived from a Scottish placename.

Lornah, Lorrna, Lorrnah

Lorraine (French) from the region, Lorraine; (Latin) sorrowful.

Larain, Laraine, Larrain, Larraine, Lora, Lorain, Loraina, Loraine, Lorayne, Lorein, Loreine, Lori, Lorine, Lorrain, Lorraina, Lorrainah, Lorrayn, Lorrayne, Lorrein, Lorreine

Losa (Polynesian) rose.

Losah, Rosa, Rose

Lotte (French) little, strong woman, a form of Charlotte.

Lote, Lotee, Lotey, Loti, Lotie, Lotta, Lottee, Lottey, Lotti, Lottie, Lotty

Lotu (African) admired.

Lotus (Greek) the flower of the lotus tree.

Lottus

Louam (Ethiopian) sleep well.

Louama

Louella (American) combination of Louise and Ella.

Louellah, Luella, Luellah

Louise (German) famous warrior, feminine form of Louis.

Aloisa, Aloise, Aloisia, Aloysia, Eloisa, Eloise, Eloisia, Heloise, Lawis, Lawisa, Lawisah, Lawise, Leweese,

Leweez, Loisa, Loisah, Loise, Lou, Louisa, Louisah, Louisetta, Louisette, Louiz, Louiza, Louizah, Louize, Louyz, Louyza, Louyzah, Louyze, Luis, Luisa, Luisah, Luise, Luiz, Luiza, Luizah, Luize, Luys, Luysa, Luysah, Luyse, Luyz, Luyza, Luyzah, Luyze

Lourdes (French) from the pilgrimage town in southern France, a unisex name.

Lourd, Lourde, Lourds

Love (English) loved one, love, kindness.

Lovelace, Lovelea, Loveleah, Lovely, Lovlea, Lovleah, Lovlee, Lovlie, Lovlier

Luca (Latin) bringer of light, a form of Lucy, a unisex name.

Lucah, Lucca, Luccah, Lucka, Luckah, Luka, Lukah

Lucetta (Spanish, English) light, a form of Lucy.

Lucia (Italian, Spanish) light, a form of Lucy.

Luciah, Luceea, Luceeah, Luciana, Lucya, Lucyah

Lucianna (Spanish) light, a form of Lucy.

Luciana, Lucianah, Luciannah

Lucinda (Latin) light, a form of Lucy.

Cindi, Cindie, Cindy, Loucind, Loucinda, Loucindah, Loucinde, Luci, Lucida, Lucidah, Lucind, Lucindah, Lucinde, Lucindea

Lucretia (Latin) rewarded, rich.

Lucrece, Lucrecia, Lucreciah, Lucreecia, Lucreeciah, Lucresa, Lucresha, Lucreshia, Lucreshiah, Lucreshya, Lucreshyah, Lucresia, Lucresiah

Lucy (Latin) light, bringer of light.

Loucey, Loucie, Loucy, Luca, Luce, Lucee, Lucey, Lucie, Lucinda

Ludella (Anglo-Saxon) renowned.

Ludel, Ludela, Ludelah, Ludell, Ludellah

Ludmilla (Slavonic) loved by the people.

Ludie, Ludka, Ludkah, Ludmila, Ludmilah, Ludmillah, Luydmila, Luydmilah, Luydmilla, Luydmillah, Lyuba, Lyubah

Luella (English) elflike.

Loella, Loellah, Lou, Louella, Ludella, Ludellah, Luela, Luelah, Lou-Ella, Luellah, Luelle, Lula, Lulah, Lulu

Luigia (Italian) famous battle maiden, a form of Louise.

Luisa (Italian, German, Spanish) famous warrior, a form of Louise.

Luisah, Luiza, Luizah

Lulani (Polynesian) highest point of heaven, a unisex name.

Loulanee, Loulaney, Loulani, Loulanie, Loulany, Lulanee, Lulaney, Lulanie, Lulany

Lulu (Arabic) pearl; (Native American) rabbit.

Lolo, Looloo, Loulou, Lula

Luna (Latin) moon.

Louna, Lunah, Luneta, Lunetah, Lunnet, Lunneta, Lunnetah, Lunnett, Lunnetta, Lunnettah, Lunnette

Lunetta (Italian) little moon.

Loonetta, Lounetta, Lou-Netta, Lune, Lunet, Luneta, Lunetah, Lunete, Lunett, Lunette, Lunnet, Lunneta, Lunnete, Lunnett, Lunnetta, Lunnette

Lupe (Spanish) wolf-like.
Lupa, Lupee, Lupi, Lupie, Luppi, Lupy

Lupine (Latin) wolf-like.
Lupina, Lupinah, Lupyna, Lupynah, Lupyne

Lure (Latin) one who attracts.
Lura, Lurah

Lute (Polynesian) friendly; (English) a musical instrument.

Luvena (Latin) little beloved one.
Louvena, Louvenah, Luvenah, Luvenna, Luvennah

Luyu (Native American) pecking bird.

Luz (Spanish) light.
Luzee, Luzi, Luzia, Luziah, Luzie, Luzija, Luzijah, Luzy

Lycoris (Greek) twilight.
Licoris, Licorise, Licoriss, Licorisse, Lycorise, Lycoriss, Lycorisse

Lydia (Greek) beautiful woman from Lydia, in Asia Minor.
Lidia, Lidiah, Lidya, Lydiah, Lydie, Lydya, Lydyah

Lyn/Lynn/Lynne (Anglo-Saxon) brook or pool.
Lin, Lina, Linley, Linn, Linna, Linne, Linnea, Lynlee, Lynley, Lynly, Lynna, Lynnae, Lynnah, Lynnea

Lynda (Spanish) pretty, a form of Belinda.
Linda, Lindah, Lindee, Lindey, Lindy, Linnda, Linndah, Lyndah, Lynde, Lyndee, Lyndey, Lyndy, Lynnda, Lynndah

Lyndsay/Lyndsey (Anglo-Saxon) linden trees by the water, a unisex name.
Lindsay, Lindsea, Lindsee, Lindsei, Lindsey, Lindsie, Lindsy, Linsay, Linsey, Lyndsea, Lyndsee, Lyndsei, Lyndsey, Lyndsi, Lyndsie, Lyndsy, Lyndzee, Lyndzey, Lyndzi, Lyndzie, Lynndsie

Lynette (French) linnet bird; (Celtic) little, graceful.
Linet, Lineta, Linetah, Linete, Linett, Linetta, Linettah, Linette, Linnet, Linneta, Linnetah, Linnete, Linnett, Linnetta, Linnettah, Linnette, Lynet, Lyneta, Lynetah, Lynete, Lynett, Lynetta, Lynettah, Lynnet, Lynneta, Lynnetah, Lynnete, Lynnett, Lynnetta, Lynnettah, Lynnette

Lynley (English) from the field of flax, a unisex name.
Linlea, Linleah, Linlee, Linlei, Linleigh, Linley, Linli, Linlia, Linliah, Linlie, Linly, Lynlea, Lynleah, Lynlee, Lynlei, Lynleigh, Lynli, Lynlia, Lynliah, Lynlie, Lynly

Lyra (Greek) player of the lyre.
Lira, Lirah, Lirra, Lirrah, Lyrah, Lyre, Lyrie, Lyris

Lyris (Greek) player of the lyre, harp.
Liris, Lirisa, Lirise, Liriss, Lirissa, Lirisse, Lyrisa, Lyrisah, Lyrise, Lyriss, Lyrissa, Lyrisse

Lysandra (Greek) liberator, defender of humankind, feminine form of Lysander.
Lisandra, Lisandrah, Lysandrah, Lysanna, Lysannah, Lysanne, Lyshae

Lysanne (American) combination of Lysandra and Anne.
Lisanne, Lizanne, Lyzanne

Maata (Maori) lady.
Marta, Mata

Mab (Celtic) fairy queen, joy.
Mabb, Mabbe, Mabela, Mabele, Mabell, Mabella, Mabelle, Mabrey, Mabry, Maby

Mabel (Latin) lovable.
Mabela, Mabele, Mabell, Mabella, Mabelle, Maebel, Maebela, Maebele, Maebell, Maebella, Maebelle, Maibel, Maibela, Maibele, Maibell, Maibella, Maibelle, Maybel, Maybela, Maybele, Maybell, Maybella, Maybelle, May-Belle

Mabyn (Welsh) youthful.
Mabin, Mabine, Mabyne

Macalla (Australian Aboriginal) full moon.
Macala, Macalah, Macallah, Macayla, Macaylla, Mackayla, Mackaylla

Macaria (Greek) happy.
Macariah, Macarya, Macaryah

Macawi (Native American) motherly, generous.
Macawee, Macawia, Macawie, Macawy

Mackenna (Irish) of the wise, handsome leader, a form of Mackenzie.
Mackena, Mackenah, MacKenna, Mackennah, Makena, Makenah, Makenna, Makennah,

Mackenzie (Celtic) child of the wise, handsome leader, a unisex name.
Macenzie, Mackensey, Mackensy, Mackenzee, Mackenzey, Mackenzia, MacKenzie, Mackinsy, Makenzie, McKenzie

Macra (Greek) fast growing, long living.
Macrah, Macrina, Macrinah, Macrine, Macryna, Macrynah, Macryne

Madalena (Spanish, Italian) of Magdala, a woman from the village of Magdala.
Madaleina, Madaleinie, Madalina, Maddalena, Maddalina, Madeleina, Madeleine, Magdalena

Maddison/Madison (English) good, child of Maude or Matthew, a unisex name.
Maddie, Maddisan, Maddisen, Maddisin, Maddisun, Maddyson, Maddysyn, Madisan, Madisen, Madisin, Madissan, Madissen, Madissin, Madisson, Madissyn, Madisun, Madisyn, Madsen, Madson, Madysan, Madysen, Madysin, Madyson, Madysun, Madysyn

Maddox (Welsh) lucky, generous, fortunate, feminine form of Maddock.
Madox

Madeira (Portuguese) a Portuguese island, a sweet wine.

Madeleine/Madeline (Greek) from the high tower; (English) from Magdalen.
Madalain, Madalaina, Madalaine, Madalayn, Madalayne, Madalena, Madaleina, Madaleine, Madalyna, Maddeline, Madelain, Madelaina,

Madelaine, Madelein, Madeleina, Madelena, Madaleine, Madaleina, Madelene, Madelia, Madelin, Madelina, Madelinah, Madeleyn, Madeleyna, Madella, Madelle, Madelyn, Madelyna, Madelyne, Magda, Magdalene

Madge (Greek) pearl, a form of Margaret.

Madgea, Madgee, Madgey, Madgi, Madgie, Madgy

Madhura (Sanskrit) charming, sweet.

Madhur, Madhuri

Madonna (Latin) my lady.

Madona, Madonah, Madonnah, Madrona, Madronah, Madronna, Madronnah

Madra (Spanish) mother.

Madre

Mae (English) great one.

Mai, Maia, Maie, May, Maya, Maye

Maegen (Irish) pearl, a form of Megan, Margaret.

Maegan, Maeghan, Maeghen, Maeghin, Maeghon, Maegin, Maegon, Maegyn, Megan, Megen, Meghan, Megin, Megon, Megyn, Meghen, Meghin, Meghon, Meghyn

Maeko (Japanese) honest, truthful child.

Maeki

Maeve (Irish) joyous, a pale purple colour, mauve.

Maev, Maevi, Maevie, Maevy, Maiv, Maive, Maivie, Maivy, Mayv, Mayve

Magda (Czech, Polish, Russian) from the high tower; (English) from Magdalen.

Magdah, Magdala, Maida

Magdalena/Magdalene (Czech, Polish, Russian) from the high tower; (English) from Magdalen.

Magdala, Magdalan, Magdalane, Magdaleen, Magdalina, Magdaline, Magdalyn, Magdalyna, Magdalyne, Magdalynn, Magdalynna, Magdalynne, Magdelain, Magdelaina, Magdelaine, Magdelan, Magdelana, Magdelane, Magdelen, Magdelena, Magdelene, Magdelin, Magdelina, Magdeline, Magdelyn, Magdelyna, Magdelyne

Magena (Native American) coming moon.

Maggie (Greek) pearl, a form of Margaret.

Mag, Magee, Magey, Magg, Maggee, Maggey, Maggi, Maggia, Maggy, Magi, Magie, Mags, Magy

Magnolia (Latin) magnolia flowering tree.

Magnolea, Magnoleah, Magnoliah, Magnolya, Nola

Maha (Arabic) cow-eyes.

Mahal (Filipino) love.

Mahala, Mahalah

Mahala (Arabic) tenderness; (Native American) powerful woman.

Mahalah, Mahalia, Mahaliah, Melhala, Melhalah, Melhalia, Melhaliah

Mahesa (Hindu) great lord.

Maheesa, Mahesah, Mahessa, Mahessah, Mahisa, Mahisah, Mahissa, Mahissah, Mahysa, Mahyssa

Mahila (Hindu) woman.

Mahilah, Mahyla, Mahylah

Mahina (Hawaiian) moon, glow of the moon.
Mahinah, Mahyna, Mahynah

Mahira (Hebrew) energy.
Mahirah, Mahryra, Mahryrah, Mahyra, Mahyrah

Mahla (Hebrew) polished.
Mahlah

Mahogany (Spanish) strong, rich.
Mahoganee, Mahoganey, Mahogani, Mahogania, Mahoganie

Mai (Japanese) bright; (Vietnamese) flower; (Native American) coyote.
Maie

Maia (Greek) mother, Roman goddess of spring, brightest star in the Pleiades.
Mae, Mai, Maie, Maiea, May, Maya, Maye, Mayea

Maida (English) maiden, woman.
Mada, Mady, Maide, Maidel, Maidena, Maidie, Mayda, Mayde, Maydel, Maydena, Maydie

Maija (Finnish) bitter, star of the sea, wished for, a form of Mary.
Maiji

Maimi (Japanese) smile of truth.
Maemee, Maimee, Maimey, Maimie, Maimy

Mairi (Celtic) bitter, star of the sea, wished for, a form of Mary.
Mairie, Mairy, Mairiam, Miriam

Maisha (Arabic) she who walks with a confident swinging gait; (African) life.
Maisa, Maisaha, Maishah

Maisie (Scottish) pearl, a form of Margaret, maize, sweet corn.
Maesee, Maesey, Maesi, Maesie, Maesy, Maisee, Maisey, Maisi, Maisy, Maizee, Maizey, Maizi, Maizie, Maizy, Maysee, Maysey, Maysi, Maysie, Maysy

Maitane (English) beloved.

Maja (Arabic) splendid, a form of Maijidah.
Majah, Majal

Majesta (Latin) majestic.
Magesta, Magestah, Magestic, Magestica, Magesticah, Magestiqua, Mgestique, Majestah, Majestic, Majestica, Majesticah, Majestiqua, Majestique

Majidah (Arabic) glorious, splendid.
Majeeda, Majid, Majida

Makala (Hawaiian) myrtle.
Makalae, Makalah, Makalai, Makalea, Makaleah, Makalee, Makalei, Makaleigh, Makaley, Makali, Makalia, Makaliah, Makalie, Makaly, Makalya

Makana (Hawaiian) gift.
Makanah, Makanna, Makannah

Makani (Hawaiian) wind, a unisex name.
Makanee, Makaney, Makania, Makaniah, Makanie, Makany, Makanya, Makanyah

Makayla (Hebrew, American) like God, a form of Michaela, feminine form of Michael.
Macaela, Macaila, Macala, Makaela, Makaila, Mica, Micah, Micaela, Micaelah, Micaele, Micala, Micalah, Michael, Michaela, Michalina, Michaeline, Michaella, Michaellah, Michala, Michalah, Michalina, Micheline, Michella,

Michellah, Michelle, Mikaela, Mikaelah, Mikala, Mycael, Mycaela, Mycaelah, Mycaele, Mycala, Mycalah, Mycale, Mychelina, Mycheline, Mychell, Mychella, Mychelle, Mykaelah, Mykayla, Mykaylah, Mykela, Mykelah

Malachie (Hebrew) angel of God, God's messenger, feminine form of Malachy.

Malachee, Malachey, Malachi, Malachia, Malachy

Malak (Arabic) angel.

Malana (Hawaiian) light.

Malanah, Malanna, Malannah

Malanie (Greek) dark-skinned, a form of Melanie.

Malanee, Malaney, Malani, Malania, Malany

Malaya (Filipino) free.

Malaia, Malaiah, Malayah

Malha (Hebrew) queen.

Malhah, Malia, Maliah, Malka, Malkah, Malkia, Malkiah, Malkie, Malkiya, Malkiyah

Mali (Thai) jasmine flower.

Malea, Maleah, Malee, Malei, Maleigh, Maley, Malia, Maliah, Malie, Maly, Malya, Malyah

Malia (Native American) bitter, star of the sea, wished for, a form of Mary.

Malea, Maleeya, Maleeyah, Maleia, Maleiah, Maleya, Maleyia, Maleyiah, Maliah, Malie, Maliea, Mallea, Malleah, Malleia, Malleiah, Malleya, Mallia, Malliah, Mallya, Malya, Malyah

Malika (Arabic) queen, feminine form of Malik; (Hungarian) hard working.

Maalika, Maleeka, Malikah,

Malikee, Maliki, Malikia, Malyka, Malykah

Malinda (Greek) gentle.

Malena, Malenda, Malina, Malinde, Mallie, Mally, Melina, Melinda, Melinde, Lindy

Malini (Hindu) gardener.

Malinee, Malinia, Maliniah, Malinie, Maliny, Malinya, Malynee, Malyni, Malynia, Malyniah, Malynie, Malyny, Malynya

Mallory (French) wild duck, unlucky; (German) army counsellor, a unisex name.

Mal, Malary, Maleri, Malery, Mallari, Mallarie, Mallary, Malleri, Mallerie, Mallery, Malloree, Mallori, Mallorie, Maloree, Malori, Malorie, Malory

Malu (Hawaiian) peacefulness.

Maloo

Malulani (Hawaiian) under a peaceful sky.

Malulanea, Malulanee, Malulaney, Malulania, Malulanie, Malulany

Malva (Greek) soft and slender, a form of Melba.

Malba, Malbah, Malvah, Malvina, Melba, Melbah, Melva, Melvah, Melvina

Malvina (Celtic) cultured, armoured chief, smooth brow, a form of Melvina.

Mal, Malva, Malvie, Malvine, Mel, Melva, Melvie, Melvina, Melvine

Mamie (French, American) my love.

Maimee, Maimey, Maimi, Maimie, Maimy, Mamee, Mamey, Mami, Mamy, Maymee, Maymey, Maymi, Maymie, Maymy

Mamo (Hawaiian) saffron flower, yellow bird, a unisex name.
Maamaoh, Maamo, Maamoh, Mamoh

Manaal (Arabic) attainment, achievement.
Manal

Manar (Arabic) guiding light.
Manara

Manda (Spanish) warrior.
Mandah

Mandara (Hindu) calm.
Mandarah

Mandi (Latin) lovable, a form of Amanda.
Mandee, Mandie, Mandy

Mandisa (African) sweet.
Mandisah, Mandissa, Mandissah, Mandysa, Mandysah, Mandyssa, Mandyssah

Manette (French, Hebrew) bitter, wished for, star of the sea, a form of Mary.
Manet, Maneta, Manete, Manett, Manetta

Mangena (Hebrew) melody, song.
Mangina, Mangyna

Mani (Chinese) a prayer or mantra for understanding.
Manee, Maney, Manie, Many

Manilla (Australian Aboriginal) winding river.
Manila, Manilah, Manillah, Manille, Manyla, Manylah, Manylla, Manyllah

Manpreet (Punjabi) mind full of love.
Manpret, Manprit

Mansi (Native American) plucked flower.
Mancee, Mancey, Manci, Mancie, Mancy, Mansee, Mansey, Mansie, Mansy

Manuela (Spanish) God is with us, feminine form of Emmanuel.
Emanuel, Emanuela, Emanuele, Emanuell, Emanuella, Emanuelle, Emmanuel, Emmanuela, Emmanuele, Emmanuell, Emmanuella, Emmanuelle, Manuel, Manuela, Manuele, Manuell, Manuella, Manuelle

Mara (Hebrew) bitter, a form of Mary.
Marah, Maralina, Maraline, Maraline, Maralyn

Maraam (Arabic) aspiration, objective.

Marcella (Latin) warlike, martial, feminine form of Marcel.
Marcela, Marcele, Marcell, Marcelle, Marcellina, Marcelline, Marcey, Marcie, Marcile, Marcilla, Marcille, Marcy

Marcia (Latin) warlike, martial.
Marcela, Marcella, Marcelle, Marcelline, Marcey, Marchita, Marcie, Marcile, Marcille, Marcy, Marquita, Marsha, Marsia, Marsie, Marsy

Mardi (French) born on a Tuesday.
Mardea, Mardee, Mardey, Mardia, Mardie, Mardy

Marelda (German) battle maiden.
Mareldah, Marella, Marellah, Marilda, Marildah

Margaret (Greek) pearl.
Greta, Gretal, Gretchen, Grete, Gretel, Gretta, Grettal, Griet, Madge, Mag, Maggie, Mairghread, Marg, Margalo,

Margareta, Margarete, Margarethe, Margarita, Marget, Margette, Margory, Margot, Marguerite, Marj, Marje, Marjorie, Marjory, Meg, Peg, Peggy, Rita

Margarita (Spanish) pearl, a form of Margaret.

Margareta, Margaretta, Margarida, Margaritis, Margaritta, Margereta, Margeretta, Margharita, Margherita, Margheritta, Margrieta, Margrietta, Margrita, Margritta, Margurita, Marguritte

Margaux (French) pearl, a form of Margaret.

Margau, Margeau, Margeaux, Margo, Margot

Margherita (Italian) pearl, a form of Margaret.

Margherite, Margheritta, Margheritte

Margot (French) pearl, a form of Margaret.

Mago, Marget, Margetta, Margette, Margalo

Marguerite (French) pearl, a form of Margaret.

Margarite, Margerite, Marguareta, Marguarete, Marguaretta, Marguarette, Marguarita, Marguarite, Marguaritta, Marguaritte, Marguereta, Marguerete, Marguerett, Margueretta, Marguerette, Marguerita, Margueritta, Margueritte, Margurita, Margurite, Marguritta, Marguritte

Mari (Japanese) ball; (Hebrew) wished for, star of the sea, bitter, a form of Mary.

Marea, Maree, Maria, Mariah, Mary

Maria (Hebrew, Italian, Spanish) wished for, star of the sea, bitter, a form of Mary.

Marea, Mareah, Maree, Marie, Mariesa, Mariessa, Marya

Mariabella (Italian) combination of Mary and Bella.

Mariabelle

Mariam (Hebrew) wished for, star of the sea, bitter, a form of Miriam.

Mariamm, Maryam, Maryamm

Marian (English) wished for, star of the sea, bitter, a form of Mary.

Mariana, Marianah, Mariane, Mariann, Marianna, Marianne, Marien, Mariena, Marienah, Mariene, Marienn, Marienna, Marienne, Marion, Marrian, Marriana, Marriane, Marriann, Marianna, Marianne, Maryann, Maryanna, Maryanne

Marianna (Italian, Spanish) wished for, star of the sea, bitter, a form of Marianne.

Mariana

Marianne (English) wished for, star of the sea, bitter, graceful, a form of Mary-Ann.

Mariann

Maribel (French) beautiful; (English) combination of Maria and Bel or Isabel.

Mareabel, Mareabela, Mareabele, Mareabell, Mareabella, Mareabelle, Mariabella, Mariabelle, Maribela, Maribelah, Maribele, Maribell, Maribella, Maribellah, Maribelle, Marybel, Marybela, Marybelah, Marybele, Marybell, Marybella, Marybellah, Marybelle

Marie (French) wished for, star of the sea, bitter, a form of Mary.

Maira, Maire, Mara, Mare, Maree, Mari, Maria, Mariam, Marion, Marri

Marietta (Italian) wished for, star of the sea, bitter, a form of Marie.

Maretta, Marette, Mariet, Marieta, Mariett, Mariette, Marriet, Marrieta, Marriete, Marriett, Marrietta, Marriette

Marigold (English) Mary's gold flower with yellow and orange petals.

Marigolde, Marrigold, Marygold

Marikka (Dutch, Slavic) wished for, star of the sea, bitter, a form of Mary.

Mareeka, Marica, Maricka, Marieca, Marieka, Marieke, Marika, Marikah, Marike, Marikia, Marikkah, Mariqua, Marique, Marrica, Marricah, Marrika, Marrikah, Marrike, Merica, Mericah, Merika, Merikah, Meriqua, Merique

Mariko (Japanese) circle.

Mareako, Mareecko, Mareeco, Mareeko, Maricko, Marico

Marilla (Hebrew, German) wished for, star of the sea, bitter, a form of Mary.

Marella, Marelle, Marila, Marilah, Marillah, Marille, Maryla, Marylah, Marylla, Maryllah

Marilyn (Hebrew) Mary's descendants or line.

Maralin, Maralina, Maraline, Maralyn, Maralyna, Maralyne, Maralynn, Maralynna, Maralynne, Marelyn, Marielin, Marielina, Marieline, Marilena, Marilene, Marilin, Marilina, Mariline, Marillin, Marillyn, Marrilin, Marrilyn, Marylyn

Marina (Latin) of the sea.

Mareena, Mareenah, Mareenna, Mareennah, Marena, Marenah, Marinah, Marinna, Marinnah

Marini (African) healthy, pretty.

Marinee, Mariney, Marinie, Mariny, Marynee, Maryney, Maryni, Marynie, Maryny

Marion (Hebrew) wished for, star of the sea, bitter, a form of Mary, a unisex name.

Marian, Marien, Mariene, Marrian

Mariposa (Spanish) butterfly.

Mariquita (Spanish) wished for, star of the sea, bitter, a form of Mary.

Maris (Latin) sea.

Marisa, Marisah, Marissa, Marissah, Marris, Marrisa, Marrisah, Marrissa, Marrissah

Marisol (Spanish) sunny sea.

Marisola, Marizol, Marizola, Marysol, Marysola, Maryzol, Maryzola

Marissa (Latin) sea.

Mareesa, Marisa, Marisah, Marissah, Marrisa, Marrisah, Marrissa, Marrissah

Marita (Spanish) sea, a form of Marissa.

Maritah, Maryta, Marytah

Maritza (Arabic) blessed.

Maritsa, Maritsah, Maritzah, Marytsa, Marytsah, Marytza, Marytzah

Marjan (Persian) coral.

Marjana, Marjanah, Marjane, Marjanna, Marjannah

Marjolaine (French) marjoram.

Marjolain, Marjolaina, Marjolana, Marjolane, Marjolayn, Marjolayna, Marjolayne

Marjorie (Scottish) pearl, a form of Margaret.

Marge, Margerie, Margery, Margorie, Margory, Marj

Marlee (Hebrew) from the high tower, a form of Madeline or Marlene.

Marleigh, Marley, Marli, Marlie, Marly

Marlene (Greek) from the high tower, a form of Madeline, (German) combination of Maria and Magdalene, used by actress Marlene Dietrich.

Marlana, Marlane, Marlayna, Marlayne, Marlen, Marlena, Marleen, Marleena, Marlein, Marleine

Marlo (English) wished for, star of the sea, bitter, a form of Mary.

Marlon, Marlona, Marlonah, Marlone

Marmara (Greek) shining.

Marmarah, Marmee

Marquise (French) noble, feminine form of Marquis.

Makeese, Makese, Marquees, Marquese, Marquice, Marquies, Marquiese, Marquisa, Marquisee, Marquisse, Marquiste

Marsala (Latin) warlike, martial, from the Roman god of war.

Marcella, Marcelle, Marcey, Marcia, Marcie, Marcy, Marsali, Marsella, Marselle, Marsey, Marsia, Marsie, Marsy

Marta (Italian, English) a lady, sorrowful, lady of sorrow.

Maarta, Maartah, Martah, Marte, Mata, Matah

Martha (Aramaic) a lady, sorrowful, lady of sorrow.

Maartha, Maarthah, Marth, Marthah, Marthe, Marta

Martina (Latin) warlike.

Martaina, Martainah, Martana, Martanah, Martanna, Martannah,
Martayna, Martaynah, Marteana, Marteanah, Marteena, Marteenah, Marthena, Marthenah, Marthina, Marthinah, Martinah, Martine, Martinia, Martinique, Martyna, Martynah

Maru (Japanese) round.

Maroo

Marva (Hebrew) sweet sage.

Marvah

Marvella (Latin) miracle, wondrous, feminine form of Marvell.

Marvela, Marvele, Marvell, Marvella, Marvellah, Marvelle, Marvyl, Marvyla, Marvyle, Marvyll, Marvylla, Marvylle

Mary (Hebrew) wished for, star of the sea, bitter, mother of Jesus, English monarch.

Mae, Mai, Maida, Maidie, Maidy, Maija, Maira, Maire, Mairie, Mairy, Mame, Mamie, Manette, Manka, Manon, Manya, Mara, Mare, Maree, Marella, Marelle, Maren, Marey, Mari, Maria, Maricara, Marice, Marie, Mariel, Mariela, Marika, Marilla, Marion, Mariquilla, Mariquita, Marisha, Marja, Marjan, Marlo, Maroula, Marree, Marrey, Marri, Marrie, Marry, Maruca, Marye, Maryla, Masha, Mavra, May, Maya, Mayme, Merane, Merey, Meridel, Merie, Merrey, Merrie, Merry, Mery, Mhairie, Mirja, Moira, Moire, Molara, Morag, Moya

Masada (Hebrew) strong base.

Masadah, Massada, Massadah

Masago (Japanese) sands of time.

Massago

Masani (African) gap in her teeth.

Masanee, Masaney, Masania, Masaniah, Masanie, Masany, Masanya, Masanyah

Mashika (African) born during the rainy season.

Mashikah, Mashyka, Mashykah, Masika, Masikah

Matana (Hebrew) gift.

Matanah, Matania, Mataniah, Matanna, Matannah, Matannia, Matanniah, Matanya, Matanyah

Mathilda (Teutonic) strong and resilient, warrior, a form of Matilda.

Maithilda, Maithilde, Maitilda, Maitilde, Matelda, Mathelda, Mathelde, Matilda, Mathilde, Matty, Tilda, Tilde, Tilly, Tillie

Matilda (German) strong and resilient, warrior.

Matelda, Matelde, Mathild, Mathilda, Mathilde, Mathildis, Mati, Matilde, Mattee, Mattie, Matty, Metild, Metilda, Metildah, Metilde, Metyld, Metylda, Metyldah, Metylde, Tilda, Tylda, Tilly

Matrika (Hindu) mother.

Matrica, Matricah, Matricka, Matrickah, Matryca, Matrycah, Matrycka, Matryckah, Matryka, Matrykah

Matsuko (Japanese) pine tree.

Mattea (Hebrew) gift from God, feminine form of Matthew.

Matea, Mateah, Mathea, Matheah, Mathia, Mathiah, Matia, Matiah, Matteah, Matthea, Mattheah, Matthia, Matthiah, Mattia, Mattiah

Maud (Teutonic) strength in battle, powerful warrior.

Maude, Maudea, Maudee, Maudey, Maudi, Maudie, Maudy, Mawd, Mawde

Maura (Celtic) dark.

Maure, Mauree, Mauri, Mauria, Maurie, Maury, Moyra, Moyrah

Maureen (Celtic, French) of dark complexion.

Maireen, Maireena, Maireene, Mairin, Mairina, Maurine, Maura, Maure, Mauree, Maureena, Maurena, Maurene, Maurin, Maurina, Maurine, Maurisa, Maurise, Maurita, Mauritah, Mauritia, Mauritiah, Maurizia, Maurya, Moira, Mora, Morah, Moreen, Moreene, Moreena, Moren, Morena, Morenah, Morene, Morin, Morina, Morinah, Morine, Moryn, Moryna, Morynah, Moryne

Mauve (Greek) pale purple colour.

Maev, Maeve, Malva, Mauv

Mavis (French) the song-thrush.

Maevis, Maviss, Mavisse

Maxine (Latin) greatest, feminine form of Maximilian.

Max, Maxeen, Maxeena, Maxeene, Maxi, Maxie, Maxima, Maxime, Maxy, Maxyn, Maxyna, Maxyne

May (Latin) great; (English) child born in May, blossom.

Mae, Mai, Maia, Maie, Maii, Maye

Maya (Hindu) God's creative power, illusion; (Greek) mother, grandmother.

Maea, Maia

Maybelle (Latin) loveable, a form of Mabel.

Mabel, Mabell, Mabelle, Maibel, Maibell, May, Maybel, Maybela, Maybele, Maybell, Maybella, Maybelle

Mayda (English) woman, maiden.

Maeda, Maida, Maydah

Maygan (Irish) pearl, a form of Megan or Margaret.

Maegan, Maegen, Maegin, Maygen, Maygin

Mayoree (Thai) beautiful.
Mayra, Mayree, Mayari, Mayaria, Mayariah, Mayary, Mayarya, Mayaryah

Mayra (Australian Aboriginal) spring wind.
Maera, Maerah, Maira, Mairah, Mayaria, Mayariah, Mayarya, Mayaryah

Maysun (Arabic) of beautiful face and body.
Maesun, Maisun, Mason, Maysoon

McKayla (American) like God, a form of Michaela.

McKenna (Irish) of the wise handsome leader, traditionally used as a surname.
Mackenna

Meadow (English) field, meadow.
Medow

Meagan (Irish) pearl, a form of Margaret.
Meagann, Meaghan, Meaghin, Meaghon, Meagin, Meg, Megan, Meghan

Meara (Irish) merry laughter.
Mara, Marah, Mearah, Miera, Mierah

Meda (Native American) priestess.
Medah

Media (Latin) middle child.
Medea, Medeah, Mediah, Medora, Medorah

Medina (Arabic) place where Muhammad's tomb lies.
Medeana, Medeanah, Medeena, Medeenah, Medinah, Medyna, Medynah

Mee (Chinese) beautiful.
Me, Mee-Mee, Mei, Mey, Mi, My

Meg (English) pearl, a form of Margaret, Megan.
Meggy

Megan (Irish) pearl, a form of Margaret.
Meaghan, Meaghin, Meegan, Meegen, Meeghan, Meeghen, Meeghin, Meeghon, Meeghyn, Meegin, Meegon, Meegyn, Meg, Meghan, Megin, Megon, Megyn

Megara (Greek) first-born child.
Megarah

Mehadi (Hindu) flower.
Mehadee, Mehadie, Mehady

Mehira (Hebrew) speedy, energetic.
Mahira, Mahirah, Mehirah, Mehyra, Mehyrah

Mei (Hawaiian) great.
Mey

Meira (Hebrew) light.
Meera, Meerah, Meirah, Mera, Merah, Meyra, Meyrah, Mira, Mirah, Myra, Myrah

Meit (Burmese) affectionate.
Meita, Meitah, Meyt, Meyta, Meytah

Meiying (Chinese) beautiful flower.
Mei

Meka (Hebrew) like God, a form of Michaela.
Mekah

Mekayla (American) like God, a form of Michaela.
Mekaela, Mekaila, Mekala, Mekayela, Mekaylia

Melanie (Greek) dark colouring.

Malainee, Malainey, Malaini, Malania, Malainie, Malainy, Malana, Malanah, Malanee, Malaney, Malani, Malania, Malaniah, Malanie, Malany, Mel, Melaina, Melainah, Melaine, Melainee, Melainey, Melaini, Melainie, Melainy, Melana, Melanah, Melane, Melanee, Melaney, Melani, Melany, Melena, Melenee, Meleney, Meleni, Melenie, Meleny, Mellanee, Mellaney, Mellani, Mellanie, Mellany, Mellenee, Melleney, Melleni, Mellenie, Melleny, Melleni, Mellenie, Melleny, Mellie, Melona, Melonah, Melonee, Meloney, Meloni, Melonia, Meloniah, Meloni, Melonie, Melony

Melantha (Greek) dark flower.

Melanthe

Melba (Greek) soft, slender; (Latin) mallow flower; (English) the famous singer Dame Nellie Melba named herself after her hometown, Melbourne, Australia.

Malba, Malbah, Malbas, Malva, Malvah, Melbah, Melva, Malvah

Mele (Hawaiian) poem, song.

Melle

Meleni (African) melon.

Melenee, Meleney, Melenia, Meleniah, Melenie, Meleny, Melenya, Melenyah

Melesse (Ethiopian) eternal.

Mellesse

Melia (Greek) nymph, daughter of Oceanus.

Meliah, Melya, Melyah

Melina (Greek) song; (Latin) canary yellow.

Malina, Malinah, Mallina, Mallinah, Melaina, Melainah, Melaine,

Melana, Melanah, Melane, Meleana, Meleanah, Meleane, Melena, Melenah, Melene, Melinah, Meline, Melinia, Meliniah, Melinna, Melinnah, Melinne, Mellina, Mellinah, Melline, Melona, Melonah, Melyna, Melynah, Melyne, Melynna, Melynnah, Melynne

Melinda (Greek) gentle one, sweet as honey.

Malinda, Malindah, Malinde, Malindea, Malindee, Malindia, Malindiah, Malynda, Malyndah, Melindah, Melinde, Melindea, Melindee, Melindia, Melindiah, Melynda, Melyndah

Melissa (Greek) honey bee.

Lissa, Malesa, Malessa, Malisa, Malissa, Mallessa, Mallissa, Melessa, Melessah, Melisa, Melisah, Melise, Melissah, Melisse, Melissia, Melitta, Melittah, Mellie, Mellissa, Melly, Melysa, Melysah, Melyssa, Melyssah, Melysse, Milisa, Milisah, Milissa, Milissah, Millicent, Millie, Millisent, Millisa, Millisah, Millissa, Millissah, Milly, Missy, Mylisa, Mylisah, Mylissa, Mylissah, Mylissia, Mylissiah

Melita (Greek) sweet as honey.

Melitah, Mellita, Mellitah

Melody (Greek) song.

Mallodie, Mallody, Malodie, Malody, Mellodie, Mellody, Meloda, Melodah, Melodea, Melodee, Melodey, Melodi, Melodia, Melodiah, Melodie

Melosa (Spanish) sweet like honey.

Malosa, Malosah, Malossa, Malossah, Melosah, Melossa, Melossah

Melva (Celtic) armoured chief.

Melvah

Mena (German, Dutch) strong.

Meana, Meanah, Meina, Meinah, Menah

Menora (Hebrew) candle holder.
Menorah, Meonora, Meonorah

Merab (Hebrew) increase of greatness.

Mercedes (Latin) reward; (Spanish) compassionate, from a title of the Virgin Mary.
Meceades, Mercedeas, Mercedees, Mersades

Mercer (English) merchant, a unisex name.
Merca, Merce, Mercee, Mercey, Merci, Mercia, Merciah, Merse, Merser

Mercia (Anglo-Saxon) ancient British kingdom.
Merciah, Mercie, Mercy

Mercy (English) compassion, pity, merciful.
Merce, Mercee, Mercey, Merci, Mercia, Merciah, Mercie, Mercina, Mercinah, Mercya, Mercyah, Mersee, Mersey, Mersi, Mersia, Mersiah, Mersie, Mersina, Mersinah, Mersy

Meredith (Celtic) protector of the sea, a unisex name.
Meredeth, Meredithe, Meredy, Meredyth, Meredythe, Meridath, Merideth, Meridie, Meridith, Merri, Merridie, Merridith, Merry

Merinda (Australian Aboriginal) pretty woman.
Merindah

Merle (French) blackbird, a unisex name.
Mearl, Mearle, Mearll, Mearlle, Merl, Merola, Meryl, Myrle

Merrina (Australian Aboriginal) grass seed.

Merina, Merinah, Meriwa, Meriwah, Merrin, Merrinah, Merriwa, Merriwah, Merryna, Merrynah, Merrywa, Merrywah, Meryn, Meryna, Merynah

Merritt (Latin) worthy of merit.
Merit, Merite, Merritte, Meryt, Meryte, Merytt, Merytte

Merry (English) festive, joyful, happy, a form of Meredith.
Merri, Merrie, Mery

Meryl (German) famous; (Irish) of the bright sea; (French, English) blackbird.
Meral, Merel, Meril, Merrall, Merrell, Merril, Merrile, Merrill, Merryl, Merryle, Merrylle, Meryle, Meryll, Merylle

Meta (Australian Aboriginal) land.

Mia (Latin, Italian) mine.
Meea, Meah, Miaa, Miah, Miya, Miyah

Miakoda (Native American) power of the moon.

Micah (Hebrew) one who is like the Lord, a form of Michael, one of the archangels, a unisex name.
Mica, Micaela, Mical, Michaela, Michaella, Michaelle, Michal, Michala, Michalina, Michaline, Michel, Michele, Michelina, Micheline, Michell, Michella, Michellah, Michelle, Miguela

Michaela (Hebrew) like God, feminine form of Michael.
Micaela, Michal, Michala, Michelle, Mickie, Micky, Miguala, Migeulaita, Mikaela, Mikaila, Mikayla

Michelle (French) who is like God, feminine form of Michael.
Machell, Machella, Machelle, Mashell, Mashella, Mashelle,

Mechel, Mechell, Mechella, Mechelle, Meshell, Meshella, Meshelle, Mica, Micaela, Michaella, Michaelle, Micah, Mical, Michal, Michalina, Michaline, Michel, Michele, Michelina, Micheline, Michell, Michella, Michellah, Miguela, Miguelita, Miquela, Miquelah, Miquella, Miquelle, Mishel, Mishela, Mishele, Mishell, Mishella, Mishellah, Mishelle, Mychel, Mychela, Mychelah, Mychele, Mychell, Mychella, Mychelle, Myshel, Myshela, Myshelah, Myshele, Myshell, Myshella, Myshellah, Myshelle

Michi (Japanese) righteous.
Miche, Michee, Michey, Michie, Michiko, Michy

Midori (Japanese) green.
Madorea, Madoree, Madorey, Madori, Madorie, Madory, Midorea, Midoree, Midorey, Midorie, Midory

Mielikki (Finnish) pleasing.
Mieliki

Mietta (French) small sweet thing.
Miet, Mieta, Mietah, Miett, Miettah, Miette

Migdana (Hebrew) gift.
Dana, Danah, Migdanna, Migdannah, Mygdana, Mygdanah

Migina (Native American) moon returning.
Migeana, Migeanah, Migeena, Migeenah, Miginah

Mignon (French) dainty, petite.
Mignona, Mignone, Mignonetta, Mignonette

Miguela (Spanish) like God, a form of Michaela.
Miguel, Miguelina, Miguelita, Miguella, Miguelle

Mikayla (Hebrew) like God, a form of Michaela.
Mahkayla, Makayla, Michaela

Mila/Milana (Italian) from Milan; (Russian) dear one.
Milah, Milanah, Mili, Milia, Milla, Millah, Millia, Myla, Mylah, Mylla, Myllah

Milagros (Spanish) miracle.
Mila, Milagrios, Milagro, Milagrosa

Mildred (English) gentle counsellor.
Mil, Mildrid, Mill, Mildred, Milldrid, Mille, Millie, Myldrid, Myldryd, Mylldred, Mylldrid, Mylldryd

Mileta (German) merciful.
Miletah, Milett, Miletta, Milettah, Milette, Milita, Militah, Millita, Millitah, Myleta, Myletah, Mylita, Mylitah, Mylyta, Mylytah

Milia (German) industrious.
Mila, Milah, Mili, Milla, Millah, Milla-Milla, Millia, Milliah, Milya, Milyah

Milla (English) strong and good worker.

Millicent (Teutonic) strong, industrious.
Melicent, Melicenta, Melisande, Melisenda, Mellicent, Milicent, Milicenta, Milisande, Milisenda, Milisent, Milissent, Millisent, Millisenta, Millie, Milly, Myllicent, Myllicenta, Myllicente

Milly (English) a form of Amelia, Camille, Melissa, Mildred, Millicent.
Milee, Milei, Miley, Mili, Milie, Mily, Millee, Millei, Milley, Milli, Millie

Mima (Burmese) woman.
Mimah, Mimma, Mimmah, Myma, Mymah, Mymma, Mymmah

Mimi (French) wished for, star of the sea, bitter, a form of Miriam.

Mimea, Mimee, Mimey, Mimie, Mimmey, Mimmi, Mimmie, Mimmy, Mimy

Mina (German) love, loved memory; (Arabic) wish; (English) protector, a form of Wilhelmina.

Meena, Meenah, Minah, Minna, Minnah, Myna, Mynah, Mynna, Mynnah

Minal (Native American) fruit.

Minala, Minalah, Mynala, Mynalah

Minda (Hindu) knowledge.

Mindee, Mindie, Mindy

Minerva (Greek) wise.

Minervah, Minervera, Mini, Minivera, Minnerva, Mynerva, Mynervah, Mynervera

Minette (French) faithful defender.

Minetta, Minitta, Minitte, Minnetta, Minnette

Minikin (Dutch) darling.

Minikina, Minikinah, Minikine, Minikyn, Minikyna, Minikynah, Minikyne

Minkie (Australian Aboriginal) daylight.

Minkee, Minkey, Minki, Minky

Minna (German) love, loved memory.

Mina, Minah, Mindy, Minetta, Minette, Minnah, Minnetta, Minnette

Minnehaha (Native American) waterfall.

Minehaha

Minore (Australian Aboriginal) white flower.

Minora, Minorah, Minoree, Mynora, Mynorah, Mynoree

Minowa (Native American) singer.

Minowah, Mynowa, Mynowah

Mio (Japanese) three times as strong.

Myo

Mira (Latin) wonderful, beautiful.

Mayra, Mirella, Mirelle, Mirra, Mirrella, Mirrelle, Myra, Myrena, Myria, Myrilla

Mirabel (Latin) beautiful, wonderful.

Mira, Mirabell, Mirabella, Mirabelle, Mirable

Mirage (English) not as it seems, elusive.

Marage, Marrage, Mirrage

Miranda (Latin) worthy of admiration, wonderful.

Maranda, Marandah, Meranda, Merandah, Miran, Mirandah, Myranda, Myrandah

Mireille (Hebrew) God has spoken; (Latin) wonderful.

Mireil, Mireila, Mirel, Mirela, Mirele, Mirelle, Miriell, Miriella, Mirielle, Mirilla, Mirille, Myrella, Myrelle, Myrilla, Myrille

Mirena (Hawaiian) loved.

Mirenah, Myrena, Myrenah

Miriam (Hebrew) wished for, star of the sea, bitter, a form of Mary.

Mimi, Minnie, Mitzie, Myriam, Myriamne, Myryam, Myryamne

Mirna (Irish) polite.

Merna, Mernah, Mirnah, Myrna, Myrnah

Mirrin (Australian Aboriginal) cloud.

Mirrina, Mirrine, Mirynn, Mirynna, Mirryn, Myrrina, Myrrine, Myrryn, Myrryna, Myrryne

Missy (English) young girl, honey bee, a form of Melissa.

Misee, Misey, Misi, Misie, Misse, Missey, Missee, Missi, Missie

Misty (Anglo-Saxon) cloudy, covered by mist.

Missty, Mistee, Mistey, Misti, Mistie, Mistin, Mistinna, Mystee, Mysti, Mystie

Mitzie (German) wished for, star of the sea, bitter, a form of Mary.

Mitz, Mitzee, Mitzey, Mitzie, Mitzy, Mytzee, Mytzey, Mytzi, Mytzie, Mytzy

Miwa (Japanese) wise eyes.

Miwah, Miwako, Mywa, Mywah, Mywako

Miya (Japanese) temple.

Miyah, Miyana, Miyanna, Mya, Myah

Miyoko (Japanese) a generation's beautiful child.

Mioko, Miyo, Miyuka, Myoko, Myyoko, Yoko

Miyuki (Japanese) snow.

Miyukee, Myyukee, Myyuki

Moana (Hawaiian) ocean.

Moanah, Moane, Moann, Moanna, Moannah, Moanne

Mocha (Arabic) chocolate flavoured coffee.

Mochah, Moka, Mokah

Modesty (Latin) modest.

Modesta, Modeste, Modesti, Modestia, Modestie, Modestine

Mohala (Hawaiian) flowering.

Moala, Moalah, Mohalah

Mohini (Hindu) enchantress.

Mohinee, Mohiney, Mohinie, Mohiny

Moira (Irish) great, wished for, star of the sea, bitter, a form of Mary.

Maira, Maura, Maureen, Moirae, Moirah, Moreen, Moyra, Moyrah, Myra, Myrah

Moledina (Australian Aboriginal) creek.

Moledin, Moledinah, Moledine, Moledyn, Moledyna, Moledynah, Moledyne

Moli (African) the colour orange.

Molea, Molee, Molei, Moleigh, Moley, Molia, Molie, Moly

Molly (Irish, English) wished for, star of the sea, bitter, a form of Mary.

Moll, Molleigh, Molley, Mollie

Momoko (Japanese) peach girl.

Mona (Greek) alone, one, single; (Irish) noble.

Moina, Moinah, Monah, Mone, Monea, Monna, Monnah, Moyna, Moynah

Monica (Latin) adviser; (Greek) solitary.

Mona, Monca, Moneeca, Moneecah, Monia, Monic, Monicah, Monice, Monicia, Monicka, Monika, Monikah, Moniqua, Monique, Monn, Monnica, Monnicah, Monnicka, Monnie, Monnyca, Monya, Monyca, Monycah, Monycka, Monyka

Monifa (African) luck.

Monifah, Monyfa, Monyfah

Monique (French) adviser; (Greek) solitary, a form of Monica.
Moniquie, Monnique

Montana (Spanish) mountain.
Monta, Montanah, Montania, Montaniah, Montanna, Montannah, Montea, Monteen, Monteena, Monteenah, Montey, Monti, Montia, Montie, Montina, Montinah, Montine, Monty, Tana

Moon (English) moon, from the moon.
Moona, Moonah, Moone

Moona (Australian Aboriginal) plenty.

Mora (Spanish) blueberry.
Morae, Morah, Morea, Moreah, Moria, Morie, Morita, Moryta, Morytah, Moryte

Morag (Gaelic) sun.
Moragg

Morgan (Welsh) from the sea, a unisex name.
Morgain, Morgaina, Morgainah, Morgana, Morganah, Morganna, Morgannah, Morgen, Morgena, Morgin, Morgina, Morgon

Moriah (French) dark skinned; (Hebrew) God is my teacher.
Moreil, Moria, Morria, Morriah, Morya, Moryah

Morie (Japanese) bay.
Morea, Moree, Morey, Mori, Mory

Morina (Irish) mermaid.
Morinah, Morinna, Morinnah, Moryna, Morynah, Morynna, Morynnah

Morit (Hebrew) teacher.
Moritt, Moritta, Morittah, Morryt, Morryta, Morrytah, Morryte, Moryt,

Moryta, Morytah, Moryte, Morytt, Morytta, Moryttah, Morytte

Morna (Gaelic) gentle, beloved.
Mornah, Mornina, Mornine, Morrna, Morrnah, Muirna, Muirne

Morowa (African) queen.
Morowah

Morrin (Irish) long-haired.
Morin, Morine, Morrine, Moryn, Moryne

Moselle (Hebrew) taken from the water, feminine form of Moses.
Mosel, Mosela, Moselah, Mosele, Mosella, Mosellah, Mozel, Mozela, Mozelah, Mozele, Mozella, Mozellah, Mozelle

Mosi (African) first-born.
Mosea, Mosee, Mosey, Mosiah, Mosie, Mosy

Mrena (Slavic) white eyes.
Mren, Mrenah

Mufida (Arabic) useful.
Mufeeda, Mufeedah, Mufidah

Muhja (Arabic) heart's blood, soul.
Muhjah

Muirne (Celtic) beloved.

Muna (Arabic) desired; (Basque) saint.
Munah, Mona, Monah

Munira (Arabic) illuminating, shedding light.
Muneera, Muneerah, Munirah

Mura (Japanese) village.
Murah

Muriel (Greek) fragrant; (Arabic) myrrh; (Celtic) sea-bright.
Marial, Mariel, Mariella, Marielle,

Meriel, Meriella, Merielle, Merl, Merle, Meryl, Muireall, Muirgheal, Murial, Muriell, Muriella, Murielle, Muryell, Muryella, Muryelle

Murphy (Irish) from the sea, a unisex name.

Murph, Murphee, Murphey, Murphi, Murphie

Musetta (French) little bagpipe, small muse.

Muse, Muset, Museta, Musetah, Musete, Musettah, Musette

Mushira (Arabic) giving counsel, advising.

Musheera, Musheerah, Mushirah

Musidora (Greek) beautiful muse.

Musidorah, Musidore, Musydor, Musydora, Musydorah, Musydore

Musika (African) music.

Musica, Musicah, Musicka, Musikah

Muslimah (Arabic) devout believer.

Muslima

Mya (Bumese) emerald.

Meia, Meiah, Mia, Miah, Myah

Myfanwy (Welsh) my treasure, precious.

Miff, Miffany, Miffey, Miffie, Miffy, Myff, Myffanwy, Myffany, Myffey, Myffie, Myffy, Myfina

Myla (English) merciful.

Mila, Milah, Milla, Millah, Mylah, Mylla, Myllah

Mylene (Greek) dark.

Mylaine, Mylana, Mylee, Myleen

Myra (Latin) fragrant oil; (Greek) full and abundant.

Miara, Miaria, Miarias, Mira, Mirra, Myrah, Myria, Myrra, Myrrah

Myrna (Arabic) myrrh; (Irish) gentle.

Merna, Mernah, Mirna, Mirnah, Morna, Mornah, Muirna, Muirnah, Myrnah

Myrtle (Greek) myrtle, a flower, symbol of victory.

Mertis, Mertle, Mirtle, Myrta, Myrtia, Myrtias, Myrtice, Myrtie, Myrtilla, Myrtis

Myune (Australian Aboriginal) clear water.

Miuna, Miunah, Miune, Myuna, Myunah

N

Naama (Hebrew) pleasant.

Naamah, Nama, Namah, Narma, Narmah, N'Ami, N'Ama

Nabila (Arabic) noble.

Nabilah, Nabeela, Nabeelah, Nabyla, Nabylah

Nachine (Spanish) fiery.

Nachina, Nachinah, Nachyna, Nachynah, Nachyne

Nada (Arabic) generous, a unisex name.

Nadah, Nadan, Nadana, Nadanah, Nadda, Naddah, Nade, Nadeh, Nadia, Nady, Nadya, Nadyah

Nadia (Slavic, French) hopeful.

Nadeea, Nadeeah, Nadiah, Nadie, Nadina, Nadine

Nadika (Sanskrit) river.

Nadeeka, Nadeekah, Nadikah

Nadine (Slavic, French) hopeful, a form of Nadia.

Nadan, Nadana, Nadanah, Nadane, Nadean, Nadeana, Nadeanah, Nadeane, Nadeen, Nadeena, Nadeenah, Nadeene, Nadia, Nadiah, Nadina, Nadinah, Nadine, Nadyn, Nadyna, Nadynah, Nadyne

Nadira (Arabic) rare, precious.

Nadeera, Nadeerah, Nadirah

Nafisah (Arabic) precious thing, gem.

Nafeesa, Nafeesah, Nafisa

Nafuna (African) child born feet first.

Nafunah

Nagida (Hebrew) prince, leader, noble, a feminine form of Nagid.

Nagda, Nagdah, Nageeda, Nageedah, Nagidah, Nagyda, Nagydah

Nahid (Persian) Venus, goddess of love and beauty.

Nahyd

Nahimana (Native American) mystic.

Nahima, Nahimah, Nahimanah

Naida (Greek) water nymph.

Naeda, Naedah, Naeeda, Naeedah, Naid, Naidah, Nayad, Nayada, Nayadah, Nyad, Nyada, Nyadah

Nailah (Arabic) one who succeeds, a unisex name.

Naeela, Naeelah, Naela, Naelah, Naila, Nayla, Naylah

Naima (Arabic) comfort, tranquillity, peace.

Na'ima, Na'imah, Naimah

Najah (Arabic) success.

Naja, Najaa, Najaah

Najam (Arabic) star.

Naja, Najah, Najaam, Najma

Najibah (Arabic) of noble birth.

Najeeba, Najeebah, Najiba

Najila (Arabic) of wide, brilliant eyes.

Najilah

Najwa (Arabic) secret conversation.

Najwah

Nalani (Hawaiian) calmness of the heavens.

Nalanea, Nalaneah, Nalanee, Nalaney, Nalania, Nalaniah, Nalanie, Nalany, Nalanya, Nalanyah

Nama (Australian Aboriginal) tea-tree.

Namah, Namma, Nammah

Nami (Japanese) wave.

Namee, Namey, Namie, Namika, Namiko, Namy

Nancy (English) gracious, a form of Anna, Ann.

Nan, Nance, Nancea, Nancee, Nancey, Nanci, Nancie, Nancine, Nancya, Nancyah, Nancye, Nann, Nanncea, Nanncee, Nanncey, Nannci, Nanncie, Nanncy, Nanncya, Nanncyah, Nanouk, Nansea, Nansee, Nansey, Nansi, Nansie, Nansine, Nansy, Nanuk

Nandali (Australian Aboriginal) fire.

Nandalea, Nandaleah, Nandalee, Nandalei, Nandaleigh, Nandaley, Nandalia, Nandaliah, Nandalie, Nandaly, Nandalya, Nandalyah

Nanette (French) gracious, a form of Nancy, Ann.

Nancy, Nanet, Naneta, Nanetah, Nanete, Nanett, Nanetta, Nanettah, Nannet, Nanneta, Nannetah, Nannete, Nannett, Nannetta, Nannettah, Nannette, Nanni, Nanny, Netty

Nani (Hawaiian) beautiful; (Greek) charming.

Nanee, Naney, Nania, Naniah, Nanie, Nannee, Nanney, Nanni, Nannia, Nanniah, Nannie, Nanny, Nany, Nanya, Nanyah

Naomi (Hebrew) sweet, pleasant one.

Naoma, Naomah, Naome, Naomee, Naomey, Naomia, Naomiah, Naomy, Neoma, Neome, Neomee, Neomey, Neomia, Neomiah, Neomy, Noami

Napea (Latin) girl of the valley.

Napeah, Napia, Napiah, Napya, Napyah, Napyia, Napyiah

Nara (Greek) happy; (Japanese) oak.

Narah, Narra, Narrah

Narcissa (Greek, French) daffodil, love of oneself.

Narciska, Narcissah, Narcisse, Narcissus, Narsissa, Narsissah, Narsisse, Narsissus

Narda (Latin) perfume, scented oil.

Nardah

Narella (Australian Aboriginal) woman from the sea.

Narel, Narela, Narelah, Narele, Narell, Narellah, Narelle,

Nari (Japanese) thunder.

Narea, Nareah, Naree, Narey, Naria, Nariah, Narie, Nary, Narya, Naryah

Nascha (Native American) owl.

Nashida (Arabic) student.

Nashita (Arabic) energetic, full of life.

Nashitah

Nashota (Native American) second-born twin.

Nashotah

Nashwa (Arabic) feeling of intoxication, elation.

Nashwah, Naswa, Naswah

Nasiha (Arabic) gives valuable advice.
Nasihah

Nasira (Arabic) helper, defender, feminine form of Nasir.
Naasera, Naassira, Naesera, Naesira, Naezira, Nasera, Nazera, Nazira, Nazzera, Nazzi, Nazzie, Nazzy

Nasya (Hebrew) miracle.
Nasia, Nasiah, Nasyah

Nata (Hindu) rope, dancer; (Native American) creator, speaker; (Latin) swimmer.
Naeta, Naetah, Naita, Naitah, Natah, Natia, Natiah, Natya, Natyah

Natalia (Italian, Russian) born at Christmas, feminine form of Natal.
Nasia, Nat, Natala, Natalah, Natalea, Nataleah, Natali, Nataliah, Nataliya, Nataliyah, Natalla, Natallah, Natallea, Natallia, Natalya, Natalyah, Natasha, Natelea, Nateleah, Nateli, Natelia, Nateliah, Nathala, Nathalah, Nathalea, Nathaleah, Nathali, Nathalia, Nathaliah, Nathalie, Nathaliya, Nathaliyah, Nathalya, Nathelea, Natheleah, Natheli, Nathelia, Natheliah, Natila, Natili, Natilia, Natiliah, Natlia, Natliah, Natylea, Natyleah, Natyli, Natylia, Natyliah

Natalie (Latin) born at Christmas.
Nasia, Nat, Natala, Natalae, Natalah, Natalee, Nataleh, Natalei, Nataleigh, Nataley, Natalia, Nataliee, Nataline, Natallie, Natalya, Natasha, Natela, Natelee, Natelei, Nateleigh, Nateley, Nateli, Natelie, Nately, Nathalee, Nathalei, Nathaleigh, Nathaley, Nathali, Nathalia, Nathalie, Nathaly, Nathalya, Natilee, Natilei, Natileigh, Natili, Natilie, Natily, Natlee, Natlei, Natleigh, Natley, Natli, Natlie, Natly, Natty, Natylee, Natylei, Natyleigh,

Natyley, Natyli, Natylie, Natyly

Natane (Native American) daughter.
Natana, Nateen, Nateena, Natina, Natine

Natania (Hebrew) gift of God, God is given, feminine form of Natan.
Natana, Nataniah, Nataniela, Nataniele, Nataniell, Nataniella, Natanielle, Natanya, Natanyah, Nathania, Nathaniah, Nathanya, Nathanyah, Nathenia, Natheniah, Nathenya, Nathenyah, Natonia, Natoniah, Natonya, Natonyah, Netania, Netanya, Nethania, Nethanya

Natara (Arabic) sacrifice.
Natarah, Nataria, Natariah, Natarya, Nataryah

Natasha (Russian, Latin) born at Christmas.
Nasia, Nat, Natala, Natalae, Natalia, Nataline, Natalya, Natashah, Natashy, Natashya, Natashyah, Natasia, Natasiah, Natasie, Natassa, Natassia, Natassja, Natasya, Nathali, Nathalia, Nathalie, Natty, Nettie, Netty, Noel, Noelle, Tash, Tasha

Nathania (Hebrew) gift of God, feminine form of Nathan.
Natania, Nataniah, Nataniel, Nataniela, Nataniele, Nataniell, Nataniella, Natanielle, Natanya, Natanyah, Nathaniah, Nathaniel, Nathaniela, Nathaniele, Nathaniell, Nathaniella, Nathanielle, Nathanya, Nathanyah, Nathena, Nathenah, Nathene, Natty

Nathifa (Egyptian) clean, pure.

Natividad (Spanish) the nativity.
Natividada, Natividade, Natividadia

Natsu (Japanese) summer.

Nava (Hebrew) beautiful.
Navah, Naveh, Navit, Navita, Navitah, Navyt, Navyta, Navytah

Nawal (Arabic) gift.

Nazahah (Arabic) purity, righteousness.
Nazaaha, Nazaha, Nazeeha, Naziha

Nazaret (Spanish) person from Nazareth, feminine form of Nazareth.
Nazarette, Nazari, Nazarie, Nazzi

Nea (Greek) new.
Neah, Nia, Niah

Neala (Celtic) champion, feminine form of Neil.
Nealah, Neila, Neilah, Niela, Nielah

Nebula (Latin) misty, like a vapour.
Nebulah, Nebulia, Nebuliah, Nebulla, Nebullah

Neci (Hungarian) fiery.
Necee, Necey, Necia, Neciah, Necie, Necy

Neda (Slavic) child born on a Sunday.
Nedah, Nedda, Neddah, Nedia, Nediah, Nedya, Nedyah

Neema (African) child born in a prosperous period.
Neemah

Nefertiti (Egyptian) most beautiful one.
Neferetete, Neferteti, Nefertitie, Nefertity

Nelda (English) of the elder tree.
Neilah, Neila, Neilda, Neildah, Neldah, Neldda, Nelddah, Nellda, Nelldah, Nellie, Nelly

Nell (Greek, English) light, a form of Nellie, Helen.
Nel, Nela, Nelah, Nelda, Neldah, Nelia, Nelina, Nelita, Nella, Nellah, Nelle, Nelli, Nellie, Nellis, Nelly

Nellie (Greek, English) light, a form of Helen.
Nela, Nelda, Neli, Nelia, Nelie, Nelina, Nelita, Nella, Nelle, Nelley, Nellis, Nelly

Nellwyn (English) friend of Nell.
Nellwin, Nellwina, Nellwinah, Nellwine, Nellwinn, Nellwinna, Nellwinnah, Nellwinne, Nell-Wyn, Nellwyna, Nellwynah, Nellwyne, Nellwynn, Nellwynna, Nellwynnah, Nellwynne, Nell-Wynne, Nelwin, Nelwina, Nelwinah, Nelwine, Nelwinn, Nelwinna, Nelwinnah, Nelwinne, Nelwyn, Nelwyna, Nelwynah, Nelwyne, Nelwynn, Nelwynna, Nelwynnah, Nelwynne

Nenet (Egyptian) born near the sea.
Neneta, Nenetah, Nenete, Nennet, Nenneta, Nennetah, Nennete, Nennett, Nennetta, Nennettah, Nennette

Neola (Greek) young one.
Neolah, Niola, Niolah

Neoma (Greek) new moon.
Neoma, Neomah, Neomma, Neommah, Nioma, Niomah

Nerida (Australian Aboriginal) flower or red waterlily.
Neridah, Neryda, Nerydah

Nerina (Latin) black.
Nerinah, Nerine, Neryn, Neryna, Nerynah, Neryne

Nerine (Greek) sea nymph.
Nerin, Nerina, Nerinah, Nerrin, Nerrina, Nerrinah, Nerrine, Neryn, Neryna, Nerynah, Neryne, Nerryn, Nerryna, Nerrynah, Nerryne

Nerita (Greek, Spanish) of the sea.
Neritah, Neritta, Nerittah

Neroli (Italian) orange blossom.
Nerolee, Neroley, Nerolia, Nerolie, Neroly

Nerys (Welsh) lady.
Nereace, Nerease, Nereece, Nereese, Nereice, Nereise, Nereyce, Nereyse, Nerice, Nerise, Neryce, Neryl, Neryse

Nessa/Nessie/Nessy
(Scandinavian) headland;
(English) a form of Vanessa;
(Greek) pure, a form of Agnes.
Neisa, Neisah, Nesa, Nesah, Nesia, Nesiah, Nessah, Nessi, Nessia, Nessiah, Nessya, Nessyah

Neta (Hebrew) plant.
Netah, Netai, Netia, Netiah, Netta, Nettah, Nettia, Nettiah, Nettya, Nettyah, Netya, Netyah

Netis (Native American)
trustworthy.
Netisa, Netisah, Netise, Netissa, Netissah, Netisse, Nettiss, Nettissa, Nettissah, Nettisse, Nettys, Nettysa, Nettysah, Nettyse, Netys, Netysa, Netysah, Netyse, Netyssa, Netyssah, Netysse

Neva (Spanish) white.
Nevah, Niva

Nevina (Irish) saint worshipper.
Neveen, Neveena, Neveenah, Neveene, Nevena, Nevenah, Nevinah, Nevine, Nivena, Nivenah, Nivina, Nivinah, Nivine

Neylan (Turkish) fulfilled wish.
Nealana, Nealanah, Nealane, Nealanee, Nealaney, Nealani, Nealania, Nealaniah, Nealany, Nealanya, Nealanyah, Neilana, Neilanah, Neilane, Neilanee, Neilaney, Neilani, Neilania,
Neilaniah, Neilany, Neilanya, Neilanyah, Neylana, Neylanah, Neylane, Neylanee, Neylaney, Neylani, Neylania, Neylaniah, Neylany, Neylanya, Neylanyah

Neysa (Greek) pure, a form of Agnes.
Neisa, Neisah, Nesa, Nesah, Nessa, Nessah, Neysah

Ngaire (Polynesian) flax, a native New Zealand tree.
Nairee, Nairey, Nairie, Nirie, Niree, Ngaio, Ngairey, Ngairie, Ngairy, Nyree, Nyrey, Nyrie, Nyry

Niabi (Native American) fawn.
Niabia, Niabiah, Niabie, Niaby, Niabya, Niabyah, Nyabi, Nyabia, Nyabiah, Nyabie, Nyaby, Nyabya, Nyabyah

Niamh (Irish) bright.
Niam, Niama, Niamah, Nyam, Nyama, Nyamah, Nyamh

Nibal (Arabic) arrow, a unisex name.
Nibala, Nibel, Nibela, Niebel, Niebella, Nybal, Nybala, Nybel, Nybela

Nichelle (Greek) victory of the people; (French) like God, combination of Nicole and Michelle.
Nechel, Nechela, Nechelah, Nechele, Nechell, Nechella, Nechellah, Nechelle, Nichel, Nichela, Nichelah, Nichele, Nichell, Nichella, Nichellah, Nishell, Nishella, Nishellah, Nishelle

Nichole (French) victory of the people, feminine form of Nicholas.
Nichol, Nichola, Nicholle

Nicki (American) victory of the people, a form of Nicole.
Nicci, Niccy, Nicky, Niki, Nikki, Nikky, Niky

Nicola (Italian) victory of the people, a form of Nicole, feminine form of Nicholas.

Nicala, Nicalah, Nichala, Nichalah, Nichola, Nicholah, Nickala, Nickalah, Nicki, Nickola, Nickolah, Nicolah, Nicole, Nicolea, Nicolette, Nicolla, Nikita, Nikkola, Nikola, Nikole, Nikolia

Nicole (French) victory of the people, feminine form of Nicholas.

Nica, Nichola, Nicia, Nicki, Nicky, Nicol, Nicola, Nicolette, Nicoli, Nicolia, Nicolie, Nicolina, Nicoline, Nicoll, Nicolle, Nikki, Nikkos, Nikita

Nicoletta (French) victory of the people, a form of Nicole.

Nickolet, Nickoleta, Nickoletah, Nickolete, Nickolett, Nickoletta, Nickolettah, Nickolette, Nicolet, Nicoleta, Nicoletah, Nicolete, Nicolett, Nicolettah, Nicollete

Nigella (Latin) dark-haired, black, feminine form of Nigel.

Nigela, Nigelah, Nigele, Nigell, Nigellah, Nigelle

Nike (Greek) victorious, a unisex name.

Nikki, Nyke, Nykee, Nykey, Nyky

Nikita/Nikkita (Russian) victory of the people.

Nakeita, Nakita, Nakitta, Nickeata, Nickeatah, Nickeeta, Nickeetah, Nicki, Nicola, Nicole, Nicolette, Nikeata, Nikeatah, Nikeeta, Nikeetah, Nikeita, Nikeitah, Nikitah, Nikitia, Nikitiah, Nikitta, Nikittah, Nikitte, Nikki, Nikkos, Niquita, Niquitah, Niquite, Niquitta

Nikki (American) victory of the people, a form of Nicole.

Nicci, Niccy, Nicki, Nicky, Nikky

Nila (Latin) Nile River.

Nilah, Nilesia, Nilesiah, Nyla, Nylah

Nimah (Arabic) blessing; (Hebrew) thread.

Neema, Neemah, Nema, Nemah, Niama, Niamah, Nima, Ni'mah, Nyma, Nymah

Nimeesha (African) princess.

Nimisha, Nymeeshia, Nymisha

Nina (Spanish) girl; (Russian) graceful, a form of Ann.

Neana, Neanah, Neena, Neenah, Ninah, Ninet, Nineta, Ninetah, Ninete, Ninett, Ninetta, Ninette, Ninon, Nyna, Nynah

Nirel (Hebrew) God's light.

Nirela, Nirelah, Nirele, Nirell, Nirella, Nirellah, Nirelle

Nirvelli (Hindu) water child.

Nirvelea, Nirveleah, Nirvelee, Nirvelei, Nirveleigh, Nirveley, Nirveli, Nirvelie, Nirelleah, Nirvellee, Nirvellei, Nirvelleigh, Nirvelley, Nirvelli, Nirvellie, Nirvelly, Nirvely

Nishi (Japanese) west.

Nishee, Nishey, Nishie, Nishy

Nita (Native American) bear.

Nitah, Nyta, Nytah

Nitza (Hebrew) flower bud.

Nitzah, Nitzana, Nitzanah, Nitzanit, Nitzanita

Nixie (German) water nymph.

Nixee, Nixey, Nixi, Nixy

Noelani (Hawaiian) beautiful one sent from heaven.

Noelanee, Noelaney, No'elani, Noelania, Noelaniah, Noelanie, Noelany, Noelanya, Noelanyah

Noeline (Latin) born at Christmas, feminine form of Noel.

Noela, Noelah, Noelan, Noelana, Noelanah, Noele, Noelean,

*Noeleana, Noeleanah, Noeleane,
Noeleen, Noeleena, Noeleenah,
Noeleene, Noelin, Noelina,
Noelinah, Noell, Noella, Noellah,
Noellan, Noellana, Noellanah,
Noelle, Noellin, Noellina, Noellinah,
Noelline, Noellyn, Noellyna,
Noellynah, Noellyne, Nolein,
Noleina, Noleinah, Noleine, Noleyn,
Noleyna, Noleynah, Noelyne*

Noelle (French) born at Christmas
time, feminine form of Noel.

*Noel, Noela, Noelah, Noele, Noell,
Noella, Noellah, Nowel, Nowela,
Nowelah, Nowele, Nowell, Nowella,
Nowellah, Nowelle*

Noga (Hebrew) morning light.

Nogah

Nokomis (Native American)
daughter of the Moon.

Nokoma, Nokomas, Nokomi

Nola (Latin) small bell; (Celtic)
fair-shouldered.

*Nolah, Nolia, Noliah, Nolla, Nollah,
Notlia, Nolliah*

Nolana (Irish) born at Christmas, a
form of Noeline

*Noelana, Noelanah, Noelanee,
Noelaney, Noelani, Noelania,
Noelaniah, Noelanie, Noelanna,
Noelannah, Noelanne, Noelannee,
Noelanney, Noelanni, Noelannia,
Noelanniah, Noelannie, Noelanny,
Noelannya, Noelannyah, Noelany,
Nolanah, Nolanee, Nolaney,
Nolani, Nolania, Nolaniah, Nolanie,
Nolany, Nolanya, Nolanyah*

Noleta (Latin) unwilling.

*Noleata, Noleatah, Noleeta,
Noleetah, Noletah, Nolita, Nolitah,
Nolyta, Nolytah*

Nona (Latin) ninth-born child.

*Nonah, Nonia, Noniah, Nonna,
Nonnah, Nonya, Nonyah*

Noni (Latin) respect, honesty.

*Nonee, Noney, Nonia, Noniah,
Nonie, Nony, Nonya, Nonyah, Nora,
Norah, Norra, Norrah*

Nora (Greek) light, a form of
Eleanor, Honora.

Norah, Norra, Norrah

Norberta (Teutonic) brilliant hero,
feminine form of Norbert.

*Norbertah, Norbertta, Norberttah,
Norbirta, Norbirtah, Norburta,
Norburtah*

Nori (Japanese) doctrine, religious
beliefs.

*Noree, Norey, Noria, Noriah, Norie,
Norii, Nory, Norya, Noryah*

Noriko (Japanese) doctrine child.

Noreeko

Norleen (Irish) honest.

*Norlean, Norleana, Norleanah,
Norleane, Norleena, Norleenah,
Norleene, Norlein, Norleina,
Norleinah, Norleine, Norlin, Norlina,
Norlinah, Norline, Norlyn, Norlyna,
Norlynah, Norlyne*

Norma (Latin) rule, feminine form
of Norman.

Normah, Normi, Normia, Normie

Norna (Old Norse) the goddess of
fate.

Nornah

Nouf (Arabic) peak of a mountain.

Nova (Latin) new.

*Novah, Novia, Noviah, Novya,
Novyah*

Novella (Latin) newcomer.

*Novel, Novela, Novelah, Novele,
Novell, Novellah, Novelle*

Nu (Vietnamese) girl.

Nue

Nuala (Celtic) fair-shouldered one, a form of Fionnula.

Nualah, Nualla, Nuallah, Nula, Nulah, Nulla, Nullah

Nudhar (Arabic) gold, precious.

Nudar

Numa (Arabic) beautiful, pleasant, a unisex name.

Numah

Numilla (Australian Aboriginal) lookout.

Numil, Numila, Numilah, Numile, Numill, Numillah, Numille, Numyl, Numyla, Numylah, Numyle, Numyil, Numylla, Numyllah, Numylle

Nuna (Native American) land.

Nunah

Nunzia (Italian) bearer of news, from Annunciata.

Nuncia, Nunciah, Nunciata, Nunciatah, Nunziah, Nunziata, Nunziatah

Nur/Nura (Aramaic) light.

Noor, Noora, Noorah, Nurah

Nuru (African) born during daylight hours, a unisex name.

Nydia (Latin) safe place, nest, refuge.

Nidia, Nidiah, Nydiah, Nydya, Nydyah

Nyoko (Japanese) treasure.

Nioko

Nyree (Maori) sea.

Naira, Nairee, Nairie, Nyra, Nyrie

Nyssa (Greek) to begin.

Nisa, Nisah, Nisia, Nisiah, Nisie, Nissa, Nissah, Nissia, Nissiah, Nissie, Nysa, Nysah, Nysia, Nysiah, Nysie, Nyssah, Nyssia, Nyssiah, Nyssie

Nyusha (Russian) pure, a form of Agnes.

Nusha, Nushenka, Nushka, Nyushenka, Nyushka

Nyx (Greek) night.

Nix, Nixe, Nyxe

Oake (Anglo-Saxon) near the oak trees, oak tree, a unisex name.
Oak, Oakes, Oakey, Oakie, Oaks, Oaky

Obelia (Greek) needle, strength.
Belia, Elia, Obeliah, Obelya, Obelyah, Obey

Oceana (Greek) ocean, sea.
Ocan, Ocana, Ocanah, Ocea, Oceah, Ocean, Oceanah, Oceane, Ocearn, Ocearne, Oecean, Oeceana, Oeceanah, Oshearn, Oshearna, Oshearnah, Oshearne

Octavia (Latin) eighth born child, feminine form of Octavius.
Aktavia, Aktaviah, Aktavija, Octaviah, Octavian, Octaviana, Octavianah, Octavianos, Octavie, Octaviena, Octavienah, Octavio, Octaviona, Octavionah, Octavious, Octawia, Ofeliga, Oktavia, Oktaviah, Oktavija, Ottavia, Ottaviah, Ottavya, Ottavyah, Tavie, Tavy

Oda (Scandinavian) little pointed spear.
Odah

Odda (Scandinavian) wealthy, rich.
Oda, Odah, Oddah, Oddia, Oddiah

Odeda (Hebrew) courageous, strong, brave.
Odeada, Odeadah, Odedah, Odedia, Odediah

Odele (Greek) melody, song.
Odel, Odela, Odelah, Odeli, Odelia, Odeliah, Odelie, Odell, Odella, Odellah, Odelle, Odelli, Odellia, Odelliah, Odellie

Odelette (French) little song, feminine form of Odel.
Odelatt, Odelatta, Odelattah, Odelet, Odeleta, Odeletah, Odelete, Odelett, Odeletta, Odelettah, Odellatt, Odellatta, Odellattah, Odellet, Odelleta, Odelletah, Odellete, Odellett, Odelletta, Odellettah, Odellette

Odelia (French) wealthy one; (Hebrew) praise God; (Greek) ode, melody, a feminine form of Odel.
Odel, Odela, Odelah, Odele, Odeliah, Odelina, Odelinah, Odelinda, Odeline, Odell, Odella, Odellah, Odelle, Odellia, Odelliah, Odellina, Odellinah, Odellinda, Odelline, Odett, Odetta, Odettah, Odette, Odila, Odilah, Odilia, Odiliah, Odilla, Odillah, Odille, Odyla, Odylah, Odyle, Odyll, Odylla, Odyllah, Odylle, Otha, Othelia, Othilia, Ottilie

Odessa (Greek) journey, voyage.
Dessa, Odesa, Odesah, Odessah, Odisa, Odisah, Odissa, Odissah, Odysa, Odysah, Odyssa, Odyssah, Odyssea

Odetta (French) melody, a form of Odelia.
Oddetta, Oddettah, Oddette, Odettah, Odette

Odette (French) ode, melody, wealthy, home-lover.
Oddet, Oddeta, Oddetah, Oddete, Oddett, Oddetta, Oddettah, Oddette, Odet, Odeta, Odetah, Odete, Odett, Odetta, Odettah

Odina (Native American) mountain.
Odeana, Odeanah, Odeane,

Odeen, Odeena, Odeenah, Odinah, Odine, Odyn, Odyna, Odynah, Odyne

Ofelia (Italian) helper, a form of Ophelia.

Ofeelia, Ofeliah, Ofellia, Ofilia, Ofiliah

Ofira (Hebrew) gold.

Ofara, Ofarah, Ofarra, Ofarrah, Ofirah, Ofirra, Ofirrah, Ophira, Ophirah, Ophirra, Ophirrah

Ogin (Native American) wild rose.

Ogina, Oginah, Ogyn, Ogyna, Ogynah

Ohanna (Hebrew) God's gracious gift, God is gracious.

Ohana, Ohanah, Ohannah

Okalani (Hawaiian) from heaven.

Okalana, Okalanah, Okalanea, Okalanee, Okalaney, Okalania, Okalaniah, Okalanie, Okalany, Okalanya, Okalanyah

Oksana (Russian) glory to God.

Oksanah, Oksanna, Oksannah

Ola (Scandinavian) ancestor.

Olah

Olalla (Greek) sweetly spoken.

Olallah

Olathe (Native American) beautiful.

Olanth, Olantha, Olanthah, Olanthe, Olanthia, Olanthiah, Olanthye, Olath, Olatha, Olathah, Olathia, Olathiah, Olathye

Oldina (Australian Aboriginal) snow.

Oldeena, Oldeenah, Olldena, Oldenah, Oldenia, Oldeniah, Oldinah, Oldine, Oldyn, Oldyna, Oldynah, Oldyne

Oleander (Latin) a type of flowering tree or shrub.

Oleanda, Oleandah, Oleeanda, Oleeandah, Oliana, Olianah, Olianda, Oliandah, Oliander, Oliane, Oliann, Olianna, Oliannah, Oliannda, Olianndah, Oliannde, Oliannder, Olianne, Olyana, Olyanah, Olyanda, Olyandah, Olyander, Olyane, Olyann, Olyanna, Olyannah, Olyannda, Olyanndah, Olyannder, Olyanne

Olena (Russian) light, a form of Helen.

Alena, Oleena, Oleenah, Olenah, Olenia, Oleniah, Olenka, Olenna, Olennah, Olenya, Olenyah, Olina, Olinah, Olya, Olyah, Olyena, Olyenah, Olyona, Olyonah

Oletha (Latin) truthful.

Aleathea, Aleatheah, Aletha, Alethah, Oleatha, Oleathah, Oleathea, Oleatheah, Oleathya, Oleathyah, Oleta, Oletah, Olethah

Olga (Scandinavian) holy one, a saintly woman.

Elga, Helga, Olenka, Olgah, Olgi, Olgie, Olgy, Olia, Oliah, Olive, Olivia, Olva

Oliana (Hawaiian) the flower oleander.

Olianah, Oliane, Oliann, Olianna, Oliannah, Olianne, Olyan, Olyana, Olyanah, Olyane, Olyann, Olyanna, Olyannah, Olyanne

Olina (Hawaiian), happy.

Olinah, Olyna, Olynah

Olinda (Latin) sweet smelling fragrance.

Olindah, Olinka, Olinkah, Olynda, Olyndah

Olisa (African) God.
Olisah, Olissa, Olissah, Olysa, Olysah, Olyssa, Olyssah

Olive (Latin) olive tree.
Livia, Livie, Livvia, Livvie, Olave, Olga, Olinda, Olivetta, Olivette, Oliv, Oliva, Olivah, Olivia, Oliviah, Ollie, Olly, Olva, Olyv, Olyve, Yolanda

Olivia (Italian) olive tree, a form of Olive.
Liv, Livia, Livie, Livvia, Livvie, Olevia, Olga, Olia, Oliah, Olida, Oliva, Olivah, Olive, Olivea, Oliveia, Olivetta, Olivette, Olivi, Oliviah, Oliviana, Olivianah, Oliviann, Olivianna, Oliviannah, Olivianne, Olivya, Olivyah, Oliwia, Ollie, Olly, Olva, Olyvia, Olyviah, Olyvya, Olyvyah

Olwen (Welsh) white footprints.
Olwena, Olwenah, Olwene, Olwenn, Olwenna, Olwennah, Olwenne, Olwin, Olwina, Olwinah, Olwine, Olwinn, Olwinna, Olwinnah, Olwinne, Olwyn, Olwyna, Olwynah, Olwyne, Olwynn, Olwynna, Olwynnah, Olwynne

Olympia (Greek) from Mount Olympus, heavenly one.
Olimpe, Olimpi, Olimpia, Olimpiah, Olimpias, Olimpie, Olympe, Olympi, Olympiah, Olympias, Olympie, Olympya, Olympyah, Pia

Oma (Arabic) person in charge; (Hebrew) reverent; (German) grandmother.
Omah

Omaira (Arabic) red.
Omair, Omairah, Omairi, Omairia, Omairiah, Omar, Omara, Omarah, Omari, Omaria, Omariah, Omarra, Omarrah

Omega (Greek) last-born child.
Omegah

Ona (Latin) unifying person, graceful.
Onah, Oona, Oonah, Oonagh

Onatah (Native American) daughter of the earth and the corn.
Onata

Onawa (Native American) one who is wide-awake.
Onaiwa, Onaiwah, Onawah, Onowa, Onowah

Ondine (Latin) wave, wave of water.
Ondin, Ondina, Ondinah, Ondyn, Ondyna, Ondynah, Ondyne, Undin, Undina, Undinah, Undine, Undyn, Undyna, Undynah, Undyne

Oneida (Native American) eagerly awaited.
Oneidah, Oneyda, Oneydah, Onida, Onidah, Onyda, Onydah

Onella (Hungarian) light, shining, a form of Helen.
Onela, Onelah, Onellah

Oni (African) born on holy ground.
Onee, Oney, Onie, Ony, Onye

Onora (Latin) honour.
Onorah, Onoria, Onoriah, Onorina, Onorinah, Onorine, Ornora, Ornorah, Ornoria, Ornoriah

Ontaria (Native American) beautiful lake.
Oniatario, Ontariah, Ontario, Ontarya, Ontaryah, Ontaryo

Onyx (Greek) type of black semi-precious stone.
Onix, Onixe, Onyxe

Oodgeroo (Australian Aboriginal) paper-bark tree.

Oodlawirra (Australian Aboriginal) hill and tree country.

Opa (Native American) owl.
Opah

Opal (Hindu) jewel, precious stone.
Opala, Opalah, Opalia, Opaliah, Opalina, Opalinah, Opaline, Opell, Opella, Opellah, Opelle, Opellia, Opelliah

Ophelia (Greek) helper.
Ofelia, Ofeliah, Ofilia, Ofiliah, Opheliah, Ophelie, Ophellia, Ophelliah, Ophellya, Ophellyah, Ophillia, Ophilliah, Orfelia, Orfeliah, Orfilia, Orfiliah, Orphelia, Orpheliah, Orphelie, Orphellia, Orphelliah, Orphellya, Orphellyah, Orphillia, Orphilliah, Phelia, Pheliah, Phelya, Phelyah

Ophira (Greek) gold.
Ophirah

Oprah (Hebrew) runaway, little fawn.
Opra, Orpa, Orpah, Ophra, Ophrah, Orpha, Orphah

Ora (Latin) prayer; (English) coastline; (Spanish) gold.
Aura, Aurah, Orabel, Orabelle, Orah, Orra, Orrah

Oralee (Hebrew) light, the Lord is my light.
Oralea, Oraleah, Oralei, Oraleigh, Oraley, Orali, Oralie, Oraly, Oralye

Oralia (Latin) golden, a form of Aurelia.
Oraliah, Oralie, Oralis, Oralya, Oralyah, Orelia, Oreliah, Oriel, Oriela, Orielah, Orielda, Oriele, Oriella, Oriellah, Orielle, Oriole, Orlena, Orlene

Orana (Australian Aboriginal) welcome.

Aurana, Auranah, Auranna, Aurannah, Oran, Oranah, Oranna, Orannah

Orazia (Italian) timekeeper, feminine form of Oratio.
Orazaia, Orazaiah, Oraziah, Orazya, Orazyah, Orzaya, Orzayah

Orea (Greek) from the mountains.
Oreah, Oria, Oriah

Orela (Latin) announcement from the gods.
Oreal, Oreala, Orealah, Oreilla, Orel, Orelah, Orelia, Oreliah, Orell, Orella, Orellah, Orelle

Orenda (Native American) magic power.
Orendah

Oriana (Latin) dawn, to rise.
Orana, Oranah, Orane, Orania, Oraniah, Ori, Oria, Oriah, Orian, Orianah, Oriane, Orianna, Oriannah, Orianne, Oryan, Oryana, Oryanah, Oryane, Oryann, Oryanna, Oryannah, Oryanne

Oriel (Latin) fire; (French) golden.
Orial, Oriala, Orialah, Oriale, Oriall, Orialla, Oriallah, Orialle, Oriela, Orielah, Oriele, Oriell, Oriella, Oriellah, Orielle, Oryal, Oryala, Oryalah, Oryale, Oryall, Oryalla, Oryallah, Oryalle

Orina (Russian) peaceful, a form of Irene.
Orinah, Orya, Oryah, Oryna, Orynah

Orinda (Hebrew) pine tree; (Irish) light-skinned.
Orenda, Orendah, Orindah, Orynda, Oryndah

Orinthia (Irish) name invented by playwright George Bernard Shaw in The Apple Cart, 1929.

Oriole (Latin) golden, black and orange bird.
Oriola, Oriolah

Orla (Irish) golden.
Orlah

Orlenda (Russian) eagle.
Orlanda, Orlandah, Orlendah

Orli (Hebrew) light.
Orelea, Oreleah, Orlee, Orlei, Orleigh, Orley, Orlia, Orliah, Orlie, Orly

Ormanda (Latin) noble; (German) mariner, sailor.
Orma, Ormah, Ormandah, Ormandia, Ormandiah, Ormandya, Ormandyah

Ornat (Irish) green.
Ornait, Ornaita, Ornaitah, Ornaite, Ornata, Ornatah, Ornate, Orneta, Orentah, Ornete, Ornetta, Ornettah, Ornette, Ornit, Ornita, Ornitah, Ornite, Ornitt, Ornitta, Ornittah, Ornitte, Ornyt, Ornyta, Ornytah, Ornyte, Ornytt, Ornytta, Orynyttah, Ornytte

Ornice (Hebrew) cedar tree; (Irish) olive colour.
Orna, Ornah, Ornise

Orpah (Hebrew) young deer, runaway.
Orpa, Orpha, Orphah Orphie

Orsola (Italian) bear-like, a form of Ursula.
Orsolah, Orsula, Orsulah

Ortensia (Italian) gardener, a form of Hortense.
Ortensiah

Ortrude (Teutonic) golden maid.
Ortrud, Ortruda, Ortrudah

Orva (English) friend with a spear; (French) golden, worthy.
Orvah

Orwina (Hebrew) boar friend.
Orwin, Orwinah, Orwine, Orwyn, Orwyna, Orwynah, Orwyne

Osen (Japanese) one thousand.
Osena, Osenah

Oseye (African) merry, happy.
Osey

Osita (Spanish) divine strength.
Ositah, Osith, Ositha, Osithah, Osithe, Osyta, Osytah, Osyte, Osyth, Osytha, Osythah, Osythe

Osma (English) divine protector.
Osmah, Ozma, Ozmah

Othilia (Teutonic) rich.
Othiliah, Ottilia, Ottiliah

Ottavia (Italian) eighth-born child, a form of Octavia.
Otavia, Otaviah, Otavya, Otavyah, Ottaviah, Ottavya, Ottavyah

Ovia (Latin, Danish) egg.
Ova, Ovah, Oviah, Ovya, Ovyah

Ove (Norse) the spears tip, a unisex name.

Owena (Welsh) young warrior, of noble birth.
Owenah, Owina, Owinah, Owyna, Owynah

Oya (Native American) called forward.
Oia, Oiah, Oyah

Ozara (Hebrew) treasure.
Ozarah, Ozarra, Ozarrah

Ozera (Hebrew) helper.
Ozerah, Ozira, Ozirah, Ozyra, Ozyrah

P

Pabla (Spanish) small, a form of Paula.
Pablah

Paca (Spanish) free person, a form of Pancha.
Paka

Pacifica (Spanish) peaceful.
Pacificah, Pacifyca, Pacifycah

Padma (Hindu) lotus.
Padmah, Padmar

Padmani (Sri Lankan) flower.
Padmanee, Padmaney, Padmania, Padmaniah, Padmanie, Padmany, Padmanya, Padmanyah

Pagan (Latin) of the country, a unisex name.
Paegan, Paegen, Paegin, Paegon, Paegyn, Pagen, Pagin, Pagon, Pagun, Pagyn, Paigan, Paigen, Paigin, Paigon, Paigyn

Paige (Anglo-Saxon) youthful assistant, young child, a unisex name.
Padget, Padgett, Page, Paget, Pagi, Payg, Payge

Paisley (Scottish) patterned fabric.
Paislay, Paislea, Paislee, Paisleigh, Paisliann, Paislianna, Paislianne, Paizlay, Paizlea, Paizlee, Paizleigh, Paizley, Pazley

Paiton (English) place of a warrior.
Paitan, Paiten, Paitin, Paitonn,

Paityn, Paityne, Paiyton, Paten, Patton

Paka (African) catlike.
Pakah

Pakuna (African) bounding deer.
Pakunah

Pala (Native American) water.
Palah, Palla, Pallah

Pallas (Greek) goddess of wisdom in Greek mythology.
Pallass, Pallassa, Pallis, Pallissa

Palma (Latin) palm tree.
Palmah, Palmar, Palmara, Palmarah, Palmira, Parlma,

Paloma (Spanish) dove.
Palloma, Palomah, Palomar, Palomara, Palomarah, Palomaria, Palomariah, Peloma, Pelomah

Pamela (Greek) honeyed.
Pam, Pamala, Pamalah, Pamalia, Pamaliah, Pamalla, Pamallah, Pamalya, Pamalyah, Pamelah, Pamelia, Pameliah, Pamella, Pamellah, Pamelya, Pamelyah, Pamee, Pamey, Pami, Pamie, Pamm, Pammee, Pammey, Pammie, Pammie, Pammy, Pamy

Pana (Native American) partridge bird.
Panah, Panna, Pannah

Pancha (Spanish) free person, feminine form of Pancho.
Paca, Panchah, Panchika, Panchikah, Panchita, Panchitah

Pandora (Greek) talented one.
Pandi, Pandorah, Pandorra, Pandorrah, Pandy, Panndora, Panndorah, Panndorra, Panndorrah

Pania (Maori) mythological sea-maiden.

Panea, Paneah, Paniah, Panya, Panyah, Panyia, Panyiah

Pansofia (Greek) knowledgeable, wise.

Pansofee, Pansofey, Pansoffee, Pansoffey, Pansoffi, Pansoffia, Pansoffie, Pansoffy, Pansoffya, Pansoffyah, Pansofi, Pansofiah, Pansofie, Pansofy, Pansofya, Pansofyah, Pansophee, Pansophey, Pansophi, Pansophia, Pansophiah, Pansophie, Pansophy, Pansophya, Pansophyah

Pansy (Greek) flower; (French) thoughtful.

Pansea, Panseah, Pansee, Pansey, Pansi, Pansie, Pansya, Pansyah

Panthea (Greek) of all the gods.

Pantheah, Panthia, Panthiah, Panthya, Panthyah

Paola (Italian) small, a form of Paula.

Paolah, Paoli, Paolina, Paolinah, Paula

Paolina (Italian) small, a form of Paulina.

Paola, Paoleena, Paolinah

Papina (Native American) ivy, vine on oak tree.

Papinah, Papyna, Papynah

Paramita (Hindu) perfect, good.

Paramitah, Paramyta, Paramytah

Paris/Parris (French) from Paris, capital of France; (Greek) the Trojan warrior who abducted Helen and started a war, a unisex name.

Paras, Paree, Pares, Paresa, Parese, Parice, Parie, Parisa, Parise, Parish, Parisha, Pariss, Parissa, Parisse, Parras, Parree, Parres, Parresa, Parrese, Parris, Parrisa, Parrise, Parrish, Parrisha, Parrys, Paryse, Parryss, Parrysse, Parys, Paryss, Parysse

Parthenia (Greek) a virgin.

Partheenia, Parthena, Parthene, Partheniah, Parthenie, Parthenya, Parthenyah, Parthia, Parthienne, Parthinia

Parvati (Hindu) mountain climber.

Parvatee, Parvatey, Parvatia, Pavatiah, Parvatie, Parvaty

Parveneh (Persian) butterfly.

Pasang (Tibetan, Sherpa) child born on a Friday.

Pascale (Hebrew) born at Easter, feminine version of Pascal.

Pascal, Pascala, Pascalelle, Pascalia, Pascalina, Pascaline, Pascalle, Pascalline, Pascelle, Paschal, Paschala, Paschale, Paschalia, Paschalina, Paschaline, Paschalle, Paschalline, Paschelle, Pasqua, Pasquah, Pasquale

Passion (Latin) passionate.

Pashion, Pashonne, Pasion, Pasionette, Passionae

Patam (Hindu) city.

Patem, Patim, Patom, Pattam, Pattem, Pattim, Pattom, Pattym, Patym

Patia (Spanish) leaf.

Patiah, Patya, Patyah

Patience (English) patience, one of the seven virtues.

Patia, Patiencia, Patienna, Patienne, Patishia

Patricia (Latin) noble woman, feminine form of Patrick.

Pat, Patia, Patrece, Patresa,

Patrese, Patrice, Patricea, Patrickia, Patriece, Patrisa, Patrise, Patrisha, Patrisia, Patrizia, Patsi, Patsy, Pattrice, Pattsy, Patty, Payten, Payton, Peyten, Tissia, Tric, Tricia, Triciah, Trish, Trisha, Trishia, Trishiah

Paula (Latin) small, feminine form of Paul.

Pabla, Palika, Paliki, Paola, Paulette, Paulina, Pauline, Paulla, Paulle, Pavia, Pavla, Polly

Paulette (Latin) small, a form of Paula.

Paulet, Paulett, Pauletta, Paulita

Paulina (Spanish) small, a form of Paula.

Pabla, Paola, Paula, Pauleen, Pauleena, Paulena, Paulene, Paulenia, Paulette, Pauliana, Pauliane, Paulianna, Paulianne, Paulien, Pauliena, Paulin, Pauline, Paullena, Paullene, Paulyna, Paulyne, Paulynn, Paulynna, Paulynne, Polena, Polina, Polinia, Pouline

Pauline (French) small, a form of Paula.

Pabla, Paola, Paula, Pauleen, Paulena, Paulenia, Paulene, Paulette, Paulien, Paulin, Paulina, Paulyn, Paulyne, Paulynn, Paulynne, Pouline

Pavla (Slavic) small, a form of Paula.

Pavlah, Pavlina, Pavlinka

Payge (English) youthful assistant, young child.

Page, Paige

Payton (Irish) noble warrior's farm, a form of Patricia, a unisex name.

Paitan, Paiten, Paitin, Paiton, Paton, Paytan, Payten, Paytin, Peytan, Peyten, Peytin, Peyton

Paz (Spanish) peace, a unisex name.

Pazz

Pazia (Hebrew) golden child.

Paz, Paza, Pazah, Pazi, Paziah, Pazie, Pazise

Peace (Latin) tranquillity, peaceful child.

Pease, Peece, Peese

Peach (English) stone fruit that is soft and furry on the outside and sweet inside.

Peacha, Peachee, Peachey, Peachia, Peachy

Pearl (Latin) pearl, gem of the sea.

Pearla, Pearlah, Pearle, Pearlea, Pearleah, Pearlee, Pearlei, Pearleigh, Pearley, Pearli, Pearlie, Pearlina, Pearline, Pearly, Peri, Perl, Perla, Perlah, Perle, Perlea, Perleah, Perlee, Perlei, Perleigh, Perley, Perli, Perlie, Perlina, Perline, Perly

Peata (Maori) bringer of joy.

Peatah, Peeta, Peetah, Peita, Peitah, Peyta, Peytah, Pita, Pitah

Peggy (Greek) pearl, a form of Margaret.

Peg, Pegey, Pegg, Peggey, Peggi, Peggie, Pegi, Pegie, Pegy

Pelagia (Greek) sea.

Pelaga, Pelage, Pelageia, Pelagiah, Pelagie, Pelga, Pelgah, Pelgia, Pelgiah

Penda (African) loved.

Pendah

Penelope (Greek) weaver, penny coin.

Pena, Penah, Penee, Penelopa, Penelopea, Penelopee, Penelopey, Penelopi, Penelopia, Penelopiah, Penelopie, Penelopy, Peney, Peni,

Penia, Penie, Penna, Pennah, Pennee, Pennelopa, Pennelopea, Pennelopee, Pennelopey, Pennelopi, Pennelopia, Pennelopiah, Pennelopie, Pennelopy, Penney, Penni, Pennia, Pennie, Penny, Peny

Penny (Greek) weaver, a form of Penelope.

Peney, Peni, Penie, Penney, Penni, Pennie, Peny

Penthea (Greek) fifth-born child.

Pentheah, Penthia, Penthiah, Penthya, Penthyah

Peony (Greek) flower.

Peonee, Peoney, Peoni, Peonie

Pepita (Spanish) God shall add, increase, a form of Josephine.

Pepeeta, Pepeetah, Pepi, Pepida, Pepidah, Pepitah, Pepy, Pepyta, Pepytah

Pepper (Latin) from the pepper plant.

Pepa, Pepah, Pepi, Pepie, Peppa, Peppah, Peppar, Peppi, Peppie, Peppy, Pepy

Perdita (Latin) lost.

Perdi, Perdida, Perdie, Perditah, Perdy

Perfecta (Spanish) perfect one.

Perfect, Perfectah

Peri (Greek) mountain dweller.

Perea, Peree, Perey, Peria, Periah, Perie, Perita, Perrea, Perree, Perrey, Perri, Perria, Perriah, Perrie, Perry, Pery

Peridot (French) yellow-green gem.

Peridota, Peridotah, Perydot, Perydota, Perydotah

Perla (Spanish) pearl.

Perlah

Perpetua (Latin) constant.

Perpetea, Perpethea, Perpethia, Perpethua, Perpetia

Perri/Perry (Greek) small rock; (French) pear tree.

Peree, Peri, Perie, Perre, Perree, Perrie, Perrya, Perryah, Pery, Perya, Peryah

Persephone (Greek) goddess of the underworld.

Perci, Persefone, Persefoni, Persefonie, Persefonni, Persefonnie, Persephani, Persephanie, Persephany, Persephoni, Persephonie, Persi, Persofni, Persophany

Persis (Greek) from Persia, a unisex name.

Persi, Persian, Persiana, Persiann, Persianna, Persianne, Persys

Peta (Greek) rock, feminine form of Peter.

Peeta, Peetah, Peita, Peitah, Petah, Petra, Petrah, Petrea, Petreah

Petra (Greek) small rock, feminine form of Peter.

Patra, Peta, Petah, Petena, Peterina, Petrah, Petrann, Petranna, Petranne, Petrice, Petrina, Pier, Pierce, Pietra, Petrina

Petronella (Greek) small rock, a form of Petra.

Pernella, Pernelle, Peternella, Peternelle, Petronelja, Petronelle, Petronellia, Petronilla

Petula (Latin) seeker.

Petulah

Petunia (Latin) petunia flower.

Petuniah, Petunya, Petunyah

Peyton (English) noble warrior's town, a form of Patricia, a unisex name.

> Paeden, Paiten, Peyden, Peydon, Peyten

Phaedra (Greek) bright.

> Fay, Faye, Phadra, Phadrah, Phae, Phaedrah, Phaedre, Phaidra, Phaidrah, Phaidre, Phaie, Phay, Phaydra, Phaydrah, Phaydre, Phe, Phedra, Phedrah, Phedre

Phelia (Greek) immortal wisdom.

> Felia, Feliah, Felya, Felyah, Pheliah, Phelya, Phelyah

Philana (Greek) lover of humankind, feminine form of Philander.

> Phila, Philanna, Philanne, Philina, Philine, Phillina, Philline, Phylana, Phylanah, Phylane, Phyllan, Phyllana, Phyllanah, Phylane

Philantha (Greek) lover of flowers.

> Phila, Philanthe, Philanthia, Philena, Philene, Philina, Philine, Phinena

Philberta (English) brilliant, intelligent, feminine form of Philbert.

> Filberta, Filbertah, Filberte, Philbertah, Philberte, Phylbert, Phylberta, Phylbertah, Phylberte, Phyllberta, Phyllbertah, Phyllberte

Philippa (Greek) horse lover, feminine form of Philip.

> Felipa, Felipe, Felippa, Filipa, Filippa, Philipa, Philipah, Philippe, Philippina, Phillipa, Phillipah, Phillipe, Phillippa, Phylipa, Phylipah, Phyllipa, Phyllipah, Phyllypa, Phyllypah

Phillida (Greek) loving.

> Phillidah, Phillyda, Phillydah, Phyllida, Phyllidah

Philomela (Greek) lover of songs.

> Filomela, Filomelah, Philomelah, Phylomela, Phylomelah

Philomena (Greek) she is loved.

> Filamena, Filamina, Fillamena, Fillamina, Fillomena, Fillomene, Filomena, Filomene, Filomina, Filominah, Filominia, Filominiah, Filomyna, Filomynah, Filomyne, Mena, Phillomena, Phillomene, Philomenah, Philomene, Philomenia, Philomeniah, Philomina, Philominah, Philomine, Philominia, Philominiah

Phoebe (Greek) shining bright.

> Febe, Feebea, Feebee, Fibee, Phaebe, Pheba, Phebe, Phebea, Phebee, Pheby, Pheebea, Pheebee, Pheebey, Pheebie, Pheeby, Phoebea, Phoebee, Phoebey, Phoebie, Phoeby

Phoenix (Greek) an immortal bird who rose from its ashes every 500 years, a unisex name.

> Feenix, Foenix, Pheenix, Phenix, Phynix

Photina (Greek) light.

> Fotina, Fotinah Fotine, Photinah, Photine

Phyllis (Greek) green branch.

> Philis, Philise, Phillis, Phillise, Phylis, Phylise, Phyliss, Phylisse, Phyllise, Phylliss, Phyllisse

Pia (Italian) holy and prayerful, feminine form of Pius.

> Piah, Pya, Pyah

Piedad (Spanish) devoted.

Pier (French) small rock, feminine form of Pierre, Peter.

Pierette (French) small rock, feminine form of Pierre, Peter.

> Perett, Peretta, Perette, Pieret,

Pierett, Pieretta, Pierin, Pierina, Pierine, Pieryn, Pieryna, Pieryne

Pilar (Latin) pillar, column, a unisex name.
Peela, Peelah, Peelar, Peeler, Pilla, Pillar, Pylar, Pyllar

Pililani (Hawaiian) near to heaven.
Pililanee, Pililaney, Pililanie, Pililany

Pina (Spanish) pine.
Peena, Peenah, Pinah

Pineki (Hawaiian) peanut.
Pinekee, Pinekey, Pinekie, Pineky

Ping (Chinese) duckweed; (Vietnamese) peaceful.

Pinga (Hindu) bronze.
Pingah

Pinterry (Australian Aboriginal) star.
Pinterree, Pinterrey, Pinterri, Pinterrie

Piper (Anglo-Saxon) pipe player, a unisex name.
Pipa, Pipar, Pippa, Pipper, Pippor, Pypa, Pypah, Pyper, Pyppa, Pyppah

Pipipa (Australian Aboriginal) sand piper.
Pipipah, Pipypa, Pipypah, Pipyper, Pypipa, Pypipah, Pypiper

Pippa (Greek) horse lover, a form of Philipa.
Pipa, Pipah, Pipee, Pipey, Pipie, Pippah, Pippee, Pippen, Pippey, Pippie, Pippin, Pippy, Pipy

Pippi (French) rosy cheeks.
Pipee, Pipey, Pipi, Pipie, Pippee, Pippey, Pippie, Pippin, Pippy, Pipy

Pita (African) fourth-born child.
Peeta, Peetah, Pitah, Pyta, Pytah

Pixie (English) fairy or sprite.
Pixee, Pixey, Pixi, Pixxee, Pixxey, Pixxi, Pixxie, Pixxy, Pixy

Placida (Latin) calm, serene.
Placidah, Placide, Placidea, Placidia, Placidiah, Placyda, Placydah

Platona (Greek) broad, strong shoulders, feminine form of Plato.
Platonah, Platonia, Platoniah, Platonya, Platonyah

Pleasance (French) agreeable.
Pleasa, Pleasann, Plesanse, Pleaza, Pleazance, Pleazann, Pleazanse

Pocahontas (Native American) playful.
Pocohonta

Poeta (English) poetry.
Poetah, Poetrea, Poetree, Poetri, Poetria, Poetriah

Polly (English) small, a form of Paula.
Pal, Pali, Pauli, Paulie, Paullie, Paully, Pauly, Pol, Polea, Poleah, Polee, Polei, Poleigh, Poley, Poli, Polie, Poll, Pollea, Polleah, Pollee, Pollei, Polleigh, Polley, Polli, Pollie, Poly

Pollyanna (English) combination of Polly and Anna.
Poliana, Polianna, Polliana, Pollianna, Pollyana, Polyana, Polyanna

Poloma (Native American) bow.
Polomah, Polome

Polyxena (Greek) welcoming.
Polyxeena, Polyxeenah, Polyxenah, Polyxina, Polyxinah, Polyxyna, Polyxynah, Polyzeena, Polyzeenah,

*Polyzena, Polyzenah, Polyzina,
Polyzinah, Polyzyna, Polyzynah*

Pomona (Latin) apple.
*Pomma, Pommah, Pomme, Pommi,
Pommona, Pommonah, Pommone,
Pomonah, Pomone*

Poni (African) second-born child.
*Ponee, Poney, Ponie, Ponnee,
Ponney, Ponni, Ponnie, Ponny, Pony*

Poppy (Latin) red poppy flower.
*Popea, Popeah, Popee, Popey,
Popi, Popie, Poppea, Poppeah,
Poppee, Poppey, Poppi, Poppie,
Popy*

Pora (Hebrew) fruitful.
Porah, Poria, Poriah, Porya, Poryah

Portia (Latin) offering.
*Porcha, Porchah, Porche, Porcia,
Porscha, Porschah, Porsche,
Porschia, Porschiah, Porsha,
Porshah, Porshay, Porshe, Porshia,
Porshiah, Porteia, Porzia*

Posy (English) bunch of flowers.
*Poesee, Poesey, Poesi, Poesia,
Poesiah, Poesie, Poesy, Posee,
Posey, Posi, Posia, Posiah, Posie*

Preciosa (Latin) precious.
*Preciosah, Precious, Prescious,
Preshious, Preshus*

Premilla (Hindu) loving girl.
*Premila, Premilah, Premillah,
Premyla, Premylah, Premylla,
Premyllah*

Prima (Latin) first-born child,
feminine form of Primo.
*Preema, Prema, Primalia, Primetta,
Primina, Priminia*

Primavera (Italian, Spanish)
springtime, a child of the spring.
Primaverah

Primrose (English) primrose flower.
Primrosa, Primula

Princess (English) daughter of
queen and king.
*Princesa, Princessa, Princesse,
Pryncess, Pryncessah, Pryncesse*

Priscilla (Latin) ancient.
*Cilla, Precila, Precilla, Prescila,
Prescilla, Presila, Presilia, Presilla,
Presillia, Pressila, Pressilia, Pressilla,
Pressillia, Priscela, Priscella, Priscill,
Priscille, Priscillia, Priscillie, Prisella,
Prisellia, Prisila, Prisilla, Prissila, Prissilla*

Priya (Hindu) beloved,
sweet-natured.
Preeya, Preeyah, Pria, Priah, Priyah

Prospera (Latin) favourable,
prosperous, feminine form of
Prosper.
*Prosperah, Prosperia, Prosperiah,
Prosperitee, Prosperitey, Prosperiti,
Prosperitie, Prosperity*

Prudence (Latin) virtue, cautious,
discreet.
*Prudencia, Prudens, Prudense,
Prudensia, Prudenza, Prudy, Prue*

Prunella (Latin) plum-colored.
*Prunel, Prunela, Prunelah, Prunele,
Prunell, Prunellah, Prunelle*

Psyche (Greek) soul.
*Psychee, Psychey, Psychie, Psychy,
Psyke*

Pua (Hawaiian) flower.
Puah

Pualani (Hawaiian) heavenly
flower.
*Pualanee, Pualaney, Pualania,
Pualaniah, Pualanie, Pualany*

Pulcheria (Latin) great beauty.
Pulcheriah, Pulcherie

Purity (English) purity.

Puritee, Puritey, Puriti, Puritia,
Puritiah, Puritie, Puritya, Purityah

Pythia (Greek) high priestess,
prophet.

Pithea, Pitheah, Pithia, Pithiah,
Pithya, Pithyah, Pythea, Pytheah,
Pythiah, Pythya, Pythyah

Qadesh (Egyptian) Egyptian goddess.

Qadesha, Qadeshah, Quedesh, Quedesha, Quedeshah

Qadira (Arabic) powerful.

Kadira, Kadirah, Qadirah, Qadyra, Qadyrah

Qamra (Arabic) moon.

Kamra, Kamrah, Qamrah, Qammra, Qammrah

Qi (Chinese) jade, fine and distinguished.

Qing (Chinese) blue.

Qing Yuan (Chinese) clear spring, deep water.

Qitara (Arabic) fragrant.

Kitara, Kitarah, Qitarah, Qytara, Qytarah

Quaashie (African) born on a Sunday.

Quaashi, Quaashy, Quashi, Quashie, Quashy

Quanika (American) combination of prefix Qu and Nika.

Quanikah, Quanikka, Quaniqua, Quanique, Quannika, Quannikki, Quantenique, Quanyka, Quanykki, Quanyque, Quawanica, Quawanyca, Queenika, Queenique

Quarralia (Australian Aboriginal) star.

Quaralia, Quaraliah, Quaralya, Quaralyah, Quarraliah, Quarralya, Quarralyah

Quartas (Latin) fourth child.

Quarta, Quartah

Quartilla (Latin) fourth child.

Quantila, Quantilla, Quartila, Quartilah, Quartile, Quartillah, Quartille, Quartyla, Quartylah, Quartyle, Quartylla, Quartyllah, Quartylle

Qubilah (Arabic) agreeable.

Quabila, Quabilah, Quabilla, Quabillah, Quabyla, Quabylah, Quabylla, Quabyllah, Qubila, Qubilla, Qubillah, Qubyla, Qubylah, Qubylla, Qubyllah

Queena (English) form of the royal English title, queen.

Queenah, Queenee, Queenia, Queeniah, Queenie, Queeny

Queenie (English) queen.

Quean, Queana, Queanee, Queaney, Queani, Queania, Queaniah, Queanie, Queany, Queanya, Queanyah, Queen, Queena, Queenee, Queeneste, Queenetta, Queenette, Queeney, Queeni, Queenia, Queeniah, Queenika, Queenique, Queeny, Queenya, Queenyah, Quenna

Quella (English) to pacify.

Quela, Quelah, Quele, Quellah, Quelle

Quenby (Scandinavian) feminine.

Queenbea, Queenbee, Queenbey, Queenbi, Queenbie, Queenby, Queenbye, Quenbea, Quenbee, Quenbey, Quenbi, Quenbie, Quenbye

Quenisha (American) combination of Queenie and Aisha.

Quanecia, Quanesha, Quanesia, Quanisha, Quanishia, Quansha, Quarnisha, Queeneesha, Queisha, Queniesha, Quenisha, Quenishia, Quennisha, Qynisha

Querida (Portuguese, Spanish) beloved, much loved.
Quereeda, Queridah

Questa (French) one who seeks.
Questah

Queta (Spanish) ruler of the house.
Quetah

Quiana (American) combination of prefix Qu and Anna.
Quianah, Quiane, Quiani, Quiann, Quianna, Quiannah, Quianne, Quyana, Quyanah, Quyane, Quyann, Quyanna, Quyannah, Quyanne

Quinby (Scandinavian) estate of the queen.
Quinbea, Quinbee, Quinbey, Quinbi, Quinbia, Quinbie, Quynbea, Quynbee, Quynbey, Quynbi, Quynbia, Quynbie, Quynby

Quincy (Irish, Latin) fifth, a unisex name.
Quincee, Quincey, Quinci, Quincia, Quincie, Quinncee, Quinncey, Quinnci, Quinncia, Quinncie, Quinncy, Quinsey, Quyncee, Quyncey, Quynci, Quyncia, Quyncie, Quyncy, Quynncee, Quynncey, Quynnci, Quynncia, Quynncie, Quynncy, Quynsy

Quinlan (Irish) well-formed, very strong, athletic, a unisex name.
Quinlann, Quinlanne, Quinlanna, Quinlen, Quinlena, Quinlin, Quinlina, Quinlyn, Quinlyna

Quinn (Latin) fifth; (German) queen; (Celtic) advisor, counsellor; a unisex name.
Quin, Quina, Quinah, Quinna, Quinnah, Quinne, Quinnee, Quinney, Quinnie, Quinny, Quiyn, Quyn, Quynn

Quinta (Latin) fifth child.
Quintah, Quintana, Quintanah, Quintane, Quintann, Quintanna, Quintannah, Quintanne, Quintila, Quintilah, Quintile, Quintilla, Quintillah, Quintille, Quintyla, Quintylah, Quintyle, Quintylla, Quintyllah, Quintylle, Quynta, Quyntah, Quyntana, Quyntanah, Quyntann, Quyntanna, Quyntannah, Quyntanne, Quyntila, Quyntilah, Quyntile, Quyntilla, Quyntillah, Quyntille, Quyntyla, Quyntylah, Quyntyle, Quyntylla, Quyntyllah, Quyntylle

Quintessa (Latin) essence.
Quintaysha, Quintesa, Quintesah, Quintesha, Quintessah, Quintesse, Quintessia, Quintice, Quinticia, Quintisha, Quintissa, Quintosha, Quyntessa, Quyntessah, Quyntesse

Quintrell (American) combination of Quinn and Trella.
Quintrela, Quintrella, Quintrelle

Quipolly (Australian Aboriginal) water full of fish.
Quipoly, Quypolly, Quypoly

Quiteria (French, Latin) tranquil.
Quita, Quitah, Quiteree, Quiteri, Quiteriah, Quiterie, Quitery, Quyteree, Quyteri, Quyteria, Quyteriah, Quyterie, Quytery

Quoba (Australian Aboriginal) good.
Quobi, Quobie, Kwobi

R

Raanana (Hebrew) fresh, feminine form of Raanan.
Raananah, Ranana, Rananah

Rabab (Arabic) white cloud.
Rababa, Rababah

Rabi (Arabic) fragrant breeze, a unisex name.
Rabbi, Rabee, Rabeeh, Rabeh, Rabia, Rabiah, Rabie, Rabih, Raby, Rabya, Rabyah

Rabia (Arabic) born in springtime.
Rabbia, Rabbiah, Rabiah, Rabi'ah

Rachael/Rachel (Hebrew) ewe, lamb, wife of Jacob and mother of Joseph.
Rach, Racha, Rachal, Rachala, Racheal, Racheala, Rachela, Rachelah, Rachele, Rachella, Rachelle, Racquel, Rae, Raecha, Raechah, Raechel, Raechela, Rahel, Rahela, Rahil, Rahila, Raiche, Raichel, Raichela, Raquel, Raquela, Rashel, Rashelle, Ray, Raycel, Raycene, Raychel, Raychelle, Reichal, Reichel, Rey, Reychel, Ruchel

Rachelle (French) ewe, lamb, a form of Rachael.
Rachal, Rachale, Rachall, Rachalle, Rachel, Rachele, Rachell, Rachella, Raechell, Raechelle, Raeshel, Raeshele, Raeshell, Raeshelle, Rashel, Rashele, Rashell, Rashelle, Raychel, Raychele, Raychell, Raychelle, Rayshel, Rayshele, Rayshell, Rayshelle, Ruchelle

Racquel (French) ewe, lamb, a form of Rachael.
Rackel, Racquela, Racquele, Racquell, Racquella, Racquelle, Raquel, Raquela, Raquele, Raquell, Raquella, Raquelle

Rada (Slavic) glad, happy.
Radah

Radella (English) an adviser, counsellor.
Radela, Radelah, Radelia, Radeliah, Radellah, Radelle, Radyla, Radylah, Radylla, Radyllah, Radyllya, Radyllyah, Radylya, Radylyah

Radeyah (Arabic) content, satisfied.
Radeeya, Radeeyah, Radeya, Radhiya, Radhiyah, Radia, Radiah, Radiya, Radiyah

Radha (Hindu) success.

Radinka (Slavic) joyful, active, playful.
Radinkah, Radinki, Radynka, Radynkah

Radmilla (Slavic) hard worker for the people.
Radmil, Radmila, Radmilah, Radmile, Radmill, Radmillah, Radmille

Radwa (Arabic) mountain.
Radwah

Rae (English) doe, a form of Rachel, Raelene.
Raeh, Raeniece, Raeniesha, Raesha, Ray, Raya, Raye, Rayette, Rayma, Rey

Raeanna (American) combination of Rae and Anne.
Raea, Raean, Raeana, Raeanah,

Raeannah, Raeanne, Raeona, Reanna, Reannah, Reanne

Raelene (English) a form of Rae, an invented name.

Raelean, Raeleana, Raeleanah, Raeleane, Raeleen, Raeleena, Raeleenah, Raeleene, Raeleigh, Raelien, Raelina, Raeshia, Railean, Raileana, Raileanah, Raileane, Raileen, Raileena, Raileenah, Raileene, Raileigh, Railien, Railiena, Railina, Railine, Ralean, Raleana, Raleanah, Raleane, Raleen, Raleena, Raleenah, Raleene, Raleigh, Ralien, Raliena, Ralin, Ralina, Ralinah, Raline, Raylean, Rayleana, Rayleanah, Rayleane, Rayleen, Rayleena, Rayleenah, Rayleene, Rayleigh, Raylena, Raylenah, Raylene, Raylien, Rayliena, Raylina, Rayline

Raelyn (American) combination of Rae and Lyn.

Rae, Raelin, Raelina, Raelinda, Raeline, Raelynda, Raelyne, Raelynne

Raeven (English) black bird, a form of blackbird.

Raevan, Raevin, Raevon, Raevonne, Raewyn, Raivan, Raiven, Raivin, Raivon, Raivonne, Raiwyn, Ravan, Raven, Ravin, Ravon, Ravonne, Rawyn, Rayvan, Rayven, Rayvin, Rayvon, Rayvonne, Raywyn

Rafa (Arabic) prosperous, happy.
Rafah, Raffa, Raffah

Rafaela (Hebrew) God has healed, blessed healer, feminine form of Rafael.

Rafaele, Rafaella, Rafaelle, Raffeala, Raffeale, Raffealla, Raffealle, Raphaela, Raphaele, Raphaella, Raphaelle

Ragan (Irish) little ruler, a form of Reagan.

Ragean, Rageanne, Rageen, Ragen, Ragena, Ragene, Rageni, Ragenna, Raggan, Raygan, Raygen, Raygene, Raygin

Rahab (Hebrew) wide, spacious.

Raheema (Arabic) merciful, compassionate, feminine form of Rahim.

Raheem, Raheemah, Rahima, Rahimah

Rahel (Hebrew) ewe, lamb, a form of Rachael.
Rahela, Rahelah

Raidah (Arabic) leader, ruler, feminine form of Raid.

Raeda, Raedah, Raida, Ra'idah, Raiida, Raiidah

Raina (German) mighty ruler.

Raeina, Raeinna, Raena, Raenah, Raheena, Rain, Rainah, Rainai, Raine, Rainea, Rainee, Rainey, Raini, Rainie, Rainna, Rainy, Reanna, Reyne

Rainbow (English) array of bright colours, rainbow.

Raenbo, Raenbow, Rainbeau, Rainbeaux, Rainbo, Raynbow

Raisa (Hebrew) rose.

Raisah, Raissa, Raissah, Raisse, Raiza, Raizah, Rasa, Rasah, Raysa, Rayza, Razia

Raizel (Hebrew) rose.

Raisah, Raisal, Raissa, Raissal, Raiza, Raizal, Rayza, Rayzal, Razil, Rayzil, Reizel, Resel

Raja (Arabic) hopeful.
Raia, Rajaa, Rajaah, Rajae, Rajah, Rajai

Rajani (Hindu) evening, of the night.

Rajanee, Rajaney, Rajanie, Rajany

Rakel (Scandinavian) ewe, lamb, a form of Rachael.

Rakele, Rakell, Rakelle

Raku (Japanese) pleasure.

Ramla (African) one who predicts the future.

Ramlah

Ramona (Spanish) a wise protector, the feminine form of Ramon, Raymond.

Raemona, Raemonah, Raimona, Raimonah, Raimone, Ramana, Ramanah, Ramonah, Ramonda, Raymona, Raymonah, Romona, Romonah, Romonda

Ramosa (Latin) branch.

Ramosah, Ramose

Ramya (Hindu) beautiful, elegant.

Ramia, Ramiah, Ramyah, Ramyia, Ramyiah, Remia, Remiah, Remya, Remyah

Ran (Japanese) water lily; (Scandinavian) sea goddess.

Rann, Ranne

Rana (Hindu) royal.

Raena, Rahna, Rahni, Ranah, Rani, Rayna

Ranait (Irish) graceful.

Ranaita, Ranaitah, Ranaite, Ranayt, Ranayta, Ranaytah, Ranayte

Randa (Arabic) tree.

Randah

Randa/Randi/Randie (English) wolf, shield, a form of Miranda, feminine form of Randall.

Rande, Randee, Randeen, Randey, Randii, Randy

Rane (Scandinavian) queen.

Raen, Raena, Raenah, Raene, Raenia, Rana, Ranah, Ranee, Rania, Rayn, Rayna, Raynah, Rayne, Raynia

Rangi (Maori) heaven or the sky, a unisex name.

Rangee, Rangey, Ranghi, Rangia, Rangiah, Rangie, Rangy

Rani/Rania (Hindu) a queen.

Raen, Raena, Raenah, Raene, Raenee, Raeney, Raeni, Raenia, Raeniah, Raenie, Raeny, Raenya, Raenyah, Rain, Raina, Rainah, Raine, Rainee, Rainey, Raini, Rainia, Rainiah, Rainie, Rainy, Rainya, Rainyah, Rana, Ranah, Rane, Ranee, Raney, Rania, Raniah, Ranie, Rany, Ranya, Ranyah, Rayn, Rayna, Raynah, Rayne, Raynee, Rayney, Rayni, Raynia, Rayniah, Raynie, Rayny, Raynya, Raynyah

Ranita (Hebrew) my song of happiness, joyful song, feminine form of Rani.

Raneat, Raneata, Raneatah, Raneate, Raneatt, Raneatta, Raneattah, Raneatte, Raneet, Raneeta, Raneetah, Raneete, Raneett, Raneetta, Raneettah, Raneette, Raniita, Raniitah, Ranit, Ranitah, Ranite, Ranitt, Ranitta, Ranittah, Ranitte, Ranta, Rantah, Rantta, Ranttah, Ranyta, Ranytah, Ranyte, Ranytta, Ranyttah, Ranytte

Raniyah (Arabic) gazing.

Ranee, Raney, Rani, Raniya, Rany, Ranyia, Ranyiah

Rapa (Hawaiian) moonbeam.

Rapah

Raphaela (Hebrew) the divine healer, healed by God, feminine form of Raphael.

Raefaela, Raefaella, Raefaelle, Raephaela, Raephaella, Raephaelle, Rafaela, Rafaella, Rafaelle, Rafela, Rafella, Rafelle,

Raphaella, Raphaelle, Raphela, Raphella, Raphelle, Raphiela, Raphiella, Raphielle

Raquel (French) ewe, lamb, a form of Rachael.

Rakel, Rakhil, Rakhila, Raqueal, Raqueala, Raquela, Raquell, Raquella, Raquelle, Rickelle, Rickquel, Rickquella, Rickquelle, Ricquel, Ricquella, Ricquelle, Rikell, Rikelle

Rasa (Slavic) morning dew.

Rasah, Rasi

Rasha (Arabic) young gazelle.

Rashae, Rashah, Rashai, Rashea, Rashi, Rashia

Rashida (Arabic) wise, righteous, a unisex name.

Rashda, Rashdah, Rashea, Rasheda, Rashedah, Rasheeda, Rasheedah, Rasheedia, Rashidah, Rashidi, Rashieda

Rashieka (Arabic) descended from royalty.

Rasheeka, Rasheekah, Rasheika, Rasheikah, Rasheka, Rashekah, Rashika, Rashikah

Rasia (Greek) rose.

Rasi, Rasiah, Rassi, Rassia, Rassiah, Rassy, Rassya, Rassyah

Rata (Australian Aboriginal) plant.

Rataana, Ratah, Rataj

Ratana (Thai) crystal.

Ratanah, Ratania, Rataniah, Ratanya, Rattan, Rattana, Ratttanah, Rattane, Rattanya

Rati (Hindu) love.

Ratee, Ratey, Ratie, Ratii, Raty

Ratna (Hindu) a precious jewel.

Ratnah

Ratri (Hindu) night.

Ratree, Ratrey, Ratria, Ratriah, Ratrie, Ratry, Ratrya, Ratryah

Raula (French) wolf counsellor, feminine form of Raoul.

Raola, Roalah, Raole, Raolla, Raollah, Raolle, Raoula, Raoulah, Raoule, Raoulla, Raoullah, Raoulle, Raulah, Raule, Raulla, Raullah, Raulle

Raven (English) raven, blackbird, a unisex name.

Raevan, Raeven, Raevin, Raevon, Ravee, Raveen, Raveena, Raveenah, Revena, Ravenah, Ravenn, Ravenna, Ravennah, Ravenne, Ravi, Ravin, Ravina, Ravinah, Ravine, Ravinn, Ravinna, Ravinnah, Ravinne, Ravion, Ravyn, Ravyna, Ravynah, Ravynn, Ravynna, Ravynnah

Rawnie (Romanian) fine lady.

Rawna, Rawnah, Rawnee, Rawney, Rawni, Rawnia, Rawniah, Rawnii, Rawny, Rawnya, Rawnyah, Rhawna, Rhawnah, Rhawnee, Rhawney, Rhawni, Rhawnia, Rhawniah, Rhawnie, Rhawnii, Rhawny, Rhawnya, Rhawnyah

Raya (Hebrew) friend.

Rae, Raia, Raiah, Raiya, Raiyah, Rayah, Rayya, Rayyah

Rayanne (American) combination of Rae and Anne.

Raeana, Raenanah, Rae-Ann, Raeann, Raeanna, Raeanne, Rayana, Rayanah, Rayane, Rayann, Ray-Ann, Rayanna, Reana, Reanah, Reane, Reann, Reanna, Reannah, Reanne, Reiana, Reianah, Reiane, Reianna, Reiannah, Reianne, Reyana, Reyanah, Reyane, Reyann, Reyanna, Reyannah, Reyanne

Raymonde (German) wise protector, feminine form of Raymond.

Rayma, Raymae, Raymah, Raymie, Raymonda

Rayna (Scandinavian) mighty; (Hebrew) pure.

Rayana, Rayanah, Raynah, Rayne, Raynelle, Rayni, Raynia, Rayniah, Raynie, Rayny, Raynya, Raynyah, Reina, Reinah, Reyna, Reynah

Razi (Aramaic) secret.

Razie, Razy, Razz, Razzi, Razzie, Razzy

Raziya (African) agreeable.

Razia, Raziah, Raziyah

Rea (Greek) poppy flower.

Reah, Rhea

Reagan (Irish) little ruler, a unisex name.

Raygan, Raygen, Raygene, Rayghan, Raygin, Raygine, Raygon, Raygyn, Reagen, Reagene, Reaghan, Reagin, Reagine, Reagon, Reagyn, Reigan, Reigana, Reiganah, Reigane, Reygan, Reygana, Reyganah, Reygane

Reba (Hebrew) bound, faithful, a form of Rebecca, fourth-born child, fourth part.

Reaba, Reabah, Rebah, Rebecca, Rebekah, Reeba, Reebah, Reiba, Reibah, Reyba, Reybah

Rebecca (Hebrew) bound, faithful, one who is emotionally tied for life, wife of Isaac in the Bible.

Bec, Beca, Becca, Beck, Becky, Rabbeca, Rabbecah, Rabbecca, Rabbeccah, Rabeca, Rabecah, Rabecca, Rabeccah, Reba, Rebbeca, Rebbecah, Rebbecca, Rebbeccah, Rebeca, Rebecah, Rebeccah, Rebeccea, Rebecckah, Rebecha, Rebechah, Rebecka, Rebeckah, Rebecqua, Rebecquah, Rebecque, Rebeka, Rebekah, Rebekka, Rebekkah, Rebekke, Rebequa, Rebequah, Rebeque, Riva, Rivah, Rivka, Rivkah

Rebekah (Hebrew) bound, faithful, one who is emotionally tied for life, a form of Rebecca.

Bec, Beca, Becca, Beck, Becky, Rabbeca, Rabbecah, Rabbecca, Rabbeccah, Rabeca, Rabecah, Rabecca, Rabeccah, Reba, Rebbeca, Rebbecah, Rebbecca, Rebbeccah, Rebeca, Rebecah, Rebecca, Rebeccah, Rebeccea, Rebecckah, Rebecha, Rebechah, Rebecka, Rebeckah, Rebecqua, Rebecquah, Rebecque, Rebeka, Rebekka, Rebekkah, Rebekke, Rebequa, Rebequah, Rebeque, Riva, Rivah, Rivka, Rivkah

Rebel (Latin) rebellious one, a unisex name.

Rebal, Rebala, Reball, Reballa, Rebell, Rebella, Rebelle, Rebyl

Redempta (Latin) redeemed.

Reena (Greek) peaceful.

Rean, Reana, Reanah, Reane, Reen, Reenah, Reene, Reenia, Reeniah, Reenie, Reenya, Reina, Reinah, Reine, Rena, Renah, Rene, Reyna, Reynah, Reyne, Rina, Rinah

Reese (Welsh) ardent, enthusiastic, a unisex name.

Reece, Rees, Reis, Reise, Rhys, Rhyse, Rys, Ryse

Reet/Reeta (Slavic) pearl, a form of Margaret.

Reat, Reata, Reatah, Reate, Reath, Reatha, Reathe, Reetah, Reete, Reit, Reita, Reitah, Reite, Reta, Retah, Retha, Rethah, Reyt, Reyta, Reytah, Reyte

Regan (Irish) little ruler, a form of Reagan, a unisex name.

Raegan, Raegane, Reagann, Reaganne, Reagan, Reagana, Reaganah, Reagane, Regana, Reganah, Regane, Regann, Reganne, Reghan

Regina (Latin) royal queen.

Gina, Jean, Jeana, Jenny, Jina, Rane, Ranee, Rania, Rega, Regan, Regana, Reganah, Regane, Regeana, Regeanah, Regeane, Regeena, Regeenah, Regeene, Regenna, Regennah, Regennie, Reggie, Regi, Regia, Regiah, Regin, Reginah, Regine, Regis, Reina, Rena, Reygin, Reygina, Reyginah, Reygine, Reygyn, Reygyna, Reygynah, Reygyne, Reyna, Reynah

Rei (Japanese) well-behaved, polite.

Reiko (Japanese) grateful.

Reilly (Irish) valiant, a form of Riley, a unisex name.

Reilee, Reiley, Reilie, Reillee, Reilley, Reily, Rhilee, Rhiley, Rhilie, Rhillee, Rhilley, Rhillie, Rhilly, Rhily, Rhylee, Rhyley, Rhylie, Rhyllee, Rhylley, Rhyllie, Rhylly, Rhyly, Rilee, Rilie, Rillee, Rilley, Rillie, Rylee, Ryley, Rylie, Ryllee, Rylley, Ryllie, Rylly, Ryly

Reina (Spanish) ruler, queen.

Rain, Raina, Rayn, Rayna, Reana, Reanah, Reane, Reena, Reenah, Reene, Rein, Reinah, Reine, Reiny, Rene, Renia, Reniah, Reyna, Reyne

Reine (Latin, French) queen.

Rain, Raine, Rein, Reina, Reinah, Reinie, Renina, Reinna, Reiona, Rina

Reka (Maori) sweet.

Rekah

Rekha (Hindu) fine, thin line.

Reka, Rekah, Rekia, Rekiah, Rekiya

Remy (French) from Rheims, France.

Remee, Remi, Remie, Remmi, Remmie, Remmy

Ren (Japanese) beautiful lotus, water lily.

Rene, Renn, Renne

Rena (Greek) joyous song, peaceful, a form of Irene.

Reana, Reanah, Reanna, Reannah, Reena, Reenah, Reenna, Reennah, Reina, Reinah, Reinna, Reinnah, Rina, Rinah, Rinna, Rinnah

Renae (French) reborn, a form of Renee.

Ranata, Ren, Rena, Renah, Renai, Renaia, Renaiah, Renata, Renatah, Renate, Renatta, Renay, Renaya, Renayah, Renaye, Rene, Renea, Reneah, Renee, Renita, Renitah, Renite, Renitta, Renittah, Renitte, Renna, Rennah, Rennae, Rennah, Rennay, Rennaya, Rennaye, Renne, Rennea, Renneah, Rinada, Rinata

Renata (French) born again.

Ranata, Reinet, Reineta, Reinetah, Reinete, Reinett, Reinetta, Reinettah, Reinette, Renada, Renadah, Renatah, Renate, Renatta, Renattah, Rennie

Rene (French) reborn, a form of Renee; (Greek) peace, a form of Irene, a unisex name.

Reen, Reenie, Renay, Renee, Reney, Renie, Rennay, Renne, Rennee, Rennie

Renee (French) reborn.

Ranae, Ranata, Ren, Rena, Renae, Renah, Renai, Renaia, Renaiah, Renata, Renatah, Renate, Renatta, Renay, Renaya, Renayah, Renaye, Rene, Renea, Reneah, Renita, Renitah, Renite, Renitta, Renittah, Renitte, Renna, Rennae, Rennah, Rennay, Rennaya, Rennaye, Renne, Rennea, Renneah, Rinada, Rinata

Renita (French) reborn, a form of Renata.

Ranata, Reinet, Reineta, Reinete, Reinett, Reinetta, Reinettah, Reinette, Reinita, Reinite, Renada, Renatah, Renate, Renatta, Renattah, Reneeta, Renetta, Renettah, Renette, Renitah, Renite, Renitza, Rennie

Rennie (English) born again, a form of Renata.

Reni, Renie, Renni, Renny, Reny

Rere (Maori) watchful.

Reree

Reseda (Spanish) mignonette flower.

Reseada, Reseadah, Resedah, Reseeda, Reseedah, Resida, Residah, Resyda, Resydah

Resi (German) harvester, a form of Theresa.

Resee, Resey, Resia, Resie, Ressa, Resse, Ressee, Ressey, Ressi, Ressia, Ressie, Ressy, Resy, Reza, Rezee, Rezey, Rezi, Rezie, Rezka, Rezy

Reta (African) shaken.

Reata, Reatah, Reate, Reatee, Reatey, Reati, Reatie, Reatta, Reattah, Reaty, Reeta, Reetah, Reita, Reitah, Reitta, Reittah, Retah, Retee, Retta, Rettah, Reyta, Reytah, Reytta, Reyttah, Rheata, Rheatah, Rheta, Rhetah, Rhetta, Rhettah

Reubena (Hebrew) behold a daughter, feminine form of Reuben.

Reubana, Reubanah, Reubania, Reubaniah, Reubenah, Reubenia, Reubeniah, Reubina, Reubinah, Reubinia, Reubiniah, Rubana, Rubanah, Rubania, Rubaniah, Rubena, Rubenah, Rubenia, Rubeniah, Rubina, Rubinah, Rubine, Rubinia, Rubiniah

Reva (Latin) renewed strength, revived.

Ree, Reeva, Riva, Revia, Revida

Rewa (Polynesian) slender.

Rewah

Rewuri (Australian Aboriginal) spring.

Rewuree, Rewurey, Rewurie, Rewury

Rexanne (American) queen, royalty.

Rex, Rexan, Rexana, Rexann, Rexanna

Reyhan (Turkish) sweet smelling flower.

Reihan, Reihana, Reihanah, Reihane, Reyhana, Reyhanah, Reyhane

Reynalda (Anglo-Saxon) advisor to the king, feminine form of Reynold.

Reynaldia, Reyann, Reyanne

Rez (Slavic) auburn hair.

Rezz

Rhea (Greek) flowing brook, stream, the mother of Zeus.

Rhealin, Rheana, Rheanah, Rheann, Rheanna, Rheanne, Rhia, Rhiana

Rhedyn (Welsh) fern.

Readan, Readen, Readin, Readon, Readyn, Reedan, Reeden, Reedin, Reedon, Reedyn, Rheadan, Rheaden, Rheadin, Rheadon, Rheadyn, Rhedan, Rheden, Rhedin, Rhedon, Rheedan, Rheeden, Rheedin, Rheedon, Rheedyn

Rhiannon (Welsh) goddess, nymph, sorceress.

Rheanan, Rheanin, Rheannan, Rheannin, Rheannon, Rheanon,

Rhian, Rhianan, Rhianen,
Rhiannan, Rhiannen, Rhianon,
Rhianyn, Rhinnon, Rhyanan,
Rhyanen, Rhyanna, Rhyannan,
Rhyannen, Rhyannon, Rhyanon,
Riana, Rianan, Rianen, Riannan,
Riannen, Riannon, Rianon, Ryanan,
Ryanen, Ryanin, Ryanon, Ryanyn

Rhoda (Greek) a beautiful rose.

Rhod, Rhode, Rhodee, Rhodi,
Rhodie, Rhodina, Rhody, Roda,
Rodee, Rodi, Rodie, Rodina

Rhona (Celtic) rough island,
powerful, mighty.

Rhonae, Rhonna, Rhonnae,
Rhonnie, Rona, Ronna, Rowna,
Rownna

Rhonda (Celtic) grand.

Rhondda, Ronda, Ronnette

Rhonwen (Welsh) white lance,
white hair, white skirt.

Rhonwyn, Ronwen, Ronwyn

Ria (Spanish) river.

Rhia, Rhiah, Rhya, Rhyah, Riah, Rya,
Ryah

Rianna (Irish) virtuous, a form of
Briana.

Reann, Reanna, Reanne, Rhianna,
Rhianne, Rhyanna, Rhyanne,
Riana, Riane, Rianah, Rianne

Rica (Spanish) shortened form of
names ending in 'rica', for example
Erica, Frederica.

Ricah, Ricca, Rieca, Rieka, Riecka,
Rika, Rikka

Ricarda (Teutonic) powerful ruler,
feminine form of Richard.

Rica, Ricah, Ricardah, Ricardia,
Ricca, Riccah, Riccarda,
Riccardah, Riccardia, Richa,
Richarda, Richardah, Richardia,
Richardina, Richi, Rickarda,
Rickardah, Ricki, Rikarda, Rikardah,

Rikki, Ritcharda, Ritchardia,
Rycarda, Rycardah, Ryccarda,
Ryccardah, Ryckarda, Ryckardah,
Rykarda, Rykardah

Richelle (German, French)
powerful ruler, feminine form of
Richard.

Richel, Richela, Richelah, Richele,
Richell, Richella, Richellah, Richi,
Rishel, Rishela, Risehelah, Risehele,
Rishell, Rishella, Rishellah, Rishelle

Rickma (Hebrew) woven.

Rickmah, Ricma, Ricmah, Ryckma,
Ryckmah, Rykma, Rykmah

Rida (Arabic) favoured by God.

Ridah, Ruda, Ryda, Rydah

Rihana (Arabic) sweet basil.

Rika (Swedish) ruler.

Rhica, Rhicah, Rhicca, Rhiccah,
Rhika, Rhikah, Rhikka, Rhikkah,
Rica, Ricah, Ricca, Riccah, Ricka,
Rickah, Rikah, Rikka, Rikkah, Riqua,
Riquah, Ryca, Rhycah, Rycca,
Ryccah, Rycka, Ryckah, Ryka,
Rykah, Rykka, Rykkah

Rikki (American) a form of names
ending with 'rica', e.g. Erica,
Frederica.

Rica, Ricci, Riccy, Rickee, Rickie,
Ricky, Riki, Rikita, Rikke, Rikkie, Riko

Riley (Irish) valiant, a unisex name.

Raleigh, Reilee, Reiley, Reilie,
Reillee, Reilley, Reilly, Reily, Rhilee,
Rhiley, Rhilie, Rhillee, Rhilley, Rhillie,
Rhilly, Rhily, Rhylee, Rhyley, Rhylie,
Rhyllee, Rhylley, Rhyllie, Rhylly,
Rhyly, Rielee, Rielle, Riely, Rilee,
Rilie, Rillee, Rilley, Rillie, Rylee, Reilly,
Ryley, Rylie, Ryllee, Rylley, Ryllie,
Rylly, Ryly

Rilla (Teutonic) small brook.

Rhila, Rhilah, Rhilla, Rhillah, Rhyla,
Rhylah, Rhylla, Rhyllah, Rila, Rilah,
Rillah, Rille, Ryla, Rylah, Rylla, Ryllah

Rim (Arabic) white antelope, a form of Rima.

Reem, Rheem, Rhim

Rima (Arabic) white antelope.

Reama, Reamah, Reem, Reema, Reemah, Rema, Remah, Reyma, Reymah, Rheama, Rheamah, Rheema, Rheemah, Rhema, Rhemah, Rheyma, Rheymah, Rhima, Rhimah, Rhime, Rhyma, Rhymah, Rimah, Rimm, Ryma, Rhymah

Rimona (Hebrew) pomegranate.

Reamona, Reamonah, Reamone, Reemona, Reemonah, Reemone, Remona, Remonah, Remone, Rheemona, Rheemonah, Rheemone, Rhemona, Rhemonah, Rhemone, Rhimona, Rhimonah, Rhimone, Rhymona, Rhymonah, Rhymone, Rimonah, Rimone, Rymona, Rymonah, Rymone

Rin (Japanese) park.

Rini, Rinn, Ryn, Ryni, Rynn, Rynni

Rina (Hebrew) happy, joyful, a form of names ending in Rina, eg, Marina.

Reena, Reenah, Riena, Rienah, Rinah

Rinah (Hebrew) joyful.

Rina, Ryna, Rynah

Rio (Spanish) river, a unisex name.

Ryo

Riona (Irish) queen, saint.

Reaona, Reaonah, Reeana, Reeanah, Reeona, Reeonah, Reiona, Reionah, Reona, Reonah, Reyona, Reyonah, Rheaona, Rheaonah, Rheeona, Rheeonah, Rheiona, Rheionah, Rheona, Rheonah, Rheyona, Rheyonah, Rhiona, Rhionah, Rhyona, Rhyonah, Rionah, Ryona, Ryonah

Risa (Latin) laughter.

Reasa, Reasah, Reesa, Reesah,

Reisa, Reisah, Resa, Resah, Risah, Rysa, Rysah

Risha (Hindu) born during solar month of Vrishanha or Taurus.

Rishah, Rysha, Ryshah

Rishona (Hebrew) first.

Rishon, Rishonah, Ryshona, Ryshonah

Rita (Greek) pearl, a form of Margherita, Margarita, Margaret.

Reata, Reatha, Reathas, Reda, Reeta, Reida, Reita, Reitha, Rheta, Rhita, Riet, Rieta, Ritah, Ritamae

Riva (French) riverbank.

Rivalee, Rivana, River, Rivi, Rivva, Rivvi

River (Latin) stream of water, river bank, a unisex name.

Riva, Rivana, Rivanah, Rivane, Rivanna, Rivannah, Rivanne, Rivers, Riviana, Riviane, Rivianna, Rivianne, Ryvana, Ryvanah, Ryvane, Ryvanna, Ryvannah, Ryvanne, Ryver, Ryvera

Rivka (Hebrew) bound, faithful, a form of Rebecca.

Rivca, Rivcah, Rivkah

Roberta (German) bright and famous, feminine form of Robert.

Roba, Robbi, Robbie, Robena, Robenah, Robenia, Robeniah, Robertah, Robertha, Robertina, Robett, Robetta, Robette, Robettia, Robettiah, Roben, Roburta, Roburtah

Robin/Robyn (English) small bird, a unisex name.

Roban, Robana, Robanah, Robane, Robann, Robanna, Robannah, Robanne, Robban, Robbana, Robbanah, Robbane, Robben, Robbena, Robbenah, Robbene, Robbin, Robbina, Robbinah, Robbine, Robbon,

*Robbyn, Robbyna, Robbynah,
Robbyne, Robeen, Robeena,
Robeenah, Robeene, Roben,
Robena, Robenah, Robene,
Robenia, Robeniah, Robian,
Robiana, Robianah, Robiane,
Robina, Robinah, Robine, Robinn,
Robyna, Robynah, Robyne*

Rochelle (French) the little rock,
from La Rochelle, a French fishing
port.

*Reshelle, Roche, Rochel, Rochela,
Rochele, Rochell, Rochella,
Rockella, Rockelle, Roshel, Roshela,
Roshele, Roshell, Roshella, Roshelle*

Rocio (Latin) dewdrops.

Rocyo

Roderica (Teutonic) famous ruler,
feminine form of Roderick.

*Rica, Rika, Roderick, Rodericka,
Roderik, Roderika, Roderiqua,
Roderique, Rodrick, Rodricka,
Rodrik, Rodrika, Rodriqua,
Rodrique*

Rodne (English) island of reeds,
island clearing, feminine form of
Rodney.

Rodna, Rodnah, Rodnai, Rodnay

Rohana (Hindu) sandalwood,
feminine form of Rohan.

*Rohanah, Rohanna, Rohannah,
Rohena, Rohenah, Rohenna,
Rohennah*

Rohini (Hindu) woman.

*Roheeni, Rohinee, Rohiney,
Rohinie, Rohiny*

Roisin (Irish) rose.

*Roisina, Roisinah, Roisine, Roisyn,
Roisyna, Roisynah, Roisyne,
Rosheen, Rosheena, Rosheenah,
Rosheene, Roshyn, Roshyna,
Roshynah, Roshyne*

Rolanda (German) renowned

throughout the land, feminine
form of Roland.

*Rolandah, Rolandia, Rolandiah,
Rolande, Rolena, Rolenah,
Rolene, Rolinda, Rolindah, Rolleen,
Rolonda, Rolonde*

Roma (Latin) from Rome, feminine
form of Roman.

*Ramma, Romah, Romai, Rome,
Romeka, Romella, Romelle,
Romilla, Romille, Romina, Romine,
Romini, Romma, Romola, Romonia*

Romaine (Latin) from Rome,
feminine form of Roman.

*Ramain, Roma, Romah, Romaina,
Romainah, Romaine, Romana,
Romanah, Romanda, Romane,
Romanel, Romanela, Romanele,
Romanell, Romanella, Romanelle,
Romania, Romanique, Romayna,
Romaynah, Romayne, Romilda,
Romina, Rominah, Romine, Romy,
Romyn, Romyna, Romynah,
Romyne*

Romia (Hebrew) praised.

Romiah, Romya, Romyah

Romilda (Teutonic) a glorious
warrior maiden.

Milda, Millie, Romi, Romildah

Romy (Latin) from Rome, a form of
Romaine.

*Romee, Romei, Romi, Rommee,
Rommei, Rommi, Rommy*

Rona (Scandinavian, Scottish)
brave and powerful ruler, king's
advisor, feminine form of Ronald;
(Irish) seal; (Hebrew) song of joy.

*Rhona, Ronah, Ronna, Rondi,
Ronna, Ronnah, Ronnai, Ronnay,
Ronne, Ronni, Ronsy*

Ronalda (Scandinavian, Scottish)
brave and powerful ruler, king's
advisor, feminine form of Ronald.

Rhonalda, Rhonaldah, Rhonaldia,
Rhonaldiah, Ronaldah, Ronaldia,
Ronaldiah, Ronalla, Ronalle,
Ronelda, Ronella, Ronelle, Ronnella

Roneisha (American)
combination of Rona and Aisha.

Ronaisha, Ronecia, Ronee,
Roneesha, Ronesa, Ronesha,
Ronessa, Roniece, Roniese,
Ronisha

Roni (American) a form of names
that have 'Ron' in them, such as
Veronica.

Rona, Rone, Ronee, Roney, Ronie,
Ronna, Ronnee, Ronney, Ronni,
Ronnie

Ronli (Hebrew) happy.

Ronlea, Ronleah, Ronlee, Ronlei,
Ronleigh, Ronley, Ronlia, Ronliah,
Ronlie, Ronly, Ronnlea, Ronnleah,
Ronnlee, Ronnlei, Ronnleigh,
Ronnley, Ronnli, Ronnliah, Ronnlie,
Ronnly

Rori/Rory (Irish) brilliant, famous
ruler, ruddy one, red ruler, a unisex
name.

Roree, Rorey, Roria, Roriah, Rorya,
Roryah

Ros (Latin) rose, a form of Rosa,
Rosalind, Rosamund.

Rosi, Rosie, Ross, Rossi, Rossie, Rossy,
Rosy, Roz, Rozi, Rozie, Rozy, Rozz,
Rozzi, Rozzie, Rozzy

Rosa (Italian) rose.

Rosah, Rosan, Rosana, Rosanah,
Rosane, Rosann, Rosanna,
Rosannah, Rosanne, Rosea,
Roseah, Rosean, Roseana,
Roseanah, Roseane, Roseann,
Roseanna, Roseannah, Roseanne,
Rosey, Rosia, Rosiah, Rosie, Rosy,
Rosya, Rosyah, Roza, Rozah

Rosabel/Rosabell/Rosabelle
(Latin) beautiful rose.

Rosabela, Rosabelah, Rosabele,
Rosabelia, Rosabeliah, Rosabella,
Rosabellah, Rosabellia,
Rosabelliah, Rosebel, Rosebela,
Rosebelah, Rosebele, Rosebell,
Rosebella, Rosebellah, Rosebelle,
Rosebellia, Rosebelliah, Rozabel,
Rozabela, Rozabelah, Rozabele,
Rozabelia, Rozabeliah, Rozabell,
Rozabella, Rozabellah, Rozabelle,
Rozabellia, Rozabelliah, Rozebel,
Rozebela, Rozebelah, Rozebele,
Rozebell, Rozebella, Rozebellah,
Rozebelle, Rozebellia,
Rozebelliah

Rosalba (Latin) white rose.

Rosalbah, Roselba, Roselbah

Rosalie (Latin) beautiful rose, a
form of Rosalind.

Rosalea, Rosalee, Rosaleen,
Rosaleigh, Rosalene, Rosali,
Rosalia, Roselea, Roselee,
Rosealey, Roseley, Roseli, Rosely,
Rosleia, Rosleiah, Rosli, Rozalea,
Rozalee, Rozaleen, Rozaleigh,
Rozalene, Rozali, Rozalia, Rozalie,
Rozelee, Rozealey, Rozele, Rozeley,
Rozeli, Rozely, Rozleia, Rozleiah,
Rozli

Rosalind/Rosalinda (Latin,
Spanish) beautiful rose,
Shakespeare's heroine in *As You
Like It*.

Linda, Ros, Rosalean, Rosaleana,
Rosaleanah, Rosaleane,
Rosaleen, Rosaleena, Rosaleenah,
Rosaleene, Rosalindah, Rosalinde,
Rosaline, Rosalyn, Rosalyna,
Rosalynah, Rosalynd, Rosalynda,
Rosalyndah, Rosalynde, Rosalyne,
Roseann, Roselean, Roseleana,
Roseleanah, Roseleane, Roseleen,
Roseleanah, Roseleenah, Roselin,
Roselina, Roselinah, Roselinda,
Roselindah, Roselinde, Roseline,
Roselyn, Roselyna, Roselynah,
Roselynda, Roselyndah, Roselynde,
Roselyne, Rosie, Roslan, Roslana,
Roslanah, Roslane, Roslain,
Roslaina, Roslainah, Roslaine,

Roslana, Roslanah, Roslane,
Roslin, Roslina, Roslinah, Rosline,
Roslinia, Rosliniah, Roslyn, Roslynd,
Roslynda, Roslyndah, Roslynde,
Roslyne, Roz, Rozalean, Rozaleana,
Rozaleanah, Rozaleane,
Rozaleen, Rozaleena, Rozaleenah,
Rozaleene, Rozalind, Rozalinda,
Rozalindah, Rozalinde, Rozaline,
Rozalyn, Rozalyna, Rozalynah,
Rozalynd, Rozalynda, Rozalyndah,
Rozalynde, Rozalyne, Rozeann,
Rozelean, Rozeleana, Rozeleanah,
Rozeleane, Rozeleen, Rozeleena,
Rozeleenah, Rozelin, Rozelina,
Rozelinah, Rozelinda, Rozelindah,
Rozelinde, Rozeline, Rozelyn,
Rozelyna, Rozelynah, Rozelynda,
Rozelyndah, Rozelynde, Rozelyne,
Rozie, Rozlan, Rozlana, Rozlanah,
Rozlane, Rozlain, Rozlaina,
Rozlainah, Rozlaine, Rozlana,
Rozlanah, Rozlane, Rozlin, Rozlina,
Rozlinah, Rozline, Rozlinia, Rozliniah,
Rozlyn, Rozlynd, Rozlynda,
Rozlyndah, Rozlynde, Rozlyne

Rosamond (Latin) rose of the
world, rose of purity; (Teutonic)
horse, guardian.

Rosamonda, Rosamondah,
Rosamonde, Rosamund,
Rosamunda, Rosamundah,
Rosemond, Rosemonda,
Rosmondah, Rosemonde,
Rosemund, Rosemunda,
Rosemundah, Rozamond,
Rozamonda, Rozamondah,
Rozamonde, Rozamund,
Rozamunda, Rozamundah,
Rozemond, Rozemonda,
Rozmondah, Rozemonde,
Rozemund, Rozemunda,
Rozemundah

Rosanna (English) combination of
Rose and Ann.

Ranna, Roanna, Rosana, Rosanah,
Rosannah, Rosanne, Roseana,
Roseanah, Roseane, Roseann,
Roseanna, Roseannah, Roseanne,
Rozana, Rozanah, Rozanna,
Rozannah, Rozanne, Rozeana,
Rozeanah, Rozeane, Rozeann,

Rozeanna, Rozeannah, Rozeanne

Rosaria (Italian) rosary.

Rosariah, Rosarya, Rosaryah,
Rozaria, Rozariah, Rozarya,
Rzoaryah

Rose (Latin) rose.

Rada, Raisa, Raisina, Rois, Roise,
Ros, Rosa, Rosah, Rosalind, Rosalyn,
Rosea, Roseanne, Rosella, Roses,
Rosetta, Rosie, Rosina, Rosse

Roselani (Hawaiian) heavenly
rose.

Roselana, Roselanah, Roselanea,
Roselanee, Roselaney, Roselania,
Roselaniah, Roselanie, Roselany,
Roselanya, Roslana, Roslanah,
Roslanea, Roslanee, Roslaney,
Roslani, Roslania, Roslaniah,
Roslanie, Roslany, Roslanya

Rosemarie (English) combination
of Rose and Marie.

Rosa-Maree, Rosa-Maria, Rosa-
Marie, Rose-Maree, Rose-Maria,
Rose-Marie, Rosemaria, Rosemary

Rosemary (English) a fragrant
herb, symbol for remembrance,
combination of Rose and Mary.

Rosemaree, Rosemarey,
Rosemaria, Rosemarie, Rosemarya,
Rosemaryah, Rosemerri, Rosemerry

Rosetta (Italian) rose.

Roseta, Rosette

Roshan (Hindu) light, a unisex
name.

Roshaina, Roshainah, Roshaine,
Roshana, Roshanah, Roshane,
Roshani, Roshania, Roshaniah,
Roshanie, Roshany, Roshanya,
Roshanyah

Rosie/Rosy (English) rose, a form
of Rose.

Rosa, Rosalia, Rosamond, Rosee,
Rosene, Rosheen, Rosi, Rosia

Rosina (English) rose, a form of Rose.

Rosalie, Roseen, Roseena, Roseenah, Roseene, Rosena, Rosenah, Rosene, Rosinah, Rosine, Rosyna, Rosynah, Rosyne, Rozena, Rozina

Rosita (Spanish) rose, a form of Rose.

Roseat, Roseata, Roseatah, Roseate, Roseet, Roseeta, Roseetah, Roseete, Roseta, Rosetah, Rosete, Rosetta, Rosettah, Rosette, Rosit, Rositah, Rosite, Rositt, Rositta, Rosittah, Rositte, Rosyt, Rosyta, Rosytah, Rosyte, Rozet, Rozeta, Rozete, Rozetta, Rozettah, Rozette, Rozita, Rozitah, Rozitta, Rozittah

Roslyn (Latin) rose, a form of Rosalind.

Rosalyn, Rosalynn, Rosalynne, Roselyn, Roselynn, Roselynne, Roslynn, Roslynne

Rowan (English) mountain ash tree, tree with red berries, a unisex name.

Rhoan, Rhoana, Rhoanah, Rhoane, Rhoann, Rhoanna, Rhoannah, Rhoanne, Rhoen, Rhoena, Rhoenah, Rhoene, Rhoenn, Rhoenna, Rhoennah, Rhoenne, Rhoin, Rhoina, Rhoinah, Rhoine, Rhoinn, Rhoinna, Rhoinnah, Rhoinne, Roane, Rohan, Rohana, Rohanah, Rohane, Rohann, Rohanna, Rohannah, Rohanne, Rowana, Rowanah, Rowane, Rowen, Rowena, Rowenah, Rowene

Rowena (Celtic) slender and fair; (Anglo-Saxon) well-known friend.

Rana, Ranah, Ranna, Rannah, Rohena, Rohenah, Rohenia, Rowan, Rowana, Rowanah, Rowanna, Rowannah, Rowe, Roweana, Roweanah, Roweena, Roweenah, Rowein, Roweina,

Roweinah, Rowen, Rowenah, Rowenna, Rowennah, Rowina, Rowinah, Rowyna, Rowynah, Rowyne, Rowynn, Rowynna, Rowynnah, Rowynne

Roxanne (Perisan) sunrise.

Roxan, Roxana, Roxanah, Roxane, Roxann, Roxanna, Roxannah, Roxannia, Roxanniah, Roxannie, Roxanny, Roxi, Roxie, Roxy

Roxy (Perisan) sunrise, a form of Roxanne.

Roxi, Roxie

Royale (French) regal one, feminine form of Roy.

Royal, Royala, Royalene, Royall, Royalle, Royel, Royela, Royelah, Royele, Royell, Royella, Royelle, Roylea, Roylee, Roylene, Ryal, Ryall, Ryalle, Ryell, Ryelle

Roz (English, Spanish) rose, a form of Rosalind.

Roza, Rozalie, Rozel, Rozelli, Rozsi, Rozz, Rozza, Rozzie

Rozena (Native American) rose.

Razina, Razinah, Razine, Rozeana, Rozeanah, Rozeane, Rozeena, Rozeenah, Rozeene, Rozenah, Rozina, Rozinah, Rozine, Rozyn, Rozyna, Rozynah, Rozyne

Ruby (Latin) precious red stone.

Ruba, Rube, Rubea, Rubee, Rubey, Rubi, Rubia, Rubiah, Rubiann, Rubie, Rubina, Rubinah, Rubine, Rubinia, Rubiniah, Rubis, Rubyann, Rubye, Rubyn, Rubyna, Rubynah, Rubyne

Ruchi (Hindu) a wish to please.

Ruchee, Ruchey, Ruchie, Ruchy

Rudelle (Teutonic) famous.

Rudel, Rudela, Rudelah, Rudele, Rudelia, Rudeliah, Rudell, Rudella, Rudellah, Rudellia, Rudelliah

Ruel (English) path.

Rual, Ruala, Rualah, Ruale, Ruall, Rualla, Ruallah, Ruela, Ruelah, Ruele, Ruell, Ruella, Ruellah

Rudi/Rudy (German) famous wolf, a unisex name.

Rudee, Rudey, Rudia, Rudiah, Rudie

Rudra (Hindu) seeds.

Rud, Rudrah

Rue (English) aromatic medicinal plant.

Ru, Ruey

Rufina (Italian) red-haired, feminine form of Rufus.

Rufeana, Rufeanah, Rufeane, Rufeena, Rufeenah, Rufeene, Rufena, Rufenah, Rufene, Rufinah, Rufine, Rufinia, Rufiniah

Rui (Japanese) loving.

Ru

Rukan (Arabic) steady, confident.

Rukana, Rukanah, Rukane, Rukann, Rukanna, Rukannah, Rukanne

Rukmini (Hindu) gold, wife of Lord Krishna.

Rukimi, Rukminy, Rukmyny, Rukymi, Rukymy

Rula (Latin) ruler, feminine form of Rule.

Ruela, Ruelah, Ruella, Ruellah, Rulah, Rular, Rule, Ruler, Rulla, Rullah

Rumer (English) gipsy.

Rouma, Roumah, Roumar, Roumer, Ruma, Rumah, Rumar, Rumi, Rumor

Runa (Old Norse) secret.

Runah, Rune

Ruqayyah (Arabic) charming, daughter of the prophet Muhammad.

Ruqaya, Ruqayah, Ruqayya

Ruri (Japanese) emerald.

Ruree, Rurie, Ruriko

Ruth (Hebrew) compassionate friend.

Rueth, Rutha, Ruthalma, Ruthana, Ruthann, Ruthanna, Ruthe, Ruthee, Ruthi, Ruthie, Ruthina, Ruthine, Ruthven

Ruza (Slavic) rose.

Ruzah, Ruzha, Ruzsa

Ryan (Irish) little ruler, a unisex name.

Raian, Raiane, Raiann, Raianne, Rayan, Rayana, Rayane, Rhian, Rhiana, Rhiane, Rhyan, Rhyann, Rian, Riana, Riane, Riann, Rianna, Rianne, Ruana, Ryana, Ryann, Ryanna, Ryanne, Ryen, Ryena, Ryenn, Ryenna, Ryenne

Rylee (Irish) valiant, a form of Riley.

Riley, Rye, Ryelea, Ryelee, Ryeleigh, Ryeley, Ryeli, Ryelie, Ryelin, Ryelina, Ryelleigh, Ryellie, Rylea, Ryleigh, Ryley, Ryli, Rylie, Rylin, Rylina, Rylleigh, Ryllie

S

Saada (Hebrew) one who helps and supports.
Saadah, Sada, Sadah

Saarah (Arabic) princess, a form of Sarah.
Saara, Sara, Sarah, Sarra, Sarrah

Saba (Arabic) morning; (Greek) woman from Sheba.
Sabaa, Sabaah, Sabah, Sabba, Sabbah

Sabi (Arabic) young girl.
Sabee, Sabie, Sabih, Saby, Sahbee, Sahbi, Sahby

Sabina/Sabine (Italian) woman of ancient Italian culture, a tribe living in central Italy during the establishment of Rome.
Bina, Binnie, Sabienna, Sabienne, Sabinah, Sabinn, Sabinna, Sabinnah, Sabinne, Sabyna, Sabyne, Sabynn, Sabynna, Sabynne, Savina, Savinda, Savindah, Savine, Savyna, Savynah, Savyne, Sebina, Sebinah, Sebine, Sebyn, Sebyna, Sebynah, Sebyne

Sabiya (Arabic) morning eastern wind.
Sabaya, Sabayah, Sabea, Sabeah, Sabia, Sabiah, Sabiyah, Sabya, Sabyah

Sable (English) sleek, soft fur, black.
Sabel, Sabela, Sabelah, Sabella, Sabellah, Sabelle

Sabra (Hebrew) thorny cactus fruit, hard on the outside and soft on the inside.
Sabrah, Sabre, Sabrea, Sabreah, Sabree, Sabreea, Sabri, Sabria, Sabriah, Sebra, Sebrah

Sabrina (Latin) boundary; (English) princess.
Sabra, Sabrana, Sabre, Sabreen, Sabreena, Sabrena, Sabrene, Sabrinah, Sabrinas, Sabrine, Sabrinn, Sabrinna, Sabrinne, Sabryna, Sabryne, Sabrynna, Sabrynne, Sebree, Sebrena, Sebrene, Sebrina, Sebrine, Subreana, Subreane, Subrina, Subrine

Sacha (Greek) helper and defender of humankind.
Sachah, Sache, Sahsha, Sascha, Saschae, Saschia, Sasha, Sashah, Sashana, Sashel, Sashia, Sashiah, Sashira, Sashisha, Sashya

Sachi (Japanese) blessed child.
Saachi, Sachie, Sachiko

Sada (Anglo-Saxon) seed.
Sadah, Sadda, Saddah

Sade (Hebrew) princess, a form of Sarah.
Sadae, Sadai, Saday, Sadea, Sadee, Shadae, Shadai, Shaday, Shade, Shadea Shadee

Sadella (American) combination of Sade and Ella.
Sadel, Sadela, Sadelah, Sadele, Sadell, Sadellah, Sadelle, Saedell, Saedella, Saedelle, Sarella, Sarelle, Sydel, Sydela, Sydell, Sydella, Sydelle

Sadhana (Hindu) devoted.
Sadhanah, Sadhanna, Sadhannah, Sedhana, Sedhanah

Sadie (English) princess, a form of Sarah.

Saddie, Sadee, Sadeh, Sadi, Sadia, Sady, Sadye, Saida, Saidah, Saide, Saidee, Saidia, Saidy, Sally, Sara, Sarah, Seidee, Seidie, Seidy, Siedie

Sadira (Arabic) star.
Sadeera, Sadeerah, Sadirah, Sadra, Sadrah, Sadre

Sadiya (Arabic) lucky child.
Sadi, Sadia, Sadiah, Sadiyah, Sadya, Sadyah

Safa (Arabic) pure.
Safak, Safeya, Saffa, Saffra, Safiya, Safiyah, Safra

Saffi (Danish) wise.
Safee, Safey, Saffee, Saffey, Saffie, Saffy, Safie, Safy

Saffron (English) yellow, a plant used as a spice.
Saffrona, Saffronah, Saffrone, Safron, Safrona, Safronah, Safrone, Safronna, Safronnah, Safronne, Saphron, Saphrona, Saphronah, Saphrone

Safiya (Arabic) untroubled, serene, pure, best friend.
Safeia, Safeya, Safiyah, Safiyya, Safiyyah

Sagara (Hindu) ocean.
Sagarah, Segara, Segarah

Sage (French) herb, wise person, a unisex name.
Saige, Saje, Sayg, Sayge

Sahar (Arabic) dawn.
Sahara, Saharah

Sahara (Arabic) wilderness, desert.
Sahar, Saharah, Sahari, Saheer, Saheera, Saheerah, Saher, Sahera, Saherah, Sahira, Sahirah, Sahra, Sahrah

Sai (Japanese) talented.
Saiko, Say

Saida (Arabic) happy; (Hebrew) princess, a form of Sarah.
Saeda, Saedah, Said, Saidah, Saide, Saidea

Sakae (Japanese) one who is prosperous.
Saka, Sakai, Sakay

Sakari (Hindu) sweet.
Sacari, Sackari, Sakara, Sakarah, Sakarrah, Sakarri, Sekari

Saki (Japanese) rice wine, cloak.
Sakee, Sakia, Sakiah, Sakie, Saky, Sakya, Sakyah

Sakina (Arabic) peace of mind, tranquillity; (Hindu) friend.
Sakeena, Sakeenah, Sakinah

Sakti (Hindu) full of energy.
Saktea, Saktee, Saktey, Saktia, Saktiah, Saktie, Sakty, Saktya, Saktyah, Shatki

Sakuna (Native American) bird.
Sakunah

Sakura (Japanese) cherry blossom, prosperous, rich.
Sakurah

Sala (Hindu) a sacred Hindu tree.
Salah, Salal, Salla, Sallah

Salali (Native American) squirrel.
Salalea, Salaleah, Salalee, Salalei, Salaleigh, Salalia, Salaliah, Salalie, Salaly, Salalya, Salalyah

Salama (Arabic) peaceful, a feminine form of Salamon.
Lama, Salamae, Salamah, Salamee, Selama, Selamah

Salena (Latin) salty.

Salana, Salanah, Salane, Salean, Saleana, Saleanah, Saleane, Saleen, Saleena, Saleenah, Saleene, Salen, Salenah, Salene, Salenna, Salennah, Salenne, Salin, Salina, Salinah, Salinda, Salindra, Saline, Salineh, Sallena, Sallenah, Sallene, Salleena, Salleenah, Salleene, Sallin, Sallina, Sallinah, Salline, Sallyn, Sallyna, Sallynah, Sallyne, Zalean, Zaleana, Zaleanah, Zaleane, Zaleena, Zaleenah, Zaleene, Zalena, Zalenah, Zalene, Zalina, Zalinah, Zaline, Zalyna, Zalynah, Zalyne

Salida (Hebrew) happy.

Salidah

Salima (Arabic) peaceful, safe and healthy, feminine form of Salim.

Saleema, Saleemah, Salema, Salemah, Salim, Salimah, Salma, Salyma, Salymah

Salina (Latin) solemn.

Salana, Salanah, Salane, Salean, Saleana, Saleanah, Saleane, Saleen, Saleena, Saleenah, Saleene, Salen, Salena, Salenah, Salene, Salinah, Saline, Salinee, Salleen, Salleena, Salleenah, Salleene, Sallin, Sallina, Sallinah, Salline, Sallyn, Sallyna, Sallynah, Sallyne, Sallynee, Salyn, Salyna, Salynah, Salyne, Zalean, Zaleana, Zaleanah, Zaleane, Zaleen, Zaleena, Zaleenah, Zaleene, Zalena, Zalenah, Zalene, Zalina, Zalinah, Zaline, Zalyna, Zalynah, Zalyne

Sally (English) princess, a form of Sarah.

Sadie, Salaide, Salea, Saleah, Salee, Salei, Saleigh, Saley, Sali, Salia, Saliah, Salie, Sallea, Salleah, Sallee, Sallei, Salleigh, Salletta, Sallette, Salley, Salli, Sallia, Salliah, Sallie, Sallya, Sallyah, Sallye, Saly, Salya, Salyah, Salye, Sara

Salma (Arabic) safe and healthy, a form of Salima.

Salmah

Salome (Hebrew) peaceful.

Salaome, Saloma, Salomah, Salomea, Salomee, Salomey, Salomi, Salomia, Salomiah, Salomya, Salomyah

Salvadora (Spanish) saviour, saved, feminine form of Salvador.

Salvadorah

Salvia (Latin) herb, wise person, a form of Sage; (Spanish) strong, healthy.

Sallvia, Sallviah, Salviah, Salviana, Salvianah, Salviane, Salvianna, Salviannah, Salvianne, Salvina, Salvinah, Salvine, Salvinna, Salvinnah, Salvinne, Salvyna, Salvynah, Salvyne

Sam (Hebrew) God has asked me, listener, a form of names beginning with Sam, such as Samantha, a unisex name.

Sami, Samm, Sammi, Sammy

Samala (Hebrew) God has asked me.

Samalah, Samale, Samalla, Samallah, Sammala, Sammalah, Sammale, Sammalla, Sammallah

Samantha (Aramaic) listener.

Sam, Samana, Samanah, Samanatha, Samanitha, Samanithia, Samanta, Samantah, Samanth, Samarra, Samatha, Samathia, Samathiah, Sami, Sammana, Sammantha, Sammanthia, Sammanthiah, Sammara, Sammi, Samora, Zamantha, Zamathia, Zamanthiah, Zammantha, Zammanthia, Zammanthiah, Zammanthya, Zammanthyah

GIRLS

Samar (Arabic) evening conversationalist.

> Samara, Samarah, Samarr, Samarra, Samarrah

Samara (Hebrew) watched over by God.

> Saimara, Samaira, Samar, Samarah, Samaree, Samari, Samaria, Samariah, Samarie, Samarra, Samary, Samera, Sameria, Samira, Sammar, Sammara, Samora

Sameh (Arabic) forgiving, a unisex name; (Hebrew) listener.

> Samaiya, Samaya

Samina (Hindu) happiness.

> Saminah, Samyna, Samynah

Samira (Arabic) entertaining companion.

> Sameera, Samirah, Samire, Samiria, Samirra, Samyra

Samuela (Hebrew) asked of God, God has heard, feminine form of Samuel.

> Samala, Samalah, Samelia, Sameliah, Samella, Samellah, Sami, Samiella, Samiellah, Samielle, Samilla, Samillah, Samille, Sammila, Sammilah, Sammile, Samuelah, Samuele, Samuella, Samuellah, Samuelle, Zamuel, Zamuela, Zamuelah, Zamuele, Zamuell, Zamuella, Zamuellah, Zamuelle

Sana (Arabic) resplendent brilliance, mountain top.

> Sanaa, Sanaah, Sanae, Sanah, Sanee

Sancia/Sanchia (Spanish) saintly, sacred, sanctified, holy, feminine form of Sancho.

> Sancaria, Sanceska, Sancha, Sanchah, Sancharia, Sanche, Sanchiah, Sanchie, Sanchya, Sanchyah, Sanciah, Sancie, Sancya, Sancyah, Sanzia, Sanziah, Sanzya, Sanzyah

Sandhya (Hindu) sunset.

> Sandhia, Sandhea

Sandra (Greek) defender, helper of humankind, a form of Cassandra.

> Sandea, Sandee, Sandey, Sandi, Sandia, Sandiah, Sandie, Sandrea, Sandreah, Sandreana, Sandreanah, Sandreane, Sandreen, Sandreena, Sandreenah, Sandreene, Sandreia, Sandreiah, Sandreina, Sandreinah, Sandreine, Sandrenna, Sandrennah, Sandrenne, Sandria, Sandriah, Sandrina, Sandrinah, Sandrine, Sandryna, Sandrynah, Sandryne, Sandy, Zandea, Zandee, Zandey, Zandi, Zandia, Zandiah, Zandie, Zandrea, Zandreah, Zandreen, Zandreena, Zandreenah, Zandreene, Zandreina, Zandreinah, Zandreine, Zandrina, Zandrinah, Zandrine, Zandryna, Zandrynah, Zandryne, Zandy

Sandy (Greek) defender, helper of humankind, a form of Sandra, Cassandra.

> Sandee, Sandey, Sandi, Sandie, Sanndee, Sanndi, Sanndie, Zandee, Zandey, Zandi, Zandie, Zandy, Zanndi

Sangmu (Tibetan, Sherpa) kind-hearted one.

> Sangma, Sangmae

Sanjana (Hindu) conscience, feminine form of Sanjay.

> Sandjana, Sanjanah, Sanjaya, Sanjayah, Senjaya, Sonjana

Sanne (Dutch) lily, a form of Susan.

> Sanea, Saneen, Saneh, Sanna, Sannea, Sanneh

Santa (Italian) saint, feminine form of Santo.

Sainta, Saintah, Santah, Santina, Santo

Santana (Spanish) saint, a unisex name.

Santa, Santah, Santanah, Santaniata, Santanna, Santannah, Santanne, Santena, Santenah, Santenna, Santennah, Shantana, Shantanah

Santina (Spanish) little saint, feminine form of Santos.

Santin, Santinah, Santine, Santinia, Santiniah, Santyn, Santyna, Santynah, Santyne

Sanura (African) little kitten.

Sanira, Sanirra, Sanora, Sanorra, Sanurra

Sanuye (Native American) red clouds at sunset.

Sanuie

Sanya (Hindu) born on Saturday.

Sanyah, Sanja, Sanjae, Sania, Saniah, Sanyia, Sanyiah

Sanyu (African) happy, a unisex name.

Saoirse (Irish) freedom.

Saoirsa, Saoirsah

Sapata (Native American) dancing bear.

Sapatah

Sapphira/Sapphire (Greek) deep blue sapphire jewel.

Saffir, Saffira, Saffirah, Saffire, Saffyr, Saffyra, Saffyrah, Safir, Safira, Safirah, Safire, Safyr, Safyra, Safyrah, Saphera, Sapherah, Sapheria, Saphir, Saphira, Saphirah, Saphire, Saphyra, Saphyrah, Saphyre, Sapphir, Sapphirah, Sapphyr, Sapphyra, Sapphyrah, Sapphyre

Sara (Hebrew) princess, a form of Sarah.

Saara, Saarah, Sahra, Sahrah, Salli, Sallie, Sally, Sarah, Sarra, Sarrah

Sarah (Hebrew) princess, wife of Abraham and mother of Isaac.

Saara, Saarah, Sada, Sadah, Sadel, Sadela, Sadelah, Sadele, Sadell, Sadella, Sadellah, Sadelle, Sadea, Sadee, Sadey, Sadi, Sadia, Sadiah, Sadie, Sahra, Sahrah, Sahria, Sahriah, Sahrya, Sahryah, Sallea, Sallee, Salley, Salli, Sallia, Salliah, Sallie, Sally, Sara, Sarae, Saraha, Sarahana, Sarahanah, Sarahann, Sarahanna, Sarahannah, Sarahi, Sarai, Saraia, Saraiah, Saray, Saraya, Sarayah, Saree, Sareeka, Sareka, Sari, Saria, Sariah, Sarika, Sarita, Sarra, Sarrah, Sarri, Sarrie, Sary, Sarya, Saryah, Sarye, Sasa, Sasha, Sayra, Sayrah, Sayria, Sayriah, Sera, Serah, Serra, Serrah, Zahra, Zahrah, Zahria, Zahriah, Zara, Zarah, Zarra, Zarrah

Saraid (Celtic) excellent.

Saraida, Saraidah

Sarala (Hindu) honest.

Saralah, Saralla, Sarallah, Saralle, Sarella, Sarellah, Sarelle

Sarila (Turkish) waterfall.

Sarilah, Sarilla, Sarillah, Saryla, Sarylah, Saryle, Sarylla, Saryllah, Sarylle

Sarina (Hebrew) princess, a form of Sarah.

Sareana, Sareanah, Sareane, Sareen, Sareena, Sareenah, Sareene, Saren, Sarena, Sarenah, Sarene, Sarenn, Sarenna, Sarennah, Sarenne, Sarin, Sarinah, Sarine, Sarinn, Sarinna, Sarinnah, Sarinne, Saryna, Sarynah, Saryne, Sarynna, Sarynnah, Sarynne, Zareana, Zareanah, Zareane, Zareen, Zareena, Zareenah, Zareene, Zaren, Zarena, Zarenah, Zarene, Zarenn, Zarenna, Zarennah, Zarenne, Zarin, Zarina,

Zarinah, Zarine, Zarinn, Zarinna, Zarinnah, Zarinne, Zaryna, Zarynah, Zaryne, Zarynna, Zarynnah

Sarisha (Sanskrit) charming.
Sareesha, Sariesha, Sarishah

Sarita (Hebrew) princess, a form of Sarah.
Sareata, Sareatah, Sareate, Sareatta, Sareattah, Sareatte, Sareeta, Sareetah, Sareete, Saretta, Sarettah, Sarette, Sarit, Saritah, Saritta, Sarittah, Saritte, Saryta, Sarytah, Saryte, Sarytta, Saryttah, Sarytte

Saroja (Hindu) born near a lake.

Sarotte (French) princess, a form of Sarah.
Sarot, Sarota, Sarotah, Sarote, Sarott, Sarotta, Sarottah

Sasha (Russian) defender, helper of humankind, a form of Sandra.
Sacha, Sachsha, Sahsha, Sasa, Sascha, Saschae, Sashae, Sashah, Sashai, Sashana, Sashay, Sashea, Sashel, Sashenka, Sashey, Sashi, Sashia, Sashira, Sasjara

Saskia (Dutch) a Saxon.
Saskiah, Sassie, Sassy

Satara (American) combination of Sarah and Tara.
Sartarah, Sataria, Satariah, Satarra, Satarrah, Satarya, Satryah, Satera, Saterah, Sateria, Sateriah, Saterra, Saterrah, Saterria, Saterriah

Satin (English) smooth, silky, shiny.
Satanne, Satean, Sateane, Sateen, Sateena, Sateene, Satina, Satinah, Satine, Satinda, Satinn, Satinna, Satinne, Satten, Sattena, Sattene, Satyn, Satyna, Satynah, Satyne

Satinka (Native American) sacred dancer.
Satinkah

Sato (Japanese) sweet, sugar.
Satoko, Satu

Saturna (Latin) of Saturn, feminine form of Saturn, the Roman god of agriculture.
Saturnah

Saundra (English, Greek) defender, helper of humankind, a form of Sandra.
Saunda, Saundah, Saundea, Saundee, Saundi, Saundie, Saundrah, Saundrea, Saundreah, Saundree, Saundrey, Saundri, Saundria, Saundriah, Saundrie, Saundry, Saundrya, Saundryah

Saura (Hindu) worshipper of the sun.
Saurah, Saurie

Savanna/Savannah (Spanish) treeless plain, open grassland.
Sahvana, Sahvanah, Sahvanna, Sahvannah, Savan, Savana, Savanah, Savanha, Savania, Savann, Savannha, Savannia, Savanniah, Savhana, Savhanah, Savhanna, Savhannah, Savona, Savonah, Savonna, Savonnah, Savonne, Sevana, Sevanah, Sevanna, Sevannah, Svana, Svanah, Svanna, Svannah, Zavana, Zavanah, Zavanna, Zavannah, Zevana, Zevanah, Zevanna, Zevannah

Savina (Latin) woman of ancient Italian culture, a tribe living in central Italy during the establishment of Rome, a form of Sabina.
Savean, Saveana, Saveanah, Saveane, Saveen, Saveena, Saveenah, Saveene, Savinah, Savine, Savyn, Savyna, Savynah, Savyne

Sawa (Japanese) swamp; (Native American) stone.
Sawah

Sawson (Arabic) lily.
Sawa, Sawae, Sawsan, Sawsen, Sawsenn, Sawsenne, Sawsonn, Sawsonne

Saxon (English) of the Saxons, or people of the sword, a unisex name.
Sax, Saxa, Saxan, Saxana, Saxen, Saxena, Saxona

Sayo (Japanese) born at night.
Saio

Scarlet (English) brilliant red colour, the heroine in Margaret Mitchell's *Gone with the Wind*.
Scarleta, Scarletah, Scarlete, Scarlett, Scarletta, Scarlettah, Scarlette

Scholastica (Latin) student.
Scholasticah, Scholastique

Schuyler (Dutch) scholar, shelter, protection, a unisex name.
Schuylar, Schuylor, Schular, Schyler, Schylor, Sky, Skye, Skyelar, Skyeler, Skyelor, Skylar, Skyler, Skylor

Scottie (Scottish) from Scotland.
Scota, Scoti, Scotia, Scotta, Scotti, Scottia, Scotty

Seanna (Celtic) God is gracious, feminine form of Sean.
Seana, Seanae, Seanah, Seane, Seann, Seannah, Seanne, Seante, Sian, Siana, Siann, Sianna, Sina, Sinah, Shawna, Shawnah, Shawne

Season (Latin) season.
Seasan, Seasann, Seasanne, Seasen, Seazon, Seazonne

Sebastienne (Greek) revered, honoured by all, feminine form of Sebastien.
Sebasteen, Sebasteena, Sebasteenah, Sebasteene, Sebastena, Sebstene, Sebastenia, Sebastia, Sebastiana, Sebastianna, Sebastianne, Sebastiena, Sebastienna

Seble (Eithopian) born in autumn.
Seebie, Seeble

Secilia (Latin) blind, a form of Cecilia.
Sacelia, Saselia, Sasilia, Seela, Selia, Siela, Silea, Silia

Secunda (Latin) second-born child.
Seconda, Secondah, Secondea, Secondee, Secondia, Secondiah, Secundah, Secundea, Secundee, Secundia, Secundiah

Seda (Armenian) hearer of forest voices.
Sedah

Sedna (Inuit) well-fed.
Sednah

Seiriol (Welsh) the sparkling bright one.
Seirial, Seirian, Seiriola, Seiriole

Seki (Japanese) wonderful.
Seka, Sekah, Sekee, Sekey, Sekia, Sekiah, Sekie, Seky

Sela (Hebrew) rock.
Selah, Siela, Sielah

Selam (Eithopian) peaceful.
Selama, Selamah

Selda (Anglo-Saxon) rare.
Seldah, Selde, Sellda, Selldah, Zelda

Selena (Greek) moon, heavenly.
*Celeana, Celeanah, Celeane,
Celeen, Celeena, Celeenah,
Celeene, Celena, Celenah,
Celene, Celina, Celinah, Celine,
Celyn, Celyna, Celynah, Celyne,
Saleena, Salenna, Salina, Sela,
Selah, Selana, Selean, Seleana,
Seleanah, Seleen, Seleena,
Seleenah, Seleene, Selen, Selenah,
Selene, Selenia, Seleniah, Selenie,
Selenna, Selennah, Selenne, Selia,
Seliah, Selie, Selin, Selina, Selinah,
Seline, Selinda, Selini, Selinia,
Selinka, Selyn, Selyna, Selynah,
Selyne, Sylena, Zelean, Zeleana,
Zeleanah, Zeleane, Zeleen,
Zeleena, Zeleenah, Zeleene,
Zelen, Zelena, Zelenah, Zelene,
Zelin, Zelina, Zelinah, Zeline, Zelyn,
Zelyna, Zelynah, Zelyne*

Selima (Hebrew) peace.
Seleema, Seleemah, Selimah

Selma (Scandinavian) divinely
protected; (Celtic) fair; (Arabic)
secure.
Sellma, Sellmah, Selmah, Zelma

Sema (Turkish) divine omen.
Semah, Semja

Sen (Japanese) magical forest fairy.
Senn, Senne

Senalda (Spanish) sign.
Sena, Senaldah, Sendfa, Senna

Senga (Scottish) slender, holy, its
popularity derives from the fact it
is Agnes spelled backwards.
Sengah

Senta (German) assistant.
Sentah

Septima (Latin) seventh-born child.
*Septime, Septym, Septyma,
Septyme*

Sequoia (Native American)
redwood tree.
*Sequoi, Sequoiah, Sequoira,
Sequoiya, Sequora, Sequoya,
Sequoyra, Sikoya*

Serafina (Hebrew) burning,
ardent, Seraphim are the highest
order of the angels in the Bible,
feminine form of Serafin.
*Sarafin, Sarafina, Sarafine,
Serafeen, Serafeena, Serafeene,
Serafin, Serafinah, Serafine,
Serapheen, Serapheena,
Serapheene, Seraphin, Seraphina,
Seraphinah, Seraphine, Seraphyn,
Seraphyna, Seraphynah,
Seraphyne*

Serena (Latin) calm, serene,
tranquil, feminine form of Sereno.
*Rena, Sareina, Sarena, Sarina,
Saryna, Seraina, Serana, Sereen,
Sereena, Serenah, Serene, Serenia,
Serin, Serina, Serine, Serreena,
Serren, Serrena, Serrin, Serrina*

Serenity (Latin) peaceful.
*Serenidy, Serenitae, Serenitee,
Sereniti, Serenitie, Serrenitae,
Serrenitee, Serreniti, Serrenitie,
Serrenity*

Serica (Greek) silky to touch.
*Sereeca, Sereeka, Sereica, Sereika,
Sericah, Sericka, Serika, Serikah,
Seryca, Serycah, Seryka, Serykah*

Serilda (Germanic) armed
maiden of war.
*Sarilda, Sarildah, Serildah, Serylda,
Seryldah*

Serina (Latin) calm, serene, a form
of Serena.
*Sereena, Sereenah, Sereene,
Serin, Serinah, Serine, Serreena,
Serreenah, Serreene, Serrin, Serrina,
Serrinah, Serrine, Serryn, Serryna,
Serrynah, Serryne, Seryn, Seryna,
Serynah, Seryne*

Sestia (Latin) sixth-born child.
Sestiah

Severina (Latin) severe, feminine form of Severin.
Severana, Severanah, Severeena, Severeenah, Severinah, Sevrina, Sevrinah

Sevilla (Spanish) the name of a city in Spain.
Sevillah, Seville

Shaba (Spanish) rose.
Shabah, Shabana, Shabanah, Shabina, Shabinah, Shabine, Shabyna, Shabynah, Shabyne

Shada (Native American) pelican.
Shadae, Shadah, Shaday, Shade, Shadea, Shadeana, Shadee, Shadi, Shadie, Shadiya, Shaida, Shaidah, Shaiday, Shaide, Shaidea, Shaideana, Shaidee, Shaidi, Shaidie, Shaidiya, Shayda, Shaydah

Shadiyah (Arabic) singer.
Shadeeah, Shadeeyah, Shadiah

Shae/Shay (Irish) from the fairy palace.
Shaeen, Shaeena, Shaeina, Shaeine, Shaela, Shaelaine, Shaelana, Shaelanna, Shaelanne, Shaelea, Shaeleah, Shaelee, Shaeleigh, Shaelene, Shaeli, Shaelie, Shaely, Shaelyn, Shaena, Shaenah, Shaenel, Shaeya, Shah, Shai, Shaiah, Shailea, Shaileah, Shailee, Shailei, Shaileigh, Shailey, Shaili, Shailia, Shailiah, Shailie, Shaily, Shaya, Shayah, Shayla, Shaylah, Shaylea, Shayleah, Shaylee, Shaylei, Shayleigh, Shayli, Shaylia, Shayliah, Shaylie, Shayly

Shaelisa (American) combination of Shae and Lisa.
Shaelesa, Shaelese, Shaelise, Shaelissa, Shaelisse, Shalesa,
Shalese, Shaleze, Shalisa, Shalise, Shalissa, Shalisse, Shaliza, Shalizza

Shaella (American) combination of Shae and Ella.
Shaela, Shaele, Shaelie, Shaelle, Shaellie, Shaelly, Shaely

Shaelona (American) combination of Shae and Lona.
Shaelone, Shalona, Shalonda, Shalonde, Shalondra Shalone, Shalonia, Shalonna, Shalonne

Shafira (African) well-known and highly thought of.
Shafeera, Shafeerah, Shafirah

Shah (Persian) fit for the king, a unisex name.
Sha

Shahar (Arabic) born on a moonlit night.
Shahara, Shaharah, Shaharia, Shahariah, Shaharr, Shaharra Sharhara, Sharharah, Sharharia, Sharhariah

Shahina (Arabic) falcon.
Shaheen, Shaheena, Shaheenah, Shaheene, Shahi, Shahia, Shahiah, Shahie, Shahin, Shahinah, Shahine

Shahla (Afghanistan) beautiful eyes.
Shaela, Shaelah, Shahlah, Shaila, Shailah, Shalah

Shahnaz (Persian) the pride of the emperor.
Shahnez

Shahrazad (Arabic) city-born, fictional story-teller of the *Tales of 1001 Nights*.
Scheherazad, Scheherazada, Scheherazade, Shahrazada, Shahrazade, Shahrazadia, Sharhad, Sharhada

Shaina (Hebrew, Irish) beautiful.

*Shaena, Shaenah, Shaene,
Shaenna, Shaennah, Shaenne,
Shainah, Shaine, Shainna,
Shainnah, Shainne, Shane, Shania,
Shaniah, Shanie, Shayna, Shaynah,
Shayne, Sheina, Sheinah, Sheine*

Shajauna (American)
combination of Shae and Juanita.

*Shajana, Shajanah, Shajuan,
Shajaune, Shajuanna, Shajuannah,
Shajaunne*

Shakara (American) combination
of Shae and Kara.

*Shacara, Shacarah, Shacari,
Shacaria, Sharcariah, Shacarra,
Shacarrah, Shaka, Shakah,
Shakarah, Shakari, Shakaria,
Shakariah, Shakarra, Shakarrah,
Shakarya, Shakaryah, Shikara*

Shakeena (American)
combination of Shae and Kena.

*Shakean, Shakeana, Shakeanah,
Shakeane, Shakeen, Shakeenah,
Shakeene, Shakein, Shakeina,
Shakeinah, Shakeine, Shakina,
Shakinah, Shakine, Shakyna,
Shakynah, Shakyne*

Shakeita (American) combination
of Shae and Keita.

*Shakeata, Shakeatah, Shakeate,
Shakeeta, Shakeetah, Shakeete,
Shakeetia, Shakeetiah, Shakeitah,
Shakeite, Shaketa, Shaketah,
Shakete, Shakeyta, Shakeytah,
Shakeyte, Shakita, Shakitah,
Shakite, Shakitra, Shakitrah,
Shekeita, Shekeitah, Shekeite,
Shekita, Shekitah, Shekieta,
Shekietah*

Shakia (American) combination
of Shae and Kia.

*Shaekea, Shaekeea, Shaekeeia,
Shaekia, Shakea, Shakeea,
Shakeeia, Shakeeiah, Shakeia,
Shakeiah, Shakiya, Shakiyah,*
*Shakya, Shakyah, Shekia, Shekiah,
Shekya, Shekyah*

Shakila (Arabic) pretty girl.

*Chaka, Chakaela, Chakayla,
Chakela, Chakila, Chekila, Shaka,
Shakaela, Shakail, Shakaila, Shakala,
Shakayla, Shakeela, Shakela,
Shakilah, Shekila*

Shakira (Arabic) thankful.

*Chakierra, Chakira, Shakeer,
Shakeera, Shakeerah, Shakiera,
Shakierah, Shakierra, Shakierrah,
Shakir, Shakirah, Shakirra, Shakirrah,
Shaquera, Shikira, Shikirah, Shikyra,
Shikyrah*

Shakti (Hindu) the powerful divine
woman.

*Sahkti, Sakti, Shaka, Shakah,
Shakhi, Shakhu, Shaki, Shaktee,
Shaktey, Shaktia, Shaktiah, Shaktie,
Shakty, Sita*

Shakuntala (Hindu) bird.

Shalana (American) combination
of Shae and Lana.

*Shaelana, Shaelanah, Shaelane,
Shaellana, Shaellanah, Shaellane,
Shalaina, Shalainah, Shalaine,
Shalanah, Shalane, Shalanna,
Shalannah, Shalanne, Shalena,
Shalenah, Shalene, Shallan,
Shallana, Shallanah, Shallane,
Shaylaina, Shaylainah, Shaylaine,
Shalayna, Shalaynah, Shalayne,
Shelena, Shelenah, Shelene,
Shellana, Shellanah, Shellane,
Shellena, Shellenah, Shellene*

Shaleah (American) combination
of Shae and Leah.

*Shaelea, Shaelee, Shaeleigh,
Shaelia, Shaeliah, Shalea, Shalee,
Shalia, Shaliah*

Shalena (American) combination
of Shae and Lena.

*Shaelina, Shaelinah, Shaelinda,
Shaelindah, Shaelyn, Shaelyna,*

Shaelynn, Shaelynna, Shaelynne, Shalean, Shaleana, Shaleanah, Shaleane, Shaleen, Shaleena, Shaleenah, Shaleene, Shalenah, Shalene, Shalenna, Shalennah, Shalina, Shalinah, Shalinda, Shalindah, Shaline, Shalini, Shalyn, Shalyna, Shalynn, Shalynna, Shalynne

Shalita (American) combination of Shae and Lita.

Shaeleda, Shaeleta, Shaelita, Shaleata, Shaleatah, Shaleda, Shaleeta, Shaleetah, Shaleta, Shaletah, Shaletta, Shalettah, Shalitah, Shalyta, Shalytah, Shalyte

Shamara (Arabic) ready to do battle.

Shaemara, Shaemarea, Shaemaree, Shaemari, Shaemaria, Shaimara, Shaimarea, Shaimaree, Shaimari, Shaimaria, Shamar, Shamarah, Shamare, Shamarea, Shamaree, Shamari, Shamaria, Shamariah, Shamora, Sharmara, Sharmaria, Sharmoriah, Shamorria

Shamika (American) combination of Shae and Meika.

Shaimeaker, Shaimecha, Shaimeeker, Shaimekah, Shaimeke, Shaimica, Shaimicka, Shaimieka, Shaimiekah, Shameaker, Shamecha, Shameeker, Shamekah, Shameke, Shamica, Shamicka, Shamieka, Shamiekah, Shamikah, Shamikia

Shamira (Hebrew) precious stone.

Shameer, Shameera, Shamir, Shamirah, Shamiria, Shamiriah, Shamirra, Shamirrah, Shamyra, Shamyrah, Shamyria, Shamyriah

Shanae (Hebrew) God is gracious, feminine form of Shane.

Chana, Shana, Shanay, Shane, Shanea

Shaneisha (American) combination of Shane and Aisha.

Shaneisa, Shaneisah, Shanesha, Shaneshia, Shanessa, Shanesse, Shaneysa, Shaneysah, Shanisha, Shanissha, Shanysha

Shaneka (Russian) precious gift belonging to God.

Shaneaca, Shaneacah, Shaneacka, Shaneackah, Shaneaka, Shaneakah, Shaneaqua, Shaneaquah, Shaneaque, Shaneca, Shanecah, Shanecka, Shaneckah, Shaneeka, Shaneekah, Shaneeker, Shaneika, Shaneikah, Shaneikia, Shaneikiah, Shanekah, Shanequa, Shanequah, Shaneque, Shanica, Shanicah, Shanicka, Shanickah, Shanika, Shanikah, Shanikia, Shanikiah, Shaniqua, Shaniquah, Shanique, Shanyca, Shanycah, Shanyka, Shanykah

Shani/Shany (African) wonderful.

Shanee, Shanie, Sharnee, Sharni, Sharnie, Sharny

Shania (Native American) I'm on my way.

Shanee, Shani, Shanie, Shanya, Sharnee, Sharnia, Sharnie, Sharyna

Shanika (American) combination of Shane and Nika.

Shaenica, Shaenicah, Shaenicka, Shaenickah, Shaeniqua, Shaenique, Shaneaca, Shaneacah, Shaneacka, Shaneackah, Shaneaka, Shaneakah, Shaneaqua, Shaneaque, Shaneca, Sharecah, Shanecka, Shaneckah, Shaneika, Shaneikah, Shaneka, Shanekah, Shanica, Shanicah, Shanikah, Shanike, Shanikia, Shanikiah, Shanikie, Shaniqua, Shanique

Shanita (American) combination of Sha and Nita.

Shanitah, Shanitra, Shanitrah,

Shanitt, Shanitta, Shanittah,
Shanitte, Shanyt, Shanyta,
Shanytah, Shanyte, Shanytt,
Shanytta, Shanyttah, Shanytte

Shanley (Irish) hero's child.

Shanlea, Shanleah, Shanlee,
Shanlei, Shanleigh, Shanli, Shanlie,
Shanly

Shannelle (French) channel.

Schanel, Schanelle, Schannel,
Shanell, Shanella, Shanelle,
Shanelli, Shanelly

Shannon (Irish) little wise one, the name of a river, a unisex name.

Shanan, Shaneen, Shanen, Shann,
Shanna, Shannan, Shannen,
Shannie, Shanon

Shanta (French) song, a form of Chantal.

Shantae, Shantah, Shantai,
Shantal, Shantea, Shantee,
Shantel

Shantara (American) combination of Sha and Tara.

Shantarah, Shantaria, Shantariah,
Shantarra, Shantarrah, Shantarria,
Shantarriah, Shantarya,
Shantaryah, Shantyra, Shantryah

Shantel (French) song, a form of Chantal.

Chantal, Chantale, Chantall,
Chantel, Chantele, Chantell,
Shanntell, Shanta, Shantae,
Shantal, Shantale, Shantall,
Shantel, Shantele, Shantell,
Shantella, Shantelle, Shontal,
Shontella, Shontelle

Shanti (Hindu) the tranquil one.

Shantee, Shantie, Shanty

Shappa (Native American) red thunder.

Shapa, Shapah, Shappah

Sharai (Hebrew) princess.

Shara, Sharae, Sharah, Sharaia,
Sharaiah, Sharay, Sharaya

Sharan (Hindu) one who will protect.

Sharen, Sharran, Sharrann, Sharren,
Sharrenn

Shardae (Punjabi) charitable and good; (Arabic) runaway; (African) honoured by royalty.

Shada, Shadah, Shadai, Shaday,
Sade, Shadee, Sharda, Shar-Dae,
Shardai, Shar-Dai, Sharde, Shardea,
Shardee, Shardei, Shardey

Shari (French) beloved one.

Cherie, Shara, Sharee, Sharia,
Shariah, Shariann, Sharianne,
Sharie, Sharra, Sharree, Sharri,
Sharrie, Shary, Sheree, Sherry

Sharifah (Arabic) noble, honourable, distinguished, feminine form of Sharif.

Shareefa, Shareefah, Sharifa

Sharik (African) child of God.

Sharika, Sharikah, Sharike, Sharyka,
Sharykah, Sharyke

Sharmila (Hindu) the protected one.

Shameela, Shameelah, Shameella,
Sharmilah, Sharmilla

Sharnae (Hebrew) from the plains.

Sharna, Sharnai, Sharnay, Sharne,
Sharnea, Sharnee, Sharnetta,
Sharnie, Sharnise, Sharny

Sharon (Hebrew) from the plains.

Shaaron, Shara, Sharai, Sharan,
Shareen, Sharen, Shari, Sharin,
Sharira, Sharna, Sharona, Sharonda,
Sharone, Sharron, Sharrona,
Sharronda, Sharyn, Sherren, Sheron,
Sheronda, Sherondah

Sharona (Hebrew) from the plains, a form of Sharon.

Sharonah, Sharone, Sharonia, Sharonna, Sharony, Sharronna, Sharronnah, Sharronne, Sheron, Sherona, Sherron, Sherrona, Sherronah, Sherronne, Shirona

Shasta (Native American) three.

Shastah, Shasti

Shatara (Arabic) good and industrious.

Shatarah, Shatari, Shataria, Shatarra, Shatarrah, Shataura, Shateira, Shatera, Shateria, Shatiera, Shatira, Shatiria

Shavonne (American) combination of Shae and Yvonne.

Schavon, Schavonne, Schevon, Schevonne, Shavana, Shavanna, Shavaun, Shavon, Shavona, Shavone, Shavonn, Shavonna, Shavonni, Shavonte, Shivonne

Shawna (Irish) God is gracious, a form of Jane, feminine form of Sean, Shaun.

Schaun, Schauna, Schaunah, Schaune, Schaunee, Schawn, Schawna, Schawnah, Schawne, Schawnee, Seana, Seanah, Seane, Seanee, Shaun, Shauna, Shaunah, Shaundel, Shaundell, Shaundelle, Shaune, Shaunee, Shaunta, Shauntae, Shauntah, Shaunte, Shauntei, Shauntrell, Shauntrelle, Shawn, Shawna, Shawnah, Shawndel, Shawndell, Shawndelle, Shawne, Shawnee, Shawney, Shawni, Shawnie, Shonta, Siana, Sianah, Sianna, Siannah, Sion, Syon

Shawnee (Irish) God is gracious, a form of Shawna.

Shaunee, Shauni, Shaunie, Shaunta, Shaunty, Shauny, Shawneea, Shawni, Shawnie, Shawnta, Shawntae, Shawnte, Shawntelle, Shonta

Shay (Irish) hawk-like, majestic, admirable, fairy palace, a form of Shea.

Cheye, Shae, Shaie, Shaye, Shey, Sheye

Shayla (Irish) fairy palace, a form of Shea.

Shaela, Shaelah, Shaeleigh, Shaelin, Shaelyn, Shaelynne, Shaylah, Shaylea, Shayleah, Shaylei, Shayleigh, Shayley, Shayli, Shaylie, Shaylin, Shaylynne, Shaylla

Shayna (Hebrew) beautiful one from the fairy palace.

Shaena, Shaenah, Shaina, Shainah, Shanae, Shaylee, Shaynae, Shaynah, Shayne, Shaynee, Shayney, Shayni, Shaynia, Shaynie, Shayny, Sheana, Sheanna

Shea (Irish) hawk-like, majestic, admirable, fairy palace, a unisex name.

Cheye, Shae, Shaie, Shay, Shaya, Shayah, Shayda, Shaye, Shayla, Shey, Sheye

Sheba (Hebrew) promise, a form of Bathsheba.

Shebah, Sheeba, Sheebah

Sheela (Hindu) of good character.

Sheena (Irish) God is gracious, a form of Jane, Scottish feminine form of John.

Sheana, Sheanah, Sheenah, Sheina, Sheinah, Shena, Shenah, Sheyna, Sheynah

Sheila (Latin) blind, a form of Cecilia.

Sheela, Sheelagh, Sheelah, Sheilah, Shela, Shelah, Shiela, Shielah

Sheina (Hebrew) God's gift.

Sheana, Sheanah, Sheena, Sheenah, Sheinah, Shena, Shenah

Shelby (English) dweller at the estate by the ledge, a sheltered town, a unisex name.

Chelby, Schelbe, Schelbee, Schelbi, Schelbie, Schelby, Selbee, Selbi, Selbie, Selby, Shelbe, Shelbee, Shelbi, Shelbie, Shelee, Sheli, Shelie, Shellbi, Shellbie, Shellby

Shelley (English) from the meadow's ledge, like God, a form of Michelle, a unisex name.

Shelee, Sheleen, Shelena, Sheley, Sheli, Shelia, Shelicia, Shelie, Shelina, Shelinda, Shelisa, Shelise, Shelita, Sheliza, Shellee, Shellen, Shellena, Shelli, Shellia, Shellicia, Shellie, Shellina, Shellinda, Shellisa, Shellise, Shellita, Shelly, Shellzia, Shely

Shenandoa (Native American) beautiful star.

Shenandoah

Shera (Aramaic) light.

Cher, Sheera, Sheerah, Sherae, Sherah, Sheralee, Sheray, Sheraya, Sherelle

Sheree (French) beloved, loved one, a form of Cherie.

Cheree, Cheri, Cherie, Cherree, Cherrie, Cherry, Sheerie, Shere, Shereena, Sherene, Sheri, Sherie, Sherree, Sherrie, Sherry,

Sheri (French) beloved.

Sheree, Sherey, Sherie, Sherree, Sherrey, Sherri, Sherrie, Sherry, Shery

Sherian (American) combination of Sheri and Anne.

Sheriana, Sherianna, Sherianne, Sherina, Sherrian, Sherrianna, Sherrianne, Sherrina

Sherice (French) beloved.

Cherice, Cherise, Scherice,
Scherise, Shereece, Shericia, Sherise, Sherissa, Sherisse, Sheryse*

Sheridan (Irish) wild, a unisex name.

Sheraden, Sheradin, Sherida, Sheridane, Sheriden, Sheridon, Sheridyn, Sherridan, Sherriden, Sherridon, Sherridyn, Sherrydan, Sherydan

Sherika (Punjabi) relative; (Arabic) easterner.

Shereika, Sherikah

Sherilyn (American) combination of Sheryl and Lyn.

Sherilin, Sherillyn, Sherillynn, Sherilynn, Sherolin, Sherrilyn, Sherrilynn, Sherrilynne, Sherryline, Sheryline

Sheryl (Welsh) beloved, a form of Cheryl.

Cheril, Sharilyn, Sharyll, Sherell, Sheril, Sherrell, Sherrelle, Sherril, Sherryl, Sheryll

Shiane (Native American) from the tribal name Cheyenne.

Shian, Shiana, Shiann, Shianna, Shianne, Shienn, Shienna, Sian

Shifra (Hebrew) beauty.

Shifrah

Shika (Japanese) deer.

Sheeca, Sheeka, Shi, Shikah, Shikha

Shilo (Hebrew) God's gift.

Shiloh

Shina (Japanese) virtuous, good.

Shinae, Shinay, Shine, Shinna

Shino (Japanese) bamboo stalk.

Shyno

Shira (Hebrew) my song.

Shara, Sheerah, Shirah

Shirin (Persian) charming.
Shirah, Shiran, Shiray, Shiree, Shireen, Shiren, Shirit, Shyra

Shirley (English) bright meadow.
Sherlee, Sherley, Sherli, Sherlie, Sherly, Shirl, Shirlee, Shirlene, Shirli, Shirlie, Shirline, Shirly, Shirlynn

Shivani (Hindu) life and death, feminine form of Shiva.
Shiva, Shivane, Shivanee, Shivanie, Shivanna, Shivanne, Shivannee, Shivannie

Shizu (Japanese) silent one.
Shizue, Shizuka, Shizuki

Shobhana (Hindu) the beautiful one.
Shobhanah

Shona (Irish) God is gracious, a form of Jane, Shawna, feminine form of John.
Shana, Shauna, Shawna, Shonah, Shondel, Shondell, Shondelle, Shonie, Shonna, Shonnah, Shonta

Shoshana (Hebrew) lily, a form of Susannah.
Shosha, Shoshahi, Shoshan, Shoshanah, Shoshann, Shoshanna, Shoshannah, Shoshane, Shoshona, Shoshonah

Shu (Chinese) gentle, kind.

Shula (Arabic) bright flame.
Shulah

Shulamith (Hebrew) peaceful.
Shula, Shulamit, Sula, Sulamith

Sian (Irish) God is gracious, a form of Jane.
Siana, Sianae, Siann, Sianna, Siannah, Sianne, Sianni, Siena, Sienna

Sibilla (Greek) prophet, wise woman, a form of Sibyl.
Sibel, Sibela, Sibil, Sibila, Sibyl, Sibyla, Sibyll, Sibylla, Sybel, Sybell, Sybella, Sybelle, Sybil, Sybill, Sybilla, Sybille

Sibyl (Greek) prophet, wise woman.
Sibel, Sibela, Sibell, Sibella, Sibelle, Sibil, Sibila, Sibill, Sibilla, Sibille, Sibla, Sibley, Sibyla, Sibyll, Sibylla, Sibylle, Sybel, Sybell, Sybella, Sybelle, Sybil, Sybill, Sybilla, Sybille

Sidonia (Greek) fine linen cloth.
Sidiana, Sidona, Sidonah, Sidonee, Sidoney, Sidoni, Sidoniah, Sidonie, Sidony, Sydiana, Sydona, Sydonah, Sydonee, Sydoney, Sydoni, Sydonia, Sydoniah, Sydonie, Sydony

Sidra (Latin) child of the stars.
Sidrah, Sidras

Sienna (Italian) reddish brown, a place name in Tuscany, Italy.
Ciena, Cieni, Cienna, Siena, Seini

Sierra (Spanish) mountain, saw-toothed; (Irish) black.
Seara, Searia, Searra, Searria, Seera, Seira, Seirra, Siara, Siarra, Siera, Sierrah, Sierre, Sierrea, Sierria, Sierriah

Sigfreda (German) peaceful victory, feminine from of Siegfried.
Sigfreeda, Sigfreida, Sigfrida, Sigfrieda, Sigfryda

Signe (Latin) sign, victorious; (Scandinavian) conquering guardian.
Signa, Signee, Signey, Signi, Signie, Signy, Singna, Singne, Singnee, Signey, Singni, Singnie, Singny, Sygna, Sygne, Sygnee, Sygney, Sygni, Sygnie, Sygny

Sigourney (English) victorious conqueror.

Signe, Signorrie, Signorry, Signoury, Sigournee, Sigourni, Sigournie, Sigourny, Sygournee, Sygourney, Sygourni, Sygournie, Sygourny

Sigrid (Old Norse) beautiful victory.

Siegrid, Siegrida, Siegritt, Sigrida, Sigritt, Sygrid, Sygrida, Sygritt, Sygryd, Sygryda

Sigrun (Old Norse) secret victory.

Sygrun

Siham (Arabic) arrow.

Syham

Sihu (Native American) flower.

Syhu

Silvana (Latin) from the forest, feminine form of Silvanus.

Silvanah, Silvane, Silvania, Silvaniah, Silvanie, Silvanna, Silvannah, Silvanne, Silvannia, Silvanniah, Silvannie, Silvanny, Sylvana, Sylvanah, Sylvane, Sylvania, Sylvaniah, Sylvanie, Sylvanna, Sylvannah, Sylvanne, Sylvannia, Sylvanniah, Sylvannie, Sylvanny

Silver (English) silver, a valuable metal, silversmith.

Silva, Silvee, Silvi

Silvestra (Latin) from the forest, feminine form of Silvester.

Silvesta, Silvestah, Silvestrah, Silvia, Sylvesta, Sylvestah, Sylvestra, Sylvestrah, Sylvia

Silvia (Latin) from the forest, silver.

Silva, Silvah, Silvea, Silvee, Silvi, Silviah, Silvie, Silvy, Silvya, Silvya, Sylva, Sylvah, Sylvea, Syvee, Sylvi, Sylvia, Sylvie, Sylvy, Sylvya, Sylvyah

Simcha (Hebrew) happiness, joyful, a unisex name.

Simchah, Simmy, Symcha, Symchah, Symmy

Simone (Hebrew, French) good listener, feminine form of Simon.

Saimon, Saimona, Saimone, Samon, Samona, Samone, Semoan, Semmoan, Semmon, Semmona, Semmone, Semon, Semona, Semonah, Semone, Simoan, Simoana, Simoane, Simmona, Simmone, Simona, Simonna, Simonne, Simonetta, Simonette, Symon, Symona, Symone, Ximena, Ximenia, Ximoan, Ximoana, Ximon, Ximona, Ximone, Xymon, Xymona, Xymone, Zimon, Zimona, Zimone, Zymon, Zymona, Zymone

Sina (Irish) God is gracious.

Seana, Seanah, Sinah

Sindy (American) moon, a form of Cindy.

Cindee, Cindey, Cindi, Cindie, Cindy, Sinda, Sindal, Sindee, Sindey, Sindi, Sindia, Sindie, Synda, Syndal, Syndee, Syndey, Syndi, Syndie, Syndy

Sinead (Irish) God is gracious, a form of Jane.

Seonaid, Sine, Sined, Sineade

Siobhan (Irish) God is gracious, a form of Jane.

Shavaugn, Shavaughn, Shavon, Shavona, Shavonah, Shavone, Shavonn, Shavonna, Shavonnah, Shavonne, Shibahn, Shibahna, Shiban, Shibana, Shibani, Shibhan, Shibhana, Shiobhan, Shiobhana, Shobha, Shobana, Shyvon, Shyvona, Shyvonah, Shyvone, Shyvonn, Shyvonna, Shyvonnah, Shyvonne, Siobahn, Siobahna, Siobhana, Siobhann, Siobhon, Sioned, Siovaun

Siran (Armenian) alluring.
Sirana, Sirann, Siranna, Siranne, Siren, Sirena, Sirenn, Sirenna, Sirenne, Sirienna, Sirienne

Sirena (Greek) temptress.
Sireen, Sireena, Sireenah, Sirene, Sirena, Sirine, Syrena, Syrenna

Sisika (Native American) songbird.
Sisikah, Sisiki

Sissy (English) blind, a form of Cecelia.
Sisey, Sisi, Sisie, Sissey, Sissie, Sisy

Sita (Hindu) furrow, trench.

Sitara (Hindu) morning star.
Sita, Sitah, Sitarah, Sitha, Sithah, Sithara, Sitharah

Sithembile (African) trust.

Siv (Old Norse) bride, wife of Thor.

Skye (English) island off the Scottish coast.
Skie, Skiy, Sklair, Sky, Skya, Skyla, Skylar, Skylark, Skylea, Skylee

Sloane (Celtic) warrior, a unisex name.
Sloan, Sloann, Sloanne

Socorro (Spanish) helper.
Socoro

Sofia (Latin) wisdom, a form of Sophia.
Sofea, Sofee, Sofeea, Sofeeia, Sofey, Soffea, Soffee, Soffeea, Soffeeia, Soffey, Soffi, Soffia, Soffie, Soffija, Soffy, Soffya, Sofi, Sofie, Sofija, Sofka, Sofy, Sofya, Zofea, Zofee, Zofey, Zoffea, Zoffee, Zoffey, Zoffi, Zoffia, Zoffie, Zoffy, Zoffya, Zofi, Zofia, Zofiah, Zofie, Zofy, Zofya, Zophea, Zophee, Zophey, Zophi, Zophia, Zophie, Zophy

Sol (Latin) the sun, a unisex name.
Solee, Solie, Soll, Sollee, Sollie, Solly, Soly

Solace (Latin) comfort.
Solas, Solase

Solada (Thai) listener.
Soladah

Solana (Spanish) sunshine.
Solande, Solanna, Solena, Solende, Solenna, Soliel, Solina, Solinda, Solinna

Solange (French) dignified, solemn.
Solang

Soledad (Spanish) alone.
Solaine, Sole, Soleda, Soleil, Solene, Solenna, Solenne, Solina, Soulle

Solita (Latin) lonely one, accustomed.
Soleata, Soleatah, Soleeta, Soleetah, Soleete, Soleita, Soleitah, Solitah, Solite, Solitta, Solittah, Solitte, Solyta, Solytah, Solytta, Solyttah, Solytte

Solveig (Old Norse) strong house, healing drink, heroine of Henrik Ibsen's play *Peer Gynt*.
Solvig

Soma (Hindu) moon, born during lunar month of Cancer.
Somah, Somar

Sonia (Greek) wise.
Soniah, Sonica, Sonida, Sonita, Sonja, Sonjae, Sonjah, Sonna, Sonni, Sonnia, Sonnie, Sonny, Sonnya, Sonya, Sonyae, Sunya

Sophia/Sophie (Greek) wisdom.
Sofeea, Sofeeia, Sofeeiah, Soffia, Soffiah, Soffie, Soffy, Sofi, Sofia, Sofiah, Sofie, Sofy, Sofya, Sofyah,

Sophea, Sopheea, Sopheia, Sopheiah, Sophey Sopheya, Sopheyah, Sophi, Sophiah, Sophy, Sophya, Sophyah, Zofea, Zofee, Zofey, Zoffea, Zoffee, Zoffey, Zoffy, Zoffya, Zofi, Zofia, Zofiah, Zofie, Zofy, Zofya, Zophea, Zophee, Zophey, Zophi, Zophia, Zophie, Zophy

Sora (Native American) singing bird soars.

Sorah

Soraya (Persian) princess.

Soraha, Soraia, Soraiah, Sorayah

Sorrel (French) bitter, from the name of the herb, red-brown colour, a unisex name.

Sorel, Sorela, Sorelah, Sorele, Sorell, Sorella, Sorellah, Sorelle, Sorrell, Sorrella, Sorrelle, Soryl, Soryla, Soryle, Sorryl, Sorryla, Sorryle

Soso (Native American) chubby-cheeked baby.

Souzan (Persian) burning fire.

Sousan, Sousana, Sousann, Sousanna, Sousanne, Souzana, Souzann, Souzanna, Souzanne

Sparrow (English) a bird.

Spica (Latin) ear of wheat, the name of a star in Virgo.

Spicah

Spirit (Latin) spiritual, lively.

Spiritt, Spiryt

Spring (English) springtime.

Spryng

Stacey/Stacia (Greek) resurrection, a form of Anastasia, a unisex name.

Stace, Stacea, Stacee, Staci, Staciah, Stacie, Stacy, Staice, Staicea, Staicee, Staici, Staicia, Staiciah, Staicie, Staicy, Stasea, Stasee, Stasey, Stasi, Stasia, Staisiah, Stasie, Stasy, Stasya, Stasyah, Stasha, Stasje, Stayce, Staycea, Staycee, Staycey, Stayci, Staycia, Stayciah, Staycie, Staycy, Staysi, Staysia

Star (English) star, a unisex name.

Starea, Staree, Staria, Starie, Starika, Starisha, Starla, Starleen, Starlena, Starlene, Starlet, Starletta, Starlette, Starlia, Starlight, Starlyn, Starr, Starri, Starrla, Starry, Stary, Starynite

Starling (English) small bird.

Starlin

Stefannia (Greek) crowned, feminine form of Stephan.

Estephanie, Panya, Stefane, Stefanee, Stefaney, Stefani, Stefania, Stefanie, Stefanni, Stefannia, Stefanny, Stefanya, Stefeni, Stefenie, Steffi, Steffine, Stefka, Stephena, Stephene, Stepheney, Stepheni, Stephenia, Stephenie, Stepheny, Stephenya, Stephine, Stephne, Stephney, Stephni, Stephnia, Stephnie, Stesha, Steshka, Stevanee, Stevie, Zephania, Zephannia

Stella (Latin) star.

Estel, Estela, Estelah, Estele, Estell, Estella, Estellah, Estelle, Stela, Stelah, Stellah

Stephanie (Greek) crowned, feminine form of Stephan.

Stefanea, Stefanee, Stefaney, Stefani, Stefania, Stefaniah, Stefanie, Stefany, Stefanya, Stefanyah, Steffanea, Steffanee, Steffaney, Steffani, Steffania, Steffaniah, Steffanie, Steffany, Steffanya, Steffanyah, Stephanea, Stephanee, Stephaney, Stephani, Stephania, Stephaniah, Stephany, Stephanya, Stephanyah, Stephaija, Steva, Stevana, Stevee, Stevi, Stevy

Stockard (English) stockyard, a unisex name.
Stocard, Stocarde, Stockarde, Stokard, Stokarde, Stokkard, Stokkarde

Storm (English) storm, tempest, a unisex name.
Storme, Stormee, Stormey, Stormi, Stormie, Stormy

Suchin (Thai) beautiful thoughts.

Sue (English) lily, a form of Susan.
Soo, Sou, Su

Sue-Ellen (English) combination of Sue and Ellen.
Sooellen, Soo-Ellen, Souelen, Souellen, Sou-Ellen, Suella, Suelle, Suellen, Su-Ellen

Sugar (American) sweet as sugar.
Sugarh, Sugarr

Suha (Arabic) star.
Suhah

Sujata (Hindu) of noble birth.
Sujatah

Suki (Japanese) beloved child.
Sukie, Sukii

Sula (Scandanavian) large soaring seabird; (Greek) little bear, a form of Ursula.
Soula, Soulah, Sulah, Suleta, Sulia, Suliana

Sulwen (Welsh) bright as the sun.
Sully, Sulwyn, Sulwynn, Sulwynne

Suma (African) asked for.
Sumah

Sumalee (Thai) beautiful flower.
Sumilee, Sumili, Sumilie, Summeile

Sumi (Japanese) elegant.
Sumii

Summer (English) born during summer.
Sumadai, Sumatym, Summa, Summabreze, Summadae, Summadai, Summadaiz, Summahaze, Summalee, Summar

Sun (Korean) obedient.
Sundai, Sundance, Sundee, Sundi, Sundip, Suni, Sunnee, Sunta, Sunya

Sunee (Thai) good.
Sun-Hi, Suni

Suni (Native American) member of our tribe.
Sunie, Sunita, Suniti, Sunne, Sunni, Sunnie

Sunita (Hindu) of good conduct.
Sunitah

Sunniva (Scandinavian) gift of the sun.
Suniva, Sunivah, Sunnivah

Sunny (English) bright, cheerful, sunshine, a unisex name.
Sonee, Soney, Soni, Sonie, Sonni, Sonnie, Sonny, Sunee, Suney, Suni, Sunie, Sunn, Sunni, Sunnie, Suny

Sunshine (English) sunny-natured, sunshine.
Sunshyn, Sunshyne

Surata (Pakastani) blessed joy.
Suratah

Surya (Hindu) sun, a unisex name.
Suria, Suryah

Susan (Hebrew) lily.
Santje, Shoshan, Shoshana, Shushan, Siusan, Siusann, Soosan, Soosana, Soosanah, Soosane,

Sosan, Sosana, Sosanah, Sosane, Sosann, Sosanna, Sosannah, Sousan, Sousana, Sousanah, Sousane, Sousann, Sousanna, Sousannah, Sousanne, Suann, Suanna, Suannah, Suanne, Sue, Suella, Suelle, Suesan, Suesana, Suesanah, Suesane, Suesann, Suesanna, Suesannah, Suesanne, Sus, Susana, Susanah, Susane, Susanka, Susann, Susanna, Susannah, Susanne, Sussan, Sussana, Sussanah, Sussane, Sussann, Sussanna, Sussannah, Sussanne, Suzan, Suzana, Suzanah, Suzane, Suzann, Suzanna, Suzannah, Suzanne, Suze, Suzie, Suzzan, Suzzana, Suzzanah, Suzzane, Suzzann, Suzzanna, Suzzannah, Suzzanne, Suzetta, Suzette

Susanna/Susannah (Hebrew) lily, a form of Susan.

Soosana, Soosanah, Sosana, Sosanah, Sosanna, Sosannah, Sousana, Sousanah, Sousanna, Sousannah, Sousanne, Suanna, Suannah, Sue, Suesana, Suesanah, Suesanna, Suesannah, Sus, Susana, Susanah, Suzana, Suzanah, Suzanna, Suzannah, Suze, Suzie, Suzzana, Suzzanah, Suzzanna, Suzzannah, Suzetta, Suzette

Susanne (Hebrew) lily, a form of Susan.

Susane, Susann, Suszanne, Suzane, Suzann, Suzanne, Suzzanne

Susette/Suzette (French) lily, a form of Susan.

Susetta, Suzetta, Suzzetta, Suzzette

Suzu (Japanese) little bell.

Suzue, Suzuko

Svea (Swedish) woman of Sweden.

Sveah

Svetlana (Russian, Slavic) bright star.

Svata, Svatochka, Svetlanah

Swana (English) swan.

Swania, Swanna, Swannie, Swanny

Swanhilda (Teutonic) swan battle maiden.

Swanhilde

Sya (Chinese) summer.

Sia, Siah, Syah

Sybil (Greek) prophet.

Cebel, Cebele, Cebell, Cebelle, Cibal, Cibel, Cibell, Cibelle, Cibil, Cibyl, Cybal, Cybel, Cybele, Cybell, Cybelle, Cybil, Cybill, Cybyl, Cylbel, Cylbell, Cylbelle, Sibal, Sibeale, Sibel, Sibell, Sibelle, Sibette, Sibil, Sibila, Sibill, Sibilla, Sibille, Sibillie, Sibillina, Sibla, Sibley, Sibyle, Sibyll, Sibylle, Sibyllina, Sevilla, Sevillia, Sybal, Sybel, Sybell, Sybelle, Sybill, Sybyl, Sylbel, Sylbell, Sylbelle

Sydelle (Hebrew) princess.

Sidela, Sidele, Sidella, Sidelle, Sydel, Sydela, Sydell, Sydella

Sydney (French) from St-Denis in France, a unisex name.

Sid, Sidel, Sidell, Sidelle, Sidnay, Sidni, Sidnie, Sidny, Signee, Syd, Sydel, Sydell, Sydelle, Sydnay, Sydne, Sydnea, Sydnee, Sydnei, Sydni, Sydnie, Sydny

Sying (Chinese) star.

Syke (Greek) mulberry tree.

Sylvia (Latin) from the forest.

*Silvain, Silvaine, Silvana, Silvanah,
Silvania, Silvaniah, Silvestra, Silvi,
Silvia, Silvie, Silvy, Silvya, Silvyah,
Sylvain, Sylvaine, Sylvainia, Sylvana,
Sylvanah, Sylvania, Sylvaniah, Sylvi,
Sylvian, Sylvianne, Sylvie, Sylvina,
Sylvinnia, Sylvonna, Sylvonnia,
Sylwia, Xylia, Xylvia*

Symone (Hebrew) good listener, a
form of Simone.

*Symeon, Symmone, Symoan,
Symona, Symonne*

T

Tabia (African) talented.
Tabiah, Tabya, Tabyah

Tabina (Arabic) follower of Muhammad.
Tabinah, Tabyna, Tabynah

Tabitha (Greek) gazelle.
Tabatha, Tabbatha, Tabbetha, Tabbitha, Tabbytha, Tabetha, Tabytha

Tabora (Arabic) drum or drummer, feminine form of Tabor.
Tab, Tabber, Tabbera, Tabor, Taborah, Taibor, Taibora, Taiborah, Tayber, Taybera, Tayberah, Taybor, Taybora, Tayborah

Taci (Native American) washtub.
Tacee, Tacey, Tacia, Taciah, Tacy, Tacya, Tacyah

Tacita (Latin) silent, peaceful one.
Tace, Tacea, Tacee, Taceeta, Taceetah, Taci, Tacia, Taciah, Tacie, Tasie, Tasita, Tasitah, Tayce, Taycita, Taycitah

Tafline (Welsh) beloved.
Taflina, Taflinah, Taflyn, Taflyna, Taflynah, Taflyne

Tafne (Egyptian) goddess of light.
Taffne, Taffnee, Taffney, Taffni, Taffnie, Taffny, Tafna, Tafnah, Tafnee, Tafney, Tafni, Tafnie, Tafny

Tahira (Arabic) pure, feminine form of Tahir.
Taheera, Taheerah, Tahera, Taherah, Tahirah, Tahyra, Tahyrah

Tahiti (Polynesian) rising sun.
Tahitea, Tahitee, Tahitey, Tahitia, Tahitie, Tahity

Tai (Vietnamese) talented, prosperous one.
Tae, Taie

Taima (Native American) loud crash of thunder, born during a thunderstorm, a unisex name.
Taimah, Taimy, Taimma, Taimmah, Taimmy, Tayma, Taymah, Taymi, Taymie, Taymmi, Taymmie, Taymmy, Taymy

Taimani (African) diamonds.
Taimanee, Taimaney, Taimania, Taimaniah, Taimanie, Taimany, Taimanya, Taimanyah

Tainn (Native American) new moon, a unisex name.
Tain, Taina, Tainah, Taine, Tainn, Tane, Tayn, Tayna, Taynah, Tayne

Taipa (Native American) flying quail.
Taipah

Tais (Greek) bound.
Taisa, Taisah, Tays, Taysa, Taysah

Taite (English) cheerful, happy, a unisex name.
Tait, Taita, Taitah, Taitt, Taitta, Taittah, Tayt, Tayta, Taytah, Tayte

Taja (Hindu) crown, feminine form of Taj.
Tajah, Taji

Taka (Japanese) honoured.
Takah

Takara (Japanese) treasure or precious object.
Takarah, Takaria, Takariah, Takarya, Takaryah

Takenya (Native American) falcon.
Takenia, Takeniah, Takenyah

Taki (Japanese) waterfall.
Takee, Takey, Takie, Takii, Taky

Takia (Arabic) worshipper.
Takea, Takeah, Takeia, Takeiah, Takeiya, Takeiyah, Takeya, Takeyah, Takiah, Takiya, Takiyah, Takkia, Takkiah, Takkya, Takkyah, Takya, Takyah

Tala (Native American) stalking wolf.
Talah

Talasi (Native American) corn-tassel flower, a unisex name.
Talasea, Talasee, Talasia, Talasiah, Talasie, Talasy, Talasya, Talasyah

Taleebin (Aboriginal Australian) young.
Taleabin, Taleabina, Taleabine, Taleabyn, Taleabyna, Taleabyne, Taleebina, Taleebyn, Taleebyna, Taleebyne

Talen (English, French) claw, a unisex name.
Talin, Tallen, Tallon, Talon

Talia (French, Latin) birthday, from the name Natalya; (Greek) blooming; (Hebrew) dew from heaven.
Tahlia, Tahliah, Talea, Taleah, Taliah, Taliea, Talieah, Talieya, Talieyah, Tallia, Talliah, Tallya, Tallyah, Talya, Talyah

Talibah (Arabic) seeking knowledge, intelligent, feminine form of Talib.
Taleba, Talebah, Tali, Taliba, Talyba, Talybah

Talisa (American, African) consecrated to God.
Talisah, Talissa, Talissah, Talysa, Talysah, Talyssa, Talyssah, Tahlia

Talisha (English, American) damsel arising.

Talitha (Aramaic) young woman.

Tallis (French, English) forest, woods.
Talease, Taleece, Taleese, Taleice, Taleise, Taleyce Taleyse, Talice, Taliece, Taliese, Talis, Talise, Tallas, Tallise, Talliss, Tallisse, Tallyce, Tallys, Tallyse, Talyce, Talys, Talyse, Talyss, Talysse

Tallulah (Native American) running water.
Tallula, Talula

Talma (Hebrew) small hill; (Native American) crashing thunder.
Talmah, Talmar, Talmara, Talmarah, Talmare, Talmaria, Talmariah, Talmarya, Talmaryah

Talor (Hebrew) morning dew; (English) a form of Taylor, a unisex name.
Taelor, Taelora, Talora, Talorah, Talore, Talori, Taloria, Taloriah, Talorie, Talory, Talorya, Taloryah

Tam (English) a form of names starting with Tam, such as Tamara; (Vietnamese) heart.
Tama, Tamah, Tami, Tamia, Tamiah, Tamie, Tammy, Tamya, Tamyah, Tamyh

Tama (Japanese) pearl.
Tamah

Tamaka (Japanese) bracelet.
Tamakah, Tamaki, Tamakia, Tamakiah, Tamako, Tamakya, Tamakyah

Tammy

Tamara (Hebrew) spice or palm tree, feminine form of Tamar.

Tama, Tamar, Tamarah, Tamareah, Tamaree, Tamari, Tamaria, Tamariah, Tamarie, Tamarind, Tamarra, Tamarrah, Tamarya, Tamaryah, Tamera, Tamerah, Tamerlain, Tamerlaina, Tamerlaine, Tamika, Tamma, Tamra, Tamy

Tameka (Hebrew) twin, feminine form of Thomas.

Tameca, Tamecah, Tamecka, Tameckah, Tameeca, Tameecah, Tameeka, Tameekah, Tamekah, Tamica, Tamicah, Tamicca, Tamiccah, Tamicka, Tamickah, Tamika, Tamikah, Tamikka, Tamikkah

Tamera (Hebrew) spice or palm tree, a form of Tamara.

Tamer, Tamerah, Tamerai, Tameran, Tameria, Tameriah, Tamerra, Tamerrah, Tammera, Tammerah

Tamia (Hebrew) spice or palm tree, a form of Tamara.

Tamea, Tameah, Tameea, Tameeah, Tamiah, Tamya, Tamyah

Tamika (African American) people.

Tameca, Tamecah, Tamecka, Tameckah, Tameeca, Tameecah, Tameeka, Tameekah, Tameka, Tamekah, Tamica, Tamicah, Tamicka, Tamickah, Tamikah, Tamyca, Tamycah, Tamycka, Tamyckah, Tamyka, Tamykah

Tamiko (Japanese) child of the people.

Tameeko, Tameko, Tamyko

Tamira (Hebrew) spice or palm tree, a form of Tamara.

Meera, Mira, Tameera, Tammie,

Tammy (Hebrew), palm tree, date fruit.

Tamalana, Tamalane, Tamalina, Tamalinah, Tamaline, Tamara, Tamee, Tameeka, Tameika, Tamera, Tamerah, Tamey, Tami, Tamia, Tamiah, Tamika, Tamike, Tamiko, Tamilla, Tamille, Tamira, Tamisa, Tamisha, Tamitta, Tamitte, Tamlyn, Tammee, Tammey, Tammi, Tammia, Tammiah, Tammie, Tammra, Tammrah, Tamra, Tamrah, Tamy, Tamya, Tamyah, Tema, Temah, Temara, Temarah, Temaria, Temariah, Temarya, Temaryah, Tomika, Tomyka

Tamsyn (Aramic) twin, a form of Thomasina.

Tamasin, Tamasine, Tami, Tamsin, Tamsine, Tamsyn, Tamsyne, Tamzin

Tana (Australian Aboriginal) ceremony.

Tanah

Tanaka (Japanese) swamp dweller.

Tandice (American) team.

Tandise

Tandy (English) team.

Tanda, Tandah, Tandea, Tandee, Tandey, Tandi, Tandia, Tandiah, Tandie, Tandis, Tandya, Tandyah, Tandye

Tani (Japanese) valley.

Tahnee, Tanee, Tania, Taniah, Tanie, Tanita, Tannis, Tany, Tanya, Tanyah, Tanys, Tanysa, Tanysah

Tania (Russian, Slavic) fairy queen, a form of Tatiana.

Tahna, Tahnah, Tahnee, Tahni, Tahnia, Tahniah, Tahniya, Tahniyah, Tahnya, Tahnyah, Taina, Tana, Tanae, Tanah, Tanaya, Tanea,

Tanee, Taneek, Taneisha, Tanelle, Tanhya, Taniah, Tanika, Tanique, Taniya, Taniyah, Tanja, Tanjah, Tanje, Tanneale, Tannia, Tanniah, Tannika, Tannya, Tannyah, Tanthe, Tanya, Tanyah, Tatiana, Tatianah, Tatiania, Tatianiah, Tatiann, Tatianna, Tatiannah, Tawnea, Tawnee, Tawney, Tawni, Tawnia, Tawniah, Tawnie, Tawny, Tawnya, Tawnyah, Tenaya, Teneal, Tenia, Teniah, Tenie, Tenya, Tenyah, Tonia, Toniah, Tonie, Tonya, Tonyah

Taniel (Hebrew) God is my judge, feminine form of Nathaniel.

Taniela, Tanielah, Taniele, Taniell, Taniella, Taniellah, Tanielle, Tanyel, Tanyela, Tanyelah, Tanyell, Tanyella, Tanyellah, Tanyelle

Tanika (Hindu) rope.

Nika, Nikka, Nikki, Tenika, Tyneka, Tynika

Tanith (Phoenican) goddess of love.

Tanitha, Tanithah, Tanithe, Tanyth, Tanytha, Tanythah, Tanythe

Tansy (Greek) immortality, herb.

Tancy, Tansea, Tansee, Tansey, Tansi, Tansia, Tansiah, Tansie, Tansya, Tansyah, Tanzey, Tanzy

Tanya (Russian, Slavic) fairy princess.

Tahna, Tahnah, Tahnee, Tahni, Tahnia, Tahniah, Tahniya, Tahniyah, Tahnya, Tahnyah, Taina, Tana, Tanae, Tanah, Tanaya, Tanea, Tanee, Taneek, Taneisha, Tanelle, Tanhya, Tania, Taniah, Tanika, Tanique, Taniya, Taniyah, Tanja, Tanjah, Tanje, Tanneale, Tannia, Tanniah, Tannika, Tannya, Tannyah, Tanthe, Tanyah, Tatiana, Tatianah, Tatiania, Tatianiah, Tatiann, Tatianna, Tatiannah, Tawnea, Tawnee, Tawney, Tawni, Tawnia, Tawniah, Tawnie, Tawny, Tawnya, Tawnyah, Tenaya, Teneal, Tenia, Teniah, Tenie, Tenya, Tenyah, Tonia,

Toniah, Tonie, Tonya, Tonyah

Tao (Chinese) peach, long life, a unisex name.

Tapanga (African) sweet.

Tara (Gaelic) rocky hill; (Aramic) throw or carry; (Arabic) measure.

Tarah, Taralyn, Taralynn, Taralynne, Taran, Taria, Tariah, Tarnia, Tarniah, Tarra, Tarrah, Tarya, Taryah, Taryn, Taryna, Tarynah, Taryne

Taraneh (Persian) melody.

Taran, Tarana, Taranah, Tarane

Taranga (Polynesian) a figure from legend, the mother of Maui.

Tarati (Maori) gift of God.

Taratea, Taratee, Taratey, Taratia, Taratiah, Taratie, Taraty, Taratya, Taratyah

Taree (Japanese) branch with an arch.

Tarea, Tarey, Tari, Taria, Tariah, Tarie, Tary, Tarya, Taryah

Tarika (Hindu) star.

Tarikah

Tarne (Scandinavian) mountain lake.

Tarn, Tarna, Tarnah, Tarnea, Tarnee, Tarney, Tarni, Tarnia, Tarniah, Tarnie, Tarny

Tarni (Australian Aboriginal) saltwater.

Tarne, Tarnea, Tarnee, Tarney, Tarnia, Tarniah, Tarnie, Tarny, Tarnya, Tarnyah, Tarnye

Tarra (Australian Aboriginal) creek, stream.

Tara, Tarah, Tarrah

Tarub (Arabic) merry.

Taroob

Taryn (American) combination of Tara and Karyn.

Taran, Taren, Tarin, Tarran, Tarren, Tarrin, Tarryn

Tasha (English) born on Christmas Day, a form of Natasha, from nativity.

Natasha, Tashi, Tashia, Tashiah, Tashy, Tashya, Tashyah, Tassam, Towsha

Tashi (Tibetan) lucky one.

Tasmin/Tasmyn (English) twin, feminine form of Thomas.

Tamasin, Tamasina, Tamasine, Tammi, Tammie, Tammy, Tamsin, Tamzin, Tamzina, Tasma, Tasman, Tasmen, Tasmina, Tasminah, Tasmine, Tasmyna, Tasmynah, Tasmyne, Tasmynn, Tasmynna, Tasmynnah, Tasmynne, Tassie, Tassy, Tazmin, Tazmina, Tazminah, Tazmine, Tazmyn, Tazmynah, Tazmyne, Thomasa, Thomasah, Thomasin, Thomasina, Thomasinah, Thomasine, Thomasyn, Thomasyna, Thomasynah, Thomasyne, Tomasin, Tomasina, Tomasinah, Tomasine, Tomasyn, Tomasyna, Tomasynah, Tomasyne

Tassos (Greek) harvester, a form of Theresa.

Tasos

Tatiana/Tatyana (Russian, Slavic) fairy queen.

Taitiana, Taitiann, Taitianna, Tatania, Tataniah, Tatanya, Tatanyah, Tateana, Tateanna, Tateonna, Tateyana, Tati, Tatia, Tatianah, Tatiania, Tatianiah, Tatiayana, Tatie, Tatihana, Tationna, Tatiyona, Tatiyonna, Tatyanah, Tatyanna, Tatyannah

Tatum (Anglo-Saxon) cheerful, happy, a feminine form of Tate.

Tait, Taitam, Taitem, Taitim, Taitom, Taitum, Taitym, Tata, Tatam, Tate, Tatem, Tatim, Tatom, Tayt, Taytam, Taytem, Taytim, Taytom, Taytum, Taytym

Tavie (Scottish) twin.

Tavee, Tavey, Tavia, Taviah, Tavy, Tavya, Tavyah

Tawia (African) child born after twins.

Tawiah, Tawya, Tawyah

Tawnie/Tawny (English) yellowish-brown colouring.

Tawna, Tawnah, Tawnea, Tawnee, Tawney, Tawni, Tawnia, Tawniah, Tawnya, Tawnyah, Tawnye

Taya (English) tailor of clothes, a form of Taylor.

Tayah

Tayanita (Native American) beaver.

Taianita, Taianitah, Tayanitah, Tayanyta, Tayanytah

Tayce (French) silence.

Taice, Taise, Tayse

Tayen (Native American) new moon.

Taylor (English) tailor of clothes, a unisex name.

Tahla, Tahyla, Tai, Taie, Taila, Tailah, Tailar, Tailara, Tailer, Tailor, Tailora, Tailore, Taurina, Taurine, Tay, Taya, Tayah, Taye, Tayissa, Tayla, Taylah, Taylar, Taylara, Tayler, Taylora, . Taylore

Tazu (Japanese) stork.

Taz

Teagan (Welsh) beautiful, a unisex

name.

Taegan, Taegen, Taegin, Taegon, Taegun, Taegyn, Teahgan, Teahgen, Teahgin, Teahgon, Teahgyn, Teagen, Teagin, Teagon, Teagun, Teagyn, Teegan, Teegen, Teegin, Teegon, Teegun, Teegyn, Tegan, Tegana, Teganah, Tegane, Tegen, Tegin, Tegon, Tegun, Tegyn, Teigan, Teigen, Teigin, Teigon, Teigun, Teigyn, Teygan, Teygen, Teygin, Teygon, Teygun, Teygyn, Tigan, Tigen, Tigin, Tigon, Tigun, Tigyn, Tygan, Tygen, Tygin, Tygon, Tygun, Tygyn

Teal (English) sea-green water bird, a unisex name.

Teala, Tealah, Teale, Teel, Teela, Teelah, Teele, Teil, Teila, Teilah, Teile, Teyla, Teylah

Teangi (Australian Aboriginal) earth.

Teeangi

Teanna (English) graceful.

Teana, Teanah, Teane, Teannah, Teanne, Teiana, Teianah, Teiane, Teiann, Teianna, Teiannah, Teianne, Teyan, Teyana, Teyanah, Teyane, Teyann, Teyanna, Teyannah, Teyanne, Tian, Tiana, Tianah, Tiane, Tiann, Tianna, Tiannah, Tianne, Tyan, Tyana, Tyanah, Tyane, Tyann, Tyanna, Tyannah, Tyanne

Teca (Hungarian) harvester, a form of Theresa.

Tecah, Techa, Techah, Tecka, Teckah, Teka, Tekah, Tica, Ticah, Tika, Tikah, Tyca, Tycah, Tyka, Tykah

Tegan (Welsh) beautiful, a form of Teagan.

Taegan, Taegen, Taegin, Taegon, Taegun, Taegyn, Teahgan, Teahgen, Teahgin, Teahgon, Teahgun, Teahgyn, Teagan, Teagen, Teagin, Teagon, Teagun, Teagyn, Teegan, Teegen, Teegin, Teegon, Teegun, Teegyn, Tegana,

Teganah, Tegane, Tegen, Tegin, Tegon, Tegun, Tegyn, Teigan, Teigen, Teigin, Teigon, Teigun, Teigyn, Teygan, Teygen, Teygin, Teygon, Teygun, Teygyn, Tigan, Tigen, Tigin, Tigon, Tigun, Tigyn, Tygan, Tygen, Tygin, Tygon, Tygun, Tygyn

Tegwen (Welsh) beautiful one.

Tegwyn

Tehya (Native American) precious.

Tehia, Tehiya

Telma (Greek) ambitious.

Thelma

Temima (Arabic) honest.

Tamimah, Tamyma, Tamymah, Temina, Temira

Temperance (Latin) moderate.

Tempe, Tempee, Temperanse

Tempest (French) storm, a unisex name.

Tempes, Tempesta, Tempestah, Tempeste, Tempist, Tempistt, Tempress, Tempteste

Teodora (Greek) gift from God, feminine form of Theodore.

Teodoria, Teodorsia, Theodora, Theodoria, Theodorsia

Tera (Latin) earth.

Terah, Terra, Terrah

Terena (English) earthly and tender, feminine form of Terence.

Tereena, Terenia, Terina, Terrena, Terrina

Teresa/Theresa/Therese (Greek) harvester.

Tereasa, Tereasah, Terease, Terees, Tereesa, Tereesah, Tereese, Teresah, Terese, Teresina, Teresita, Teressa, Tereza, Terezia, Tereziah,

Terezie, Teri, Teria, Teriah, Terie, Terisa, Terisah, Terise, Terrea, Terreas, Terreasa, Terreasah, Terrease, Terree, Terreey, Terris, Terrisa, Terrisah, Terrise, Terry, Terrys, Terrysa, Terrysah, Terryse, Tery, Thereas, Thereasa, Theresah, Theresia, Theresie, Theris, Therisa, Therisah, Therise, Therris, Therrisa, Therrisah, Therrise, Therrys, Therrysa, Therrysah, Therryse, Therys, Therysa, Therysah, Theryse

Teri/Terri (Greek) harvester, a form of Teresa.

Teria, Teriah, Terie, Terrie, Terry, Terrys, Tery

Terra (Latin) earth.

Tera, Terah, Teria, Teriah, Terrah, Terria, Terriah, Terrya, Terryah, Terya, Teryah

Terrene (Latin) smooth, earthly, tender, feminine form of Terence.

Terea, Tereana, Tereane, Tereen, Tereena, Tereene, Terin, Terina, Terine, Terrean, Terreana, Terreane, Terreen, Terreena, Terreene, Terrena, Terrenah, Terrin, Terrina, Terrine, Terryn, Terryna, Terryne, Teryn, Teryna, Teryne

Tertia (Latin) the third child.

Tertiah, Tertya, Tertyah

Tess (Greek) harvester, fourth-born child, a form of Therese.

Tes, Tesa, Tesah, Tesara, Tessa, Tessah, Tessara

Tetsu (Japanese) iron.

Tetsoo

Tevy (Cambodian) angel.

Tevee, Tevey, Tevi, Tevie

Thaddea (Greek) courageous, feminine form of Thaddeus.

Thada, Thadda, Thaddea, Thaddeah, Thaddia, Thaddiah,

Thaddie, Thaddina, Thaddya, Thaddyah, Thaddyna, Thaddyne, Thadea, Thaden, Thadia, Thadiah, Thadie, Thadina, Thadya, Thadyah, Thadyna, Thadyne

Thadine (Hebrew) praised.

Thadee, Thady, Thadyne

Thalia (Greek) flourishing, flowering, joyful.

Talia, Thaliah, Thalya, Thalyah

Thana (Arabic) happy occasion.

Thaina, Thainah, Thanah, Thayna, Thaynah

Thandie (African) beloved.

Thandee, Thandey, Thandi, Thandy

Thanh (Vietnamese) finished, complete, brilliant, intelligent, sky-blue, a unisex name.

Than

Thao (Vietnamese) she who respects her parents.

Thara (Arabic) wealth.

Thea (Greek) goddess.

Theah, Theia, Theiah, Theya, Theyah

Theda (Teutonic) of the people.

Theodora

Thelma (Greek) wilful.

Telma, Thelmae, Thelmah, Thelmai

Thema (African) queen.

Themah

Theodora (Greek) gift from God, feminine form of Theodore.

Teodora, Theo, Theodorah, Theodore, Theodoria, Theodoriah, Theodosia, Theodosiah, Theodra

Theodosia (Greek) gift from God, a form of Theodora.

Teodisa, Teodisah, Teodosia, Teodosiah, Teodosya, Teodosyah, Thedisa, Thedisah, Thedosia, Thedosiah, Thedosya, Thedosyah, Theodisa, Theodisah, Theodosiah, Theodosya, Theodosyah

Theola (Greek) God's name is divine.

Theolah

Theone (Greek) gift from God, godly, feminine form of Theon.

Theona, Theonah, Theondra, Theonee, Theoni, Theonie

Theophania (Greek) God has appeared, born on the Epiphany, 6th January, feminine form of Theophanus.

Theophani, Theophaniah, Theophanie, Theophano, Theophanya, Theophanyah

Theophila (Greek) loved by God.

Teofila, Teofilia, Teofiliah, Teofilie, Teophila, Teophilah, Teophilia, Teophiliah, Teophyla, Teophylah, Teophylia, Teophyliah, Theofila, Theofilah, Theofilia, Theofiliah, Theofilie, Theophilah, Theophilia, Theophiliah, Theophyla, Theophylah, Theophylia, Theophyliah

Thera (Greek) wild, untamed.

Therah

Theresa (Greek) reaper.

Terena, Teresa, Teresah, Teresia, Teresiah, Terisa, Terisah, Terysa, Terysah, Thereasa, Thereasah, Theresah, Therese, Theresia, Theresiah, Theresie, Theresita, Theressa, Theressah, Thereza, Therisa, Therisah, Therissie, Therrisa, Therrisah, Therrysa, Therrysah, Thersea, Therseah, Therysa, Therysah

Thetis (Greek) determined.

Thetisa, Thetisah, Thetise, Theriss, Thetissa, Thetissah, Thetisse, Thetys, Thetysa, Thetysah, Thetyse, Thetyss, Thetyssa, Thetyssah, Thetysse

Thi (Vietnamese) poem.

Thia, Thiah, Thy, Thya, Thyah

Thirza (Hebrew) pleasant, sweet-natured.

Thersa, Therza, Thirsa, Thirzah, Thursa, Thurza, Thyrza, Thyrzah

Thistle (English) thistle plant.

Thissel, Thissle, Thistel

Thomasina (Hebrew) twin, feminine form of Thomas.

Thomasa, Thomasah, Thomasia, Thomasiah, Thomasin, Thomasinah, Thomasine, Thomason, Thomasona, Thomassana, Thomassina, Thomassinah, Thomassine, Thomassyn, Thomassyna, Thomassynah, Thomassyne, Thomasyn, Thomasyna, Thomasynah, Thomasyne, Thomsina, Thomsinah, Tomasa, Tomasah, Tomasia, Tomasiah, Tomasin, Tomasina, Tomasinah, Tomasine, Tomasyn, Tomasyna, Tomasynah, Tomasyne, Tomina, Tominah, Tommina

Thora (Norse) thunder, feminine form of Thor, the god of thunder.

Thorah

Thorberta (Norse) the brilliance of Thor, feminine form of Thorbert.

Thorbertah, Thorbirta, Thorbirtah, Thorburta, Thorburtah, Thorbyrta, Thorbyrtah

Thordis (Scandinavian) in the spirit of Thor.

Thordia, Thordiah, Thordisa, Thordisah, Thordise, Thordiss, Thordissa, Thordissah, Thordisse, Thordys, Thordysa, Thordysah, Thordyse, Thordyss, Thordyssa, Thordyssah, Thordysse

Thyra (Norse) from Tyr, god of battles.

Thira, Thirah, Thyrah, Tyra, Tyrah

Tia (Spanish) aunt, (Greek) princess.

Teea, Teeah, Teeya, Ti, Tiah, Tya, Tyah

Tiana (English, Hebrew) graceful princess; (Russian) fairy queen, a form of Tatiana.

Tianah, Tiane, Tianee, Tianna, Tiannah, Tianne, Tiannee, Tyana, Tyanah, Tyane, Tyann, Tyanna, Tyannah, Tyanne, Tyannee, Tiani

Tiara (Latin) jewelled crown.

Tiarah, Tyara, Tyarah

Tiberia (Latin) the River Tiber in Italy, feminine form of Tiberio.

Tib, Tibbie, Tibby, Tiberiah, Tyberia, Tyberiah, Tyberya, Tyberyah

Tifara (Hebrew) happy.

Tifarah, Tifarra, Tifarrah

Tiffany (Greek) born on the Epiphany, January 6th, a form of Theophania.

Teffan, Teffani, Teffanie, Teffany, Thefania, Theophania, Thiphania, Tifainee, Tifaini, Tifainie, Tifane, Tifani, Tifanie, Tiffan, Tiffanee, Tiffaney, Tiffani, Tiffanie, Tiffini, Tiffinie, Tiffiny, Tiphane, Tiphanee, Tiphaney, Tiphani, Tiphania, Tiphaniah, Tiphanie, Tiphany, Tyffanee, Tyffaney, Tyffani, Tyffanie, Tyffany

Tigris (Irish) tiger.

Tiger, Tigrise, Tigriss, Tyger, Tygris, Tygrise, Tygriss, Tygrys, Tygryss

Tiki (Polynesian) one who is touched by a spirit after death.

Tikee, Tikey, Tikie, Tiky

Tikva (Hebrew) hope.

Tikvah

Timotea (Greek) honouring God, a form of Timothea, feminine form of Timothy.

Timatea, Timatia, Timatya, Timotia, Timotya

Timothea (Greek) honouring God, feminine form of Timothy.

Timathea, Timithea, Timythea, Tymathea, Tymithea, Tymothea, Tymythea

Tina (Spanish, American) a form for names ending in 'tine' or 'tina' such as Christina, Martine, Valentina.

Teena, Teenah, Tinah, Tyna, Tynah

Tinble (English) bell sound.

Tinbal, Tinbla, Tynbal, Tynbla, Tynble

Tinh (Vietnamese) mindful, aware.

Tinka (Australian Aboriginal) day.

Tinkah, Tynka, Tynkah

Tiponya (Native American) great horned owl.

Tiponia, Tiponiah, Tiponyah, Typonia, Typoniah, Typonya, Typonyah

Tira (Hindu) an arrow.

Tirah, Tyra, Tyrah

Tirion (Welsh) gentle.

Tirian, Tirrian, Tirrion, Tirryan, Tirryon, Tiryan, Tiryon, Tyrian, Tyrion, Tyrrian, Tyrrion, Tyrryan, Tyrryon, Tyryan, Tyryon

Tirtha (Hindu) ford.

Tirzah (Hebrew) pleasant, cypress tree.

Tierza, Tierzah, Tirza, Thirza, Thirzah, Thyrza, Thyrzah, Tyrza, Tyrzah

Tisha (Latin) joy, happiness.

Teisha, Teishah, Tish, Tishah, Tishia,

Tishiah, Tysha, Tyshah, Tyshia, Tyshiah

Tivona (Hebrew) lover of nature, feminine form of Tivon.
Tibona, Tiboni, Tivonah, Tivone, Tivoni, Tivonie, Tivony, Tyvona, Tyvonah, Tyvone

Tiwa (Native American) onion.
Tiwah, Tywa, Tywah

Tizane (Hungary) gypsy.

Tobi (African) great; (Hebrew) God is good, a unisex name.
Toba, Tobbee, Tobbey, Tobbi, Tobbia, Tobbiah, Tobbie, Tobby, Tobbya, Tobbyah, Tobe, Tobea, Tobee, Tobey, Tobia, Tobiah, Tobie, Tobit, Toby, Tobya, Tobyah

Toki (Japanese) hopeful.
Tokee, Tokey

Tomiko (Japanese) wealthy.
Tomeeko, Tomi

Tomo (Japanese) intelligent.
Tomoko

Tong (Vietnamese) fragrant.

Toni (Latin) praiseworthy, a form of Antonia.
Tonia, Toniah, Tony, Tonni, Tonnia, Tonniah, Tonny, Tonnya, Tonnyah, Tony, Tonya, Tonyah

Toorah (Australian Aboriginal) bird.
Toora

Topaz (Latin) a yellow gem.
Topaza, Topazah, Topazia, Topaziah, Topazz, Topazza, Topazzah, Topazzia, Topazziah

Tora (Japanese) tiger.
Torah, Torra, Torrah

Tori (Japanese) bird.
Torei, Torii

Toshi (Japanese) mirror reflection, a unisex name.
Toshee, Toshey, Toshie, Toshii, Toshy

Toski (Native American) squashed bug.
Toskee, Toskey, Toskie

Totsi (Native American) moccasins.
Totsee, Totsey, Totsia, Totsiah, Totsie, Totsy, Totsya, Totsyah

Tove (Hebrew) good, feminine form of Tovi.

Toya (English) plaything.
Latoya, Latoyah, Toia, Toiah, Toyah

Tracey (Irish) warrior, a unisex name.
Tracea, Traceah, Tracee, Traci, Tracia, Traciah, Tracie, Tracinda, Tracinta, Tracy, Tracya, Tracyah, Traicea, Traiceah, Traicee, Traicey, Traici, Traicia, Traiciah, Traicie, Traicy, Traicya, Traicyah, Traisea, Traisee, Traisey, Traisi, Traisia, Traisiah, Traisie, Traisy, Traisya, Traisyah, Trasea, Trasee, Trasey, Trasi, Trasia, Trasiah, Trasie, Trasy, Trasya, Trasyah, Traycea, Traycee, Traycey, Trayci, Traycia, Trayciah, Traycie, Traycy, Traycya, Traycyah, Traysea, Traysee, Traysey

Trava (Slavic) first spring grass.
Travah

Traviata (Italian) straying.
Traviatah, Travyata, Travyatah

Treasure (English) treasure, wealth, precious.
Treasur, Treasura, Treasurah

Tressa (Greek) harvester, a form of Theresa.

Tresa, Trese, Tresia, Tresie, Tresse, Tressia, Tressie

Trevina (Celtic) prudent, cautious, feminine form of Trevor.

Trevana, Trevanah, Trevanna, Treveana, Treveanah, Treveane, Treveena, Treveenah, Treveene, Trevena, Trevenah, Trevenia, Trevia, Treviana, Trevinah, Trevine, Trevinia, Treviniah

Tricia (English) of noble descent, a form of Patricia.

Trica, Triciah, Trish, Trisha, Trishah

Trifena (Greek) dainty, delicate.

Trifen, Trifenah, Trifin, Trifina, Trifinah

Trilby (Italian) singer; (English) soft hat, a unisex name.

Trilbea, Trilbee, Trilbey, Trilbi, Trilbie, Trillby

Trina (Greek) pure one.

Treana, Treanah, Treanee, Treaney, Treani, Treania, Treaniah, Treanie, Treany, Treena, Treenah, Treenee, Treeney, Treeni, Treenia, Treeniah, Treenie, Treeny, Trinah, Trinee, Triney, Trini, Trinia, Triniah, Trinie, Triny, Tryna, Trynah, Trynee, Tryney, Tryni, Trynia, Tryniah, Trynie, Tryny, Trynya, Trynyah

Trinity (Latin) blessed threefold, holy trinity, the Father, Son and Holy Spirit, a unisex name.

Trenedy, Trini, Trinidad, Trinidy, Trinitee, Trinitey, Triniti, Trinitie

Trish/Trisha (English) of noble descent, a form of Patricia.

Trishana, Trishanah, Trishann, Trishanna, Trishanne, Trishia, Trishiah, Trishna, Trissha, Trysha, Tryshah, Tryshia, Tryshiah

Trista (Latin) the melancholy one, sad, sorrowful, feminine form of Tristran.

Tristah, Tristana, Tristiana, Tristra, Tristrah, Trysta, Trystah, Trystra, Trystrah

Trixie (English) bringer of joy, a form of Beatrice.

Trixe, Trixee, Trixey, Trixi, Trixy

Trudy (English) spear maiden, a form of Gertrude.

Trudee, Trudey, Trudi, Trudia, Trudiah, Trudie

Tryne (Dutch) pure.

Trine

Tryphena (Greek) dainty, delicate, feminine form of Tryphon.

Trifena, Trifenna, Trifona, Trifonna, Triphena, Triphenna, Triphona, Triphonna, Tryfena, Tryfenna, Tryfona, Tryfonna, Tryphenna, Tryphonna, Tryphonnah

Tu (Chinese) jade.

Tuesday (English) born on a Tuesday.

Tuesdae, Tuesdai, Tuesdey

Tuhina (Hindu) snow.

Tuhinah

Tulip (Turkish) tulip, a flower.

Tullip

Tullia (Gaelic) peaceful.

Tulliah, Tullya, Tullyah

Tully (Celtic, Gaelic) peaceful one, at peace with God, a unisex name.

Tulea, Tuleah, Tulee, Tulei, Tuleigh, Tuley, Tuli, Tulie, Tullea, Tulleah, Tullee, Tullei, Tulleigh, Tulley, Tulli, Tullie, Tuly

Tulsi (Hindu) sacred herb.
Tulsia, Tulsiah, Tulsie, Tulsy, Tulsya, Tulsyah

Turi (Polynesian) the name of a famous chief.

Turquoise (French) a blue-green precious stone.
Turkois, Turkoise, Turquois

Turua (Polynesian) beautiful.
Turuah

Tuyen (Vietnamese) angelic, a unisex name.

Twyla (English) woven with double thread.
Twila, Twilla, Twylla

Tya (Australian Aboriginal) earth.
Tia, Tiah, Tyah

Tyler (English) tiler or tile-maker, a unisex name.
Tiela, Tielah, Tila, Tilah, Tilar, Tiler, Tiller, Tilor, Ty, Tye, Tyla, Tylah, Tylar, Tyle, Tylee, Tylie, Tyller, Tylor

Tyra (Scandinavian) warrior.
Tira, Tirah, Tyrah

U (Korean) gentle.

Ualani (Hawaiian) rain from heaven.

Ualana, Ualanah, Ualanea, Ualanee, Ualane, Ualania, Ualanie, Ualany

Uda (Teutonic) prosperous, rich.

Udah, Udda, Uddah, Udel

Udalrike (German) noble ruler.

Udalrika, Udalriqua, Udalrique

Udele (English) rich, wealthy, prosperous.

Uda, Udel, Udela, Udell, Udella, Udelle, Yudele, Yudelle

Ugolina (German) bright mind and spirit, intelligent, feminine form of Ugo.

Hugolina, Hugolinah, Hugoline, Hugolyna, Hugolynah, Hygolyne, Ugolin, Ugolinah, Ugoline, Ugolyna, Ugolynah, Ugolyne

Ula (Celtic) jewel of the sea.

Eula, Oola, Ulah, Uli, Ulia

Ulalia (Greek) sweet, softly-spoken.

Ulaliah, Ulalya, Ulalyah

Ulan (African) first-born twin, a unisex name.

Ulana, Ulen, Ulena, Ulin, Ulina

Ulani (Hawaiian) cheerful, light-hearted.

Ulana, Ulanah, Ulane, Ulanee, Ulaney, Ulania, Ulanie, Ulany, Ulanya, Ulanyah

Ulema (Arabic) intelligent one, wisdom.

Uleama, Uleamah, Uleema, Uleemah, Ulemah, Ulima, Ulimah, Ullema, Ulyma, Ulymah

Ulima (Arabic) astute, wise.

Uleama, Uleamah, Uleema, Uleemah, Ulema, Ulemah, Ulimah, Ullima, Ulyma, Ulymah

Ulla (Swedish) will, wilful.

Ula, Ulah, Ullah, Ulli

Ulrica (German) ruling wolf, feminine form of Ulrick.

Ula, Ulah, Ulca, Ulcah, Ulka, Ulkah, Ulla, Ullca, Ullcah, Ullka, Ullkah, Ullrica, Ullricka, Ullrika, Ulricah, Ulricka, Ulrickah, Ulrika, Ulrikah, Ulrike, Ulrique, Ulryca, Ulrycah, Ulrycka, Ulryckah, Ulryka, Ulrykah, Ulryqua

Ulrike (Scandinavian, German) wolf ruler, powerful, feminine form of Ulrick.

Ulricke, Ulryke

Ultima (Latin) the greatest, last, farthest.

Ultimah, Ultyma, Ultymah

Ululani (Hawaiian) heavenly inspiration.

Ululanee, Ululane, Ululania, Ululanie, Ululany, Ululanya

Ulva (Teutonic) wolf, brave like a she-wolf.

Ulvah

Uma (Hindu) light, peace, mother.

Umah

Umay (Turkish) hopeful.

Umai

Umeko (Japanese) plum-blossom child, patient.

Ume, Umeyo

Umiko (Japanese) child of the sea.

Umeeko

Una (Latin) one, united; (Native American) good memory.

Oona, Oonah, Unah, Unna, Unnah, Uny, Unya, Unyah

Undine (Latin) wave.

Ondine, Undeen, Undene, Undina, Undinah, Undyn, Undyna, Undynah, Undyne

Unique (Latin) only one, a unisex name.

Uniqia, Uniquia

Unity (English) together in a common cause, oneness, unity, a unisex name.

Uinita, Unita, Unite, Unitea, Unitee, Unitey, Uniti, Unitie, Unyta, Unyte, Unytea, Unytee, Unytey, Unyti, Unytie, Unyty

Unn (Norwegian) she is loved.

Un

Unna (German) woman.

Una, Unah, Unnah

Unnea (Scandinavian) linden tree.

Unea, Uneah, Unneah

Unni (Norse) modest.

Unnie, Unny

Urania (Greek) heavenly.

Uraina, Urainah, Urainia, Urainiah, Urainie, Urainiya, Urainya, Urainyah, Urana, Uranah, Uraniah, Uranie, Uraniya, Uranya, Uranyah

Urbana (Latin) belonging to the city, city dweller, feminine form of Urban.

Urbaina, Urbainah, Urbainna, Urbainnah, Urbanah, Urbanna, Urabannah, Urbena, Urbenah, Urbenna, Urbennah, Urberna, Urbernah, Urbernna, Urbernnah

Uri (Hebrew) my light, God's light, a unisex name.

Uree, Urie, Ury

Urika (Native American) useful to all.

Ureca, Urecah, Ureeca, Ureecah, Ureeka, Ureekah, Ureka, Urekah, Urica, Uricah, Uricka, Urickah, Urikah, Uriqua, Uryca, Urycah, Uryka, Urykah, Uryqua

Urit (Hebrew) light, bright.

Urice, Urita, Uritah, Uryt, Uryta, Urytah

Urith (German) worthy, deserving.

Uritha, Urithah, Urithe, Uryth, Urytha, Urythah, Urythe

Ursa (Latin, Greek) bear, feminine form of Ursus.

Ursah, Ursea, Ursela, Urselah, Ursella, Ursellah, Ursey, Ursi, Ursie, Ursila, Ursilah, Ursilla, Ursillah, Ursina, Ursinah, Ursinna, Ursinnah, Ursy, Ursyla, Ursylah, Ursylla, Ursyllah, Ursyna, Ursynah, Ursynna, Ursynnah

Ursanne (French) bear.

Ursana, Ursanah, Ursane, Ursanna, Ursannah

Ursula (Latin, Greek) little bear.

Ursala, Ursalah, Ursalla, Ursallah, Ursel, Ursela, Urselah, Ursella, Ursellah, Ursely, Urselya, Urselyah, Ursila, Ursilah, Ursilla, Ursillah, Ursillana, Ursillanah, Ursillane, Ursola, Ursolah, Ursolla, Ursollah, Ursulah, Ursule, Ursulina, Ursuline, Ursullina, Ursullinah, Ursulline, Ursullyna, Ursullynah, Ursulyna, Ursylyn, Urzula, Urzulah

Usagi (Japanese) moon.

Usagee

Usha (Hindu) sunrise.
Ushah

Ushi (Chinese) ox.
Ushee, Ushie, Ushy

Uta (German) fortunate heroine in battle.
Utah, Utako, Utta, Uttah

Ute (Teutonic) prosperity, fortunate, rich.
Utee, Utey

Utina (Native American) woman of my country.
Utahna, Uteana, Uteanah, Uteena, Uteenah, Utinah, Utona, Utonna, Utyna, Utynah

Uzuri (African) beauty.

Uzza (Arabic) strong, might.
Uza, Uzah, Uzzah

Uzzia (Hebrew) God is my strength, God is strong.
Uzia, Uziah, Uzya, Uzyah, Uzziah, Uzzya, Uzzyah

V

Vachya (Hindu) speaking.
Vachia, Vachiah, Vachyah

Vail (Anglo-Saxon) valley, a unisex name.
Vailee, Vailey, Vaili, Vailie, Vaillee, Vailley, Vailli, Vaillie, Vailly, Vaily, Vale, Valee, Valey, Valie, Valli, Vallee, Valley, Vallie, Vally, Valy

Vailea (Polynesian) talking water.
Vaile, Vaileah, Vailee, Vailei, Vaileigh, Vailey, Vaili, Vailie, Vaillea, Vailleah, Vaillee, Vaillei, Vailleigh, Vailley, Vailli, Vaillie, Vailly, Vaillya, Vaille, Vaily, Vailya, Vailyah, Vaylea, Vaylee, Vaylei, Valeigh, Vayley, Vayli, Vayly

Val (Latin) strength, a form of Valentina, Valerie, a unisex name.
Vale, Vall, Valle

Vala (German) chosen one.
Valah, Valla, Vallah

Valborga (Swedish) a powerful mountain.
Valborg, Valborgah

Valda (German) powerful, a battle heroine, famous ruler, feminine form of Valdus.
Valdah, Valida, Validah, Velda, Veldah

Valencia (Spanish) strong, brave, a place name in Spain, a form of Valentina.
Valacia, Valanca, Valance, Valancia, Valecia, Valence, Valenciah, Valencya, Valencyah, Valenica, Valenicah, Valenzia

Valentina (Latin) strong, powerful, brave, feminine form of Valentine.
Valantina, Valenteana, Valenteane, Valenteen, Valenteena, Valenteene, Valentena, Valentia, Valentiah, Valentin, Valentinah, Valentine, Valentyn, Valentyna, Valentyne, Valtina, Tina

Valerie (Latin) strong, healthy, feminine form of Valerian.
Vairy, Val, Valaree, Valari, Valarie, Valary, Vale, Valeray, Valeree, Valeri, Valeria, Valérie, Valery, Valerya, Valerye, Valka, Valleree, Valleri, Vallerie, Vallery, Valliree, Valliri, Vallirie, Valliry, Valry, Valya, Veleree, Veleri, Velerie, Velery

Valeska (Slavic) powerful ruler.
Valesca, Valese, Valeshca, Valeshia, Valeshka, Valeskah, Valezka

Valia (Latin) strong protector, brave, valiant, feminine form of Valiant.
Valiah, Vallia, Valliah, Vallya, Vallyah, Valya, Valyah

Valli (Hindu) a native plant in India.

Valonia (Latin) strong, brave, form of Valia; (Anglo-Saxon) from the shadow valley.
Valiona, Valionah, Valione, Valioney, Valioni, Valionia, Valioniah, Valionie, Valiony, Valionya, Valionyah, Vallon, Vollona, Vallonah, Vallonia, Valloniah, Vallonya, Vallonyah, Valona, Valoniah, Valonya, Valonyah, Valyona, Valyonah, Valyonia, Valyoniah, Valyony, Valyonya, Valyonyah

Valora (Latin) brave, form of Valia.
Valorah, Valore, Valoria, Valoriah, Valorya, Valoryah, Velora

Valtina (Latin) love, health.
Valentina, Valentine, Valtine

Vanda (German) wanderer.
Vandah, Vandana, Vandetta, Vandi, Vannda

Vandani (Hindu) honourable.
Vandanee, Vandaney, Vandanie, Vandany

Vanessa (English) invented by Jonathan Swift as a nickname for Esther Vanhomrigh, also a genus of butterfly.
Ness, Nessa, Nessee, Nessey, Nessi, Nessie, Nessy, Van, Vana, Vanasa, Vanasha, Vanashia, Vanasia, Vanassa, Vanasse, Vanassia, Vane, Vanesa, Vanesha, Vaneshia, Vanesia, Vanesse, Vanessee, Vanessia, Vanessica, Vanetta, Vaneza, Vania, Vaniah, Vaniesa, Vaniessa, Vanija, Vanika, Vanisa, Vaniss, Vanissa, Vanisse, Vanissee, Vanita, Vanitta, Vanna, Vannah, Vannessa, Vannesse, Vannessee, Vanni, Vannia, Vanniah, Vanny, Vannysa, Vannysah, Vannyssa, Vannyssah, Vanysa, Vanysah, Vanyssa, Vanyssah

Vania (Russian) gracious gift of God, graceful, a form of Ann.
Vanea, Vaneah, Vaniah, Vannea, Vanneah, Vannia, Vanniah, Vannie, Vannja, Vannya, Vannyah, Vanya, Vanyah

Vanita (Indian) woman.

Vanity (English) vain.
Vanita, Vanitah, Vanitee, Vanitey, Vaniti, Vanitia, Vanitie, Vanitta, Vanittah, Vanittee, Vanittey, Vanitti, Vanittia, Vanittie, Vanitty, Vanyta, Vanytah, Vanytee, Vanytey, Vanyti, Vanytia, Vanytie, Vanyty

Vanora (Celtic) white wave.
Vanorah, Vanorea, Vanoree, Vanorey, Vanori, Vanoria, Vanoriah, Vanorie, Vanory, Vanorya, Vanoryah

Vara (Scandinavian) careful, cautious.
Varah, Varia, Variah

Varana (Hindu) river.
Varanah, Varanna, Varannah

Varda (Arabic) rose.
Vardia, Vardiah, Vardina, Vardinah, Vardine, Vardinia, Vardiniah, Vardis, Vardisa, Vardiss, Vardissa, Vardisse, Vardit, Vardita, Vardyn, Vardyna, Vardynah, Vardyne

Varian (Latin) variable, the changeable one, a unisex name.
Vari, Variana, Varianah, Varien, Variena, Varienah, Varyan, Varyana, Varyanah

Vasanta (Hindu) spring.
Vashanta

Vashti (Persian) beautiful.
Vashtee, Vashtie, Vashty

Veda (Hindu) sacred knowledge, sacred writings, feminine form of Ved.
Vedad, Vedah, Veida, Veleda

Vedette (Italian) sentinel.
Vedet, Vedeta, Vedetah, Vedete, Vedett, Vedetta, Vedettah

Vedis (German) forest spirit.
Vedisa, Vedise, Vediss, Vedissa, Vedisse, Vedys, Vedysa, Vedyse, Vedyss, Vedyssa, Vedysse

Vega (Arabic) falling star.
Vegah

Veleda (Teutonic) inspired wisdom.
Valeda, Valedah, Veledah

Velika (Slavic) great.
Velikah, Velyka, Velykah

Velma (English) desire to protect.
Valma, Valmah, Vallma, Vallmah, Vellma, Vellmah, Velmah, Vilma, Vilmah, Vilna, Vylma, Vylmah

Velvet (English) velvety, from the Latin for fleece.
Velveta, Velvetah, Velvete, Velvett, Velvetta, Velvettah, Velvette, Velvit, Velvyt

Venetia (Italian) woman from Venice.
Veneta, Venetiah, Venetta, Venette, Venetya, Venetyah, Venita, Venitah, Venitia, Venitiah, Vineta, Vinetia, Vinetiah, Vinita, Vinitah, Vonita, Vonitia, Vonitiah, Vynita, Vynitah, Vynyta, Vynytah

Ventura (Latin) venture, a unisex name.

Venus (Latin) love, after the Roman goddess of beauty and love.
Venis, Venusa, Venusina, Venussa, Venys, Vinny, Vynys

Vera (Latin) truth, feminine form of Vere; (Russian) faith.
Vara, Veera, Veira, Verah, Verda, Vere, Verra, Verrah, Vida, Vira

Verbena (Latin) sacred plant.
Verbeen, Verbeena, Verbeene, Verben, Verbene, Verbin, Verbina, Verbine, Verbyn, Verbyna, Verbyne

Verda (Latin) young and fresh.
Verdah, Verdi

Verdad (Spanish) truthful.
Verdada

Verena (Latin) sacred wisdom, true.
Vera, Verana, Veranah, Veradis, Verean, Vereana, Vereane, Vereen, Vereena, Vereene, Verenah, Verene, Verina, Verine, Verita, Verity, Veryn, Veryna, Veryne, Virna, Virnah, Vyrna, Vrynah

Verity (Latin, Italian) truth.
Verita, Veritah, Veritea, Veritee, Veritey, Veriti, Veritie, Veryta, Verytah, Verytea, Verytee, Verytey, Veryti, Verytie, Veryty

Verna (Latin) youthful, spring time, feminine form of Vernon.
Verda, Verena, Vernah, Verne, Vernia, Verniah, Vernice, Vernis, Virna, Virnah, Vyrna, Vyrnah

Veronica (Latin) true image, like her mother.
Ronica, Ronicah, Ronika, Ronikah, Ronnie, Varonica, Varonicah, Varonicca, Varoniccah, Vee, Vera, Verinica, Verona, Veronic, Veronicah, Veronice, Veronicka, Veronika, Veronike, Veronique, Veronnica

Vesna (Slavic) goddess of spring.
Vesna, Vessna, Vessnah

Vespera (Latin) an evening star.
Vesperah

Vesta (Latin) of the home, after the Roman goddess of the hearth.
Vest, Vestah, Vestea, Vestee, Vestey

Vevay (Welsh) white wave.
Vevae, Vevah, Vevau, Vevaya

Vevila (Irish) harmonious, melodious.
Vevilah, Vevilia, Veviliah, Vevilla,

Vevillah, Vevillia, Vevilliah, Vevyla, Vevylah, Vevyle, Vevylla, Vevyllah, Vevylle

Vevina (Celtic) sweet lady, pleasant.

Vevin, Vevinah, Vevine, Vevyn, Vevyna, Vevynah, Vevyne

Vi (Latin, French) violet, a flower, a form of Viola.

Vie, Violet, Viola, Vy, Vye

Victoria (Latin) victory, the victorious one, feminine form of Victor.

Vicki, Vickie, Vickee, Vicky, Victoriah, Victorria, Victorriah, Victorya, Victoryah, Viki, Vikki, Vikky, Viktoria, Viktoriah, Viktorya, Vitoria, Vyctoria, Vyctoriah

Vida (Hebrew) the beloved one; a form of Davida, feminine version of David.

Veeda, Veedah, Vidah, Vyda, Vydah

Vidal (Latin) vital, lively, life, a unisex name.

Vidala, Vidalia, Vital, Vitala, Vitalia, Vydal, Vydala, Vydalia, Vytal, Vytala, Vytalia

Vidonia (Portuguese) vine-branch.

Vedonia, Vidoniah, Vidonya, Vidonyah, Vydonia, Vydoniah, Vydonya, Vydonyah

Vidya (Hindu) knowledge, wisdom.

Vidyah

Vienna (Latin) the capital of Austria.

Vena, Venah, Venia, Venna, Vennah, Vennia, Viennah, Vienne

Vigilia (Latin) alert, vigilant, watching.

Vigila, Vigilah, Vigiliah, Vigilla, Vigillah, Vigillia, Vigill, Vijilia, Vijiliah

Vignette (French) little wine.

Vignet, Vigneta, Vignete, Vignett, Vignetta, Vygnet, Vygneta, Vygnett, Vygnetta, Vygnette

Vijaya (Hindu) victory, feminine form of Vijay.

Veejaya, Veejayah, Vijayah

Vimala (Hindu) pure.

Vina (Hindu) a stringed instrument carried by goddess of wisdom; (Spanish) from the vineyard.

Veena, Veenah, Viña, Vinah, Vinesha, Vinessa, Vinisha, Vinna, Vinnah, Vyna, Vynah, Vynna, Vynnah

Vincenta/Vincentia (Latin) conqueror, victor, feminine form of Vincent.

Vicenta, Vicentena, Vincenna, Vincennah, Vincenne, Vincensa, Vincensah, Vincensia, Vincensiah, Vincentah, Vincentena, Vincentiah, Vincentina, Vincentine, Vincenza, Vincenzah, Vincenzia, Vincenziah, Vincy, Vinnie

Vinna (Spanish) from the vineyard.

Vina, Vinia, Vinni, Vinnia, Vinniah, Vinnie, Vinny, Vynna, Vynnah

Vinvella (French) excellent, like good wine.

Viola (Latin) violet, a musical instrument.

Violah, Viole, Vyoila, Vyoilah, Vyola, Vyolah

Violet/Violetta (French) violet flower.

Vi, Viola, Violeta, Violete, Violett, Violette

Virgilia (Latin) staff bearer, feminine form of Virgil.

Virgila, Virgilah, Virgilea, Virgileah, Virgilee, Virgileigh, Virgili, Virgilie, Virgilla, Virgillah, Virgillia, Virgily, Virgilya

Virginia (Latin) maidenly, pure, honorific for the Virgin.

Verginia, Verginya, Virge, Virgen, Virgene, Virgenia, Virgenya, Virige, Virgina, Virgine, Virginie, Virginnia, Virginnya, Virginya, Virgy

Viridis (Latin) youthful and blooming; (Italian) green.

Viridisa, Viridiss, Viridissa, Viridys, Viridysa, Viridyss, Viridyssa, Vyridis, Vyridisa, Vyridiss, Vyridissa

Virtue (Latin) pure, virtuous.

Vertue, Virtu

Vita (Latin) alive, lively, full of life, feminine form of Vitalis.

Veeta, Vitah, Vitala, Vitaliana, Vitalione, Vitalla, Vitel, Vitella, Vitia, Vitta, Vyta, Vytah, Vytta, Vyttah

Vitoria (Spanish) the victorious one, a form of Victoria.

Vitoriah, Vitorya, Vitoryah, Vittoria, Vittoriah, Vittorya, Vittoryah, Vytoria, Vytoriah, Vyttoria, Vyttoriah

Vivian (Latin) gracious in life or lively, full of life, a unisex name.

Viv, Viva, Vivi, Vivia, Viviana, Viviann, Vivianne, Vivien, Viviena, Vivienna, Vivienne, Vivina, Vivyan, Vivyann, Vivyanne, Vyvan, Vyvann, Vyvanne

Volante (Latin) one who is born to fly.

Volanta, Volantah

Voleta (French) veiled woman.

Volet, Voletah, Volett, Voletta, Volettah, Volette, Volita, Volitah, Volyta, Volytah, Volyte, Volytt, Volytta, Volyttah, Volytte

Vulpine (English) like a fox.

Vulpina, Vulpinah, Vulpyna, Vulpynah, Vulpyne

Wadd (Arabic) beloved.
Wad

Wafiya (Arabic) loyal, faithful, trustworthy.
Wafiyah, Wafiyya, Wafiyyah

Wahalla (Scandinavian) immortal.
Valhalla, Walhallah

Wainani (Hawaiian) beautiful water.
Wainanee, Wainanie, Wainany

Wakana (Japanese) plant.
Wakanah

Wakanda (Native American) magic power.
Wakandah

Walad (Arabic) newborn child.
Walada, Waladah, Walida, Walidah, Walyda, Walydah

Walda (Teutonic) to wield power and reign, famous, powerful warrior, feminine form of Waldo.
Waldah, Waldina, Waldine, Walida, Walidah, Wallda, Walldah, Waldyna, Waldyne, Welda, Weldah, Wellda, Welldah

Walker (English) cloth walker, cloth cleaner, a unisex name.
Wallker

Wallis (English) foreigner from Wales, a unisex name.

Walice, Walise, Wallice, Wallise

Waltraud (German) strong ruler.
Valtrada, Valtraud, Valtraude, Valtraute, Waltrada, Waltraude, Waltraute

Wan (Chinese) gentle and gracious.

Wanda (German) wanderer.
Vanda, Wahnda, Wandah, Wandie, Wandis, Wandja, Wannda, Wanndah, Wonda, Wondah, Wonnda, Wonndah

Waneta (Native American) charger.
Waneata, Waneatah, Waneeta, Waneetah, Waneita, Waneitah, Wanetah, Wanete, Wanita, Wanitah, Wanite, Wanneata, Wanneatah, Waneeta, Wanneetah, Wanneita, Wanneitah, Wanneta, Wannetah, Wannete, Wauneta, Waunita, Woneta, Wonita, Wonnita, Wonnitah, Wonyta, Wonytah, Wonyte

Wanetta (English) pale and delicate.
Wanette, Wannetta, Wannette, Wonnitta, Wonnitte, Wonytta, Wonyttah, Wonytte

Wanika (Hawaiian) God is gracious, a form of Juanita.
Waneeka, Wanikah, Wanyka, Wanykah

Warda (English) guardian, watchman, feminine form of Ward.
Wardah, Wardeh, Wardena, Wardenia, Wardia, Wardine, Warrinah, Wordah

Washi (Japanese) eagle.
Washee, Washie, Washy

Wasila (English) healthy, good.
Wasilah, Wasilla, Wasillah, Wasylla, Wasyllah

Wattan (Japanese) homeland.
Watan

Wauna (Native American) snow goose.
Waunah

Waverly (English) from the windy meadow of aspens, a unisex name.
Waverlea, Waverlee, Waverley, Waverli, Waverlie

Waynette (English) wagon maker, feminine form of Wayne.
Wainet, Waineta, Wainetah, Wainete, Wainetta, Wainettah, Wainette, Waynet, Wayneta, Waynetah, Waynete, Waynetta, Waynettah

Weeko (Native American) pretty girl.
Weiko, Weyko

Weemala (Australian Aboriginal) long view, distant view.

Wei (Chinese) precious and valuable, great, a unisex name.

Wen (Chinese) cultured, ornamental, refined, a unisex name.

Wenda (Welsh) fair one, light-skinned.
Wendah, Wendaina, Wendainah, Wendaine, Wendalin, Wendalina, Wendalinah, Wendayn, Wendayna, Wendayne, Wendi, Wendy

Wendelle (English) wanderer, a feminine form of Wendel.
Wendalin, Wendalina, Wendalinah, Wendaline, Wendall, Wendalla, Wendallah, Wendalle, Wendalyn, Wendalyna, Wendalynah, Wendalyne, Wendelin, Wendelina, Wendeline, Wendell, Wendella,
Wendellah, Wendelle, Wendelyn, Wendelyna, Wendelynah, Wendelyne

Wendy (Welsh) fair one, light-skinned.
Wenda, Wendea, Wendee, Wendey, Wendi, Wendia, Wendiah, Wendie, Wendya, Wendyah, Wendye

Wenona (Native American) first-born daughter.
Wenonah, Winona, Winonah, Wynona, Wynonah

Wesisa (African) foolish.
Wesisah, Wesysa, Wesysah

Weslea (English) west meadow, feminine form of Wesley.
Wes, Wesla, Weslah, Wesleah, Weslee, Weslei, Wesleigh, Wesley, Wesli, Weslia, Wesliah, Weslie, Wesly, Weslya, Weslyah

Whalley (English) woodland clearing near a round hill, a surname.
Whalea, Whaleah, Whalee, Whalei, Whaleigh, Whaley, Whali, Whalia, Whaliah, Whalie, Whallea, Whalleah, Whallee, Whallei, Whalleigh, Whalli, Whallia, Whallie, Whally, Whallya, Whaly, Whalya

Whetu (Maori) star.

Whitley (English) white meadow, a unisex name.
Whitely, Whitlea, Whitleah, Whitlee, Whitlei, Whitleigh, Whitli, Whitlia, Whitlie, Whitly, Whitlya, Whittley, Whittleigh, Whittlie, Whittly, Whytlea, Whytleah, Whytlee, Whytlei, Whytleigh, Whytley, Whytli, Whytlia, Whytlie, Whytly, Whytlya

Whitney (English) white island, a unisex name.

Whitani, Whiteney, Whitne, Whitnee, Whitni, Whitnie, Whitny, Whitnye, Whittaney, Whittanie, Whittany, Whitteney, Whittenie, Whitteny, Whittnay, Whittney, Whittnie, Whittny, Whytne, Whytnee, Whytney, Whytni, Whytnie, Whytny, Witney

Whoopi (English) happy.

Whoopee, Whoopey, Whoopie, Whoopy

Widad (Arabic) love.

Wila (Hawaiian) loyal, faithful.

Wilah, Wyla, Wylah

Wilda (English) wild and untamed.

Wildah, Willda, Willdah, Wylda, Wyldah

Wilfreda (English) peacemaker, desiring peace, feminine form of Wilfred.

Freda, Wilfrida, Wilfrieda, Wilfryda, Willfreda, Willfrida, Willfrieda, Willfryda

Wilhelmina (German) the resolute protector, determined guardian, feminine form of Wilhelm.

Wilamina, Wilaminah, Wilamine, Wilemina, Wileminah, Wilemine, Wilhelminah, Wilhelmine, Wiliamina, Wiliaminah, Wiliamine, Willamina, Willaminah, Willamine, Willemina, Willeminah, Willemine, Williamina, Williaminah, Williamine, Willma, Willmina, Willminah, Willmine, Wilma, Wilmina, Wilminah, Wilmine, Wylhelmin, Wylhelmina, Wylhelminah, Wylhelmine, Wylhelmyn, Wylhelmyna, Wylhelmynah, Wylhelmyne, Wyllhelmin, Wyllhelmina, Wyllhelminah, Wyllhelmine, Wyllhelmyn, Wyllhelmyna, Wyllhelmynah, Wyllhelmyne

Willa (German) resolute, determined guardian, a feminine form of Will.

Wila, Wilah, Willah, Wyla, Wylah, Wylla, Wyllah

Willow (English) willow tree.

Willo, Willough, Wyllo, Wyllow, Wyllough

Wilma (German) desire to protect, guardian, form of Wilhelmina.

Williemae, Willma, Wilmah, Wilmaya, Wilmetta, Wilmette, Wilmina, Wilmine, Wilmyna, Wilmyne, Wylma, Wylmah

Wilona (English) desired.

Willona, Willone, Wilonah, Wilone

Winda (African) hunter.

Winema (Native American) female chief.

Winemah, Wynema, Wynemah

Winifred (German) friend of peace, feminine form of Winfred.

Winafred, Winefred, Winefrid, Winefride, Winefried, Winfred, Winfreda, Winfried, Winfrieda, Winifrid, Winifryd, Winifryda, Winnafred, Winnafreda, Winnefred, Winniefred, Winnifred, Winnifreda, Winnifrid, Winnifrida, Wynafred, Wynafreda, Wynafrid, Wynafrida, Wynefred, Wynefreda, Wynefryd, Wynifred, Wynnifred

Winna (African) friend.

Wina, Winnah, Wyna, Wynah, Wynna, Wynnah

Winona (Native American) first-born daughter.

Wanona, Wanonah, Wenona, Wenonah, Winonah, Wynona, Wynonah

Winsome (English) attractive, charming.

Winsom, Wynsom, Wynsome

Winter (English) born in winter, a unisex name.

Wintr, Wynter

Wren/Wrena (English) wren bird; (Welsh) ruler, chief, a unisex name.

Renn, Wrenah, Wrenee, Wrenie, Wrenn, Wrenna, Wrennah, Wrennee, Wrennie, Wrenny, Wreny

Wyanet (Native American) of great beauty, legendary beauty.

Waianeta, Waianetta, Waianita, Waianitta, Wianet, Wianeta, Wianete, Wianett, Wianetta, Wianette, Wyaneta, Wyanete, Wyanett, Wyanetta, Wyanette, Wyanita

Wynne (Celtic) fair, light-skinned, a form of Winifred.

Win, Winetta, Winette, Winn, Winne, Wyn, Wyna, Wyne, Wynet, Wyneta, Wynetah, Wynete, Wynett, Wynetta, Wynettah, Wynette, Wynn

Xandra (Spanish) defender, a
form of Alexandra; (Greek) a form
of Sandra.
Xander, Xandrah

Xanthe (Greek) golden-haired,
blonde, feminine form of Xanthus.
*Xantha, Xanthah, Xanthia,
Xanthiah, Xanthus, Zantha, Zathah,
Zanthe, Zanthia, Zanthiah*

Xara (Hebrew) princess, a form of
Sarah.
*Xarah, Xari, Xaria, Xariah, Xarie,
Xarra, Xarrah, Xarri, Xarria, Xarriah,
Xarrie, Xarry, Xary, Xarya, Xaryah,
Zara, Zarah*

Xaviera (Arabic) bright, brilliant;
(Spanish) of the bright new house,
feminine form of Xavier.
*Xavia, Xavierah, Xaviére, Xavyera,
Xavyerah, Xavyere*

Xena (Greek) welcoming.
*Xeena, Xenah, Xene, Xina, Xinah,
Xyna, Xynah*

Xenia (Greek) hospitable.
*Xeenia, Xeeniah, Xenea, Xeniah,
Xenya, Xenyah, Xinia*

Xenosa (Greek) stranger, feminine
form of Xenos.
*Xenos, Xenosah, Zenos, Zenosa,
Zenosah*

Xia (Chinese) sunrise glow.
Xiah

Xiang (Chinese) fragrant.
Xeang, Xeeang, Xyang

Ximena (Spanish) heard, listener, a
form of Simona.
*Ximenah, Ximene, Ximenia,
Ximeniah, Ximona, Ximonah,
Ximone, Ximonia, Ximoniah,
Xymena, Xymenah, Xymenia,
Xymeniah, Xymona, Xymonah
Xymonia, Xymoniah*

Xiu Mei (Chinese) beautiful plum.

Xuan (Vietnamese) spring.
Xuana, Xuanah, Zuan, Zuanah

Xuxa (Spanish) a queen or ruler,
feminine form of Xerxes.
Xera, Xerah, Xuxah, Yuxa, Yuxah

Xylia (Greek) of the woods, forest,
feminine form of Xylon.
*Xila, Xilah, Xilia, Xiliah, Xilina, Xilinah,
Xilya, Xilyah, Xilyna, Xilynah, Xyla,
Xylah, Xyliah, Xylina, Xylinah,
Xylya, Xylyah, Xylyna, Xylynah,
Zila, Zilah, Zilia, Ziliah, Zilina, Zilinah,
Zylia, Zyliah, Zylina, Zylinah, Zylyna,
Zylynah*

Xylina (Greek) of the woods,
forest.
*Xylin, Xylinah, Xyline, Xylona,
Xylonah, Xylyn, Xylyna, Xylynah,
Xylyne, Zilin, Zilina, Zilinah, Zilyna,
Zilynah, Zylin, Zylina, Zylinah, Zylyn,
Zylyna, Zylynah*

Xylona (Greek) of the woods,
forest.
*Xilon, Xilona, Xilonah, Xilone,
Xilonia, Xiloniah, Xilonya, Xilonyah,
Xylon, Xylonah, Xylone, Xylonia,
Xyloniah, Xylonya, Xylonyah*

Xylophila (Greek) lover of the
woods.
*Xilophia, Xilophiah, Xilophila,
Xilophilah, Xylophia, Xylophiah,
Xylophilah, Zilophia, Zylophia*

Y

Yachne (Hebrew) gracious, hospitable.
Yachnee

Yael (Hebrew) mountain goat, a unisex name.
Jael, Jaela, Jaelah, Jaele, Jaell, Jaella, Jaellah, Jaelle, Yaela, Yaelah, Yaele, Yaell, Yaella, Yaellah, Yaelle

Yaffa (Hebrew) beautiful, lovely.
Yaffah

Yakini (African) truth.

Yakira (Hebrew) precious, honoured, feminine form of Yakir.
Yakirah, Yakyra, Yakyrah

Yalena (Russian) shining light, a form of Helen.
Yalan, Yalana, Yalanah, Yalane, Yaleana, Yaleanah, Yaleane, Yaleena, Yaleenah, Yaleene, Yalen, Yalenah, Yalina, Yalinah, Yaline, Yalyna, Yalynah, Yalyne, Yelan, Yelana, Yelanah, Yelane, Yeleana, Yeleanah, Yeleane, Yeleena, Yeleenah, Yeleene, Yelen, Yelena, Yelenah, Yelina, Yelinah, Yeline, Yelyna, Yelynah, Yelyne

Yaminah (Arabic) right and proper.
Yamina, Yamyna, Yamynah

Yamka (Native American) blossom.
Yamkah

Yamuna (Hindu) sacred river.
Yamunah

Yana (Slavic) God is gracious, feminine form of Yanni.
Yane, Yanah, Yanay, Yanaye, Yanesi, Yaney, Yania, Yaniah, Yanina, Yanis, Yanisha, Yanitza, Yanna, Yannah, Yannia, Yanniah, Yannica, Yannina, Yannya, Yannyah, Yannyna

Yanaba (Native American) brave.
Yanabah

Yancy (Native American) Englishman, a unisex name.
Yance, Yancee, Yancie, Yankee

Yang (Chinese) sun.

Yani (Australian Aboriginal) peace, peaceful.
Yanee, Yaney, Yanie, Yannee, Yanney, Yanni, Yannie, Yanny, Yany

Yannick (French) the Lord is gracious, a form of John, a unisex name.
Yanic, Yanick, Yanik, Yann, Yannic, Yanig, Yannik

Yannis (Hebrew) gift of God.
Janice, Janis, Jannis, Yanice, Yanis, Yannys, Yanys

Yarkona (Hebrew) green.
Yarkonah

Yarmilla (Slavic) trader.
Yarmila, Yarmilah, Yarmillah, Yarmille, Yarmyla, Yarmylah, Yarmylla, Yarmyllah, Yarmylle

Yasmeen (Persian) fragrant jasmine flower.
Yasmeene, Yasmen, Yasmene, Yasmenne, Yasmin, Yassmeen, Yyassmeene, Yassmen, Yassmin

Yasmin (Persian) fragrant jasmine flower, a form of Jasmine.
Jasmin, Jasmine, Jasmyn, Yasmeen, Yasmina, Yasmine, Yasmyn, Yasmyna, Yasmyne

Yasu (Japanese) peaceful, calm.
Yasuko, Yasuyo, Yazoo

Yates (English) gate keeper, guard of the gate, a unisex name.
Yaetes, Yaites

Yayoi (Japanese) spring.

Yedda (German) singer.
Jedda, Jeddah, Yeda, Yedah, Yeddah, Yedya, Yedyah

Yedida (Hebrew) dearest friend.
Jedida, Yedidah, Yedyda, Yedydah

Yehudit (Hebrew) praised, a form of Judith.
Yehudita, Yehuditah, Yudit, Yudita, Yudyta, Yudytah

Yei (Japanese) flourishing.

Yeira (Hebrew) light.
Yeirah, Yeyra, Yeyrah

Yelena (Latin) lily blossom, shining light, a form of Helen.
Jelena, Lena, Yelen, Yelenah, Yelene, Yelenn, Yelenna, Yelennah, Yelenne, Yelin, Yelina, Yelinah, Yelinn, Yelinna, Yelinnah, Ylen, Ylena, Ylenah, Ylenia, Yleniah, Ylenn, Ylenna, Ylennah

Yelisabeta (Russian) holy, sacred to God, a form of Elizabeth.
Yelisabet, Yelisabeth, Yelisavet, Yelisaveta, Yelizabet, Yelizabeta, Yelizabeth, Yelizavet, Yelizaveta

Yemena (Arabic) from Yemen.
Yemenah, Yemina, Yeminah, Yemyna, Yemynah

Yemina (Hebrew) right hand, feminine form of Yamin.
Yemeena, Yemeenah, Yeminah

Yen (Chinese) yearning, desirous.
Yeni, Yenie, Yenih, Yenn, Yenny

Yenene (Native American) shaman.
Yenena, Yenenah, Yenina, Yeninah, Yenyna, Yenynah, Yenyne

Yeo (Korean) mild.
Yee

Yepa (Native American) winter girl, snow girl.
Yepah, Yeppa, Yeppah

Yetta (English) ruler of the house, giving, a form of Henrietta.
Jetta, Yeta, Yetah, Yettah, Yette

Yeva (Ukrainian) life, life-giving.
Yevah

Yevgenia (Russian) noble, a form of Eugenia, feminine form of Yevgeni.
Yevgena, Yevgenah, Yevgeniah, Yevgenya, Yevgenyah, Yevgina, Yevginah, Yevginia, Yevginiah, Yevginya, Yevginyah, Yevgyna, Yevgynah

Yin (Chinese) silver.
Yinn

Yi Ze (Chinese) happy person.

Ynes (Spanish) pure, a form of Agnes.
Ines, Inez, Ynez, Ynnes, Ynnez

Ynez (Spanish) pure, a form of Agnes.
Ines, Inez, Ynes, Ynesita, Yness, Ynesse, Ynnes, Ynness

Yoanna (Hebrew) God is gracious, a form of Joanna.
Yoana, Yoanah, Yoane, Yoannah, Yoanne, Yohana, Yohanah, Yohane, Yohanka, Yohanna, Yohannah, Yohanne

Yoi (Japanese) born in the evening.

Yoki (Native American) bluebird.
Yokie, Yoko, Yoky

Yoko (Japanese) positive and determined woman.
Yo

Yolanda (Greek) violet flower.
Yolaina, Yolainah, Yolaine, Yolana, Yolanah, Yolandah, Yolande, Yolandee, Yolane, Yolanna, Yolanne, Yolantha, Yolanthe, Yolette, Yolie, Yolonda, Yulonda

Yoluta (Native American) summer flower.
Yolutah

Yon (Burmese) rabbit; (Korean) lotus blossom.
Yona, Yonna

Yone (Japanese) rice, wealth.
Yonee, Yoney, Yoni, Yonie, Yony

Yonina (Hebrew) dove.
Jona, Jonah, Jonati, Jonatia, Jonatiah, Jonina, Joninah, Jonnya, Jonyah, Jonyta, Jonytah, Yona, Yonah, Yonati, Yonatia, Yonatiah, Yonee, Yoney, Yoni, Yonie, Yoninah, Yonita, Yonitah, Yony, Yonyna, Yonynah, Yonyta, Yonytah

Yoome (Native American) star.
Yome, Yoom, Yoomee

Yordana (Basque) descendant.
Yordanah, Yordanna, Yordannah

Yori (Japanese) reliable.
Yoriko, Yoriyo

Yoshe (Japanese) a beauty, lovely.
Yoshee

Yoshi (Japanese) quiet, respected, a unisex name.
Yoshee

Yovela (Hebrew) rejoicing, joyful.
Yovelah, Yovele, Yovella, Yovellah, Yovelle

Ysabel (Spanish) consecrated to God, a form of Elizabeth.
Isabel, Isabell, Isabella, Isabelle, Ysabela, Ysabelah, Ysabele, Ysabell, Ysabella, Ysabelle, Ysbel, Ysbela, Ysbelah, Ysbele, Ysbell, Ysbella, Ysbellah, Ysabelle, Ysobel, Ysobela, Ysobelah, Ysobele, Ysobell, Ysobella, Ysobellah, Ysobelle

Ysann (American) combination of Ysabel and Anne.
Ysande, Ysanna, Ysannah, Ysanne

Yseult (Gaelic) light-skinned; (German) ice ruler.
Isault, Iseult, Isold, Isolde, Isolt, Ysault, Yseulte, Yseultt, Yseultte, Ysold, Ysolde, Ysolt

Yudita (Russian) praised, a form of Judith.
Yudit, Yuditah, Yudith, Yuditt, Yuditta, Yudittah

Yuki (Japanese) snow, lucky, a unisex name.
Yukee, Yukey, Yukie, Yukiko, Yuky

Yulia (Russian) youthful, a form of Julia.
Yula, Yulah, Yulenka, Yuliah, Yulie, Yulinka, Yulka, Yulya, Yulyah

Yuliana (Spanish) youthful, a form of Juliana.

Yulian, Yulianah, Yuliane, Yuliani, Yuliania, Yulianiah, Yuliann, Yulianna, Yuliannah, Yulianne, Yulien, Yuliena, Yulienah, Yuliene

Yumi (Japanese) beauty.

Yumee, Yumii

Yumiko (Japanese) arrow child.

Yumyko

Yuri (Japanese) lily.

Yuree, Yuriko, Yuriyo, Yury

Yuriko (Japanese) child of the lillies.

Yuryko

Yusra (Arabic) wealthy.

Yusrah

Yvanna (Slavic) God is gracious, a form of Ivana.

Yvana, Yvanah, Yvane, Yvania, Yvaniah, Yvannah, Yvanne, Yvannia, Yvanniah, Yvannya, Yvannyah

Yvette (French) little archer, a form of Yvonne, feminine form of Yves.

Yavetta, Yavette, Yevett, Yevetta, Yevette, Yvet, Yveta, Yvetah, Yvete, Yvett, Yvetta, Yvettah

Yvonne (French) little archer; (Scandinavian) yew tree.

Evonn, Evonne, Vonn, Vonnee, Vonnie, Vonny, Yavanda, Yavanna, Yavannah, Yavanne, Yavonda, Yavonna, Yavonnah, Yveline, Yvonn, Yvonna, Yvonnah, Yvonnie, Yvonny

Z

Zabrina (English) princess; (Latin) boundary, a form of Sabrina.

Zabreana, Zabreanah, Zabreane, Zabreena, Zabreenah, Zabreene, Zabreenia, Zabreeniah, Zabrinah, Zabrine, Zabrinia, Zabriniah, Zabrinie, Zabrinna, Zabrinnah, Zabrinne, Zabryna, Zabrynah, Zabryne

Zacharie (Hebrew) God remembers, feminine form of Zachariah.

Zac, Zacara, Zacarah, Zacaree, Zacarey, Zacari, Zacaria, Zacariah, Zaccara, Zaccarah, Zaccaree, Zaccarey, Zaccari, Zaccaria, Zaccariah, Zacchara, Zacchari, Zaccharie, Zachara, Zacharah, Zacharee, Zacharey, Zachari, Zacharia, Zachariah, Zack, Zackery,Zakaria, Zakariah, Zakarie, Zakary, Zakarya, Zakaryah, Zakaya, Zakayah, Zaria, Zary, Zechara, Zecheri, Zecherie

Zada (Arabic) lucky one.

Sada, Zadah, Zaida, Zayda, Zayelda

Zafina (Arabic) triumph.

Zafana, Zafanah, Zafeena, Zafeenah, Zafena, Zafenah, Zafinah, Zafyna, Zafynah

Zafirah (Arabic) victory, victorious, feminine form of Zafir.

Zafara, Zafarah, Zafeera, Zafeerah, Zafera, Zaferah, Zafira, Zafire, Zafyra, Zafyrah, Zafyre

Zahar (Hebrew) dawn.

Zahara, Zaharah, Zaher, Zahera,

Zaherah, Zahir, Zahira, Zahirah, Zahyr, Zahyra, Zahyrah

Zahara (African) flower.

Sahara, Saharah, Zaharah

Zahava (Hebrew) gold.

Zahavah, Zachava, Zachavah, Zaheva, Zahevah, Zeheva, Zehevah, Zehaava, Zehaavah

Zahra (Arabic) white; (African) flower.

Sahra, Zahraa, Zahrah, Zahreh, Zahria, Zahriah

Zaida (Arabic) fortunate.

Sada, Saida, Sayda, Zada, Zaidah, Zayda

Zaira (Arabic) rose.

Zairah

Zakelina (Russian) God remembers, a form of Zacharie.

Zakelean, Zakeleana, Zakeleanah, Zakeleane, Zakeleen, Zakeleena, Zakeleenah, Zakeleene, Zakelin, Zakelinah, Zakeline, Zakelyn, Zakelyna, Zakelynah, Zakelyne

Zakia (Arabic) pure; (African) intelligent.

Zakea, Zakeia, Zakeya, Zakiah, Zakiya, Zakiyah, Zakiyaa, Zakiyya

Zali (Polish) princess, a form of Sarah.

Zalea, Zaleah, Zalee, Zalei, Zaleigh, Zaley, Zalia, Zaliah, Zalie, Zaly, Zalya, Zalyah

Zalika (African) well-born into royalty.

Salika, Zalik, Zalikah, Zalyka, Zalykah

Zaltana (Native American) high mountain.

Zaltanah

Zan (Chinese) praise.

Zana (Persian) womanly; (Hebrew) God is gracious, a form of Jane.
Zanah, Zanha, Zania, Zaniah, Zanie, Zsaine, Zsane

Zandra (Greek) defender of humankind, a form of Sandra.
Zahndra, Zandrah, Zandria, Zandriah, Zandrie, Zandrya, Zandryah, Zandry, Zanndra, Zanndrah, Zondra, Zondrah

Zaneta (Hebrew) God is gracious, a form of Jane.
Saneta, Sanetah, Sanete, Sanett, Sanetta, Sanette, Zaneata, Zaneatah, Zaneeta, Zaneetah, Zanetah, Zanete, Zanett, Zanetta, Zanettah, Zanette, Zanita, Zanitah, Zanyta, Zanytah

Zanna (English) lily, a form of Suzanna; (Spanish) God is gracious, a form of Jane.
Zaina, Zainah, Zainna, Zainnah, Zana, Zanah, Zanella, Zanelle, Zanetta, Zanette, Zannah, Zannetta, Zannette, Zannia, Zanniah, Zannie, Zannya, Zannyah

Zanta (African) beautiful girl.
Zantah

Zara/Zarah (Hebrew) princess, a form of Sarah, dawn brightness.
Zahrah, Zahreh, Zarea, Zareea, Zareena, Zaira, Zari, Zaria, Zarra, Zarrah, Zarya, Zaryia

Zaria (Arabic) rose; (Latin) princess.
Zariah

Zarifa (Arabic) successful.
Zarifah, Zaryfa, Zaryfah

Zarina (African) golden.
Zareana, Zareanah, Zareena,
Zareenah, Zarinah, Zaryna, Zarynah

Zarita (Hebrew) princess, a form of Sarah.
Zareata, Zareatah, Zareate, Zareeta, Zareetah, Zareete, Zaritah, Zarite, Zaritta, Zarittah, Zaritte, Zaryt, Zaryta, Zarytah, Zaryte

Zasha (Russian) defender of humankind, a form of Sasha.
Zascha, Zaschah, Zashah, Zashenka, Zashka, Zasho

Zaviera (Spanish) bright new house, a form of Xaviera.
Zavier, Zavierah, Zavyera, Zavyerah, Zavyiera, Zavyierah

Zawati (African) gift.
Zawatia, Zawatiah, Zawaty, Zawatya, Zawatyah

Zayit (Hebrew) olive.
Zaya, Zayah, Zayeet, Zayeeta, Zayita, Zayitah

Zaza (Hebrew) movement.
Saza, Zah, Zazah, Zazu

Zea (Latin) ripened grain.
Sea, Seah, Sia, Siah, Zeah, Zia, Ziah, Zya, Zyah

Zehava (Hebrew) golden.
Sehara, Sehari, Sehava, Zehara, Zehari, Zehavah, Zehavi, Zehavia, Zehaviah, Zehavya, Zehavyah

Zelah (Hebrew) side.
Zela

Zelda (German, Jewish) grey-haired woman warrior.
Selda, Seldah, Zeldah, Zelde, Zella, Zellah

Zelene (English) sunshine.
Zeleen, Zeleena, Zeleenah, Zeleene, Zelen, Zelena, Zelenah,

Zelin, Zelina, Zelinah, Zeline, Zelyn, Zelyna, Zelynah, Zelyne

Zelia (Spanish) sunshine.
Zeelia, Zeeliah, Zele, Zelene, Zeliah, Zelie, Zelina, Zelya

Zelma (German) protected, secure, a form of Selma.
Selma, Selmah, Zelmah

Zemira (Hebrew) song of joy.
Semir, Semira, Semirah, Zemir, Zemirah, Zemyr, Zemyra, Zemyrah, Zimira, Zimirah, Zymira, Zymirah

Zena (Persian) woman.
Sena, Senah, Senia, Seniah, Senya, Senyah, Syhna, Xena, Xenah, Xihna, Xihnah, Xina, Xinah, Xyhnah, Xyna, Xynah, Zanae, Zanah, Zeena, Zeenat, Zeenet, Zeenia, Zeenya, Zein, Zeina, Zenah, Zenana, Zenea, Zenia, Zeniah, Zenna, Zennah, Zennia, Zenya Zenyah, Zihna, Zihnah, Zina, Zinah, Zyhna, Zyhnah, Zyna, Zynah

Zenaida/Zenaide (Greek) dove.
Zenaidah, Zenayda, Zenaydah, Zenayde, Zenochka

Zenda (Persian) sacred, feminine.
Senda, Sendah, Zendah

Zenobia (Greek) bright sky, given life by Zeus, father's ornament, feminine form of Zenobias.
Senobe, Senobia, Senobie, Senovia, Sizi, Xenobia, Xenobiah, Xenobya, Xenobyah, Zeba, Zeeba, Zena, Zenaida, Zenavia, Zenda, Zenia, Zenna, Zenobah, Zenobe, Zenobea, Zenobee, Zenobiah, Zenobie, Zenobya, Zenobyah, Zenovia, Zizi, Zyzy

Zephania (Greek) crowned, a form of Stephanie; (Hebrew) the Lord has hidden, protected treasure of God, feminine form of Zephan.

Zepania, Zepaniah, Zepanie, Zephaniah, Zephanie, Zephanua, Zephany

Zephyr (Greek) west wind, a unisex name.
Zefer, Zeffer, Zeffyr, Zefirryn, Zefyr, Zepher, Zephir, Zephire, Zephra, Zephria, Zephrina, Zephrine, Zephyer

Zera (Hebrew) seeds.
Sera, Serah, Zerah

Zerdali (Turkish) wild apricot.
Zerdalia, Zerdaliah, Zeradaly, Zeradalya

Zerlina (Hebrew) beautiful dawn.
Serlin, Serlina, Serlinah, Serlinda, Serline, Serlyn, Serlyna, Serlynah, Serlynda, Serlyne, Zearla, Zerla, Zerlean, Zerleana, Zerleanah, Zerleane, Zerlee, Zerleen, Zerleena, Zerleenah, Zerleene, Zerlin, Zerlinah, Zerlinda, Zerlindah, Zerline, Zerlyn, Zerlyna, Zerlynah, Zerlynda, Zerlyndah

Zerrin (Turkish) golden.
Zerran, Zerren, Zerron, Zerryn

Zeta (Hebrew) olive.
Seta, Sita, Syta, Xeta, Xetah, Xita, Xitah, Xyta, Xytah, Zayit, Zetah, Zetana, Zetta, Zita, Zitah, Zyta, Zytah

Zetta (Portuguese) rose.
Zeta, Zita

Zeva (Hebrew) wolf.
Seva, Sevah, Zevah, Zevia, Zeviah, Zevya, Zevyah

Zevida (Hebrew) gift.
Sevida, Sevidah, Zevidah, Zevyda, Zevydah

Zhana (Slavic) God is gracious, a form of Jane.
Zhanae, Zanah, Zhanay, Zhanaya,

Zhane, Zhanea, Zhanee, Zhaney, Zhani, Zhanna, Zhannia

Zhen (Chinese) chaste, precious.
Zen, Zenn, Zhena

Zia (Arabic) light, a unisex name.
Sia, Zea, Ziah, Zya, Zyah

Zigana (Hungarian) gypsy girl.
Ziganah, Zigane

Zihna (Native American) top spinner.
Zihnah, Ziohnah, Zyhna, Zyhnah

Zilla (Hebrew) shade or a shadow.
Zila, Zilla, Zylla

Zilya (Russian) harvester, a form of Theresa.
Zilyah, Zylya, Zylyah

Zimra (Hebrew) song of joy, praise, a unisex name.
Zemara, Zimraa, Zimrah, Zimri, Zimria, Zimriah, Zymria, Zymriah, Zymrya, Zymryah

Zina (African) secret spirit.
Zeena, Zinah, Zine, Zyhna, Zyna, Zynah

Zinerva (Italian) fair-haired.
Zinervah, Zynerva, Zynervah

Zinnia (Latin) zinnia flower with colourful flowers.
Zinia, Ziniah, Zinniah, Zinny, Zinnya, Zinya

Zippora (Hebrew) a little bird.
Zipora, Ziporah, Zipporah, Zipporia, Ziproh

Zisel (Hebrew) sweet.
Sisel

Zita (Spanish) rose.
Zeeta, Zeta, Zyta, Zytka

Ziva (Hebrew) bright, radiant.
Zeeva, Ziv, Zivanka, Zivi, Zivit

Zizi (Hungarian) dedicated to God, a form of Elizabeth.
Zsi, Zsizsi

Zlatka (Slavic) gold.
Zlatanne, Zlatenne, Zlatkah

Zoe (Greek) gift of life.
Zoë, Zoela, Zoelah, Zoee, Zoelie, Zoeline, Zoella, Zoellah, Zoelle, Zoey, Zoi, Zoie, Zowe, Zowey, Zowie, Zoya

Zofia (Greek) wisdom, a form of Sophia.
Zofea, Zofee, Zofey, Zofi, Zofiah, Zofie, Zofy, Zofya, Zofyah, Zophea, Zophee, Zophey, Zophi, Zophia, Zophiah, Zophie, Zophy, Zophya, Zophyah, Zsofia, Zsofiah, Zsofie, Zsofy, Zsophee, Zsophey, Zsophi, Zsophia, Zsophiah, Zsophie, Zsophy

Zohar (Hebrew) brilliant, shining.
Zoehra, Zoera, Zoeri, Zohara, Zoharah, Zohera, Zoherah, Zohra

Zohreh (Persian) happy.
Zohra, Zohrah, Zohre, Zora, Zorah, Zore, Zoreh

Zola (Latin) mound of earth; (German) prince, a unisex name.
Zoela, Zoila, Zolah, Zolla, Zollah

Zona (Greek) girdle.
Sona, Sonah, Zonah

Zora (Slavic) aurora, dawn, morning star, feminine form of Zorya.
Zara, Zahreh, Zohra, Zohrah, Zorah, Zorana, Zoranah, Zoreen, Zoreena, Zorna, Zorra, Zorrah, Zorya

Zorina (Slavic) gold.
Zorana, Zoranah, Zorean, Zoreana,

Zoreanah, Zoreane, Zoreen,
Zoreena, Zoreenah, Zoreene,
Zori, Zorie, Zorinah, Zorine, Zorna,
Zornah, Zory, Zoryn, Zoryna,
Zorynah, Zoryne

Zosima (Greek) lively, wealthy,
feminine form of Zosimus.

Sosima, Sosimah, Sosyma, Sosymah,
Zosimah, Zosyma, Zosymah

Zsa Zsa (Hungarian) lily, a form of
Susan.

Zhazha, Zsa, Zsa-Zsa, Zsuzsa,

Zsuzsanna (Hungarian) lily, a form
of Susan.

Zsusanna, Zsuska, Zsuzsa, Zsuzsi,
Zsuzsika, Zsuzka, Zuzanny

Zudora (Indian) labourer,
industrious.

Zudorah

Zula (African) from an African
tribe, the Zulus.

Zulah

Zuleika (Persian) brilliant.

Suelia, Sueliah, Suleika, Zeleeka,
Zuelia, Zueliah, Zuelya, Zuelyah, Zul,
Zulay, Zuleikah, Zuleka, Zulekha,
Zuleyka, Zulu

Zulema (Arabic, Hebrew) peace.

Sulema, Sulima, Zulemah, Zuliema,
Zulima, Zulyma, Zyta

Zurafa (Arabic) lovely.

Ziraf, Zirafa, Zirafah, Ziruf, Zirufa,
Zirufah, Zurafah

Zuri (African) beautiful.

Zuria, Zurie, Zurisha, Zury

Zusa (Slavic) lily, a form of Susan.

Zusah, Zusanka, Zusanna, Zusia,
Zuska, Zusu, Zuzanka, Zuzanna,
Zuzia, Zuzka, Zuzu

Zuwena (African) good.

Zuwina

Zytka (Slavic) rose.

Zitka, Zitkah, Zytkah

BOYS' NAMES

Aakarshan (Hindu) attraction.
Akaarshan, Akarshan

Aaron (Hebrew) enlightened; (Arabic) messenger, the brother of Moses in the Bible.
Aaharon, Aahron, Aaran, Aaranos, Aarek, Aaren, Aarenos, Aari, Aarin, Aarinos, Aaronke, Aaronos, Aarran, Aarranos, Aarren, Aarrenos, Aarrin, Aarrinos, Aarron, Aarronos, Aarryn, Aarrynos, Aaryn, Aeron, Aharon, Ahron, Aran, Aranos, Arek, Aren, Arenos, Ari, Arin, Arinos, Aron, Aronek, Aronos, Arran, Arranos, Arren, Arrenos, Arrin, Arrinos, Arron, Arronos, Arryn, Arrynos, Aryn

Abadi (Arabic) eternal.
Aabaadi, Aabadi, Abaadi

Aban (Persian) water figure.
Aabaan, Aaban, Abaan

Abasi (African) stern.
Aabaasi, Aabasi, Abaasi, Abasy

Abba (Aramaic) father; (Hebrew) God.
Aba, Abbas, Abbe

Abban (Latin) white.
Abben, Abbin, Abbine, Abbon

Abbas (Arabic) stern.
Aabbas, Abbaas

Abbott (Hebrew) father of the abbey.
Ab, Abad, Abba, Abbah, Abban, Abbe, Abbé, Abbet, Abbett, Abbey, Abboid, Abbot, Abett, Abott

Abbud (Arabic) devoted.
Aabbud, Aabud, Abud

Abdel (Arabic) servant, a form of Abdul.
Aabdel

Abdiel (Hebrew) servant of God.
Aabdiel

Abdul (Arabic) servant.
Aabdal, Aabdel, Aabdeel, Aabdoul, Aabdoula, Aabdoulah, Aabdual, Aabdul, Aabdull, Aabdulla, Aabdullah, Aabul, Abdal, Abdel, Abdeel, Abdoul, Abdoula, Abdoulah, Abdual, Abdull, Abdulla, Abdullah, Abul

Abdulaziz (Arabic) servant of the mighty one.
Aabdelazim, Aabdelaziz, Aabdellazim, Aabdellaziz, Aabdulazaz, Aabdulazez, Aabdulazeez, Aabdulaziz, Aabdullazaz, Aabdullazez, Aabdullazeez, Aabdullaziz, Abdelazim, Abdelaziz, Abdellazim, Abdellaziz, Abdulazaz, Abdulazez, Abdulazeez, Abdullazaz, Abdullazez, Abdullazeez, Abdullaziz

Abdullah (Arabic) servant of Allah.
Aabdala, Aabdalah, Aabdalla, Aabdallah, Aabduala, Aabdualah, Aabdualla, Aabduallah, Aabdula, Aabdulah, Aabdulahi, Aabdulha, Aabdulla, Aabdullah, Aabdullahi, Aabdullha, Abdala, Abdalah, Abdalla, Abdallah, Abduala, Abdualah, Abdualla, Abduallah, Abdula, Abdulah, Abdulahi, Abdulha, Abdulla, Abdullahi, Abdullha

Abdulrahman (Arabic) servant of the merciful one.
Aabdellrahim, Aabdellrahman, Aabdelrahim, Aabdelrahman,

Aabdirahman, Aabdirrahman,
Aabdollrahem, Aabdollrahim,
Aabdollrahman, Aabdolrahem,
Aabdolrahim, Aabdolrahman,
Aabdolrrahem, Aabdularahman,
Aabdullaraham, Aadullarahmon,
Aabdulraham, Aabdurahman,
Aabduram, Aabdurrahman,
Aabdurram, Abdellrahim,
Abdellrahman, Abdelrahim,
Abdelrahman, Abdirahman,
Abdirrahman, Abdollrahem,
Abdollrahim, Abdollrahman,
Abdolrahem, Abdolrahim,
Abdolrahman, Abdolrrahem,
Abdularahman, Abdularrahman,
Abdullraham, Abdullrahman,
Abdulraham, Abdurrahman,
Abdurram

Abe (Hebrew) father of the
multitudes, founder of the Hebrew
people, a form of Abraham.

Aabbe, Aabbie, Aabe, Aabie,
Aabraham, Aabram, Abbe, Abbie,
Abie, Abraham, Abram

Abel (Hebrew) breath of fresh air,
son of Adam and Eve in the Bible.

Ab, Abb, Abbe, Abe, Abele,
Abeles, Abell, Able

Abelard (German) born of high
nobility, resolute, ambitious.

Abalard, Abalarde, Abalardo,
Abalhard, Abelarde, Abelardo,
Abelhard, Abilard, Abilarde,
Abilardo, Abilhard, Adalard,
Adelard, Adilard

Abernethy (Scottish) mouth of a
river.

Abarnathi, Abarnathy, Abarnethi,
Abarnethy, Abernethi

Abhay (Hindu) no fear.

Aabhay

Abi (Turkish) elder brother.

Aabi, Abbe, Abbee, Abbey, Abbi,
Abbie, Abby, Abee, Abie, Aby

Abiah (Hebrew) the Lord is my
father.

Aabiah, Abia

Abidan (Hebrew) father of
judgement.

Abiden, Abidin, Abidon, Abidyn,
Abydan, Abyden, Abydin, Abydon,
Abydyn

Abie (Hebrew) father of the
multitudes, founder of the Hebrew
people, a form of Abraham.

Aabi, Aabie, Aaby, Abi, Aby

Abiel (Hebrew) the Lord is my
father, a form of Abiah.

Aabiel

Abijah (Hebrew) the Lord is my
father.

Aabijah

Abir (Hebrew) strong.

Aabir

Abisha (Hebrew) God's gift.

Aabbija, Aabbijah, Aabbisha,
Aabbishai, Aabija, Aabijah,
Aabisha, Aabishai, Abbija,
Abbisha, Abbishai, Abija, Abijah,
Abishai

Abner (Hebrew) father of light.

Aabna, Aabnah, Aabner, Aavner,
Ab, Abna, Abnah, Avner, Ebner,
Evner

Abraham (Hebrew) father of the
multitudes, founder of the Hebrew
people.

Aabaran, Aabarran, Aabe,
Aaberham, Aabey, Aabie,
Aabrahaim, Aabraham,
Aabrahame, Aabrahamo,
Aabrahan, Aabraheem,
Aabraheen, Aabrahem, Aabrahim,
Aabrahm, Aabram, Aabramo,
Aabran, Aabrano, Aabrao,
Aabriham, Aarram, Aavram,

Abaran, Abarran, Abe, Aberham,
Abey, Abie, Abrahaim, Abrahame,
Abrahamo, Abrahan, Abraheem,
Abraheen, Abrahem, Abrahim,
Abrahm, Abram, Abramo, Abran,
Abrano, Abrao, Abriham, Arram,
Avram, Bram, Ibraham, Ibrahim

Abram (Hebrew) father of the
multitudes, founder of the Hebrew
people, a form of Abraham.

Aabram, Aabrama, Aabramah,
Aabramo, Abrama, Abramah,
Abramo

Absalom (Hebrew) father of
peace, son of King David in the
Bible.

Aabasalaam, Aabasalam,
Aabsalom, Aabsalon, Aabselon,
Aabsolum, Abasalaam, Abasalam,
Absalon, Abselon, Absolum

Abu (Arabic) father.

Aabu

Acar (Turkish) bright.

Ace (Latin) at one with
humankind, unity.

Acee, Acer, Acey, Acie, Ayce,
Aycee, Aycer, Aycey, Aycie

Acel (French) noble.

Ace, Aceel, Acelin

Achilles (Greek) without lips, a
figure in Greek mythology.

Achill, Achille, Achillea, Achilleas,
Achillee, Achillees, Achillios, Akil,
Akili, Akilles

Ackerley (English) dweller in the
oak-tree meadow.

Accerley, Accerly, Ack, Acker,
Ackerlea, Ackerlee, Ackerleigh,
Ackerlsey, Ackerly, Acklea, Acklee,
Ackleigh, Ackley, Ackly

Acton (English) from the
settlement with oak trees.

Actonn, Akton, Aktonn

Acucio (Latin) sharp.

Acuzio

Adahy (Native American) in the
woods.

Adair (Scottish) from the oak tree
near the ford.

Adaire, Adare, Adayre, Addair,
Addaire, Addare, Adderr

Adalard (Teutonic) noble, brave.

Adalarde, Adalardo, Adelard,
Adelarde, Adelardo

Adalgiso (Teutonic) noble
hostage.

Adallgiso

Adalrico (German) noble chief.

Adelric, Adelrich, Adelricho,
Adelrick, Adelricko, Adelrik, Adelriko,
Adelryk, Adelryko, Aldo, Rico

Adam (Hebrew) man of the red
earth, the first man according to
the Bible.

Aadam, Adama, Adamec,
Adamek, Adamh, Adamik, Adamka,
Adamko, Adamok, Adamm,
Adamo, Adams, Adas, Addam,
Addama, Addams, Addee,
Addham, Addhamm, Addie, Addis,
Addy, Adem, Ademm, Adham,
Adhamh, Adhamm, Adné, Adok,
Adom, Adoma, Adomas, Ade

Adamson (Hebrew) son of Adam.

Adams, Adamsson, Addams,
Addamson

Adar (Syrian) ruler; (Hebrew)
noble.

Aadar, Aaddar, Addar

Addison (English) son of Adam.

Addis, Addisan, Addisen, Addisun,
Addyson, Adisan, Adisen, Adison,
Adisson, Adyson, Adysonn,
Adysson, Addyssonn

Ade (African) royal.
Ad

Adel (Teutonic) noble.
Addel, Addell, Adel, Adell

Adelard (German) noble, brave,
form of Adalard.
Adelarde, Adelardo

Adelbert (German) bright, noble.
*Adelbertt, Adelbirt, Adelbirtt,
Adelburt, Adelburtt*

Adelino (German) noble.

Adelmo (German) noble
protector.
Adelemo

Adelphos (Greek) brother.
Adalphos, Adelphio, Adelpho

Ademaro (German) glorious in
battle.
*Adamar, Adamaro, Ademar,
Adhemar, Adimar, Adimaro*

Aden (Irish) fiery one.
*Adan, Adin, Adon, Adyn, Aedan,
Aeden, Aedin, Aedon, Aedyn,
Aidan, Aiden, Aidin, Aidon, Aidyn*

Adeodatus (Latin) given by God.
Adeodato, Adeodatos

Adham (Arabic) black.

Adhamh (Irish) man of the red
earth, the first man according to
the Bible, a form of Adam.

Adiel (Hebrew) adorned by the
Lord.
Addiel

Adil (Arabic) wise, just.
Adill, Adyl, Adyll

Adir (Hebrew) noble, majestic.
Adirr, Adyr

Adiran (Latin) of the Adriatic Sea.
Adirran, Adyran

Aditya (Hindu) sun.
Adittya

Adiv (Hebrew) gentle, pleasant.
Adeev, Adev

Adlai (Hebrew) my witness,
refuge; (Arabic) acting justly.

Adler (Teutonic) eagle.
Ad, Addlar, Addler, Adlar

Adley (Hebrew) just.
*Adlea, Adlee, Adleigh, Adli, Adlie,
Adly, Adlye*

Admon (Hebrew) peony.

Adnan (Arabic) pleasant.
Adnaan, Adnane

Adney (English) dweller on the
island.
Adnee, Adni, Adnie, Adny, Adnye

Adolph (German) noble wolf.
*Ad, Addof, Addoff, Addofo, Adof,
Adoffo, Adofo, Adolf, Adolfo,
Adolfus, Adolph, Adolphe,
Adolpho, Adolphus, Dolf, Dolfe,
Dolfi, Dolph, Dolphe, Dolphi*

Adom (African) God will help.

Adon (Hebrew) sacred name for
the Lord.
Adonn

Adoni (Australian Aboriginal) sunset.
Adonee, Adoney, Adonie, Adony

Adonis (Greek) the handsome
youth loved by Venus, according
to myth; (Hebrew) lord.
Adoni, Adony, Adonys

Adri (Pakastani) rock.

Adrian (Latin) dark one; (Greek) rich, black, mysterious.
Adraen, Adriaen, Adriano, Adrianus, Adrien, Adriene, Adrienus, Adrin, Adrino, Adrinus, Adryan, Adryen, Adryn

Adriel (Hebrew) from God's congregation.
Adrial, Adriale, Adriall, Adriele, Adriell, Adryel, Adryele, Adryell

Adwin (African) creative.
Adwyn

Aeneas (Greek) the praised one, hero of *The Aeneid* by Virgil.
Eneas, Enne

Aeolus (Greek) the ruler of the winds, according to myth.
Aolus

Afif (Arabic) chaste, modest.
Afeef, Affif, Afiff

Afram (African) a river in Ghana, Africa.

Afton (English) from Afton, England.
Aftan, Aften, Aftin, Aftyn

Agamemnon (Greek) resolute.
Agaimemnon, Agame, Aygamemnon

Agni (Hindu) god of fire.

Agrippa (Latin) born feet first.
Agripa, Agripah, Agrippah, Agrypa, Agrypah, Agryppa, Agryppah

Agu (African) leopard.

Agustin (Spanish) venerable, the exalted one, a form of Augustine, Augustus.
Agustine, Agustinn, Agustus, Augustin, Augustine, Augustinn, Augustus

Ahab (Hebrew) uncle.

Ahanu (Native American) he who laughs.

Ahdik (Native American) deer, caribou.
Adic, Adick, Adik, Adyc, Adyck, Adyk, Ahdic, Ahdick, Ahdyc, Ahdyck, Ahdyk

Ahearn (Celtic) owner or lord of many horses.
Ahearne, Aherin, Ahern, Aherne, Hearne, Heren, Herin, Herne, Heron, Herri, Herron

Ahmad (Arabic) most highly praised, a form of Muhammad.
Ahmed

Ahren (German) eagle.
Ahrenn, Ahrenne, Ehren, Ehrenne

Aidan (Irish) little fiery one.
Adan, Aden, Adin, Adian, Adon, Adyn, Aiden, Aidian, Aidin, Aidon, Aidyn, Aydan, Ayden, Aydian, Aydin, Aydon, Aydyn, Eden

Aiken (English) made of oak.
Aicken, Aickin, Aikin

Aimon (French) house.
Aimonn, Aymon, Eamon

Aindrea (Celtic) strong, brave, a form of Andrew.
Anders, Andie, Andre, Andreas, Andres, Andrew, Andy, Aundrae, Aundray, Aundre, Aundrea, Aundrey, Aundry, Drew

Ainsley (Scottish) my meadow, my own place, my field, from the clearing, a unisex name.
Aineslea, Aineslee, Ainesley, Aineslie, Ainslie, Ansley, Anslie, Ansly

Ajala (African) potter.
Ajalah

Ajax (Greek) eagle.

Ajay (Punjabi) victorious.
AJ, Ajae, Ajai, Ajaie, Ajaye

Akando (Native American) ambush.

Akar (Turkish) stream.
Akara, Akare

Akash (Hindu) sky.
Aakash, Aakasha, Aakashay, Akasha, Akashay

Akbar (Arabic) great.
Achbar, Achbara, Akbara, Akbare, Akbarr

Akemi (Japanese) dawn.
Ackeem, Ackeemi, Akeam, Akeami, Akee, Akeem, Akeemi, Akeim, Akeimi, Akeme, Akemie, Akemy

Akil (Arabic) intelligent, thoughtful, one who uses reason.
Akile, Akill, Akyl, Akyle, Akyll

Akins (African) brave.
Akin, Akyn, Akyns

Akio (Japanese) bright.
Akyo

Akira (Japanese) bright, intelligent, a unisex name.
Akeera, Akio, Akirah, Akiyo, Akyra, Akyrah

Akmal (Arabic) perfect.
Achmal, Ackmal

Akram (Arabic) most generous.

Akshay (Hindu) sky, a form of Akash.

Akule (Native American) he looks up.
Akool, Akul, Akull, Akulle

Al (English) a form of Alan, Albert, Alexander.

Ala (Arabic) excellent.

Aladdin (Arabic) nobility, excellence of faith.
Al, Ala, Alaadin, Aladin, Alladin, Alladdin

Alaire (French) joyful.
Alair, Alare, Alayr, Alayre

Alam (Arabic) universe.
Alame, Allam

Alan (Irish) handsome, noble, peaceful.
Ailan, Ailean, Ailin, Al, Alain, Alaine, Aland, Alen, Alin, Alind, Allen, Allin, Allyn, Alyn

Alaric (German) ruler of all.
Alarich, Alaricho, Alarick, Alaricko, Alarico, Alarik, Alaryc, Alarych, Alaryck, Alaryk, Alric, Alrich, Alrick, Alrik

Alastair (Scottish) helper or defender of humankind, a form of Alexander.
Alastaire, Alaster, Alastir, Alastire, Alec, Alistair, Alistaire, Alister, Alistir, Alistire, Allastair, Allaster, Allastir, Allastire, Allistaire, Allistar, Allister, Allistir, Allistire, Elastair, Elastaire

Alban (Latin) white.
Albany, Alben, Albeny

Alberic (German) wise, intelligent ruler.

Alberich, Alberick, Alberik, Alberyc, Alberych, Alberyck, Alberyk

Albern (German) noble, courageous.

Alberne, Alburn, Alburne

Albert (German) noble, bright and illustrious.

Ailbert, Al, Albee, Alberte, Alberto, Albie, Albirt, Albrecht, Alburt, Alby, Adalbert, Adelbert, Bert, Bertie, Berty, Elbert

Albion (Latin) white.

Alcott (English) old stone house.

Alcot, Alkot, Alkott, Allcot, Allcott, Allkot, Allkott

Alden (English) old and wise friend.

Aldan, Aldin, Aldwan, Aldwen, Aldwin, Aldwyn, Aldyn, Eldan, Elden, Eldin, Eldwan, Eldwen, Eldwin, Eldwyn, Eldyn

Alder (English) alder tree.

Aldar, Aldare, Aldere

Aldis (English) old house.

Aldiss, Aldos, Aldous, Aldus, Eldis, Eldiss, Eldos, Eldous, Eldus

Aldo (Teutonic) old, wise.

Aldred (Anglo-Saxon) old, wise councellor.

Alldred

Aldrich (Teutonic) old, wise ruler.

Aldric, Aldrick, Alric, Alrich, Alrick, Audric, Audrich, Audrick, Eldric, Eldrich, Eldrick

Aldwin (English) old and wise friend, a form of Alden.

Aldwan, Aldwen, Aldwon, Aldwyn

Alec (English) helper or defender of humankind, a form of Alexander, Alastair.

Al, Alech, Aleck, Alecko, Aleic, Aleich, Aleick, Aleik, Alek, Alekk, Alekko, Aleko, Alex

Aled (Welsh) offspring.

Aelad, Aeled, Alad, Elad, Eled

Alejandro (Spanish) helper or defender of humankind, a form of Alexander.

Alastair, Alec, Alej, Alejanda, Alexander, Janda, Jandro

Alem (Arabic) wise man.

Alim, Alym

Aleron (Latin) with wings.

Alerone, Aleronn, Aleronne, Alleron, Allerone, Alleronn, Alleronne, Eleron, Elerone, Eleronn, Eleronne, Elleron, Ellerone, Elleronn, Elleronne

Alex (Greek) helper or defender of humankind, a form of Alexander.

Al, Alec, Alech, Aleck, Alecko, Aleic, Aleich, Aleick, Aleik, Aleix, Alek, Alekk, Alexa

Alexander (Greek) helper or defender of humankind, Alexander the Great was the Macedonian world conqueror who died in 323 BC.

Alasander, Alasdair, Alassander, Alastair, Alec, Alecsander, Alecksander, Alejandro, Alejo, Aleksander, Aleksei, Aleksi, Aleksy, Alesander, Alessander, Alessandre, Alessandro, Alex, Alexa, Alexandre, Alexandro, Alexei, Alexi, Alexio, Alexis, Alister, Alsandair, Alsandar, Sander, Sandy, Saunders, Sondy, Xander, Zanda, Zandy, Zondy

Alfonse (Spanish) noble, ready, a form of Alphonse.
Alfonso, Alfonze, Alfonzo, Alphonse, Alphonso, Alphonze, Alphonzo

Alfred (English) wise judge, elf counsellor.
Ailfred, Ailfrid, Alf, Alfie, Alfredo, Alfrid, Allfred, Fred

Alger (Teutonic) spearman.
Algar

Algernon (French) one with a moustache.
Al, Algie, Algy

Algis (German) spear.
Algiss

Ali (Arabic) the highest, greatest.
Aliy, Aly

Alim (Arabic) wise or learned scholar.
Alym

Allambee (Australian Aboriginal) quiet place.
Alambee, Alambey, Alambi, Alambie, Alamby, Allambee, Allambey, Allambi, Allambie, Allamby

Allard (English) noble, brave.
Alard

Allen (Irish) handsome, noble, peaceful.
Alan, Alen, Alin, Alyn, Allan, Allin, Allyn

Allison (English) Alice's son, noble birth, a unisex name.
Al, Alisen, Alisin, Alison, Alisun, Allisen, Allisin, Allisun, Allysen, Allysin, Allyson, Allysun, Alysen, Alysin, Alyson, Alysun, Elison, Ellison

Almeric (Teutonic) great ruler.
Almerich

Almo (Anglo-Saxon) noble, famous.

Almon (Hebrew) widower.
Alman, Almen, Almin, Almyn

Alon (Hebrew) oak.
Alonn, Allon, Allonn

Alonso (Spanish) noble, ready, a form of Alphonse.
Allonse, Allonso, Allonze, Allonzo, Alons, Alonse, Alonz, Alonze, Alonzo

Aloysius (German) famous warrior, a form of Louis.
Aloys, Alewis, Alouis, Lewis, Louis, Ludwig

Alphonse (German) noble, ready.
Alfons, Alfonse, Alonso, Alphonsus

Alroy (Spanish) the king.
Alroi

Alston (English) from the old village, from the noble town.
Alstan, Alsten, Alstin, Alstun, Alstyn

Altair (Arabic) the flying eagle.
Altayr, Altayre

Altman (German) old, wise man.
Altmann, Altmen, Altmenn

Alton (English) of the old town.
Altan, Alten, Altin, Altun, Elton

Alun (Welsh) handsome, noble, peaceful, a form of Alan.
Alan, Alen, Alin, Allan, Allen, Allin, Allun

Alvern (Latin) spring.
Alverne

Alvis (Scandinavian) wise.
Alviss

Alwyn (Anglo-Saxon) noble, old, friend.
Allwin, Allwyn, Alwin

Amadeus (Latin) loved by God.
Amadeo, Amado, Amando, Amandos

Amal (Hebrew) hard-working; (Arabic) hopeful.
Amahl

Amar (Punjabi) eternal, immortal; (Arabic) builder.
Amare, Amario, Amaris, Amaro, Amarr

Amasa (Hebrew) burden bearer.
Amasah, Amassa, Amassah, Emasa, Emasah, Emassa, Emassah

Amato (French) loved.
Amat, Amatt, Amatto

Ambert (Teutonic) bright light.
Amerto, Ambirt, Ambirto, Amburt, Amburto

Ambrose (Greek) divine, immortal.
Ambroise, Ambros, Ambrosi, Ambrosio

Ameer (Arabic) prince, a form of Amir.
Ameere, Amere, Amir, Emeer, Emeere, Emere, Emir

Amerigo (Italian) hardworking ruler.
Ameri, America, Americo, Ameriga, Amierca, Amierco, Amierga, Amierigo, Emery, Emmery, Emmett, Emric, Emrik

Ames (French) friend.
Amess

Amiel (Hebrew) God of my people.
Amiell, Amyel, Amyell

Amin (Arabic, Hebrew) trustworthy, loyal, honest.
Ameen, Amyn

Amir (Arabic) prince.
Amirr, Amyr, Amyrr

Amiri (Maori) east wind.

Amit (Punjabi) unfriendly; (Arabic) highly praised.
Amita, Amitan, Amrit, Amrita, Amritan, Amryt, Amryta, Amrytan, Amyt

Amjad (Arabic) glorious.

Ammar (Arabic) builder, constructor, a form of Amar.
Ammare, Ammario, Ammaris, Ammaro

Ammon (Egyptian) hidden.

Amon (Hebrew) trustworthy, faithful.
Aman, Amen, Amin, Amyn

Amory (Latin) love; (Teutonic) divine ruler.
Amerie, Amerrie, Amery, Amorie, Amorrie

Amos (Hebrew) burdened.
Amose, Amoss

Amram (Hebrew) mighty nation.
Amariem, Amarien, Amram, Amran, Amrem, Amren, Amrym, Amryn

An (Chinese) peaceful.

Anan (Arabic, Hebrew) clouds, a unisex name.

Anand (Hindu) happiness, bliss.
Ananda, Anant, Ananth

Anastasius (Greek) resurrection.
Anastacio, Anastacios, Anastacius, Anastas, Anastase, Anastasi, Anastasio, Anastasios, Anastatius, Anastice, Anastis, Anastisis

Anatole (Greek) from the east.
Anatol, Anatole, Anatoli, Anatolie, Anatolio, Anatoly

Ancel (German) god; (Latin) servant.
Ancelin

Anchali (Native American) painter.
Anchalee, Anchaley, Anchalie, Anchaly

Ande (African) pillar.

Anders (Swedish) strong, courageous, manly, a form of Andrew.
Aindrias, Ander, Andie, Andrea, Andree, Andres, Andrias, Andy

Andrei (Russian) strong, courageous, manly, a form of Andrew.
Aindre, Aindrea, Aindreas, Andre, Andreas, Andree, Andrei, Andres, Andreus

Andrew (Greek) strong, courageous, manly, patron saint of Scotland.
Aindreas, Anders, Andie, Andre, Andrei, Andreas, Andres, Andreus, Andy, Drew

Andrey (Russian) strong, courageous, manly, a form of Andrew.
Andri, Andrie, Andry

Aneurin (Welsh) truly golden, Honourable.
Aneuryn

Angel (Greek, Latin) heavenly messenger, a unisex name.
Angell, Angello, Angellos, Angellus, Angelo, Angelos, Angelous, Angelus, Angiolo, Anglico, Aniello, Anjel, Anjell, Anjello, Anjelo

Angus (Scottish) exceptional qualities.
Gus

Angwyn (Welsh) handsome.
Angwin, Angwine

Anh (Vietnamese) safety, peace.
An

Anil (Hindu) god of wind.
Aniel, Aniello, Anielo, Anill, Anillo, Anilo, Anyl, Anyll, Anyllo, Anylo

Anis (Arabic) close friend.

Annan (Celtic) from the stream.
Annen, Annin, Annon, Annun, Annyn

Anoke (Native American) actor.
Anokee, Anokey, Anoki, Anokie, Anoky

Ansel (French, German) wearer of a helmet, with God's protection, follower of a nobleman.
Ansele, Ansell, Anselle

Anselm (German) wearer of a helmet, with God's protection, follower of a nobleman.
Anse, Ansel, Anselmi, Anshel, Anshelm

Ansley (English) from the meadow.
Anslee, Ansleigh, Ansli, Anslie, Ansly

Anson (English, Hebrew) Ann's son.
Aenson, Ansan, Ansen, Ansin, Ansyn

Anstice (Greek) resurrected one.
Anstise, Anstiss, Anstisse

Antares (Greek) star.

Anthony (Latin) priceless, praiseworthy; (Greek) flourishing.
Anntoin, Anthonee, Anthoney, Anthoni, Anthonie, Antin, Antoin, Antoine, Anton, Antone, Antonee, Antoney, Antoni, Antonie, Antonio, Antonius, Antony, Toni, Tony

Antoine (French) priceless, a form of Anthony.
Anthony, Antoin, Anton, Antonio

Antonio (Italian) priceless, a form of Anthony.
Anthony, Anton, Antonius, Antony, Antonyo, Toni, Tony

Anwar (Arabic) light ray.

Anwell (Welsh) beloved, dearest.
Anwel, Anwil, Anwill, Anwyl, Anwyll

Apiatan (Native American) wooden lance.

Apollo (Greek) the ancient Greek god of the sun.

Aquila (Latin) eagle.
Aquil, Aquill, Aquilla

Arafat (Arabic) mountain of recognition.
Arrafat

Araldo (Spanish) great leader of the army, a form of Harold.
Arald, Arrald, Arroldo

Aram (Syrian) high, exalted.
Arem, Arim, Arram, Arrem, Arrum, Arrym, Arum, Arym

Aran (Thai) forest.
Arane

Archard (French) powerful.

Archer (English) bowman.
Archar

Archibald (German) very bold, brave.
Arch, Archaimbaud, Archibaldo, Archie, Archimbald, Archy

Ardell (Latin) eager.
Ardall, Ardel

Arden (Latin) fiery; (English) dwelling place, ardent and sincere, valley of the eagles, a unisex name.
Ard, Ardan, Ardane, Ardean, Ardeane, Ardene, Ardent, Ardin, Ardn, Ardun, Ardyn

Ardley (English) ardent meadow.
Ardlea, Ardlee, Ardleigh, Ardli, Ardlie, Ardly

Ardon (Hebrew) bronzed.
Ardan, Arden, Ardin, Ardun, Ardyn

Aren (Danish) eagle, ruler.
Aaran, Aaren, Aarin, Aaron, Aaryn, Aran, Arin, Aron, Arran, Arren, Arrin, Arron, Arryn, Aryn

Ares (Greek) Greek god of war.

Argus (Greek) giant with 100 eyes, according to myth; (Scandinavian) watchful, vigilant.
Arguss

Argyle (Irish) from Ireland.
Argile, Argy

Aric (English) brave ruler, a form of Eric, Frederick.
Arick, Arik, Eric, Erick, Erik, Frederick, Ric, Rick, Rickie, Ricky

Ariel (Hebrew) lion of God.
Aariel, Airal, Airel, Arel, Areli, Ariele, Ariell, Aryel, Aryell, Aryl, Aryll, Arylle, Eariel

Aries (Latin) ram, the first sign of the zodiac.

Arif (Arabic) knowledgeable.
Aryf

Aristotle (Greek) best thinker, the Greek philosopher.
Aris, Aristitle, Aristitol, Aristo, Aristotal, Aristotel, Aristotol, Aristotyl, Arystotle

Arkady (Russian) bold.
Arkadee, Arkadey, Arkadi, Arkadie

Arkin (Norwegian) son of the eternal king.
Arkeen, Arken, Arkyn

Arlen (Irish) pledge, promise.
Arlan, Arlann, Arlenn, Arlin, Arlinn, Arlon, Arlonn, Arlyn, Arlynn

Arley (English) of the hare's meadow, a form of Harley.
Arlea, Arlee, Arleigh, Arli, Arlie, Arly, Harley

Armand (Latin, German) warrior, a form of Herman.
Arman, Armande, Armando, Armin, Armind, Arminde, Armindo

Armstrong (Anglo-Saxon) strong armed.
Armstron

Arnaud (French) powerful like an eagle, a form of Arnold.
Arnaude, Arne, Arnie, Arnold, Arny

Arne/Arni (Teutonic) powerful like an eagle, a form of Arnold.
Arnee, Arney, Arni, Arnie, Arny

Arnett (English) little eagle.
Arnatt, Arnatte, Arnette, Arnott, Arnotte

Arnold (Teutonic) powerful like an eagle.
Arn, Arnald, Arnalde, Arnaldo, Arnaud, Arnaude, Arne, Arnie, Arnolde, Arnoldo, Arnyld, Arnylde

Arnon (Hebrew) rushing river.
Arnan, Arnen, Arnin, Arnyn

Aroon (Thai) dawn.
Aroone

Arran (Scottish) island dweller.
Aran, Aren, Arin, Aron, Arren, Arrin, Arron, Arryn, Aryn

Arrio (Spanish) warlike.
Ario, Arryo, Aryo

Arsenio (Greek) manly, virile.
Arsen, Arsene, Arseneo, Arsenius, Arsinio

Arsha (Persian) venerable.
Arshah

Art/Artie (Welsh, Celtic) strong as a bear; strong as a rock, a form of Arthur.
Artee, Arty

Artemas (Greek) gift of Artemis the goddess.
Artemo

Arthfael (Welsh) bear, strength.

Arthur (Welsh, Celtic) strong as a bear; strong as a rock.
Art, Artair, Artur, Arturo, Artus, Arty

Arturo (Spanish) strong as a bear; strong as a rock, a form of Arthur.
Arthur, Arty, Art

Arun (Hindu) sun rising.

Arundel (English) eagle valley.
Arundle

Arvad (Hebrew) wanderer.
Arval, Arved, Arvel, Arvid, Arvil, Arvyd, Arvyl

Arve (Norwegian) heir.
Arv

Arvel (Welsh) wept over.
Arval, Arvalis, Arvelis

Arvin (German) friend of the people.
Arvan, Arven, Arvon, Arvyn, Arwan, Arwen, Arwin, Arwon, Arwyn

Aryeh (Hebrew) lion.
Arye

Arziki (African) prosperity.

Asa (Hebrew) healer.
Asaa, Asaah, Asah

Asad (Arabic) lion.
Asaad, Assad

Asadel (Arabic) most prosperous one.
Asadul, Asadyl, Aael

Ascot (English) of the eastern cottage.
Ascott

Ash (English, Hebrew) from the ash tree.
Ashby, Ashburn, Ashe, Ashford, Ashley, Ashly

Asher (Hebrew) fortunate, happy.
Ashar, Ashir, Ashur, Ashyr

Ashford (English) ash tree ford.
Ashforde

Ashley (English) from the meadow, from the grove of ash trees, a unisex name.
Ash, Ashe, Asher, Ashlee, Ashlei, Ashleigh, Ashli, Ashlie, Ashly

Ashon (African) seventh-born child.
Ashan, Ashen, Ashin, Ashyn

Ashraf (Arabic) most honourable.

Ashton (English) at the ash tree town.
Ashtan, Ashten, Ashtin, Ashtown, Ashtyn, Astan, Asten, Astin, Aston, Astown, Astyn

Ashur (Hebrew) black.

Ashwin (Hindu) star.
Ashwan, Ashwen, Ashwon, Ashwyn

Asiel (Hebrew) created by God.
Asim, Asyel, Asym

Asif (Arabic) forgiveness.
Aseef, Asyf

Asim (Arabic) protector, defender.
Aseem

Asker (Turkish) warrior, soldier.
Aske

Asoka (Hindu) without sorrow, the name of a flower.
Asokah

Aspen (English) flower from Brittany, aspen tree, a unisex name.
Aspin, Aspine

Astley (Greek) starry field.
Asterlea, Asterlee, Asterleigh,

Asterley, Asterli, Asterlie, Asterly, Astlea, Astlee, Astleigh, Astli, Astlie, Astly

Aswad (Arabic) black.

Ata (African) twin.
Atah

Athan (Greek) immortal.
Athen, Athin, Athon, Athyn

Atherton (English) town by the stream, spring.
Atharton, Athartown, Athertown

Athol (Celtic) from Ireland.
Atholl, Atol, Atoll

Atid (Thai) sun.
Atyd

Atif (Arabic) compassionate, sympathetic.
Atyf

Atley (English) at the meadow.
Atlea, Atlee, Atleigh, Atli, Atlie, Atly, Attlea, Attlee, Attleigh, Attley, Attli, Attlie, Attly

Attis (Greek) handsome boy.
Atis, Atiss, Attiss

Atwell (English) at the spring, well.
Attwel, Attwell, Atwel

Atwood (English) at the wood.
Attwood

Atworth (English) at the farm.
Attworth

Aubin (French) fair, white.
Aubine

Aubrey (German) noble, bright; (English, French) elf ruler, a unisex name.
Aubary, Aubery, Aubray, Aubury

Auburn (English) reddish-brown colour.
Abirn, Abirne, Aburn, Aburne, Abyrn, Abyrne, Aubern, Auberne, Aubin, Aubirn, Aubirne, Aubun, Auburne, Aubyrn, Aubyrne

Auden (English) old friend.
Audan, Audin, Audon, Audyn

Audon (French) old, rich.
Auden

Audric (English) wise ruler.
Audrick, Audrik

Audun (Scandinavian) deserted.
Audan, Auden, Audin, Audon, Audyn

August (Latin) venerable, the exalted one, a form of Augustine, Augustus.
Auguste, Augustin, Augustine, Augustus, Gus

Augustine (Latin) venerable, the exalted one.
August, Auguste, Augusteen, Augustein, Augustin, Augustino, Augusto, Augustus, Augustyn, Augustyne, Gus

Augustus (Latin) venerable, the exalted one.
August, Auguste, Augusteen, Augustein, Augustin, Augustine, Augustino, Augusto, Augustyn, Augustyne, Gus

Aukai (Hawaiian) seafarer.
Aukay

Aulay (Scandinavian) family descendant.
Auley

Aundre (Greek) strong, courageous, manly, a form of Andrew.

Aundrae, Aundray, Aundrea,
Aundree, Aundrey, Aundry

Aure (Greek) breeze, soft air.

Aurelius (Latin) golden.
Arelian, Areliano, Arelias, Aurel,
Aurele, Aureli, Aurelian, Aureliano,
Aurelias, Aurelio, Aurellio, Aurelien,
Aurellius, Aurey, Auriel, Aury

Aurick (German) protector, ruler.
Aurec, Aureck, Aurek, Auric, Aurik

Auryn (Welsh) gold.
Aurryn, Aurynn

Austin (Latin) venerable, the
exalted one, a form of Augustine.
Astan, Asten, Astin, Astine, Aston,
Austan, Austen, Austine, Auston,
Austun, Austyn, Austyne, Oistin,
Oistyn, Ostin, Ostyn

Avel (Greek) breath.
Avell

Avenall (French) dweller at the
oat field.
Avernal, Avenel, Avenell

Averill (English) slayer of the boar,
boar-like, a unisex name.
Averel, Averell, Averiel, Averiell,
Averil, Averille, Averyl, Averyll, Avrel,
Avrell, Avril, Avrill, Avryl, Avryll

Avery (English) elf ruler, a form of
Aubrey.
Avary, Aveary, Avere, Averey, Averi,
Averie, Avrey, Avry

Avi (Hebrew) my father.
Aavi, Aavian, Aavidan, Aavidor,
Aaviel, Aavion, Avian, Avidan,
Avidor, Aviel, Avion

Aviv (Hebrew) youth.
Aaviv, Aaveev, Aveev

Avshalom (Hebrew) father of
peace.
Abshalom, Absalom, Avsalom

Awan (Native American) person
of significance.
Awen, Awin, Awon, Awun, Awyn

Axel (Latin) axe; (German) source
of all life; (Scandinavian) father of
peace, a form of Avshalom.
Aaxel, Aaxell, Aaxelle, Aksel, Aksell,
Ax, Axell, Axelle, Axe, Axil, Axill, Axl,
Axle, Axll, Axlle

Axton (English) sword sharpener's
stone.
Axtan, Axten, Axtin

Aydin (Turkish) intelligent.
Aidan, Aiden, Aidin, Aidon, Aidyn,
Aydan, Ayden, Aydon, Aydyn

Ayers (English) heir to a fortune.
Aiers

Ayinde (African) praise.
Aayinde

Aylmer (English) noble, famous, a
form of Elmer.
Aillmer, Ailmer, Allmer, Almer, Ayl,
Ayle, Ayllmer

Aylwin (English) noble friend.
Ailwan, Ailwen, Ailwin, Ailwyn,
Alwan, Alwen, Alwin, Alwyn,
Aylwan, Aylwen, Aylwon, Aylwyn

Ayman (Arabic) lucky, right-
handed.
Aayman

Aymon (French) mighty, wise
protector, a form of Raymond.
Aiman, Aimen, Aimin, Aimon,
Aimyn, Ayman, Aymen, Aymin,
Aymyn

Ayo (African) happy.
Aayo

Azad (Turkish) free.
Aazad

Azeem (Arabic) defender.
Aazeem, Aazim, Azim

Azel (Hebrew) noble.
Aazel

Azhar (Arabic) shining, luminous.
Aazhar

Azi (Nigerian) young.
Aazi, Aazee, Azee

Azim (Arabic) defender.
Aazim, Azeem, Aazeem

Aziz/Azizi (African) precious.
Aaziz, Aazizi, Azez, Azezi, Ezez, Ezezi

Azriel (Hebrew) God is my aid.
Aazriel, Aazrielle, Aazzriel, Aazzrielle, Azrielle, Azzriel, Azzrielle

Azuriah (Hebrew) aided by God.
Aazaria, Aazariah, Aazuria, Aazuriah, Azaria, Azariah, Azuria

Azzam (Arabic) determined, resolved.
Aazam, Aazzam, Azam, Ezam, Ezem, Ezzam, Ezzem

B

Baako (African) first-born child, a unisex name.

Babak (Persian) little father.

Babu (African) grandfather.

Baden (German) bath.
Badin, Badon, Badyn, Baeden, Baedin, Baedon, Baedyn, Bayden, Baydin, Baydn, Baydon, Baydyn

Badr (Arabic) full moon, a unisex name.

Badrick (Anglo-Saxon) axe ruler.
Badric, Badrik, Badryc, Badryck, Badryk

Badru (African) born at the full moon.

Baez (Welsh) boar.

Baha (Arabic) brilliant, magnificent.

Bahir (Arabic) dazzling, brilliant.
Baheer, Bahur

Bahman (Persian) good mind.

Bailey (English, Old French) bailiff, one who keeps guard, a unisex name.
Bail, Bailee, Baileigh, Baili, Bailie, Bailio, Baillee, Bailleigh, Bailley, Bailli, Baillie, Baillio, Baily, Baylee, Bayleigh, Bayley, Bayli, Baylie, Baylio, Bayly

Bain (Irish) bridge over white water, a form of Bainbridge.
Baine, Bane, Baynn, Baynne

Bainbridge (Irish) bridge over white water.
Bain, Bane, Banebridge, Baynbridge, Bayne, Baynebridge

Baird (Celtic) a wandering minstrel who sings ballads.
Bairde, Bard, Barde

Bairn (Celtic) child.
Bairne

Bakari (African) noble promise.
Bacari, Bacarie, Baccari, Bakarie, Bakkari

Baker (English) baker.
Bayker

Bal (Hindu) child born with lots of hair.

Balasi (Basque) flat footed.

Balbo (Latin) indistinct speaker, stammerer.
Balbi, Bailby, Balby

Baldemar (German) bold, famous prince.
Baldemaro, Baldemer, Baldomero, Baumar, Baumer

Balder (Anglo-Saxon) brave army leader.
Balda, Baldar, Baldur, Baudier

Baldovino (Italian) brave friend, a form of Baldwin.
Baldovin

Baldric (German) brave princely ruler.
Baldrick, Baldrik, Baudric, Baudrick, Baudrik

Baldwin (German) brave friend.
Bald, Baldewin, Baldewyn, Baldovino, Balduin, Baldwinn, Baldwyn, Baldwynn, Baudoin, Baudoiun

Balfour (Scottish) far hill or pasture.
Balfor, Balfore

Balin (Hindu) mighty warrior.
Baline, Balyn, Balyne, Baylen, Baylin, Baylon

Ballard (German) brave, strong.
Balard, Ballarde

Balraj (Hindiu) strongest.

Balthasar (Greek) God save the King, one of the three wise men who brought gifts for baby Jesus.
Baldassar, Baldassare, Baltasar, Baltazar, Balthasaar, Balthazar, Balthazzar, Baltsaros, Belshazar, Belshazzar, Boldizar

Banan (Irish) white.
Banen, Banin, Bannan, Banon, Banyn

Bancroft (English) bean field.
Ban, Bancrofft, Bank, Bankroft, Bankrofft, Banky

Bandi (Hungarian) strong, courageous, manly, a form of Andrew.
Bandee, Bandey, Bandie, Bandit

Bandit (English) robber.
Bandet, Bandett, Banditt, Bandyt, Bandytt

Bane (Hawaiian, Hebrew) son of the ploughman, a form of Bartholomew.
Baen, Baene, Bain, Baine, Bayn, Bayne

Banner (English, Scottish) flag bearer.
Bannor, Banny

Banning (Irish) little blond one.
Bannie, Banny

Bao (Chinese) treasure.

Baptist (Greek) to baptise.
Baptista, Bapttista, Batist, Batista, Battista

Baqi (Arabic) enduring.

Baradine (Australian Aboriginal) small kangaroo.
Baradin, Baradyn, Baradyne

Barak (Hebrew) flash of light.
Barack, Barrack, Barrak

Baram (Hebrew) son of the people.
Barem, Barim, Barom, Barym

Baran (Russian) ram.
Baren, Barin, Baron, Barran, Barren, Barrin, Barron, Barryn, Baryn

Barasa (African) meeting place.
Barasah

Barclay (English) meadow of the birch tree.
Bar, Barcklae, Barcklaey, Barcklai, Barcklaie, Barcklay, Barcklie, Barclae, Barclaey, Barclai, Barclaie, Barclie, Barklae, Barklaey, Barklai, Barklaie, Barklay, Barklie, Barrclay, Berkeley

Bard (Celtic) poet, singer.
Bar, Barde, Baird, Bairde, Bardia, Bardiya, Barr

Barden (English) barley valley.
Bairdan, Bairden, Baridin, Bairdon, Bairdyn, Bardan, Bardin, Bardon, Bardyn

Bardolf (Teutonic) bright wolf.
Bardolph, Bardou, Bardoul, Bardoulf, Bardoulph, Bardulf, Bardulph

Bardrick (Teutonic) axe ruler.
Bardric, Bardrik

Baringa (Australian Aboriginal) light.

Baris (Turkish) peaceful.
Barris, Barrys, Barys

Barlow (Anglo-Saxon) bald hill.
Baerhloew, Baerloew, Baerlow, Barlowe, Barrlow, Barrlowe

Barnabas (Aramaic, Greek, Hebrew) son of consolation, son of prophecy.
Barna, Barnaba, Barnabe, Barnaby, Barney, Barnie, Barny

Barnard (English, German) bold as a bear.
Barn, Barney, Barnie, Barny, Bern, Bernard, Berney, Bernie, Berny, Nardo

Barnes (English) bold as a bear, a form of Barnard.
Barns

Barnett (English) nobleman, leader.
Barn, Barnet, Barnete, Barnette, Barney, Baronet, Baronett, Barrie, Barron, Barry, Boernet

Barney (English) bold as a bear, a form of Barnard.
Barnard, Barnee, Barnie, Barny, Bern, Bernard, Bernee, Bernie, Berny, Nardo

Barnum (English) noble one's stone house.

Baron (English, German) nobleman, baron.
Baaron, Barin, Barion, Baronie, Barrin, Barrion, Barron, Barryn, Baryn, Bayron, Berron

Barr (Anglo-Saxon) gateway.
Bar, Barre

Barrett (German) strong like a bear.
Bar, Barat, Baret, Barrat, Barratt, Barret, Barrin, Barrion, Baron, Baryn, Berret, Berrett, Berrit, Berritt

Barric (English) grain farm.
Barrick, Barrik, Beric, Berick, Berik, Berric, Berrick, Berrik

Barrington (English, French) fenced town.
Barington

Barris (Welsh) son of Harry.
Baris, Barrys, Barys

Barry ((Irish) spear, marksman.
Bari, Barree, Barrey, Barrie, Barris, Bary, Baz, Bazza

Bart (English) son of the ploughman, a form of Bartholomew.
Barrt, Bartee, Bartel, Bartey, Barth, Bartie, Barty, Bat

Bartholomew (Hebrew) son of the ploughman.
Balta, Bane, Bart, Bartek, Barth, Barthel, Barthelemy, Barthelmy, Bartho, Bartholo, Bartholomaus, Bartholome, Bartholomeo, Bartholomeus, Bartholomieu, Bartimous, Bartlet, Barto, Bartolome, Bartolomew, Bartolommeo, Bartome, Bartz, Bat

Barton (Anglo-Saxon) barley town.
Bart, Bartan, Barten, Bartin, Bartyn

Bartram (English) bright raven, a form of Bertram.
Barthram

Baruch (Hebrew) blessed.
Barucha, Boruch, Borucha

Baruti (Egyptian) teacher.

Barwon (Australian Aboriginal) magpie.

Basam (Arabic) smiling.
Basem, Basim, Bassam, Bassem, Bassim

Basil (Latin) royal, like a king.
Basile, Basilio, Basilius, Basill, Basille, Basillio, Basillius, Basyl, Basyle, Basylio, Basylius, Basyll, Basylle, Basyllio, Basyllius, Vasil, Vasile, Vasilio, Vasilius, Vassily

Basilio (Italian) royal, like a king, a form of Basil.
Basylio

Basir (Turkish) discerning, clever; (Arabic) seer.
Basar, Baseer, Bashar, Basheer, Bashir, Bashiyr, Bashyr, Basiyr, Basyr, Bechir, Bhasheer, Bhasir

Bassett (English) little person.
Baset, Basett, Basit, Basitt, Basset, Bassit

Bastiano (Greek, Italian) venerable; (Latin) revered, a form of Sebastien.
Bastian

Bastien (Greek) venerable; (Latin) revered, a form of Sebastien.
Bastern, Bastiaan, Bastian, Bastilen, Baston, Sebastien

Bat (English) son of the plough-man, a form of Bartholomew.

Battista (Italian) to baptise, a form of Baptist.
Baptist, Baptista, Battist

Baul (Gypsy) snail.

Bavol (Gypsy) wind, air.
Baval, Bavel, Bavil, Bavyl

Baxter (English) baker.
Bax, Baxie, Baxtar, Baxtie, Baxtir, Baxtor, Baxy

Bay (Vietnamese) seventh son, (French, English) chestnut- brown colour, evergreen tree.
Bai, Baye

Bayard (English) red-brown hair.
Bae, Baiard, Baiardo, Bay, Bayardo, Bayrd, Bayrdo, Biaiard, Biaiardo

Bayley (English, Old French) bailiff, one who keeps guard, a form of Bailey.
Bailey, Baylee, Bayleigh, Baylie, Bayly

Beacan (Irish) small.
Beacen, Beacon, Becan, Becen, Becon

Beacher (English) near the beech trees.
Beach, Beachy, Beech, Beecher, Beechy

Beagan (Irish) little one.
Bea, Beagan, Beagen, Bee, Beegen

Beal/Beale (French, English) handsome one.
Beall, Bealle, Beel, Beele, Beell, Beelle

Beaman (English) bee-keeper.
Bea, Bee, Beeman

Beamer (English) trumpeter.
Beemer

Beasley (English) pea field.
Beaslea, Beaslee, Beasleigh, Beasli, Beaslie, Beasly, Beeslea, Beeslee, Beesleigh, Beesley, Beesli, Beeslie, Beesly

Beattie (Latin) bestower of blessings.
Beatey, Beatie, Beatty, Beattey, Beaty, Beetea, Beetee, Beetey, Beety

Beau (French) handsome.
Bo, Beale, Beaux

Beaufort (French) handsome, beautiful fort.
Beauford, Beauforde, Beauforte

Beaumont (French) beautiful mountain.

Beauregard (French) handsome guard.
Beau, Boregard

Beaver (English) beaver.
Beav, Beavo, Beavor, Beever, Beevor, Beve, Bevo

Bebe (French) baby.

Beck (Old Norse) small brook.
Bec, Bek

Bede (English) prayerful.
Beed, Beede

Bedir (Turkish) full moon.
Bedeer, Bedire, Bedyr, Bedyre

Bela (French) handsome.

Beldan (English, French) pretty valley.
Belden, Beldin, Beldon, Belldan, Bellden, Belldon

Belen (Greek) arrow.
Belenan

Bell (French) handsome; (English) bell ringer.
Bel

Bellamy (French) handsome friend.
Belamey, Belami, Belamie, Belamy, Bell, Bellamey, Bellami, Bellamie, Bellemy

Bello (African) helpful one.

Belmiro (Portugese) good looking, attractive.
Belmyro

Belveder (Italian) beautiful.
Belvder, Belvedear, Belvedere, Belvidear, Belvider, Belvidere

Bem (African) peace.
Behm

Bemus (Latin) platform.
Bemis

Ben (Hebrew) son of the right hand, a form of Benjamin.
Behn, Behnn, Behnne, Behnno, Benio, Benn, Benne, Benno

Ben-Ami (Hebrew) son of my people.
Baram, Barami, Benami

Benedetto (Italian) blessed, a form of Benedict.

Benedict (Latin) blessed.
Ben, Benard, Benci, Bendic, Bendick, Bendict, Bendino, Bendix, Bendrick, Bendrict, Benedect, Benedett, Benedetto, Benedick, Benedicti, Benedictus, Benedikt, Bengt, Benito, Benjamen, Benjamin, Benji, Bennett, Benoit

Benedikt (German, Slavic) blessed, a form of Benedict.
Bendek, Bendik, Benedek, Benedekt, Benedik

Bengt (Scandinavian) blessed, a form of Benedict.
Beng, Benke, Bent

Beniam (Ethiopia) son of the right hand, a form of Benjamin.
Beneyam, Beniamin, Beniamino, Benyam

Benito (Italian) blessed, a form of Benedict.
Benedo, Beneno, Beneto, Benido, Benino, Benno, Beno, Betto, Beto

Benjamen (Hebrew) son of the right hand, a form of Benjamin.
Benejamen, Benjarmen, Benjermen, Benjimen, Benjjmen

Benjamin (Hebrew) son of the right hand.
Beathan, Behnjamin, Bejamin, Bemjiman, Ben, Benejaminas, Bengamin, Beniam, Benja, Benjahmin, Benjaim, Benjam, Benjamaim, Benjaman, Benjamen, Benjamine, Benjaminn, Benjamino, Benjamon, Benjamyn, Benjamynn, Benjemin, Benjermain, Benjermin, Benji, Benjie, Benjiman, Benjimen, Benjy, Bennjamin, Benny, Benyamin, Benyamino, Binyamin

Benjiman (Hebrew) son of the right hand, a form of Benjamin.
Benjimain, Benjimin, Benjimon, Benjmain

Benjiro (Japanese) enjoys peace.

Bennett (English) little blessed one.
Benet, Benett, Benit, Benitt, Bennet, Bennit, Bennitt, Bennyt, Bennytt, Benyt, Benytt

Benny (Hebrew) son of the right hand, a form of Benjamin.
Benney, Benni, Bennie

Beno (Hebrew) son.
Benno

Benoit (French) blessed, a form of Benedict.

Benoite, Benoitt, Benoyt, Benoyte, Benoytt

Benoni (Hebrew) son of my sorrow, the son of Jacob and Rachel in the Bible.

Benson (English, Hebrew) son of Benjamin.
Ben, Benji, Benny, Bensan, Bensen, Bensin, Sonny

Bentley (English) moor, grass meadow.
Bent, Bentlea, Bentlee, Bentleigh, Bentlie, Benty, Lee

Benton (English) Ben's town, town on the moors.

Benzi (Hebrew) son of Zion, a form of Ben-Zion.

Ben-Zion (Hebrew) son of Zion.
Benson, Benzi, Benzion

Beppe (Italian) God shall increase, a form of Joseph.
Bepe, Bepee, Beppee, Beppy, Bepy

Ber (Hebrew) bear.
Berr

Beredei (Russian) bright mind, bright spirit, a form of Hubert.
Berdrei, Berdry, Berdy, Beredej, Beredy

Berenger (Teutonic) bear spear.
Beringer

Beresford (English) from the barley ford.
Beresforde

Berg (German) mountain.
Berdj, Berge, Bergh, Berj, Berje

Bergen (German) mountain dweller.
Bergin, Birgen, Birgin

Berger (French) shepherd.

Bergren (Scandinavian) mountain stream.
Berg

Berk (Turkish) solid, rugged.
Birk, Burk

Berkeley (English) birch meadow.
Berkelea, Berkelee, Berkeleigh, Berkeli, Berkelie, Berkely, Berklea, Berklee, Berkleigh, Berkley, Berkli, Berklie, Berkly

Berl (German) wine servant; (English) tree with a knot, a form of Burl.
Berle, Berlie, Berlin, Berlyn, Birl, Birle, Burl, Burle

Bern (German) bold as a bear, a form of Bernard.
Berne, Bernie, Bernn, Bernne, Berny, Nardo

Bernal (German) strong as a bear.
Bernald, Bernaldo, Bernel, Bernhal, Bernhald, Bernhold, Bernold

Bernard (German) bold as a bear.
Barnard, Barney, Barnir, Bear, Bearnard, Benek, Ber, Berend, Bern, Bernabe, Bernadal, Bernadas, Bernal, Bernardin, Bernardo, Bernardus, Bernardyn, Bernarr, Bernat, Berne, Bernek, Bernel, Bernerd, Berngard, Berngards, Bernhard, Bernhards, Bernhardt, Bernie, Berny, Bjorn, Burnard, Nardo

Bernardo (Spanish) bold as a bear, a form of Bernard.
Barnardino, Barnardo, Barnhardo, Benardo, Bernardino, Bernhardo, Berno, Burnardo, Nardo

Bernie (German) bold as a bear, a form of Bernard.
Berney, Berni, Berny, Birney, Birnie, Birny, Burney, Burny

Bernstein (German) amber stone.
Bernsteen, Bernsteyn, Bernsteyne

Bert (English) a form of Herbert, Bert, Albert, Bertram.
Bertee, Bertie, Berty

Berthold (German) brilliant ruler.
Bert, Bertholdi, Berthooud, Bertie, Bertold, Bertoldi, Bertooud

Bertil (Scandinavian) bright.
Bertyl, Birtil, Birtyl, Burtil, Burtyl

Bertin (Spanish) special, honoured friend.
Bertyn, Burtin, Burtyn

Berton (English) brilliant one's town.
Bert, Bertan, Berten, Bertie, Bertin

Bertram (English) bright raven.
Beltram, Beltran, Bertran, Bertrand, Bertrando

Berwick (English) barley farm.
Berwic, Berwik, Berwyc, Berwyck, Berwyk

Berwyn (Welsh) white head.
Berwin

Beval (English) windy.
Bevel, Bevil, Bevyl

Bevan (Welsh) son of Evan.
Beavan, Beaven, Beven

Beverly (English) from the stream of the beaver, near the meadow of beavers, a unisex name originally derived from a surname.
Bev, Beverlea, Beverlee, Beverleigh,

Beverley, Beverli, Beverlie, Bevleigh, Bevley, Bevlie, Bevly

Bevis (Latin) ox.
Beauvis, Bevvis

Bhagwandas (Hindu) servant of God.
Bhagwanda

Bharat (Hindu) maintainer.
Barat

Bhaskar (Hindu) light.
Baskar

Bickford (English) axeman's ford.
Bick, Bickforde

Bijan (Persian) ancient hero.
Bijann, Bijon, Bijonn, Byjan, Byjann, Byjon, Byjonn

Bilal (Arabic) chosen one.
Bila, Bilaal, Bilale, Bile, Bilel

Bill (German) determined guardian, a form of William.
Billee, Billey, Billi, Billie, Billy

Binah (Hebrew) understanding, wise.
Bina, Byna, Bynah

Bing (German) hollow tree.

Binh (Vietnamese) peace.
Bin

Bink (English) dweller at the slope.
Binka, Binke, Binkee, Binki

Birch (English) birch tree.
Berch, Berche, Berk, Birche, Birk

Birin (Australian Aboriginal) cliff.
Biryn, Byrin, Byryn

Birkitt (English) birch-tree headland.
Berket, Berkett, Berkit, Berkitt, Birk, Birket, Birkett, Birkit, Burket, Burkett, Burkit, Burkitt

Birley (English) birch tree meadow.
Birlee, Birleigh, Birlie, Burlee, Burleigh, Burley, Burlie

Birney (English) birch-tree island.
Birnie, Burney, Burnie

Birtle (English) hill with birds.

Bishop (English) bishop.

Bjorn (Norse) bear.
Bjorne

Blackburn (Scottish) black stream.
Blackbern, Blackberne, Blackburne

Blade (English) sword of good fortune.
Blaid, Blaide, Blayd, Blayde

Blaine (Irish) thin, lean.
Blain, Blane, Blayn, Blayne, Bleyn, Bleyne

Blair (Scottish) field, battleground; (Irish) field or plain dweller, a unisex name.
Blaire, Blayr, Blayre

Blaise (English) flame; (Latin) stammerer.
Blaize, Blase, Blaze

Blake (Anglo-Saxon) attractive, dark, a unisex name.
Blaik, Blaike, Blayk, Blayke

Blakeley (English) dark meadow.
Blakelea, Blakelee, Blakeleigh, Blakeley, Blakely

Blanco (Spanish) white.
Blanko

Bland (Latin) gentle.
Blande

Blane (Irish) thin, lean, a form of Blaine.
Blain, Blaine, Blayn, Blayne, Bleyn, Bleyne

Blaze (English) flame, a unisex name; (Latin) stammerer, a form of Blaise.
Blais, Blaise, Blas, Blasien, Blasius, Blayze

Bledig (Welsh) like a wolf.

Bliss (Anglo-Saxon) joy, blissful, a unisex name.
Blis, Blisse, Blys, Blyss

Bly (Native American) high, tall.
Bli, Bligh

Blythe (English) happy, cheerful, gentle, a unisex name.
Blith, Blithe, Blyth

Bo (Chinese) precious, a unisex name.
Beau, Boe, Bowe

Boaz (Hebrew) swift, fast, strong.
Boas, Booz, Bos, Boz

Bob (English) famous, brilliant, a form of Robert.
Bobbie, Bobby

Bobo (African) born on a Tuesday.

Boden (French) messenger; (Scandinavian) shelter.
Beauden, Bodin, Bowden

Bodil (Norwegian) strong ruler.
Bodill, Bodyl, Bodyll

Bodua (African) animal tail.
Boduah

Bogart (French) strong as a bow.
Bo, Bogar, Bogey, Bogie

Bohdan (Ukrainian) ruler of the world, proud leader, a form of Donald.
Bohdane, Bohden, Bohdon

Bomani (African) strong warrior.

Bonamy (French) good friend.
Bonamie

Bonar (Latin) good, kind, gentle.
Bonnar, Bonne, Bonner, Bonnie

Bonaro (Spanish, Italian) good friend.
Bona, Bonar, Bonero, Bonnar

Bonaventure (Italian) good adventure.
Bonadventure

Bond (English) soil tiller.
Bondie, Bondon, Bonds, Bondy

Boniface (Latin) one who does well for mankind, handsome face.
Bonifacio, Bonifacius

Bono (Latin) good.
Bon, Bonno, Bonus

Booker (English) one who reads books, including the Bible.
Bookie, Bookker, Books, Booky

Boone (Latin) good.
Bon, Bone, Boon, Boonie, Boony

Booth (English) hut; (Scandinavian) temporary shelter.
Boot, Boote, Boothe

Borak (Arabic) lightning.
Borac, Borack

Borden (English) valley of the boars.
Board, Boardan, Boarden, Boardie, Boardin, Boardon, Boardy, Boardyn, Bord, Bordan, Bordie, Bordin, Bordon, Bordy, Bordyn

Borg (Scandinavian) castle; (Norse) from the settlement.
Borge

Boris (Slavic) warrior.
Borris, Borrys, Borys

Borka (Russian) warrior.
Borkah

Boseda (African) born on a Sunday.
Bosedah

Bosley (English) grove of trees.
Boslea, Boslee, Bosleigh, Bozlea, Bozlee, Bozleigh, Bozley

Boswell (English) boar enclosure next to the stream.
Boswel, Bozwel, Bozwell

Bosworth (English) boar enclosure.
Bozworth

Boulus (Arabic) small, a form of Paul.
Boulos

Bourey (Cambodian) country.
Bouree, Bourie, Boury

Bourne (English) stream.
Born, Borne, Bourn

Bowen (Welsh) son of Owen.
Bow, Bowan, Bowe, Bowie, Bowin, Bowon, Bowyn

Bowie (Irish) fair-haired.
Bowee, Bowey, Bowi, Bowy

Boyce (French) woodland, forest.
Boice, Boise, Boycey, Boycie, Boyse, Boysey, Boysie

Boyd (Celtic) fair-haired.
Boydan, Boyde, Boyden, Boydin, Boydon, Boydyn

Boyne (Irish) white cow.
Boin, Boine, Boyn

Brac (Welsh) free.
Brach, Brack, Bracke, Brak

Brad (English) broad meadow.
Bradd, Bradford, Bradlee, Bradley, Bradlie, Bradly

Bradburn (English) broad stream.
Bradbern, Bradberne, Bradborn, Bradborne, Bradbourn, Bradbourne, Bradburne

Braden (English) broad valley.
Bradin, Bradon, Braeden, Braedin, Braedon, Brayden, Braydin, Braydon

Bradford (English) broad ford.
Brad, Bradd, Braddford, Bradforde

Bradley (English) broad meadow.
Brad, Bradd, Bradlea, Bradlee, Bradleigh, Bradlie, Bradly, Lee

Bradshaw (English) broad forest.
Brad, Braddshaw, Bradshawe

Brady (Irish) spirited; (English) broad island.
Brad, Bradey, Bradie, Brady, Braedey, Braedie, Braedy

Braedan (English) broad valley, a form of Braden.
Bradan, Braden, Bradyn, Braedan, Braedyn, Braydan, Brayden

Bragi (Scandinavian) poet.
Brage

Braham (Hindu) creator.
Braheem, Braheim, Brahiem, Brahm

Brahma (Hindu) prayer.

Bram (Hebrew) father of the multitudes, founder of the Hebrew people, a form of Abraham.
Bramm

Bramwell (English) bramble stream.
Bramwel

Bran (Celtic) raven.
Brann

Branch (Latin) tree branch.

Brand (English) firebrand, torch, beacon.
Bran, Brande

Brandon (English) gorse-covered hill; (Celtic) raven.
Bran, Brand, Brandan, Branden, Brandin, Brant, Brantan, Branten, Brantin, Branton

Brandy (Dutch, Anglo-Saxon) brandy, burnt wine, a unisex name.
Brandie

Brant (English) proud one.
Brante

Brawley (English) hill on the meadow.
Brawlea, Brawlee, Brawleigh, Brawli, Brawlie, Brawly

Braxton (English) Brock's town.
Brax, Braxdon, Braxston, Braxtan, Braxten, Braxtin, Braxtyn

Brayden (English) broad valley, a form of Braden.
Braden, Braeden

Breck (Irish) freckled.
Brec, Breik, Brek, Brekk

Brecon (Welsh) a group of mountains in South Wales.
Breckon, Brekon

Brede (Scandinavian) iceberg.
Bred

Brendan (Celtic) little raven, sword.
Breandan, Breanden, Breandon, Bren, Brenden, Brendin, Brendon, Brendyn, Brenn

Brennan (Celtic) little raven, a form of Brendan.
Bren, Brenan, Brendan

Brent (English) steep hill.
Brentan, Brenten, Brentin, Brenton, Brentyn

Brett (English) from Britain.
Bret, Bretain, Breton, Britain, Briton, Britt

Brewster (English) one who brews beer.
Brewer, Bruer, Bruster

Brian (Celtic) strong, honourable; (Irish) hill.
Brant, Brent, Briant, Briano, Brien, Brient, Brion, Briont, Bryan, Bryant

Briar (French) heather; (English) thorny rose, a unisex name.
Brear, Brier, Bryar

Brice (Celtic) ambitious, quick.
Brise, Bryce, Bryse

Brick (English) bridge.
Bric, Bricker, Brik, Bryc, Bryck, Brycker, Bryk

Bridger (English) bridge builder.
Bridgar, Bridge, Bridges

Brigham (English) covered bridge.
Brig, Brigam, Brigg, Briggs, Bryg, Brygg, Bryggs, Brygham

Brinley (Anglo-Saxon) burning wood.
Brinleigh, Brinly

Brion (Celtic) strong, honourable; (Irish) hill, a form of Brian.
Brian, Brien, Bryan, Bryen

Brishan (Gypsy) born during the rain.
Brishen, Brishin, Brishon, Brishyn, Bryshan, Bryshen, Bryshin, Bryshon, Bryshyn

Briton (English) British.
Brett, Britt, Brittan, Britton, Bryton, Brytt, Brytton

Brock (English) badger.
Broc, Broch, Brockie, Brok

Broderick (Welsh) son of Roderick.
Broderic, Broderik, Brodrick, Brodrik

Brodie/Brody (Irish) ditch, canal builder.
Brodey

Brogan (Irish) work shoe.
Broggan

Bromley (English) brushwood meadow.
Bromlea, Bromlee, Bromleigh, Bromli, Bromlie, Bromly

Bronson (English) son of Brown.

Bron, Bronniw, Bronnson, Bronny, Bronsan, Bronsen, Bronsin, Bronsun, Bronsyn

Bronte (Greek) thunder; (English) the surname of the Brontë sisters, novelists Charlotte, Emily and Anne; a unisex name.
Brontee, Brontey, Brontie

Brook (English) brook, stream.
Brooke

Bruce (French) dense shrubs, forest.
Brooce, Broose, Brucey, Brucy, Brue, Bruis, Bruse

Bruno (Italian) brown-haired.
Braun

Brutus (Latin) brute, coarse.

Bryan (Celtic) strong, honourable; (Irish) hill.
Brant, Brent, Brian, Briant, Briano, Brien, Brient, Brion, Bry, Bryant, Bryen, Bryent

Bryant (Celtic) strong, honourable; (Irish) hill, a form of Bryan.
Brent, Brian, Briant, Brient, Bryent

Bryce (Celtic) ambitious, quick, a form of Brice.
Brice, Bryse

Brychan (Welsh) freckled.
Brichan, Brinach, Brynach

Bryn (Welsh) mountain.
Brin, Brinn, Brinne, Bryne, Brynn, Brynne

Brynmor (Welsh) large mountain.
Brinmor, Brinmore, Brynmore

Bryson (Welsh) Bryce's son.
Brysan, Brysen, Brysin, Brysun

Buck (Anglo-Saxon) male deer.
Buc, Buk

Buckley (English) deer meadow.
Bucklea, Bucklee, Buckleigh, Buckli, Bucklie, Buckly, Buclea, Buclee, Bucleigh, Bucley, Bucli, Buclie, Bucly, Buklea, Buklee, Bukleigh, Bukley, Bukli, Buklie, Bukly

Bud (English) friend.
Budd, Budde, Buddie, Buddy, Budie, Budy

Buell (German) one who lives at the hill.
Buel, Buele

Bundy (Anglo-Saxon) free.
Bundee, Bundey, Bundie

Bunyan (Autralian Aboriginal) pigeon home.
Bunyen, Bunyin, Bunyon, Bunyn

Burchard (English) strong, fortified castle.
Burckard, Burckart, Burckhard, Burckhardt, Burgard, Burgaud

Burdett (French) small shield.
Berdet, Berdett, Burdet

Burgess (English) townsman.
Berges, Bergess, Burge, Burges

Burian (Ukrainian) lives close to weeds.
Berian, Beriane, Beryan, Beryane, Birian, Biriane, Biryan, Biryane, Buriane, Buryan, Buryane, Byrian, Byriane, Bryryan, Byryane

Burke (German) fortress.
Berk, Berke, Birk, Birke, Bourke, Burk

Burl (German) wine servant; (English) tree with a knot.
Berl, Berle, Burle, Byrl, Byrle

Burnaby (Norse) warrior's estate.
Birnabee, Birnabey, Birnabi, Birnabie, Birnaby, Burnabee, Burnabey, Burnabi, Burnabie, Byrnabee, Byrnabey, Byrnabi, Byrnaie, Byrnaby

Burnett (English) burnt nettle.
Bernet, Bernett, Birnet, Birnett, Burnet

Burr (Swedish) young; (English) prickly plant.
Berr, Burre

Burril (Australian Aboriginal) wallaby.
Bural, Burel, Buril, Burol, Burral, Burrel, Burrol, Burryl, Buryl

Burt (English) a form of Herbert, Bert, Albert, Bertram, Burton.
Bert, Bertee, Bertie, Bertt, Berty, Burtee, Burtie, Burtt, Burty

Burton (English) fortified town.
Birton, Birt, Burt

Busby (Scottish) village in the thicket.
Busbee, Busbey, Busbie

Butcher (English) butcher.
Butch

Butler (English) wine steward, head servant.
Butlar, Buttlar, Buttler

Butrus (Arabic) rock, a form of Peter.

Byram (English) cattle shed.
Biram

Byrd (English) like a bird.
Bird, Birdie, Byrdie

Byron (English) cow shed.
Biron, Byrne, Byrone

Cable (French, English) maker of rope.
Cabel, Cabell, Caible, Cayble

Cadby (English) warrior's settlement.
Cadbee, Cadbey, Cadbi, Cadbie

Caddock (Welsh) keen in battle.
Caddoc, Caddok, Cadoc, Cadock, Cadok

Cade (Celtic) battle, a form of Cadell.
Cady, Caid, Caide, Cayd, Cayde

Cadell (Celtic) battle.
Cadel, Caddell, Caede, Caedel, Caedell

Cadeyrn (Welsh) battle king.
Cadern

Cadfan (Welsh) battle peak.
Cadfen, Caedfan, Caidfan, Caydfan

Cadman (Irish) warrior.
Cadmen, Caedman, Caidman, Caydman

Cadmar (Irish) brave warrior.
Cadmer, Cadmir, Caedmar, Caidmar, Caydmar

Cadmus (Greek) eastern.

Cadogan (Welsh) honour in battle.

Caesar (Latin) long-haired, emperor.
Caesare, Casar, Casare, Cesar, Cesare

Cahil (Turkish) young, naïve.
Cahill

Cain (Hebrew) spear, possession, first son of Adam and Eve who killed his brother, Abel.
Caine, Cane, Cayn, Cayne, Kain, Kaine, Kane, Kayn, Kayne

Cairbre (English) strong man.

Cairn (Welsh) landmark containing a pile of stones.
Cairne, Cairnes, Cairns, Carn, Carne, Carnes, Carns

Calbhach (Irish) bald.
Calbach

Calder (English) river of stones.
Caldar

Caldwell (English) cold well.
Caldwell

Cale (Hebrew) faithful.
Cael, Caele, Caell, Cail, Caile, Caill, Calle, Cayl, Cayle, Cayll, Kael, Kaele, Kaell, Kail, Kaile, Kaill, Kale, Kalle, Kayl, Kayle, Kayll

Caleb (Hebrew) bold dog, faithful.
Caelab, Caeleb, Cailab, Caileb, Calab, Calabe, Calebe, Calyb, Calybe

Caley (Gaelic) slender.
Calie, Caylie, Kaley, Kalie, Kaylie

Calhoun (Irish) warrior of the forest.
Calhoon, Colhoun, Kalhoon, Kalhoun, Kolhoun

Calisto (Greek) most beautiful.
Callisto, Kalisto, Kallisto

Calix (Greek) most beautiful.
Caliks, Callix

Callan (Australian Aboriginal) sparrow-hawk bird.
Callen, Callin, Callon, Callyn

Callis (Latin) cup, chalice.
Calis, Calise, Caliss, Calisse, Callise, Calliss, Callisse, Chalis, Chaliss, Challis, Challise, Challiss, Kallis

Callum (Irish) dove, peacemaker.
Calam, Calem, Callam, Callem, Callym, Calum, Calym, Kallam, Kallem, Kallum

Calum (Irish) dove, peacemaker, a form of Callum.
Calam, Calem, Callam, Callem, Callym, Calum, Calym, Kallam, Kallem, Kallum

Calvert (English) herder of calves.
Cal, Calvart, Calven, Kal, Kalvart, Kalven, Kalvert

Calvin (Latin) bald.
Cal, Calvan, Calven, Calvine, Calvino, Calvyn, Kal, Kalvan, Kalven, Kalvin, Kalvine, Kalvino, Kalvyn

Cam (Gypsy) beloved; (Scottish) crooked nose, a form of Cameron.
Cameron, Camm, Kam

Camden (English) winding, windy valley.
Cam, Camdan, Camdene, Camdin, Camdon, Camdyen, Camdyn, Kam, Kamdan, Kamden, Kamdene, Kamdin, Kamdon, Kamdyen, Kamdyn

Cameron (Scottish) crooked nose.
Cam, Cameran, Camerin, Camerran, Camerren, Camerron, Camerryn, Cameryn, Camiron, Kam

Camilo (Latin) child born to freedom.
Camiel, Camillo, Camilow, Camillus, Chamiel, Chamillo, Chamillus, Chamilo, Chamilow

Campbell (Scottish) wry, crooked mouth; (French) beautiful field.
Cam, Cambell, Camp, Kampbell

Cannon (French) church official, gun.
Canen, Canin, Cannen, Cannin, Cannyn, Canon, Canyn

Canute (Scandinavian) knot; (Latin) white-haired.
Canut, Knute, Knut

Canyon (Latin) grand craggy valley, canyon.
Cannyon, Canyan, Canyen, Canyin, Kanyon

Cappi (Gypsy) good fortune, prosperity.
Cappee, Cappey, Cappie, Cappy

Caradoc (Welsh) beloved, aimable.
Cardoc

Carden (Irish) from the black fortress; (French) wool comber.
Cardan, Cardin, Cardon, Cardyn

Cardew (Welsh) black fort.

Carel (French) strong, a form of Charles.
Carell, Carrel, Carrell, Karel, Karell, Karrel, Karrell

Carey (Welsh) from the castle; (Greek) pure.
Carry, Cary, Karey, Kary, Kerry

Carl (English) strong, courageous, manly, a form of Charles.

Carleton, Carlisle, Carlos, Carlton, Charles, Charlie, Charlton, Chase, Karl

Carleton (English) Carl's town.
Carlton

Carlin (Irish) little champion.
Carlan, Carlen, Carli, Carling, Carlino, Carlon

Carlo (Italian) strong, courageous, manly, a form of Carl.
Karlo

Carlos (Spanish) strong, courageous, manly, a form of Charles.
Carleton, Carlisle, Carlton, Charles, Charlie, Charlton, Chase, Karl, Karlos

Carlton (English) Carl's town.
Carleton, Carlten, Carltin, Carltyn, Karleton, Karlten, Karltin, Karlton, Karltyn

Carmichael (Scottish) friend, follower of Michael.

Carmine (Latin) song, crimson, a unisex name.
Carman, Carmen, Carmon

Carney (Irish) brave, victorious warrior.
Carnee, Carnie, Carny, Cearny, Cearney, Kearny, Kearney

Carr (Scandinavian) from the marsh.
Car, Karr, Kerr

Carrick (Irish) rock.
Carek, Carreck, Karek, Karreck, Karrick

Carrington (English) town where goods are loaded, rocky town, town of the marsh, a unisex name.

Carroll (Celtic) champion.
Carol, Caroll, Carrol, Karol, Karoll, Karrol, Karroll

Carson (English) son of Carr.
Carsan, Carsen, Carsun, Carsyn, Karsan, Karsen, Karson

Carter (English) cart maker, cart driver, a unisex name.
Cart, Carta, Cartar, Kart, Karta, Kartar, Karter

Cartwright (English) cart maker, cart builder.
Cartright

Carver (English) sculptor, wood carver.
Carvar, Carvir, Carvor, Karvar, Karver, Karvir, Karvor

Carwyn (Welsh) blessed love.
Carie, Cary, Cerwyn, Karwyn, Kerwyn, Wyn

Cary (Welsh) from the castle; (Greek) pure.
Carey, Carrie, Karey, Karry, Kary, Kerry

Case (Irish) brave, a form of Casey.

Casey (Irish) brave, Irish surname, a unisex name.
Cacey, Cacy, Caisey, Casee, Casi, Casie, Cassee, Cassey, Cassi, Cassie, Casy, Kacey, Kacy, Kasey

Cash (Latin) vain.
Cashe

Cashlin (Irish) little castle.
Cashlind, Cashlyn, Cashlynd, Kashlin

Casimir (Slavic) peace announcement.
Cazimir, Kasimir, Kazimir

Casper (Persian) treasurer.
Cash, Caspar, Cass

Cassidy (Celtic) clever, curly-haired, a unisex name.
Casidy, Cassady, Cassedy, Cassidee, Cassidey, Cassidi, Cassidie, Kassady, Kassedy, Kassidey, Kassidy

Cassius (Latin) vain.
Casius

Casta (Greek) purity.

Castor (Greek) beaver.
Castar, Caster, Castir, Caston, Kastar, Kaster, Kastir, Kaston, Kastor

Cater (English) supplier of household goods.
Cat, Cate, Catey, Cati, Caty, Kat, Kater

Cathal (Irish) wise, mighty.
Cathel, Cathol, Kathal

Cathmor (Irish) great warrior.
Cathmoor, Cathmoore, Cathmore

Cato (Latin) knowledgeable, wise.
Kato

Caton (Latin) knowledgeable, wise, a form of Cato.
Calton, Katon

Cavan (Irish) handsome.
Cavenn, Kavan, Kavenn,

Cavell (French) little active one.
Caevel, Cavel, Kaevel, Kavel, Kavell

Cawley (Scottish) ancient; (Anglo-Saxon) cow meadow.
Cawlea, Cawlee, Cawleigh, Cawli, Cawlie, Cawly

Cecil (English) blind.

Cece, Cecelio, Cecile, Cecilio, Cecilius, Cecill, Cecille, Cecyl, Cecyll

Cedar (English) evergreen tree.
Ceeda

Cedric (Anglo-Saxon) battle chief.
Ced, Cedrec, Sedric

Celerino (Latin) fast.
Celerinio, Celeryno

Celestine (Latin) heavenly one, little moon.
Celestin, Celestino, Celestyn, Celestyne

Cemal (Arabic) beautiful, handsome.

Cephas (Latin) rock.
Cepheus, Cephus

Cerdic (Welsh) beloved.
Cerdig, Ceredic, Ceredig, Ceretic

Cerek (Polish) lord.
Cerik

Cesar (Latin) emperor, long-haired.
Caesar, Caesare, Casar, Casare, Cesare, Cesareo, Cesario, Cesaro

Chad (English) warlike, warrior.
Chaad, Chadd, Chaddi, Chaddie, Chaddy, Chade, Chado, Chadwick, Chady

Chadwick (English) town of the warrior.
Chaddwick, Chadwik, Chadwyc, Chadwyck, Chadwyk

Chago (Spanish) replacer, a form of Jacob.
Chango

Chaim (Hebrew) life.
Caim, Caym, Cayme, Chai, Chaym, Chayme

Chal (Gypsy) boy, son.

Chale (Spanish) strong, youthful.

Chalmers (Scottish) son of the lord.
Chalmer, Chalmr

Champak (Hindu) tree, flower.

Chan (Hindu) shining.
Chann, Chano

Chanan (Hebrew) cloud.
Chanen, Chanin, Channan, Channen, Channin, Channon, Channyn, Chanon, Chanyn

Chance (English) luck, fortune, chance.
Chancey, Chancie, Chaunce, Chauncey, Chauncie

Chancellor (Latin) record keeper.
Chance, Chancelen, Chancelor, Chaunce

Chander (Hindu) moon.
Chand, Chandan, Chandany, Chandon

Chandler (French) candle maker, a unisex name.
Chandelar, Chandlan, Chandlar, Chandlier, Chandlor

Chaney (French) oak.
Chany

Channing (English) wise; (French) church official.
Chan, Chanen, Chanin, Chaning, Chann, Chanon, Channen, Channin, Channon, Channyn, Chanyn

Chante (French) singer.
Chant, Chantry

Chapin (French) clergyman.
Chaplin

Chapman (English) merchant.
Chap, Chapmann, Chapmen, Chapmin, Chapmyn, Chappie

Charles (English) strong, courageous, manly.
Cahil, Carel, Carl, Carleton, Carlie, Carling, Carlisle, Carlo, Carlos, Carlson, Carlton, Carlyle, Carol, Caroll, Carolle, Carolus, Carrol, Carroll, Carry, Cary, Caryl, Cathal, Chad, Chaddie, Chaddy, Char, Charlea, Charleah, Charlee, Charleigh, Charlet, Charley, Charli, Charlie, Charlton, Charly, Chase, Karl, Karol, Karole, Karoley, Karolius, Karoll, Karoly, Karroll, Siarl, Tearlach

Charlie (English) strong, courageous, manly, a form of Charles.
Charley, Charly

Charlton (English) Charles' town.
Charleton

Charro (Spanish) horse rider.
Charo

Chase (French) hunter.
Chacier, Chaise

Chaska (African) first-born son.
Chaskah

Chatham (English) warrior's cottage, house.
Chathem, Chathim, Chathom, Chathym

Chauncey (Latin) chancellor, church official.
Chaiton, Chancellor, Chaunce, Chauncee, Chauncer, Chaunci, Chauncie, Chauncy

Chayton (Native American) falcon.

Chay, Chaiton, Chey, Cheyton

Chaz (English) strong, courageous, manly, a form of Charles.

Carleton, Carlisle, Carlos, Carlton, Charles, Charlie, Charlton, Chas, Chase, Chazz, Karl

Che (Spanish) God shall add, a form of Joseph.

Chey

Chen (Chinese) great, vast.

Chencho (Spanish) crown of laurel leaves, victory.

Chenco

Cheney (French) oak forest.

Chenee, Cheni, Chenie, Cheny, Chesnee, Chesney, Chesni, Chesnie, Chesny, Cheynee, Cheyney, Cheyni, Cheny

Cheng (Chinese) correct, righteous.

Chen

Chepe (Spanish) God shall add, a form of Joseph.

Cheph, Chephe

Cherokee (Native American) tribal name for people with a different speech.

Cheroki

Cherub (English) little angel.

Cher, Cherr, Cherrub, Cherubin, Cherrubin, Cherubyn, Cherubyno

Cherubino (Italian) little cherub, angel.

Cherub, Cherubin, Cherubyno

Chesmu (Native American) abrasive, rough.

Chesmue

Chester (English) fortified camp, a form of Rochester.

Castar, Caster, Castor, Chesleigh, Chesley, Cheslie, Chestan, Chestar, Chesten, Chestin, Chestir, Cheston, Chestor

Chevalier (French) knight.

Chevallier, Chevalyer, Chevee, Chevelier, Chevellier, Chevey, Chevi, Chevie, Chevy

Chevy (French) knight, a form of Chevalier.

Chev, Chevee, Chevee, Chevi, Chevie, Chevvy

Cheyenne (Native American) tribal name.

Chi (African) guardian angel; (Chinese) young.

Chico (Spanish) boy.

Chicho, Chiko

Chike (African) power of God.

Chik, Chyk, Chyke

Chilton (English) children's farm by the spring.

Chillton

Chim (Vietnamese) bird.

Chym

Chioke (African) gift of God.

Chyoke

Chipo (African) gift.

Chippia (Australian Aboriginal) duck.

Chipia, Chippya, Chipya

Chiram (Hebrew) noble, exalted.
Chyram

Christian (Greek) carrier of Christ, anointed, follows Christ.
Chris, Chrissy, Christiano, Christie, Christy, Chrystian, Kristian

Christopher (Greek) Christ-bearer, carrier of Christ, anointed, follows Christ.
Chris, Chrissy, Christiano, Christie, Christof, Christofer, Christoffer, Christoph, Christophorus, Christy, Kit, Kristian, Kristofer, Kristoffer, Kristopher

Christos (Greek) Christ-bearer, carrier of Christ, anointed, follows Christ, a form of Christopher.
Chrystos, Kristos, Krystos

Chrysander (Greek) golden.
Chrisander, Chrisandor, Chrisandre, Chrysandor, Chrysandre, Crisander, Crisandor, Crysander, Crysandor

Chui (African) leopard.

Chul (Korean) firm.

Chumo (Spanish) twin, a form of Thomas.

Chung (Chinese) the wise one.

Churchill (English) church hill.
Churchil

Cian (Irish) ancient.
Cein, Ciann, Cienn

Cicero (Latin) chickpea.
Ciceron, Cicerone, Ciceroni, Ciro, Cycero, Cyceron, Cycerone, Cyro

Cid (Spanish) lord.
Cidd, Cyd, Cydd, Sid

Ciro (Persian) the sun, a form of Cyrus.
Ciero, Kiero, Kiro

Clancy (Irish) red-headed soldier, a unisex name.
Clance, Clancee, Clancey, Clancie, Clanse, Clansee, Clansey, Clansi, Clansie, Clansy

Clarence (Latin) clear, bright, illustrious.
Clair, Clairis, Claral, Clarance, Clare, Clarin, Clarince, Claron, Claronce, Claryn, Clarynce

Clark (French) cleric, scholar.
Clarke, Clerk, Clerke

Claude (Latin) lame.
Claud, Claudan, Claudanus, Claudel, Claudell, Claudey, Claudi, Claudian, Claudie, Claudien, Claudin, Claudio, Claudius, Claudy

Claudio (Italian) lame, a form of Claude.

Claus (German) victory of the people, a form of Nicholas.
Claas, Clause, Klaas, Klaus, Klause

Clay (English) clay, earth.
Clae, Clai, Claye

Clayborne (English) made from clay.
Clae, Claeborn, Claeborne, Claebourn, Claebourne, Claeburn, Claeburne, Clai, Claiborn, Claiborne, Claibourn, Claibourne, Claiburn, Claiburne, Clay, Clayborn, Claybourn, Claybourne, Clayburn, Clayburne

Clayton (English) town established on clay.
Clay, Clayten, Cleyton

Cleary (Irish) scholar.
Clearie

Cledwyn (Welsh) rough, blessed.
Cledwin

Clement (Latin) gentle, merciful.
*Clem, Clemen, Clemens,
Clemente, Clementius, Clemmy,
Clim, Climent, Klemins, Klemens,
Klement*

Cleon (Greek) famous.
Cleone, Kleon, Kleone

Cletus (Greek) illustrious.
*Cleatis, Cleatos, Cleatus, Cleeitis,
Cleetos, Cleetus, Cleotis, Cleotos,
Cleotus, Cletis, Cletos, Cleytis,
Cleytos, Cleytus*

Cleveland (English) land close to
cliffs.
*Cleaveland, Cleavelend,
Cleavland, Cleavlend, Clevelend*

Clifford (English) cliff at the river
ford.
*Clif, Cliford, Cliff, Clyf, Clyff, Clyfford,
Clyford*

Clifton (English) town by the cliff.
*Clif, Cliff, Clifft, Clifften, Cliffton, Clift,
Cliften, Clyf, Clyff, Clyfft, Clyfften,
Clyffton, Clyft, Clyften, Clyfton*

Clinton (English) hill town.
*Clint, Clintan, Clinten, Clintin, Clynt,
Clyntan, Clynten, Clyntin, Clynton*

Clive (English) cliff.
Cleve, Clyve

Clovis (German) famous warrior.
Clovvis, Clovvys, Clovys

Cluny (Irish) meadow, resting place.
*Clunee, Cluney, Cluni, Clunie,
Clunies*

Clyde (Celtic) heard from afar.
Cleit, Clwyd, Clyd

Coburn (English) meeting place
of two streams.
*Cobern, Coberne, Cobirn, Cobirne,
Cobourn, Cobourne, Coburne,
Cobyrn, Cobyrne, Koburn*

Coby (English) replacer, a form of
Jacob.
Cobee, Cobey, Cobie, Kobie, Koby

Cody (English) cushion, pillow, a
unisex name.
Codee, Cadey, Codie, Kodie, Kody

Coen (Australian Aboriginal)
thunder.
Koen

Coffie (African) born on a Friday.
Cofi, Cofie

Cola (Celtic) victory of the
people, a form of Nicholas.
*Coela, Colah, Colar, Koela, Kola,
Kolah, Kolar*

Colbert (Latin) brilliant seafarer.
*Calbert, Calburt, Colburt, Colvert,
Culbert, Culburt*

Colby (English) coal town, dark-
haired.
Colbee, Colbey, Colbie

Cole (English) black, dark, swarthy;
(Celtic) promise, victory of the
people, a form of Nicholas.
Coel, Col, Koel, Kole

Colin (Irish) dove, young child.
*Cailean, Col, Colan, Coll, Collan,
Collin, Coln, Kolen, Kolin, Koln*

Collier (English) miner.
*Colier, Colis, Collis, Collyer, Colyer,
Koelier, Kollier*

Colm (Irish) dove.

Colon (Latin) dove.

Colt (English) young horse.
Colte

Colter (English) colt herder.

Colton (English) black-coal town.
Coltan, Colten, Coltin, Coltyn, Koltan, Kolten, Koltin, Kolton, Koltyn

Columba (Latin, Irish) dove, the name of an Irish saint.
Colum, Columb, Columbah, Columbias, Columbas, Columbus

Coman (Arabic) noble; (Irish) bent.
Camen, Comen, Comin, Comyn

Compton (Anglo-Saxon) town in the valley.

Conan (Scottish) wise, intelligent; (Irish) praised.
Conant, Conary, Connan, Connen, Connon, Conon, Konan

Cong (Chinese) intelligent, clever, a unisex name.

Coniah (Hebrew) gift sent from God.
Conia, Conya, Conyah

Conlan (Irish) hero.
Colenn, Conlen, Conlin, Conlon, Conlyn, Konlan

Conn (Celtic) high.
Con

Conner (Scottish) wise, intelligent; (Irish) praised, a form of Connor.
Coner, Connor, Conor, Konner, Konnor

Connor (Scottish) wise, intelligent; (Irish) praised.

Coner, Conner, Conor, Konner, Konnor

Conrad (German) brave counseller.
Comrade, Con, Cort, Curt, Koenraad, Kon, Konrad, Kort, Kurt

Conroy (Irish) wise man.
Conroi, Conry, Roy

Constantine (Latin) constant, firm.
Consadine, Considine, Constadine, Constandine, Constantino, Constandios, Constantin, Constantinos, Constantinus, Constantios, Constintine, Konstantine, Konstantin, Konstant

Consuelo (Spanish) consolation, a unisex name.

Conway (Irish) hound of the plains; (Welsh) holy water.
Conwai

Cook (English) chef, cook.
Cooke, Cooki, Cookie, Cooky

Cooper (English) barrel maker, a unisex name.
Coop, Couper

Corban (Greek) raven.
Corben, Corbin, Corby

Corbett (Latin) raven.
Corbet, Corbin, Corby

Corbin (French) raven.
Corben, Corbet, Corbett, Corby, Korban, Korben, Korbin, Korbyn

Corcoran (Irish) of reddish complexion.

Cordell (French) rope-maker.
Cordale, Cordel

Cordero (Spanish) little lamb.
*Cordaro, Cordeal, Cordeara,
Cordearo, Cordeiro, Cordelro,
Corder, Cordera, Corderro,
Cordiaro, Cordy*

Corey (Irish) hollow.
Cory

Cormac (Irish) chariot boy.
Cormack, Cormick, Kormak

Cornelius (Latin) horn colour,
cornel tree.
*Cornal, Cornall, Cornealous,
Corneili, Corneilius, Corneille,
Corneilus, Cornel, Cornelias,
Corneliaus, Cornelious, Cornelis,
Corneliu, Cornell, Cornellious,
Cornellis, Cornellius, Cornellus,
Cornelous, Corneluis, Cornelus,
Corney, Cornie, Cornielius,
Corniellus, Corny*

Corrigan (Irish) spear carrier.
*Carrigan, Carrigen, Corigan,
Corigen, Corogan, Corogen,
Corrigon, Corrigun, Corrogun*

Cort (German) bold.

Corwin (Anglo-Saxon) friend of the
heart.
*Corwen, Corwinn, Corwyn,
Corwynn, Corwynne*

Cosmo (Greek) universal order.
*Cosimo, Cosma, Cosmas, Cosme,
Cosmos, Kosmo, Kosmos*

Costa (Greek) constant, firm, a
form of Constantine.
Costah, Coastas, Costes, Kosta

Coty (French) slope.
*Cote, Cotee, Cotey, Coti, Cotie,
Cotte, Cottee, Cottey, Cotti,
Cottie, Cotty, Cottye, Cotye*

Courtland (English) dweller in court.
Cortlan, Cortland, Courtlan

Courtney (French) short nose;
(English) from the court, a unisex
name.
*Cortnay, Cortney, Cortnie, Cortny,
Court, Courten, Courtenay,
Courtene, Courteney, Courteny,
Courtnay, Courtnee*

Coyle (Irish) leader in battle.
Coil, Coile, Coyl

Craddock (Welsh) love, beloved.
*Caradoc, Caradog, Caradok,
Craddoc, Craddoch, Craddok,
Cradoc, Cradoch, Cradock, Cradok*

Craig (Scottish) crag, stony hill.
*Craeg, Craege, Craegg, Crag,
Craige, Craigen, Craigg, Crayg,
Crayge, Craygg*

Cramer (English) full.
Kramer

Crandall (English) valley of the
cranes.
*Cran, Crandal, Crandel, Crandell,
Crandle*

Crane (English) crane bird.
Crain, Craine, Crayn, Crayne

Cranog (Welsh) a heron.
*Craenn, Craenog, Crannog,
Kraenn, Kraennog, Kraenog*

Crawford (English) ford of the
crows.
Craw, Crow, Crowford

Creed (Latin) I believe.
Credo

Creighton (English) town near rocks.
*Craighton, Crayton, Creight,
Creightown, Creyton, Crichton,
Chrichtyn*

Crevan (Irish) fox.
Creven, Crevin, Crevon, Crevyn

Crisiant (Welsh) crystal.
Crisient, Crisyant, Crysiant, Crysient, Crysyant, Crysyent

Crispin (Latin) curly-haired.
Crepin, Crespin, Crispian, Crispino, Crispus, Krispin

Cristo (Spanish) Christ-bearer, carrier of Christ, anointed, follows Christ, a form of Christopher.
Christo, Christos, Cristos

Cromwell (English) winding spring.
Cromwel, Cromwill, Cromwyl, Cromwyll

Cronan (Irish) dark-haired.
Cronnan

Crosby (English) dweller near the town crossing; (Scandinavian) village with a cross.
Crosbey, Crosbie, Krosbey, Krosbie Krosby

Crosley (English) meadow with the cross.
Croslea, Croslee, Crosleigh, Crosli, Croslie, Crosly

Cruz (Portuguese, Spanish) cross.
Cruze, Cruzz, Kruz

Csaba (Hungarian) shepherd.

Cullen (Irish) handsome.
Cull, Cullan, Cullin, Kullen

Culley (Irish) forest.
Culea, Culeah, Culee, Culeigh, Culey, Culi, Culie, Cullea, Cullee, Culleigh, Culli, Cullie, Cully, Culy, Kulley

Culver (English) gentle dove.
Colver, Colfre

Curran (Irish) hero.
Curren, Currey, Currie, Currin, Curry, Kurran, Kurrie

Curt (French) courteous, a form of Curtis.
Kert, Kurt

Curtis (French) courteous.
Curt, Curtiss, Kurt, Kurtis, Kurtiss

Cuthbert (English) famous, brilliant.
Cuthberte, Cuthburt, Cuthburte

Cyan (English) blue colour, a unisex name.

Cynan (Welsh) chief.
Cinan, Cinen, Cinin, Cinon, Cinyn, Cynen, Cynin, Cynon, Cynyn

Cyprian (French) from Cyprus.
Cyprien

Cyrano (Latin) from Cyrene.
Cyranno

Cyril (Greek) lordly ruler.
Ciril, Cirile, Cirill, Cirille, Cirillo, Cirilo, Cyrile, Cyrill, Cyrille, Cyrillus, Cyrilus,

Cyrus (Persian) sun.
Ciro, Cy, Kiro, Ky, Sirus

Dabi (Basque) beloved, a form of David.
Dabee, Dabey, Dabie, Daby

Dacey (Irish) southerner, a unisex name.
Dacee, Daci, Dacie, Dacy, Daice, Daicee, Daicey, Daici, Daicie, Daicy, Dayc, Dayce, Daycee, Daycey, Dayci, Daycie, Daycy

Dafydd (Welsh) beloved, a form of David.
Dafid, Dafidd, Dafyd

Dag (Scandinavian) bright day.
Daegen, Dagen, Dagenn, Dagg, Dagon

Dagan (Hebrew) earth, grain.
Daegan, Daegen, Daegin, Daegon, Dagen, Dagin, Dagon, Daygan, Daygen, Daygin, Daygon

Dagwood (Anglo-Saxon) the shining one's wood.

Dai (Japanese) large; (Welsh) beloved, a form of David.
Dae, Daie, Day, Daye

Daibhi (Irish) beloved, a form of David.

Dakarai (African) happiness.
Dakara, Dakarah

Daku (Australian Aboriginal) sand.

Dakota (Native American) friend, tribal place name, a unisex name.

Dak, Dakotah, Dekoda, Dekodah, Dekota, Dekotah, Dekotha, Takota, Takotah

Dalal (Hindu) broker.

Dalbert (Anglo-Saxon) from the bright valley.
Dalby, Dolby

Dale (English) valley, dale, a unisex name.
Dael, Dail, Daile, Dal, Daley, Dalton, Daly, Dayl, Dayle

Dallas (Irish) wise; (Scottish) valley of the water, a city in Texas, a unisex name.
Dailaess, Dallis, Dallus, Dallys

Dallin (English) people's pride.
Daelin, Dalin, Dallaen, Dallan, Dallen, Dallyn, Dalyn

Dalton (English) town near the valley.
Dal, Dalltan, Dallten, Dalltin, Dallton, Dalltyn, Dalt, Daltan, Dalten, Daltin, Daltyn

Dalziel (Scottish) small field.
Dalzil, Dalzyel, Dalzyl

Damek (Czech) earth, a form of Adam.
Dameck, Damick, Damik, Damyk

Damian (Greek) tamer.
Daemian, Daemien, Daemion, Daemiyn, Daimian, Daimien, Daimion, Damaien, Damaun, Damayon, Damean, Damen, Damiane, Damiann, Damiano, Damianos, Damion, Damiyan, Damon, Damyan, Damyen, Damyin, Daymian, Daymien, Daymion, Daymiyn

Damiano (Italian) tamer, a form of Damian.

Damon (Greek) tamer, constant; (Latin) spirit.

Daemian, Daemien, Daemion, Daemiyn, Daimian, Daimien, Daimion, Daman, Damen, Damian, Damien, Damin, Damion, Damone, Daymian, Daymien, Daymion, Daymiyn

Dan (Hebrew) God is my judge, a form of Daniel.

Dann, Danny

Dana (English) from Denmark, bright as day, a unisex name.

Daena, Danale

Danby (English) from the Dane's settlement, a form of Denby.

Dandin (Hindu) holy man.

Dandan, Danden, Dandon, Dandyn

Dane (Danish) from Denmark.

Daen, Daene, Dain, Daine, Dana, Dayn, Dayne

Daniel (Hebrew) God is my judge, an Old Testament prophet.

Dan, Dane, Daneel, Danial, Daniell, Danil, Danilo, Dann, Dannal, Danne, Danneel, Dannel, Danniel, Danniell, Dannil, Dannol, Danny, Danyel, Danyell, Danyil, Danyill, Danyl, Danyll

Danior (Gypsy) born with teeth.

Danyor

Danny (Hebrew, English) God is my judge, a form of Daniel.

Dan, Dane, Danee, Dani, Danie, Daniel, Danil, Dann, Danne, Dannee, Danni, Dannie, Dannil, Dany

Dante (Italian) lasting, enduring, a form of Durante, named after the poet and philosopher, a unisex name.

Dantae, Dantee, Danton

Darby (Irish) free; (Scandinavian) a deer estate, a unisex name.

D'arby, Darb, Darbe, Darbee, Darbey, Darbi, Darbie, Dairmaid, Derb, Derbe, Derbee, Derbey, Derbi, Derbie, Derby

Darcy (Irish) dark; (French) from the fortress.

D'arcy, D'Arcy, Darc, Darce, Darcee, Darcel, Darcey, Darci, Darcie, Darcio, Darius, Darse, Darsee, Darsey, Darsi, Darsie, Darsy

Dard (Greek) son of Zeus.

Daren (African) born at night.

Darin, Darren, Darryn, Daryn, Dearan, Dearun

Dario (Spanish) affluent.

Darian, Darien, Darion, Daryo

Darius (Greek) affluent.

Darien, Darieus, Dario, Darios, Dariuse, Dariuss, Darrus, Darus, Daryos, Daryus

Darrell/Daryl (French) beloved, darling, from the grove of oak trees, a unisex name.

Daral, Darale, Darall, Daralle, Darel, Darele, Darell, Darelle, Daril, Darile, Darill, Darille, Darral, Darrel, Darril, Darryl, Daryle, Daryll, Darylle

Darren/Darrin (Irish) great; (English) rocky hill.

Daran, Daren, Darian, Darien, Darin, Daron, Darran, Darrian, Darrien, Darrine, Darron, Darryn, Daryn, Deran, Deren, Derin, Deron, Derran, Derren, Derrin, Derron, Derryn, Deryn, Doran, Doren, Dorin, Doron, Dorran, Dorren, Dorrin, Dorron, Dorryn, Doryn

Darshan (Hindu) one of the Hindu gods.

Darshen, Darshin, Darshon, Darshyn

Dartagnan (French) from Artagnan, France.

Darton (English) deer estate or town.
Dartan, Dartel, Darten, Dartin, Dartyn

Darwin (English) beloved friend.
Darwen, Darwyn, Derwin, Derwyn

Da'ud (Arabic) beloved, a form of David.
Dawud

Dave (Hebrew, English) beloved, a form of David.
Daeve, Daive, Dayve

Davey (Hebrew, English) beloved, a form of David.
Daivey, Daivie, Daivy, Davie, Davy, Dayvey, Dayvie, Dayvy

David (Hebrew) beloved, famous Israelite king of the Bible and the patron saint of Wales.
Daeved, Daevid, Daevyd, Dafydd, Dai, Daibidh, Daived, Daivid, Dave, Daved, Daveed, Davey, Davidd, Davidde, Davide, Davie, Davyd, Davydd, Davydde, Davyde, Dayvid

Davide (Italian) beloved, a form of David.
Davidino, Davy

Davidson (Welsh) son of David, beloved, a form of David.
Davidsen

Davin (Scandinavian) bright, happy one from Finland.
Daven, Davyn

Davis (Welsh) son of David.
Davies

Da-wa (Tibetan, Sherpa) born on a Monday.

Dawson (English) son of David.
Dawsan, Dawsen, Dawsin, Dawsyn

Deacon (Greek) hard-working servant.
Daicon, Daycon, Deakin, Deicon, Deycon

Dean (English) one who lives in the valley; (Latin) religious leader.
Deane, Deannane, Deen, Deene, Dein, Deine, Dene

Deandre (English) combination of Dean and Andre.
Deenandre, Deiandre, Dayandre

Decker (Belgian) roofer.
Deker

Declan (Irish) prayerful, name of a 5th-century bishop.
Daclan, D'clan, Declyn, Deklyn, Dyclan

Dedric (German) ruler of the people.
Deadric, Deadrick, Deadrik, Dederic, Dederick, Dederik, Dedrick, Dedrik, Diedric, Diedrick, Diedrik

Deepak (Hindu) little lamp or light, a form of Dipak.

Dein (Hebrew) God is my judge, a form of Daniel; (English) one who lives in the valley; (Latin) religious leader, a form of Dean.
Deine

Deiondre (French) valley, a unisex name.

Delaney (Irish) challenger's descendant; (Latin) of the elder tree grove, a unisex name.

*D'Laney, D'Lanee, D'Lanie,
Dalaney, Dalanie, Dalany, Dalene,
Daleney, Dallany, Dallene,
Dalleney, Del, Delainey, Delane,
Delayne, Dell, Dellainey, Dellane,
Dellany, Dellayne*

Delano (French) of the night;
(Latin) of the elder tree grove.
Dalan, Dalano, Delan

Delbert (English) bright as day.
Bert, Delbirt, Delburt

Deli (Chinese) virtuous.

Dell (English) dell, hollow.
Del

Delmar/Delmore (Latin) of the sea.
*Delma, Delmah, Delmare,
Delmario, Delmarr, Delmarre,
Delmer, Delmere, Delmerr,
Delmerre, Delmor, Delmorr,
Delmorre*

Delroy (French) belonging to the king.
Dalroi, Dalroy, Delroi

Delsin (Native American) he is so.
Delsan, Delsen, Delson, Delsyn

Delwyn (Welsh) friend from the valley, a unisex name.
Delwen, Delwin

Deman (Dutch) man.
Demann

Demas (Greek) popular.
Demos

Demetrio (Italian, Greek) lover of the earth, a form of Demetrius.
*Demeter, Demeteri, Demeterio,
Demetre, Demetrei, Demetri,
Demetrie, Demetrius, Demetry,
Dimetrei, Dimetri, Dimetrie, Dimetry,
Dimitrei, Dimitri, Dimitry*

Demetrius (Greek) lover of the earth.
*Demeitrius, Demeterious,
Demetreus, Demetrias, Demetriu,
Demetrois, Demetrus, Demetryus,
Demtrius, Demtrus, Dimetrias,
Dimetrius, Dymetrius, Dymetryus*

Demos (Greek) of the people.
Demmos, Demmous, Demous

Dempsey (Irish) proud.
*Demp, Demps, Dempsi, Dempsie,
Dempsy, Demsea, Demsey*

Dempster (English) the judge.
Dempstar, Demster

Demyan (Russian) a true friend.
Demian

Denby (Norse) of the Danish settlement.
Denbee, Denbie

Dene (English) one who lives in the valley; (Latin) religious leader, a form of Dean.
Dean, Deane, Deen, Deene

Denham (English) homestead in the valley.
Denhem

Denis/Dennis (Greek) follower of Dionysus, the Greek god of wine.
*Denas, Denes, Deney, Denie,
Dennas, Dennes, Denny, Dennys,
Deny, Denys, Dion, Dione Dionne,
Dionysio, Dionysios, Dionysus*

Denman (Anglo-Saxon) of the dell, valley.
Denmann

Denton (English) from the valley estate.

Denver (Anglo-Saxon) dweller by the valley.
Denvor

Denzil (Celtic) high stronghold.
Densel, Densell, Densil, Densill, Denzel, Denzell, Denzill

Deo (Greek) godlike.
Dio

Deorsa (Scottish) farmer, a form of George.

Derain (Australian Aboriginal) of the mountains.

Derby (Irish) free; (Scandinavian) a deer estate, a form of Darby.
Darbie, Darby, Derbie, D'erby

Derek (German) ruler of the people, a form of Theodoric.
Darec, Dareck, Darek, Daric, Darick, Darik, Darric, Darrick, Darrik, Darryc, Darryck, Darryk, Derac, Derack, Derak, Derec, Dereck, Deric, Derick, Derik, Derk, Derric, Derrick, Derrik, Deryek, Deryc, Deryck, Deryk, Dirk

Dermot (Irish) free of envy; (Hebrew) God will uplift, a form of Jeremiah.
Der, Dermond, Dermont, Dermott, Diarmid, Diarmit

Derron (Irish) great.
Derran, Derren, Derrin, Derryn, Deryn

Derry (Irish) red-haired.
Deri, Derie, Derri, Derrie, Dery

Derward (English) deer-keeper.
Derwood, Dirward, Dirwood, Durward, Durwood

Derwent (English) valley thick with oaks, oak river, name of rivers in England and Tasmania.

Derwin (English) dear friend, a form of Darwin.
Derwyn

Derwood (English) of the deer wood.
Derward, Durward, Durwood

Desiderio (Spanish) desired.
Desi, Desidero

Desmond (Irish) from south Munster, Ireland.
Des, Desmund

Dev (Hindu) godlike.

Devdan (Hindu) gift of the gods.

Deven (Hindu) for God.
Deaven

Deverell (English) riverbank.
Devarell, Deveril

Devin (Irish) poet, a unisex name.
Deavin, Dev, Devein, Deven, Devinn, Devyn, Devynn

Devlin (Irish) heroic, brave.
Devlan, Devlen, Devlyn

Devon (English) poet, from Devonshire, a unisex name.
Devin, Devonn, Devyn

Dewey/Dewy (Welsh) beloved, a form of David.
Dewi, Dewie

Dewitt (Flemish) blond.
Dewit, Dewyt, Dewytt

Dexter (English) dyer of cloth; (Latin) dexterous, skilful, right-handed.
Dex, Dextar, Dextor

Diamante (Spanish) like a diamond, a form of Diamond, a unisex name.
Diamonte

Diamond (Latin) precious jewel, shining protector, a unisex name.
Diaman, Diamand, Diamande, Diamonde, Diamund, Dmond, Dymond

Dian (Indonesian) candle.
Dyan

Diarmad (Scottish) without envy.
Diarmid

Dick (English, German) powerful ruler, a form of Richard, Frederick.
Dic, Dicken, Dickie, Dicky, Dik

Dickson (English) son of Dick, Richard.
Dickenson, Dickinson, Dixen, Dixon

Didier (French) desired one.

Diego (Spanish) supplanter, a form of James.
Diaz, Santiago

Dieter (German) army of the people.
Deirhard, Deyter, Diehardt, Dihard, Dihardt, Dyeter

Dietrich (German) ruler of the people, a form of Theodoric.
Deitrich, Deitrick, Deitrik, Diedrich, Diedrick, Diedrik, Dieterich, Dieterick, Dieterik, Dietric, Dietrick

Digby (Norse) from the settlement by the dyke, ditch.
Digbe, Digbee, Digbey, Digbi, Digbie

Diggory (Cornish) lost or strayed.
Diggorey, Diggori, Diggorie, Digorey, Digori, Digorie, Digory

Dilip (Hindu) protector.
Dillip

Dillon (Welsh) from the sea, a form of Dylan.
Dilan, Dilen, Dilin, Dilion, Dillan, Dillen, Dillin, Dillion, Dilon, Dylan, Dylen, Dylin, Dylion, Dyllan, Dyllen, Dyllin, Dyllion, Dyllon, Dylon

Dimitri (Greek) a form of Demeter, goddess of harvest, the earth Mother and goddess of fertility.
Demetrei, Demetri, Demetrie, Demitrei, Demitri, Dimetri, Dimetrei, Dimetric, Dimetrie, Dimetrios, Dimetrius, Dimetrus, Dimitr, Dimitrei, Dimitric, Dimitricus, Dimitrie, Dimitrios, Dimitris, Dimitrius, Dimitry, Dymiter, Dymitri, Dymitr, Dymitry, Dymyter

Dinesh (Hindu) lord of the day.

Dino (Italian) from the valley, a form of Dean.
Dinos, Dyno, Dynos

Dinsdale (Welsh) born on Sunday.

Diomedes (Greek) thoughts of Zeus.
Dyomedes

Dione (Greek) lover of wine, a form of Dionysus, the Greek god of wine.
Dennis, Deon, Deone, Dio, Dion, Dionis, Dionn, Dionne, Dyon, Dyone, Dyonn, Dyonne

Dionysus (Greek) the Greek god of wine.
Dion, Dionesios, Dionesius, Dionisos, Dionusios, Dionysios, Dionysius, Dionysos, Dyonisios, Dyonisus

Dipak (Hindu) little lamp or light.
Deepak

Dirk (German) ruler of the people, a form of Theodore.
Dereck, Derek, Derk, Derrick, Dirke

Dixon (English) Richard's son, son of the powerful ruler, a form of Richard.
Dickson, Dikson, Dixan, Dixen, Dixin, Dixyn, Dyxon

Dmitri (Greek) a form of Demeter, goddess of harvest, the earth Mother and goddess of fertility, a form of Dimitri.
Dmetri, Dmetriy, Dmitiri, Dmitiry, Dmitriy

Dobry (Polish) good.
Dobri, Dobrie

Dodd (German) of the people.

Dolan (Irish) black-haired.
Dolin, Dollan, Dolon, Dolyn

Dolf (German) noble wolf, a form of Adolf.
Dolfe, Dolph, Dolphe

Dom (Latin) belonging to God, a form of Dominic.
Domm, Domo

Domenico (Latin) belonging to God, a form of Dominic.
Domenik, Dominic

Domingo (Spanish) born on Sunday.

Dominic (Latin) belonging to God.
Dom, Domeni, Domenic, Domenick, Domenie, Domenik, Domini, Dominie, Dominick, Dominik, Dominique, Dominy, Domm, Domminic, Domminick, Domonic, Nic, Nick

Don (Scottish) ruler of the world, proud leader, a form of Donald.
Donn

Donahue (Irish) dark-haired warrior.
Donahe, Donahugh, Donehue, Donehugh, Donohue, Donohugh

Donald (Scottish) ruler of the world, proud leader, mighty.
Don, Donal, Donalds, Donall, Donel, Doneld, Donell, Donil, Donild, Donill, Donnald, Donni, Donny, Donyl, Donyld

Donatien (French) gift.
Donathan, Donathon, Donato

Donato (Latin) gift from God.
Don, Doneto, Donito

Donegal (Irish) fort of foreigners.

Donnell (Irish) dark brave one.
Donel, Donele, Donell, Donelle, Donnel, Donnele, Donnelle, Donniel, Donnyl, Donyl

Donnelly (Irish) dark brave one, a form of Donnell.
Donelly, Donlee, Donley

Donnie/Donny (Scottish) ruler of the world, proud leader, a form of Donald.
Donee, Doney, Doni, Donie, Donnee, Donney, Donni, Dony

Donoghue (Irish) dark-haired warrior.
Donahue, Donohue

Donovan (Irish) dark-haired warrior.
Donavan, Donaven, Donavin, Donavon, Donavyn, Donevan, Doneven, Donevin, Donevon, Donoven, Donovin, Donovon, Donyvan, Donyven, Donyvin, Donyvon

Dooley (Irish) dark hero.
Doolee, Dooleigh, Dooli, Doolie, Dooly

Dorak (Australian Aboriginal) lively.
Dorek, Dorik, Doryk

Doran (Irish) wanderer, stranger;
(Greek) gift.
*Doren, Dorin, Doron, Dorran,
Dorren, Dorrin, Dorron, Dorryn,
Doryn*

Dorian (Greek) belonging to the
Dorian tribe, one of the ancient
Greek tribes, Oscar Wilde used
this name for his character in *The
Picture of Dorian Gray*.
*Dore, Dorey, Dorie, Dorien, Dorrian,
Dorrien, Dorryan, Dorryen, Dorryn,
Dory, Doryan, Doryen*

Dorjee (Tibetan, Sherpa)
thunderbolt.

Doron (Greek) gift, masculine form
of Dora.
*Doren, Dorren, Dorron, Dorryn,
Doryn*

Dory (French) golden.
Doree, Dorey, Dori, Dorie

Doug (Celtic) from the dark
stream, a form of Douglas.
Dougie, Douglas, Douglass

Dougal (Celtic) dark stranger.
Dougall, Dugald

Douglas (Celtic) from the dark
stream.
*Doug, Douglass, Dugald, Duglas,
Duglass*

Dov (Hebrew) bear, beloved, a
form of David.
Dove, Dovi, Dovid

Dover (Hebrew) of the waters,
speaker.

Dow (Irish) black-haired.

Doyle (Irish) dark stranger.
*Doial, Doiale, Doiall, Doialle,
Doil, Doile, Doyal, Doyale, Doyel,
Doyele, Doyell, Doyelle, Doylle*

Dragan (Slavic) dear one.
Dragen, Dragin, Dragon, Dragyn

Drake (English) dragon.
Draek, Draik, Draike, Drayk, Drayke

Draper (Anglo-Saxon) seller of
cloth, cloth maker.
Draeper, Draiper, Drayper, Draypr

Drew (Celtic) wise, courageous,
strong, a unisex name.
Drewe, Dru, Drue

Driscoll (Celtic) interpreter.
Driscol

Drostan/Drystan (English) noisy
one, a form of Tristam.
Dristan

Drummond (Scottish) druid's
mountain.
Drummund, Drumond, Drumund

Drury (French) dear one, a
sweetheart.
*Druce, Druec, Druree, Drurey, Druri,
Drurie*

Dryden (English) from the dry
valley.
*Dridan, Driden, Dridin, Dridan,
Dridyn, Drydan, Drydin, Drydon,
Drydyn*

Duane (Irish) dark one.
*Dewain, Dewaine, Dewan,
Dewane, Dewayn, Dewayne,
Duain, Duaine, Duwain, Duwaine,
Duwane, Duwayn, Duwayne,
Dwain, Dwaine, Dwayn, Dwayne*

Duarte (Portuguese) prosperous
guardian, a form of Edward.
Duart

Dudley (English) from the meadow.
Dud, Dudd, Dudlea, Dudlee, Dudleigh, Dudli, Dudlie, Dudly

Duff (Scottish) dark complexion, dark-haired.
Duffy

Dugal (Celtic) dark stranger, a form of Dougal.
Dougal, Dougald, Dougall, Dougan, Dugald, Dugall, Dugan, Duglas

Dugan (Irish) dark-haired.
Doogan, Doogen, Dougan, Dougen, Duggan, Douggen, Dugen

Duha (Arabic) forenoon, morning, a unisex name.
Dhuha

Duke (French) leader.

Duman (Turkish) smoke or mist.
Dumen, Dumin, Dumon, Dumyn

Dunbar (Celtic) dark branch.

Duncan (Scottish) dark–haired warrior.
Dunc, Duncen, Duncun, Dunkan

Dunley (English) from the brown hilly meadow.
Dunlee, Dunleigh, Dunli, Dunlie, Dunly

Dunmore (Scottish) from the fortress on the hill.
Dunmoor, Dunmoore, Dunmor

Dunn (Celtic) brown-haired.
Dun, Dunne

Dunstan (English) from the dark stone or hill.
Dunsten, Dunstin, Dunston, Dunstyn

Dural (Australian Aboriginal) hollow tree on fire.
Durall, Durral, Durrall

Durand (Latin) enduring, steadfast, a form of Durant.
Durande, Durant, Durante, Durrand

Durant (Latin) enduring, steadfast.
Durand, Durande, Durante, Durrant

Durham (English) hilly peninsula.

Durward (English) gatekeeper.
Derward, Derwood, Durwood, Ward

Durwin (English) beloved friend, a form of Darwin.
Durwyn

Dusan (Czech) spirited.
Dusen, Dusin, Duson, Dusyn

Dustin (German) valiant fighter, dark stone.
Dust, Dustain, Dustan, Dusten, Duston, Dustyn

Dutch (Dutch) from Holland.
Dutchie

Dwaine/Dwayne (Irish) dark one, a form of Duane.
Duane, Duayne, Dwane, Dwayne

Dwight (English) blond, a form of DeWitt.

Dyami (Native American) eagle.
Dynami

Dyer (English) colourer of cloths.

Dyfan (Welsh) constant, tamer; (Latin) spirit, a form of Damon.
Difan

Dylan (Welsh) from the sea, a
unisex name.

Dilan, Dilen, Dilin, Dilion, Dillan,
Dillen, Dillin, Dillion, Dillon, Dilon,
Dylen, Dylin, Dylion, Dyllan, Dyllen,
Dyllin, Dyllion, Dyllon, Dyllyn

Eachan (English) horseman, works with horses.
Eachen, Eachin, Eachon, Eachyn

Eamon (Irish) prosperous protector, a form of Edmund.
Eaman, Eamen, Eamin, Eamman, Eammen, Eammin, Eammon, Eammun, Eammyn, Eamun, Eamyn

Ean (English, Scottish) God is gracious, a form of Ian.
Eaen, Eann, Eon, Eyan, Eyen, Eyon, Eyyn, Ian

Earl (Irish) pledge, promise; (English) of high rank, nobleman.
Airle, Earle, Earli, Earlie, Early, Erl, Erle, Erral, Errel, Erril, Errol, Erryl, Eryl

Earnest (English) sincere, a form of Ernest.
Earn, Earneste, Earnesto, Earnie, Eyrnest

Eaton (English) from the riverside village.
Eatton, Eton, Etton, Eyton

Eben (Hebrew) rock, stone.
Eaban, Eaben, Eban, Ebhan, Ebhen, Ebin, Ebon, Ebyn

Ebenezer (Hebrew) stone foundation.
Ebeneeser, Ebeneezer, Ebenesar, Ebeneser, Ebenezar

Eberhard (German) courageous boar.

Ebba, Eber, Eberard, Eberardo, Eberhardo, Eberhardt

Ebo (African) born on a Tuesday.

Ed (English) a form of Edward, Edgar.
Edd, Eddie, Eddy, Ned, Ted

Edan (Celtic) fiery flame.
Eadan, Eaden, Eadin, Eadon, Eadyn, Eden, Edin, Edon, Edyn

Edbert (English) brilliant, wealthy.
Edbirt, Edburt

Eddie (English) a form of Edward, Edgar.
Ed, Edd, Eddy, Ned, Neddy, Ted, Teddy

Edel (German) noble.
Adel, Adell, Edell

Eden (Hebrew) paradise, delightful, enchanting, a unisex name.
Aedenn, Eaden, Eadin, Eadon, Eadyn, Edan, Edin, Edon, Edyn

Eder (Hebrew) flock.
Edar, Edir, Edor, Edyr

Edgar (English) great spearman.
Eadgar, Edek, Edgaras, Edgard, Edgardo, Edgars, Edger, Edgir, Edgor, Edgy

Edgardo (Spanish) great spearman, a form of Edgar.

Edison (English) son of Edward.
Eddisen, Eddison, Eddisyn, Eddysen, Eddyson, Edisen, Edisyn, Edysen, Edyson

Edmondo (Italian) rich, happy, prosperous protector, a form of Edmund.

Edmund (English) rich, happy, prosperous protector.
Eamon, Ed, Eddie, Eddy, Edman, Edmand, Edmon, Edmond, Edmun, Mundy

Edoardo (Italian) prosperous guardian, a form of Edward.
Eduardo

Edred (English) rich counsel.
Eddred, Eddrid, Edrid

Edric (English) prosperous ruler.
Eddric, Eddrick, Eddrik, Eddryc, Eddryck, Eddryk, Ederic, Ederick, Ederik, Ederyc, Ederyck, Ederyk, Edreece, Edreese, Edrice, Edrick, Edrik, Edris, Edryc, Edryck, Edryk, Edrys

Edsel (English) deep thinker, from the rich man's house.

Edson (English) son of Edward, a form of Edison.
Addison, Eddison, Edison, Edisen, Edsen

Eduardo (Spanish) prosperous guardian, a form of Edward.

Edur (Basque) snow.
Edure

Edwald (Anglo-Saxon) prosperous ruler.

Edward (English) prosperous guardian.
Ed, Eddie, Eddy, Edoard, Eduard, Edvard, Edvood, Edwardo, Edwards, Edzio, Etzio, Ewart, Ned, Ted, Teddy

Edwin (English) prosperous friend.
Eadwin, Eadwinn, Edik, Edlin, Eduin, Eduino, Edwinn, Edwyn, Edwynn

Efrain (Hebrew) fruitful.

Efraine, Efrayn, Efrayne, Efren, Efrin, Efryn

Efrat (Hebrew) honoured, distinguished.

Efrem (Hebrew) fruitful, a form of Ephraim.
Efraim, Efram, Ephram, Ephraim, Ephrem

Egan (Irish) fiery.
Aegen, Eagan, Eagen, Eagon, Egen, Egon

Egbert (English) bright sword.
Egbirt, Egburt, Egbryt

Egidio (Italian) shield of goat skin, a form of Giles.

Egil (Norwegian) awe-inspiring.
Egel, Egyl, Eygel, Eygil

Eginhard (German) sword of power.
Eginhardt, Einhard, Einhardt

Egor (Russian) farmer, a form of George.
Igor

Ehren (German) honourable.
Eren

Eikki (Finnish) ever-powerful.
Eiki

Einar (Norse) leader in battle; (Scandinavian) individual.
Einer, Einhar, Einher

Eitan (English) strong, firm, enduring, a form of Ethan.
Eithan, Eithon, Etan, Ethan, Eton

Ekon (African) strong.

Elam (Hebrew) highlands.
Elame

Elan (Native American) the friendly one; (Hebrew) tree.
Elann

Elbert (English) noble, brilliant.
Albert, Egbert, Elbirt, Elburt, Elbyrt, Ellbert

Elden (Anglo-Saxon) old and wise friend, a form of Alden.
Aldan, Alden, Aldon, Aldyn, Eldan, Eldon, Eldyn

Eldon (English) hill.
Eldan, Elde, Elden

Eldred (English) old, wise counsellor.
Eldrid, Eldryd

Eldridge (English) old, wise ruler.
Eldred, Eldredge, Eldrege, Eldrid, Eldrige

Eldwin (English) old friend.
Aldwin, Aldwyn, Eldwyn

Eleazar (Hebrew) God helps.
Elasar, Elasaro, Elazar, Elazaro, Eleasar, Eleasaro, Elezaro

Elgar (English) noble spearman.
Elger

Elgin (English) noble, white.
Elgan, Elgen, Elgon, Elgyn

Eli (Hebrew) uplifting, the Lord is my God, a form of Elijah.
Elias, Elija, Elijah, Ely

Elia (Hebrew) uplifting, the Lord is my God, a form of Elijah.
Eli, Eliah, Elija, Elijah

Elias (Hebrew) uplifting, the Lord is my God, a form of Elijah.
Elia, Elis, Eliyas, Ellias, Ellis, Elyas, Elyes

Elijah (Hebrew) the Lord is my God.
Elia, Eliah, Elias, Elija, Elijuo, Eliot, Eliott, Eliya, Eliyahu, Eljah, Ellija, Ellijah, Elliot, Elliott, Ellis, Ellyjah, Ellys, Elys

Eliot (English) the Lord is my God, a form of Elliot.
Elija, Elijah, Elliott

Elisha (Hebrew) God is my salvation.
Elish, Elishe, Elisher, Elishia, Elishua, Elsih, Elsiher, Elysha, Elysher, Elyshja, Elysha

Eljon (Syrian) going up.

Elk (English) large deer.
Elke

Elkan (Hebrew) God is jealous.
Elkana, Elkanah, Elkin, Elkins, Elkyn, Elkyns

Elki (Native American) hanging over.
Elkie, Elky

Ellard (German) sacred, brave.
Allard, Allerd, Alleri, Ealhard, Elari, Elarie, Elard, Elerd, Elery, Ellari, Ellarie, Ellary, Ellerd, Elleri, Ellerie, Ellery

Ellery (English) from the elder-tree island, a unisex name.
Elari, Elarie, Elery, Ellari, Ellarie, Ellary, Ellerey, Elleri, Ellerie

Elliot (English) uplifting, the Lord is my God, a form of Elijah.
Elija, Elijah, Eliot, Eliott, Eliud, Elliott, Ellis, Ellyot, Ellyott, Elyot, Elyott

Ellis (English) uplifting, the Lord is my God, a form of Elias.
Elia, Eliah, Elias, Elija, Elijah, Elijuo, Elis, Elishjsha, Eliya, Eliyahu, Ellija, Ellijah, Elliott, Ellison, Ellyjah, Ellys, Ellyson, Elys, Elyson

Ellison (English) son of Ellis.
Elison, Elleson

Elman (English) elm tree.
Almen, Ellman, Ellmen, Elmen

Elmer (English) famous
nobleman.
*Almer, Aylmar, Aylmer, Ellmar, Ellmer,
Ellmoar, Ellmoor, Ellmoore, Ellmor,
Ellmore, Elmoar, Elmar, Elmoor,
Elmoore, Elmor, Ulmer*

Elmo (Greek) amiable, friendly.

Elmore (English) elm-tree moor.
*Ellmoar, Ellmoor, Ellmoore, Ellmor,
Ellmore, Elmoar, Elmoor, Elmoore,
Elmor, Ulmer*

Elonzo (Spanish) noble, ready, a
form of Alonso.
Alonz, Alonzo, Elons, Elonso, Elonz

Eloy (Latin) chosen one.
Eloi, Eloye

Elrad (Hebrew) God rules.
Ellrad, Ellradd, Elradd

Elroy (Latin) royal, like a king.
Elroi, Elroye

Elsdon (English) noble one's hill.
Elsden, Elsdin, Elsdyn

Elson (English) son of Ellis.
Ellson, Elsen, Elsin

Elston (English) noble one's town.
Ellsten, Ellston, Elsden, Elsdon, Elsten

Elsu (Native American) soaring
swooping falcon.

Elsworth (English) noble one's
estate.
Ellsworth

Elton (English) old town.

*Alton, Ellton, Eltan, Elten, Eltin,
Eltyn*

Elvern (English) spring, a form of
Alvern.
Alvern, Elver, Elverne

Elvin (English) elf friend.
*Elvinn, Elvyn, Elvynn, Elwin, Elwinn,
Elwyn, Elwynn*

Elvio (Spanish) blond-haired.

Elvis (Scandinavian) wise.
El, Elviss, Elvys, Elvyss

Elvy (English) elf warrior.
Elvi, Elvie

Elwell (English) old stream.
Ellwell

Elwin (English) friend of the elves.
*Elvin, Elvinn, Elvyn, Elvynn, Elwinn,
Elwyn, Elwynn*

Elwood (English) old forest.
Ellwood

Emerson (German) son of the
industrious one.
Emersen

Emery (German) industrious ruler.
*Emeree, Emeri, Emerie, Emmeree,
Emmeri, Emmerie, Emmery*

Emil (German) industrious; (Latin)
flatterer.
*Emiel, Emiell, Emile, Emilio, Emill,
Emille, Emyl, Emyll, Emylle*

Emilio (Spanish, German)
industrious; (Latin) flatterer, a form
of Emil.
Emile

Emlyn (Welsh) waterfall.
Emelen, Emelyn, Emlen

Emmanuel (Hebrew) God is with us.

Emanual, Emanuel, Emanuele, Emanuell, Emmanual, Emmanuele, Emmanuell, Imanual, Imanuel, Imanuele, Imanuell, Immanual, Immanuel, Immanuele, Immanuell, Mannie, Manny, Manual, Manuel

Emmett (Teutonic) hard-working, strong; (English) ant.

Emmet, Emmit, Emmitt, Emmot, Emmott

Emre (Turkish) brother.

Emra, Emreson

Emrick (German) industrious ruler, a form of Emery.

Emery, Emory, Emre, Emrik, Emrys

Emry (Welsh) honourable.

Emree, Emrey, Emri, Emrie

Enan (Welsh) hammer.

Enen, Enin, Enon, Enyn

Engelbert (German) bright angel.

Engelbirt, Engelburt, Englebert, Englebirt, Engleburt, Ingelbert, Ingelbirt, Ingelburt, Inglebert, Inglebirt, Ingleburt

Ennis (Greek) mine; (Celtic) island.

Enis

Enoch (Hebrew) dedicated or consecrated.

Enoc, Enock, Enok, Henoch

Enos (Hebrew) man.

Ennos

Enrico (Spanish) ruler of the home, a form of Henry.

Enric, Enrique

Enright (Irish) attacker's son.

Enrite, Enryght, Enryte

Enver (Turkish) bright, handsome.

Enyeto (Native American) walks like a bear.

Enzi (African) powerful.

Enzie, Enzy

Eoin (Irish) God is gracious, a form of John.

Owen

Ephraim (Hebrew) fruitful.

Effraim, Efram, Efrem, Ephram, Ephrem

Eran (Hebrew) vigilant.

Eren, Erin, Eron, Eryn

Erasmus (Greek) amiable, lovable, desired, from Eros the god of love.

Erbert (German) excellent soldier, a form of Herbert.

Ebert, Eberto, Ebirt, Ebirto, Eburt, Eburto, Ebyrt, Ebyrto, Erberto, Erbirt, Erbirto, Erburt, Erburto, Erbyrt, Erbyrto

Ercole (Italian) wonderful gift.

Ercoal, Ercol

Eric (Scandinavian) powerful ruler; (English) brave ruler.

Ehric, Ehrich, Ehrik, Enrich, Enrick, Enrik, Erich, Erick, Erico, Erie, Erik

Erland (English) nobleman's land.

Earlan, Earland, Earlen, Earlend, Erlan, Erlen, Erlend

Erling (English) noble one's son.

Earling, Eorling, Erlin

Erminio (Italian, German) warrior; (Latin noble) a form of Herman.

Ermanio, Ermos, Herman

Ernest (English) sincere, earnest.

Earnest, Earnesto, Eirnest, Eranest, Erneste, Ernist, Ernst, Ernyst, Eyrnest

Ernesto (Spanish) sincere, a form of Ernest.

Ernie (English) sincere, a form of Ernest.
Earnee, Earni, Earnie, Earny, Ernee, Ernest, Erney, Erni, Erny

Ernst (German) sincere, a form of Ernest.
Earnest, Ernest, Ernesto

Eros (Greek) love, the god of love.

Errol (Latin) wanderer.
Eral, Erel, Eril, Erol, Erral, Errall, Errel, Errell, Erril, Errill, Erroll, Erryl, Erryll, Eryl, Eryll

Erroman (Basque) from Rome.
Eroman

Erskine (Scottish) height of the cliff.
Erskin, Erskyn, Erskyne

Eruera (Maori) prosperous guardian, a form of Edward.

Erwin (English) friend of the sea.
Erwan, Erwann, Erwinn, Erwyn, Erwynn

Esau (Hebrew) hairy.

Esbern (Danish) holy bear.
Esberne, Esbirn, Esbirne, Esburn, Esburne, Esbyrn, Esbyrne

Esmond (English) wealthy protector.
Esmonde, Esmund, Esmunde

Essien (African) sixth-born son.
Esien

Este (Italian) from the east.
Estes

Esteban (Spanish) crowned, a form of Stephen.
Esteben, Estefan, Estefano, Estefen, Estefeno, Estephan, Estephano, Estephen, Estepheno

Estevan (Spanish) crowned, a form of Stephen.
Esteban, Esteben, Estefan, Estefano, Estefen, Estefeno, Estephan, Estephano, Estephen, Estepheno, Estevano, Esteven, Esteveno

Ethan (Hebrew) firm, strong, steadfast.
Eathan, Eathen, Eathin, Eathon, Eathyn, Eithan, Eithen, Eithin, Eithon, Eithyn, Ethaen, Ethen, Ethian, Ethin, Ethon, Ethyn

Ethelred (Anglo-Saxon) noble counsel.
Althelred

Etienne (French) crowned, a form of Stephen, a unisex name.
Etian, Etianne, Étienn, Etienn, Étienne

Ettore (Italian) reliable, steadfast.
Etor, Etore, Ettor

Etu (Native American) sunny.

Eugene (Greek) well-born, noble.
Eugean, Eugeane, Eugen, Eugenio, Eugine, Eustache, Eustatius, Gene

Eurwyn (Welsh) fair-haired, golden.
Eurwin

Eusebius (Greek) pious.
Eusebio

Eustace (Greek) fruitful, productive; (Latin) calm.
Eustacee, Eustache, Eustacio, Eustachius, Eustasio, Eustasius, Eustatius

Evan (Welsh) young warrior, well born, God is gracious, a form of John.
Even, Ewan, Ewen, Owen

Evander (Greek) preacher.
Evandar

Evelyn (English) life, a unisex name.
Evelynn, Evlyn, Evlynn

Everett (English) mighty like a boar.
Everard, Everarde, Everet, Everete, Everette, Everit, Everitt

Everly (English) meadow where boars live.
Everleigh, Everlie

Ewald (German) always powerful.

Ewan (Celtic) young warrior, well born, God is gracious, a form of John, Evan.
Ewen

Ewert (English) shepherd.
Ewart

Ewing (English) friend of the law.
Ewin, Ewyn, Ewyng

Eyota (Native American) great one.
Eiota

Ezar (Hebrew) helper, a prophet, a form of Ezra.
Ezra, Ezzar

Ezekiel (Hebrew) strength of God.
Ezechiel, Ezechiele, Ezeck, Ezeckiel, Ezeckiele, Ezekeil, Ezekeile, Ezekial, Zeke

Ezra (Hebrew) helper, a prophet.
Esdras, Esera, Esra, Esrah, Ezer, Ezera, Ezrah

Faas (Scandinavian) wise counsellor.
Fas

Fabian (Latin) bean grower.
Faba, Fabar, Fabean, Faber, Fabia, Fabiano, Fabien, Fabio, Fabir, Fabius, Fabyan, Fabyr

Fabiano (Italian) bean grower, a form of Fabian.
Fabianno

Fabrice (French) works with the hands, a unisex name.
Fabriano, Fabritius

Fabrizio (Italian) one with skilful hands, craftsman.
Fabricio, Fabricius, Fabrizius

Fabron (French) little blacksmith.
Fabre, Fabrizio, Fabroni

Fadi (Arabic) redeemer.
Fadee, Fadhi

Fadil (Arabic) generous.
Fadal, Fadeel, Fadel

Fagan (Irish) fiery one.
Faegan, Faegen, Faegin, Faegon, Faegyn, Fagen, Fagin, Fagon, Fagyn, Faigan, Faigen, Faigin, Faigon, Faigyn, Faygan, Faygen, Faygin, Faygon, Faygyn

Fahd (Arabic) lynx.
Fahaad, Fahad

Fairfax (English) fair-headed.
Fax, Fayrfax

Faisal (Arabic) decisive.
Faidal, Faidel, Faidil, Faisel, Faisil, Faisl, Faiyaz, Faiz, Faizal, Faize, Faizel, Faizi, Fasel, Fasil, Faysal, Fayzal, Fayzel

Fakhir (Arabic) excellent.
Fakher, Fakir

Fakih (Arabic) one who reads the Koran.

Falco (Latin) falconer.
Falcko, Falckon, Falcon, Falconn, Falconner, Falconnor, Falko, Falkon

Fane (English) joyful.
Faine, Fayne, Feyne

Faraji (African) consolation.

Farand (German) attractive.

Farid (Arabic) unique.
Farad, Fared, Fareed, Farod, Faryd

Faris (Arabic) horseman.
Fares, Faress, Fariss, Farres, Farress, Farris, Farriss, Farrys, Farryss, Farys, Faryss

Farlane (English) far lane.
Farlaen, Farlaene, Farlain, Farlaine, Farlayn, Farlayne

Farley (Anglo-Saxon) from the far meadow, a unisex name.
Farlee, Farleigh, Farli, Farlie, Farly

Farman (Old Norse) traveller.
Farnell, Farold

Faroh (Latin) ruler.
Faro, Farro, Farroh, Farrow, Pharo, Pharoh, Pharro, Pharroh

Farquhar (Celtic) friendly.
Farquar, Farquahr

Farr (English) traveller.
Faer, Far

Farrar (Anglo-Saxon) blacksmith.
Farar, Farer, Farrer

Farrell (Irish) man of valour and heroism.
Faral, Farel, Faril, Farol, Farral, Farrall, Farrel, Farril, Farrill, Farrol, Farroll, Farryl, Farryll, Faryl

Farrow (English) piglet.
Farow

Faruq (Arabic) one who distinguishes truth from falsehood.
Farok, Farook, Farooq, Faroq

Faste (Norwegian) firm.
Fast

Fath (Arabic) victorious.

Fatin (Arabic) clever.
Faeten, Faeteen, Faetin, Faetyn, Fateen, Faten, Fatyn

Faust (Latin) auspicious, lucky, fortunate.
Fauste, Fausto, Faustus

Favian (Latin) understanding.
Favien, Favion, Favyon

Faxon (German) long-haired.
Faxan, Faxen, Faxin, Faxyn

Fay (Irish) raven.
Fae, Fah, Fai, Feyet, Feyette

Fazio (Italian) good worker.
Fazyo

Federico (Spanish) peaceful ruler, a form of Frederick.
Federic, Federigo, Fred, Frederic, Frederick, Frederico, Frederigo

Fedor (Russian) gift of God, a form of Theodore.
Fedore, Fidor, Fidore, Fiodor

Feivel (Hebrew) God will aid.
Feyvel

Felice (Italian) fortunate, happy, a form of Felix.
Feliciano, Felicio, Feliziano, Felizio

Felipe (Spanish) lover of horses, a form of Philip.
Felip, Fellip, Fellipe

Felix (Latin) fortunate, happy.
Fee, Felic, Felice, Felik, Feliz, Felizio, Filix, Filyx, Fylix, Fylyx

Felton (English) town in the fields.
Feltan, Felten, Feltin, Feltyn

Feodor (Russian) gift of God, a form of Theodore.
Feador, Feadore, Feaodor, Feaodore, Fedar, Fedor, Fedore, Feedor, Feedore, Feeodor, Feeodore, Fidor, Fidore, Fiodor, Fiodore, Fyodor, Fyodore

Feoras (Greek) smooth rock.
Feora

Ferd (German) horse.
Ferda, Ferde, Ferdi, Ferdie, Ferdy

Ferdinand (German) courageous, adventurous.
Ferd, Ferdie, Ferdinan, Ferdinando, Fernand, Fernando, Hernando

Ferdinando (Italian) courageous, adventurous, a form of Ferdinand.
Ferdinand

Fergus (Irish) strong man, man of choice.
Feargus, Fergie, Fergusen, Ferguson, Firgus, Firgusen, Firguson,

Furgus, Furgusen, Furguson,
Furgussen, Furgusson

Ferguson (Celtic) son of Fergus.
Fergusen, Fergussen, Fergusson,
Furgus, Furgusen, Furguson,
Furgussen, Furgusson

Fermin (Spanish) firm, strong.
Ferman, Fermyn, Firman, Firmin,
Firmyn, Furman, Furmin, Furmyn

Fernando (Spanish) courageous,
adventurous, a form of Ferdinand.
Ferdinand, Ferdinando, Fernand,
Fernandez

Ferran (Arabic) baker.
Faran, Farran, Farren, Feran, Feren,
Ferin, Feron, Ferren, Ferrin, Ferron,
Ferryn, Feryn

Ferris (Irish) rock,a form of Peter.
Faris, Farris, Feriss, Ferrys, Ferys

Feroz (Persian) fortunate.
Firoz

Festus (Latin) joyful, happy.
Festys

Fidel (Latin) faithful.
Fidele, Fidelio, Fidell

Fielding (English) field.
Fielder

Filbert (English) brilliant one.
Filberte, Filberti, Filberto, Filbirt,
Filbirte, Fillbert, Fillberte, Fillbirt,
Fillbirte, Philbert, Philberti, Philberto,
Philbirt, Phibirte

Filemon (Greek) lover of horses.
Filemone, Philemon, Philemone

Filip (Spanish) lover of horses, a
form of Phillip.
Filipe, Fillip, Fillipe, Fillipp, Fillippe

Filmore (English) famous one.
Fillmer, Fillmor, Fillmore, Filmer,
Filmor, Fyllmer, Fyllmore, Fylmer,
Fylmore, Philmore

Finbar (Celtic) fair-haired leader.
Finbarr, Finnbar, Fynbar, Fynbarr,
Fynnbar

Findlay (English) fair-haired warrior.
Fin, Findlea, Findlee, Findleigh,
Findley, Findly, Finlay, Finlea, Finlee,
Finleigh, Finley, Finly, Finn, Finnlay,
Finnlea, Finnlee, Finnleigh, Finnley,
Finnly, Lee

Fingal (Celtic) fair warrior.
Finngal

Finlay (Irish) fair-haired soldier.
Fin, Findlay, Findley, Finley, Finn, Lee

Finn (Celtic) fair-haired.
Fin, Finne, Fyn, Fynn, Fynne

Finnegan (Irish) fair-haired.
Finegan, Fynegan, Fynnegan

Firas (Arabic) persistent.
Fira, Firah, Fyra, Fyrah, Fyras

Firdus (Arabic) paradise.

Firman (French) strength, firm.
Firmyn, Furman, Furmyn, Fyrman

Firoz (Arabic) successful.
Firoze, Firuz

Fisher (English) fisherman.
Fischer

Fiske (English) fish.
Fisk, Fysk, Fyske

Fitch (English) weasel.

Fitz (English, Celtic) son of, for
example, Fitzpatrick is the son of
Patrick.
Fits, Fytz

Fitzgerald (English, Celtic) son of Gerald.
Fitsgerald, Fitsgeraldo, Fitzgeraldo, Fytzgerald, Fytzgeraldo

Fitzhugh (English, Celtic) son of Hugh.
Fitshue, Fitshugh, Fitzhue, Fytzhue, Fytzhugh

Fitzpatrick (English, Celtic) son of Patrick.
Fitspatric, Fitspatrick, Fitzpatric, Fytzpatric, Fytzpatrick

Fitzroy (English) son of Roy.
Fitsroi, Fitsroy, Fitzroi, Fytzroi, Fytzroy

Flann (Irish) red-haired.
Flan, Flanan, Flanen, Flanin, Flannan, Flannen, Flannin, Flannon, Flannyn, Flanon, Flanyn

Flavian (Latin) yellow-haired.
Flaviane, Flaviano, Flavien, Flavius, Flavyan

Flavio (Latin) yellow-haired, a form of Flavian.
Flabio, Flabious, Flavious, Flavius, Flavyo

Fleming (English) from Denmark.
Flemming

Fletcher (English) arrow maker.
Fletch

Flint (English) stream, flint stone.
Flinte, Flynt, Flynte

Floranz (Latin) flowering.
Floranzo, Florence, Florenz, Florenzo

Florian (Latin) blooming.
Florean, Florien

Floyd (English) grey-haired, a form of Lloyd.
Floid, Floyde, Lloyd, Lloyde, Loyd, Loyde

Flynn (Irish) son of the red-haired man.
Flin, Flinn, Flyn

Folant (Welsh) strong, powerful, brave, a form of Valentine.

Foluke (African) given to God.
Foluk

Fontaine (French) fountain.
Fontain, Fontayn, Fontayne, Fountain, Fountaine, Fountayn, Fountayne

Forbes (English) prosperous man of the fields.
Forbs

Ford (English) river crossing.
Forde

Fordon (German) destroyer.
Fordan, Forden, Fordin, Fordyn

Forest/Forrest (English) dweller in the forest, forester, guardian of the lord's forest, a unisex name.
Foreste, Forreste, Forrestt

Forester/Forrestor (English) dweller in the forest, forester, guardian of the lord's forest.
Forestor, Forrester

Fortino (Italian) fortunate, lucky.
Fortin, Fortine, Fortunatus, Fortyn, Fortyne

Foster (English) guardian of the forest, environment.
Forest, Forester, Forestor, Forrest, Forrester, Forrestor, Forster, Forstor, Fostor

Fouad (Lebanese) heart.
Foad

Fowler (English) gamekeeper of birds.

Francesco (Italian) free, from France, a form of Francis.
Francis, Francisco, Franco, Frank

Francis (Latin) free, from France.
Franc, Frances, Francesco, Francisco, Francois, Francys, Frank, Frankie, Frans, Fransis, Franz

Francisco (Spanish) free, from France, a form of Francis.

Franco (Latin) free, from France, a form of Francis.
Franko

Frank (English) free, from France, a form of Francis.
Franc, Franck, Francke, Frang, Franke, Franko

Franklin (English) free.
Frank, Frankie, Franklyn, Francklin, Francklyn

Franz (German) free, from France, a form of Francis.
Fransz, Franzen, Franzie, Franzl, Franzy

Fraser (French) strawberry; (English) curly-haired.
Frasier, Frasyer, Frazer, Frazier, Frazyer

Frayne (French) ash tree; (English) stranger.
Fraine, Frayn, Frean, Freen, Freyn, Freyne

Frazer (French) strawberry; (English) curly-haired, a form of Fraser.
Frazier, Frazyer

Fred (German) peaceful ruler, a form of Frederick.

Frederick (German) peaceful ruler.
Fred, Freddie, Freddy, Frederic, Frederico, Frederik, Frederiko, Fredric, Fredrico, Fredrik, Friedrich, Friedrik

Frederico (Spanish) peaceful ruler, a form of Frederick.
Frederigo

Freeborn (English) child of freedom.
Freborn

Freeman (English) free.
Freedman, Freiman, Freman

Fremont (German) protector of freedom.
Freemont, Freemonte, Fremonte

Frewin (English) free, noble friend.
Frewen

Frey (Scandinavian, English) noble, the masculine form of Freya, a goddess of love.
Frai, Fray, Frei

Frick (English) bold.
Frik, Frike, Fryck, Fryk, Fryke

Fridolf (English) peaceful wolf.
Freydolf, Freydolph, Freydolphe, Freydulf, Freydulfe, Fridolph, Fridolphe, Fridulf, Fridulfe, Friduwolf, Friduwulf, Fridwolf, Fridwulf, Friedolf, Friedolfe, Frydolph, Frydolphe, Frydulf, Frydulfe

Frisco (Spanish) free, from France, a form of Franciso.

Fritz (German) peaceful ruler, a form of Frederick.

Frits, Fritson, Fritt, Fritzchen, Fritzl, Frytson, Frytz, Frytzon

Frode (Norwegian) wise.

Frod

Fulbert (German) shining bright.

Fulberto, Fulbirt, Fulbirto, Fulburt, Fulburto

Fuller (Anglo-Saxon) clothing presser.

Fuler

Fulton (English) field near the town.

Faulton, Folton, Fulton

Funsoni (African) requested.

Funsony

Fyfe (Scottish) from Fife, Scotland.

Fife, Fyffe

Fynn (African) river name in Ghana.

Fin, Finn, Finne, Fyn, Fynne

Gabe (Hebrew) devoted to God, God's messenger, a form of Gabriel.
Gab

Gabriel (Hebrew) devoted to God, God's messenger.
Gabe, Gabie, Gabby, Gable, Gabreal, Gabreale, Gabrial, Gabriale, Gabriele, Gabriell, Gabrielle, Gabriello, Gabrielo

Gabriele (Italian, Hebrew) devoted to God, God's messenger, a form of Gabriel.
Gabby, Gabe

Gad (Arabic) lucky.
Gadd, Gadi, Gadie, Gady

Gadi (Arabic) God is my wealth, fortune.
Gad, Gadd, Gaddi, Gaddie, Gaddy, Gadie, Gadiel, Gadil, Gady

Gael (Irish) Gaelic.
Gaelic

Gage (French) pledge, promise, a unisex name.
Gager, Gaig, Gaige, Gayg, Gayge

Gair (Irish) short one.
Gaer, Gairr, Gayr, Geir, Geirr

Gaius (Latin) one who is happy and rejoices.
Gayus

Galahad (Welsh) hawk.

Galbraith (Irish) Scotsman living in Ireland.
Gailbraith, Gailbraithe, Gailbrayth, Gailbraythe, Galbraithe, Galbrayth, Galbraythe

Galen (Greek) healer, calm; (Irish) little, lively, a unisex name.
Gaelan, Gaelen, Gaelin, Gaelyn, Galan, Gale, Galeno, Galin, Galyn, Gaylen

Galeus (Greek) lizard.

Gali (Hebrew) fountain or spring on a hill, a unisex name.
Galie, Galli, Gallie

Gallagher (Celtic) eager helper.
Galaher, Galagher, Gallaher

Galt (Norwegian) high ground.

Galvin (Irish) sparrow.
Gal, Gall, Gallvan, Gallven, Gallvin, Gallvyn, Galvan, Galven, Galvyn

Gamal (Arabic) beautiful camel.
Gamail, Gamel, Gamil, Jamal

Gamaliel (Hebrew) the Lord is my reward.
Gamalielle, Gamiell, Gamielle

Gamba (African) warrior.
Gambah

Gamlyn (Scandinavian) little elder.
Gamlin

Gan (Chinese) adventurous.

Ganan (Australian Aboriginal) west.
Ganen, Ganin, Ganon, Ganyn

Gandolf (German) wolf's progress, fierce wolf.
Gandolfo

Ganesh (Hindu) son of the god Shiva and goddess Parvati, fortunate, god of good luck and wisdom.
Ganesha

Gannon (Irish) of fair complexion.
Ganan, Ganen, Ganin, Gannan, Gannen, Gannin, Gannyn, Ganon, Ganyn

Gar (English) a form of Gareth, Garnet, Garvin.
Garr

Garcia (Spanish) spear carrier, a form of Gerald.
Garcias, Garcya, Garcyah, Garcyas, Garsia, Garsias, Garsya, Garsyah, Garsyas

Gardiner (Anglo-Saxon) gardener.
Gardener, Gardner

Garek (Polish) great spearman, a form of Edgar.
Garak, Garik, Garok, Garyk

Gareth (Welsh) gentle.
Gar, Garethe, Garith, Garithe, Garreth, Garrethe, Garrith, Garrithe, Garth, Garthe, Garyth, Garythe, Gath, Gathe

Garfield (English) battlefield, field of spears.
Garfielde, Garfyld, Garfylde

Garland (French) wreath of flowers, a unisex name.
Garlan, Garlande, Garlane, Garlond, Garlonde

Garman (English) spearman.
Garmann, Garrman, Garrmann, Garmyn, Garmynn, Garmynne, Garrmyn

Garner (French) guard.

Garnar, Garnier, Garnierr, Garrnar, Garrner, Garrnier

Garnet (Latin) dark red gem, a unisex name.
Gar, Garnete, Garnett, Garnette, Garnie, Garny, Garnye, Garr

Garnock (Welsh) dweller by the alder tree river.
Garnoc, Garnok

Garren (English) guardian.
Garan, Garen, Garin, Garion, Garon, Garran, Garrett, Garrin, Garrion, Garron, Garry, Garyn, Garynn, Garynne, Gerron, Gerryn

Garrett (English, Irish) spear carrier, a form of Gerald.
Garit, Garrard, Garrat, Garratt, Garret, Garritt, Garyt, Garytt, Gerret, Gerrot

Garrick (English) spear power, oak spear.
Gaerick, Gaerik, Gareck, Garek, Garick, Garik, Garreck, Garrek, Garric, Garrik, Garryck, Garryk, Gerreck, Gerrick

Garrie (Australian Aboriginal) sleepy emu.
Gaerie, Gaerrie, Garie

Garrison (French) troops in a battle; (Anglo-Saxon) Gary's son.
Garis, Garison, Garisson, Garris, Garrisson

Garroway (English) spear fighter.
Garaway, Garoway, Garraway, Garway

Garry (English) spear carrier, a form of Gary.
Garee, Garen, Garey, Gari, Garie, Garree, Garren, Garrey, Garri, Garrie, Garrin, Garron, Gary

Garson (English) son of Gar.

Garth (Scandinavian) from the garden, enclosure.
Gar, Gareth, Gart, Garthe

Garton (Old English) triangular-shaped town.
Garaton, Garatun, Gartun, Garrton, Garrtun

Garvey (Irish) peace.
Garrv, Garrvan, Garrvee, Garrvey, Garrvi, Garrvie, Garrvy, Garv, Garvan, Garvee, Garvi, Garvie, Garvy

Garvin (English) friend in battle.
Garvinn, Garwin, Garwinn

Gary (English) spear carrier.
Garee, Garey, Gari, Garie, Garree, Garrey, Garri, Garrie, Garry

Gaspar (Persian) treasurer, a form of Casper.
Caspar, Casparo, Casper, Caspero, Gaspard, Gaspare, Gaspari, Gasparo, Gasper, Gaspero, Gazsi, Jaspar, Jasper, Kaspar, Kasper, Kaspero

Gaston (French) from Gascony, France.
Gascon, Gasconn, Gasconne, Gastan, Gastaun, Gasten, Gastin, Gastonn, Gastonne, Gastyn

Gaute (Norwegian) great.
Gaut, Gautt, Gautte

Gautier (French) army ruler, a form of Walter.
Galteiro, Galtero, Gaultier, Gaultiere, Gaultiero, Gauthier, Gauthiere, Gauthiero, Gautiere, Gautiero

Gavin (Welsh) white hawk.
Gav, Gavan, Gaven, Gavinn,

Gavino, Gavn, Gavohn, Gavon, Gavyn, Gavynn, Gawain

Gavra (Slavic) hero of God.
Gavrah, Gavril, Gavrill

Gavrie (Russian) belonging to God.
Gavri, Gavry

Gavriel (Hebrew) man of God.
Gav, Gavi, Gavrel, Gavri, Gavriele, Gavrielo, Gavril, Gavrile, Gavrilo, Gavrilushka, Gavy, Gavyel

Gawain (Welsh) white hawk, a form of Gavin.
Gawaine, Gawayn, Gawayne, Gawen, Gwayn, Gwayne

Gayadi (Australian Aboriginal) platypus.
Gaiadi

Gaylord (French) merry nobleman.
Gaillard, Gallard, Gayelord, Gaylar, Gayler, Gaylor, Gaylorde

Gaynor (Irish) fair, child of the fair one, a unisex name.
Gainar, Gainer, Gainor, Gaynar, Gayner, Gaynnar, Gaynner, Gaynnor

Geary (English) changes.
Gearey, Gery

Geert (Dutch) spear carrier, a form of Gerard.
Geart, Gearte, Geerte, Gert, Gerte

Gene (Greek) well-born, noble, a form of Eugene.
Gena, Genek

Gennaro (Italian) born in January.

Geoffrey (English) gentle, kind, God's peace, divinely peaceful.

*Geffrey, Geofery, Geoff, Geoffery,
Geoffre, Geoffrie, Geoffroi,
Geoffroy, Geoffry, Geofri, Geofry,
Jeff, Jeffery, Jeffrey*

George (Greek) farmer.
*Georas, Geordie, Georg, Georga,
Georgas, Georges, Georget,
Georgi, Georgie, Georgii, Georgio,
Georgios, Georgiy, Georgy, Gevork,
Gheorghe, Goerge, Goran, Gorge,
Gorje, Gorya, Griogio, Grzegorz,
Gyorgy, Jorg, Jorge, Jorgen, Jorgis,
Jorin, Joris, Jur, Jurgis, Yorge, Yorgos*

Geraint (Welsh) old man.
Gerainte, Gerraint, Gerrainte

Gerald (German) spear carrier.
*Garald, Garaldo, Garold, Garoldo,
Garolds, Gearalt, Gellert, Geralde,
Geraldo, Gerale, Geraud, Gerick,
Gerik, Gerlado, Gerold, Geroldo,
Gerrald, Gerrell, Gerrild, Gerrin,
Gerrit, Gerrold, Gerry, Geryld, Girald,
Giraldo, Giraud, Girauld*

Geraldo (Italian) spear carrier, a
form of Gerald.

Gerard (German) spear carrier.
*Garhard, Garrard, Garrat, Garratt,
Garret, Garrett, Gearard, Gerad,
Gerar, Gerardo, Geraro, Geraud,
Gerd, Gerek, Gerhard, Gerhardi,
Gerhardt, Gerhart, Gerhort,
Gerhordt, Gerrard, Gerrit, Gerry,
Gherard, Gherardo, Girard,
Girardo*

Gerardo (Italian) spear carrier, a
form of Gerard.
Gherardo

Geraud (French) spear carrier, a
form of Gerard.
Gerad, Gerrad, Gerraud

Gerber (German) tanner of
leather.

Gerek (Polish) spear carrier, a form
of Gerard.
Gerik, Gerrek, Gerrik

Geremia (Hebrew) exalted,
chosen by God.
*Geremiah, Gerimia, Gerimiah,
Geromia, Geromiah*

Gerik (Polish) great spearman, a
form of Edgar.
Geric, Gerick, Gerrik

Germain (French) from Germany.
*Germaine, Germane, Germano,
Germayn, Germayne*

Geronimo (Italian, Spanish)
sacred name, holy, a form of
Jerome.
Gerome, Geronemo, Jerome

Gershom (Hebrew) exiled.
Gersh, Gersham, Gershon

Gervaise (French) spear carrier, a
unisex name.
*Gervais, Gervase, Jervais, Jervaise,
Jervase*

Gervasio (Italian) spear carrier, a
form of Gervais.

Gerwyn (Welsh) fair love.
Gerwen, Gerwin

Gethin (Welsh) dark-skinned.
Gethyn

Geysa (Hungarian) chief.
Geisa, Geiza, Gesa, Geyza, Geza

Ghalib (Arabic) victor.
Ghaalib

Ghassan (Arabic) young.
Ghaassan, Ghasan

Ghazi (Arabic) conqueror.

Gi (Korean) brave.

Gia (Vietnamese) family.
Giaa, Giaah, Giah

Giacinto (Portuguese) hyacinth.
Giacintho

Giacomo (Italian) replacer,
supplanter, a form of Jacob.
*Gaimo, Giacamo, Giaco,
Giacobbe, Giacobo, Giacop*

Gian (Italian) God is gracious, a
form of John.
*Giann, Giannes, Gianni, Giannis,
Gianno, Giannos, Giano, Ghian,
Ghiann, Ghiannes, Ghianni,
Ghiannis, Ghianno, Ghiano,
Ghianos*

Gian-Carlo (Italian) combination
of Gian and Carlo.
*Giancarol, Giancarlos, Gianncarlo,
Gianncarlos*

Gian-Luca (Italian) combination
of Gian and Luca.
Gian-Lucas

Gianni (Italian) God is gracious, a
form of John.
Giani, Gioni, Gionni, Johnny

Giano (Italian) God is gracious, a
form of John.

Gianpaolo (Italian) combination
of Gian and Paolo.
*Giannpaolo, Gian-Paolo,
Gianpaulo, Gian-Paulo*

Gib (English) brilliant pledge
trustworthy, a form of Gilbert.
Gibb, Gibbe, Gibbie, Gibby

Gibor (Hebrew) strong, powerful.
Gibbor

Gibson (English) son of Gilbert.

*Gibbon, Gibbons, Gibbs, Gilson,
Gillson*

Gideon (Hebrew) tree cutter.
*Gedeon, Gedeone, Gideone,
Gidon, Hedeon, Hedeone, Hideon,
Hideone*

Gifford (Teutonic) bold giver.
*Gif, Giff, Giffard, Gifferd, Giffie, Giffy,
Gyf, Gyff, Gyffard, Gyfferd, Gyffie,
Gyfford, Gyffy*

Gig (English) horse-drawn
carriage.

Gil (Greek) shield bearer;
(Hebrew) happy; (English) brilliant
pledge, trustworthy, a form of
Gilbert.
*Gilbert, Gilberto, Gilchrist, Gili, Gill,
Gilli, Gillis, Gilly, Gily, Gyl, Gyli, Gyll,
Gylli*

Gilad (Arabic) camel hump.
Giladi, Giladie, Gilead

Gilamu (Basque) determined
guardian, a form of William.

Gilbert (English) brilliant, pledge,
trustworthy, bright.
*Gib, Gil, Gilberto, Gilburt, Gilburto,
Giselbert, Giselberto, Giselbertus,
Guilbert, Guilburt, Gylbert, Gylburt*

Gilberto (Italian) brilliant pledge,
trustworthy, a form of Gilbert.
Gilburto

Gilby (Scandinavian) hostage's
estate; (Irish) blond boy.
*Gilbee, Gilbey, Gilbie, Gillbee,
Gillbey, Gillbie, Gillby*

Gilchrist (Irish) servant of Christ.
*Ghil, Ghilchrist, Ghill, Ghilley,
Ghillie, Ghilly, Gil, Gilcrist, Gill, Gilley,
Gillie*

Gilen (Basque) illustrious pledge.
Gylen

Giles (French) goat-skin shield.
Gilles, Gide, Gyles, Gylles

Gillean (Scottish) servant of St John.
Gilan, Gilean, Gilen, Gilian, Gillan, Gillen, Gillian

Gillespie (Irish) son of the bishop's servant.
Gill, Gillespy

Gilmer (English) famous hostage.
Gillmer, Gillmere, Gilmere

Gilmore (Irish) devoted servant of Mary.
Gillmor, Gillmore, Gillmour, Gillmoure, Gilmor, Gilmour, Gilmoure

Gilon (Hebrew) circle.
Gillon, Gillonn, Gilonn

Gilroy (Irish) devoted to the king.
Gilderay, Gilderoy, Gildray, Gildroy, Gillray, Gillroy, Gilray, Gyllray, Gyllroy, Gylray, Gylroy

Gino (Italian) well-born, noble a form of Eugene.
Geeno, Ginno, Ginnoh, Ginoh

Gioacchino (Italian) God will establish, a form of Joachim.
Joachim

Giona (Italian) dove, a form of Jonah.
Gionah, Gyona, Gyonah

Giordano (Italian) flowing down, descending, a form of Jordan.
Giordan, Giordana, Giordin, Girdino, Girodina, Guordan, Guordana, Guordano, Guordin, Guordina, Guordino

Giorgio (Italian) farmer, a form of George.
Giorg, Giorge, Giorgi

Giorgos (Greek) farmer, a form of George.
Georgios, Giorgios

Giosia (Italian) God is my salvation, a form of Joshua.
Giosiah, Giosya, Giosyah, Gyosia, Gyosiah, Gyosya, Gyosyah

Giotto (Italian) gentle, kind, God's peace, divinely peaceful, a form of Geoffrey.

Giovanni (Italian) God is gracious, a form of John.
Geovan, Geovani, Geovann, Geovanne, Geovannee, Geovannhi, Geovanni, Geovannie, Geovanny, Geovany, Gian, Gianino, Gianni, Giannino, Giovan, Giovani, Giovann, Giovannee, Giovannhi, Giovannie, Giovanno, Giovanny, Giovonni, Giovonnia, Giovonnie, Givonni

Gipsy (English) wanderer.
Gipsi, Gipson, Gypson, Gypsy

Girish (Hindu) mountain lord, the Hindu god Shiva.
Giris

Girvin (Irish) little rough one.
Garbhan, Girbhan, Girbhen, Girbhin, Girvan, Girven

Gitano (Spanish) gypsy.

Giuliano (Italian) youthful, a form of Julius.
Giulano, Giulino, Guillano, Giulliano, Giullino

Giulio (Italian) youthful, a form of Julius.
Giullio, Giullo, Giulo

Giuseppe (Italian) God shall increase, a form of Joseph.

Giuseppe, Giuseppi, Giuseppie, Giusseppe, Guisseppe, Guiseppi, Guiseppino

Giustino (Italian) just, a form of Justin.

Giusto, Giustiniano, Justinian

Given (English) one who is given.

Givan, Givon, Givun, Givyn, Gyvan, Gyven, Gyvon

Givon (Hebrew) hill heights.

Givan, Given, Givin, Givyn

Gladwin (English) cheerful, happy.

Gladd, Gladdie, Gladdwin, Gladdy, Gladwinn, Gladwinne, Gladwyn, Gladwynn, Gladwynne

Glanville (English) village with oak trees.

Glanvil, Glanvill, Glanvyl, Glanvyll, Glanvylle

Glen/Glenn (Celtic) from the valley.

Glean, Glenis, Glenne, Glennis, Glennon, Glenon, Glenton, Glyn, Glynis, Glynn, Glynn, Glynnon, Glynon

Glendon (Scottish) fortress in the glen.

Glenden, Glendin, Glennden, Glenndin, Glenndon, Glennten, Glenntin, Glennton, Glenten, Glentin, Glenton

Glenrowan (Irish) valley with rowan trees.

Glennrowan, Glennrowen, Glennrowin, Glennrowon, Glennrowyn, Glenrowan, Glenrowen, Glenrowin, Glenrowon, Glennrowyn, Glynnrowan, Glynnrowen, Glynnrowin, Glynnrowon, Glynnrowyn,

Glynrowan, Glynrowen, Glynrowin, Glynrowon, Glynrowyn

Glyn (Welsh) from the valley, a form of Glen.

Glin, Glinn, Glean, Glenn, Glennis, Glennon, Glenon, Glenton, Glyn, Glynnis, Glynnon, Glynon, Glynton

Goddard (German) firm in God.

Godard, Godart, Goddart, Godhadrt, Godhart, Goddhart, Gothard, Gothart, Gotthard, Gotthardt, Gotyhart

Godfrey (German) gentle, kind, God's peace, divinely peaceful, a form of Geoffrey.

Giotto, Godefroi, Godfree, Godfry, Godofredo, Godofroi, Godrey, Gofredo, Goraidh, Gorry, Gothfraidh, Gottfri

Godric (Anglo-Saxon) divine, powerful ruler.

Godrick, Godrik

Godwin (English) friend of God.

Godewin, Godewinn, Godewyn, Godewynn, Godwinn, Godwyn, Godwynn, Goodwin, Goodwinn, Goodwinne, Goodwyn, Goodwynn, Goodwynne

Goel (Hebrew) redeemer, to regain.

Goffredo (Italian) gentle, kind, God's peace, divinely peaceful, a form of Godfrey.

Gofredo

Goldwin (English) golden friend.

Golden, Goldewin, Goldewinn, Goldewinne, Goldewyn, Goldewynn, Goldewynne, Goldwinn, Goldwinne, Goldwyn, Goldwynn, Goldwynne

Goliath (Hebrew) revealing, the giant beaten by David in the Bible.

Golliath, Golyath, Gully

Gomda (Native American) wind.
Gomdah, Gommda, Gommdah

Gomer (Hebrew) to finish.
Gome, Gomme, Gommer

Gomez (Spanish) man.
Gomaz

Gonza (African) to love.
Gonnza, Gonnzah, Gonzah

Gonzalo (Spanish) wolf.
Goncalve, Goncalves, Gonsalee, Gonsales, Gonsalo, Gonsolo, Gonzales, Gonzelee, Gonzolo

Goodman (English) good man.
Godman

Goodwin (English) good friend.
Godwin

Goraidh (Irish) gentle, kind, God's peace, divinely peaceful, a form of Godfrey.
Goraid

Goran (Swedish) farmer, a form of George.
Gorran

Gordon (English) great three-cornered, triangular-shaped hill.
Gerodan, Gerodann, Gerodian, Gerodin, Geordon, Gordan, Gordann, Gorden, Gordian, Gordie, Gordin, Gordun, Gordy, Gordyn, Jorden, Jordon

Gore (English) triangular-shaped plot.

Gorman (Irish) little blue-eyed one.
Gormann, Gorrman, Gorrmann

Goro (Japanese) fifth-born child.

Goronwy (Welsh) figure from Celtic mythology.

Gosheven (Native American) great leaper.

Gottfried (German) gentle, kind, God's peace, divinely peaceful, a form of Geoffrey.
Gotfrid, Gotfrids, Gotfried, Gottfirds, Gottfrid, Gottfrids

Gotzon (German) angel.

Gough (Welsh) red-haired.
Gof, Goff, Goph

Govert (Dutch) heavenly peace.

Gower (Welsh) one with great purity.
Gowyr

Gozol (Hebrew) soaring bird.

Grady (Irish) illustrious, noble, a surname, a unisex name.
Gradee, Gradeigh, Gradey, Graidey, Gradleigh, Graidy, Greadea

Graeme (Anglo-Saxon) from the grey house, a form of Graham.
Graeham, Graehame, Graehme, Graem, Graham, Grahame, Grahamm, Grahamme, Grayem, Grayeme, Grayham, Grahm, Grahme, Gram, Grame, Gramm

Graham (Anglo-Saxon) from the grey house.
Graeham, Graehame, Graehme, Graem, Graeme, Grahame, Grahamm, Grahamme, Grayem, Grayeme, Grayham, Grahm, Grahme, Gram, Grame, Gramm

Grande (Portuguese) large, grand.
Grand

Granger (Anglo-Saxo) farmer.
Grainge, Grainger, Grange

Grant (French) great, grand.
Grantley, Grand

Grantland (English) from the grand land.
Granlan, Granland, Grantlan

Granville (French) large, grand village.
Gran, Granvil, Granvile, Granvill, Granvel, Granvell, Granvelle, Granvil, Granvill, Grenvel, Grenvell, Grenvelle, Grenvil, Grenvill, Grenville, Grevill, Greville

Gray (English) grey colour.
Grae, Graye, Grey, Greye

Grayson (English) judge's son, bailiff's son.
Graysen, Greysen, Greyson

Greeley (English) grey meadow.
Greelea, Greeleah, Greeleigh, Greeli, Greelie, Greely

Greenwood (English) green forest, woods.
Green, Greene, Greenewood

Greer (Scottish) watchful, guardian, from a Gaelic form of Gregory, a unisex name.
Grear, Grier

Gregor (Scottish) watchful, vigilant, a form of Gregory.
Greg, Gregour

Gregorio (Italian) watchful, vigilant, a form of Gregory.
Gregorios, Gregorious

Gregory (Latin) watchful, vigilant.
Greg, Greagor, Greagory, Gregar, Gregary, Greger, Gregery,
Gregger, Greggery, Greggory, Gregogroy, Gregor, Gregorey, Gregori, Gregorie, Gregors, Gregos, Gregrey, Gregroy

Griffin (Latin) hooked nose.
Grifen, Griffen, Griffon, Griffyn, Griffynn, Grifon, Grifyn, Gryffyn, Gryphen, Gryphon

Griffith (Welsh) powerful lord.
Griff, Griffeth, Griffie, Griffy, Griffyth, Gryf, Gryff, Gryffith, Gryffyth, Gryfith, Gryfyth,

Grigori (Russian) watchful, vigilant, a form of Gregory.
Grigore, Grigorio, Grigorios, Grigoriv, Grigoi, Grigory, Grisha

Griogair (Scottish) watchful, vigilant, a form of Gregory.

Griswold (German, French) grey forest.
Griswald, Grizwald, Grizwold

Grosvenor (French) mighty huntsman.

Grover (English) of the grove.
Grove

Guadalupe (Spanish) wolf valley; (Arabic) river of black stones, a unisex name.
Guadalup, Guadalop, Guadalope

Gualberto (Spanish) army general, a form of Walter.
Gualbert, Gualterio

Gualtiero (Italian) army general, a form of Walter.
Gualtero, Gualtiero

Guglielmo (Italian) determined guardian, a form of William.
Gugliellmo, Guglielmin, Gugliemo

Guido (Italian, German) warrior, wide wood; (French) guide; (Hebrew) valley, a form of Guy.
Guedo

Guilford (English) ford with yellow flowers.
Guildford, Guildforde, Guilforde

Guilherme (Portuguese) determined guardian, a form of William.
Giulherm, Giulherme, Guilherm

Guillaume (French) determined guardian, a form of William.
Guilaume, Guilem, Guillaums, Guilleaume, Guillem, Guyllaume

Guillermo (Spanish) determined guardian, a form of William.
Guillerrmo

Guir/Guire (Irish) beige.

Gunnar (Scandinavian) battle army, bold warrior, a form of Gunther.
Gunar, Guner, Gunner

Guntero (Italian) battle army, bold warrior, a form of Gunther.
Gunteros

Gunther (Scandinavian) battle army, bold warrior.
Guentar, Guenter, Guenthar, Guenther, Gun, Guntar, Gunter, Gunthar

Guotin (Chinese) strong, polite leader.

Gur (English) lion cub.
Gurr

Gurion (Hebrew) young lion.
Guriel, Gurriel, Gurrian, Gurryon, Guryon

Gurpreet (Hindu) devoted to the prophet.
Gurjeet, Gurmeet, Gurprit, Gurujeet, Gurumeet, Gurupreet, Gururprit

Gurvir (Indian) warrior of the guru.
Gurveer

Gus (Scandinavian) a form of Angus, Augustine, Gustave.
Guss, Gussee, Gussi, Gussie, Gussy, Gustee, Gusti, Gustie, Gustree, Gustri, Gustrie, Gustry, Gusty

Gustave (Scandinavian) staff of the Goths.
Gustaaf, Gustaafe, Gustaf, Gustafe, Gustaff, Gustaffe, Gustaof, Gustav, Gustava, Gustaves, Gustavo, Gustavs, Gustavus, Gustik, Gustus, Gusztav

Gustavo (Italian) staff of the Goths, a form of Gustave.

Guthrie (German) war hero; (Irish) from the windy place.
Guthree, Guthrey, Guthry

Gutierre (Spanish) army ruler, a form of Walter.
Gutiere

Guy (German) warrior, wide wood; (French) guide; (Hebrew) valley.
Gie, Gui, Guye, Guyon

Guyapi (Native American) truthful.

Gwidon (Polish) life.
Gwydon

Gwilym (Welsh) determined guardian, a form of William.

Gwyn (Welsh) fair-haired, blond.
Gwin, Gwinn, Gwinne, Gwynn, Gwynne

Gwynfor (Welsh) fair lord.
Gwinfor

Gyasi (African) baby.

Gyorgy (Russian) farmer, a form of George.
Gyoergi, Gyoergy, Gyorgi, Gyuri, Gyurka

Gyula (Hungarian) young.
Gyala, Gyuszi

H

Haakon (Norse) useful.
Haacon, Hacon, Hakon

Haamid (Arabic) grateful, thankful.
Hamid

Habib (Arabic) beloved one.
Haabib, Haabyb, Habyb

Hacket (German) little woodsman.
Hackett, Hackit, Hackitt, Hakket, Hakkett, Hakkit, Hakkett

Hadad (Arabic) blacksmith.
Haddad

Hadar (Hebrew) glory.

Hadden/Haddon (English) heather-filled valley, heather-covered valley.
Hadan, Haddan, Haddyn, Haden, Hadon, Hadyn

Hadi (Arabic) guiding to the right.
Hadd, Haddi, Haddee, Haddie, Haddy, Hadee, Hadie, Hady

Hadley (English) of the heath-covered meadow, a unisex name.
Haddlee, Haddleigh, Haddley, Haddlie, Haddly, Hadlee, Hadleigh, Hadlie, Hadly, Lee, Leigh

Hadrian (Latin, Scandinavian) dark one.
Adrian, Adrien, Hadrien

Hadwin (Anglo-Saxon) friend during war.

Hadwen, Hadwenn, Hadwinn, Haddwinne, Hadwyn, Hadwynn, Hadwynne

Hafiz (Arabic) one who remembers.
Hafyz

Hagan (German) strong defence; (Irish) ruler of the home.
Hagen, Haggan, Haggen

Hagar (Hebrew) forsaken, a unisex name.
Hager, Hagir, Haggar, Hagor, Hagyr

Hagen (Irish) young.
Hagan, Haggen, Hagin, Hagon, Hagun, Hagyn

Hahnee (Native American) beggar.

Hai (Vietnamese) sea.

Haidar (Arabic) lion.
Haider

Haig (English) from the hedged field.
Haeg, Hage, Haige

Hailama (Hawaiian) famous brother.
Hailamah, Hailaman, Hilama, Hilamah

Haines (English) from a vined cottage.
Hanes, Haynes, Hayns, Heines

Haji (African) born during Mecca pilgrimage.

Hakan (Native American) fiery.
Haken, Hakin, Hakkan, Hakon, Hakyn

Hakeem (Arabic) wise ruler.
Hakem, Hakim

Hakim (Eithopian) doctor.
Hakeem, Hakiem, Hakym

Hakon (Scandinavian) of Nordic ancestry.

Haakan, Haaken, Haakin, Haakon, Haeo, Hak, Hakan, Haken, Hakin, Hako

Hal (English) a form of Halden, Hall, Harold.

Halcyon (Greek) tranquil, peaceful.

Halcion

Halden (Scandinavian) half-Dane.

Hal, Haldan, Haldane, Halfdan, Halfden, Hall, Halvdan, Halvden

Hale (English, German) hardy, hearty.

Hail, Haile, Haille, Hayl, Hayle, Haylle, Heall

Haley (English) from the meadow of hay; (Scandinavian) hero; (Irish) clever, ingenious, a unisex name.

Hailee, Haileigh, Hailie, Haily, Hailey, Hale, Haleigh, Halley, Harley, Hayleigh, Hayley, Hayli, Haylie

Halford (English) valley ford.

Haleford, Haleforde, Halforde

Hali (Greek) sea.

Halea, Haleah, Halee, Haleigh, Haley, Halie, Haly

Halian (Native American) young.

Halyan

Halifax (Anglo-Saxon) from the holy field.

Halyfax

Halil (Turkish) dear friend.

Halill

Halim (Arabic) mild, gentle, patient.

Haleem, Halym

Hall (English) dweller at the manor, hall.

Hal, Hallstead, Hallsted, Halstead, Halsted

Hallam (English) from the hill slope, valley.

Halam, Halem, Halum, Hallem, Hallum

Hallan (English) dweller at the hall.

Hailan, Halan, Halen, Halin, Hallen, Hallene, Hallin, Hallon, Hallyn, Halon, Halyn, Haylan

Halley (English) holy meadow, meadow near the hall.

Halea, Haleah, Halee, Haleigh, Haley, Halie, Hallea, Halleah, Hallee, Halleigh, Hallie, Hally, Haly

Halliwell (English) holy well.

Halewell, Haliwel, Haliwell, Hallewell, Halli, Halliwel, Hallywel, Hallywell, Halywel, Halywell, Hellewell, Helliwell, Liwell

Halse (English) neck of land.

Halsey, Halsted

Halvor (Norwegian) rock, protector.

Halvar, Halvard, Halvord

Ham (Hebrew) hot, warm, one of Noah's sons.

Hamm

Hamal (Arabic) bright star in the constellation of Aries, lamb.

Hahmal, Hahmel, Hamel, Hamil, Hammal, Hammall, Hammel, Hammil, Hammill

Haman (Hebrew) magnificent.

Hamdan (Arabic) the praised one.

Hamed (Arabic) praised, thankful to God, a form of Hamid.
Hameed, Hammed

Hamid (Arabic) praised, thankful to God, a form of Muhammad.
Haamid, Hamaad, Hamadi, Hamayd, Hamd, Hamdrem, Hamdren, Hamed, Hamedo, Hameed, Hamidi, Hammad, Hammed, Hammid

Hamilton (English) proud town, crooked mountain.
Hameltan, Hamelten, Hamelton, Hameltun, Hamiltan, Hamilten, Hamiltun, Hamylton

Hamish (Scottish) the supplanter, a form of Jacob, James.
Ham, Hamm, Hammish, Hammysh, Hamysh

Hamisi (African) born on a Thursday.

Hamlet (German French) small village, little home.
Hammlet

Hamlin (French, German) little home lover.
Hamblin, Hamelen, Hamelin, Hamlen, Hamlyn, Lin

Hammond (English) village.
Hammon, Hammund, Hamon, Hamond, Hamp, Hamund

Hampton (English) little town.

Hamza (Arabic) powerful.
Hamz, Hamzah, Hamze, Hamzeh, Hamzia

Hanan (Hebrew) grace.
Hannan

Hanbal (Arabic) purity.
Hanbel, Hanbil

Handel (German, English) God is gracious, a form of John.
Handal, Handil, Handol, Handyl

Hani (Arabic) happy, delighted, content.

Hanif (Arabic) true believer.
Hanef, Haneff, Haniff, Hanyf, Hanyff

Hank (German) ruler of the estate, a form of Henry.

Hanley (English) from the high meadow.
Hanlea, Hanlee, Hanleigh, Hanlie, Hanly, Henlea, Henlee, Henleigh, Henley, Henlie, Henly

Hannibal (Phoenician) grace of God.
Anibel, Hanibal, Hannybal, Hanybal

Hans (Scandinavian) God is gracious, a form of John.
Hanschen, Hansel, Hants, Hanz

Hansel (Scandinavian) God is gracious, a form of Hans.
Haensel, Hansell, Hansl, Hanzel, Hanzell

Hanuman (Hindu) monkey god.
Hanumant

Hara (Hindu) seizer, the destroyer, a name for the god Siva, a unisex name.
Harra

Harald (Scandinavian) great leader of the army, a form of Harold.
Haraldo, Haralds, Harapos, Harold

Harb (Arabic) warrior.

Harbin (German) bright little warrior.
Harban, Harben, Harbon, Harbyn

Harcourt (Anglo-Saxon) hawker's cottage; (French) fortified, armed dwelling.
Cort, Cours, Harcort, Harcorte, Harcourte

Harden (English) from the hare valley.
Hardan, Hardie, Hardian, Hardin, Harding, Hardon, Hardun, Hardy, Hardyn

Harding (English) resolute son of a hero.
Hardin

Hardwin (English) brave friend.
Hardwen, Hardwenn, Hardwinn, Hardwyn, Hardwynn

Hardy (German) brave hero, courageous.
Hardee, Hardi, Hardie

Hare (Maori) manly, strong, a form of Charles.

Harel (Hebrew) mountain of God.
Harell, Hariel, Hariell, Harrel, Harrell, Harriel, Harriell, Haryel, Haryell

Harford (English) ford of the hares.
Hareford

Hargrove (English) grove of hares.
Haregrove, Hargreave, Hargreaves

Hari (Hindu) tawny.
Hariel, Harin

Harith (Arabic) ploughman, cultivator.
Haryth

Harkin (Irish) dark red.

Harkan, Harken, Harkon, Harkyn

Harlan (Anglo-Saxon) from the hare or stag meadow.
Harland, Harlen, Harlend, Harlenn, Harlin, Harlind, Harlon, Harlond, Harlyn, Harlynd, Harlynn

Harley (English) of the hare or stag meadow, a unisex name.
Arley, Arly, Harlea, Harlee, Harleigh, Harlie, Harly

Harlow (English) battle hill.
Arlo, Arlow, Harlo

Harmon (German) man of the army.
Harm, Harman, Harmen, Harmond, Harms

Harold (Scandinavian) great leader of the army.
Arald, Araldo, Hal, Harald, Haraldo, Hari, Harie, Haroldo, Harri, Harrie, Harrold, Harry, Hary, Hassa, Haz, Hazza, Herold, Heronim, Herrick, Herryk

Haroun (Arabic) lofty, exalted.
Haarun, Harin, Haron, Harron, Harun

Harper (English) harp player or maker, a unisex name.
Harp, Harpa, Harpo

Harpreet (Punjabi) devoted to God, a unisex name.
Hardee, Hardeep, Harpee, Harpreete, Harprit, Harprite

Harrington (English) from Harry's town.
Harringtown

Harris (English) son of Harry, a form of Harrison.
Haris, Harrys, Harys, Heris, Herris, Herrys, Herys

Harrison (English) son of Harry.
*Haris, Harison, Harris, Harryson,
Haryson*

Harrod (Hebrew) conquering hero.
Harod

Harry (English) great leader of the
army, a form of Harold.
*Harey, Hari, Harie, Harrey, Harri,
Harrie, Hary*

Harshad (Hindu) joy giver.

Hart (English) deer meadow, a
form of Hartley.
Harte, Hartley, Hartlie

Hartford (English) from the hare's
ford.
Hartforde

Hartley (English) deer meadow.
*Hartlea, Hartlee, Hartleigh, Harlie,
Hartly*

Hartman (German) big, strong.
Hartmen

Hartwood (English) deer forest.
Harwood, Woodie, Woody

Haru (Japanese) born in the spring.
Harue

Harun (Arabic) praised highly.
Haroun

Harvey (German) army warrior.
*Harv, Harvay, Harve, Harvie, Harvy,
Hervay, Herve, Hervey, Hervie,
Hervy*

Hasad (Turkish) harvester.
Hassad

Hasan (Arabic) beautiful, good.
*Haasan, Hasaan, Hasaun,
Hashaan, Hashan, Hason, Hassan*

Hasani (African) handsome.
*Hasan, Hasanni, Hasen, Haseni,
Hassan, Hassani, Hassanni, Hassen,
Hassian, Husan, Husani, Hussan,
Hussani*

Hashim (Arabic) destroyer of evil.
*Haashim, Hasham, Hasheem,
Hashem*

Hasin (Hindu) laughing.
*Haseen, Hasen, Hassin, Hazen,
Hazin, Hesen*

Haskel (Hebrew) God is mighty,
God strengthens, a form of Ezekiel.
Haske, Haskell

Haslett (English) from the hazel
tree.
*Hasel, Haslet, Haslit, Haslitt, Haze,
Hazel, Hazlet, Hazlett, Hazlit, Hazlitt*

Hassan (Arabic) beautiful,
handsome.
*Hasan, Hasen, Hason, Hassen,
Hasson*

Hassel (English) witches' corner.
Hasel, Hasell, Hassell

Hastin (Hindu) elephant.
Hastan, Hasten, Hastyn

Hastings (German) swift one;
(Latin) spear.
Hastie, Hasty

Hatim (Arabic) judge.
Hateem, Hatem

Hauk (Scandinavian) hawk.
*Hauke, Haukly, Hawk, Hawke,
Hawkeye, Hawleigh, Hawly*

Havelock (Scandinavian) battle
at sea.
*Haveloc, Haveloch, Havloche,
Havlocke, Havelok, Haveloke*

Haven (English) refuge, a safe place, a unisex name.
Haeven, Hagan, Hevan, Hevin, Hevon, Hogan

Havika (Hawaiian) beloved, a form of David.
Havyka

Hawley (English) from the hedged meadow.
Hawlea, Hawleah, Hawlee, Hawleigh, Hawli, Hawlie, Hawly

Hawthorne (English) hawthorn tree.
Hawthorn

Hayden (English) valley with hedges.
Haydan, Haydann, Haydenn, Haydin, Haydinn, Haydyn, Haydynn, Heydan, Heyden, Heydin, Heydyn, Heydon, Heydyn

Hayes (Irish) valley with hedges.
Hais, Haise, Haiz, Haize, Hays, Hayse, Hayze

Haytham (Arabic) proud.
Haitham

Hayward (German) hedged wood.
Haward, Hawood, Haywood, Heyward, Heywood

Heath (English) heath.
Heathe, Heith, Hethe

Heathcliff (English) cliff with heather, the hero of Emily Brontë's novel *Wuthering Heights*.
Heathclif, Heathcliffe, Heathclyf, Heathclyff, Heathclyffe

Heber (Hebrew) partner, associate.
Hebar, Hebber, Hebe

Hector (Greek) anchor, steadfast.
Hecktar, Heckter, Hecktir, Hecktor, Hecktore, Hectar, Hectir, Hectore, Hektar, Hekter, Hektir, Hektor, Hektore

Heddwyn (Welsh) friend of blessed peace.
Heddwen, Heddwenn, Heddwin, Heddwinn, Heddwynn, Hedwen, Hedwenn, Hedwin, Hedwinn, Hedwyn, Hedwynn

Hedley (English) heather filled meadow.
Headley, Headly, Hedly

Hedwig (German) fighter, warrior, a unisex name.
Heddvig, Heddvyg, Heddwig, Heddwyg, Hedvig, Hedvyg, Hedwyg

Heinrich (German) ruler of the household, a form of Henry.
Heiandric, Heiandrick, Heiandrik, Heiner, Heinreich, Heinric, Heinrick, Heinrik, Henric, Henrich, Henrick, Henrik, Hinrich

Heinz (German) ruler of the household, a form of Henry.

Helaku (Native American) sunny day.

Helge (Russian) holy.
Helg

Heli (Greek) sun.
Helli, Helly, Hely

Helier (Latin) happy.
Hellier

Helki (Native American) touch.

Helmut (German) famous courage.
Hellmut, Hellmuth, Helmuth

Heman (Hebrew) faithful.
Hemen, Herman, Hermen

Hemi (Maori) the supplanter, a form of James.

Henderson (English) son of Henry.
Hendrie, Hendries, Hendron, Henrison, Henryson

Hendrick (Dutch, German) ruler of the house, a form of Henry.
Hendrich, Hendricks, Hendrik, Hendriks, Hendrikus, Hendrix, Heniek, Henier, Henning

Henoch (Hebrew) initiator.
Enoch, Henoc, Henock, Henok

Henri (French) ruler of the house, a form of Henry.
Henrie, Henrik

Henry (German) ruler of the house.
Hank, Heike, Heinrich, Heinz, Hendrick, Henery, Heniek, Henning, Henraoi, Henri, Henrich, Henrick, Henrim, Henrique, Henroi, Henrry, Heromin, Hersz

Hepetipa (Maori) one of the Maori prophets.

Herb (German) excellent soldier, a form of Herbert.
Herbe, Herbee, Herbi, Herbie, Herby

Herbert (German) excellent soldier, great warrior.
Bert, Erbert, Erberto, Erbirt, Erbirto, Eburt, Eburto, Harbert, Hebert, Heberto, Hebet, Herb, Herberto, Herbie, Herby, Hurbert, Hurberto

Hercules (Latin, Greek) glorious gift of strength, a Greek hero.
Heracles, Herakles, Herc, Hercule, Herculie, Herculies

Heremon (Irish) handsome, fair; (English) friend of the sea, boar friend; (Welsh) green river, a form of Irving.

Herman (German) warrior; (Latin) noble.
Harmon, Hermaan, Hermann, Hermie, Hermin, Hermino, Hermon, Hermy, Heromin

Hermes (Greek) messenger of the gods in Greek mythology.

Hernando (Spanish) prepared for the journey, an adventurer or traveller, a form of Ferdinand.
Herandes, Herandez, Hernades, Hernadez, Hernado, Hernandes, Hernandez

Herod (Greek) protector.
Harod, Harrod, Herrod

Herric (German) army chief.
Herrick, Herrik

Herschel (Hebrew) deer.
Hersch, Herschell, Hirsch, Hirschel, Hirschell

Hertz (Hebrew) my strife.
Herzel

Hesperos (Greek) evening star.
Hespero

Hew (Welsh) bright mind, bright spirit, a form of Hugh.
Hewe, Hewey, Hewie, Hewy, Huw, Huwe, Huwey, Huwie

Hewney (Irish) green like the fields.
Hewnee, Hewni, Hewnie, Hewny, Huenee, Hueney, Hueni, Huenie, Hueny

Hezekiah (Hebrew) God gives strength.
Ezekiah, Hazikia, Hazikiah, Hazz, Hazzie, Hezekia, Hezekya,

Hezekyah, Hezikya, Hezikyah, Hezz, Hezzie

Hiamovi (Native American) high chief.

Hiatt (English) from the high gate.
Hiat, Hiatte, Hyat, Hyatt, Hyatte

Hiawatha (Native American) river creator, a unisex name.
Hyawatha

Hibah (Arabic) gift, a unisex name.
Hiba, Hibab, Hyba, Hybah

Hideaka (Japanese) smart, clever.
Hedeaka, Hideeka, Hideo

Hieu (Vietnamese) respectful.
Hyeu

Hilary (Latin) cheerful, a unisex name.
Haillery, Hallarius, Hi, Hilair, Hilairy, Hilarey, Hilarie, Hilario, Hillaire, Hillary, Hille, Hillerie, Hillery, Hilliary, Hillie

Hildebrand (German) battle-sword.
Hildebrande, Hildo, Hildobrand, Hildobrande

Hilel (Arabic) new moon.
Hylel

Hillel (Hebrew) greatly praised and acclaimed.
Hilel, Hylel, Hyllel

Hilliard (German) war guardian.
Hilard, Hiliard, Hilier, Hilierd, Hillard, Hille, Hiller, Hillier, Hillierd, Hillyer, Hilyer

Hilmar (Swedish) noble, famous.
Hillmar, Hyllmer, Hylmer

Hilton (English) town on the hill.
Hilten, Hylten, Hylton

Hinto (Native American) blue.
Hineen, Hinin, Hintin, Hinton, Hintun, Hinun

Hinun (Native American) spirit of the storm.
Hynun

Hippocrates (Greek) ancient Greek physician after whom the Hippocratic Oath is named.

Hiram (Hebrew) noble, exalted.
Hi, Hirom, Hirum, Hyram, Hyrom, Hyrum

Hiroshi (Japanese) generous.
Hyroshi

Hisham (Arabic) generosity.

Hisoka (Japanese) reserved and shy.
Hysoka

Hiu (Hawaiian) bright mind, bright spirit, a form of Hugh.
Hyu

Ho (Chinese) goodness.

Hoang (Vietnamese) final one, finished.

Hobart (German) Bart's hill, bright of mind, bright of spirit, a form of Hubert.
Bart, Hob, Hobard, Hobb, Hobbard, Hobbart, Hobbie, Hobby, Hobie, Hobey, Hoebard, Hoebart

Hobson (English) son of Robert.
Hob, Hobb, Hobbs, Hobbson, Hobs

Hoc (Vietnamese) studious.
Hock, Hok

Hoffman (German) one who influences.
Hoffmen, Hofman, Hofmen

Hogan (Irish) young.
Haegan, Haegen, Hogean, Hogen, Hogin, Hogyn

Holbrook (English) valley brook.
Brook, Brooke, Holbrooke

Holden (English) hollow in the valley.
Holdan, Holdin, Holdon, Holdun, Holdyn

Holic (Czech) barber.
Holick, Holik, Holyc, Holyck, Holyk

Hollace (English) near the valley.
Hollice, Hollis

Hollis (English) holly tree, a unisex name.
Holice, Holise, Hollie, Holliss, Holisse, Holly, Hollys, Hollyse, Hollyss, Hollysse

Holmes (English) island by the river.
Holm, Holme, Holms

Holt (English) from the forest.
Hol, Holtan, Holten, Holtin, Holton, Holtyn

Homer (Greek) pledge, promise, the name of an ancient Greek poet.
Homa, Homar

Hondo (African) warrior.

Honi (Hebrew) gracious.
Chonee, Choni, Honee

Honon (Native American) bear.
Honnon

Honore (Latin) honoured.
Honner, Honnor, Honnore, Honnour, Honnoure, Honor, Honoray, Honorio, Honorius, Honour, Honoure

Honovi (Native American) strength.

Honza (Czech) God is gracious, a form of John.

Hop (Chinese) agreeable.

Hopkin (English) son of Robert.
Hopkins

Horace (Latin) keeper of the clock, timekeeper.
Horacio, Horatio, Horatius, Horazio, Oratio, Orazio, Orocio

Horst (German) leap, thicket.
Horstt

Horton (Latin) gardener.
Hartan, Horten, Hortin, Hortun, Hortyn

Horus (Egyptian) god of the sky.
Horrus, Horuss

Hosea (Hebrew) salvation.
Hose, Hoseah, Hoseia, Hoseiah, Hoshea, Hosheah, Hosheia, Hosheiah

Hotah (Native American) white.
Hota

Hoto (Native American) whistler.
Hototo

Houston (English) Hugh's town, the hill town.
Houstan, Housten, Houstin, Houstun, Houstyn, Hustan, Husten, Hustin, Huston, Hustun, Hustyn

Howard (English) guardian, watchman.
Howerd, Howie, Ward

Howe (German) of high birth, distinguished.
Howey, Howi, Howie, Howy

Howell (Welsh) eminent, bright, alert.
Hoel, Hoell, Howal, Howall, Howel, Hywel, Hywell

Howi (Native American) dove.
Howee, Howey, Howie, Howy

Howin (Chinese) loyal swallow.

Hu (Chinese) tiger.
Hugh, Huh, Hulah

Hua (Chinese) flower, a unisex name.
Huah

Huatare (Maori) a famous chief.

Hubert (German) bright mind, bright spirit.
Bert, Hobart, Hubard, Hubart, Hubbard, Hubbart, Hubbert, Hube, Huber, Huberto, Hubi, Hubie, Huey, Hugh, Huibert, Humbert, Humberto

Hud (Arabic) one of the prophets.
Houd

Hugh (English, German) bright mind, bright spirit, a form of Hubert.
Hew, Hewe, Hu, Hughe, Hughey, Hughie, Hughs, Hughy, Hui

Hugo (Latin) bright mind, bright spirit, a form of Hugh.
Ugo

Hula (Native American) eagle.
Hulah

Humam (Arabic) courageous, generous.

Humbert (German) brilliant, strong giant.
Hum, Humbart, Humberto, Humbirt, Humburt, Humbyrt, Umbert, Umberto

Hume (German) home-lover.
Huime

Humphrey (German) peaceful protector of the home.
Hum, Humfery, Humfredo, Humfrey, Humfrid, Humfried, Humfry, Hump, Humph, Humphery, Humphries, Humphry, Onofrio, Onufry

Hung (Vietnamese) brave.

Hunter (English) huntsman, a unisex name.
Hunt, Hunte, Huntingdon, Huntington, Huntlea, Huntlee, Huntley, Huntly, Huntter, Huntur

Hurley (Irish) tide; (English) clearing.
Hurlee, Hurleigh, Hurlie

Husam (Arabic) sword.
Hussam

Hush (Hebrew) quick.

Huslu (Native American) hairy bear.

Husni (Arabic) beauty.

Hussein (Arabic) little handsome one.
Hasien, Hassein, Hosein, Hossein, Housien, Houssein, Husayn, Husein, Husian, Husien, Husin, Huss, Hussain, Hussayn, Hussien, Hussin

Hute (Native American) star.

Huxley (English) Hugh's meadow.
Hux, Huxlea, Huxlee, Huxleigh, Huxli, Huxlie, Huxly

Huy (Vietnamese) glorious.

Hy (Vietnamese) hopeful.
Hi, Hye

Hyatt (English) from the high gate.
Hiat, Hiatt, Hiatte, Hyat, Hyatte

Hyde (English) a measurement of land.

Hyder (English) tanner of animal hides.
Hide, Hider, Hyde

Hyman (Hebrew) life.
Haim, Hayim, Hyam

Hywel (Welsh) eminent, bright, alert, a form of Howell.
Hywell

I

Iago (Spanish) replacer, supplanter, a form of James, Jacob.
Jago

Iain (Scottish) God is gracious, a form of Ian.
Iaine

Iakobos (Greek) replacer, supplanter, a form of Jacob.
Iakob, Iakobas, Jakov, Jakovas, Jakovos, Jakovs

Iakona (Hawaiian) healer.
Iakina, Iakinah, Iakonah

Ian (Scottish) God is gracious, a form of John.
Iain, Iaine, Iane, Iann, Ianne

Ianos (Czech) God is gracious, a form of John.
Ianis, Iannis, Iannos

Iban (Basque) God is gracious, a form of John.
Eban, Ebon, Evan, Evon, Ibon, Ivan, Ivon

Ibrahim (Arabic) father of the multitudes, founder of the Hebrew people, a form of Abraham.
Abraham, Abriheim, Ibrahaim, Ibraham, Ibraheem, Ibrahem, Ibrahiim, Ibrahmim, Ibram, Ibrehaim, Ibreham, Ibreheem, Ibrehem, Ibrehiim, Ibrehim, Ibrehmim, Ibrem

Ibsen (German) archer's son.
Ibsan, Ibsin, Ibson, Ibsyn

Ichabod (Hebrew) glory has departed.
Icabod

Ichiro (Japanese) first-born child.

Iden (Anglo-Saxon) wooded pasture.
Idan, Idin, Idon, Idun, Idyn

Idi (African) born during the festival.
Iddi

Idris (Arabic) one of the prophets; (Welsh) fiery, eager lord, a unisex name.
Idreas, Idrease, Idrees, Idres, Idreus, Idriece, Idriss, Idryis, Idrys

Idwal (Welsh) lord of the wall or rampart.
Idwall

Iestin/Iestyn (Welsh) just, fair, a form of Justin.
Iustin, Iusten

Ievan (Welsh) God is gracious, a form of John.
Evan, Ieuan, Owen

Igasho (Native American) traveller, wanderer, seeker.
Igashu

Iggi (African) only son.
Iggey, Iggie, Iggy

Iggy (Greek) fiery, a form of Ignatius.
Iggey, Iggi, Iggie

Ignatius (Greek) fiery.
Iggie, Iggy, Ignac, Ignace, Ignacio,

Ignacius, Ignasco, Ignatio, Ignatios, Ignatz, Ignaz, Ignazio, Ignazios, Iganazius, Nat, Nate

Igor (Norse, Russian) hero.
Igner, Ignor, Igorok, Ingvar, Yegor, Ygor

Ihorangi (Polynesian) rain.
Rangi

Ihsan (Arabic) benevolence, charity.
Isan

Ike (Hebrew) he laughes, a form of Isaac.
Ikee, Ikey, Iki, Ikie, Iky, Isaac

Ilan (Hebrew) tree.
Iilan

Ilar (Welsh) cheerful, a form of Hilary.
Hilar, Hillar, Ilary, Illar, Illary

Ilbert (German) distinguished warrior.
Ilberto, Ilbirt, Ilbirto, Ilburt, Ilburto, Ilbryt, Ilbyrto

Ilias (Latin) the Lord is my God, a form of Elijah.
Elias, Ellias, Ellyas, Elyas, Illias, Illyas, Illyes, Ilyas, Ilyes

Ilom (African) he has many enemies.
Illom

Ilya (Russian) the Lord is my God, a form of Elijah.
Ilia, Ilie, Ilja, Illia, Illie, Ilja, Illya

Imad (Arabic) support, pillar.
Imaad, Imaed

Imam (Indonesian) religious leader.
Immam

Iman (Hebrew) God is with us, a form of Emmanuel.
Imani, Imann, Imanni

Imbert (German) poet.
Imbirt, Imburt, Imbryt

Immanuel (Hebrew) God is with us, a form of Emmanuel.
Iman, Imanol, Imanual, Imanuel, Immanual, Immanuale, Immanuele, Immuneal

Imran (Arabic) host.
Imraan, Emran

Imre (German) industrious ruler, a form of Emery.
Imer

Imri (Hebrew) tall.
Imric, Imrie, Imry

Inay (Hindu) godlike.

Ince (Hungarian) innocent.

Incencio (Spanish) white.
Incencios, Incencius

Inder (Hindu) godlike.
Inderbir, Inderji, Inderjit, Inderpal, Inderveer, Indervir, Indra, Indradeer, Indradir, Indraji, Indrajit

Indiana (Hindu) from India.
Indi, Indy, Indyana

Indra (Hindu) god of the firmament.
Indrah

Inek (Welsh) handsome, a form of Irving.
Innek

Inger (Norse) son's army.
Ingar

Inglebert (German) bright like an angel.

Engelbert, Engelberte, Engelberto, Engelbirt, Engelbirte, Engelbirto, Engelburt, Engelburte, Engelburto, Engelbyrt, Englebert, Engleberte, Engleberto, Englebirt, Englebirte, Englebirto, Engleburt, Engleburte, Engleburto, Englebyrt, Ingelbert, Ingelberte, Ingelberto, Ingelbirt, Ingelbirte, Ingelbirto, Ingelburt, Ingelburte, Ingelburto, Ingelbyrt, Ingleberte, Ingleberto, Inglebirt, Inglebirte, Inglebirto, Ingleburt, Ingleburte, Ingleburto, Inglebyrt

Inglis (Scottish) English.

Ingliss, Inglys, Inglyss

Ingmar (Scandinavian) famous son, Ing's son.

Ingar, Ingemar, Inger, Inmar

Ingram (English) angel.

Inglis, Ingra, Ingrim

Inigo (Greek) fiery, a form of Ingnatius.

Inaki, Inego, Iniego, Innego, Innigo

Inir (Welsh) honourable.

Innir

Innes (Celtic) island; (Scottish) strength, a unisex name.

Inness, Innis, Inniss

Innocent (Latin) harmless, innocent.

Innocente, Innocenti, Innocentio, Innocenty, Innosente, Innosenti, Innosentio, Inocente, Inocenti, Inocentio, Inosente, Inosenti, Inusentio

Inteus (Native American) no shame.

Iokia (Hawaiian) healed by God.

Iokiah, Iokya

Ioakim (Russian) God will establish, a form of Joachim.

Ioachem, Ioachim, Ioane, Ioanes, Ioanis, Ioaniss, Ioanne, Ioannes, Ionel, Ionne, Joachim

Iokepa (Hawaiian) God shall increase, a form of Joseph.

Iokeo, Keo, Kepa

Iolo (Welsh) worthy lord.

Iolyn (Welsh) handsome lord.

Iolin, Iolo, Iorweth

Ion (Romanian) God is gracious, a form of John; (Greek) moon man.

Ionakana (Hawaiian) gift of God, a form of Jonathon.

Iosif (Russian) God shall increase, a form of Joseph.

Iosef, Ioseph, Iosiph

Ipyana (African) graceful.

Ira (Hebrew) watchful, a unisex name.

Irah

Iram (English) shining bright.

Irram

Irfan (Arabic) thankfulness.

Irmin (German) strong.

Irman, Irmen, Irmun, Irmyn

Irving (English) handsome.

Erving, Irv, Irvin, Irvine, Irwin, Irwine, Irwing

Irwin (English) handsome, a form of Irving.

Irwine, Irwinn, Irwyn

Isa (Hindu) lord; (Hebrew) God is my salvation, a form of Isaiah.

Eisa, Eisia, Eisiah, Isaa, Isaah, Issia, Issiah

Isaac (Hebrew) he laughs, son of Abraham.

Aizak, Aizik, Icek, Ike, Ikey, Ikie, Isaack, Isaaco, Isaak, Isaakio, Isaakios, Isaic, Isiacc, Ishaq, Issac, Issie, Itzac, Itzak, Izaac, Izaak, Izac, Izak, Izzie, Izzy

Isaiah (Hebrew) God is my salvation.

Isa, Isai, Isaia, Isaid, Isaih, Isais, Isaish, Isaya, Isayah, Ishaiah, Ishaq, Isia, Isiah, Issiah, Izahia, Izaia, Izaiah, Izaya, Izayha, Izayiah, Izeyah, Izeyha

Isam (Arabic) safeguard.

Isaam, Issam

Isambard (Greek) iron giant.

Isambart

Isas (Japanese) meritorious.

Isham (English) home of the iron one.

Isam

Ishan (Hindu) direction.

Isan, Isaun, Ishaan, Ishaun

Ishaq (Arabic) he laughs, a form of Isaac.

Isaak, Isak, Isaq, Ishaak, Ishak

Ishmael (Hebrew) the Lord listens.

Ishail, Ishamail, Ishma, Ishmail, Ishmale, Ishmeal, Ishmeil, Ishmel, Isail, Isamail, Isma, Ismael, Ismail, Ismeal, Ismeil, Ismel, Ismil

Isidore (Greek) gift of Isis.

Isador, Isadore, Isidor, Issy, Ixidor, Izador, Izadore, Izydor, Izzy

Ismail (Arabic) the Lord listens, a form of Ishmael.

Ismael

Israel (Hebrew) prince of God.

Isreal, Isrell, Isser, Issie, Izrael, Rael, Raelph, Yisrael, Ysrael

Issa (African) God is our salvation.

Istu (Native American) sugar pine.

Istvan (Hungarian) crowned, a form of Stephen.

Isti

Itamar (Hebrew) palm grove island.

Ittamar

Itzak (Hebrew) he laughs, a form of Isaac.

Itzac, Yitzac, Yitzak, Ytzac, Ytzak

Iukini (Hawaiian) well-born, noble, a form of Eugene.

Kini

Ivan (Russian) God is gracious, a form of John.

Iban, Ibhan, Iben, Iv, Iva, Ivanchik, Ivann, Ivano, Ivas, Iven, Ivhan, Ivin, Ivyn, Yban, Yvan

Ivar (Scandinavian) archer.

Ivan, Iven, Iver, Ives, Ivey, Ivon, Ivor, Yvan, Yvar, Yven, Yver, Yvey, Yvon, Yvor

Ivo (German) archer, a form of Yves.

Ives, Ivon, Ivor, Yves, Yvon, Yvor

Iye (Native American) smoke.

Iy

Izak (Czech) he laughs, a form of Isaac.

Itzhak, Itzhik, Izik, Izsak, Izzak

Izod (Irish) fair.
Izad, Ized, Izid, Izyd

Izzy (Hebrew) he laughs, a form of Isaac.
Isi, Isie, Issi, Issie, Issy, Isy, Izi, Izie, Izy, Izzi, Izzie

J

Ja (Korean) magnetic, attractive personality.
Jah

Jaafar (African) small river.
Ja'far, Jafar, Jafari, Jaffar, Jaffari, Jaffer, Jafur

Jaali (African) powerful.
Jali

Jaan (Estonian) follower of the prophet Jesus, a Christian.
Jan

Jaap (Dutch) supplanter, a form of Jim.
Jape

Jabari (African) brave, fearless.
Jabaar, Jabaari, Jabahri, Jabar, Jabarae, Jabaree, Jabarei, Jabarie, Jabarri, Jabarrie, Jabbaer, Jabbar, Jabbari, Jabier, Jaboori, Jabore, Jabori

Jabbar (Arabic) mighty repairer.
Jaba, Jabar, Jabba

Jabez (Hebrew) born in sorrow.
Jabe, Jabes, Jabesh

Jabilo (African) medicine man.

Jabin (Hebrew) God has created.
Jabain, Jaban, Jabien, Jabon, Jabyn

Jabir (Arabic) consoler, comforter.
Jabiri, Jabori, Jabyr

Jabril (Arabic) mighty archangel.
Jabral, Jabrail, Jabree, Jabreel, Jabrel, Jabrell, Jabrelle, Jabri, Jabrie, Jabriel, Jabriell, Jabrielle, Jabrile, Jabrill, Jabrille

Jabulani (African) happy.

Jacan (Hebrew) trouble.
Jachan, Jachin, Jacin

Jace (American) healer, a form of Jason, combination of the initials J and C.
Jaaicee, JC, Jacee, Jacey, Jaice, Jaicee

Jacinto (Portuguese) lovely, beautiful, colourful flower with fragrance, a form of Hyacinth, masculine form of Jacinta.
Jacind, Jacindo, Jacint, Jacynd, Jacyndo, Jacynt, Jacynto

Jack (English) God is gracious, a form of John, supplanter, a form of James.
Jaac, Jaack, Jaak, Jac, Jacke, Jacko, Jak, Jake, Jakk, Jakke, James, John, Jon, Jonathon

Jackson (English) son of Jack.
Jackman, Jakman, Jakson

Jacob (Hebrew) the supplanter, a form of James.
Iacob, Iakob, Jaacob, Jaap, Jachob, Jachub, Jack, Jackob, Jackub, Jaco, Jocob, Jacobb, Jacobe, Jacobi, Jacobie, Jacobo, Jacoby, Jacolbi, Jacolbie, Jacolby, Jacques, Jacub, Jaecob, Jago, Jaicob, Jaime, Jalu, Jake, Jako, Jakob, Jakov, Jasha, Jaycob, Jecis, Jeks, Jeska, Jim, Jimmy, Jocek, Jock, Jokubas, Yacob, Yakob

Jacobson (English) son of Jacob.
Jacobsen, Jakobsen, Jakobson

Jacorey (American) combination of Jacob and Corey.

Jacari, Jacarie, Jacori, Jacoria, Jacorie, Jacorien, Jacoris, Jacorrey, Jacorrie, Jacorrien, Jacorry, Jacoruis, Jacory, Jacouri, Jacourie, Jakari, Jakaria

Jacques (French) God is gracious, a form of John, supplanter, a form of James.

Jackque, Jackques, Jackquese, Jacot, Jacquan, Jacque, Jacquees, Jacquese, Jacquess, Jacquet, Jacquett, Jacquez, Jacqui, Jacquis, Jacquise, Jacqyuay, Jaquez, Jaqueze, Jaqueuz, Jaqueuze, Jaquiz, Jaquize, Jarquz, Jaquze, Jarque, Jarques, Jarquis, Jocque, Jocques, Jocquez, Jocqui, Joqueuz, Joqueuze, Joquez, Joqueze, Joquiz, Joquize, Joquz, Joquze

Jacy (Native American) moon.

Jace, Jacee, Jacey, Jaci, Jacie, Jaece, Jaecee, Jaecey, Jaeci, Jaecie, Jaecy, Jaice, Jaicee, Jaicey, Jaici, Jaicie, Jaicy, Jayce, Jaycee, Jaycey, Jayci, Jaycie, Jaycy

Jade (Spanish) green gemstone, jade, a unisex name.

Jaed, Jaeid, Jaid, Jaide, Jayd, Jayde

Jaden (Hebrew) God has heard.

Jadee, Jadeen, Jadeenn, Jadenn, Jadeon, Jadin, Jadine, Jadinn, Jadon, Jadone, Jadonn, Jadyn, Jadyne, Jadynn, Jaeden, Jaedenn, Jaedin, Jaedine, Jaedinn, Jaedon, Jaedone, Jaedonn, Jaedyn, Jaedyne, Jaedynn, Jaiden, Jaidenn, Jaidin, Jaidine, Jaidinn, Jaidon, Jaidone, Jaidonn, Jaidyn, Jaidyne, Jaidynn, Jayden, Jaydenn, Jaydin, Jaydine, Jaydinn, Jaydon, Jaydone, Jaydonn, Jaydyn, Jaydyne, Jaydynn

Jadrien (American) combination of Jay and Adrien.

Jad, Jada, Jadar, Jadd, Jader, Jadrian

Jaegar (German) hunter.

Jaagar, Jaager, Jaagur, Jaeger, Jaegur, Yaegar, Yaeger, Yaegur

Jaehwa (Korean) rich, prosperous.

Jae-Hwa, Jae-Hwaa, Jaehwaa

Jael (Hebrew) mountain goat, a unisex name.

Jaele, Jaell, Jaelle, Yael, Yaele

Jafar (Hindu) a little stream.

Ja'far, Ja'Far, Jaffar

Jagger (English) carter, teamster.

Jaggar, Jagar, Jager

Jago (Australian Aboriginal) complete.

Jaguar (Spanish) jaguar.

Jagguar, Jagguare, Jaguare

Jahan (Hindu) world.

Jahi (African) man of dignity.

Jahee

Jai (Thai) heart; (Hebrew) God has enlightened.

Jae, Jaie, Jaii, Jay

Jaiden (Hebrew) God has heard, a form of Jaden.

Jaedan, Jaeden, Jaedev, Jaedin, Jaedon, Jaedyn, Jaidan, Jaider, Jaidin, Jaidon, Jaidyn, Jaydan, Jayden, Jaydev, Jaydin, Jaydon, Jaydyn

Jaidev (Hindu) victory.

Jaedev, Jaydev

Jaimini (Hindu) victory.

Jaemin, Jaemini, Jaimin, Jaymin, Jaymini

Jair (Hebrew) God enlightens, a form of Jairo.

Jairus, Jayr

Jairo (Spanish) God enlightens.

Jair, Jairas, Jairo, Jairos, Jairus, Jarius, Jaro, Jayr, Jayro, Jayrus

Jaja (African) honoured.

Jajah

Jake (Hebrew) supplanter, a form of Jacob, James.

Jaacob, Jacob, Jaek, Jaeke, Jaik, Jaike, Jakob, James, Jaycob, Jayk, Jayke

Jakeem (Arabic) uplifted.

Jakeam, Jakim

Jakome (Basque) supplanter, a form of James.

Jakom

Jal (Gypsy) wanderer.

Jall

Jalal (Arabic) glorious, majestic.

Jahlaal, Jahlal, Jalaal, Jallal

Jalil (Hindu) god, godlike.

Jahlaal, Jahlaall, Jahlal, Jahlall, Jahlee, Jahleel, Jahleell, Jahleil, Jahleill, Jahlel, Jahlell, Jahliel, Jahlil, Jalaal, Jalaall, Jalal, Jalall, Jalee, Jaleel, Jaleell, Jaleil, Jaleill, Jalel, Jalell, Jaliel

Jalon (Hebrew) one who dwells.

Jaelan, Jaeleen, Jaelein, Jaelen, Jaelene, Jaelin, Jaellen, Jaelon, Jaelone, Jaeloni, Jaelun, Jaelyn, Jailan, Jaileen, Jailein, Jailen, Jailene, Jailin, Jaillen, Jailon, Jailone, Jailoni, Jailun, Jailyn, Jalan, Jaleen, Jalein, Jalen, Jalene, Jalin, Jallen, Jalone, Jaloni, Jalun, Jalyn, Jaolan, Jaoleen, Jaolein, Jaolen, Jaolene, Jaolin, Jaollen, Jaolon, Jaolone, Jaolun, Jaolyn, Jaylan, Jayleen, Jaylein, Jaylen, Jaylene,

Jaylin, Jayllen, Jaylon, Jaylone, Jayloni, Jaylun, Jaylyn

Jamaine (Arabic, French) from Germany, a form of Germain.

Jamain, Jamayn, Jamayne

Jamal (Arabic) handsome, beautiful.

Jahmaal, Jahmael, Jahmahl, Jahmail, Jahmaile, Jahmal, Jahmale, Jahmall, Jahmalle, Jahmar, Jahmaul, Jahmeel, Jahmel, Jahmele, Jahmell, Jahmelle, Jahmill, Jahmmal, Jahmmel, Jahmor, Jahmual, Jahmuel, Jahmul, Jamaal, Jamael, Jamahl, Jamail, Jamaile, Jamale, Jamall, Jamalle, Jamar, Jamaul, Jameel, Jamel, Jamele, Jamell, Jamelle, Jamill, Jammal, Jammel, Jamor, Jamual, Jamuel, Jamul, Jarmaal, Jarmael, Jarmahl, Jarmal, Jarmel, Jaumal, Jaumell, Jehmal, Jemal, Jermal, Jhimell, Jimell, Johmal, Johmall, Jomal, Jomall

Jamar (Arabic, American) handsome.

Jahmaar, Jahmaari, Jahmahrae, Jahmair, Jahmar, Jahmara, Jahmaras, Jahmaraus, Jahmare, Jahmari, Jahmarl, Jahmarr, Jahmarre, Jahmarrea, Jahmarri, Jahmarvis, Jahmaur, Jahmer, Jahmir, Jahmire, Jahmiree, Jahmmar, Jahmmarree, Jahrmar, Jahrmarr, Jahumar, Jamaar, Jamaari, Jamahrae, Jamair, Jamara, Jamaras, Jamaraus, Jamare, Jamari, Jamarl, Jamarr, Jamarre, Jamarrea, Jamarri, Jamarvis, Jamaur, Jamer, Jamir, Jamire, Jamiree, Jammar, Jammarree, Jarmar, Jarmarr, Jaumar, Jehmaar, Jehmar, Jemaar, Jemar, Jihmar, Jimar, Johmar, Jomar

James (Hebrew) supplanter, an English monarch, one of the apostles in the New Testament.

Dago, Diego, Gaymes, Giacobbe, Giacopo, Giacomo, Hamish, Iachamo, Iachimo, Iachomo, Iago, Jaa, Jaako, Jack, Jackson, Jaemes, Jagli, Jago, Jahu, Jaime, Jaimee, Jaimes, Jaimey, Jaimie, Jaimito, Jaimse, Jaimy, Jakab, Jakez, Jakobus, Jakome, Jakov, Jalm, Jameal, Jameel, Jamelia, Jamese, Jamesie, Jamesy, Jameyel, Jamez, Jameze, Jami, Jamia, Jamiah, Jamian, Jamie, Jamile, Jamille, Jamin, Jamm, Jamme, Jammee, Jammes, Jammie, Jammy, Jamse, Jamy, Jamye, Jamyee, Jamyle, Jamyse, Jamze, Jas, Jasha, Jay, Jayme, Jaymee, Jaymes, Jaymie, Jeames, Jem, Jemes, Jim, Jimmie, Jimmy, Seamus, Seumas, Shamus

Jameson (English) son of James.
Jaemeson, Jaemison, Jaemyson, Jaimeson, Jaimison, Jaimyson, Jamerson, Jamesyn, Jamison, Jamyson, Jaymeson, Jaymyson

Jamie (Hebrew) supplanter, a form of James.
Jaemi, Jaemie, Jaemy, Jaim, Jaime, Jaimee, Jaimey, Jaimi, Jaimy, Jamee, Jamey, Jami, Jamy

Jamil (Arabic) handsome, beautiful.
Jameal, Jameel, Jamiel, Jamiell, Jamielle, Jamile, Jamill, Jamille, Jamyl, Jamyle, Jamyll, Jarmil, Jarmill, Jarmille

Jamison (English) son of James.
Jamiesen, Jamieson, Jamis, Jamisen, Jamysen, Jamyson

Jamnu (Hindu) a sage.

Jamond (American) combination of James and Raymond.
Jamod, Jamonde, Jamont, Jamonta, Jamontae, Jamontay, Jamonte, Jarmod, Jarmonde, Jarmont, Jarmonta, Jarmontae, Jarmontay, Jarmonte

Jamsheed (Persian) man from Persia.
Jamshaid, Jamshed

Jan (Hebrew) God is gracious, a form of John, a unisex name.
Jaan, Jane, Jann, Janne, Jano, Jansen, Janson, Jenda, Yan

Janco (Czech) God is gracious, a form of John.
Jancsi, Janke, Janko

Jando (Spanish) helper or defender of humankind, a form of Alexander.
Janda, Jandino, Jandoh

Janeil (American) combination of the prefix Ja and Neil.
Janaielle, Janail, Janal, Janeile, Janel, Janell, Janelle, Janiel, Janiell, Janile, Janille

Janek (Polish) God is gracious, a form of John.
Janak, Janaka, Janeka, Janik, Janika, Janka, Jankiel, Janko

Janis (Latvian) God is gracious, a form of John, a unisex name.
Ansis, Jancis, Zanis, Zansis

Janne (Finnish) God is gracious, a form of John.
Jann, Jannes

Janos (Hungarian) God is gracious, a form of John.
Jancsi, Jani, Janis, Janko, Jankia, Jano

Jansen (Scandinavian) son of Jan.
Jaan, Jaansen, Jaanson, Jane, Jann, Janne, Jannsen, Jannson, Jano, Janse, Jansin, Janson, Janssen, Jansun, Jantzen, Janzen, Jenda, Jensen, Jenson, Yaan, Yane, Yann, Yanne, Yano, Yanse, Yansen, Yansin,

Yanson, Yanssen, Yansun, Yantzen, Yanzen, Yenda, Yensen, Yenson

Janus (Latin) gate, passageway, born in January, after the Roman God of doors and gateways.

Jannes, Jannese, Jannus, Januario, Januaro, Janusz

Jaquan (American) combination of prefix Ja and Quan.

Jaequan, Jaequon, Jaiquan, Jaiquon, Jaqawn, Jaquaan, Jaquain, Jaquan, Jaquane, Jaquann, Jaquanne, Jaquavius, Jaquawn, Jaquin, Jaquinn, Jaquoin, Jaquon, Jaquone, Jaqune, Jaqwon

Jarah (Hebrew) sweet as honey.

Jara, Jarra, Jarrah, Jera, Jerah, Jerra, Jerrah

Jared (Hebrew) the descendant.

Jahred, Jaired, Jarad, Jaredd, Jareid, Jarid, Jarod, Jarred, Jarrod, Jarryd, Jaryd, Jered, Jerod, Jerrad, Jerred, Jerrod, Jerryd

Jarek (Slavic) born in January.

Jarec, Jaric, Jarik, Jarrec, Jarrek, Jarric, Jarrik

Jarell (Scandinavian) spear carrier, a form of Gerald.

Jairall, Jairell, Jarael, Jaral, Jarall, Jareil, Jarel, Jarrell, Jarryl, Jayryl, Jerel, Jerell, Jerrell, Jhairall, Jhairell, Jharael, Jharal, Jharall, Jhareil, Jharel, Jharell, Jharrell, Jharryl, Jhayryl, Jherel, Jherell, Jherrell

Jareth (American) combination of Jared and Gareth.

Jarreth, Jereth, Jerreth

Jariath (Hebrew) tributary Lord.

Jarl (Scandanavian) noble.

Jarlea, Jarleah, Jarlee, Jarleigh, Jarley, Jarli, Jarlie, Jarly

Jarlath (Latin) in control.

Jarman (Teutonic) from Germany.

Jerman

Jaron (Hebrew) he will sing.

Jaaron, Jairon, Jaren, Jarone, Ja Ronn, Jaronn, Jarren, Jarron, Jarryn, Jaryn, Jatronn, Jayron, Je Ronn, Jeronn, J'ron

Jaroslav (Czech) glory of spring.

Jaraslav, Jarda, Jarislav, Jaryslav

Jarrah (Australian Aboriginal) mahogany gum tree.

Jarra

Jarrell (English) spear carrier, a form of Gerald.

Jaerel, Jaerell, Jaeryl, Jaeryll, Jairel, Jairell, Jairyl, Jairyll, Jareil, Jarel, Jarell, Jarrel, Jarryl, Jarryll

Jarvey (Irish) coach driver.

Jarvie, Jarvy

Jarvis (German) conqueror, war leader.

Gervais, Gervaise, Gervase, Gervice, Jarus, Jaruss, Jarvice, Jarvise, Jarvyc, Jarvyce, Jarvys, Jarvyse, Jary, Javaor, Javar, Javaras, Javare, Javares, Javari, Javarias, Javaries, Javario, Javaris, Javarius, Javaro, Javaron, Javarous, Javarre, Javarreis, Javarri, Javarris, Javarrius, Javarro, Javart, Javarus, Javor, Javorious, Javoris, Javorius, Javouris, Javrous, Jerve, Jervice, Jervis, Jervise, Jervyc, Jervyce, Jervys, Jeryse

Jas (Polish) God is gracious, a form of John.

Jasio, Jass

Jasha (Russian) supplanter, a form of James.

Jascha

Jashawn (American) combination of prefix Ja and Shawn.
Jasean, Jashan, Jashaun, Jashion, Jashon

Jaskaran (Hindu) praises the Lord.
Jaskaren, Jaskarin, Jaskarn, Jaskiran

Jason (Greek) healer.
Jaasan, Jaasen, Jaasin, Jaason, Jaasun, Jaasyn, Jaesan, Jaesen, Jaesin, Jaeson, Jaesun, Jaesyn, Jahsan, Jahsen, Jahsin, Jahson, Jahsun, Jahsyn, Jaisan, Jaisen, Jaisin, Jaison, Jaisun, Jaisyn, Jasan, Jasen, Jasin, Jasson, Jasun, Jasyn, Jaysan, Jaysen, Jaysin, Jayson, Jaysun, Jaysyn

Jasper (English) red, brown or yellow semi-precious stone, a unisex name.
Jaspar, Jazpar, Jazper, Jespar, Jesper, Jezpar, Jezper

Javan (Hebrew) clay.
Jaewan, Jahv, Jahva, Jahvan, Jahvante, Jahvaon, Jahvaughan, Jahven, Jahvian, Jahvien, Jahvin, Jahvine, Jahvon, Jahvona, Jahvone, Jahvonte, Jaivon, Jarus, Jaruss, Jarvice, Jarvise, Jarvyc, Jarvyce, Jarvys, Jarvyse, Jary, Jav, Java, Javaon, Javante, Javen, Javin, Javian, Javien, Javin, Javine, Javon, Javona, Javone, Javonte, Jawan, Jayvion, Jayvon, Jehvan, Jehvon, Jerve, Jervice, Jervis, Jervise, Jevan, Jevon

Javas (Hindu) swift, quick.
Jav, Java, Jayvas, Jayvis

Javier (Spanish) owner of the bright new house.
Jabier, Javeer, Javer, Javere, Javiar, Javiere, Javy, Xaviar, Xavier, Xiggy

Jawad (Arabic) generous.

Jawhar (Arabic) jewel.

Jay (French) blue jaybird.
Jae, Jai, Jaie, Jave, Jayd, Jayde, Jeay, Jeays, Jeye, Jeyes

Jaya (Hindu) name of a god, victory, a unisex name.
Jaea, Jaia, Jaiah, Jayah

Jayant (Hindu) victorious.
Jayanta

Jaydon (Hebrew) God has heard.
Jaedan, Jaeden, Jaedev, Jaedin, Jaedon, Jaedyn, Jaidan, Jaiden, Jaidev, Jaidin, Jaidon, Jaidyn, Jaydan, Jayden, Jaydev, Jaydin, Jaydyn

Jazz (American) improvised music of Afro-American roots, jazz music, a unisex name.
Jaz, Jazze, Jazzman, Jazzmin, Jazzmion, Jazzmon, Jazztin, Jazzton, Jazzy

Jean (French) God is gracious, a form of John.
Gean, Gene, Jeane, Jeann, Jeannot, Jeano, Jeanot, Jene

Jebediah (Hebrew) friend, beloved of the Lord.
Jeb, Jebadia, Jebadiah, Jebadya, Jebadyah, Jebb, Jebe, Jebedia, Jebedya, Jebedyah, Jebidia, Jebidiah, Jebidya, Jebidyah, Jebodia, Jebodiah, Jebodya, Jebodyah, Jebydia, Jebydiah, Jebydya, Jebydyah, Jededia, Jedediah, Jedidia

Jed (Hebrew) friend of God, a form of Jedidiah.
Jedd

Jedidiah (Hebrew) friend of God.
Jebadia, Jebadiah, Jebidia, Jebidiah, Jebidya, Jebodiah, Jebydia, Jebydiah, Jebydya, Jebydyah, Jedadia, Jedadiah,

Jedadya, Jedadyah, Jededia,
Jedediah, Jededya, Jededyah,
Jedidia, Jedidya, Jedidyah,
Jedodia, Jedodiah, Jedodya,
Jedodyah, Jedydia, Jedydiah,
Jedydya, Jedydyah

Jedrek (Polish) strong, manly.
Jedrec, Jedric, Jedrik, Jedrus

Jedynak (Slavic) one who has an only son.
Jedinak

Jeff (English) divinely peaceful, a form of Jeffrey.
Geff, Geoff, Jef, Jeffer, Jeffers

Jefferson (Anglo-Saxon) son of Jeffrey.
Jefarson, Jeferson, Jeffarson, Jeffers

Jeffrey (English) divinely peaceful.
Geffrey, Geofery, Geoff, Geoffery,
Geoffrie, Geoffry, Geofry, Jeff,
Jefferie, Jefferies, Jeffery, Jeffre,
Jeffree, Jeffrery, Jeffrie, Jeffries,
Jeffry, Jefre, Jefrey, Jefri, Jefrie,
Jefry, Jeoffroi, Joffa, Joffre, Joffrey

Jehan (French) God is gracious, a form of John.
Jehann

Jehiel (Hebrew) God lives.

Jehu (Hebrew) Jehovah is He.
Yehu

Jelani (African) mighty.
Jel, Jelan, Jelanie, Jelaun, Jelauni

Jem (English) a form of James, Jeremiah.
Jemmie, Jemmy

Jemond (French) worldly.
Jemon, Jemonde, Jemone,
Jesmon, Jesmond, Jesmonde,
Jesmone

Jen (Chinese) able.

Jenkin (Flemish) little John.
Jenken, Jenkens, Jenkins, Jenkyn,
Jenkyns, Jennings

Jeno (Hungarian) well-born, noble, a form of Eugene.
Jenci, Jency, Jenoe, Jensey, Jensi,
Jensie, Jensy

Jens (Danish) God is gracious, a form of John.
Jenns, Jennson, Jense, Jensen,
Jenson, Jenssen, Jensy, Jentz

Jensi (Hungarian) noble, well-born.
Jensee, Jensey, Jensie, Jensy

Jeovanni (Italian) God is gracious, a form of Giovanni, John.
Giovani, Giovanni, Jeovani,
Jeovanie, Jeovanni, Jeovannie,
Jeovanny, Jeovany

Jequan (American) combination of prefix Je and Quan.
Jequann, Jequon

Jerald (English) spear carrier, a form of Gerald.
Jeraldo, Jerold, Jeroldo, Jerrald,
Jerraldo, Jerrold, Jerroldo

Jerara (Australian Aboriginal) water falling.

Jeremiah (Hebrew) God has uplifted.
Jere, Jeree, Jeremy, Jeremya,
Jeremyah, Jeri, Jerimia, Jerimiah,
Jerimy, Jerimya, Jerimyah, Jerree,
Jerri, Jerrie, Jerry, Jery, Miah

Jeremy (Hebrew) God has uplifted, a form of Jeremiah.
Jere, Jeree, Jeremee, Jeremey,
Jeremi, Jeremie, Jeri, Jerimee,
Jerimey, Jerimi, Jerimie, Jerimy,

Jerree, Jerremy, Jerri, Jerrie, Jerrimy, Jerry, Jery

Jeriah (Hebrew) God has seen.
Jeria, Jerria, Jerriah, Jerrya, Jerryah, Jerya, Jeryah

Jericho (Arabic) moon city.
Jeric, Jerico, Jerric, Jerricho, Jerrico

Jeriel (Hebrew) vision of God.

Jermal (Arabic) handsome, beautiful, a form of Jamal.
Jermael, Jermail, Jermall, Jermayl

Jerome (Greek) sacred name of God.
Jerom, Jeromino, Jeromo, Jeronim, Jeronimo

Jerry (English) sacred name of God, a form of Jerome.
Geree, Gerey, Geri, Gerie, Gerree, Gerrey, Gerri, Gerrie, Gerry, Gery, Jeree, Jerey, Jeri, Jerie, Jerree, Jerrey, Jerri, Jerrie, Jery

Jerzy (Polish) farmer, a form of George.
Jersey, Jersy, Jerszy, Jerzey, Jurek

Jesse (Hebrew) wealthy.
Jes, Jesee, Jesey, Jesie, Jess, Jessee, Jessey, Jessie, Jessy, Jesy, Jez

Jesus (Hebrew) God is my salvation, a form of Joshua, the Son of God.
Jecho, Jesu, Jessus, Josu

Jet (Latin) to throw.
Jete, Jett, Jette

Jethro (Hebrew) abundant.
Jeth, Jethroe, Jetro

Jett (English) black.

Gett, Gette, Jet, Jete, Jetson, Jette

Jibben (Gypsy) life.
Jiben

Jibril (Arabic) archangel of Allah.
Jabril, Jibreel, Jibriel, Jibrill

Jie (Chinese) wonderful.
Jai, Jye

Jilt (Dutch) money.
Gilt, Jilte

Jim (Hebrew) supplanter, a form of James.
Jimee, Jimey, Jimi, Jimie, Jimm, Jimmee, Jimmey, Jimmi, Jimmie, Jimmy, Jimy

Jimiyu (African) born in the dry season.

Jimoh (African) born on a Friday.

Jin (Chinese) golden.

Jinan (Arabic) garden.
Jinen, Jinnan, Jinon, Jinnon, Jinnyn, Jinyn

Jindra (Czech) great leader of the army, a form of Harold.

Jing-Quo (Chinese) ruler.

Jirair (Armenian) hard-working, strong.

Jiri (Czech) farmer, a form of George.
Jirie

Jiro (Japanese) second-born male.

Jivin (Hindu) to give life.
Jivan, Jivanta, Jivinta

Jnana (Hindu) knowledge.

Joab (Hebrew) God is my father.
*Joabe, Joabee, Joabert, Joabey,
Joabi, Joabie, Joaby, Jobe, Jobee,
Jobert, Jobey, Jobi, Jobie, Joby*

Joachim (Hebrew) God will
establish.
*Joacheim, Joakim, Joakin,
Joaquem, Joaquen, Joaquim,
Joaquin, Jocheim, Jochim, Jokim,
Jokin, Joquem, Joquen, Joquim,
Joquin*

Joao (Portuguese) God is
gracious, a form of John.

Job (Hebrew) distressed, afflicted.
*Jobb, Jobbe, Jobe, Jobert, Jobey,
Jobie, Joby*

Joben (Japanese) clean.
Joban, Jobin

Jobo (Spanish) God will increase,
a form of Joseph.

Jock (Scottish) supplanter, a form
of Jacob.
*Jacoby, Jacolby, Jocko, Joco,
Jocoby, Jocolby, Joko, Jokoby,
Jokolby*

Jody (Hebrew) God will increase,
a form of Joseph, a unisex name.
*Jodee, Jodey, Jodi, Jodie, Joedee,
Joedey, Joedi, Joedie, Joedy,
Johdee, Johdey, Johdi, Johdie,
Johdy*

Joe (Hebrew) God will increase, a
form of Joseph.
Jo, Joey, Jow

Joel (Hebrew) God is willing.
Joele, Joell, Yoel

Johann (German) God is
gracious, a form of John.
*Johan, Johanan, Johane,
Johanne, Johannes, Johansen,
Johanson*

Johar (Hindu) jewel.

John (Hebrew) God is gracious.
*Jac, Jack, Jacko, Jacs, Jacsi,
Jahn, Jan, Janak, Janco, Janek,
Janis, Jann, Janne, Janos, Jansen,
Janssen, Jantje, Jantzen, Jaque,
Jaques, Jas, Jeahan, Jean, Jen,
Jenkin, Jenkyn, Jens, Jhan, Jhanick,
Jhon, Jian, Joao, Jock, Joen,
Johan, Johann, Johnle, Johnlee,
Johnni, Johnnie, Johnnson, Johnny,
Jon, Jonam, Jonas, Jonathan,
Jonathon, Jone, Jones, Joni, Jonie,
Jonni, Jonnie, Jonny, Jonson, Jonte,
Jony, Jovan, Juan, Juhan, Juhana,
Seamus, Sean, Yannick*

Joji (Japanese) farmer, a form of
George.

Jojo (African) born on a Monday.
Joejoe, Johjoe, Johjoh

Jokim (Basque) God will establish,
a form of Joachim.

Jolon (Native American) valley of
the dead oaks.

Jomei (Japanese) spreading light.
Jomey

Jonah (Hebrew) dove.
Jona

Jonas (Hebrew) accomplisher,
God is gracious, a form of John.
Jonass, Jonaus, Jonnas, Jonys

Jonathan/Jonathon (Hebrew) gift
of the Lord.
*Johnathan, Johnathaon,
Johnathen, Johnathin, Johnathon,
Johnothan, Johnothaon,
Johnothen, Johnothin, Johnothon,
Jonathen, Jonathin, Jonaton,
Jonethan, Jonethen, Jonethin,
Jonethon, Jonnathan, Jonnathen,
Jonnathon, Jonnothan, Jonnothon,
Jonothan, Jonothon*

Joost (Dutch) just.

Jorah (Hebrew) autumn rain.
Jora

Joram (Hebrew) God is praised, exalted.

Jordan (Hebrew) flowing down, descending, a unisex name.
Giordan, Giordane, Giordano, Gordan, Gorden, Gordon, Jordain, Jordaine, Jorden, Jordin, Jordon, Jordyn, Joryn, Jourdain

Jorell (American) he who saves.
Jorel, Jorrel, Jorrell

Jorg (Spanish) farmer, form of George.
Jorge, Jorgi, Jorgie, Jorj, Jorja, Jorje, Jorji, Jorjie

Jorin (Hebrew) child of freedom.

Jose (Spanish) God will increase, a form of Joseph, a unisex name.
José, Josea, Joséa, Josee, Josée, Josey, Josie, Josy

Joseph (Hebrew) God will increase, the father of Jesus and husband of Mary.
Jo, Joesef, Joeseph, Joey, Jose, Josef, Joseff, Josif, Josiff, Josiph, Jossef, Josseff, Josseph, Jossif, Jossiff, Jossiph, Jusepe, Jusuf, Pepito, Seph

Josh (Hebrew) God is my salvation, form of Joshua.
Johusa, Jos, Jose, Josha, Joshah, Joshau, Joshaua, Joshauh, Joshawa, Joshawah, Joshe, Joshee, Joshi, Joshia, Joshu, Joshua, Joshuaa, Joss

Josha (Hindu) satisfaction.

Joshi (African) to gallop.
Joshee, Joshey, Joshie, Joshy

Joshua (Hebrew) God is my salvation.
Johusa, Jos, Jose, Josh, Josha, Joshah, Joshau, Joshaua, Joshauh, Joshawa, Joshawah, Joshe, Joshee, Joshi, Joshia, Joshu, Joshuaa, Joshuah, Joshuea, Joshula, Joshus, Joshusa, Joshwa, Joshwah, Joshy, Joshywa, Joss, Josua, Josue, Jousha, Jozshua, Jozsua, Jozua, Jushua, Shua, Yasser, Yusha

Joss (Chinese) luck, fate.
Jos, Joz

Jotham (Hebrew) God is perfect.

Jovan (Latin) majestic; (Slavic) God is gracious, a form of John.
Jovaan, Jovaann, Jovani, Jovann, Jovanni, Jovanny, Jovany

Jovi (Latin) happy.
Jovee, Jovey, Jovie, Jovy

Joyce (Latin) joyful, a unisex name.
Joice, Joise, Joyse

Juan (Spanish) God is gracious, a form of John.
Juane, Juann, Juanne

Juan Carlos (Spanish) combination of Juan and Carlos.
Juan-Carlos, Juancarlos, Juan Karlos, Juan-Karlos, Juankarlos

Jubah (African) ant hill.
Juba

Jubal (Hebrew) source of joy.

Judah (Hebrew) praised.
Juda, Judas, Judda, Juddah

Judas (Hebrew) praised, a form of Judah.
Juddas

Judd (Hebrew) praised, a form of Judah.
Jud, Juda, Judah, Judda, Juddah, Jude

Jude (Latin) right with the law.
Jood, Joode, Jud

Judson (English) son of Judd.
Juddson

Jules (French) youthful.
Jule, Yule, Yules

Julian (Latin) young.
Gulian, Guliane, Jule, Jules, Julie, Julio, Julius, Jullian, Jullyan, Julyan

Julio (Spanish) youthful.
Juleo, Julyo, Juri

Julius (Latin) youthful with a beard.
Julias, Julious, Jullias, Jullious, Jullius, Julluis, Juluis

Jumaane (African) born on a Tuesday.

Jumah (African) born on a Friday.

Jumoke (African) loved by all.
Jumok

Jun (Chinese) truth, truthful, a unisex name.

Junior (Latin) young.
Jr, Junius, Junor

Jupp (German) God will increase, a form of Joseph.
Jup

Jur (Czech) farmer, a form of George.
Jurr

Jurgen (German) farmer, a form of George.
Gurgan, Gurgen, Jurgan, Yurgan, Yurgen

Jurgis (Lithuanian) farmer, a form of George.
Jurgiss

Juro (Japanese) long life.

Jurrien (Dutch) God will uplift.
Jurian, Jurien, Jurion, Jurrian, Jurrion, Jurryan, Jurryen, Jurryin, Jurryon, Juryan, Juryen, Juryin, Juryon

Justin (Latin) just.
Justean, Justen, Justice, Justis, Justus, Justyn

Juvenal (Latin) young.
Juvon, Juvone

Jyoti (Hindu) sun's light, a unisex name.
Jioti, Jioty, Jyotis, Jyotsua, Jyoty

K

Kabil (Turkish) spear gatherer.
Cabelle, Cabil, Kabel, Kabelle, Kabill, Kabille

Kabir (Hindu) a Hindu mystic.
Cabier, Cabir, Kabar, Kabeer, Kabier

Kabito (African) born while dignitaries are visiting.
Kabiito, Kabyto

Kabonesa (African) difficult delivery of baby.
Kabonesha

Kacey (Irish) eagle-eyed, brave; (American) combination of the initials K.C., a unisex name.
Casee, Casey, Casie, Kace, Kacee, Kaci, Kacy, Kaesy, Kase, Kasey, Kasie, Kasy, Kaycee

Kadar (Arabic) powerful.
Kaddah, Kaddar, Kedar

Kade (Scottish) wetlands.
Kadee, Kady, Kaid, Kaide, Kayd, Kayde, Kaydee

Kaden (Arabic) friend, companion, a form of Kadin.
Caden, Kadan, Kadein, Kadin, Kaedan, Kaeden, Kaedin, Kaidan, Kaiden, Kaidin, Kaydan, Kayden, Kaydin

Kadin (Arabic) friend, companion.
Kadeem, Kadeen, Kadim, Khadeem, Khadeen, Khadim, Khadin

Kadir (Arabic) spring.
Kadeer, Kaedeer, Kaedir, Kaydeer, Kaydir

Kado (Japanese) gateway.

Kael (Irish) mighty warrior.
Cael, Cale, Calen, Kale, Kalen

Kaelan (Irish) mighty warrior.
Cael, Caelan, Caelen, Caelin, Caelyn, Kael, Kaelen, Kaelin, Kaelyn

Kaemoon (Japanese) joyful.
Kaemon, Kaymon

Kafele (African) worth dying for.
Kafelle

Kaga (Native American) writer.
Kagah

Kahale (Hawaiian) home.
Kahail, Kahaile

Kahana (Hawaiian) priest.
Kahanah, Kahanna, Kahannah

Kahil (Turkish) young, naïve.
Cahil, Kaheel, Kale, Kalil, Kayle, Khahil, Khalil

Kahlil (Arabic) young, naïve, a form of Kahil.
Kahleal, Kahlee, Kahleel, Kahli, Kahliel, Kahlill, Kalel, Kalil

Kaholo (Hawaiian) runner.

Kai (Welsh) keeper of keys; (Hawaiian) sea or sea water, a unisex name.
Kae, Kaie, Kaii

Kaili (Hawaiian) religious deity, a unisex name.
Kaeli, Kaely, Kailli

Kainoa (Hawaiian) special name.
Cainoa, Kaenoa, Kaenowa

Kaipo (Hawaiian) sweetheart.

Kaiser (German) long-haired, a form of Caesar.
Caesar, Caiser, Kaesar, Kaeser, Kaezar, Kaezer, Kaisar, Kaizar, Kaizer

Kaiven (American) handsome, a form of Kevin.
Kaivan, Kaivin, Kaiwan

Kaj (Danish) earth.

Kakar (Hindu) grass.

Kala (Hindu) black, name for the god Siva, a unisex name.
Kalah

Kalama (Hawaiian) the flaming torch, a unisex name.
Kalam

Kalameli (African) caramel.
Kalamelie, Kalamely

Kalan (Hawaiian) heavenly chief, a form of Kalani.
Kalane, Kalen, Kallan

Kalani (Hawaiian) sky, heavenly chief, a unisex name.
Kalan, Kalanee, Kalaney, Kalanie, Kalany, Kalonee, Kaloney, Kaloni, Kalonie, Kalony

Kale (Hawaiian) strong, courageous, manly, a form of Carl; (Arabic) young, naïve, a form of Kahil.
Cale, Calen, Kail, Kaile, Kalee, Kalen, Kaley, Kalle, Kayl, Kayle

Kalea (Hawaiian) bright, clear, joyful, happy, a unisex name.
Kalee, Kalei, Kaleigh, Kaley, Kali, Kalie, Kaly

Kalevi (Scandinavian) hero.
Kaelevi, Kaleivi

Kali (Arabic) young, naïve, a form of Kahil.
Cali, Calli, Kalli

Kalil (Arabic) good friend.
Kahlil, Kaleel, Kalel, Kalell, Kali, Kaliel

Kaliq (Arabic) creative.
Kalic, Kalick, Kalik, Kaliqu, Kalique, Khaliq, Khaliqu, Khalique

Kalkin (Hindu) tenth.
Kalki, Kalkyn

Kalle (Scandinavian) strong, courageous, manly.
Kal, Kale, Kall

Kallen (Irish) mighty warrior.
Kalan, Kalane, Kalen, Kall, Kallan, Kallane, Kallon, Kallyne, Kalon, Kalyne

Kalmin (Scandinavian) manly.
Kalman, Kalmen, Kalmon, Kalmyn

Kaloosh (Armenian) blessed event.

Kalti (Australian Aboriginal) spear.

Kalvin (Latin) bald, a form of Calvin.
Calvan, Calvin, Calvon, Calvyn, Kal, Kall, Kallvan, Kallvin, Kallvyn, Kalvan, Kalvon, Kalvyn, Vinnie, Vinny

Kamaka (Hawaiian) face.

Kamakani (Hawaiian) wind.
Kamakanee, Kamakaney, Kamakanie, Kamakany

Kamal (Arabic) perfect one; (Hindu) lotus.
Kamaal, Kamaall, Kamahl,

Kamahll, Kamall, Kamel, Kamell,
Kamil, Kamill, Kamyl, Kamyll

Kamau (African) quiet warrior.

Kameron (Scottish) crooked nose,
a form of Cameron.
Cam, Cameren, Cameron, Camm,
Cammeron, Kam, Kameren,
Kameryn, Kamm, Kammeron,
Kammy, Kamoryn, Kamran, Kamron

Kami (Hindu) loving.
Kamee, Kamey, Kamie, Kamy

Kamil (Arabic) perfect one, a
form of Kamal.
Kameel

Kamuela (Hawaiian) God has
asked me, listener, a form of
Samuel.
Kamuel, Kamuelah

Kamuzu (African) medicine.

Kana (Hawaiian) a god;
(Japanese) powerful.

Kanaiela (Hawaiian) God is my
judge, a form of Daniel.
Kana, Kanaiel, Kaneii, Kaniel

Kane (Japanese) golden;
(Irish) tribute; (Welsh) beautiful;
(Hawaiian) eastern sky.
Cahan, Cain, Caine, Cane, Cayne,
Kahan, Kain, Kaine, Kayne

Kaniel (Hebrew) stalk.
Kaniell, Kannyel, Kanyel

Kannon (Hindu) a name for the
god, Krishna.
Kanaan, Kanan, Kanen, Kanine,
Kannan, Kannen, Kanon

Kanoa (Hawaiian) free.
Kano, Kanoan, Kanon

Kantu (Hindu) happy.

Kanu (African) wildcat.

Kanya (Australian Aboriginal) rock.
Kania, Kaniah, Kanyah

Kaori (Japanese) strong.
Kaoru

Kapali (Hawaiian) cliff.
Kapalee, Kapalie, Kapaly

Kapila (Hindu) ancient prophet.
Kapil, Kapilah

Kapono (Hawaiian) righteous.
Kapana, Kapani

Kardal (Arabic) mustard seed.
Karandal, Kardall, Kardel, Kardell

Kare (Scandiavian) large, enormous.
Karee

Kareem (Arabic) noble, exalted.
Karem, Kareme, Karim, Karrem,
Karriem, Karrim, Karrym, Karym

Karel (Czech) strong, courageous,
manly, a form of Carl.
Karell, Karil, Karill, Karl, Karrell,
Karrill

Karey (Greek) pure.
Carey, Cary, Karee, Kari, Karie,
Karry, Kary

Kari (Australian Aboriginal) smoke.

Karif (Arabic) born in autumn.
Kareef, Karreef, Karrif

Karim (Arabic) generous, noble.
Kareem, Karem

Karima (African) generous, noble,
a unisex name.
Karimah, Kareema

Karl (German, English) strong, courageous, manly, a form of Charles.

Carl, Carlo, Carlos, Kaarl, Kaarle, Kaarlo, Kaarlos, Kaarrlo, Kale, Kalman, Karci, Karel, Kari, Karlan, Karle, Karlen, Karlik, Karlin, Karlis, Karlitis, Karll, Karllo, Karllos, Karllus, Karlo, Karlos, Karlton, Karlus, Karol, Kjell

Karmel (Hebrew) vineyard of the Lord, masculine form of Carmel.

Carme, Carmel, Karme

Karson (English) son of Carr, a form of Carson.

Carson, Karsen

Karsten (Greek) blessed, anointed one, a unisex name.

Carsten, Kaarstan, Kaarsten, Kaarston, Karstan, Karston

Karu (Hindu) cousin.

Karun

Kaseem (Arabic) divided.

Kasceem, Kaseam, Kaseym, Kasim, Kasseem, Kassem, Kassim, Kazeem, Kazim

Kasem (Thai) happiness.

Kasam, Kaseam, Kaseme, Kaseom, Kasim, Kasom, Kassam, Kassem, Kassom

Kasen (Latin) head protected with a helmut.

Kasan, Kasean, Kasene, Kaseon, Kasin, Kason, Kassen, Kassin, Kasson, Kasyn

Kasey (Irish) brave and honourable, a form of Casey, a unisex name.

Casey, Kaese, Kaesy, Kaisey, Kassey, Kaysay

Kashawn (American) combination of prefix Ka and Shawn.

Cash, Cashawn, Kasean, Kash, Kashain, Kashan, Kashaun, Kashean, Kashen, Kashon

Kasib (Arabic) fertile.

Kaseeb

Kasim (Arabic) divided, a form of Kaseem.

Kashim, Kasimi, Kazim, Kazmer, Kazner

Kasiya (African) separate.

Kasiyah

Kaspar (Persian) treasurer, a form of Caspar.

Caspa, Caspah, Casper, Jaspar, Jasper, Kaspa, Kaspah, Kasper, Kaz

Kass (German) blackbird.

Kaes, Kaese, Kaess, Kasch, Kase

Kateb (Arabic) writer.

Kato (African) second-born twin.

Katriel (Hebrew) God is my crown, a unisex name; (Arabic) peace.

Katryel

Kaufman (German) merchant.

Kauffman, Kauffmann, Kaufmann

Kauri (Polynesian) tree.

Kavan (Irish) handsome.

Canan, Kavanagh, Kavaughn, Kavaugn, Kaven, Kavenagh, Kayvan

Kaveh (Persian) hero.

Kava, Kavah

Kavi (Hindu) poet.

Kavee, Kavey, Kavie, Kavy

Kawika (Hawaiian) beloved, a form of David.

Kay (German) fort; (Greek) rejoice, a unisex name.
Kai, Kaie, Kaycee, Kaye

Kayden (Arabic) friend, companion, a form of Kadin.
Kaden, Kadin, Kayde, Kaydin, Kaydn, Kaydon

Kayin (African) celebrated, longed-for child.
Kaein

Kayle (Hebrew) faithful.
Kail, Kaile, Kayl

Kayne (Hebrew) spear, possession, a form of Cain.
Cain, Cane, Kain, Kane, Kayn

Kayode (African) he brought joy.
Kayod

Kazuo (Japanese) peaceful.

Keahi (Hawaiian) flames the fire, a unisex name.

Keaka (Hawaiian) God is gracious, a form of Jack.

Kealoha (Hawaiian) fragrant perfume.
Ke'ala, Keala, Kealohah, Keela, Keelah

Keane (English) keen, sharp-witted.
Kanan, Kean, Keanen, Keani, Keanie, Keanin, Keany, Keen, Keenan, Keene, Keenen, Keenin, Kein, Keine, Keyan, Keyen, Keyin, Keyon, Kienan, Kienen, Kienin

Keanu (Hawaiian) breeze from the sea.
Keanew, Keani, Keano, Keanue, Keeno, Keenu, Kianu

Kearn (Irish) dark-haired.
Kearne, Kern, Kerne, Kerrn, Kerrne

Kearney (Irish) brave, victorious soldier, a form of Carney.
Cahney, Carney, Carnie, Kahney, Karney, Karnie, Kearnee, Kearny

Keaton (English) from the town where hawks fly.
Keatan, Keaten, Keatin, Keatun, Keatyn, Keetan, Keeten, Keetin, Keeton, Keetun, Keetyn, Keitan, Keiten, Keitin, Keiton, Keitun, Keityn

Keawe (Hawaiian) strand.

Keb (Egyptian) earth.
Kebb, Kebbe

Kedar (Hindu) mountain lord; (Arabic) powerful.
Kadar, Keder

Kedem (Hebrew) ancient.

Keefe (Irish) handsome.

Keegan (Irish) small, fiery one, a unisex name.
Kaegan, Keagan, Keagen, Keagin, Keagon, Keegen, Keegin, Keegon, Kegan, Kegen, Keghan, Keghen, Kegun, Kegyn, Keigan, Keigen, Keigin, Keigon, Keigun, Keigyn, Keygan, Keygen, Keygin, Keygon, Keygyn

Keelan (Irish) small, slender.
Keelin, Keelyn, Keilen, Kelan

Keeley (Gaelic) handsome, beautiful, a unisex name.
Kealey, Kealy, Keeli, Keelian, Keelie, Keely

Keenan (Irish) small, ancient one.
Cianan, Keanan, Keanen, Keannan, Keannen, Keenon, Kenan, Keynan, Keynen, Keynin

Keene (English) wise; (German) bold, sharp.

Kean, Keane, Keen, Keenan, Keenen, Keenin, Keenon, Kein, Keine, Kennan, Keyn, Keyne

Kehind (African) second-born twin.

Keiffer (German) cooper, barrel-maker.

Keef, Keefer, Keeff, Keeffer, Keeth, Keif, Keifer, Keiff, Keiffer, Keith, Keithe, Keyf, Keyfer, Keyff, Keyffe, Keyffer, Keyth

Keiji (Japanese) cautious ruler.

Keir (Scottish) small, dark child.

Keiran (Irish) little, dark, a form of Kieran.

Keiren, Keirin, Keiron, Kerin, Kerrin, Ceiren, Ceirin

Keitaro (Japanese) blessed.

Kieto

Keith (Celtic) forest.

Keef, Keefer, Keeff, Keeffer, Keif, Keife, Keifer, Keiff, Keiffer, Keithe, Keyf, Keyfe, Keyff, Keyffe, Keyth, Keythe

Kekoa (Hawaiian) bold, courageous.

Kekoah

Kelby (German) farm near the spring.

Kelbee, Kelbey, Kelbi, Kelbie, Kellbee, Kellbey, Kellbi, Kellbie, Kellby

Kelham (Norse) ridge.

Kellham

Kelile (Eithopian) protected.

Kell (Norse) from the well.

Kel

Kellen (Irish) mighty warrior.

Keillan, Keillen, Keillin, Kellan, Kellin

Keller (Irish) little companion warrior.

Keeler

Kelly (Celtic) battle warrior of the woods, brave warrior, a unisex name.

Callie, Kele, Kelee, Keleigh, Keley, Keli, Kelie, Kellee, Kelleigh, Kelley, Kelli, Kellie, Kely

Kelmen (Basque) merciful.

Kellman, Kellmen, Kelman

Kelsey (Sandinavian) island of ships, a unisex name.

Kelcey, Kelcy, Kelse, Kelsea, Kelsi, Kelsie, Kels, Kelsley, Kelsy

Kelvin (Irish) narrow stream.

Kelvan, Kelven, Kelvon, Kelvyn, Kelwan, Kelwin, Kelwyn

Kelwin (Anglo-Saxon) friend from the ridge.

Kelwen, Kelwenn, Kelwinn, Kelwyn, Kelwynn, Kelwynne

Kemal (Turkish) highest honour.

Kemel

Kembla (Australian Aboriginal) blessings.

Kemen (Basque) strong.

Keeman, Keemen, Keman

Kemp (English) champion fighter.

Kempe

Ken (English) handsome, a form of Kenneth.

Kena, Kenn, Keno

Kenan (Hebrew) to attain, to acquire.

Kenen, Kenin, Kenon, Kenyn

Kenaz (Hebrew) bright.

Kendall (Celtic) ruler of the valley.
Kendaale, Kendal, Kendale, Kendel, Kendell, Kendyl, Kendyll

Kendrick (Celtic) royal ruler, son of Henry.
Ken, Kenderic, Kenderich, Kenderick, Kenderik, Kendric, Kendrich, Kendrick, Kendrik, Kendrix, Kendryk, Kenric, Kenrick, Kenrik, Keondric, Keondrick, Keondrik

Kenelm (Anglo-Saxon) brave, defender of his relations.

Kenji (Japanese) second-born son.
Kenjee, Kenjie, Kenjy

Kennan (Scottish) little Ken.
Kenan, Kenen, Kenna, Kennen, Kennon, Kenon

Kennedy (Irish) helmeted chief, a unisex name.
Kenedy, Kenidy, Kennady, Kennedee, Kennedey, Kennedie, Kennidy

Kenneth (Irish) handsome; (English) royal oath.
Ken, Keneith, Keneth, Keni, Kenith, Kenneith, Kennet, Kennethen, Kennieth, Kennith, Kenny, Kennyth, Kenyth, Kineth, Kinneth, Kinny

Kenrick (Welsh) chief hero.
Kennric, Kennrick, Kennrik, Kenric, Kenricks, Kenrik

Kent (Welsh) white, bright.

Kentaro (Japanese) big boy.

Kentigern (Celtic) lord.

Kenton (English) from Kent, from the royal town.
Kent, Kenten, Kentin, Kentonn

Kentrell (English) king's estate.
Kentrel

Kenward (Anglo-Saxon) brave warrior.

Kenya (Hebrew) animal horn.
Kenyatee, Kenyatta, Kenyatti, Kenyotta

Kenyon (Irish) blond-haired.
Kenyan, Kenyn, Kenynn, Keon, Keonyan, Keonyon

Kenzie (Scottish) wise leader.
Kensi, Kensie, Kensy, Kenzi, Kenzy

Keoki (Hawaiian) farmer, a form of George.

Keola (Hawaiian) life.

Keon (Irish) young warrior, well-born, a form of Ewan.
Keeon, Keeonn, Keeonne, Keion, Keione, Keionn, Keionne, Keondre, Keone, Keonn, Keonne, Keonta, Keontay, Keonte, Keontez, Keontre, Keontrey, Keontyre, Keony, Keyon, Kian, Kion

Keoni (Hawaiian) God is gracious, a form of John.
Keonee, Keonie, Keony

Kerel (African) young.
Kerell

Kerem (Turkish) kind.
Kareem, Karem, Kereem

Kerey (Gypsy) homeward bound.
Keree, Keri, Kerie, Kery

Kerman (Basque) from Germany.
Kermen, Kerrman, Kerrmen

Kermit (Irish) free.
Kermitt, Kermyt, Kermytt

Kerr (Scandinavian) from the marsh, a form of Carr.
Carr, Karr, Ker

Kerrick (English) king's rule.
Keric, Kerick, Kerik, Kerric, Kerrik,

Kerry (Irish) dark-haired, a unisex name.
Keary, Keiry, Keree, Kerey, Keri, Kerie, Kerree, Kerrey, Kerri, Kerrie

Kers (Hindu) plant.

Kersen (Indonesian) cherry.
Kersan, Kersin, Kerson, Kersyn

Kerwin (Irish) dark-haired friend; (English) friend of the marshlands.
Kervin, Kervinn, Kervyn, Kerwinn, Kerwyn, Kirwin, Kirwinn, Kirwyn

Keshawn (American) combination of prefix Ke and Shawn.
Kaeyshaun, Keshan, Keshaun, Keshean, Keshen, Keshon, Keshun, Keyshan, Keyshon, Keyshun, Kishan, Kishaun, Kishawn, Kishen, Kishon, Kyshon, Kyshun

Kesin (Hindu) long-haired beggar.

Kesse (African) bonnie, chubby baby.
Kess, Kessey, Kessi, Kessie, Kessy

Kester (English) Christ-bearer, carrier of Christ, anointed, follows Christ, a form of Christopher.
Kess, Kesstar, Kesster, Kestar

Kestrel (English) falcon, a unisex name.
Kestrell

Keung (Chinese) universe.

Kevin (Irish) handsome.
Kaiven, Keaven, Keevon, Keivan,

Kev, Kevan, Keven, Keveon, Kevern, Keverne, Kevian, Kevien, Kevinn, Kevins, Kevis, Kevn, Kevron, Kevvy, Kevyn, Kevyon, Kewon, Kewone, Keyan, Keyin, Keyon, Kivon, Kyven, Kyvin

Khaldun (Arabic) forever.
Khaldoon

Khalid (Arabic) eternal.
Khaled, Khalida

Khalil (Arabic) friend.
Kalil, Khalee, Khaleel, Khaleil, Khali, Khaliel, Khalill

Khaliq (Arabic) creative.
Kaliq, Kalique, Khalique

Khamisi (African) born on a Thursday.
Kham

Khan (Turkish) prince.
Kahn, Kham, Khanh

Kharald (Russian) mighty spearman, a form of Gerald.
Karald, Khaarald

Khayru (Arabic) benevolent.
Kayru, Khiri, Khiry, Kiry

Khoury (Arabic) priest.
Khory

Khristian (Greek) carrier of Christ, anointed, follows Christ, a form of Christian.
Khris, Khristan, Khristin, Khriston, Khrystian, Kris, Kristan, Kristian, Kristin, Kriston, Krystian

Khristopher (Greek) Christ-bearer, carrier of Christ, anointed, follows Christ, a form of Christopher.
Khristofer, Khristophar, Kristofer, Kristophar, Kristopher

Khristos (Greek) Christ-bearer, carrier of Christ, anointed, follows Christ, a form of Christopher.
Khris, Khristo, Khristophe, Kris, Kristo, Kristophe, Kristos

Kibo (African) wise.
Kybo

Kibuuka (African) brave warrior.
Kibuka

Kidd (English) young goat, kid.
Kid, Kidde, Kido, Kyd, Kydd, Kydde

Kiefer (German) cooper, barrel-maker, a form of Keiffer.
Kief, Kiefar, Kieffer, Kiefor, Kiffer, Kiiefer

Kiele (Hawaiian) gardenia, fragrant blossom, a unisex name.
Kielle, Kyele, Kyelle

Kienan (Irish) small, ancient one, a form of Keenan.
Kiernan

Kieran (Irish) little, dark.
Keiran, Keirin, Keiron, Kiaran, Kiarin, Kiaron, Kier, Kierian, Kierin, Kiernan, Kiernin, Kiernon, Kieron, Kierr, Kierran, Kierre, Kierren, Kierron, Kyrn, Kyran

Kiet (Thai) honour.
Kyet

Kifeda (African) boy among girls.

Kiho (African) born on a foggy day.
Kyho

Kijika (Native American) walks quietly.

Kika (Hawaiian) forest, a form of Keith.
Kikah, Kyka, Kykah

Kiki (Spanish) ruler of the house, a form of Henric.

Kiley (Irish) narrow land, strait, a unisex name, a form of Kyle.
Kiel, Kilan, Kile, Kilee, Kilen, Kilie, Kily, Kyel, Kyele, Kylan, Kylar, Kyle, Kylee, Kylen, Kyler, Kylie, Kylon

Killara (Australian Aboriginal) permanent.

Kim (English) chief, a unisex name.
Kimie, Kimm, Kimmie, Kimmy, Kym, Kyme, Kymm, Kymme

Kimbal (Greek) hollow vessel; (English) warrior chief.
Kimball, Kimbel, Kimbell, Kimble

Kimo (Hawaiian) supplanter, a form of James.

Kin (Japanese) golden.

Kincaid (Scottish) battle chief.
Kincade, Kincaide, Kinkaid, Kinkaide

Kindin (Basque) fifth.
Kindyn, Kyndin, Kyndyn

King (English) ruler, king.

Kingsley (English) from the king's meadow.
King, Kings, Kingslay, Kingslea, Kingslee, Kingsleigh, Kingslie, Kingsly, Kingzlee, Kinslea, Kinslee, Kinsley, Kinslie, Kinsly

Kingston (English) from the royal residence, king's estate.
Kinston

Kinnard (Irish) high slope.
Kinard, Kynard, Kynnard

Kinsey (English) victorious king.

Kinsee, Kinsi, Kinsie, Kinsy, Kynsee, Kynsey, Kynsi, Kynsie, Kynsy

Kioshi (Japanese) quiet.

Kip (English) peak, pointed hill.
Kipp

Kir (Bulgarian) sun, a form of Cyrus.
Kirr

Kiral (Turkish) supreme leader, king.
Kirall, Kyral, Kyrall

Kiran (Hindu) ray, beam of light, a unisex name.
Kearan, Kearen, Kearin, Kearon, Keeran, Keeren, Keerin, Keeron, Keiran, Keiren, Keirin, Keiron, Kiren, Kirin, Kiron, Kirun, Kyran, Kyren, Kyrin, Kyron, Kyryn

Kirby (English) church in the village or farm, a unisex name.
Kerbee, Kerbey, Kerbie, Kerby, Kirbee, Kirbey, Kirbie, Kirkby

Kiri (Cambodian) mountain.
Kiry

Kiril (Slavic) lordly ruler, a form of Cyril.
Kirill, Kiryl, Kiryll, Kyrillos

Kiritan (Hindu) one who wears a crown.

Kirk (Scandinavian) in the house of worship.
Kirke

Kirkland (English) church land.
Kirklan, Kirklen, Kirklin, Kirkline, Kirklind, Kirkloun, Kirklun, Kirklyn, Kirklynd, Kirklynn

Kirkley (English) church meadow.
Kirklea, Kirklee, Kirkleigh, Kirkli, Kirklie, Kirkly

Kirkwell (English) church well.
Kerkwell, Kyrkwell

Kirton (English) church town.
Kerton

Kistna (Hindu) sacred.

Kistur (Gypsy) skilled rider.
Kystur

Kit (Greek) Christ-bearer, carrier of Christ, anointed, follows Christ, a form of Christopher, Christian.
Kitt, Kitts

Kito (African) precious child, precious jewel.
Kitto, Kyto, Kytto

Kitwana (African) pledge to live.

Kiva (Hebrew) supplanter, a form of Jacob.
Kiba, Kivi, Kiwa, Kyba, Kyra

Kiyoshi (Japanese) quiet, peaceful.

Kizza (African) born after twins.
Kiza, Kizzy

Kjell (Swedish) strong, courageous, manly, a form of Karl.
Kjel

Klaus (German) victory of the people, a form of Nicholas.
Clas, Claus, Clause, Klaas, Klaes, Klas, Klause

Kleef (Dutch) cliff.
Kliff

Kleng (Norwegian) claw.

Knight (English) warrior, knight.
Knights

Knoton (Native American) wind.
Knotton, Noton, Notton

Knowles (English) grassy slope.
Knolls, Knowls, Knowlls, Knowlles, Nowles

Knox (Irish) from the hills.

Knute (Scandinavian) knot; (Latin) white-haired, a form of Canute.
Kanut, Kanute, Knud, Knut

Koby (Polish) supplanter, a form of Jacob.
Coby, Kobby, Kobe, Kobey, Kobi, Kobia, Kobie

Kofi (African) born on a Friday.

Kohana (Native American) swift.

Koi (Hawaiian) water, a form of Troy.
Koy

Kojo (African) born on a Monday.

Koka (Hawaiian) Scotsman.

Kokayi (African) gathered.

Kolby (English) coal town, dark-haired, a form of Colby.
Koalby, Koelby, Kohlbe, Kohlby, Kolbe, Kolbey, Kolbi, Kolbie, Kolebe, Koleby, Kollby, Kelby

Kole (English) victory of the people, a form of Cole.
Koel, Kohl, Kohle, Koll, Kolle

Kolet (Australian Aboriginal) dove.
Kolett

Kolin (English) dove, young child, a form of Colin.
Kolen, Kollen, Kollin, Kollyn, Kolyn

Kolya (Australian Aboriginal) winter.

Kona (Hawaiian) ruler of the world, proud leader, a form of Don.
Konala

Konane (Hawaiian) bright moonlight.
Konan

Kondo (African) war.

Kong (Chinese) glorious sky.

Kono (Native American) squirrel eating pine nuts.

Konol (Australian Aboriginal) sky.
Konnol

Kontar (African) only child.
Kontor

Koora (Australian Aboriginal) day.

Koorong (Australian Aboriginal) canoe.

Korb (German) basket.
Corb, Corbe, Korbe

Kornel (Latin) horn colour, cornel tree, a form of Cornelius.
Korneil, Korneli, Kornelisz, Kornelius, Kornell, Kornellius, Krelis

Korudon (Greek) helmeted one.

Kosey (African) lion.
Kosee, Kossee, Kossey

Kosti (Finnish) staff of the Goths, a form of Gustave.
Costi, Kostee, Kostie, Kosty

Kosumi (African) spear fisher.

Koukalaka (Hawaiian) from the dark stream, a form of Douglas.

Kovit (Thai) expert.
Kovyt

Krikor (Armenian) watchful, vigilant, a form of Gregory.
Grigor, Krikory

Krischnan (Greek) carrier of Christ, anointed, follows Christ, a form of Christian.
Krishnan, Krisnan

Krishna (Hindu) delightful, pleasurable.
Kistna, Kistnah, Krisha, Krishnah, Krysha, Kryshna, Kryshnah, Kystna, Kystnah

Kuba (Czech) supplanter, a form of Jacob.
Cuba, Kubo, Kubus

Kueng (Chinese) universe.

Kugonza (African) love.

Kuiril (Basque) lord.
Kuirill, Kuirril, Kuirrill

Kulan (Australian Aboriginal) possum.
Kullan

Kunle (African) home of honours.

Kuper (Yiddish) copper.
Kupor, Kupper

Kuruk (Native American) bear.

Kwabena (African) born on a Tuesday.

Kwach (African) morning.
Kwacha

Kwakou (African) born on a Wednesday.
Kwako, Kwaku

Kwam (Native American) God is gracious, a form of John.
Kwan

Kwame (African) born on a Saturday.
Kwaim, Kwaime

Kwan (Korean) strong.
Kwane

Kwasi (African) born on a Sunday.

Kwayera (African) dawn.

Kwende (African) call to go.
Kwend

Ky (Irish) from the strait, from the narrow land, a form of Kyle.
Kai, Kaie, Ki, Kie, Kye

Kyan (Irish) little king, a form of Ryan.
Kian, Kien, Kyen

Kyele (Scottish) from the strait, from the narrow land, a form of Kyle.
Kiel, Kilan, Kile, Kilen, Kylan, Kyel, Kylan, Kylar, Kyle, Kylen, Kyler, Kylon

Kyle (Irish) from the strait, from the narrow land.
Kiel, Kilan, Kile, Kilen, Kiley, Kylan, Kyel, Kyele, Kylan, Kylar, Kylen, Kyler, Kylon

Kyloe (Anglo-Saxon) from the meadow of cows.
Kilo, Kiloe, Kilow, Kilowe, Kylow, Kylowe

Kynan (Welsh) chief.
Keynan, Keynen, Keynin, Keynon, Keynyn, Kienan, Kienen, Kienin, Kienon, Kienyn, Kynen, Kynin, Kynon, Kynyn

Kyne (Anglo-Saxon) royal.
Kian, Kiane, Kyn

Kyros (Greek) master.
Kiro, Kiros, Kyro

Laban (Hebrew) white.
Labban, Labben, Labbin, Labbon, Labbyn, Laben, Labin, Labon, Labyn

Labhrainn (Irish) one who has been crowned with a laurel, a form of Laurence.
Labhrain, Labrain, Labrainn

Labib (Arabic) sensible, intelligent.
Labid, Labyb, Labyd, Lhabib, Lhabid

Lachlan (Scottish) land of the lakes.
Lachie, Lachlann, Lachlen, Lachlin, Lachlon, Lachlyn, Lachunn, Lajuan, Lakelan, Lakeland, Lauchlan, Lauchlen, Lauchlin, Lauchlon, Lauchlyn, Laughlan, Laughlen, Laughlin, Laughlon, Laughlyn, Lochlan, Lochlann, Lochlen, Lochlin, Lochlon, Lochlyn, Lochy, Lockie, Locky

Ladd (English) young attendant, page.
Lad, Ladde, Laddey, Laddie, Laddy

Ladislav (Czech) army ruler, a form of Walter.
Laco, Lada, Ladislaus

Lado (African) second-born son.

Lafayette (French) faith, name of a French nobleman who supported the American revolution.
Lafaiete, Lafaiette, Lafayett, Lafette, Laffyette

Laidley (English) path by the slushy meadow.
Laedlea, Laedlee, Laedleigh, Laedley, Laedli, Laedlie, Laedly, Laidlea, Laidlee, Laidleigh, Laidli, Laidlie, Laidly, Laydlea, Laydlee, Laydleigh, Laydley, Laydli, Laydlie, Laydly

Laird (Scottish) land owner.

Lais (Arabic) lion.

Lajos (Hungarian) holy.
Laji, Lajo, Lajsci, Lajsi

Lake (English) lake, pond.
Lakan, Lakane, Lakee, Laken

Lakin (English) found treasure.
Lacin, Lackin, Laecin, Laeckin, Laekin, Laycin, Layckin, Laykin

Lal (Hindu) beloved.
Lall

Lall (Latin) one who has been crowned with a laurel, shortened form of Laurence.
Lal, Larry, Laurance, Lawrence, Loreto

Lamar (German) famous through the land; (French) the sea.
Lamair, Lamare, Lamario, Lamaris, Lamarr, Lamarre, Larmar, Lemair, Lemar

Lambert (German) bright land.
Lamarr, Lamarre, Lambard, Lambart, Lamberd, Lamberto, Lambirt, Lampard, Larmar, Lemar

Lamond (French) the world.
Lammond, Lamon, Lamonde, Lamondo, Lamund, Lemond

Lamont (French) mountain; (Scandinavian) lawyer.
Lammont, Lammonte, Lamonte

Lance (French) knight's attendant, a form of Lancelot.

Lanse, Launce

Lancelot (French) knight's attendant.

Lancelott, Lancilot, Lancilott, Lancylot, Lancylott, Launcelot, Launcelott

Landan (English) lives on the open land.

Landen, Landon, Landyn, Llandan, Llanden, Llandon, Llandyn

Lander (English) owner of the grassy plain.

Ander, Anders, Landers, Landis, Landys

Landric (German) ruler of the land.

Landrick, Landrik, Landryc, Landryck, Landryk

Landry (English, French) ruler of the land.

Landre, Landrey, Landri, Landrie

Lane (English) narrow road, a unisex name.

Laen, Laene, Laine, Laney, Lani, Lanie, Layn, Layne

Lang (Scandinavian) tall one.

Langar, Lange, Langer

Langdon (English) from the long hill.

Langdan, Langden, Langdin, Langdun, Langsdan, Langsden, Langsdin, Langsdon, Langsdun, Langstan, Langsten, Langstin, Langston, Langstun

Langford (English) from the long ford.

Laingford, Langforde

Langley (English) from the long meadow.

Lainglea, Lainglee, Laingleigh, Laingley, Laingli, Lainglie, Laingly, Lang, Langlea, Langlee, Langleigh, Langli, Langlie, Langly

Langston (English) long narrow town.

Laingston, Laingstown, Langsdon, Langsdown, Langstone, Langstown

Langundo (Native American) peaceful.

Lani (Hawaiian) heavenly sky, a unisex name.

Lanee, Laney, Lanie, Lannie, Lanny, Lany

Lann (Celtic) sword.

Lan, Lanne, Lannie, Lanny

Lanu (Native American) running around a pole.

Lanzo (Teutonic) land servant.

Lap (Vietnamese) independent.

Lapidos (Hebrew) torches.

Laramie (French) crying tears of love.

Laramey, Larami, Laramy, Laremey, Laremi, Laremie, Laremy

Larkin (Irish) fierce.

Larkan, Larken, Larklan, Larklen, Larklin, Larklyn, Larkyn

Larrimore (French) armorer.

Larimor, Larimore, Larmer, Larmor

Larron (French) thief.

Laran, Laren, Larin, Laron, Laronn, Larran, Larren, Larrin, Larrun, Larryn, Larun, Laryn

Larry (English) one who has been crowned with a laurel, a form of Lawrence.

Larey, Lari, Larie, Larrey, Larri, Larrie, Lary

Lars (Scandinavian) one who has been crowned with a laurel, a form of Lawrence.

Laris, Larris, Larrs, Larrse, Larse, Larson

Lasalle (French) hall.

Lasall

Lash (German) famous warrior, a form of Louis.

Lashi, Lasho

Lasse (Finnish) victory of the people, a form of Nicholas.

Lass, Lassey, Lassie, Lassy

Laszlo (Hungarian) famous ruler.

Laco, Lacko, Laslo, Lazlos

Lateef (Arabic) gentle, pleasant.

Lateif, Latif, Latyf

Latham (Scandinavian) barn; (English) district.

Laitham, Laithe, Laithem, Lathe, Lathem

Lathrop (English) barn.

Lathe, Lathorp, Lathorpe, Lathrope, Layth

Latif (Arabic) gentle, kind, pleasant, friendly.

Lateef

Latimer (French) language teacher, interpreter.

Lat, Latimar, Latimor, Lattie, Lattimar, Lattimer, Lattimor, Latty, Latymer

Laudalino (Portuguese) praised.

Lauda, Laudalin, Laudalinos, Lino

Laughlin (Irish) saint's servant.

Lachlan, Lachlen, Lachlin, Lachlon, Lachlyn, Lauchlan, Lauchlen, Lauchlin, Lauchlon, Lauchlyn, Lauchy, Laughlan, Laughlen, Laughlon, Laughlon, Leachlin, Leachlinn, Lochy

Laurence/Lawrence (Latin) one who has been crowned with a laurel.

Labhruinn, Labrenics, Labrentsis, Labrhas, Lal, Lanny, Larry, Lauran, Laurance, Laureano, Lauren, Laurencho, Laurencio, Laurens, Laurense, Laurent, Laurentia, Laurentij, Laurentios, Laurentius, Laurentz, Laurentzi, Laurie, Laurin, Lauris, Laurits, Lauritz, Laurnet, Laurnt, Lauro, Laurus, Laury, Lavrenti, Lawran, Lawrance, Lawrans, Lawranse, Lawren, Lawrens, Lawrense, Lawri, Lawrie, Lawry, Luarnce

Lavalle (French) valley.

Lavail, Laval, Lavale, Lavalei, Lavall, Lavel, Lavele, Lavell, Lavelle, Levele, Levell, Levelle

Lavan (Hebrew) white.

Lavane, Lavaughan, Lavaughn, Laven, Lavon, Levan, Levaughan, Levaughn

Lave (Italian) lava; (English) lord.

Laev, Laeve, Laiv, Laive, Lav, Layv, Layve

Lavi (Hebrew) lion.

Lavee, Lavey, Lavie, Lavy

Lawford (English) low ford on the hill.

Lawforde

Lawler (Irish) one who mutters.

Lalor, Lallor, Lawller, Lawllor, Lawlor, Lollar, Loller

Lawson (English) son of Lawrence.

Lawton (English) town on the hill.

Lazarus (Hebrew) God helps, a form of Eleazar, a biblical figure who was raised from the dead.
Lazar, Lazare, Lazarillo, Lazarito, Lazarius, Lazaro, Lazaros, Lazorus, Lazzaro, Lazzarus

Leaf (English) leaf from a tree.
Leefe, Leif, Leife, Leyf, Leyfe

Leal (English) loyal, faithful friend.
Leale, Leall, Lealle

Leander (Greek) lion man.
Leanda, Leandar, Leandre, Leandrew, Leandro, Leandros

Leben (Yiddish) life.
Lebben

Lebna (Ethiopian) spirit.

Lech (Polish) forest spirit.
Leach, Leache, Leche, Leich, Leiche

Lee (English) meadow or clearing, a unisex name.
Lea, Leigh, Li

Leggett (French) delegate.
Legat, Legate, Legatt, Legatte, Legette, Legget, Leggete, Leggette, Leggitt, Liggett

Legrand (French) the great one.
Legrande

Lei (Chinese) thunder; (Hawaiian) king, a form of Ray.
Lai, Lay, Ley

Leib (Yiddish) roaring lion.

Leif (Scandinavian) dearly loved.
Laif, Laife, Lief, Liefe

Leigh (English) meadow or clearing, a form of Lee, a unisex name.
Lee, Lei

Leighton (English) meadow town.
Layland, Layton, Lealan, Lealand, Leelan, Leigh, Leighlan, Leighland, Leighton, Lelan, Letant, Leylan, Leyland, Leyton

Leith (Scottish) wide river.
Leeth, Leethe, Leithe, Lethe

Lek (Thai) small.
Lec, Lech, Leck, Lekk

Lekeke (Hawaiian) powerful ruler.

Leks (Estonian) helper or defender of humankind, a form of Alexander.
Leksik, Lekso, Lex

Lel (Gypsy) one who takes.
Lell

Leland (English) lives in the meadow.
Laylan, Layland, Layton, Lealan, Lealand, Leaton, Leelan, Leeland, Leeton, Leighlan, Leighland, Leighton, Lelan, Letant, Leylan, Leyland, Leyton

Lemuel (Hebrew) devoted to God.
Lamual, Lamuel, Lemual

Len (Native American) flute; (English) brave like a lion, a form of Leonard.
Lenn, Lennee, Lenney, Lennie, Lenny

Lenard (German) brave like a lion, a form of Leonard.
Lenerd, Lennard, Lennerd

Lenno (Native American) man.
Leno

Lennon (Irish) cloak.
Lenan, Lenen, Lennan, Lennen, Lenon, Leonan, Leonen, Leonon

Lennor (Gypsy) springtime.
Lenor

Lennox (Celtic) field of elm trees.
Lenix, Lennix, Lenox

Leo (Latin) lion.
*Leaho, Leao, Leeo, Leigho, Leio,
Leodis, Leon, Leonard, Leondaus,
Leone, Leonid, Leonidas, Leonis, Lev,
Lio, Lion, Lyo, Lyon, Nardex, Nardo*

Leon (German, Greek) brave
like a lion, a form of Leonard,
Napoleon.
*Leeon, Leeone, Leonas, Leonce,
Leoncio, Leondris, Leone, Leonek,
Leoni, Leonid, Leonida, Leonides,
Leonidis, Leonn, Leonne, Leons,
Leontes, Leontrae, Lion, Lione,
Liutras, Lyon, Lyone*

Leonard (German) brave like a lion.
*Leaho, Leao, Leeo, Leigho,
Leio, Lenard, Lenardo, Lennard,
Lennardo, Leo, Leodis, Leon,
Leonarde, Leonardo, Leondaus,
Leone, Leonerd, Leonid, Leonidas,
Leonird, Leonis, Leonyrd, Lev, Lio,
Lion, Lionard, Lionerd, Lionird,
Lionyrd, Lyo, Lyon, Lyonard,
Lyonerd, Lyonird, Lyonyrd, Nardex,
Nardo*

Leonardo (Italian) brave like a
lion, a form of Leonard.
*Leander, Lenardo, Lennardo,
Leo, Leondardo, Lionardo, Lionel,
Lyonardo*

Leone (Italian) brave like a lion, a
form of Leon.
Leonne

Leonel (English) little lion cub.
Leonal, Lional, Lionel

Leonidas (Greek) brave like a lion,
a form of Leonard.
Lionidas

Leopold (German) brave people.
*Leopolde, Leopoldo, Leorad,
Liopold, Liopolde, Liopoldo, Lipot,
Lopolda, Lopolde, Lopoldo,
Loupold, Luepold, Luitpold, Poldi*

Leor (Hebrew) light.
Leore, Lior, Liore

Lequinton (American)
combination of prefix Le and
Quinton.
*Laquenten, Laquenton, Laquin,
Laquinn, Laquinten, Laquinton,
Lequenten, Lequenton, Lequin,
Lequinn, Lequinten*

Leron (French) circle.
*Leeron, Le Ron, Lerone, Lerron,
Lerrone, Liron, Lyron*

Leroy (French) king.
*Lee, Leeroi, Leeroy, Lee Roy, Leigh,
Leighroy, Lerai, Leroi, LeRoi, LeRoy,
Roy*

Les (Scottish) grey fortress, a form
of Leslie.
Lessie

Lesharo (Native American) chief.

Leshawn (American) combination
of prefix Le and Shawn.
*Lashan, Lashawn, Lesawn, Lesean,
Leshaun, Leshean, Leshon, Leshun*

Leslie (Scottish) grey fortress, a
unisex name.
*Lee, Leigh, Les, Leslee, Lesleigh,
Lesley, Lesli, Lesly, Lez, Lezlie, Lezz*

Lester (Latin) chosen camp.
Leicester, Leister, Les, Lestar

Lev (Hebrew) heart; a form of Levi,
Leverett.
Leb, Leba, Leva, Levka, Levko

Levant (Latin) rising.
Lavant, Lavante, Levante

Leverett (French) young hare.
*Lev, Leveret, Leverette, Leverit,
Leveritt, Leveritte*

Levi (Hebrew) joined in harmony.
*Leavi, Leavy, Leevi, Leevie, Lev,
Levey, Levie, Levin, Levitis, Levy,
Lewi, Lewvi*

Levin (English) beloved friend.

Lewis (English) famous warrior, a
form of Louis.
*Lew, Lewes, Lewie, Lewy, Lewys,
Llewellin, Llewlyn, Llywellyn, Lou,
Louis*

Lex (English) defender or helper of
humankind, a form of Alexander.
*Lexi, Lexie, Lexin, Lexus, Lexx,
Lexxus, Lexxy, Lexy*

Leyati (Native American) shaped
like an abalone shell.
Leyatie, Leyaty

Li (Chinese) strength.
Lee, Lei, Ly

Liam (Irish) wilful, a form of William.
*Bill, Billie, Leam, Leame, Leamm,
Liame, Liamm, Liem, Lieme, Liemm,
Lliam, Lliame, Lliamm, Lyam,
Lyame, Lyamm, Will, William, Willie*

Lian (Chinese) graceful willow;
(Irish) protector, a unisex name.
Liann, Lyan

Liang (Chinese) excellent.

Lias (English) rock.
Leas, Leass, Liass

Liberio (Portuguese) freedom.
*Libero, Liberto, Lyberio, Lybero,
Lyberto*

Liddon (English) shelter.
Lidden, Liddyn, Liden, Lidon, Lidyn

Lieb (German) love.
Leib, Leibe, Leibel, Liebe, Liebel

Ligongo (African) who is this?
Lygongo

Liko (Chinese) protected by
Buddha; (Hawaiian) flower bud.
Lika, Like

Lin (Burmese) bright.
Linh, Linn, Linny, Lyn, Lynn

Lincoln (English) settlement by the
pool.
*Linc, Lincon, Link, Linkoln, Linkon,
Lync, Lyncoln, Lyncon*

Lindberg (German) hill with linden
trees.
*Linberg, Linbergh, Linburg,
Linburgh, Lindbergh, Lindburg,
Lindburgh, Lindy*

Lindell (English) valley of the
linden trees.
*Lendal, Lendale, Lendall, Lendel,
Lendell, Lindel, Lyndal, Lyndale,
Lyndall, Lyndel, Lyndell*

Linden (English) valley of the
linden trees, protective shield, a
unisex name.
*Lin, Lindan, Lindin, Lindon, Lyndan,
Lyden, Lydin, Lyndon*

Lindley (English) from the
meadow, a unisex name.
Lindly

Lindon (English) hill of the linden
trees.
Lyndon

Lindsay (English) linden trees by
the water, a unisex name.
*Lindsie, Lindsy, Linsay, Linsee,
Lindsee, Lindsey, Linsey, Linsie, Linsy,
Lyndsay, Lyndsee, Lyndsey, Lyndsy*

Linfred (German) peaceful, calm.
Fred, Linn, Linnfred, Lynfred, Lynnfred

Linley (English) from the field of flax, flax meadow, a unisex name.
Linlee, Linleigh, Linly, Lynley

Linton (English) flax town.
Lintonn, Lynton, Lyntonn

Linu (Hindu) lily.

Linus (Greek) flaxen-haired.
Linas, Linnas, Linnus, Linux, Lynas, Lynnas, Lynnus, Lynus

Lio (Hawaiian) lion cub.
Leno, Leo, Leon, Lerin, Lerond, Lerrin, Leryn

Lionel (French) young lion.
Leonal, Leonel, Lional, Lionall, Lionallo, Lionell, Lionello, Lyonal, Lyonel, Lyonell, Lyonello

Liron (Hebrew) my song.
Lyron

Lise (Native American) salmon's head out of the water.
Liese, Liesse, Lisse

Lisimba (African) lion.
Lasimba, Lasymba, Lisymba, Lysimba, Lysymba, Simba, Symba

Lister (English) cloth dyer.
Lyster

Lius (Polish) light.
Liuz, Lyus, Lyuz

Liwanu (Native American) growling bear.
Liwani

Llewellyn (Welsh) lion-like.
Lewellyn, Lewelyn, Lewys, Ljudevit, Llewelyn

Lleyton (English) meadow town.
Layten, Layton, Leyton, Llaytan, Llayten

Lloyd (English) grey-haired.
Lloid, Lloide, Lloyde, Loid, Loide, Loy, Loyd, Loyde, Loydie

Lobo (Spanish) wolf.

Lochlain (Irish, Scottish) land of lakes.
Lachlain, Lachlan, Lachlin, Laughlain, Laughlan, Laughlin, Lochlan, Lochlann, Lochlin, Locklain, Lacklan, Locklin, Locklyn

Locke (English) forest.
Lock, Lockwood

Lockie (Scottish) land of the lakes, a form of Lachlan.
Lachie, Lachlen, Lachlin, Lachlyn, Lachy, Lajuan, Locklen, Locklin, Locklyn, Locky

Lodovico (Italian) famous warrior, a form of Louis.

Loe (Hawaiian) king, a form of Roy.

Logan (Irish) from the hollow.
Llogan, Llogen, Loagan, Loagen, Logann, Logen, Loggan, Loghan, Loghen, Login, Logon, Logn, Logun, Logunn, Logyn

Lok (Chinese) happy.

Lokela (Hawaiian) famous spearman, a form of Roger.

Lokni (Native American) rain dripping through the roof.

Loman (Slavic) sensitive; (Irish) bare.
Lomman

Lombard (Latin) long-bearded.
Bard, Barr, Lombardo

Lon (Spanish) noble, ready, a form of Alonso; (Irish) strong, fierce.
Loni, Lonie, Lonn, Lonni, Lonnie, Lonny, Lony

Lonan (Native American) cloud.
Lonen, Lonin, Lonnan, Lonon, Lonyn

Lonato (Native American) flint stone.

London (English) fierce, the flowing river, capital city of Britain.
Londen, Londun, Londyn, Lunden, Lundon, Lundun

Long (Chinese) dragon; (Vietnamese) hair.

Loni (Spanish) noble, ready, a form of Alonso; (Irish) strong, fierce.
Lon, Lonie, Lonn, Lonni, Lonnie, Lonny, Lonso, Lony

Lono (Hawaiian) god of farming.

Lonzo (Spanish) noble, ready, a form of Alonso.
Lonsie, Lonso, Lonzie

Lootah (Native American) red.
Loota

Lopaka (Hawaiian) famous, brilliant, a form of Robert.

Lorant (Hungarian) one who has been crowned with a laurel, a form of Laurence.
Laurant, Laurent, Lorent

Lorcan (Irish) little, fierce.
Lorcen, Lorcin, Lorcon, Lorcyn, Lorkan

Lord (English) noble one, with a title.

Lorenzo (Italian) one who has been crowned with a laurel, a form of Laurence.

Lawrence, Loren, Lorenc, Lorence, Lorenco, Lorencz, Loreno, Lorens, Lorenso, Lorentz, Lorenz, Lorenza, Loreto, Loretto, Lorin, Lorinc, Lorins, Lorinso, Lorinzo, Loritz, Lorren, Lorrenzo, Lorrin, Lorrinzo, Lorryn, Loryn, Renzo, Zo

Loretto (Latin, Italian) one who has been crowned with a laurel, a form of Laurence.
Lal, Larry, Laurence, Lawrence, Loreto, Loris, Lorito, Loritto, Loritz, Lorreto, Lorretto, Lorrie, Lorrito, Lorritto, Lorry, Lory

Lorimer (French) saddler, maker of spurs.
Lori, Lorie, Lorri, Lorrie, Lorrimer, Lorrymer, Lorymer

Loring (German) son of the famous warrior.
Lorring

Loris (Dutch) clown.
Lorris, Lorrys, Lorys

Lorne (Latin) one who has been crowned with a laurel, a form of Laurence.
Laurn, Laurne, Lorn, Lornie

Lot (Hebrew) hidden; according to the Bible, Lot fled from Sodom, but his wife looked back and was turned into salt.
Llot, Llott, Lotte

Loudon (German) low valley.
Lewdan, Lewden, Lewdin, Lewdon, Lewdyn, Loudan, Louden, Loudin, Loudyn, Lowdan, Lowden, Lowdin, Lowdon, Lowdyn

Louis (German) famous warrior.
Alois, Aloisio, Alouis, Aloysius, Clovis, Lash, Lashi, Lasho, Lewes, Lewis, Lidek, Lou, Louie, Louies, Lucho, Lude, Ludirk, Ludis, Ludko, Ludwig,

Lui, Luigi, Luigio, Luis, Luiz, Luki, Lutek

Lourdes (French) from Lourdes in France, a unisex name.
Lou, Lourd, Lourde, Lourds

Louvain (English) vain.
Louvin

Lowell (English) loved; (French) wolf.
Lovel, Lovell, Lowel

Loyal (English, French) faithful.
Loy, Loyall, Loye, Lyal, Lyall, Lyel, Lyell

Lubomir (Polish) lover of peace.

Luc (French) bringer of light, a form of Luke.
Luca, Lucas, Luce, Luk

Luca (Italian) bringer of light, a form of Luke, a unisex name.
Louca, Louka, Lucca, Lucius, Luka, Lukka

Lucas (German, Irish) bringer of light, a form of Luke.
Loucas, Loukas, Luc, Luca, Lucais, Lucano, Lucca, Luccas, Lucio, Lucis, Luk, Luka, Lukas, Lukaz, Luke, Lukela, Luken, Luki, Lukis

Lucian (Latin) bringer of light, a form of Luke.
Loucian, Lucan, Lucanas, Lucas, Lucianas, Luciano, Lucianus, Lucias, Lucien, Lucjan, Luiz, Lukian, Lukianas, Lukyan, Luviano

Lucio (Italian) bringer of light, a form of Lucius.
Laucca, Loucio, Luca, Lucas, Luce, Lucien, Luke, Lusio

Lucky (English) fortunate, lucky.
Lucki, Luckie, Lukey, Luki, Lukie, Luky

Ludlow (English) hill of the prince.

Ludwig (German) famous warrior.
Ludovic, Ludovico, Ludvig

Luigi (Italian) famous warrior, a form of Louis.
Lui, Luiggi, Luigino, Luigy

Luis (Spanish) famous warrior, a form of Louis.
Lew, Lewis, Lewys, Ljudevit, Llewelyn, Llwellyn, Lodde, Lodewyck, Lodoe, Lood, Lou, Louis, Ludwik, Lui, Luigi, Luiz, Luthais

Luka (Italian) bringer of light, a form of Luke.
Luca

Luke (Latin) bringer of light.
Luc, Luca, Lucais, Lucano, Lucas, Lucca, Lucio, Luka, Lukas, Lukaz, Lukela, Luken, Luki, Lukk, Lukka

Luki (Basque) famous warrior.
Luc, Luca, Lucais, Lucano, Lucas, Lucca, Lucio, Luk, Luka, Lukas, Lukaz, Luke, Lukela, Luken

Lukman (Arabic) prophet.
Luqman

Lulani (Hawaiian) highest point in heaven, a unisex name.
Lulanee, Lulaney, Lulanie, Lulany

Lumo (African) born face down.

Lunn (Irish) warlike.
Lun, Lunni, Lunnie, Lunny, Luny

Lunt (Swedish) grove.

Lupus (Latin) as fierce as a wolf.

Luqman (Arabic) prophet.

Lusila (Hindu) one possesses leadership ability.

Lusio (African) light.
Aloys, Aloysius, Elois, Lajos, Lasho, Lewellen, Lewes, Lucio

Lutalo (African) warrior.

Lutfi (Arabic) kind, friendly.

Luther (German) renowned warrior.
Lothar, Lothario, Lother, Lothor, Lutero, Luthar, Luthario, Luthor

Luyu (Native American) head shaker.

Luzian (Russian) bringer of light, a form of Lucian.

Lyle (French) island.
Lisle, Ly, Lysl, Lysle

Lynch (Irish) mariner.
Linch, Linche, Lynche

Lyndon (English) linden tree hill.
Lin, Linden, Lindon, Lyden, Lydon, Lyn, Lynden, Lynn

Lyndsay (English) linden tree island.
Lindsee, Lindsey, Linsay, Linsee, Linsey, Lyndsee, Lyndsey

Lynley (English) from the field of flax, a unisex name.
Linlie, Linly, Lynlie, Lynly

Lynn (Anglo-Saxon) brook or pool, a unisex name.
Lin, Linn, Lyn, Lynard, Lynell, Lynette, Lynne, Lynoll

Lysander (Greek) liberator, emancipator.
Lisander, Lizander, Lyzander, Sander, Zander

Lytton (English) town by the loud stream.
Liton, Litton, Llyton, Llytton, Lyton

Maarten (Dutch) of the Roman god Mars.
Maartin, Marten, Martin

Mabon (Welsh) son.

Mac (Scottish) son.
Mack, Macke, Mackey, Mackie, Macklin, Macks, Macky

Macabee (Hebrew) hammer.
Maccabee, Mackabee, Makabee

Macadam (Scottish) son of Adam.
Mackadam, Makadam

Macaire (Greek) happy, a form of Makarios.
Macairo, Macario, Makario, Makarios

Macalister (Irish) son of Allister.
Macalaster, Macalister, MacAlister, Macallaster, Macallister, McAlaster, McAlister, McAllaster, McAllister

Macalla (Australian Aboriginal) full moon.
Macala, Macalah, Macallah

Macario (Spanish) happy, blessed, a form of Makarios.
Macaryo, Makario, Makaryo

Macarthur (Irish) son of Arthur.
MacArthur, McArthur

Macauley (Scottish) son of righteousness.
Macaulee, Macaulei, Macauleigh, MacAuley, Macauli, Macaulie, Macaullee, Macaulleigh, Macaulley, Macaullie, Macaully, Macauly, Maccauley, Mackaulee, Mackaulei, Mackauleigh, Mackauley, Mackauli, Mackaulie, Mackauly, Macualay, Macualey, McCauley

Macbeth (Scottish) son of Beth, Elizabeth.
MacBeth, Makbeth, McBeth

Macbride (Scottish) son of the follower of St Brigid.
MacBride, Macbryde, MacBryde, Mcbride, McBride, McBryde

MacCoy (Irish) son of Coy.
Maccoy, MacCoi, Mackoi, Mackoy, MacKoy, Macoy, Makcoi, Makcoy, McCoi, Mccoy, McCoy

Maccrae (Irish) son of grace.
MacCrae, Maccray, MacCray, Macrae, Macray, Makrae, Makray, McCrae, McCray, McCrea

MacDonald (Scottish) son of Donald.
Macdonald, MacDonel, MacDonell, MacDonna, MacDonnel, MacDonnell, McDonald, Mcdonald, McDonel, McDonell, McDonna, McDonnel, McDonnell

MacDougal (Scottish) son of Dougal.
Macdougal, MacDougall, McDougal, Mcdougal, McDougall

Mace (French) club.
Macey, Macon, Macy, Maice, Mayce

MacFarlane (English) son of Farlane.
Macfarlan, MacFarlan, Mackfarlan, Mackfarlane, Macpharlan, Macpharlane, Makfarlan,

*Makfarlane, Makpharlan,
Makpharlane, Mcfarlan, Mcfarlane,
Mcpharlan, Mcpharlane*

MacGregor (Scottish) son of
Gregor.

*Macgregor, MacGregorr, McGregor,
McGregorr*

Macharios (Greek) happy,
blessed.

*Macarios, Macarius, Macaryos,
Macharius, Macharyos, Makarios,
Makcarius, Makcaryos*

Machas (Polish) like God, a form
of Michael.

MacKenzie (Celtic) son of Kenzie,
child of the wise, handsome
leader, a unisex name.

*Macensie, Macenzie, Mackensie,
Mackensey, MacKensey, Mackensy,
MacKensy, Mackenze, MacKenze,
Mackenzey, MacKenzey, Mackenzi,
MacKenzi, Mackenzie, Mackenzly,
MacKenzly, Mackiensy, MacKiensy,
Mackinsy, MacKinsy, McKensey,
McKensy, McKiensy, McKinsy,
McKenze, Mckenzie, McKenzly*

MacKinnley (Irish) son of Kinley.

*Mackinley, MacKinley, Mackinnley,
McKinley, McKinnley*

MacMahon (Irish) son of Mahon.

Macmahon, Mcmahon, McMahon

MacMurray (Irish) son of Murray.

Macmurray, Mcmurray, McMurray

MacNair (Scottish) son of Nair.

Macknair, Macnair, Mcnair, McNair

Maco (Hungarian) God is with us,
a form of Emmanual.

Macon (German, Anglo-Saxon)
creator, maker.

Maccon, Macconn, Maconn

Maddock (Welsh) lucky, generous,
fortunate.

*Maddocks, Maddok, Maddoks,
Maddox, Maddux, Madoc,
Madog, Madok, Madoks, Madox*

Madison (English) good, child
of Maude or Matthew, a unisex
name.

*Maddisan, Maddisen, Maddison,
Maddy, Madisan, Madisen,
Madisson, Madisyn, Madsen*

Madongo (African)
uncircumcised.

Madu (African) people.

Magar (Armenian) attendant of
the groom.

Magee (Irish) son of Hugh.

*MacGee, Magey, Magie, Magy,
McGee*

Magen (Hebrew) protector.

Magnar (Norwegian) strong,
warrior.

Magna, Magne, Magner

Magnus (Latin) great.

*Maghnus, Magnes, Mahgnus,
Manius, Manus*

Magomu (African) younger of
twins.

Maguire (Irish) son of Guire.

*MacGuire, Macguire, Macgwire,
MacGwire, Magguire, Maggwire,
Magwire, McGuire, McGwire*

Mahdi (Arabic) guided, directed
to the right path.

Mahde, Mahdee, Mahdie, Mahdy

Mahesa (Hindu) great god.

Maahesa

Mahiai (Hawaiian) farmer, a form of George.

Mahi'ai, Mahi'Ai

Mahir (Arabic, Hebrew) excellent, industrious.

Maher, Mahyr

Mahkah (African) earth.

Mahka, Makah

Mahmoud (Arabic) the praised one, a form of Muhammad.

Mahamed, Mahamood, Mahamoud, Mahamud, Mahamuod, Mahamut, Mahmed, Mahmmet, Mahmmood, Mahmmoud, Mahmmud, Mahmmuod, Mahmmuot, Mahmmut, Mahmood, Mahmud, Mahmuod, Mahmut

Mahon (Irish) strong bear.

Mahpee (African) sky.

Mapee

Maimon (Arabic) lucky.

Maimonn, Maimun, Maimunn

Maitland (English) dweller in the meadowlands.

Maetie, Maetlan, Maetland, Maetlen, Maetlon, Maety, Mait, Maitey, Maitlan, Maitlen, Maitlon, Mate, Matey

Majid (Arabic) glorious.

Majd, Majdi, Majdy, Majed, Majeed, Majiid

Major (Latin) great.

Majar, Maje, Majer, Mayer, Mayjer, Mayjor, Mayor

Makaio (Hawaiian) gift of God, a form of Matthew.

Mataio

Makalani (African) writer.

Makalanee, Makalaney, Makalanie, Makalany

Makani (Hawaiian) wind, a unisex name.

Makanie, Makany

Makarios (Greek) happy, blessed.

Macario, Macarios, Maccario, Maccarios, Makario

Makin (Arabic) strong.

Makyn

Makis (Greek) like God, a form of Michael.

Makys

Makoto (Japanese) sincere.

Maks (Hungarian) form of Max, Maximilian, Maxwell.

Maksz, Makszi, Makz, Max

Maksim (Russian) greatest, a form of Maximilian.

Maksima, Maksimus, Maksym, Maksymilian, Maksymus, Maxim

Makya (Native American) eagle hunter.

Makyah

Malachy (Hebrew) angel of God, God's messenger.

Malachai, Malachey, Malachi, Malachie, Malakai, Malake, Malakey, Malaki, Malakie, Malchija, Malechai, Malechey, Malechi, Malechie, Malechy, Malik, Malikey, Maliki, Malikie

Malajitm (Hindu) garland of victory.

Malajit

Malcolm (Arabic) dove; (Scottish) follower of St Columba.

Malcalm, Malcohm, Malcolme, Malcolum, Malcom, Malcome,

Malcum, Malkolm, Malkolme, Malkom, Malkum

Maldon (English) covered meeting place in the wood.
Maldan, Malden, Maldin, Maldyn

Maleko (Hawaiian) warrior, warlike, from Mars, the god of war, a form of Mark.

Malik (Arabic) king.
Maalik, Mailic, Mailik, Malac, Malak, Malec, Maleca, Maleak, Maleec, Maleek, Maleic, Maleik, Malek, Maleka, Maleke, Malic, Malick, Malicke, Maliek, Maliik, Malike, Malikh, Maliq, Malique, Mallec, Malleck, Mallek, Mallic, Mallick, Mallik, Malyc, Malyck, Malyk, Malyq

Malin (English) little warrior.
Mallin, Mallon, Malon, Mallyn, Malyn

Mallory (French) wild duck, unlucky; (German) army counsellor, a unisex name.
Mal, Maleri, Malerie, Malery, Malleri, Mallerie, Mallery, Mallori, Mallorie, Malori, Malorie, Malory, Marlerie

Malone (Irish) servant of St John.
Mallone

Maloney (Irish) devoted to attending church.
Mallone, Malloney, Mallonie, Mallony, Malone, Malonie, Malony, Mollone, Molloney, Mollonie, Mollony, Molone, Moloney, Molonie, Molony

Malvern (Welsh) bare hill.
Mallvern, Mallverne, Malverne

Mamo (Hawaiian) yellow bird, saffron flower, a unisex name.
Maamaoh, Maamo, Maamoh, Mamoh

Manchu (Chinese) pure.

Manco (Peruvian) leader.

Mandala (African) flowers.
Mandal, Mandalah, Mandel, Mandela, Mandelah

Mandeep (Punjabi) mind filled with light.
Mandiep, Mandip

Mandel (German) almond.
Mandele, Mandell, Mandelle

Mander (Gypsy) from me.

Mandu (Australian Aboriginal) sun.

Manford (English) small ford, river crossing.
Manforde

Manfred (Anglo-Saxon) man of peace.
Mandred, Mandrid, Manferd, Manfredo, Manfret, Manfried, Maniferd, Manifred, Manifredo, Manifret, Manifried, Manfryd, Mannferd, Mannfred, Mannfredo, Mannfried, Mannfryd

Mango (Spanish) God is with us, a form of Emmanuel, Manuel.
Mungo

Manheim (German) servant.
Manheimm, Mannheim, Mannheimm

Manipi (Native American) wonderous living man.

Manius (Scottish) great, a form of Magnus.
Magnius, Magnus, Manus, Manyus

Manly (German, English) manly.
Manley, Manlie, Manne, Mannlie, Mannly, Manny

Mann (German) man, masculine.
Man, Manne

Manning (English) son of Mann.
Maning

Mannix (Irish) monk.
Manicks, Manics, Maniks, Manix, Mannicks, Mannics, Manniks, Mannocks, Mannocs, Mannoks, Mannox, Mannyx, Manox, Manyx

Manny (German, Spanish) God is with us, a form of Manuel.
Mani, Manie, Manni, Mannie, Many

Mano (Hawaiian) shark.
Manno, Manolo

Manoj (Hindu) cupid.

Mansa (African) king.

Mansel (English) home of the holy man.
Manse, Mansell, Mansle

Mansfield (English) hero's field, masculine one's field.
Mannsfeld, Mannsfield, Mansfeld

Mansur (Arabic) divinely helped.
Mansoor, Mansour

Manton (English) man's town.
Manten, Mannten, Mannton

Manu (Hindu) maker of laws of conduct; (Hawaaian) bird; (African) second-born son.

Manuel (Spanish) God is with us, a form of Emmanuel.
Manni, Mannie, Mannual, Mannuel, Manny, Mano, Manolon, Manual, Manuale, Manue, Manuele, Manuelli, Manuelo, Manyuli, Minel

Manville (French) worker's village; (English) hero's village.
Mandeville, Mandville, Manvel, Manvell, Manvil, Manvill

Manzo (Japanese) third-born son.

Maona (Native American) creator.

Mapira (African) millet, grass.

Marama (Polynesian) moon.

Marar (Native American) dust.
Marare, Mararr, Mararre, Marrar, Marrare

Marc (French) warrior, warlike, from Mars, the god of war, a form of Mark.
Marcas, Marcel, Marcell, Marcellin, Marcello, Marcellus, Marco, Marcus, Mark

Marcas (Irish) warrior, warlike, from Mars, the god of war, a form of Mark.
Marc, Marcus, Mark

Marcel/Marcell (Latin) warrior, warlike, from Mars, the god of war.
Marc, Marcello, Marcellus, Marco, Marcus, Mark

Marcelino (Italian) warrior, warlike, from Mars, the god of war, a form of Marcel.
Marcel, Marcelin, Marceline, Marcelinus, Marcellin, Marcelline, Marcellino, Marcellinus, Marciano

Marcellus (Latin) warrior, warlike, from Mars, the god of war.
Marc, Marcel, Marcell, Marcello, Marcellus, Marcelo, Marcelus, Marco, Marcus, Mark

March (English) boundary dweller.

Marcilka (Hungarian) warrior, warlike, from Mars, the god of war, a form of Marcel.

Marcin (Polish) warrior, warlike, from Mars, the god of war, a form of Martin.
Maarcin, Marcian

Marco (Spanish) warrior, warlike, from Mars, the god of war, a form of Marcus.
Marc, Marcos, Marcus, Marius, Martin

Marcus (Latin) warrior, warlike, from Mars, the god of war.
Marc, Marcas, Marcel, Marcell, Marcello, Marcelo, Marcis, Marco, Marcos, Mark

Marek (Czech) warrior, warlike, from Mars, the god of war, a form of Marcus.
Marrek

Maren (Basque) sea.
Maran, Marin, Maron, Marran, Marren, Marrin, Marron, Marryn, Maryn

Mareo (Japanese) uncommon.

Marid (Arabic) rebellious.
Marrid

Marin (French) sailor.
Marian, Mariane, Mariano, Marine, Mariner, Marino, Marinos, Marinus, Mario, Marrian, Marriane, Marrin, Marrine, Marriner, Marrino, Marrinos, Marrinus, Marrio

Mario (Italian) warrior, warlike, from Mars, the god of war.
Marcus, Mariius, Marios, Marious, Marius, Marrio, Marrios

Marion (French) wished for, star of the sea, bitter, masculine form of Mary, a unisex name.
Mareon, Marian, Mariano, Marien, Mariene, Marrion

Marius (Latin) warrior, warlike, from Mars, the god of war, a form of Mario.
Mario, Marios, Marious

Mark (Latin) warrior, warlike, from Mars, the god of war.
Marc, Marcas, Marcel, Marcell, Marcello, Marcelo, Marco, Marcos, Marcus, Marek, Marian, Marion, Marius, Markas, Marke, Markee, Markel, Markess, Markey, Marko, Markus, Marque, Marques, Marqus, Martial, Marx

Markese (French) nobleman, a form of Marquis.
Markees, Markei, Markeis, Markes, Markez, Markeze, Markiece, Markis, Markise

Marlin (English) deep-sea fish.
Marlen, Marlien, Marlion, Marlyn

Marlon (French) little falcon.
Marlin, Marlyn, Merlin, Merlon, Merlyn

Marlow (English) from the lake by the hill.
Mar, Marlo, Marlowe, Marrlow, Marrlowe

Marmaduke (Irish) servant of Madoc; (Anglo-Saxon) noble, mighty.
Duke, Marmeduke, Marmiduke, Marmie, Marmy

Marmion (French) tiny; (Irish) sea bright.
Marmi, Marmione, Marmionn, Marmionne, Marmy, Mars

Marnin (Hebrew) one who sings and brings joy.
Marnyn

Maro (Japanese) myself.
Marow, Marro, Marrow

Marquan (American) combination of Mark and Quan.
Marquane, Marquante

Marquel (American) warrior, warlike, from Mars, the god of war, a form of Marcel.
Markual, Markuel, Marlea, Marleigh, Marly, Marqueal, Marquelis, Marquell, Marquiel, Marquil, Marquill, Marquillus, Marqwel, Marrley

Marques/Marquez (Portuguese) nobleman.
Markes, Markqes, Markques, Markquese, Markquez, Marqez, Marquess, Marquezz, Marquies, Marquiez, Marquillis, Marqus

Marquis (French) nobleman.
Marcius, Marcuis, Markes, Markis, Markius, Markqes, Markques, Markquese, Markquis, Markquise, Markuis, Marqez, Marques, Marquess, Marquez, Marquezz, Marquiez, Marquillis, Marquise, Marquiss, Marquisse, Marquiz, Marquize, Marquizz, Marqus

Marr (Spanish) divine.
Mar

Marsalis (Italian) warrior, warlike, from Mars, the god of war, a form of Marcellus.
Marsalius, Marsallis, Marsallius, Marsallus, Marsalus, Marselis, Marsellis, Marsellus, Marselus

Marsden (English) marsh valley, warrior's valley.
Marsdan, Marsdin, Marsdon, Marsdyn

Marsh (English) flooded low-land, marsh.
Marsch, Marshall, Marshe

Marshal/Marshall (French) caretaker of the horses.
Marschal, Marschall, Marschat, Marschel, Marschell, Marsh, Marshel, Marshell

Marshawn (American) combination of Mark and Shawn.
Marsean, Marshaine, Marshaun, Marshean, Marshon, Marshun

Marston (English) town by the lake, warrior's town.
Marstan, Marsten, Marstin, Marstyn

Martell (English) one who wields the hammer.
Martel, Martele, Martelis, Martelle, Martellis

Marten (Dutch) warrior, warlike, from Mars, the god of war, a form of Martin.
Maarten, Maartin, Maartyn, Marcen, Marcin, Marcyn, Martin, Martyn

Martez (Spanish) warrior, warlike, from Mars, the god of war, a form of Martin.
Martaz, Martaze, Martee, Martes, Martese, Marteze, Martice, Martie, Martiece, Marties, Martiese, Martiez, Martieze, Martines, Martinez, Martinus, Martis, Martise, Martiz, Martize

Martin (Latin) warrior, warlike, from Mars, the god of war.
Maarten, Maartin, Maarty, Maartyn, Mairten, Mairtin, Marcel, Marcell, Marcello, Marcelo, Marcen, Marcin, Marco, Marcus, Marcyn, Martain, Martainn,

Martan, Marten, Martez, Marti, Martie, Martijn, Martins, Marto, Marton, Marttan, Martten, Marttin, Martton, Marttyn, Marty, Martyn, Mattin, Mertin, Morten, Moss

Martino (Italian) warrior, warlike, from Mars, the god of war, a form of Martin.

Marcel, Marcell, Marcello, Marco, Marcus, Martinius, Martinos, Martinus

Marty (Latin) warrior, warlike, from Mars, the god of war, a form of Martin.

Maarten, Maarty, Marcel, Marcell, Marcello, Marco, Marcus, Martie, Martin

Marut (Hindu) god who controls the wind.

Marvell (Latin) miracle, wondrous.

Marv, Marve, Marvel, Marvele, Marvelle, Marvello, Marvelo, Marvyn, Mervyn

Marvin (English) famous friend, friend of the sea.

Marv, Marvein, Marven, Marvion, Marvn, Marvon, Marvyn, Marwen, Marwin, Marwyn, Merven, Mervin, Mervyn

Marwan (Arabic) history.

Marwen, Marwin, Marwon, Marwyn

Marzuq (Arabic) blessed by God, fortunate.

Masaccio (Italian) twin.

Masacio, Masaki, Masakio, Masakkio

Masahiro (Japanese) broadminded.

Masamba (African) leaving.

Masao (Japanese) righteous.

Masato, Masayo

Mashama (African) surprising.

Mashamah

Maska (Native American) powerful.

Maslin (French) little twin, little Thomas.

Maslan, Maslen, Maslon, Maslyn

Mason (Latin) stone worker.

Maasen, Maasin, Maason, Mace, Maisen, Maisin, Maison, Masen, Masin, Massan, Massin, Masson, Massun, Massyn, Masun, Masyn, Sonny

Masou (Native American) fire god.

Massey (English) twin.

Masi, Massi, Massie, Massy, Masy

Massimiliano (Italian) greatest, a form of Maximilian.

Masimilian, Masimiliano, Masimillian, Masimilliano, Massimilian, Massimillian, Massimilliano

Massimo (Italian) greatest, a form of Max.

Masimo, Massymo, Masymo

Masud (African) fortunate one, lucky.

Masood, Masoud, Mhasood, Mhasoud, Mhasud

Matai (Slavic, Hebrew) gift of God, a form of Matthew.

Mate, Matei

Matareka (Polynesian) the face that always smiles.

Mateen (Arabic) polite.

Matteen

Mateo (Spanish) gift of God, a form of Matthew.
Matei, Mateusz, Matias, Mattei, Matteo, Mattius

Mateusz (Slavic) gift of God, a form of Matthew.
Matejs, Mateus, Matteus, Matteusz

Mathe (German) gift of God, a form of Matthew.
Math, Matheu, Matth, Mattheu

Mather (English) powerful army.

Mathew (Hebrew) gift of God, a form of Matthew.

Mathias (German) gift of God, a form of Matthew.
Maitias, Mathi, Mathia, Mathis, Matias, Matthia, Mattgieus, Mattia, Mattias, Mattus, Matus

Mathieu (French) gift of God, a form of Matthew.
Mathie, Mathieux, Mathiew, Matthiew, Mattieu, Mattieux

Mato (Native American) brave.

Matope (African) our last-born child.
Matop

Matteo (Italian) gift of God, a form of Matthew.
Matei, Mateo, Mateusz, Matias, Mattei, Matteusz, Mattias

Matthew (Hebrew) gift of God.
Macias, Macie, Macisk, Mado, Mafew, Maffew, Mafthew, Mat, Mata, Mataus, Matausas, Mate, Matej, Mateo, Mateos, Mateoz, Mateus, Mateusz, Matfei, Mathes, Mathew, Mathia, Mathias, Mathies, Mathieu, Mathiew, Matius, Matsu, Matt, Matta, Mattaus, Matte, Mattea, Matteo, Matteos, Matteoz, Matteus, Matteusz, Mattey,

Matthes, Matthias, Matthies, Matthieu, Matthiew, Matti, Mattia, Mattias, Mattie, Mattis, Mattius, Matty, Matui, Maty, Matya, Matyas

Matu (Native American) brave warrior.
Mattu

Matus (Slavic) gift of God, a form of Matthew.
Maitais, Maitius, Mathi, Mathia, Mathias, Mathis, Matias, Matius, Mattia, Mattias, Mattius, Mattus

Matvey (Russian) gift of God, a form of Matthew.
Matka, Matvie, Matviko, Matviy, Matvy, Matya, Matyash

Mauli (Latin, Hawaiian) dark-skinned man from the moor, a form of Maurice.
Maulli

Maurice (Latin) dark-skinned man from the moor.
Mauli, Maur, Maurace, Maurance, Maurece, Maurell, Maurence, Maureo, Mauricio, Maurids, Maurie, Mauriece, Maurikas, Maurilio, Maurillio, Maurin, Maurino, Maurise, Maurisse, Mauritz, Maurius, Maurize, Maurizio, Mauro, Maurrys, Maurtel, Maurys, Moris, Moritz, Morrel, Morrice, Morrie, Morries, Morris, Morrys, Morys

Maurilio (Italian) dark-skinned man from the moor.
Maurice, Mauricio, Maurie, Maurillio, Maurillo, Maurilo, Maurizio, Moris, Morrie, Morris

Mauro (Italian) dark-skinned man from the moor, a form of Maurice.

Mawuli (African) God is real.

Max (Latin) a form of Maximilian, Maxwell.

Mac, Mack, Macks, Macs, Maks, Maxe, Maxim, Maxin, Maxx, Maxxy, Maxy

Maxfield (English) Mack's field.

Macfield, Macfyld, Mackfield, Mackfyld, Makfield, Makfyld, Maxfyld

Maximilian (Latin) greatest.

Mac, Mack, Macks, Macs, Maixam, Maixim, Mak, Makhew, Maks, Maksam, Maksim, Maksym, Max, Maxamili, Maxamilian, Maxamilion, Maxamillian, Maxamillion, Maxamillon, Maxemilian, Maxemilion, Maxemillian, Maxmillion, Maxi, Maxie, Maximilean, Maximilia, Maximilion, Maximillean, Maximillian, Maximillion, Maxmilan, Maxmilian, Maxmilion, Maxmillian, Maxmillion

Maximos (Greek) greatest, a form of Maximilian.

Maximo, Maximus

Maxwell (English) great spring.

Mac, Mack, Mackswell, Macswell, Max, Maxi, Maxie, Maxwel

Mayer (German) dairy worker; (Hebrew) light.

Magnus, Mahyar, Maier, Maiyer, Major, Mayeer, Mayor, Mayur

Mayes (English) field.

Mayo, Mays

Mayhew (English) gift of God, a form of Matthew.

Maehew, Maihew, Meyhew

Maynard (Teutonic) powerful.

May, Mayne, Maynhard, Maynor, Meinard, Meinhard, Menard, Meynard, Meynhard

Mayo (Irish) plain of the yew trees.

Mayes, Mays

Mazin (Arabic) proper.

Mazen, Mazenn, Mazinn, Mazzen, Mazzin

Mazzi (African) gentleman, sir.

Mazi

Mbita (African) born on a cold night.

Mbwana (African) master.

McKay (Irish) son of Kay.

Mackae, Mackai, Mackay, MacKay, Macky, McKae, McKai

McKenzie (Irish) son of Kenzie.

Mackennsie, Mackennzie, Mackensey, Mackensie, Mackensy, Mackenzey, Mackenzie, Mackenzy, McKennson, McKensey, McKensie, McKenson, McKensy, McKenzi, McKenzy, McKinsie, McKinsy

Mead/Meade (English) from the meadow.

Meed, Meede

Medgar (German) great spearman, a form of Edgar.

Edgar, Medger

Medric (English) flourishing meadow.

Mead, Meade, Meadric, Medrick, Medrik, Medryc, Medryck, Medryk

Medwin (English) good, worthy friend.

Medwen, Medwyn

Mehtar (Hindu) prince.

Mehta

Meinhard (German) firm, strong.

Meinhardt, Meinhart, Meinke,

Meino, Meinrad, Mendor, Menhard, Menhardt, Menhart

Meir (Hebrew) he who shines, brightens.
Mayer, Meyer, Meyr, Muki, Myer

Meka (Hawiaiian) eyes.

Mekari (Australian Aboriginal) new.

Mel (Irish) Mel's friend; (English) counsel friend, mill friend, a form of Melvin.
Mell

Melbourne (English) from the mill stream.
Melborn, Melborne, Melbourn, Melburn, Melburne, Melby, Milborn, Milborne, Milburn, Milburne

Meldon (English) mill close to the hill.
Malden, Maldon, Melden

Meldrick (English) strong, powerful mill.
Meldric, Meldrik, Meldryc, Meldryck, Meldryk

Melvern (Native American) great chief.
Melverne, Melvirn, Melvirne, Melvyrn, Melvyrne

Melville (English) mill village.
Mellville, Milville

Melvin (Irish) Mel's friend; (English) counsel friend, mill friend.
Mal, Malvin, Malvinn, Malvyn, Malvynn, Mel, Melwin, Melvinn, Melwyn, Melvyn, Melvynn

Menachem (Hebrew) comforter.
Menacheme, Menachen, Menachene, Menahem, Nachman

Menassah (Hebrew) reason to forget.
Manessa, Manessah, Manesse, Manesseh, Menasha, Menashah, Menashe, Menasheh, Menashi, Menashia, Menashiah, Menassa, Menasse, Menasseh, Menassi, Menassia, Menassiah

Mengesha (Eithopian) kingdom.

Menico (Spanish) belonging to God, a form of Dominic.
Minico

Mensah (African) third-born son.
Mensa

Mercer (Latin) merchant, a unisex name.
Merca, Merce, Merse

Meredith (Celtic) protector of the sea, a unisex name.
Meredeth, Meredithe, Meredyth, Meredythe, Meridath, Merideth, Meridith, Merry

Merit (English) of great value, merit.
Meret, Merett, Meritt, Merrett, Merritt

Merle (French) blackbird, a unisex name.
Mearle, Merl

Merlin (English) hawk, falcon; (Welsh) fort or hill by the sea, falcon.
Merle, Merlen, Merlinn, Merlon, Merlyn, Merrlen, Merrlin, Merrlon, Merrlyn

Merrick (English) ruler of the sea.
Mereck, Merek, Meric, Merick, Merik, Merric, Merrik, Meryck, Meryk, Meyrick, Meyrik, Myruc

Merrill (Irish) bright sea.
> Merel, Merell, Meril, Merill, Merle, Merrell, Meryl, Meryll

Merton (English) town by the sea.
> Mertan, Merten, Mertin, Mertyn, Murton

Merv (English) famous friend, a form of Mervyn.

Mervin/Mervyn (English) famous friend.
> Marvin, Marvyn, Merv, Merve, Merven, Mervinn, Mervynn, Merwin, Merwinn, Merwyn, Merwynn, Murven, Murvin, Murvyn, Myrven, Myrvin, Myrvyn

Meshach (Hebrew) artist.

Mesut (Turkish) happy.

Methuselah (Hebrew) man of the ages.
> Methusela

Meyer (German) farmer.
> Mayer, Meier, Myer

Mhina (African) delightful.

Micah (Hebrew) one who is like the Lord, a form of Michael, one of the archangels, a unisex name.
> Makeira, Maki, Mica, Mical, Michal, Micheal, Michean, Michel, Michele, Mick, Mike, Mitchel, Mitchell

Michael (Hebrew) like God.
> Meikal, Meikel, Meikil, Meikyl, Mekal, Mekel, Mekele, Mekil, Mekyl, Mic, Mica, Micah, Michail, Michal, Michale, Michan, Micheil, Michel, Michele, Mick, Micki, Mickie, Micky, Miekal, Miekel, Miekil, Miekyl, Miguel, Mihael, Mik, Mika, Mikael, Mikail, Mike, Mikel, Mikhail, Miki, Mikie, Mikkel, Miklos, Mikol, Mikos, Miky, Mischa,

Misshael, Mitchel, Mitchell, Myc, Mychael, Mychal, Myck, Myckael, Myckaele, Myckaell, Myckaelle, Mycki, Myckie, Mycky, Mykael, Mykaele, Mykaell, Mykaelle, Mykai, Myke, Mykey, Mykhas, Myki, Mykie, Mykil, Mykill, Mykyl, Mykyle, Mykyll, Mykylle

Michail (Russian) like God, a form of Michael.
> Mihas, Mikail, Mikale, Misha

Michal (Polish) like God, a form of Michael.
> Michale, Michalek, Michall, Michalle, Michas

Micheal (Irish) like God, a form of Michael.

Michel (French) like God, a form of Michael.
> Michaud, Miche, Michee, Michele, Michell, Michelle, Michon

Michelangelo (Italian) Michael the angel.
> Micelangelo, Michelange, Miguelangelo, Mikelangelo

Michele (Italian) like God, a form of Michael.
> Michel, Michelino

Michio (Japanese) one with the strength of three thousand.

Miguel (Spanish) like God, a form of Michael.
> Migeal, Migel, Migual, Miguale, Miguall, Migualle, Miguele, Miguell, Miguelle, Miui, Myguel, Myguele, Myguell, Myguelle

Mika (Native American) racoon; (Russian) like God, a form of Michael.
> Mikah, Myka, Mykah

Mikasi (Native American) coyote.
Mykasi

Mike (English) like God, a form of Michael.
Mick, Michel, Mik, Mitchel, Myke

Mikhail (Greek, Russian) like God, a form of Michael.
Mekhail, Mihali, Mihaly, Mikael, Mikeil, Mikhael, Mikhale, Mikhalis, Mikhalka, Mikhall, Mikheil, Mikhel, Mikhos

Miki (Japanese) tree.
Mikio

Mikkel (Scandinavian) like God, a form of Michael.
Mikel, Mikell, Mikka, Mikkael, Mikko, Mikkol, Mikle, Mikmol, Miko

Miksa (Slavic) greatest, a form of Maximilan.
Miks, Myksa

Milan (Slavic) loveable.
Milaan, Milano, Milen, Millaan, Millan, Millen, Mylan, Mylon

Milap (Native American) giving.

Milburn (English) mill stream.
Milborn, Milborne, Milbourn, Milbourne, Milburne, Millborn, Millborne, Millbourn, Millbourne, Millburn, Millburne

Milek (Polish) victory of the people, a form of Nicholas.
Millek, Mylek

Miles (Latin) soldier; (German) merciful.
Milas, Milles, Milo, Myles, Mylles, Mylo

Milford (English) mill near the ford.
Milforde, Millford, Mylford, Myllford

Mililani (Hawaiian) heavenly caress.
Mililanee, Mililaney, Mililanie, Mililany

Milko (German) industrious; (Latin) flatterer, a form of Emil.
Milkins

Millard (English) caretaker of the mill.
Milard, Mill, Millar, Miller, Millward, Milward, Myller

Miller (English) grain grinder, miller.
Mellar, Millar, Millard, Millen, Myller

Mills (English) mill keeper, of the mill.
Millard, Miller, Milward, Mylls, Mylward

Milo (Latin) soldier; (German) merciful, a form of Miles.
Mylo

Milos (Greek) pleasant.
Milo, Mylo, Mylos

Miloslav (Slavic) covered with glory.
Milloslav, Myloslav

Milton (English) mill town.
Millton, Myllton, Mylton, Nillton, Nilton, Nyllton, Nylton

Milward (English) mill keeper.
Millard, Miller, Mills, Millward, Myllward, Mylward

Mimis (Greek) lover of the earth, a form of Demetrius.
Mymis

Min (Burmese) king.
Mina

Miner (English) worker in the mine.
Minah, Myn, Myna, Mynah, Myner

Minet (French) delightful.
Minett, Mynet, Mynett

Ming (Chinese) named after a dynasty.
Mingh, Minhduc, Minhtong, Minhu

Mingan (Native American) grey wolf.
Myngan

Minkah (African) just, fair.
Minka, Mynka, Mynkah

Minor (Latin) youngest, smallest, junior.
Mynor

Minoru (Japanese) fruitful.

Miron (Polish) peace.
Mirron, Myron, Myrron

Miroslav (Czech) peace, glory.
Myroslav

Mirwais (Afghan) noble ruler.

Misha (Russian) like God, a form of Michael.
Misa, Mischa, Mischael, Mishael, Mishal, Misho, Misi, Misik, Miska, Misko, Miso, Missael

Mister (English) mister.
Mista, Mistar, Mistur, Mysta, Mystar, Myster, Mystur

Misu (Native American) rippling water.
Mysu

Mitchell (English) like God, a form of Michael.
Mick, Michel, Mike, Mitch, Mitchael, Mitchal, Mitchall, Mitchel, Mitchil, Mitchill

Mitford (English) river crossing.
Mitforde

Modesto (Latin) modest.
Modeste, Modesti, Modestie, Modesty

Modred (Latin) to consume, bite.
Modrid

Moe (English) drawn out of the water, saved, a form of Moses.
Mo

Moffatt (Celtic) long plain.
Mofat, Mofatt, Moffat

Mogens (Dutch) powerful.
Mogan, Mogans, Mogen

Mohammed (Arabic) the praised one, name of the Prophet.
Mahamed, Mahomet, Mohamed, Mohammad, Mohommad, Mohommed, Muhamed, Muhammed

Mohan (Hindu) delightful.

Moki (Australian Aboriginal) cloudy.
Mokee, Mokey, Mokie, Moky

Monahan (Irish) monk.
Monaghan, Monoghan, Monohan

Mongo (African) famous.

Monroe (English) the River Roe.
Monro, Munro, Munroe

Montague (French) pointed mountain.
Montagne, Montagu

Montana (Spanish) mountain.
Montanah

Monte (Latin) mountain.
Montee, Montey, Monti, Montie, Monty

Montez (Spanish) one who lives at the mountain.
Monteiz, Monteze, Montise, Montiz, Montize, Montyz, Montyze

Montgomery (English) wealthy man's mountain.
Montgomerey, Montgomerie, Montie, Monty

Montre (French) show.

Montreal (French) royal mountain.
Montrail, Montral, Montrale, Montrall, Montreale, Montrel, Montrell, Montroyal, Montroyale

Montsho (African) black.

Monty (English) wealthy man's mountain, a form of Montague.
Montee, Montey, Monti, Montie

Mordecai (Hebrew) martial, warlike.
Mordekai

Mordred (Latin) pain, painful.
Modred, Mordrid

Morel (French) mushroom.
Morell, Morrel, Morrell

Moreland (English) moor, marshland.
Morelan

Morgan (Welsh) from the sea, a unisex name.
Morgain, Morgen, Morgin, Morgon, Morgun, Morgyn

Morio (Japanese) woods, forest.
Moryo

Morley (English) meadow near the moor, marsh.
Morlea, Morlee, Morleigh, Morli, Morlie, Morly

Morrison (English) son of Morris.
Morisen, Morison, Morrisen

Mortimer (French) still water.
Mort, Morty, Mortymer

Morton (English) town by the moor, marsh.
Morten

Morven (Scottish) mariner.
Morvan, Morvin, Morvon, Morvyn

Moses (Hebrew) drawn out of the water, saved.
Moise, Moises, Mos, Mose, Mosse, Mosses, Moyse, Moyses, Moz, Mozes

Mosi (African) first-born child.
Mosee, Mosey, Mosie, Mosy

Mostyn (Welsh) field of the fortress.
Mostin

Moswen (African) light in colour.
Moswin, Moswyn

Motega (Native American) new arrow.

Mozart (Italian) breathless.
Motzart, Mozar

Mu'adh (Arabic) protected.
Muad, Muadh

Mu'awiyah (Arabic) young fox.
Muawiya, Muawiyah

Mubarak (Arabic) happy, blessed.
Mubarrak

Mufid (Arabic) useful.
Mufeed

Muhammed (Arabic) the praised one, name of the Prophet.
Mahomed, Mahomet, Mehemet,

Mehmet, Mohamed, Mahammad, Mohammad, Mohammed, Muhamed

Muhanned (Arabic) sword.
Muhanad, Muhaned, Muhannad

Muhsin (Arabic) beneficent, charitable.
Musin

Muhtadi (Arabic) rightly guided.
Mutadi

Muir (Scottish, Anglo-Saxon) moor, marsh.
Muer, Muire, Muyer, Muyr, Muyre

Mujahid (Arabic) fighter in the way of Allah.

Mukasa (African) God's chief administrator.

Mukhtar (Arabic) chosen.
Muktar

Mukul (Hindu) bud, blossom, the soul.

Mulogo (African) wizard.

Mundan (African) garden.
Mundana

Mungo (Scottish) friendly, lovable.
Mungoe

Munir (Arabic) brilliant.
Muneer

Munny (Cambodian) wise.
Munee, Muney, Muni, Munie, Munnee, Munney, Munni, Munnie, Muny

Muntasir (Arabic) victorious.
Muntassir

Muraco (Native American) white moon.
Muracco

Murali (Hindu) flute player.
Muralli

Murat (Turkish) wish come true.
Murrat

Murdoch (Scottish) wealthy mariner.
Murdoc, Murdock, Murdok

Murphy (Irish) from the sea, a unisex name.
Murph, Murphee, Murphey, Murphi, Murphie

Murray (Scottish) sailor.
Murae, Muray, Murrae, Murrai, Murree, Murrey, Murri, Murrie, Murry

Murtadi (Arabic) satisfied.
Murtadhi, Murtadhy, Murtady

Musa (Arabic) drawn out of the water, saved, a form of Moses.
Moosa, Moses

Mus'ad (Arabic) unfettered camel.
Musad

Mustafa (Arabic) chosen one.
Mostafa, Mostafah, Mostaffa, Mostaffah, Moustafa, Moustafah, Moustaffa, Moustaffah, Mustafah, Mustaffa, Mustaffah

Muti (Arabic) obedient.

Muwaffaq (Arabic) successful.
Muwafaq

Myall (Australian Aboriginal) drooping acacia.
Mial, Miall, Myal

Myer (Hebrew) light.
Meier, Mier, Mire, Mires, Myers

Myles (Latin) soldier.
Miles, Mieles, Mylles

Myron (Greek) sweet fragrant oil.
Miron

N

Naal (Irish) birth.

Naaman (Hebrew) pleasant.
Naman

Nabiha (Arabic) intelligent.
Naabeeha, Naabeha, Naabiha, Nabeeha, Naebeha, Naebeeha, Naebiha

Nabil (Arabic) noble prince.
Nabeel, Nabiel, Naebel, Naebil, Naebiel

Nachman (Hebrew) comforter, a form of Menachem.
Nach, Nachie, Nachum, Naechem, Nahum

Nada (Arabic) generous, a unisex name.
Nadah, Nadan, Nadav, Nadda, Nade, Nadeh, Nadiv

Nader (Arabic) dear, rare, a form of Nadir.
Nadar, Nayder

Nadim (Arabic) friend.
Nadeem

Nadir (Arabic) dear, rare.
Nader, Nadyr

Nadisu (Hindu) beautiful river.

Naeem (Arabic) kind, benevolent.
Naem, Naim, Naiym, Nayeem, Nieem, Nyeem

Nagaraj (Hindu) king of serpents.

Nagendra (Hindu) a name for the serpent god Sesh.
Nagesh

Nagid (Hebrew) prince, leader, noble.
Nagyd

Naham (Hebrew) consoling, sighing.
Nahum

Nahele (Hawaiian) forest.
Nahel, Nahell, Nahelle

Nahma (Native American) sturgeon fish.
Nama

Nailah (Arabic) one who succeeds, a unisex name.
Naela, Naila, Nayla, Naylah

Naim (Arabic) ease, tranquillity.
Naym

Nairn (Scottish) alder tree river.
Nairne

Naji (Arabic) safe.
Najae, Najee, Najei, Najie

Najib (Arabic) of noble descent.
Najeeb, Najibb

Najjar (Arabic) carpenter.
Najar

Najji (African) second-born child.
Naji

Najm al Din (Arabic) star of the faith.

Nakia (Arabic) pure.
Nakai, Nakee, Nakeia, Naki, Nakiah, Nakii

Nakos (Native American) wise sage.

Nam (Vietnamese) to scrape off.

Namaka (Hawaiian) eyes.

Namid (Native American) star dancer.
Named

Nando (Spanish) courageous, adventurous, a form of Ferdinando.
Nandor, Nandos, Nandu

Nangila (African) child born while his parents travel.
Nangilah, Nangyla, Nangylah

Nansen (Swedish) son of Nancy.
Nansan, Nansin, Nanson, Nansyn

Nantai (Native American) chief.
Nantay

Nantan (Native American) spokesman.
Nanten, Nantin, Nanton, Nantyn

Naoko (Japanese) honest, straightforward.

Napashni (Native American) he is courageous and does not flee.
Napaeshni, Napyashni, Napasni

Napier (Greek) from the new city.
Naper, Napyer, Neper, Nepier, Nepyer

Napoleon (Italian) from the city of Naples; (Greek) lion of the woods.
Leon, Nap, Napol, Napoleone, Napolion, Napolione, Nappie, Nappy

Naquan (American) combination of prefix Na and Quan.
Naqawn, Naquain, Naquawn, Naquen, Naquon

Narain (Hindu) protector, guardian, a name for the god Vishnu.
Narayn, Narian, Naryan

Narasimha (Hindu) incarnation of the god Vishnu.
Narasima

Narayan (Hindu) son of man, way of man.
Narayana

Narcissus (Greek) daffodil, self-love, the young man who fell in love with his own reflection, according to Greek myth.
Narcis, Narcisco, Narcisse, Narcisus, Narkis, Narkisso

Nard (Persian) chess player.
Narde

Nardo (German) strength; (Spanish) bold as a bear, a form of Bernardo.
Barnard, Barney, Barny, Bern, Bernard, Bernie, Nard, Narde, Nardos

Narendra (Hindu) king.

Narrie (Australian Aboriginal) bushfire.
Narree, Narrey, Narrie, Narry

Narve (Dutch) healthy, strong.
Narv

Nashashuk (Native American) loud thunder.

Nashoba (Native American) wolf.
Nash, Nasho, Nashobi, Obi, Shobi

Nasim (Persian) fresh air, breeze.
Naseem, Nasym

Nasir (African) helper, defender.

Naaser, Naasir, Naazer, Naazir, Naeser, Naesir, Naezer, Naezir, Naser, Nazer, Nazir, Nazzer, Nazzie, Nazzir, Nazzy

Nasir al Din (Arabic) protector of the faith.

Nasser (Arabic) victorious.
Naseer, Naser, Nasier, Nasir, Nasr, Nassir, Nassor

Nat (English) gift from God, a form of Nathan, Nathaniel.
Natt, Nattie, Natty

Natal (Spanish) born at Christmas, a form of Noel.
Naital, Naitale, Naitel, Nat, Natale, Natalino, Natalio, Nate, Naytal, Naytale, Naytel

Natan (Hebrew) gift of God, God has given.
Natane, Nate, Naten, Nathan, Nathen, Nathon, Naton

Nataraj (Hindu) king of dance.

Nate (Hebrew) gift of God, a form of Nathan, Nathaniel.
Naet, Naete, Nait, Naite, Nat, Nath, Nayt, Nayte

Nathan (Hebrew) gift of God, a form of Nathaniel.
Naethan, Naithan, Nat, Nate, Nath, Nathaen, Nathann, Nathen, Nathian, Nathin, Nathon, Nathyn, Natthan, Naythan, Nethan, Niel, Than

Nathaniel (Hebrew) gift of God.
Nat, Natanael, Nataniel, Nate, Nathan, Nathanael, Nathanal, Nathaneal, Nathaneil, Nathanel, Nathanial, Nathanil, Nathanile, Nathannal, Nathannial, Nathanniel, Nathannil, Nathanual, Nathanyal, Natheneol, Nathenial, Natheniel, Natty, Nethaniel, Thaniel

Natividad (Spanish) the nativity.
Natividade, Natividadio

Navarro (Spanish) plains.
Nava, Navar, Navare, Navaro, Navarr, Navarre, Varr, Varro

Naveen (Hindu) new, modern.
Navene, Navin, Navine, Navyn, Navyne

Navin (Hindu) new.
Navyn

Nayati (Native American) wrestler.

Naylor (English) nail maker.
Nailor, Naylar, Nayler

Nazareth (Hebrew) person of Nazareth.
Nazaire, Nazaret, Nazarie, Nazario, Nazim, Nazir, Naziret, Nazireth, Nazz, Nazzareth

Nazih (Arabic) pure, chaste.
Nazeeh, Nazeem, Nazeer, Nazi, Nazieh, Nazim, Nazir, Nazz

Ndale (African) trick.
Ndal, Ndall, Ndalle

Neal (Irish) champion.
Neale, Neall, Nealle, Nealon, Nealy, Neel, Neele, Neil, Neile, Neill, Neille, Nial, Niale, Niall, Nialle, Niel, Niele, Niell, Nielle, Nile, Niles, Nyal, Nyale, Nyall, Nyalle, Nyle, Nyles, Nyll, Nylle

Nectarios (Greek) a Greek saint.
Nectaire, Nectar, Nectare, Nectario

Ned (English) prosperous guardian, a form of Edward.
Nedd, Neddey, Neddie, Neddy

Neerim (Australian Aboriginal) long.

Nehemiah (Hebrew) compassion of God.
Nehemia, Nehemie, Nehemya, Nehemyah, Nihimia, Nihimiah, Nehmia, Nehmiah

Nehru (Hindu) canal.
Neru

Neil (Irish) champion.
Neal, Neale, Neall, Nealle, Nealon, Nealy, Neel, Neele, Neile, Neill, Neille, Nial, Niale, Niall, Nialle, Niel, Niele, Niell, Nielle, Nile, Niles, Nyal, Nyale, Nyall, Nyalle, Nyle, Nyles, Nyll, Nylle

Neka (Native American) wild goose.
Neke, Neika

Nelek (Polish) horn colour, cornel tree, a form of Cornelius.
Corrnelek, Cornie, Nelius, Nellek, Nelley, Nelson, Nelly

Nelo (Spanish) God is my judge, a form of Daniel.
Nello

Nels (Scandinavian) a form of Nelson, Neil.
Neal, Neil, Neles, Nells, Nelson, Niles, Nils, Nyls, Nyles

Nelson (Scandinavian, English) son of Neal.
Nealson, Neilsen, Neilson, Nellie, Nels, Nelsen, Nelssen, Nelsson, Nilson, Nilsson

Nemo (Greek) of the valley.
Neemo, Nimo, Nymo

Nemuel (Hebrew) sea of God.
Nemual, Nemuale, Nemuall, Nemualle, Nemuele, Nemuell, Nemuelle

Nen (Egyptian) ancient waters.
Nenn

Neo (Greek) new.
Nio, Nyo

Neptune (Latin) ruler of the sea, the Roman god of the sea.

Nero (Latin) black; (Spanish) stern.
Neero, Neerone, Neron, Nerro, Nerron

Nerville (French, Irish) sea village.
Nervil, Nervile, Nervill, Nervyl, Nervyle, Nervyll, Nervylle

Nesbit (English) river bend which is nose-shaped.
Nesbet, Nesbett, Nesbitt, Nesbyt, Nesbytt, Nisbet, Nisbett, Nisbit, Nisbitt, Nysbet, Nysbett, Nysbit, Nysbitt

Nester (Greek) wise traveller.
Nesta, Nestar, Nestor

Nethaniel (Hebrew) gift from God, a form of Nathaniel.
Naethaniel, Naethanyel, Netania, Netaniah, Nethania, Nethaniah, Netana, Netanel, Netanial, Netaniel, Netanya, Netanyal, Nethanel, Nethania, Nethanial, Nethaniel, Nethanyal

Neto (Spanish) earnest, a form of Ernest.
Nesto, Netto

Nevada (Spanish) snow-clad.
Navada, Nevade

Nevan (Irish) holy.
Nevean, Nivan

Neville (French) from the new village.
Naville, Nev, Nevil, Nevile, Nevill, Nevyl, Nevyle, Nevyll, Nevylle

Nevin (English) nephew; (Irish) little saint.

Neven, Nevins, Nevyn, Niven,
Nivens, Nivyn

Newell (English) new spring.
Newal, Newale, Newall, Newalle,
Newel, Newele, Newelle, Newyl,
Newyle, Newyll, Newylle

Newman (English) newcomer.
Neiman, Neimen, Neuman,
Neumen, Newmen, Numan, Numen

Newton (English) new town.
Newtan, Newten, Newtin,
Newtown, Nueton, Nuetown

Ngai (Vietnamese) herb.

Nghia (Vietnamese) forever.
Ngia

Ngozi (African) blessed.

Ngu (Vietnamese) sleep.

Nhean (Cambodian) self-knowledge.
Nean

Niall (Irish) champion, a form of Neil.
Nial, Niale, Nialle, Nyal, Nyale,
Nyall, Nyalle

Nibal (Arabic) arrow, a unisex name.
Nibel, Niebel, Nybal, Nybel

Nibaw (Native American) stands tall.
Nybaw

Nicandro (Greek) man of victory.
Nicanda, Nicander, Nicando,
Nickanda, Nickander, Nickando,
Nickandro, Nikkanda, Nikkander,
Nikkando, Nikkandro

Nicholas (Greek) victory of the people.

Nic, Nicalas, Nicalaus, Nicalos,
Niccalas, Niccalaus, Niccalos,
Niccolas, Niccolaus, Niccolos,
Nich, Nichaalos, Nichalas,
Nichalaus, Nichalos, Nichele,
Nichlas, Nichlaus, Nichloas,
Nichlos, Nichol, Nichola, Nicholaes,
Nicholaus, Nicholese, Nicholl,
Nichollas, Nichollos, Nicholoas,
Nicholos, Nicjlos, Niclaus, Niclos,
Nick, Nickalas, Nickalaus, Nickalos,
Nickalous, Nicklas, Nicklaus,
Nicklos, Nickolas, Nickolaus,
Nickolos, Nicky, Nicolas, Nicolos,
Nikalas, Nikalaus, Nikalos, Nike,
Nikhil, Niki, Nikki, Nikky, Niklas,
Niklaus, Niklos, Niko, Nikolai,
Nikolas, Nikolos, Niky, Niocal, Niocal

Nicholson (English) son of Nicholas.
Nicholes, Nicholeson, Nicholis,
Nicholisson, Nicholsen, Nickelsen,
Nickelson, Nickoles

Nick (English) victory of the people, a form of Nicholas.
Nic, Nich, Nicho, Nichy, Nicko, Nicky,
Nico, Nik, Niki, Nikki, Nikko, Niko,
Nikky, Niky

Nicodemus (Greek) victory of the people.
Nicodem, Nikodem, Nikodemus,
Nikodimus, Nikodium

Nicol (English, Scottish) victory of the people, a form of Nicholas.
Nicholl, Nicholas, Nickol, Nickoll,
Nicoll, Nikol, Nikolas, Nikoll, Nikolos

Nicolai (Slavic) victory of the people, a form of Nicholas.
Nicholai, Nickolai, Nicolaj, Nicolau,
Nicolay, Nicolei, Nicolus, Nicoly

Nicolas (Italian) victory of the people, a form of Nicholas.
Nic, Nicholas, Nick, Nicolo, Niocal,
Niocalas, Nike

Niels (Scandinavian) champion, a form of Neil.
Niel, Niell, Niells, Nielsen, Nielson, Niles, Nils

Nien (Vietnamese) year.

Nigel (Latin) dark-haired, black.
Niegel, Niel, Nigal, Nigale, Nige, Nigele, Nigell, Nigelle, Nigiel, Nigil, Nigile, Nigill, Nigille, Nigle, Nijel, Nijil, Nye, Nygel, Nygell, Nyje

Nika (African) ferocious.

Nike (Greek) victorious, a unisex name.
Nikee, Nikey, Niki, Nikie, Nikka, Nikke, Nikkee, Nikkey, Nikki, Nikkie, Nikky, Niky

Nikhil (Hindu) complete, whole.
Nikil

Nikita (Russian) victory of the people, a form of Nicholas.
Nakita, Nakitis, Nekita, Niki, Nikia, Nikiah, Nikkie, Nikula, Nykei, Nykey, Nykita

Nikiti (Native American) round, smooth like the abalone shell.
Nikitie, Nikoe, Nykiti, Nyko

Nikolai (Russian) victory of the people, a form of Nicholas.
Nikolas, Nikolei

Nila (Hindu) blue.
Nilah, Nyla, Nylah

Niles (English) son of Neil.
Niel, Niels, Nile, Nyle, Nyles

Nimrod (Hebrew) fiery rod, great hunter.

Nino (Spanish) young child.

Niran (Thai) eternal.

Niren, Nirin, Niron, Niryn, Nyran, Nyren, Nyrin, Nyron, Nyryn

Nishan (Armenian) sign, cross.
Nyshan

Nishant (Hindu) dawn.
Nyshant

Nissan (Hebrew) sign, emblem.
Nison, Nysan, Nyssan

Nitis (Native American) friend.
Netis

Nixon (English) son of Nicholas.
Niksan, Nixan, Nixen, Nixin, Nixyn

Nizam (Arabic) leader.

Nkunda (African) loves those who despise him.
Nkundah

N'namdi (African) the father lives on in the son.
Namdi

Noah (Hebrew) long rest, peaceful, according to the biblical account, Noah built the ark which survived the Great Flood.
Naoch, Naoh, Noak, Noa, Noe, Noi

Noam (Hebrew) sweet, pleasant friend.

Noble (Latin) noble.
Nobel

Nodin (Native American) wind.

Noe (French) long rest, peaceful, a form of Noah.
Noeh

Noel (French) born at Christmas.
Noele, Noell, Noelle, Nowel, Nowele, Nowell, Nowell

Nohea (Hawaiian) handsome.
Naha, Noho, Nokoni

Nolan (Irish) famous, descended from nobility.
Noland, Nolande, Nolane, Nolen, Nolin, Nollan, Nolland, Nollande, Nollane, Nolyn

Nollie (Scandinavian) kind; (French, Latin) olive tree, a form of Oliver.
Noll, Nolli, Nolly

Norbert (Scandinavian) brilliant hero.
Bert, Norberto, Norbertt, Norbertto, Norbie, Norburt, Norburto, Norburtto, Norby

Norm (English) man from the north, a form of Norman.
Normie, Normy

Norman (French) man from the north.
Norm, Normand, Normen, Normend, Normie, Normy

Normand (English) man from the north, a form of Norman.
Normend

Norris (French) northerner.
Noreys, Noreyse, Norice, Norie, Noris, Norreys, Norreyse, Norrie, Norry

Northcliff (English) northern cliff.
Northclif, Northclife, Northcliffe, Northclyf, Northclyfe, Northclyff, Northclyffe

Northrop (English) northern farm.
North, Northup

Northville (English) northern village.
Northvil, Northvile, Northvill, Norvil, Norvile, Norvill

Norton (English) northern town.
Northton, Northtown, Nortown

Norwood (English) northern forest.
Northwood

Notaku (Native American) growling bear.

Nowles (English) grassy slope, a form of Knowles.
Nowls

Nsoah (African) seventh-born child.

Numa (Arabic) beautiful, pleasant, a unisex name.
Numah

Numair (Arabic) panther.

Nuncio (Italian) messenger.
Nunc, Nunci, Nunz, Nunzi, Nunzio

Nur al Din (Arabic) brightness, light of the faith.

Nuri (Hebrew) fire.
Nori, Nory, Nury

Nuriel (Hebrew) fire of the Lord.
Nori, Nury, Nuryel

Nuru (African) born during daylight hours, a unisex name.

Nusair (Arabic) bird of prey.
Nusa, Nusar

Nwa (African) my son.

Nwake (African) born on market day.

Nye (Anglo-Saxon) islander.
Nie, Ny

Oake (English) near the oak trees, oak tree, a unisex name.
Oak, Oakes, Oakey, Oakie, Oaks, Oaky, Ochs, Oches

Oakley (English) field of oak trees.
Oak, Oakes, Oakie, Oaklea, Oaklee, Oakleigh, Oakli, Oaklie, Oakly, Oaks

Oalo (Spanish) small.

Oba (African) king.
Obah

Obadiah (Hebrew) servant of the Lord.
Obad, Obada, Obadah, Obadia, Obadias, Obadya, Obadyah, Obadyas, Obed, Obeda, Obedah, Obedas, Obedia, Obediah, Obedias, Obedya, Obedyah, Obedyas, Obie, Ovadia, Ovadiah, Ovadya, Ovadyah

Obed (Hebrew) working, servant of the Lord, a form of Obadiah.
Obad

Oberon (German) noble, king of the fairies in Shakespeare's *A Midsummer Night's Dream*.
Oberan, Oberen, Oberin, Oberron, Oberyn

Obert (German) wealthy, bright.
Obirt, Oburt

Obie (English) servant of the Lord, a form of Obadiah.
Obee, Obey, Obi, Oby

Ocan (African) hard times.
Okan

Ocean (English) sea, ocean.
Ocan, Ocea, Oceane, Ocearn, Ocearne, Oecean, Ohshen, Oshearn, Oshearne

Oceanus (Greek) god of the sea.
Ocan, Ocanus, Ocea, Ocean, Oceana, Oceane, Oceanis, Oceanius, Oceanos, Oceanous, Oceanys, Ocearn, Ocearne, Ocearnus, Oshearn, Oshearne, Oshearnus

Octavius (Latin) eighth-born child.
Octavian, Octaviano, Octavias, Octavien, Octavio, Octavious, Octavo, Octavos, Octavus, Ottavian, Ottaviano, Ottovias, Ottavien, Ottavious, Ottavio, Ottavius, Ottavo, Ottavos, Ottavus, Tavius

Odakota (Native American) friendly.
Oda

Odd (Norwegian) point.
Od, Odo, Oddo, Oddvar

Ode (Greek) ode, melody, a form of Odel; (African) born on the road during travel.
Odel, Odell, Odey, Odie, Ody

Oded (Hebrew) encouraging.

Odel (Greek) ode, melody.
Dell, Odal, Odall, Ode, Odell

Odin (Scandinavian) ruler, a god in Norse mythology.
Oden, Odenn, Odinn, Odyn, Odynn, Wodan, Wodanaz, Woden, Wodin

Odion (African) first-born twin.
Odeon, Odyon

Odo (Anglo-Saxon, Norwegian) rich, a form of Otto.
Oddo

Odolf (German) prosperous wolf.
Odolff, Odolph, Odulf, Odulff, Odulph

Odom (African) oak tree.

Odon (Hungarian) wealthy protector.
Oden, Oddon, Odi, Odin, Odonn, Odonne

Odran (Irish) pale green.
Odhran, Odren, Odrin, Oran, Oren, Orin, Orran, Orren, Orrin

Odwin (German) noble friend.
Odwen, Odwenn, Odwinn, Odwyn, Odwynn

Odysseus (Greek) full of wrath, hero of Homer's epic poem, *The Odyssey*.
Odyseus, Olysseus, Oulixeus, Oulixes, Ulysses, Ulixes

Ofer (Hebrew) young deer.
Ofar

Ogbay (Eithopian) do not take this child away.
Ogbae, Ogbai

Ogbonna (African) the child looks like his father.
Bonna, Ogbonnia

Ogden (English) lives beside the oak valley.
Ogdan, Ogdin, Ogdon, Ogdyn

Ogilvie/Ogilvy (Celtic) from the high peak.
Ogilvey

Ogima (Native American) chief.
Ogimah, Ogyma, Ogymah

Ogun (African) god of war.
Ogeun, Oegun

Ohanko (Native American) restless.
Oanko

Ohannes (Turkish) God is gracious, a form of John.
Ohan, Ohane, Ohanes, Ohann, Ohanne

Ohanzee (African) shadowy one who brings comfort.
Hanze, Hanzee, Ohanze

Ohin (African) chief.
Ohan, Ohyn

Ohitekah (African) brave.
Ohiteka, Ohitee, Tekah, Tekkah

Oisin (Irish) little deer.
Oisyn, Oysin, Oysyn

Oistin (Celtic) venerable, the exalted one, a form of Austin.
Osten, Ostenn, Ostinn, Ostyn, Ostynn

Ojo (African) difficult delivery.
Oja, Ojay

Okapi (African) a red-brown coloured animal with horns and a long neck.
Okapy

Oke (Hawaiian) divine spearman, a form of Oscar.
Okee, Okey, Oki, Okie, Oky

Okechuku (African) God's gift.
Okech, Okeche, Okechu

Okeke (African) born on market day.
Okek, Okorie

Okie (American) from Oklahoma.
Okee, Okey, Oky

Oko (African) god of war.

Okpara (African) first-born son.

Ola (African) wealthy.
Olah, Olla, Ollah

Olaf (Norse) relics of the ancestors.
Olaff, Olafur, Olav, Ole, Olef, Oleff, Olev, Ollaf, Ollaff, Ollav, Oloff, Olov, Olof, Oluf, Oluff, Oluv

Olamina (African) this child is my wealth.
Olam, Olumin, Olaminah, Olumina

Ole (Scandinavian) relics of the ancestors, a form of Olaf.
Olay, Oleh, Oley, Olle

Oleg (Slavic) holy.
Olezka, Olleg

Oleksandr (Russian) helper or defender of humankind, a form of Alexander.
Olek, Oleksanda, Oleksandar, Oleksander, Olesanda, Olesandar, Olesander, Olesandr, Olesko, Olexanda, Olexandar, Olesander, Olexandr

Olin (English) holly.
Olen, Ollin, Olney, Olyn

Olisholo (African) God has blessed me with this child.
Olishalo, Olusholo

Oliver (French, Latin) olive tree; (Scandinavian) kind.
Nollie, Olihibhear, Olivar, Oliverio, Oliverios, Olivero, Oliveros, Olivier, Olivierio, Oliwa, Ollie, Olliver, Ollivor, Olly, Olvan

Oliviero (Italian) olive tree; (Scandinavian) kind, a form of Oliver.
Olivero, Oliveros, Oliveras, Oliverio, Oliverios, Olivieras, Olivieros

Oliwa (Hawaiian) olive tree; (Scandinavian) kind, a form of Oliver.
Olliwa

Ollie (English) olive tree; (Scandinavian) kind, a form of Oliver.
Oley, Olie, Olle, Olley, Olly, Oly

Olo (Spanish) famous, renowned in the land, a form of Orlando.
Ollo

Olubayo (African) this child gives the highest joy.

Olufemi (African) wealth and honour is mine.

Olujimi (African) God gave me this child.

Omar (Arabic) first-born son, eloquent speaker, follower of the prophet.
Omair, Oman, Omare, Omari, Omarr, Omarre, Omer, Umar

Omari (African, Arabic) first-born son, eloquent speaker, follower of the prophet, a form of Omar.
Omare, Omaree, Omarey, Omarie, Omary

Omer (African, Arabic) first-born son, eloquent speaker, follower of the prophet, a form of Omar.
Omeer, Omero, Omerr, Omeo

Omkar (Hindu) holy sound and letter.

Omolara (African) child who is born at the expected time.
Omolar

Omparkash (Hindu) the light of God.

Omran (Arabic) solid structure.

On (Chinese) peace.

Onan (Turkish) prosperous.
Nan, Nani, Nany, Onen, Onin, Onnan, Onon, Onyn

Onani (African) looking quickly.
Onanee, Onaney, Onanie, Onany

Onaona (Hawaiian) pleasant fragrance.
Onaonah

Ondro (Slavic) strong, courageous, manly, a form of Andrew.
Ondra, Ondre, Ondrea, Ondrew, Ondrey

O'Neil (Irish) son of Neil.
Oneal, O'Neal, O'Neale, O'Neel, O'Neill, O'Neille, Onel, Oniel, O'Niel, O'Niell, Onil, Onill

Onofrio (German) peaceful protector of the home, a form of Humphrey.
Oinfre, Onfre, Onfrio, Onofre, Onofredo, Onofrios

Onslow (Anglo-Saxon) hill of the enthusiastic one.
Enslo, Onsloe, Onslowe, Ounslow

Onur (Turkish) honour.

Ophir (Hebrew) faithful.
Ophyr

Opio (African) first born of twin boys.
Opyo

Oran (Irish) green.
Odhran, Odran, Ora, Orane, Orann, Oren, Ori, Oron, Orran, Oryn

Orane (Greek) rising.

Oratio (Latin) timekeeper, a form of Horace.
Horatio, Oracio, Oracyo, Oratyo, Orazio, Orazyo

Orban (Hungarian) urban, from the city.
Orbane, Urban, Urbane

Ordell (Latin) beginning.
Orde, Ordel, Ordele, Ordelle

Orel (Russian) eagle; (Latin) listener.
Oreel, Orele, Orell, Orelle, Orrel, Orrele, Orrell, Orrelle

Oren (Hebrew) pine tree; (Celtic) pale-skinned.
Oran, Orin, Oris, Orono, Orren, Orrin

Orestes (Greek) mountain climber.
Aresty, Orest, Oreste, Orreste, Orrestes

Ori (Hebrew) light, my light.
Oree, Orey, Orie, Orri, Ory

Oriel (French) golden.
Oree, Ori, Orie, Oro, Orri, Ory

Orien (Latin) visitor from the east.
Oren, Orian, Orin, Orion, Oris, Oron, Orono, Orrin, Oryn

Orion (Greek) son of fire.
Orrion, Orryon, Oryon

Orji (African) mighty tree.

Orlando (German) famous, renowned in the land, a form of Roland.
Lando, Olando, Olandos, Olandres, Olo, Orlan, Orland, Orlanda, Orlandis, Orlandos, Orlandras, Orlandus, Orlo, Orlondas, Orlondo, Orlondon

Orleans (Latin) golden.
Orlean, Orlian, Orlians, Orlin

Orman (German) mariner.
Ormand, Ormen, Ormend

Ormond (Anglo-Saxon) bear mountain.
Ormand, Ormend, Ormonde

Oro (Spanish) golden.
Orro

Orrick (English) at the old oak tree.
Horrick, Oerick, Orrec, Orreck, Orric, Orryck, Orryk, Oryn, Orynn

Orrin (English) river.
Oren, Orin, Oris, Orren, Orriss

Orris (Latin) time-keeper, a form of Horace.
Horis, Horriss, Oris, Oriss, Orriss, Orrys, Orryss, Orys, Oryss

Orry (Latin) oriental.
Oarrey, Oarrie, Oarry, Orrey, Orrie

Orsino (Latin, Italian) bear, a form of Orson.
Orsine, Orsinio, Orsyne, Orsynio, Orsyno

Orson (Latin) bear.
Ausen, Auson, Oerson, Orsan, Orsen, Orsonn, Son, Sonny, Urson

Orton (English) shore town.
Auten, Auton, Ortan, Orten, Ortin

Ortzi (Basque) sky.
Ortzy

Orunjan (African) born under the midday sun.

Orville (French) golden village.
Orv, Orval, Orvale, Orvall, Orvalle,
Orvel, Orvele, Orvell, Orvelle, Orvile, Orvell, Orvill, Orvie, Orvil, Orvile, Orvill

Orvin (English) spear friend.
Orvan, Orven, Orvinn, Orvon, Orvyn, Orwin, Owynn

Osahar (African) God has heard me.

Osaze (African) a child that God loves.
Osaz

Osbert (English) divine, bright.
Osberto, Osbirt, Osbirto, Osburt, Osburto, Osbyrt, Osbyrto

Osborn (English) warrior of God; (Scandinavian) divine bear.
Osbern, Osberne, Osbon, Osborne, Osbourn, Osbourne, Osburn, Osburne, Ossie, Oz, Ozzie

Oscar (Scandinavian) divine spearman.
Oke, Oscer, Oskar, Osker, Oszkar

Osei (African) noble.
Osee, Osey, Osi, Osie, Osy

Osgood (English) divinely good.
Os, Osgoode, Ossgood, Ossgoode, Ossie, Ossy, Oz, Ozgood, Ozzie, Ozzy

O'Shea (Irish) son of Shea.
O'Shae, O'Shai, O'Shane, O'Shaun, O'Shay, Oshaye, Oshe, Oshea, Oshean

Osman (English) servant of God; (Turkish) ruler.
Osmanek, Osmen, Osmin, Ossman, Otman, Ottman, Ottmar, Ottmor

Osmar (English) wonderful, divine.
Osmarr

Osmond (English) godly defence, divine protector.
Osmand, Osmonde, Osmondo, Osmont, Osmonte, Osmund, Osmunde, Osmundo, Ossie, Ozzie

Osric (English) divine ruler.
Osrick, Osrik, Osryc, Osryck, Osryk

Ossian (Latin) Fawn
Osian, Osien, Ossien

Ossie (Spanish, English) a form of Osborn, Oswald.
Osborn, Osgood, Osman, Osmond, Ossee, Ossey, Ossi, Ossy, Oswald, Oswaldo, Oswell, Oswin

Ostin (Latin) venerable, the exalted one, a form of Austin.
Ostan, Osten, Ostyn

Osvaldo (Spanish) divine power, God of the forest, a form of Oswald.
Osbaldo, Osbalto, Osvald, Osvalt, Osvalto, Oswald, Oswaldo, Oswalt, Oswaltt

Oswald (English) divine power, God of the forest.
Ossie, Osvall, Osvell, Oswaldo, Oswall, Oswalld, Oswalldo, Oswell, Oswold, Ozzie

Oswin (English) divine friend.
Osvin, Oswinn, Oswyn, Oswynn

Osya (Slavic) God will add, increase, a form of Joseph.
Josep, Joseph, Josya, Osip, Yosep, Yosya

Ota (Czech) prosperous.
Otah

Otadan (Native American) plentiful.

Otem (African) born away from home.
Ottem

Othello (Spanish) prosperous.
Otell, Otelle, Otello, Otelo, Othell, Othelo, Thello

Othman (German) wealthy.
Othmen, Ottman, Ottmen

Otis (Greek) one who hears well; (German) son of Otto.
Oates, Oatis, Odis, Otes, Otess, Otez, Otise, Otiss, Ottis, Ottiss, Otys, Otyss, Ottys, Ottyss

Ottah (African) thin baby.
Ota, Otah, Otta

Ottar (African) warrior who instils fear.
Otar

Ottavio (Italian) eighth.
Octavio, Octavo, Octavius, Ottavius, Ottavo

Otto (German) prosperous.
Odo, Otek, Otello, Otfried, Othello, Otho, Othon, Otik, Otilio, Otman, Oto, Oton, Otone, Ottman, Ottoe, Otton, Ottone

Ottokar (German) happy warrior.
Otocar, Otockar, Otokar, Otokars, Ottocar, Ottockar

Otu (Native American) one who collects seashells in a basket.
Ottu

Ouray (Native American) arrow.
Ourae, Ourai

Ove (Narse) the spear's tip, a unisex name

Oved (Hebrew) one who worships.
Ovid

Owen (English) well-born, noble.
Eion, Eoghan, Eoin, Eoiwn, Evan, Ewan, Owain, Owan, Owens, Owin, Owyn, Owyns, Uaine

Owney (Irish) elderly.
Onee, Oney, Oni, Onie, Ony, Ownee, Owni, Ownie, Owny

Oxford (English) where oxen cross the river.
Ford, Oxferd, Oxferde, Oxforde

Oxley (English) meadow of the oxen.
Oxlea, Oxlee, Oxleigh, Oxli, Oxlie, Oxly

Oxton (Anglo-Saxon) ox town.
Oxtan, Oxten, Oxtin, Oxtown, Oxtyn

Oz (Hebrew) strength.
Ozi, Ozz, Ozie, Ozy, Ozzi, Ozzie, Ozzy

Ozias (Hebrew) the Lord's strength.
Ozia, Oziah, Ozya, Ozyah, Ozyas

Ozseb (Hungarian) pious

Ozuru (Japanese) stork.
Ozuro

Ozzie (Spanish, English) a form of Osborn, Oswald.
Ozborn, Ozgood, Ozi, Ozie, Ozman, Ozmond, Ozvaldo, Ozwald, Ozwaldo, Ozwell, Ozwin, Ozzi, Ozzy

Paavo (Scandinavian) small, a form of Paul.
Paav, Paaval, Paavel, Paaveli

Pablo (Spanish) small, a form of Paul.
Pable, Paublo

Pace (English) born at Easter, a form of Pascal.
Pacey, Paice, Paicey, Payce, Paycey

Pacifico (Spanish) peaceful.
Pacifica, Pacific, Pacifyc, Pacifyco, Pacyfyc

Paco (Spanish) free man, a form of Francisco; (Native American) bald eagle; (Italian) pack.
Pacco, Pacho, Pacorro, Panchito, Paquito, Paquo, Pauncho

Paddy (Irish) noble, a form of Patrick.
Pad, Paddi, Paddie, Pat, Patrick, Patty

Paden (English) warrior's town, a form of Patton.
Padan, Padin, Padon, Padyn

Padrig (Celtic) noble, a form of Patrick.
Padreg

Pagan (Latin) of the country, a unisex name.
Paegan, Paegen, Paegin, Paegon, Paegyn, Pagen, Pagin, Pagon, Pagun, Pagyn, Paigan, Paigen, Paigin, Paigon, Paigun, Paigyn

Page (Anglo-Saxon) youthful assistant, young child, a unisex name.
Padget, Padgett, Paget, Pagett, Paige, Payge

Pagiel (Hebrew) worships God.
Paegel, Paegell, Paegiel, Paegiell, Pagel, Pagell, Pagiell, Paigel, Paigell, Paigiel, Paigiell, Paygel, Paygell, Paygiel, Paygiell

Paige (Anglo-Saxon) youthful assistant, young child, a unisex name.
Padget, Padgett, Page, Paget, Pagett, Pagge

Paine (Old French) country person.
Pain, Payn, Payne

Painter (Latin) artist, painter.
Paintar, Paintor, Payntar, Paynter, Payntor

Pakelika (Hawaiian) noble, a form of Patrick.

Paki (African) witness.

Pakile (Hawaiian) royal.
Pakil, Pakill, Pakille, Pakyl, Pakyle, Pakyll, Pakylle

Pal (Scandinavian) small, a form of Paul.
Pali, Palika, Pall

Palaina (Hawaiian) strong, honourable, a form of Brian.
Palain

Palaki (Polynesian) black.
Palakee, Palakey, Palakie, Palaky

Palani (Hawaiian, Latin) free man, a form of Frank.
Palanee, Palaney, Palanie, Palany

Palash (Hindu) flowery tree.

Palben (Basque) blonde.

Paley (English) small, a form of Paul.
Palee, Pali, Palie, Pallee, Palli, Pallie, Pally, Paly, Paladin, Paladon, Palaton, Paleten

Pallaton (Native American) fighter.
Palladin, Palladon, Palleten,

Palmer (English) pilgrim, palm-bearer.
Palm, Palmar

Palmiro (Latin) born on Palm Sunday.
Palmira, Palmo, Palmyro

Palti (Hebrew) God liberates.

Panas (Slavic) immortal.
Pannas

Pancho (Spanish) free man, a form of Frank.
Panchito, Pancito, Panco

Pancras (Greek) strength.
Pancrass, Pacraz, Pancrazz

Pancrazio (Italian) all powerful.
Pancrasio, Pancraso, Pancraz, Pancrazo

Panos (Greek) rock, a form of Peter.
Pan, Pane, Panio, Pano, Petro

Paolo (Italian) small, a form of Paul.
Paolio, Paolos

Paramesh (Hindu) another name for the god, Shiva.
Parames

Pardeep (Hindu) mystic light.
Pardip

Paris (French) from Paris, capital of France; (Greek) the Trojan warrior who abducted Helen and started a war, a unisex name.
Paras, Paree, Pares, Parese, Parie, Parish, Parras, Parree, Parres, Parrese, Parrie, Parris, Parrish, Parrys, Parys

Parker (English) keeper of the park.
Parc, Pakes, Park, Parkar, Parkey, Parks

Parkin (English) little Peter.
Parken, Perken, Perkin

Parley (English) speaking.
Parlay, Parlan, Parlee, Parlie, Parly

Parnell (Latin) stone.
Parle, Parnel, Parnet, Pernell

Parr (English) cattle pen, barn.
Par

Parrish (English) church district.
Parish, Parishe, Parrie, Parrishe, Parrysch, Parrysh, Parysh

Parry (English) son of Harry.
Paree, Parey, Pari, Parie, Parree, Parrey, Parri, Parrie, Pary

Parson (Latin) parish priest, minister.

Parthenios (Greek) virgin.
Parthan, Panthanios, Parthanos, Parthen, Parthenos

Pascal (French) born at Easter.
Pace, Pascale, Pascall, Pascalle, Paschal, Paschale, Paschall, Paschalle, Paschallis, Pascoe, Pascow, Pascual, Pasqual, Pasquale, Pasquall, Pasqualle

Pascha (Latin) born at Easter.
Pascale, Pasha

Pasha (Slavic) small, a form of Paul.
Pascha, Pashka

Pasi (Finnish) king, a form of Basil.
Pasee, Pasey, Pasie, Pasil, Pasy

Pasquale (Italian) born at Easter, a form of Pascal.
Pace, Pascal, Pascale, Pascall, Pascalle, Paschal, Paschale, Paschall, Paschalle, Paschallis, Pascoe, Pascow, Pascual, Pasqual, Pasquall, Pasqualle

Pastor (Latin) spiritual leader.
Parstor, Pastar, Paster, Pastir, Pastyr

Pat (English) noble, a form of Patrick.
Pati, Patie, Patt, Pattie, Patty

Patamon (Native American) raging.
Pataman, Patamen, Patamin, Patamyn

Patek (Polish) noble, a form of Patrick.
Patec, Pateck, Patick, Patik, Patric, Pattec, Patteck, Pattek

Patricio (Spanish) noble, a form of Patrick.
Patricius

Patrick (Latin) noble.
Paddy, Padelika, Padriac, Padric, Pat, Patek, Patric, Patrice, Patricio, Patricios, Patrik, Patrique, Patriz, Patrizio, Patrizius, Patryc, Patryck, Patryk, Pats, Patsy, Pattrick, Patty, Rick, Ricky

Patterson (Irish) Pat's son.
Paterson, Patteson

Pattin (Gypsy) leaf.
Patin, Pattyn, Patyn

Patton (English) warrior's town.
Patan, Paten, Paton, Patun, Pattan, Patten, Pattun, Peton, Petton

Patwin (Native American) man.
Patwen, Patwyn

Paul (Latin) small.
Paavo, Paavlo, Pablo, Pal, Pala, Pall, Paol, Paolo, Paolos, Pasha, Pasko, Pauli, Paulia, Paulin, Paulino, Paulis, Paulo, Paulus, Pavel, Pavlos, Pawel, Pawl, Pol, Poul, Saul

Pavel (Russian) small, a form of Paul.
Paavel, Pasha, Pavils, Pavlik, Pavlo, Pavlusha, Pawl

Pavit (Hindu) pious, pure.
Pavitt, Pavyt, Pavytt

Pawl (Anglo-Saxon) small, a form of Paul.
Pawel, Pawell

Pax (Latin) peaceful.
Paxx

Paxton (Latin) town of peace.
Packston, Pax, Paxon, Paxten, Paxtun

Payat (Native American) the boy is on his journey.
Pay, Payatt, Paye

Payne (Latin) rustic man, from the country.
Pain, Paine, Paynn

Paytah (African) fire.
Paye, Payta

Payton (English) warrior's farm, noble, a unisex name.
Paitan, Paiten, Paitin, Paiton, Pate, Paton, Patton, Payden, Paytan, Payten, Paytin, Peaton, Peighton,

Peytan, Peyten, Peytin, Peyton

Paz (Spanish) peace, a unisex name.
Pazz

Peadar (Irish) rock, a form of Peter.
Peader, Peedar, Peeder, Peadrus, Pedar, Peder

Pearce (English) rock, a form of Peter.
Pears, Pearse, Peirce, Peirs, Peirse, Pierce, Piers, Pierse

Pearson (English) son of Peter.
Pearse, Pehrson, Peirce, Peirson, Pierce, Pierson, Peterson

Pedr (Welsh) rock, a form of Peter.
Parkin, Peder, Peter, Pierson

Pedro (Spanish) rock, a form of Peter.
Pedrin, Pedros, Petren, Petron, Petronio

Peeter (Slavic) rock, a form of Peter.
Peet, Peeta, Peetar

Pekelo (Hawaiian) rock, a form of Peter.
Pekello, Pekka

Peleke (Hawaiian) peaceful ruler, a form of Frederick.
Pelek

Pelham (English) stream.
Pelam, Pelhe, Pelhim, Pelhon, Pelhym

Peli (Latin) happy.
Pele, Pelee, Pelie, Pely

Pelias (Greek) to lead.
Pelios, Pellias, Pello, Pelo, Peru, Piarres

Pell (English) parchment, paper.
Pall, Pel

Pello (Greek, Basque) stone.
Pelo

Pelton (English) town by a pool.
Peltan, Pelten, Peltin, Peltun, Peltyn

Pembroke (Celtic) from the headland.
Pembrock, Pembrok, Pembrook, Pembrooke

Pendle (English) hill.
Pendal, Pendel, Penndal, Penndel, Penndle

Peniamina (Hawaiian) son of the right hand, a form of Benjamin.
Peni, Peniamin, Penjamen, Penjamin, Penni, Pennie, Penny

Penley (English) enclosured meadow.
Penlea, Penlee, Penleigh, Penli, Penlie, Penly

Penn (Latin) pen, enclosure.
Pen, Penna, Penney, Pennie, Penny

Penrith (Welsh) chief ford.
Penrithe, Penryth, Penrythe

Penrod (German) esteemed commander.
Penn, Pennrod, Rod

Pepa (Czech) God shall add, a form of Joseph.
Pepek, Pepik, Peppa

Pepe (Spanish) God shall add, a form of Joseph.
Pepa, Pepey, Pepillo, Pepito, Peppe, Pequin, Pipo

Pepin (German) he who petitions.
Pepi, Peppie, Peppin, Peppy

Per (Swedish) rock, a form of Peter.
Perr

Perben (Greek, Danish) stone.
Perban, Perbin, Perbon, Perbyn

Percival (French) pierce the valley.
Parsafal, Parsaval, Parsifal, Parsival, Parzaval, Parzival, Perc, Percaval, Percavall, Perce, Perceval, Percevall, Percifal, Percy, Percyfal, Percyval, Pereduc, Persafal, Persaval, Persifal, Persival, Purcell, Pursafal

Percy (English) pierce the valley, a form of Percival.
Percey, Percie

Peredur (Welsh) pierce the valley, a form of Percival.
Peridur

Peregrine (Latin) traveller, pilgrim.
Peregrin, Perine, Perino, Perregrin, Perregrine, Perri, Perrie, Perrin, Perrine, Perry, Perryn, Perryne

Perkin (English) little Peter.
Perka, Perkan, Perkins, Perkyn, Perkyns

Perry (English) a form of Peter, Peregrine.
Parrie, Parrin, Parry, Peri, Perin, Perri, Perrin

Persis (Greek) from Persia, a unisex name.
Persys

Perth (Scottish) thorn-bush thicket.

Pervis (Latin) passage.
Pervez, Perviz, Pervys

Pesach (Hebrew) spared, another name for Passover.
Pessach

Pete (English) rock, a form of Peter.
Peat, Peet, Petey, Peti, Piet, Pit

Peter (Latin) rock, one of Christ's apostles.
Panos, Pater, Peader, Peadras, Peder, Pedro, Pedros, Peeron, Peers, Peeter, Peirce, Peirs, Peiter, Peitr, Pekelo, Per, Perico, Perkin, Perris, Perry, Petar, Pete, Peterke, Peterus, Petr, Petras, Petro, Petros, Petru, Petruno, Petrus, Petter, Peyo, Piadro, Piaras, Piater, Pierce, Piero, Pierre, Piers, Pierson, Pieter, Pietr, Pietrek, Pietro, Pioter, Piotr, Piter, Piti, Pjete, Pyoter, Pyotr

Peterson (English) son of Peter.
Peteris, Petersen

Petiri (African) here.
Petri, Petyri, Petyry

Peton (English) warrior's town, a form of Patton.
Patton, Peatoan, Peaten, Peatin, Peaton, Peatun, Peatyn, Petan, Peten, Petin, Petun, Petyn

Petroc (Welsh) rock, a form of Peter.
Petrock, Petrok

Peverell (French) one who plays the pipes.
Peveral, Peverall, Peverel, Peveril, Peverill

Peyton (English) noble, warrior's town, a unisex name.
Payton, Peyden, Peydon, Peyt, Peyten, Peython, Peytonn

Pharaoh (Latin, Egyptian) ruler.
Faraoh, Faro, Faroh, Pharo, Pharoh

Phelan (Celtic) wolf.
Felan, Feland, Pheland

Phelim (Irish) good.
Felim

BOYS

Phelix (Latin) fortunate, happy, a form of Felix.
Phelixe, Phelyx

Phelps (English) Philip's son.
Felp, Felps, Phelp

Philander (Greek) lover of humankind.
Filander, Fylander, Philandar, Phylandar, Phylander

Philart (Greek) lover of virtue.
Filart, Filarte, Fylart, Fylarte, Philarte, Phylart, Phylarte

Philbert (English) brilliant, intelligent.
Philberte, Philbirt, Philbirte, Philburt, Philburte, Phillbert, Phillberte, Phillbirt, Phillbirte, Phillburt, Phillburte, Phylbert, Phylberte, Phylbirt, Phylbirte, Phylburt, Phylburte, Phyllbert, Phyllberte, Phyllbirt, Phyllbirte, Phyllburt, Phyllburte

Philemon (Greek) kiss.
Phila, Philamen, Philamin, Philamine, Philamon, Philamyn, Philemen, Philemin, Philemone, Philemyn, Philimania, Philmon, Philmyn, Philmyne, Phylmin, Phylmine, Phylmon, Phylmyn

Philip/Phillip (Greek) lover of horses.
Filip, Filipe, Fillip, Fillipe, Phelipe, Phelippe, Phelps, Phil, Philipe, Philipp, Philippe, Philippo, Phillipe, Phillippos, Philly, Philp, Phylip, Phyllip, Pibib, Pilib, Pilipo, Pip, Pippo

Philly (American) lover of horses, a form of Philip.
Philie, Phillie

Philo (Greek) lover, friend.
Filo, Fillo, Phillo

Phineas (Hebrew) oracle; (Egyptian) dark skin.
Finean, Fineas, Finias, Finien, Finienn, Finienne, Phinean, Phinian, Phinias, Phinien, Phinienne

Phirun (Cambodian) rain.

Phoenix (Greek) an immortal bird, who rose from its ashes every 500 years, a unisex name.
Feenix, Foenix, Pheenix, Phenix, Pheonix, Phynix

Pias (Gypsy) fun loving.
Pyas

Picton (English) town by the pointed hill.
Pickton, Picktown, Picktyn, Pictan, Picten, Pictin, Pictown, Pictun, Pictyn, Piktan, Pikten, Piktin, Pikton, Piktown, Piktun, Piktyn, Pyckton, Pycton, Pyctin, Pyctyn, Pyktin, Pykton, Pyktyn

Pierce (English) rock, a form of Peter.
Pearce, Pearse, Pedro, Peirce, Peirse, Perry, Pete, Pierse, Pierre

Pierre (French) rock, a form of Peter.
Pedro, Peirce, Perry, Pete, Pier, Piere, Pierr, Pierce

Pierson (English) son of Peter.
Pierrson, Piersen, Piersun

Pietro (Italian) rock, a form of Peter.
Pedro, Pete, Peter, Pierce, Piero, Pierre, Pietr, Pietrio, Pietros, Pietruccio

Pilan (Native American) supreme essence.
Filan, Fillen, Fillene, Pillan, Pilen, Pillen, Pillene

Pilar (Spanish) pillar, column, a unisex name.
Pillar, Pylar, Pyllar

Pili (African) second-born child.
Pyli, Pyly

Pillan (Native American) supreme essence.
Pilan, Pylan, Pyllan

Pin (Vietnamese) faithful.
Pyn

Pinchas (Hebrew) oracle; (Egyptian) dark-haired.
Phineas, Pinas, Pincheas, Pinchos, Pinchus, Pincus, Pinkas, Pinkus, Pinky

Pindari (Australian Aboriginal) from the high ground.
Pyndari, Pyndary

Pino (Italian) God shall add, a form of Joseph.
Peeno

Pinon (Native American) hunter who become the constellation of Orion.
Pinnon

Pio (Latin) pure.
Pios, Pius, Pyo, Pyos

Piper (Anglo-Saxon) pipe player, a unisex name.
Pipar, Pipper, Pyper

Pippin (German) father.
Pipin, Pippyn, Pipyn

Piran (Irish) prayerful, patron saint of miners.
Peran, Pieran, Pirron

Pirrin (Australian Aboriginal) cave.
Pirran, Pirryn, Pyrrin, Pyrryn

Pirro (Spanish, Greek) flaming hair.
Piro, Pyro, Pyrro

Pita (Maori) rock, a form of Peter.
Peata, Peeta, Pieta, Piter, Piti, Pito

Pitney (English) island of the stron-willed man.
Pitnee, Pitni, Pitnie, Pitny, Pittnee, Pittney, Pittni, Pittnie, Pittny, Pytnee, Pytney, Pytni, Pytnie, Pytny

Pitt (English) hollow, pit, ditch.
Pit, Pitte

Pius (Latin) holy.
Pios, Pious, Pyos, Pyous, Pyus

Placidus (Latin) peaceful.
Placide, Placidius, Placido, Placidos, Placyd, Placydius, Placydo, Placydus

Plato (Greek) broad, strong shoulders, name of a famous philosopher.
Platan, Platen, Platin, Platon, Platto, Platun, Platyn

Platte (French) flat land.
Platt

Pol (Irish) small, a form of Paul.
Pal, Poal, Pola, Poll, Polla

Pollock (English) small, a form of Paul.
Polick, Pollick, Polloc, Polloch, Pollok, Poloc, Polock, Polok

Pollux (Greek) one of the twins in the constellation Gemini, crowned.
Pollock, Polluck, Polluk, Polux

Polo (Greek) a form of Apollo; (Tiebetan) brave wanderer.
Pollo

Pomeroy (French) apple orchard.
Pomeray, Pommeray, Pommeroy

Pompeo (Italian) to show off, showy, leader of the procession.
Pompey, Pompio, Pompyo

Ponce (Spanish) fifth-born child.

Pony (Scottish) small horse.
Ponee, Poney, Poni, Ponie

Porfirio (Greek) purple stone.
Porfyrio, Phophirio, Porphyryo

Porter (Latin) gatekeeper, carrier.
Port, Portar, Porte, Portie, Porty

Poshita (Hindu) cherished.
Posita

Poutini (Polynesian) green stone.
Poutin, Poutine, Poutinee, Poutiney, Poutiny, Poutyny

Pov (Gypsy) earth.

Powa (Native American) wealthy.

Powel (Celtic) son of Howell.
Powal, Powall, Powell

Pramad (Hindu) rejoicing, joyful.
Prahmad

Pravat (Thai) history.
Pravatt

Pravin (Hindu) capable
Prahvin, Prahvyn, Pravyn

Prem (Hindu) love.

Prentice (English) learner, apprentice.
Prent, Prentis, Prentiss, Printes, Printice, Printis, Printiss

Prescott (English) priest's house.
Prescot, Prestcot, Prestcott

Presley (English) priest's meadow.
Preslea, Preslee, Presleigh, Presli, Preslie, Presly, Prezlea, Prezlee, Prezleigh, Prezley, Prezli, Prezlie, Prezly

Preston (English) priest's town.
Prestaan, Prestan, Prestann, Presten, Prestin, Prestyn

Prewitt (French) valiant one.
Preuet, Preuit, Pruit, Pruitt, Prewet, Prewett, Prewit

Price (English) son of the ardent one.
Prise, Pryce, Pryse

Pricha (Thai) clever.

Primo (Latin) first-born child.
Preema, Premo, Prymo

Prince (Latin) chief.
Prence, Prinz, Prinze, Prynce, Pryns, Prynse

Princetown (English) princely town.
Preston, Princeton, Princton

Proctor (Latin) agent, official.
Prockter, Procktor, Procter

Prosper (Latin) fortunate.
Prospero, Prosperos, Spero

Pryce (Welsh) son of the ardent one, a form of Price.
Price

Pryderi (Welsh) care for.
Prydwyn, Prys, Prysor

Pryor (Latin) head of the monastery.
Prior

Pumeet (Hindu) pure.
Pumit

Purdy (Hindu) recluse.
Purdee, Purdi, Purdie

Purvis (Latin) supplier.
Pervis, Perviss, Purves, Purviss

Pyotr (Russian) rock, a form of Peter.
Petreenka, Petrinka, Petrusha, Petya, Pyatr, Pyoter

Pyralis (Latin) of fire.
Piralis, Pirallis, Pyrallis, Pyrhus, Pyrrhus

Qabic (Arabic) able.
Qabick, Qabik, Qabyc, Qabyck, Qabyk, Quabic, Quabick, Quabik, Quabyc, Quabuck, Quabyk,

Qabil (Arabic) able.
Qabill, Qabyl, Qabyll

Qadim (Arabic) ancient.
Qadym

Qadir (Arabic) powerful.
Qadeer, Qaader, Qaadir, Qadeer, Qader

Qamar (Arabic) moon.

Qasim (Arabic) divider.
Qasym

Qimat (Hindu) valuable.
Qymat

Quaashie (African) born on a Sunday.
Quaashi, Quashi, Quashie

Quadarius (American) combination of Quan and Darius.
Quadara, Quadarious, Quadaris, Quadaruis, Quadarus, Quaddarius, Quandarious, Quandarius

Quade (Latin) fourth.
Quadell, Quaden, Quadon, Quadre, Quadrie, Quadrine, Quadrion, Quaid, Quaide, Quayd, Quayde, Qwade

Quain (French) clever.
Quayn

Quamaine (American) combination of Quan and Jermaine.
Quamain, Quaman, Quamane, Quamayn, Quamayne, Quarmain, Quarmaine, Quaymain, Quaymaine, Quaymane

Quan (Native American) fragrant.
Quahn, Quanah

Quandre (American) combination of Quan and Andre.
Quaandre, Quanandre, Quander

Quant (Greek) how much, quantity.
Quanta, Quantae, Quantai, Quantas, Quantay, Quante, Quanteau, Quantey, Quantez

Quantavius (American) combination of Quant and Octavius.
Quantavian, Quantavias, Quantavin, Quantavious, Quantavis, Quantavius, Quantavon, Quantavus

Quashawn (American) combination of Quan and Shawn.
Quasean, Quashaan, Quashan, Quashane, Quashaun, Quashaunn, Quashon, Quashone, Quashun, Queshan, Queshawn, Queshon, Quesyn

Qudamah (Arabic) courageous.
Qudam, Qudama

Quennel (French) small oak tree.
Quenal, Quenall, Quenel, Quenell, Quennal, Quennall, Quennell, Quinel, Quinell, Quinnel, Quinnell

Quentin (Latin) fifth-born child.
Quent, Quentan, Quenten, Quentine, Quenton, Quienten, Quientin, Quintan, Quinten, Quintin, Qwentin, Qwentine

Quillan (Irish) cub.

Quilan, Quilen, Quilin, Quilon, Quilyn, Quille, Quillen, Quillin, Quillon, Quillyn

Quillon (Latin) sword.

Quilon, Quyllon, Quylon

Quimby (Norse) queen's estate.

Quembee, Quembey, Quemby, Quenbee, Quenbey, Quenby, Quimbee, Quimbey, Quinbee, Quinbey, Quinby

Quincy (French) fifth-born child, the fifth son's estate, a unisex name.

Quencey, Quencie, Quency, Quiencey, Quiencie, Quiency, Quincey, Quincie, Quinn, Quinncy, Quinnsy, Quinsey, Quinzy

Quinlan (Irish) very strong, well-formed, athletic, a unisex name.

Quenlan, Quenlen, Quenlin, Quinlen, Quinlyn, Quinnlan, Quinnlen, Quinnlin, Quinnlyn

Quinn (Latin) fifth; (Celtic) advisor, counsellor, a unisex name.

Quin, Quinne, Quinnten, Quiyn, Quyn, Quynn

Quintin (Latin) fifth-born child, a form of Quentin.

Quenten, Quentin, Quinten, Quinton, Quynten, Quynton

Quiqui (Spanish) ruler of the house, a form of Henry.

Quiquin, Quiquy, Quyquy

Quito (Spanish) fifth, a form of Quentin.

Quyto

Quon (Chinese) bright.

R

Raamah (Hebrew) thunder.
Raama, Rama, Ramah

Raanan (Hebrew) fresh.
Ranan

Rab (Scottish) famous, brilliant, a form of Robert.
Rabb

Rabi (Arabic) fragrant breeze, a unisex name.
Rabbi, Rabee, Rabeeh, Rabeh, Rabie, Rabih, Raby

Race (English) race, one who races.
Racel, Raice, Rayce

Rachamin (Hebrew) compassionate.
Racham, Rachaman, Rachim, Rachin, Rachmiel, Rachum, Raham, Rahamim

Rad (English) advisor; (Slavic) happy.
Raad, Raade, Radd, Radde, Raddie, Raddy, Rade, Radee, Radey, Radi

Radbert (Anglo-Saxon) brilliant counsellor.
Raad, Rad, Radbirt, Radburt, Radbyrt

Radburn (Anglo-Saxon) red stream.
Radborn, Radborne, Radbourn, Radbourne, Radburn, Radburne

Radcliff (Anglo-Saxon) red cliff.
Radcliffe, Radclyff, Radclyffe, Redcliff

Radek (Czech) famous ruler.
Radec, Radeck

Radford (Anglo-Saxon) red ford.
Radforde, Redford

Radley (Anglo-Saxon) red meadow.
Radlea, Radlee, Radleigh, Radly

Radman (Slavic) joyful, happy.
Radmen, Radusha, Redman

Radnore (Anglo-Saxon) red shore.
Radnor, Rednor, Rednore

Radomil (Slavic) happy, peaceful.
Radik, Rado, Radomill, Radomyl, Radzmir

Radwan (Arabic) delightful.
Raad, Rada, Radd, Radwen

Raequan (American) combination of prefix Rae and Quan.
Raequon, Raeqwon, Raiquan, Raiquon, Raquan, Raquon

Raeshawn (American) combination of prefix Rae and Shawn.
Raesean, Raeshane, Raeshaun, Raeshon, Raeshun

Rafael (Spanish, Hebrew) God has healed.
Raefael, Raefaell, Raefaello, Raefaelo, Raefel, Raefele, Raefell, Raefelle, Raefello, Rafaele, Rafaell, Rafaello, Rafaelo, Rafal, Rafe, Rafeal, Rafee, Rafel, Rafell, Rafello, Rafelo, Rafer, Raff, Raffael, Raffaele, Raffaell, Raffaello, Raffiel, Rafiel, Rafiele, Raphael, Raphaell

Rafferty (English) prosperous.
Rafarty, Rafe, Rafer, Raferty, Raffarty, Raffer

Rafi (Hebrew) God has healed, a form of Rafael; (Arabic) praised, exalted.
Rafe, Rafee, Raffe, Raffee, Raffi, Raffy, Rafy

Rafiq (Arabic) friend.
Raafiq, Rafeeq, Rafic, Rafique

Raghib (Arabic) desirable.
Ragib, Raquib

Raghnall (Irish) wise, powerful.
Raghna, Raghnal, Ragna, Ragnal, Ragnall, Ragnhild, Ragnild, Rainell, Renild, Renilde

Ragnar (Norwegian) powerful army.
Ragner, Ragnir, Ragnor

Rago (African) ram.

Rahim (Arabic) merciful, compassionate.
Raaheim, Raheam, Raheem, Raheim, Raheime, Rahein, Rahiim, Rahime, Rahium, Rahma, Rakeme, Rakim

Rahul (Arabic) traveller.

Raibeart (Scottish) famous, brilliant, a form of Robert.
Raibert, Raibirt, Raiburt

Raid (Arabic) leader, ruler.
Raidd, Raidde, Raide, Raiide

Raiden (Japanese) thunder god.
Raidan, Raydan, Rayden

Raine (English) lord, wise.
Raen, Raene, Rain, Raines, Rayn, Rayne

Rainer/Rainier (German) army adviser.
Raener, Raenier, Raine, Rainee, Rainie, Rainor, Rainyer, Rayner, Raynier, Raynor, Reiner, Reinier

Raini (Native American) god who created the world.

Raishawn (American) combination of prefix Rai and Shawn.
Raisean, Raishawne, Raishon, Raishun

Raja (Hindu) king.
Raaja, Raajah, Raajeh, Raj, Rajaah, Rajae, Rajah, Rajahe, Rajan, Raje, Raji

Rajak (Hindu) pure, clean.

Rajan (Hindu) king, a form of Rajah.
Rajaahn, Rajain, Rajen, Rajin

Rakin (Arabic) respectable.
Rakeen, Rakene

Raktim (Hindu) bright red.
Raktym

Raleigh (English) deer meadow.
Raelea, Raelee, Raeleigh, Raeley, Raely, Railea, Railee, Raileigh, Railey, Raily, Ralea, Ralee, Raley, Raliea, Rallee, Ralleigh, Ralley, Rally, Raly, Raylea, Raylee, Rayleigh, Rayley, Rayly

Ralph (Old Norse) wolf counsellor.
Rafe, Ralf, Ralfe, Randalf, Randall, Randalph, Randelf, Randell, Randelle, Randelph, Randolf, Randolff, Randolffe, Randolph, Randy, Raoul, Rendell, Rendelle, Rolf, Rolfe, Rolph

Rama (Hindu) godlike; (English) male sheep.

Ramah, Rami, Ramir, Ramma, Ramme, Ramy

Ramadan (Arabic) ninth month.

Rambert (German) brilliant.
Rambirt, Ramburt, Rambryt

Rami (Spanish) supreme judge, a form of Ramiro; (Hindu) godlike; (English) male sheep, a form of Rama.
Rame, Ramee, Ramey, Ramih, Ramy

Ramiro (Portugese, Spanish) supreme judge.
Miro, Rameer, Rameero, Ramere, Ramero, Rami, Ramme, Rammiro, Ramon, Ramos, Ray, Raymond

Ramon (Spanish) wise protector, a form of Raymond.
Ramen, Ramero, Ramin, Rammiro, Raymon, Raymond, Remon, Remone, Romone

Ramsden (English) valley of the rams.
Rammsdan, Rammsden, Rammsdin, Rammsdon, Rammsdyn, Ramsdan, Ramsdin, Ramsdon, Ramsdyn

Ramses (Egyptian) born of the sun.
Rameses, Ramesis, Ramsis

Ramsey (English) island of the rams.
Ram, Ramsay, Ramsee, Ramsie, Ramsy, Ramzee, Ramzey, Ramzie, Ramzy

Rance (English) one who has been crowned with a laurel, a form of Lawrence.
Rancel, Rancell, Rances, Rancey, Rancie, Rancy, Ranse, Ransel, Ransom

Rand (English) warrior.
Rande, Randi, Randie, Randy

Randall (English) wolf, shield, a form of Randolph.
Ralph, Randal, Randale, Randalle, Randel, Randele, Randell, Randelle, Randolf, Randolfe, Randolff, Randolffe, Randolph, Randy, Rendal, Rendale, Rendall, Rendalle, Rendel, Rendele, Rendell, Rendelle

Randolph (English) wolf, shield.
Ralph, Randal, Randall, Randel, Randell, Randelle, Randolf, Randolfe, Randolff, Randolffe, Randolphe, Randulf, Randulfe, Randulff, Randulffe, Randulph, Randy, Rendell, Rendelle

Randy (English) wolf, shield, a form of Randolph.
Ralph, Randal, Randall, Randee, Randel, Randele, Randell, Randelle, Randey, Randie, Randolf, Randolffe, Rendell, Rendelle

Ranger (French) protector, keeper of the forest.
Rainge, Rainger, Rangar, Range, Raynge, Raynger

Rangi (Maori) heaven or the sky, a unisex name.
Rangee, Rangey, Rangie, Rangy

Rangle (American) cowboy.
Rangel, Ranglar, Rangler, Wranglar, Wrangle, Wrangler

Rani (Hebrew) my song of happiness, joyful song.
Ranee, Raney, Ranie, Rannee, Ranney, Ranni, Rannie, Ranny, Rany

Ranjan (Hindu) delighted.
Jahn, Rahnjan, Ranjahn, Rhan

Rankin (Anglo-Saxon) little shield.
Ranken, Rankon, Rankyn

Ransford (English) raven's ford.
Ransforde, Ransfort, Wransford

Ransley (English) raven's field.
*Ranslea, Ransleigh, Ransly,
Ravenslea, Ravensleigh, Ravensley,
Ravensly, Wranslea, Wransleigh,
Wransley, Wransly*

Ransom (English) son of the shield.
Rance, Ransome, Ranson

Raoul (French) wolf counsellor, a
form of Ralph.
Raol, Raul, Reual, Reuel, Roul

Raphael (Hebrew) the divine
healer, healed by God.
*Rafael, Rafaele, Rafaell, Rafaelle,
Rafal, Rafale, Rafall, Rafalle, Rafel,
Rafell, Raff, Raffael, Raffaele,
Raffaell, Raffaelle, Raffaello,
Raphaele, Raphaell, Raphaelle,
Raphaello, Raphal, Raphale,
Raphall, Raphalle, Rapheal,
Rapheall, Raphel, Raphell,
Raphello, Raphiel, Ray, Rephael*

Rapier (French) sharp like a blade.
Rapiere, Rapyer

Raquan (American) combination
of the prefix Ra and Quan.
*Raaquan, Rachquan, Rachwon,
Racquan, Raekwon, Raequan,
Rahquan, Raquane, Raquon,
Raquwan, Raquwn, Raqwan,
Raqwann*

Rashad (Arabic) wise advisor.
*Raashad, Rachad, Rachard,
Rachaud, Raeshad, Raeshard,
Raishad, Rashaad, Rashard,
Rashase, Rashass, Rashaud,
Rashaude, Rasheed, Rashed,
Rashid, Rashod, Rhaashad,
Rhashaad, Rhashad, Rhishad*

Rashean (American) combination
of the prefix Ra and Sean.
*Raesean, Raeshien, Rahsaan,
Rahsean, Rahshien, Resean,
Rhashan, Rhashawn*

Rashida (Arabic) wise, righteous, a
unisex name.
*Rashda, Rasheeda, Rasheedah,
Rashedda, Rashidah, Rashidi,
Rashiod, Rashod*

Rashne (Persian) judge.

Raul (French) wolf counsellor, a
form of Ralph.
*Ralph, Randolf, Randolff, Randolffe,
Randolph, Randulf, Randulfe,
Randulff, Randulffe, Randy, Rauel,
Rauele, Rauell, Rauelle, Raule,
Raull, Raulle*

Raven (English) raven, blackbird,
black-haired, a unisex name.
*Raevan, Raeven, Raevin, Raevon,
Raevyn, Ravan, Ravean, Raveen,
Ravenel, Ravin, Ravine, Ravon,
Ravyn, Rayvan, Rayven, Rayvin,
Rayvon, Rayvyn, Reven, Rhavan,
Rhaven, Rhavin, Rhavon,
Rhavyn*

Ravi (Hindu) sun.
*Raevi, Ravee, Ravie, Ravijot, Ravvy,
Ravy, Rayvi*

Ravid (Hebrew) dew, rain.
Ravyd

Rawdon (English) rough hill.
Rawden, Rawdin, Rawdyn

Rawiri (Maori) beloved, a form of
David.
Rawiera, Rawieri, Rawira

Rawleigh (English) deer meadow.
*Raleigh, Rawle, Rawlee, Rawley,
Rawlie, Rawling, Rawly*

Ray (French) king; (English) wise protector, a form of Raymond.

Rae, Rai, Raiae, Raie, Raye, Raymond

Rayan (Irish) little king, a form of Ryan.

Raian, Rayaun

Rayburn (English) deer stream.

Raebern, Raeburn, Raibern, Raiburn, Raybern

Rayhan (Arabic) favoured by God.

Raehan, Raihan, Rayan

Raymond (English) wise protector.

Raemon, Raemond, Raemondo, Raimon, Raimond, Raimonda, Ramond, Ramonde, Ramondo, Ray, Raymand, Raymande, Raymando, Raymonde, Raymondo, Redmond, Reyman, Reymand, Reymon, Reymond, Reymonde

Read/Reade (English) red-haired.

Reed, Reid, Reide

Reagan (Irish) little king, a unisex name.

Raegan, Raegen, Reagen, Reegan, Reegen, Regan, Regen, Reghan, Reigan, Reigen, Reign, Rheagan, Rheagen

Reba (Hebrew) fourth-born child, a unisex name.

Reaba, Reiba, Reyba

Rebel (English) rebellious one, a unisex name.

Rebel, Rebale, Rebbal, Rebbe, Rebell, Rebelle

Reda (Arabic) satisfied.

Redah

Redmond (German) adviser; (English) wise protector, a form of Raymond.

Mondy, Radmond, Radmonde, Red, Redmand, Redmande, Redmonde, Redmont, Redmonte

Reece (Welsh) ardent, enthusiastic.

Rees, Reese, Reys, Reyse, Rheece, Rheese, Rhys, Rhyse

Rees/Reese (Welsh) ardent, enthusiastic, a unisex name.

Reece, Reis, Reise, Rhys, Rhyse, Rys, Ryse

Reeves (English) steward.

Reaves, Reeve, Reives, Ryvs

Regan (Irish) little king, a unisex name.

Raegan, Reagan, Reegan, Regen, Reghan, Reygan

Reginald (German) king's advisor.

Redge, Redgenald, Redginald, Reg, Regenald, Reggie, Regginald, Reggis, Reggy, Regi, Regie, Reginal, Reginalde, Reginaldo, Reginale, Reginalt, Reginaud, Reginauld, Reginel, Reginold, Reginuld, Regie, Regy, Ronald

Regis (Latin) regal.

Regiss, Regys, Regyss

Rehema (African) second-born child.

Rei (Japanese) law, rules.

Rey

Reidar (Norwegian) nest warrior.

Reydar

Remington (English) from the raven's town.

Remi, Remie, Remm, Remmi, Remmie, Remmington, Remmy, Remy

Remus (Latin) fast, according to legend, one of the brothers who founded Rome.

Reemas, Reemos, Reemus, Remas, Remos

Renato (Latin) born again.

Renata, Renatus

Rendor (Hungarian) policeman.

Rendar, Render, Rendir

Rene (French) reborn, a form of Renee; (Greek) peace, a form of Irene, a unisex name.

Reen, Reenie, Renay, Renee, Reney, Renie, Rennay, Renne, Rennee, Rennie

Renfrew (English) still river.

Renjiro (Japanese) virtuous.

Reno (Spanish) shortened form of names ending in 'eno', a city in Nevada, USA.

Reeno, Renos, Renot

Renzo (Latin) one who has been crowned with a laurel, a form of Lorenzo.

Renz, Renzy, Renzzo, Ronzo

Reshad (Arabic) wise advisor, a form of Rashad.

Reshaad, Reshade, Reshard, Resharrd, Reshaud, Reshawd, Reshead

Reshawn (American) combination of the prefix Re and Shawn.

Resean, Reshan, Reshaun, Reshaw, Reshun

Reshean (American) combination of the prefix Re and Sean.

Resean, Reshae, Reshane, Reshay, Reshawn, Reshayne, Reshea, Resheen, Reshley

Reuben (Hebrew) behold a son.

Reuban, Reubin, Reubon, Reuvan, Reuven, Reuvin, Reuvon, Rheuban, Rheuben, Rheubin, Rhuban, Rhuben, Ruban, Rube, Ruben, Rubey, Rubin, Ruby, Rueban, Rueben, Ruebin

Rex (Latin) king.

Rexx

Reyhan (Arabic) favoured by God.

Reihan

Reynard (German) brave advice; (French) fox.

Raynard, Reinard, Reinhard, Reinhart

Reynold (Anglo-Saxon) powerful, mighty; king's advisor.

Rainault, Rainhold, Ranald, Raynald, Raynaldo, Raynalt, Reenold, Reginald, Reginold, Reinald, Reinaldo, Reinaldos, Reinhart, Reinhold, Reinwald, Reinwalt, Renald, Renaldi, Renaldo, Renaud, Renauld, Rennold, Rey, Reynald, Reynaldo, Reynhard, Reynhart, Reynoi, Reynoldo, Reynolds, Rinaldo, Ronald

Rezin (Hebrew) delightful.

Rezan, Rezen, Rezon, Rezyn

Rhett (Welsh) ardent, enthusiastic, a form of Rhys.

Rett, Rhet

Rhisiart (Welsh) powerful ruler, a form of Richard.

Rhisart, Risart, Risiart

Rhodes (Greek) where the roses grow.

Rhoads, Rhodas, Rodas, Rodes

Rhodri (Welsh) ruler of the wheel.

Rodri

Rhun (Welsh) grand.

Rhyan (Irish) little king, a form of Ryan.
Rhian, Rhien, Rhyen, Rian, Rien, Ryan, Ryen

Rhydwyn (Welsh) friend by the white ford.
Rhydwen

Rhys (Welsh) ardent, enthusiastic.
Reece, Reese, Reise, Rheece, Rheese, Rheise, Rhyse, Rice, Rys, Ryse

Ricardo (Spanish) powerful ruler, a form of Richard.
Dick, Dickie, Racardo, Recard, Ricard, Ricardos, Ricaydan, Ricciardo, Richard, Richardo, Richie, Richy, Rick, Rickard, Rickardo, Rickie

Rice (English) rich, noble.
Reice, Reyce, Ryce

Richard (German) powerful ruler.
Arik, Dick, Dickie, Racard, Racardo, Recard, Ricard, Ricardo, Ricayd, Riccard, Ricchard, Ricciard, Ricco, Richar, Richards, Richardson, Richart, Richaud, Richer, Richerd, Richie, Richshard, Richy, Rick, Rickard, Rickert, Rickey, Ricki, Rickie, Ricky, Rico, Rihard, Rihardos, Rihards, Rikard, Riocard, Risa, Risardus, Rishard, Ritchard, Ritchie, Rostik, Rysio, Ryszard

Richart (German) powerful ruler, a form of Richard.

Richie (English) powerful ruler, a form of Richard.
Dick, Dickie, Rich, Richard, Richie, Richy, Rick, Rickie, Ritchi, Ritchie, Ritchy

Richmond (German) powerful protector.
Richmand, Richmande, Richmando, Richmon, Richmonde, Richmondo, Richmund, Richmunde, Richmundo

Rick (English) powerful ruler, a form of Richard.
Dick, Dickie, Richard, Richie, Richy, Rick, Ricki, Rickie, Ricky, Ritch, Ritchy

Ricker (English) powerful army.
Ricka, Rickar, Rikar, Riker, Ryckar, Rycker, Rykar, Ryker

Rickward (English) powerful guardian.
Ricward, Ryckward, Rycward

Rico (Spanish) powerful ruler, a form of Richard; (Italian) ruler of the home, a form of Enrico.
Dick, Dickie, Ricco, Richard, Richie, Richo, Richy, Rick, Rickie, Rocko

Rida (Arabic) favoured.
Ridah, Ryda, Rydar

Rider (Anglo-Saxon) knight, horse rider.
Ryder

Ridge (Anglo-Saxon) ridge.
Rydge

Rigby (English) ruler's valley.
Rigbee, Rigbey, Rigbi, Rigbie, Rygbee, Rygbey, Rygbi, Rygbie, Rygby

Rigel (Arabic) foot.
Rygel

Rigg (Anglo-Saxon) ridge.
Rig, Riggs, Rigo, Ryg, Rygg, Ryggs

Riley (Irish) valiant, a unisex name.
Reiley, Reilley, Reilly, Reily, Rhiley, Rhilley, Rhilly, Rhily, Rhylee, Rhyley, Rhyllee, Rhylly, Rhyly, Rieley, Rielley,

Reilly, Riely, Rilee, Rily, Rilye, Rylee, Ryley, Ryllee, Rylley, Rylly, Ryly

Ring (English) ring, band.
Ringe, Ringo

Ringo (English) bell ringer; (Japanese) apple.

Rio (Spanish) river, a unisex name.
Ryo

Riordan (Irish) the king's poet.
Reordan, Reorden, Riardan, Rierdan, Rierden, Rierdon

Ripley (English) strip of wood in clearing.
Riplee, Ripleigh, Riply

Rishi (Hindu) sage.
Ryshi

Ritter (German) knight.
Ritar, Riter, Rittar, Rytar, Ryter, Ryttar, Rytter

River (English) stream of water, river bank, a unisex name.
Reeva, Reever, Riva, Rivers

Roald (German) famous ruler.
Roalde

Roarke (Irish) famous ruler.
Roark, Rork, Rorke, Rourk, Rourke

Rob (German) famous, brilliant, a form of Robert.
Bob, Bobbie, Bobby, Robbie, Robbin, Robby, Robin

Robert (English) famous, brilliant.
Bob, Bobbie, Bobby, Rab, Rabbie, Rabert, Raby, Riobard, Riobart, Riobert, Rob, Robars, Robart, Robbie, Robby, Rober, Roberd, Robers, Roberte, Roberto, Robirt, Roburt, Roibeard, Rubert, Rudbert, Rupert

Robertson (English) son of Robert.
Roberson, Robeson, Robetson, Robinson, Robson

Robin (English) small bird, a unisex name.
Raban, Robban, Robben, Robbin, Robbon, Robbyn, Roben, Robyn, Robyne

Robinson (English) son of Robert.
Roberson, Robison, Robson

Rocco (Italian) rock, stone.
Rocca, Roccy, Rocki, Rockie, Rocko, Rocky, Roco

Roch (German) repose.
Roche, Rock

Rochester (English) stone fortress.
Rochestar

Rock (English) rock, stone.
Roc, Roch, Rocky

Rockley (English) rocky meadow.
Rocklea, Rocklee, Rockleigh, Rockli, Rocklie, Rockly, Rokley

Rockwell (English) rocky spring.
Roccell, Rockie, Rockwall, Rockwel, Rocky, Rocwell

Rod (English) island of reeds, island clearing, a form of Rodney; (German) famous ruler, a form of Roderick.
Rodd

Rodas (Greek) where the roses grow, a form of Rhodes.
Rhodas

Roden/Rodden (English) valley of reeds.
Roddin, Roddyn, Rodin, Rodyn

Roderick (German) famous ruler.

Radric, Radrich, Radrick, Radricki, Radrigo, Radryk, Rhoderic, Rhoderick, Rhoderik, Rod, Rodderick, Roddy, Roderic, Roderich, Roderigo, Roderik, Roderric, Roderrick, Roderrik, Roderryk, Roderyk, Rodrique, Rodryc, Rodryck, Rodryk, Roodney, Rory, Ruy

Rodney (English) island of reeds, island clearing.

Rodd, Rodde, Roderick, Roddy, Rodnee, Rodnie, Rodny

Rodrik (German) famous ruler, a form of Roderick.

Roderic, Roderick, Roderik, Rodric, Rodrick

Rodwell (English) dweller at the crucifix spring.

Roddwell, Rodwel

Roe (English) roe deer.

Rowe

Rogan (Irish) red haired.

Roegan, Roegen, Rogen, Rowgan, Rowgen

Rogelio (Spanish) famous warrior.

Rogel, Regelo, Rojel, Rojelio, Rejelo

Roger (German) famous with the spear.

Rod, Rodge, Rodger, Rodgeric, Rodgerick, Rodgerik, Rodgers, Rog, Rogelio, Rogeric, Rogerick, Rogerik, Rogerio, Rudge, Rudiger, Ruggerio, Rutger

Rohan (Irish) red-haired; (Hindu) sandalwood.

Roane, Rohen, Rowan, Rowen, Royan, Royen

Rohin (Hindu) path going up.

Rohit (Hindu) large beautiful fish.

Rahit, Raheet, Roheet

Roja (Spanish) red.

Raoja, Raojai, Rojah, Rojay

Rolan (Russian) renowned throughout the land, a form of Roland.

Rollan, Rollon, Rolon

Roland (German) renowned throughout the land.

Lorand, Orlando, Rawlins, Rodhlan, Rolan, Rolande, Rolando, Rolek, Rolend, Rolf, Rolland, Rolle, Rollend, Rollie, Rollin, Rollins, Rollo, Rolly, Rowe, Rowland, Rulan, Ruland

Rolando (Spanish) renowned throughout the land, a form of Roland.

Lando, Olo, Rolan, Roldan, Rolondo

Rolf (German) famous wolf, a form of Rudolph.

Rolfe, Rolff, Rolffe, Rolph, Rolphe, Roland, Rudolf

Rollo (English) renowned through-out the land, a form of Roland.

Roland, Rolle, Rollie, Rolly, Rolo, Rolynd

Roman (Latin) person from Rome.

Roma, Romachka, Romain, Romaine, Romane, Romann, Romanne, Romanus, Romeo, Romi, Romman, Rommie, Rommy, Romy

Romel (Latin) citizen of Rome, a form of Romulus.

Romele, Romell, Romello, Rommel, Rommelle

Romeo (Latin) man from Rome, a character in Shakespeare's Romeo and Juliet.

Roma, Roman, Rome, Romio, Rommi, Rommy, Romyo

Romero (Latin) man from Rome, a form of Romeo.

Romario, Romaro, Romer, Romere, Romerio, Romeris, Romeryo, Romiero

Romney (Welsh) curving river.

Rommi, Rommie, Rommy, Romni, Romnie, Romny

Romulus (Latin) citizen of Rome, according to legend, one of the brothers who founded Rome.

Romei, Romel, Romelus, Romolo, Romolos, Romolus, Romono, Romulo, Romulos

Romy (Italian) person from Rome, a form of Roman.

Romi, Rommi, Rommy

Ron (English, Scottish) king's advisor, a form of Ronald.

Ronn

Ronald (English, Scottish) king's advisor, a form of Reginald, Reynold.

Raghnall, Ragnald, Ranald, Ranaldo, Ranold, Rena, Renald, Renaldo, Renold, Ron, Ronal, Ronalde, Ronaldo, Ronnie, Ronnald, Ronnold, Ronny

Ronan (Irish) to make a promise, seal.

Renan, Rohnan, Rohnen, Ronat, Ronen, Ronnan, Ronnen

Rondel (French) short poem.

Rondal, Rondale, Rondall, Rondeal, Rondele, Rondell, Rondelle

Rongo (Maori) god of rain and fertility.

Roni (Hebrew) my joy, my song.

Rani, Ronee, Roneet, Ronnel, Ronnell, Ronni, Ronyell

Ronny (English, Scottish) king's advisor, a form of Ronald.

Ron, Ronney, Ronnie

Ronson (Anglo-Saxon) son of Ronald.

Ronaldson, Ronsen, Ronsin, Ronsyn

Ronte (American) combination of Ron and the suffix te.

Rontae, Rontay, Rontez

Roone (English) mystery.

Roon, Rooney, Roony, Rune, Runey, Runy

Rooney (Irish) red-haired one.

Roonie, Roony, Rowney, Rownie, Rowny

Roosevelt (Dutch) from the field of roses.

Roosevylt, Roosvelt, Roosvylt, Rosevelt, Rosevylt, Rusevelt, Rusevylt

Roper (English) rope-maker.

Roapa, Roapar, Roape, Ropar

Rory (Irish) brilliant, famous ruler, ruddy one, red king, a unisex name.

Rorey, Rorie, Rorrey, Rorrie, Rorry, Rory, Ruairdhri, Rurik

Roscoe (Scandinavian) deer forest.

Rosco, Roscow, Roscowe

Roshan (Hindu) light, a unisex name.

Roshain, Roshaine, Roshane

Ross (Scottish) peninsula; (French) red-haired; (Teutonic) famous.

Ros, Rose, Rosse, Rossell, Rosselle, Rossi, Rossie, Rossy

Rover (English) wanderer.

Rova, Rovar, Rovva, Rovvar, Rovver

Rowan (Irish) red-haired; (English) mountain ash tree, tree with red berries, a unisex name.

Rhoan, Rhoann, Rhoen, Rhoenn, Rhohan, Rhohen, Rhowan, Rhowen, Roane, Roewan, Rohan, Rowen, Rowun, Royan, Royen

Rowland (English) rough land.

Roland, Rowan, Rowe, Rowelan, Roweland, Rowen, Rowlan

Rowley (English) rough meadow.

Rowlea, Rowlee, Rowleigh, Rowli, Rowlie, Rowly

Rowson (Irish) son of a red-haired person.

Roe, Roesen, Roeson, Rowe, Rowsen

Roxbury (English) rook's fortress.

Rocksbury, Roexbury, Roksbury, Roxberry, Roxbery, Roxburie, Roxburrie, Roxburry

Roy (French) king, royal, a form of Conroy, Delroy, Fitzroy, Leroy.

Leroy, Le Roy, Le Roye, Rey, Reye, Roi, Roie, Roye

Royal (French) regal one.

Roy, Royale, Royall, Royalle, Royel, Royell

Royce (English) king's son, prince.

Roice, Roy, Royse, Royz

Royden (Anglo-Saxon) rye hill.

Royd, Roydan, Roydin, Roydon, Roydyn

Royston (Anglo-Saxo) town next to a stone cross.

Roiston

Ruben (Hebrew) son, a form of Rueben.

Reuban, Reuben, Reubin, Ruban, Rube, Rubie, Rubin, Ruby, Rueban, Rueben, Ruebin

Ruby (Hebrew) son, a form of Rueben.

Ruben, Rubey, Rubie

Ruda (Slavic) famous wolf, a form of Rudolph.

Rudar, Rude, Rudek

Rudd (English) red-coloured complexion.

Reod, Reode, Rudde, Ruddie, Ruddy, Rudyard

Rudi (Spanish) famous wolf, a form of Rudolph.

Ruedi

Rudo (African) love.

Rudolph (Teutonic) famous wolf.

Dolf, Dolph, Raoul, Rezso, Rodolf, Rodolfe, Rodolff, Rodolffe, Rodolfo, Rodolph, Rodolphe, Rolf, Rollo, Rolph, Ruda, Rudalf, Rudalph, Rudek, Rudelf, Rudelph, Rudi, Rudie, Rudolf, Rudolfe, Rudolff, Rudolffe, Rudolphe, Rudy

Rudy (English) famous wolf, a form of Rudolph.

Rudey, Rudi, Rudie, Rudolf, Rudolph

Rudyard (Anglo-Saxon) red enclosure.

Ruff (French) red-haired.

Ruffe

Rufus (Latin) red-haired.

Rayfus, Rufe, Ruff, Ruffis, Ruffus, Rufino, Rufo, Rufos, Rufous

Rugby (English) rock fortress.

Rugbee, Rugbey, Rugbi, Rugbie

Ruggerio (Italian) famous with the spear, a form of Roger.

Rogero, Ruggerios, Ruggero, Ruggiero

Ruhakana (African) one who likes to debate.

Ruland (German) renowned throughout the land, a form of Roland.

Rulan, Rulando, Rulon, Rulondo

Rule (Latin) ruler.

Regene, Regine, Regule, Ruel, Ruele, Ruell, Ruelle, Rulle

Runako (African) handsome.

Rupert (German) famous, brilliant, a form of Robert.

Rufus, Rupart, Rupe, Rupeart

Rush (French, English) red-haired, a form of Russell.

Rouche, Rousch, Rousche, Ruche, Rusch, Rusche, Rushe, Ruskin

Ruskin (French) red-haired.

Rush, Rusk, Ruske, Ruskee, Rusken, Ruskie, Rusky, Ruskyn

Russ (French) red-haired, a form of Russell.

Rusell, Russell, Rusty

Russell (French) red-haired.

Rousel, Rousell, Roussel, Roussell, Rusel, Rusell, Russ, Russel, Ruston, Rusty

Rusty (French) red-haired, a form of Russell.

Rusell, Russ, Russell, Rust, Ruste, Rustee, Rusten, Rustey, Rustin, Rustyn

Rutger (Scandinavian) famous with the spear, a form of Roger.

Rutgar, Rutj

Rutherford (English) cattle ford.

Rutherforde

Rutland (Scandinavian) red land.

Rutlan, Rutlann, Rutlen, Rutlend, Rutlenn

Rutledge (English) red ledge.

Ruttledge

Rutley (English) red meadow.

Rutlea, Rutlee, Rutleigh, Rutli, Rutlie, Rutly, Ruttlea, Ruttlee, Ruttleigh, Ruttley, Ruttli, Ruttlie, Ruttly

Ryan (Irish) little king, a unisex name.

Rayan, Rayen, Rhyan, Rhyen, Rhyne, Rian, Riann, Rien, Rienn, Ryane, Ryann, Ryaun, Ryen, Ryenn, Ryian, Ryin, Ryne, Ryon, Ryun, Ryvan

Rycroft (English) rye field.

Rycroff, Ryecroff, Ryecroft, Ryrecreff, Ryrecreft

Ryder (English) horseman.

Rhida, Rhidar, Rhider, Rhyda, Rhydar, Rhyder, Ridah, Ridar, Rider, Ryda, Rydah, Rydar

Rye (English) grain.

Rie, Ryye

Ryese (English) ardent, enthusiastic, a form of Reece.

Reyce, Reyse, Ryce, Ryece, Ryes, Ryez, Ryse

Ryland (English) land where rye grows.

Rielan, Rieland, Rilan, Riland, Ryelan, Ryeland, Ryelen, Ryelend, Ryelin, Rylan, Rylen, Rylend, Rylin, Rylynn

Ryle (Anglo-Saxon) rye hill.

Riel, Riele, Riell, Rielle, Ryal, Ryale, Ryall, Ryalle, Ryel, Ryele, Ryell, Ryelle, Rylle

Ryley (Irish) valiant, a form of Riley.
*Rillie, Rylea, Rylee, Ryleigh, Rylie,
Ryly*

Rymer (Polish) saddle-maker.
Rimer, Ryman

Ryne (Irish) little king, a form of
Ryan.
Ryein, Ryen, Ryien, Ryon

Ryton (Anglo-Saxon) rye town.
Rytan, Ryten, Ryttan, Rytten, Rytton

Saad (Arabic) lucky.
Sadd

Sabastian (Greek) venerable; (Latin) revered, a form of Sebastien.
Sabastain, Sabastan, Sabastien, Sabastin, Sabastion, Sabaston

Saber (French) sword.
Sabahr, Sabar, Sahber, Sabre,

Sabin (Italian) man of ancient Italian culture, a tribe living in central Italy during the establishment of Rome.
Sabe, Saben, Sabyn, Sahben, Sahbin, Saiben, Saibin

Sabir (Arabic) patient.
Sabeer, Sabirah

Sabiti (African) born on a Sunday.
Sabit, Sabitti, Sabitty, Sabity, Sabyti

Sabola (African) pepper.
Saboola, Saebola

Sabur (Arabic) patient.
Sabeer, Sabeerh, Sabir, Sabor, Sabure, Saburr

Saburo (Japanese) third-born child.

Sacha (Russian) helper or defender of humankind, a form of Alexander.
Saecha, Saescha, Saesha, Sascha, Sasha

Sachar (Slavic) God remembers, a form of Zachary.
Zachar

Sacheverell (French) without leather gloves.
Sacheverel

Saddam (Arabic) hard hitter.
Sadam

Sadiki (African) faithful.
Saadiq, Sadeek, Sadeeki, Sadek, Sadeki, Sadik, Sadiq, Sadique

Sadler (English) maker of saddles.
Saddla, Saddlar, Saddler, Sadla, Sadlar, Sadlia

Sadoc (Hebrew) sacred.
Sadock, Sadok

Saeed (African) happy.
Sa'eed, Sa'id, Said

Safari (African) born while travelling.
Safa, Safarin, Safary

Safford (English) ford by the willows.
Saffed, Saffud, Saford, Salford

Sage (French) herb, wise person, a unisex name.
Sagen, Sager, Saige, Saje, Sayg, Sayge

Sahale (Native American) falcon bird.
Sael, Sahail, Sahal, Sahayal, Sahayel, Sahel, Sahil, Sahiel

Sahen (Hindu) above.
Sa'en, Sahan, Sarhan, Sarhen

Sahir (Hindu) friend.
Sahyr

Sa'id (Arabic) happy.
*Sa'ad, Saaid, Saed, Sa'eed,
Saeed, Sahid, Said, Saide, Sa'ied,
Saied, Saiyed, Saiyeed, Sajid, Sajjid,
Sayed, Sayeed, Sayid, Seyed,
Seyeed, Seyid, Shadid*

Sailor (English) one who sails the sea.
Saila, Salor, Saylor

Sajag (Hindu) vigilant, watchful.
Sahjag, Saijag, Saiyd, Sajayd

Sajan (Hindu) beloved.

Saka (African) hunter.

Sakari (Scandinavian) God remembers, a form of Zachary.
*Sakarai, Sakaree, Sakarey, Sakarie,
Sakary*

Sakima (Native American) king.
Sakeema, Sakeemah, Sakimah

Sakuruta (African) sunrise.

Sal (Spanish) saviour, saved, a form of Salvador.
Salvator

Saladin (Arabic) goodness of faith.
*Saladan, Saladen, Salaidan,
Salaiden, Salaidi*

Salah (Arabic) righteousness, virtue.
Sala

Salah al Din (Arabic) righteousness of the faith.

Salamon (Italian) man of peace, a form of Solomon.
*Salaman, Saloman, Salomon,
Solaman, Solamon, Soloman,
Soloman*

Salaun (French) man of peace, a form of Solomon.
Solaun

Saleem (Arabic) peaceful, safe, a form of Salim.
Saleeme, Salim, Salime

Saleh (Indonesian) devout.
*Saelah, Saeleh, Salah, Salche,
Saleeh, Salih, Salleh*

Salene (African) good.
*Saleen, Saleene, Salen, Salin,
Saline, Salyn, Salyne*

Salih (Arabic) right, just.
Sali

Salim (Arabic, African) peaceful, safe and healthy.
*Saleem, Salem, Saliym, Salman,
Salym*

Salisbury (Anglo-Saxon) fort by the willow pool.
*Sal, Salisbery, Salle, Salsbery,
Salsbury*

Salmalin (Hindu) taloned.
*Malin, Salma, Salmal, Salmalen,
Salmalon*

Salman (Arabic) peaceful, safe, a form of Salim.
*Salmaan, Salmaine, Salmane,
Salmon*

Salmon (Hebrew) covering.
Sallmon

Salomon (Spanish) man of peace, a form of Solomon.
Saloman

Salton (English) willow tree town.
*Saelton, Saeltun, Sahlton, Saltan,
Salten, Saltyn, Saulton*

Salvador (Spanish) saviour, saved.
Salvadore, Salvadoor, Salvator, Salvatore, Salvedor, Salvedore, Salvedoor, Salvetor, Salvetore

Salvatore (Italian) saviour, saved.
Sal, Salbator, Salbatore, Sallie, Sally, Salvator, Salvatorie, Salvidor, Salvidore, Salvitor, Salvitore, Sauveur

Sam (English) asked of God, God has heard, a form of Samuel, a unisex name.
Sam, Samm, Sammy, Samsan, Samsen, Samsyn, Samy, Sem, Shem, Shmuel

Sambo (American) asked of God, God has heard, a form of Samuel.
Sambou

Sameh (Arabic) forgiving, a unisex name.
Sami, Sammeh

Sami (Arabic) high, sublime, exalted.
Saami, Saamy, Samee, Sameeh, Sameh, Sameth, Samie, Samih, Sammee, Sammey, Sammi, Sammie, Sammy, Samy

Samir (Arabic) entertaining companion.
Sameer

Samman (Arabic) grocer, supplier of food.
Saman

Samson (Hebrew) like the sun.
Sam, Sammie, Sammy, Sampsan, Sampsen, Sampson, Sampson, Samsan, Samsen, Samsyn, Sansao, Sansom, Sanson, Sansone

Samuel (Hebrew) asked of God, God has heard.
Sam, Samael, Samaru, Samauel,
Samaul, Sambo, Sameul, Sami, Samiel, Sammael, Sammail, Sammauel, Sammaul, Sammee, Sammel, Sammie, Sammuel, Sammy, Samo, Samouel, Samu, Samual, Samuael, Samuail, Samuele, Samuell, Samuello, Samuil, Samuka, Samule, Samuru, Samvel, Sanko, Saumel, Schumel, Shem, Shmuel, Simuel, Sinao, Somhaire, Zamuel

Samuele (Italian) asked of God, God has heard, a form of Samuel.
Samuelle, Samul, Samule, Samull, Samulle

Sanat (Hindu) ancient.

Sanborn (English) sandy brook.
Sanborne, Sanbourn, Sanbourne, Sanburn, Sanburne, Sandborn, Sandborne, Sandbourn, Sandbourne

Sancho (Spanish) saintly, sanctified.
Sanchez, Sanchos, Sauncho

Sandeep (Punjabi) enlightened.
Sandip

Sanders (English) son of Alexander.
Sanda, Sandar, Sander, Sanderson, Sandie, Sandy, Saunders, Saunderson

Sandon (English) sand hill.
Sande, Sanden, Sandin, Sandown, Sandy

Sandor (Slavic) helper or defender of humankind, a form of Alexander.
Sander, Sandero, Sandoro, Sandre, Sandro, Sanyi, Saundro, Shandr

Sandro (Greek, Italian) helper or defender of humankind, a form of Alexander.
Sandero, Sandie, Sandrae, Sandy

Sandy (English) helper or defender of humankind, a form of Alexander.
Sande, Sandee, Sandey, Sandi, Sandie

Sanford (English) sandy ford.
Sandy, Sanferd, Sanforde, Sanfud

Sani (Hindu) the planet Saturn.

Sanjay (Hindu) conscience.
Sanjae, Sanjai, Sanjaie, Sanjaih, Sanjaya, Sanje, Sanjey, Sanjo

Sanjiv (Hindu) will live a long time.
Sanjeev, Sanjev, Sanjive

Sankar (Hindu) another name for the god Shiva.

Sanson (Spanish) like the sun, a form of Samson.
Sansom, Sansone, Sansun, Sunny

Santana (Spanish) saint, a unisex name.
Sans, Santa, Santan, Santanah, Santanna, Santannah, Santane, Santanne, Santena, Santenna, Tana

Santiago (Spanish) St James.
Sandeago, Sandiago, Santeago, Santia, Tiago

Santino (Spanish) an American city, San Antonio, St Anthony, a form of Santonio.
Santion, Santionio, Santonio

Santo (Italian) saint.
Santos

Santon (English) sandy town.
Santan, Santen

Santonio (Spanish) an American city, San Antonio, St Anthony.
Santino, Santon, Santoni

Santos (Spanish) saint.
Santo

Santosh (Hindu) satisfied.

Sanyu (African) happy, a unisex name.

Saqr (Arabic) falcon.
Sahqr, Sahr

Saquan (American) combination of the prefix Sa and Quan.
Saquane, Saquin, Saquon, Saqwan, Saqwane

Sarad (Hindu) born in the autumn.
Saraad, Sahrad

Sargent (French, English) military man.
Sarg, Sargant, Sarge, Sargeant, Sarjant, Sergant, Serge, Sergeant, Sergent, Serjeant

Sargon (Persian) sun prince.
Sargan, Sargen, Sargin, Sargyn

Sarito (Spanish) long-haired, emperor, a form of Caesar.
Sarit

Sariyah (Arabic) clouds at night.
Sariya, Sahriah, Sareah, Saryah

Sarngin (Hindu) protector, archer.
Saarngin, Sahngen, Sahngin, Sarngen

Sarojin (Hindu) lotus-like.
Sahraj, Sahrajin, Sahrajon, Saroj, Sarojon

Sarosh (Persian) prayer.

Sasha (Slavic) helper or defender of humankind, a form of Alexander.
Sacha, Sascha, Sash, Sashak, Sashenka, Sashka, Sausha

Sasson (Hebrew) joyful, happy.
Sason

Satchel (French) small bag.
Satch, Satchle

Satordi (French) the planet Saturn.
Satordie, Satori, Satorie

Saturn (Latin) planet Saturn, the Roman god of agriculture.

Saul (Hebrew) asked for, borrowed.
Sal, Sall, Saule, Saull, Saulle, Shaul, Sol, Sollie, Solly

Saville (French) willow tree village.
Savell, Savelle, Savil, Savile, Savill, Savyl, Savyle, Savyll, Savylle, Sevil, Sevile, Sevill, Seville, Siville

Savon (American) treeless plain, open grassland, masculine form of Savannah.
Savan, Saveion, Saveon, Savhon, Saviahn, Savian, Savino, Savion, Savo, Savone, Savonn, Sayvon, Sayvone

Saw (Burmese) early.

Sawyer (English) one who saws wood.
Sawyar, Sawyere

Sawyl (Welsh) asked for or prayed for.
Sawyle, Sawyll, Sawylle, Sol, Sollie, Solly

Saxon (English) swordsman, a unisex name.
Sax, Saxan, Saxe, Saxen, Saxon, Saxton

Sayers (Welsh) carpenter.
Saye, Sayer, Sayr, Sayre, Sayres

Sayyid (Arabic) master.
Sayad, Sayed, Sayid, Sayyad, Sayyed

Schafer (German) shepherd.
Scafar, Scafer, Schaefer, Schaeffer, Schafar, Schaffar, Schaffer, Schifer, Schiffer, Shaefer, Shaeffer, Shafar, Shafer, Shaffar, Shaffer

Schmidt (German) blacksmith.
Schmid, Schmit, Schmitt, Shmid, Shmidt, Shmit, Shmitt

Schneider (German) one who works with cloth.
Schnider, Schnieder, Sneider, Snieder, Snider, Snyder

Schon (German) handsome.
Schonn, Shon

Schuman (German) shoe maker.
Schumann, Schumen, Schumenn, Shuman, Shumann, Shumen, Shumenn

Schuyler (Dutch) scholar, shelter, shield, a unisex name.
Schieler, Schiler, Schuy, Schuylar, Schuylor, Schylar, Schyler, Schylre, Scoy, Sky, Skye, Skylar, Skyler, Skylir, Skylor

Scipio (Latin) walking stick.
Cipio, Pio, Scippie, Scippio, Scippy, Skipio, Skippie, Skippio, Skippy

Scorpio (Latin) eighth sign of the zodiac, dangerous.
Scorpeo

Scot/Scott (English) of Scottish origin.
Scottie, Scotto, Scotty, Skot, Skott

Scribe (Latin) writer.
Scribner, Scrivener, Scrybe

Scully (Irish) town crier.
Scolaigh, Scolaighe, Scollie, Scolly, Sculaigh, Sculaighe, Sculley, Scullie

Seabert (English) shining sea.
Seabirt, Seaburt, Sebert, Seibert

Seabrook (English) where the brook runs into the sea.
Brook, Brooke, Seabrock, Seabrooke, Sebrock, Sebrook, Sebrooke

Seaforth (Scottish) conqueror in peace.
Seaf, Seafe, Seaforthe, Seforth, Seforthe

Seamus (Irish) God is gracious, a form of John, Sean.
Seamas, Seamis, Seumas, Shamas, Shameus, Shamus, Sheamus

Sean (Irish) God is gracious, a form of John.
Seaghan, Seanan, Seane, Seann, Seanne, Shaan, Shaine, Shane, Shaun, Shaune, Shawn, Shawne, Shayne, Shean, Shon

Seanan (Irish) wise.
Seannan, Senan, Sinan, Sinon, Sinyn

Searle (German) armed.
Searl, Searll, Searlle, Serl, Serle, Serll, Serlle

Seaton (English) sea town.
Seaten, Seatin, Seatown, Seetin, Seeton, Seten, Setin, Seton

Sebastian (Greek) venerable; (Latin) revered.
Bastiaan, Bastian, Bastien, Sabastain, Sabastian, Sabastien, Seb, Sebastain, Sebastiaan, Sebastiane, Sebastiann, Sebastien, Sebastienn, Sebastin, Sebastine, Sebastion, Sebastione, Sebb, Sebbie, Sebo

Sebastiano (Italian, Greek) venerable; (Latin) revered, a form of Sebastian.
Sabastiano

Sebastien (French, Greek) venerable; (Latin) revered, a form of Sebastian.
Sabastien, Seb, Sebasten, Sebastiaan, Sebastian, Sebastienn, Sebastyen, Sebb

Secundus (Latin) scond-born child.
Secondas, Secondus, Secundas

Sedgley (English) swordsman's meadow.
Sedge, Sedglea, Sedgleigh, Sedglie, Sedly, Seglea, Segleagh, Segleigh, Segley, Seglie, Segly

Sedgwick (English) place of the sword grass.
Sedge, Sedgewick, Segwick

Sedric (Anglo-Saxon) war chief, a form of Cedric.
Seddric, Seddrick, Seddrik, Sederic, Sederick, Sederik, Sedric, Sedrick, Sedrik, Sedriq

Seeley (English) blessed.
Sealey, Seelea, Seeleagh, Seeleigh, Seelie, Seely, Seelye, Selig

Sef (Egyptian) yesterday.
Seff

Sefton (English) place in the rushes.
Seftan, Seften, Seftin, Seftun, Seftyn

Sefu (African) sword.

Seger (English) sea warrior.
Seagar, Seager, Seegar, Seeger, Segar, Segel, Segere, Sigehere, Sighear

Segun (African) conquerer.
Segan, Segen, Segin, Segon, Segyn

Seif (Arabic) sword of religion.
Sayf, Seiff

Sein (Basque) innocent.
Seinn

Sekaye (African) laughter.
Sekay

Selby (Anglo-Saxon) willow farm.
Selbea, Selbee, Selbey, Selbie, Shelbee, Shelbey, Shelbie, Shelby

Selden/Seldon (English) valley of the willow trees.
Seldan, Selde, Seldene, Seldin, Seldyn

Selig (German) blessed.
Seligg, Seligman, Seligmann, Zelig

Selwyn (English) friend of the manor.
Selvin, Selwen, Selwin, Selwinn, Selwynn, Selwynne, Shelley, Shelly, Wyn

Semanda (African) cow.
Semandah

Semer (Ethiopian) farmer.
Semere, Semier

Semi (Polynesian) character.
Semee, Semey, Semie, Semy

Semon (Greek) he heard, listener, a form of Simon.
Semeon, Semmon

Sempala (African) born in prosperous times.

Sen (Japanese) wood fairy.
Senh

Sener (Turkish) bringer of joy.
Senner

Senior (English) lord.

Sennett (French) wise one.
Senate, Senatt, Senet, Senett, Sennet

Senon (Spanish) living.
Senan, Senen, Senin, Senyn

Senwe (African) dry grain stalk.
Senwae, Senwah

Sepp (German) God will increase, a form of Joseph.
Seph, Seppi

Septimus (Latin) seventh-born child.
Septe, Septimo

Serafin (Hebrew) burning, ardent, Seraphim are the highest order of the angels in the Bible.
Saraf, Sarafim, Sarafin, Saraph, Saraphim, Saraphin, Serafem, Serafen, Serafim, Serafimo, Serafino, Seraphim, Seraphimm, Seraphin, Serefim, Serefimo, Serefin, Serefinn, Serifino

Sereno (Latin) calm, peaceful, tranquil.
Sereen, Serene, Serenio, Serino

Serge (French) attendant, servant, a form of Sergius.
Searge, Seargeoh, Serg, Sergei, Sergi, Sergie, Sergio, Sergius, Sergiuz, Sirge, Sirgi, Sirgio

Sergio (Italian) attendant, servant.
Searge, Seargio, Serg, Serge, Sergi, Serginio, Sergio, Serjio, Sirgio, Sirjio

Sergius (French) attendant, servant.
Seargius

Serlo (Norse) armour.
Searl, Searle, Searlo, Serl, Serle

Servando (Spanish) one who serves.
Servan, Servand, Serven, Servio

Seth (Hebrew) appointed.
Sef, Seff, Sethan, Sethe, Sethen, Set, Sett, Sette, Shet, Shett, Shette, Sheth, Shethe

Setimba (African) lives by the river.

Seton (English) place by the sea.
Seatan, Seaten, Seatin, Seaton, Seatun,Seatyn, Setan, Seten, Setin, Setun, Setyn

Seumas (Scottish) supplanter, a form of James.
Seamus, Shawmas, Sheamas, Sheumus

Severin (Latin) severe.
Seve, Severan, Severen, Severian, Severien, Severo, Sevien, Sevrin

Sevilen (Turkish) beloved.
Sevilan, Sevilin, Sevilon

Seward (English) defender of the sea.
Seaward, Sewarde, Sewerd, Siward

Sewati (Native American) bear with curved claws.

Sewell (English) sea wall.
Seawall, Seawell, Sewald, Sewall, Sewel

Sexton (English) church caretaker.
Saxon, Saxton, Sexon

Sextus (Latin) sixth-born child.
Sextas, Sextis

Seymour (French) from the village of St Maur.
Seamo, Seamoor, Seamor, Seamore, Seamour, Seamoure, Seymo, Seymoor, Seymor, Seymore, Seymoure

Shadi (Arabic) singer.
Shadde, Shaddi, Shaddy, Shade, Shadee, Shadeed, Shadeeh, Shadey, Shadiah, Shadie, Shady, Shahdee, Shahdi, Shahdie,Shahdy, Shardee, Shardi, Shardie, Shadih, Shardy, Shydee, Shydi

Shadrack (Babylonian) God-like.
Chad, Shad, Shade, Shadrach, Shadrack, Shadrick, Sheddrach, Sheddrack, Shedrach, Shedrack, Shedrick, Shedrik

Shafer (Arabic) beautiful.
Shaefa, Shaefar, Shaefer, Shaeffa, Shaeffar, Shaeffer, Shafa, Shafar, Shaffa, Shaffar, Shaffer

Shafiq (Arabic) compassionate.
Shafeeq, Shafeque, Shafik, Shafique

Shah (Persian) fit for the king, a unisex name.
Sha

Shaiming (Chinese) sunshine, life.
Shaimin, Shaymin, Shayming

Shakir (Arabic) thankful.
Shakeer, Shakier, Shakire

Shakur (Arabic) grateful.
Shaekar, Shaekur, Shahkah, Shahkur, Shaka, Shakar

Shalom (Hebrew) peace.
Shallom, Shalome, Shalomm

Shalya (Hindu) born to the throne.
Shaela, Shaelya, Shaila, Shailya, Shala

Shaman (Native American) holy man.
Shahman, Shahmen, Shamaan, Shamen

Shamus (Irish) God is gracious, a form of John, Seamus.

Seamas, Seamus, Shaemus, Shamess

Shanahan (Irish) wise.

Shana, Shannahan

Shandy (English) boisterous.

Shandee, Shandey, Shandie

Shane (Irish) God is gracious, a form of John.

Chaen, Chain, Chayn, Cheyne, Shaen, Shaene, Shain, Shaine, Shayn, Shayne, Sheyn, Sheyne

Shani (Hebrew) red.

Shanee, Shaney, Shanie, Shany

Shannon (Irish) little wise one, the name of a river, a unisex name.

Shanan, Shanen, Shannan, Shannen, Shanon

Shapoor (Russian) prince.

Shah, Shahpoor, Shaphor, Shapor

Shaquille (Arabic) handsome.

Shaquil, Shaquile, Shaquill

Sharad (Pakistan) autumn.

Sharid, Sharyd

Sharif (Arabic) honest, noble, distinguished.

Shareef, Sharef, Sharreef, Sharref, Sharrif

Shavar (Hebrew) comet.

Shavara, Shaver, Shavir, Shavyr

Shaw (English) small woods, grove.

Shawe

Shawn (English) God is gracious, a form of John, Sean.

Schawn, Sean, Seane, Shawen, Shawne, Shawnn, Shean

Shea (Irish) hawk-like, majestic, admirable, fairy palace, a unisex name.

Shae, Shaie, Shay, Shaye, Sheadeagh

Sheary (Irish) peaceful.

Shearee, Shearey, Sheari, Shearie

Sheehan (Irish) peaceful, little.

Sheean, Sheehen

Sheffield (English) crooked field.

Shefeld, Sheffeld, Shefield, Sheffyeld, Shefyeld

Shelby (English) dweller at the estate by the ledge, a sheltered town, a unisex name.

Selbee, Selbie, Selby, Shelbee, Shelbie

Sheldon (English) town on the ledge, steep-sided valley.

Seldon, Sheldan, Shelden, Sheldin, Sheldyn, Sheldyne, Shelley, Shellie, Shelly, Shelton

Shelley (English) from the meadow's ledge, a unisex name.

Shelee, Sheley, Shelie, Shellee, Shellie, Shelly, Shely

Shelton (English) town on the ledge.

Sheltan, Shelten, Sheltin, Sheltyn

Shem (Hebrew) reputation.

Shemm

Shen (Chinese) meditation; (Egyptian) sacred amulet.

Chen, Schen, Shenn

Shep (Anglo-Saxon) sheep.

Schepp

Shepherd (English) shepherd.

Shep, Shephard, Shepp, Sheppard, Shepperd, Shepphard, Sheppherd

Shepley (English) sheep meadow.
Sheplea, Sheplee, Shepleigh, Shepli, Sheplie, Sheply

Sheridan (Irish) wild, a unisex name.
Sheradan, Sheraden, Sheradin, Sheriden, Sheridin, Sherradan, Sherraden, Sherradin, Sherridan, Sherriden, Sherridon

Sherill (English) shire on the hill.
Cherill, Sheril, Sherril, Sherrill, Sheryl, Sheryll

Sherlock (English) fair-haired.
Locky, Lucky, Sher, Sherlocke, Sherlok, Sherloke, Sherluck

Sherman (English) shearer.
Shearman, Sherma, Shermen, Shirman, Shyrman

Sherrod (English) land clearer.
Sherod, Sherodd, Sherrad, Sherrodd

Sherwin (English) great friend, swift runner.
Sherwen, Sherwinn, Sherwinne, Sherwyn, Sherwynne

Sherwood (English) bright forest.
Sharwood, Sher, Sherwoode, Woody

Shihab (Arabic) flame, blaze, fire.

Shilin (Chinese) intellectual.
Shilyn, Shylin, Shylyn

Shiloh (Hebrew) one who is sent, Messiah.
Shilo, Shylo, Shyloh

Shin (Korean) belief.

Shing (Chinese) victory.
Shingo, Shyng

Shipley (English) sheep meadow.
Shiplea, Shiplee, Shipleigh, Shipli, Shiplie, Shiply

Shipton (English) sheep town.
Shippton, Shiptan, Shipten, Shiptin, Shiptyn

Shiro (Japanese) fourth-born child.
Shirow, Shyro

Shiva (Hindu) life and death.
Sheeva, Shiv, Shivan, Siva

Sholto (Celtic) propagator, sower of seeds.
Scholto, Shelto, Siolta, Siolto

Shomer (Hebrew) protector, guardian.
Shomar, Shomir, Shomor, Shomyr

Shoni (Hebrew) changing.
Shonee, Shoney, Shonie, Shonni, Shony

Shunnar (Arabic) pheasant.
Shunar

Siddell (English) wide valley.
Sidael, Sidaell, Siddel, Sidel, Sidell, Syddel, Syddell, Sydel, Sydell

Siddhartha (Hindu) first name of Buddha, founder of Buddhism.
Sida, Siddartha, Siddhaarth, Siddhart, Siddharth, Sidh, Sidharth, Sidhartha

Sidney (French) from St-Denis in France, a unisex name.
Cidney, Cydney, Sid, Sidnee, Sidnie, Sidny, Sidon, Sidona, Syd, Sydney, Sydnie, Sydny

Sidwell (English) wide stream.
Siddwal, Siddwall, Siddwel, Siddwell, Sidwal, Sidwall, Sidwel, Syddwal, Syddwall, Syddwel,

Syddwell, Sydwal, Sydwall, Sydwel, Sydwell

Siegfried (German) peaceful victory.

Seifert, Seifried, Siegfred, Seigfredo, Seigfrid, Siegfrio, Siegfryd, Siffre, Sigfred, Sigfredo, Sigfrid, Sigfried, Sigfryd, Sigifredo, Sigvard, Singefrid, Sygfried, Szygfrid, Ziegfred, Ziegfried

Sigfrido (Italian) peaceful victory, a form of Sigfried.

Siffre, Sigfred, Sigfredo, Sigfrid, Sigifred, Sigifredo, Sigifrid, Sigifrido, Sigisfried, Sigisfriedo, Siguefred, Siguefredo, Sigvard

Sigmund (German) victorious protector.

Siegmund, Sig, Siggie, Sigismond, Sigismondo, Sigismun, Sigismund, Sigmand, Sigmond, Sigmunde, Sigsmond, Szygmond

Sigurd (German, Scandanavian) victorious guardian.

Sigord, Sjure, Sygurd, Syver

Sigwald (Old Norse) victorious ruler.

Siggie, Sigwaldo, Sigvald, Sigvaldo, Sygwald, Sygwaldo

Silas (Latin) of the forest.

Sailas, Si, Sias, Sielas, Sillas, Silvan, Silvanus, Silvas, Sylas

Silburn (Anglo-Saxon) blessed.

Silborn, Silborne, Silbourn, Silbourne, Silburne, Sylborn, Sylborne, Sylbourn, Sylbourne, Sylburn, Sylburne

Silvanus (Latin) from the forest.

Seilis, Silas, Silvain, Silvan, Silvanis, Silvano, Silvanus, Silvas, Silvio, Sylvanus

Silvester (Latin) of the forest.

Sailveistar, Sailvester, Silven, Silvano, Silven, Silvestre, Silvestro, Sylvan, Sylvano, Sylven, Sylvester

Silvestro (Italian) of the forest, a form of Silvester.

Silvestr, Silvestre, Silvestrio, Silvy, Sylvestr, Sylvestre, Sylvestrio, Sylvestro, Sylvy

Sim (Irish) he heard, listener, a form of Simon.

Simm, Sym, Symm

Simao (Portuguese) he heard, listener, a form of Simon.

Simba (African) lion.

Simbah, Symba

Simcha (Hebrew) happiness, joy, joyful, a unisex name.

Simmy, Symcha

Simeon (Hebrew) he heard, listener, a form of Simon.

Simeone, Simion, Simione, Symeon, Symeone

Simms (English) son of Simon.

Sim, Simm, Sims, Sym, Symm, Symms, Syms

Simmy (English) he heard, listener, a form of Simon.

Simmey, Simmi, Simmie, Symmy

Simon (Hebrew) he heard, good listener.

Saimon, Samien, Samon, Semon, Shimon, Si, Sim, Simao, Sime, Simen, Simeon, Simion, Simm, Simmon, Simmond, Simmonds, Simmons, Simms, Simmy, Simoan, Simoane, Simonas, Simone, Simson, Simyon, Siomon, Siomonn, Symon, Symone, Syzmon, Ximen, Ximene, Ximenes, Xymen, Xymene, Xymenes, Zimon, Zyman

Simpson (Hebrew) son of Simon.
Simpsan, Simpsen, Simpsin, Simpsyn, Simson, Sympsan, Sympsen, Sympsin, Sympson, Sympsyn, Symson

Sinbad (German) sparkling prince.
Sinbald, Synbad, Synbald

Sinbaldo (German) sparkling prince.
Sinbad, Sinbado, Sinbald

Sinclair (French) Saint Clair, a place name.
Sanclair, Sanclaire, Sanclare, Sinclaire, Sinclare, Synclair, Synclaire, Synclare

Sinjon (English) saint, a form of St John.
Senjin, Senjohn, Senjon, Sinjin, Sinjohn

Sion (Welsh) God is gracious, a form of John.
Sionyn, Sior, Syon

Sipatu (Native American) pulled out.

Siraj (Arabic) lamp, light.

Sisi (African) born on a Sunday.
Sisy, Sysi, Sysy

Sivan (Hebrew) born during the ninth month of the Jewish year.
Sivvan, Syvan, Syvvan

Siwili (Native American) long tail of a fox.
Siwilie, Siwilli, Siwily, Siwyli, Siwylie, Siwyly

Skeeter (English) swift one.
Skeat, Skeata, Skeate, Skeater, Skeet, Skeeta, Skeetar, Skeetes, Skeets

Skelly (Irish) story teller.
Skelea, Skelee, Skeleigh, Skeley, Skeli, Skelie, Skellea, Skellee, Skelleigh, Skelley, Skelli, Skellie, Skely

Skerry (Norse) rocky island.
Skairi, Skairie, Skairy, Skerri, Skerrie

Skipper (Scandinavian) ship master.
Skip, Skippie, Skipp, Skippy

Skipton (English) ship town.
Skippton, Skippy, Skipten, Skiptown

Slade (English) lives in the valley.
Slaed, Slaede, Slaid, Slaide, Slayd, Slayde

Slane (Czech) salty.
Slain, Slaine, Slayn, Slayne

Slater (English) roof slater.
Slaiter, Slate, Slayter

Slevin (Irish) mountaineer.
Slaven, Slevein, Sleven, Slevon

Sloan/Sloane (Irish) warrior, a unisex name.
Sloann, Sloanne

Smith (English) blacksmith.
Smithy, Smitt, Smitty, Smyth, Smythe, Smythy, Smytt, Smytty

Snowden (English) snow-capped mountain, hill.
Snowdan, Snowdin, Snowdon, Snowdyn

Socrates (Greek) wise.
Socrate, Socratis, Sokrates, Sokratis

Sofian (Arabic) devoted.
Soffian, Soffyan, Sofyan

Soja (African) soldier.
Sojah

Sol (Spanish) sun; (Hebrew) man of peace, a form of Solomon.
Sole, Solie, Soll, Solle, Sollie, Solly, Soly

Solomon (Hebrew) man of peace.
Salaman, Salamon, Salman, Saloman, Salomon, Salomone, Solaman, Solamh, Solamo, Solamon, Soloman

Solon (Greek) wise man.
Solan, Solen, Solin, Solyn

Somerled (Old Norse) summer wanderer.
Somer, Sumerled, Summer, Summerled

Somerset (English) place of the summer people.
Somer, Somersett, Sumerset, Sumersett, Summer, Summerset, Summersett

Somerton (English) summer town.
Summerton

Somerville (English) summer village.
Somer, Somervil, Somervill, Summer, Summervil, Summervill, Summerville

Son (Vietnamese) mountain; (Native American) star; (English) son.

Songan (Native American) strong.
Song

Sono (African) elephant.
Sonno

Soren (Danish) thunder, war.
Sorensen, Sorenson, Sorren, Sorrensen, Sorrenson

Sorrell (French) bitter, from the name of the herb, red-brown colour, a unisex name.

Sorel, Sorele, Sorell, Sorelle, Sorrelle, Sorryl, Sorryle, Sorryll, Sorrylle

Soterios (Greek) saviour.
Soterias, Soterio, Soteros

Southwell (English) south spring.
Southe, Southewall, Southewell, Southwall

Sovann (Cambodian) gold.
Sovan

Sowande (African) a wise healer looked for me.
Sowand

Spalding (English) divided meadow.
Spalden, Spaulden, Spaulding

Spear/Speare (English) spearman.

Speede (English) successful, fast.
Sped, Spede, Speed, Speedey, Speedie, Speedy

Spencer (English) dispenser of provisions.
Spence, Spense, Spenser

Spike (English) grain ear.
Spyke

Spiro (Greek) breath, spirit, a form of Spyridon.
Spiros, Spirydon, Spyro, Spyros

Spoor (English) spur maker.
Spoore, Spoors, Spur, Spure, Spurs

Spreckley (English) twigs.
Specklea, Specklee, Speckleigh, Speckli, Specklie, Speckly, Spreklea, Spreklee, Sprekleigh, Sprekley, Sprekli, Spreklie, Sprekly

Spyridon (Greek) breath, spirit.
Spiro, Spiros, Spyros, Spyro

Squire (English) king's attendant.
Squier, Squyre

Stacey (English) fruitful, productive, a form of Eustace, a unisex name.
Stace, Stacie, Stacy, Stasey, Stasie, Stasy

Stafford (English) ford by the landing place.
Stafforde, Staford, Staforde

Stamos (Greek) crowned, a form of Stephen.
Stammos

Stanislaus (Slavic) glorious stand.
Stanislao, Stanislas, Stanislau, Stanislav, Stanislus, Stano

Stanley (English) stony meadow.
Stan, Stanely, Stanlee, Stanleigh, Stanli, Stanlie, Stanly

Stanton (English) stony town.
Stan, Stantan, Stanten, Stantin, Stantyn

Stanway (English) stony road.
Stanwey

Stanwick (English) stone village.
Stanwicke, Stanwik, Stanwyck, Stanwycke, Stanwyk

Stanwood (English) stone forest.
Stenwood

Stark (German) strong.
Starke

Starr (English) star, a unisex name.
Star

Stavros (Greek) crowned, a form of Stephen.
Stavrios, Stavro

Steadman (English) farmstead owner.
Steadmen, Stedman, Stedmen

Steel (English) steel worker.
Steele

Stefano (Italian) crowned, a form of Stephen.
Stefan, Stephan, Stephano

Steffan (Swedish) crowned, a form of Stephen.
Stefan, Stephan

Stein (German) stone.
Stean, Steen, Steine, Stene, Steyn, Steyne

Steinar (Norwegian) stone warrior.
Stean, Steanar, Steane, Steaner, Steenar, Steene, Steener, Stein, Steine, Steiner, Steyn, Steynar, Steyne, Steyner

Steph (English) crowned, a form of Stephen.
Stef

Stephen (Greek) crowned.
Estefan, Estefen, Estephan, Estephen, Stamos, Stavros, Steafan, Steafen, Stefan, Stefano, Stefanos, Stefen, Stefeno, Stefenos, Steffan, Steffano, Steffanos, Steffen, Steffeno, Steffenos, Stenya, Stepan, Stepano, Stepanos, Steph, Stephan, Stephanas, Stephane, Stephano, Stephanos, Stephens, Stephenson, Stephfan, Stephin, Stephino, Stephon, Stepvan, Stevan, Steve, Steven, Stevie, Stevyn

Stephenson (English) son of Stephen.
Stevenson

Stepney (English) Stephen's island
Stepnee, Stepnie, Stepny

Sterling (English) silver penny, of value.
Starling, Sterlen, Sterlin, Stirlin, Stirling

Stern (German) star.
Stearn, Stearne, Sterne

Steven (Greek) crowned.
Estevan, Esteven, Steevan, Steeven, Stefan, Stephan, Stephen, Stevan, Stevano, Stevaughn, Steve, Stevean, Steveno, Stevin, Stevo, Stevon, Stevyn

Stevenson (English) son of Steven.
Stephenson, Stinson

Stewart/Stuart (English) steward.
Steward, Stewarde, Stewartt, Stewie, Stu, Stuarte, Stuartt, Stue

Stillman (English) still, quiet.
Stillmen, Stilman, Stillmen, Styllman, Styllmen, Stylman, Stylmen

Sting (English) grain spike.
Stinge, Styng

Stirling (English) silver penny, of value, a form of Sterling.

Stockard (English) stockyard, a unisex name.
Stocard, Stocarde, Stockarde, Stokard, Stokarde, Stokkard, Stokkarde

Stockwell (English) well by the tree stump.
Stockwal, Stockwall, Stockwel

Stoddard (English) horse keeper.
Stodard, Stodart, Stoddart

Stoker (English) tender of the furnace, fire.
Stoke, Stokes

Stone (English) stone.
Stonee, Stoney, Stoni, Stonie, Stony

Storm (English) storm, tempest, a unisex name.
Storme, Stormee, Stormey, Stormi, Stormie, Stormy

Stratford (English) ford on a road.
Stradford, Stratforde, Stattford

Strom (German) stream, river.

Stroud (English) thicket.
Stroude

Struthers (Irish) stream, brook.

Stud/Studd (English) rounded nail heads.
Studde

Subhi (Arabic) early morning.
Subhee, Subhie, Subi

Sudi (African) lucky.
Sud, Suud, Suudi

Sued (Arabic) chief.
Suid

Suffield (English) south field.
Sufeld, Suffeld, Sufield

Suhail (Arabic) `gentle.
Suhayl

Suhuba (African) friendly.

Sukru (Turkish) grateful, thankful.
Sukroo

Sulaiman (Arabic) man of peace, a form of Solomon.
Sulahman, Sulamain, Sulaman, Sulamon, Sulay, Sulayman, Suleiman, Sulieman, Suliman, Sulimon, Sullaiman, Sulli, Sulliman, Sulman, Suloman, Sulomon, Suluman, Sulumon, Sulyman, Sulymon

Sullivan (Irish) one with the black eyes.
Sulavan, Sulivan, Suliven, Sullavan, Sulli, Sulliven, Sully

Sultan (African) ruler.
Sultaan

Sulwyn (Welsh) fair-haired, sunny.
Sulwen

Summit (English) mountain top.
Sumeet, Sumit, Summet, Summitt, Summy

Sumner (English) one who calls, summoner.
Sumnor

Sun (Chinese) bend.

Sundeep (Punjabi) enlightened.
Sundip

Sunny (English) bright, cheerful, sunshine, a unisex name.
Soni, Sonie, Sonnie, Sonny, Suni, Sunn, Sunni

Sunreep (Hindu) pure.
Sunrip

Surya (Hindu) sun, a unisex name.
Suria, Suryah

Sutcliffe (English) south cliff.
Sutcliff, Sutclyff, Sutclyffe

Sutherland (Norse) southern land.
Sutherlan, Sutherlyn, Sutherlynd

Sutton (English) south town.
Suton, Sutten

Sven (Norse) boy, youthful.
Svein, Svenn

Swaggart (English) staggerer.
Swagart, Swagert, Swaggert

Swain (English) knight's attendant.
Swaine, Swane, Swanson, Swayn, Swayne

Sweeney (Irish) little hero.
Sweanee, Sweaney, Sweani, Sweanie, Sweany, Sweenee, Sweeni, Sweenie, Sweeny

Swindel (English) valley of the pigs.
Swindell, Swyndel, Swyndell

Swinfen (English) mud of the pigs.
Swynfen

Swinford (English) ford of the pigs.
Swinforde, Swynford

Swinton (English) pig town.
Swynton

Swithin (Teutonic) strong man.
Swithan, Swithen, Swithon, Swithyn, Swythan, Swythen, Swythwin, Swython

Sydney (French) from St-Denis in France, a form of Sidney, a unisex name.
Cidney, Cydney, Sid, Sidney, Syd, Sydnay, Sydne, Sydnee, Sydnie, Sydny

Syed (Arabic) happy.
Sied

Sying (Chinese) star.

Symon (Greek) he heard, listener, a form of Simon.
Sy, Syman, Symeon, Symion, Symman, Symmeon, Symmion, Symmon, Symmond, Symmonde, Symmonds, Symmons, Symms, Symond, Symonde, Symonds, Symone, Symons

Szygfrid (Hungarian) peaceful victory, a form of Siegfried.
Szigfrid

Szymon (Polish) he heard, listener, a form of Simon.

T

Taaveti (Finnish) beloved, a form of David.
Taavio, Taavo, Taveti

Tab (German) brilliant; (Anglo-Saxon) drummer.
Tabb, Tabbe, Tabbie, Tabby

Tabari (Arabic) remembers.
Tabahri, Tabar, Tabares, Tabarious, Tabarius, Tabarus, Tabur, Taburi

Tabberner (French) drummer.

Tabib (Turkish) physician.
Tabeeb

Tabor (Arabic) drum or drummer.
Tab, Tabber, Tabbor, Taber, Taboorus, Taibor, Taver, Tavor, Tayber, Taybor

Tadan (Native American) plentiful.
Taddan, Taden, Tadin, Tadon, Tadyn

Tadarius (American) combination of prefix Ta and Darius.
Tadar, Tadarious, Tadaris, Tadarrius

Tadashi (Japanese) serving faithfully.
Tadashee, Tadashie, Tadashy

Tadd (Welsh) father.
Tad, Tadde, Taddy, Tade, Tadek, Tadey

Taddeo (Italian) courageous, a form of Thaddeus.
Tadeo

Taddeus (Greek) courageous, a form of Thaddeus.
Taddeous, Taddeusz, Taddius, Tadeas, Tades, Tadeusz, Tadio, Tadious, Tadius

Tadeo (Spanish) praise; (English) courageous, a form of Thaddeus.
Taddeo

Tadi (Native American) wind.
Tadee, Tadey, Tadie, Tady

Tadleigh (English) poet from the meadow.
Taddleigh, Tadlea, Tadlee, Tadley, Tadli, Tadlie, Tadly

Taffy (Welsh) beloved, a form of David.
Taffie, Tafie, Taft, Tafton, Tafy

Taft (English) river.
Taffy, Tafte, Tafton

Tage (Scandinavian) day.
Tag, Tagg, Tagge, Taige

Taggart (Irish) son of the priest.
Tagart, Tagert, Taggert

Tahir (Arabic) pure.
Taheer, Taher, Tahyr

Tai (Vietnamese) talented, prosperous, weather; (Chinese) tribe.
Thai

Taima (Native American) loud crash of thunder, born during a thunder storm, a unisex name.
Tayma

Tain (Irish) stream; (Native American) new moon, a unisex name.
Taine, Tainn, Tane, Tayne

Tait (English) cheerful, happy, a unisex name.
Taite, Taitt, Tayt, Tayte

Taiwan (Chinese) island dweller.
Taewon, Taiwain, Tawain, Tawan, Tawann, Tawaun, Tawon, Taywan

Taiwo (African) first born of twins.
Taywo

Taj (Hindu) crown.
Tahj, Taje, Tajee, Tajeh, Tajh, Taji

Takeo (Japanese) strong like bamboo, strength.
Takeyo

Takis (Greek) rock, a form of Peter.
Takias, Takiss, Takius, Takkis

Takoda (Native American) friend to all.
Takota

Tal (Hebrew) dewy rain.
Taley, Tali, Talia, Talley, Talor, Taly, Talya

Talal (Arabic) nice, admirable.
Tallal

Talasi (Native American) corn-tassel flower, a unisex name.
Talasee, Talasie, Talasy

Talbert (German) bright valley.
Talberte, Talbirt, Talburt, Talbyrt

Talbot (French) boot maker.
Talbott, Tallbot, Tallbott, Tallie, Tally

Tale (African) green.
Tael, Tail, Tal, Tayl

Talen (English, French) claw, a unisex name.
Talin, Tallen, Tallon, Talon

Talfryn (Welsh) top of the hill.
Talfrin, Tallfrin, Tallfryn

Talib (Arabic) seeking knowledge, intelligent.
Taleb, Talyb

Taliesin (Welsh) radiant brow.
Talas, Talasin, Talies, Talis, Tallas, Tallis

Taliki (African) fellow.

Tallis (Persian) wise.
Talis, Tallys, Talys

Talmai (Hebrew) mound, small hill, furrow.
Talem, Talmay, Talmei

Talon (French) claw, a form of Talen.
Taelen, Taelin, Taelon, Taelyn, Talen, Talin, Tallen, Tallin, Tallon, Tallyn, Talyn

Talor (English) a form of Tal and Taylor.
Taelor, Taelur, Tailer, Tailor, Tallor, Tayler, Tayllor, Taylor, Taylour, Teylor

Tama (Maori) son.

Taman (Slavic) black, dark.
Tamann, Tamen, Tamon, Tamyn

Tamar (Hebrew) spice or palm tree.
Tamarie, Tamario, Tamarr, Tammar, Timar

Tamas (Hungarian) twin, a form of Thomas.
Tammas, Tammos, Tamos

Tambo (African) vigorous.

Tamir (Arabic) tall as a palm tree.
Tammie, Tammir, Tamyr

Tamson (Scandinavian) son of Thomas.
Tamsen, Tamzen

Tan (Burmese) million; (Vietnamese) new.
Than

Tanay (Hindu) son.
Tanai

Tancred (Teutonic) of thoughtful counsel.
Tancreda, Tancredi, Tancredie, Tancredo, Tancredy

Tane (Maori) husband.
Tain, Taine, Tainn, Tayn, Tayne, Taynn

Tanek (Greek) immortal.
Atek

Taneli (Finnish) God is my judge.
Taneil, Tanell, Tanella, Tanelli

Taner (English) leather worker who tans hides, a form of Tanner.
Tanar

Tangaroa (Polynesian) of the sea.

Tanguy (French) warrior.
Tangy

Tangwyn (Welsh) blessed peace.
Tangwen, Tangwin

Tani (Japanese) valley.
Tanee, Taney, Tanie, Tany

Taniel (Hebrew) God is my judge, a form of Daniel.
Daniel, Tanel, Tanell, Taniele, Taniell, Tanyel, Tanyell

Tanner (English) leather worker who tans hides.
Tanna, Tannar, Tannur, Tannyr

Tannin (English) tan-coloured.
Tanen, Taner, Tanery, Tann, Tannan, Tannar, Tannir, Tannon, Tannor, Tanny

Tanny (English) leather worker who tans hides, a form of Tanner.
Tana, Tannee, Tanney, Tannie, Tany

Tanton (English) by the still river.
Tantan, Tantin, Tantun, Tantyn

Tao (Chinese) peach, long life, a unisex name.

Tapani (Finnish) crowned, a form of Stephen.
Tapan, Tapann, Tapanni, Teppo

Tapko (African) antelope.

Taquan (American) combination of the prefix Ta and Quan.
TaQuan, Taquann, Taquawn, Taquon, Tarquon

Tarak (Hindu) star.
Tarrak

Taree (Australian Aboriginal) fig tree.
Tarey, Tari, Tarie, Tary

Tarif (Arabic) rare, uncommon.
Tareef, Tarreef, Tarrif

Tariq (Arabic) conquerer, hammers at the door, morning star.
Tareck, Tarek, Taric, Tarick, Tariek, Tarik, Tarikh, Tarrek, Tarrick, Tarrik, Tarryk, Taryk

Taro (Japanese) first-born boy.

Taron (American) combination of the prefix Ta and Ron.
Taeron, Tahron, Taren, Tarone, Tarrion, Tarron, Taryn

Tarquin (Latin) name of two early Roman kings.
Tarquan, Tarquen, Tarquine, Tarquinius, Tarquinus

Tarrant (Welsh) thunder.
Tarant, Tarent, Tarrane, Tarrent, Terent, Terrent, Torant, Torent, Torrant, Torrent

Tarun (Hindu) youthful.
Taran

Tarver (English) tower over the hills.
Terver

Tas (Gypsy) bird's nest.
Tass, Tassie, Tassy

Tashawn (American) combination of the prefix Ta and Shawn.
Tasean, Tashaan, Tashan, Tashaun, Tashean, Tashon, Tashun

Tasunke (Native American) horse.

Tate (English) cheerful one; (Native American) long-winded talker.
Taite, Tayte

Tatius (Latin) ruler.
Tatianus, Tatios, Tazio, Titus

Tau (African) lion.
Taue, Taur, Taure, Tor

Taurean (Latin) strong, forceful, like a bull, born under the sign of Taurus.
Tauraan, Taaurein, Taurin, Taurion, Taurone, Taurus

Tavaris (Aramaic) misfortune.
Tavar, Tavari, Tavarian, Tavarious, Tavarius, Tavarous, Tavars, Tavarus, Tavarres, Tavarri, Tavarris, Taveress, Tavor, Tevar, Tevarus

Tavey (Latin) eighth-born child, a form of Octavius.
Taevi, Taveon, Tavian, Taviann, Tavie, Tavien, Tavin, Tavio, Tavion, Tavon, Tayvon, Tavy

Tavis (Scottish) son of David.
Tav, Tavi, Taviss

Tavish (Scottish) twin, a form of Thomas.
Taviss

Tavor (Aramaic) misfortune.
Tavaris, Tavores, Tavoris, Tavorious, Tavoris

Tawfiq (Arabic) successful.
Tawfik

Tawno (Gypsy) little, tiny.

Tayib (Hindu) delicate, good.
Taeeb, Taieb, Taieeb, Tayeeb

Taylor (English) tailor of clothes, a unisex name.
Taelar, Taelor, Tailar, Tailor, Taylar, Tayler, Tayllor, Taylore

Taz (Persian) decorative cup, goblet.
Tazz

Teagan (Irish) poet, bard, a form of Teague; (Welsh) beautiful, a unisex name.
Teagen, Teagun, Teegan, Teegen, Teegun

Teague (Irish) poet, bard.
Taeg, Taege, Teagan, Teak, Tegan, Tegue, Teige, Teigue

Teale (English) sea-green, water bird, a unisex name.
Teal, Teele, Teile

Tearence (Latin) smooth, earthly, tender, a form of Terrence.
Tearance, Tearnce, Terrance. Terence

Tearlach (Celtic) strong, courageous, manly, a form of Charles.
Tearlac, Tearlache, Tearlack, Tearlak, Tearloc, Tearloch, Tearloche, Tearlock, Tearlok

Tearle (English) stern, severe.
Tearl, Terl, Terle

Teasdale (English) river dweller.
Teasdall, Teesdale, Teesdall

Teb (Spanish) crowned, a form of Stephen.

Tecwyn (Welsh) fair, white-haired friend.
Tecwen

Ted (English) a form of Edward, Theodore.
Edward, Tedd, Teddie, Teddy, Tedek, Tedik, Tedson, Theodore

Teddy (English) a form of Edward, Theodore.
Edward, Teddee, Teddey, Teddie, Tedy, Theodore

Tedmund (English) protector of the land.
Tedman, Tedmand, Tedmon, Tedmond, Tedmun

Tedorik (Scandinavian) gift from God, a form of Theodore.
Tedor, Tedore, Tedorike, Tedoryk, Tedoryke, Teodor, Teodorek, Teodorik, Theodoor

Tedrick (American) combination of Ted and Rick.
Teddrick, Tederick, Tedric, Tredrik

Tefere (Eithopian) seed.
Tefer

Tegan (Irish) poet, a form of Teague.
Taegue, Teagan, Teghan, Teigan, Tiegan

Tej (Hindu) light, lustrious.

Tejas (Hindu) sharp.

Tekle (Ethiopian) plant.
Tekel

Telek (Polish) iron worker.

Telem (Hebrew) furrow, mound.
Tel, Tellem

Telford (French) iron cutter.
Telek, Telfer, Telferd, Telfor, Telfour, Telfourd, Tellford

Teller (English) story teller.
Tell, Tella, Tellar, Telli, Tellie, Telly

Telmo (English) cultivator.

Telvin (American) combination of the prefix Te and Melvin.
Tellvan, Tellvin, Telvan

Tem (Gypsy) country.

Teman (Hebrew) on the right side.
Temani, Temanie, Temany, Temen

Tembo (African) elephant.
Tembeau

Tempest (French) storm, a unisex name.
Tempes, Tempeste

Temple (Latin) sanctuary, holy place.

Templeton (English) temple town, town by the temple.
Temp, Templeten

Tennant (English) renter.
Tenant, Tenent, Tennent

Tennessee (Native American) mighty warrior.
Tennessy, Tennesy, Tennysee

Tennyson (English) son of Denis.
Tenison, Tenney, Tenneyson, Tennie, Tennis, Tennison, Tenny, Tenson, Tenyson

Teo (Vietnamese) twin, a form of Tom.

Teodoro (Spanish) gift from God, a form of Theodore.
Teodore, Teodoros

Teppo (French) crowned, a form of Stephen.

Tequan (American) combination of the prefix Te and Quan.
Tequann, Tequen, Tequenn, Tequin, Tequinn, Tequon, Tequonn

Teremun (African) with his father's acceptance.

Terence (Latin) smooth, earthly, tender.
Tarance, Tarence, Tarrance, Tarrence, Terance, Terencio, Terrance, Terrence, Terri, Terrie, Terris, Terry, Terryal, Terrynce, Terrys, Torrence, Tracey, Tyreece, Tyreese

Terenzio (Italian) smooth, earthly, tender, a form of Terence.
Terenzo, Terenzos

Terris (Latin) son of Terry.
Terance, Terence, Terrence, Terri, Terrie, Terros, Terry, Terryal, Terrys, Tracey

Terron (American, Greek) ruler, monarch; (Irish) Owen's land, a form of Tyrone.

Tereon, Terion, Terione, Teron, Terone, Terreon, Terrion, Terrione, Terrone, Terronn, Terryon, Teryon, Tiron, Tirron

Terry (English) smooth, earthly, tender, a form of Terence.
Terance, Teree, Terence, Terree, Terrence, Terrey, Terri, Terrie, Terries, Terris, Terryal, Terrys, Thierry, Tierry, Tracey

Tertius (Latin) third-born child.
Tertio, Tertios, Tertyus

Teva (Hebrew) child of nature.

Tevel (Yiddish) beloved, a form of David.
Tevell, Tevil, Tevill, Tevyl, Tevyll

Tevin (American) combination of the prefix Te and Kevin.
Teavin, Teivon, Tevan, Tevien, Tevinn, Tevinne, Tevion, Tevohn, Tevon, Tevonne, Tevoun, Tevvin, Tevvyn, Tevyn

Tevis (Scottish) twin, a form of Thomas.

Tex (English) from Texas.
Tejas, Texas, Texx

Thabit (Arabic) firm.
Tabit, Thab

Thad (Greek) courageous, a form of Thaddeus.
Thadd

Thaddeus (Greek) courageous.
Tad, Tadd, Taddeo, Taddeus, Taddiaus, Taddis, Tadeaus, Tadeus, Tadus, Tadzio, Thadd, Thaddeo, Thaddeus, Thaddiaus, Thaddy, Thade, Thadeaus, Thadee, Thadeus, Thadus, Thady

Thai (Vietnamese) many, multiple.
Tai

Thalmus (Greek) flowering.
Thalmas, Thalmis, Thalmos, Thalmys

Thaman (Hindu) god-like.

Than (Burmese) million.
Tan, Thanh

Thane (English) attendant warrior.
Thain, Thaine, Thayn, Thayne

Thang (Vietnamese) victorious.

Thanh (Vietnamese) finished, complete, intelligent, sky-blue, brilliant, a unisex name.
Than

Thaniel (Hebrew) gift of God, a form of Nathaniel.
Nathaniel, Thaneal, Thaneel, Thaneil, Thaneyl, Thanial, Thaniall, Thaniell, Thanyel, Thanyell

Thanos (Greek) nobleman.
Thanasis, Thannos

Thatcher (English) thatcher of roofs.
Thacher, Thatch, Thaxter

Thaw (English) melting.
Thor

Thayer (French) nation's army.
Thaier, Thay

Thel (English) upper storey.
Thell

Thenga (African) bringing him.
Thengah

Theobald (German) the people's prince.
Theobaldo, Theobauld, Theobauldo, Theobault, Theobaulto, Thibald, Thibauld, Thibault, Tibalt, Tibold, Tiebold,

Tiebolt, Tiebout, Toiboid, Tybald, Tybalt, Tybault

Theodore (Greek) gift from God.
Feodor, Feodore, Feodoro, Teadoir, Teadoire, Teador, Teadore, Ted, Teddie, Teddy, Tedor, Tedorak, Tedorek, Tedoro, Telly, Teos, Tewdor, Theo, Theodor, Theodoro, Theodors, Theodorus, Tivador, Todor, Tolek, Tolor

Theodoric (German) ruler of the people.
Dedrick, Derek, Dirk, Doric, Teodoric, Teodric, Thedric, Thedrick, Theodric, Theodrick, Thierry, Till

Theon (Greek) gift from God, godly.

Theophanus (Latin) God has appeared, born on the Epiphany, 6th January.
Theophane, Theophanio, Theophanios, Theophano, Theophanos, Theophanous

Theophilus (Greek) loved by God.
Teofil, Teofilus, Thelonius, Theofilus, Theophille, Theophillus, Theopolis, Theopollis

Theron (Greek) one who hunts.
Theran, Theren, Thereon, Therin, Therion, Therrin, Therron, Theryn, Theryon

Theros (Greek) summer.
Therros

Thian (Vietnamese) smooth.
Thia, Thien

Thierry (French) ruler of the people.
Teirry, Terry, Theirry, Theorie, Theory, Tierrie, Tierry

Thies (French) gift of God.

Tho (Vietnamese) one who will live a long time.

Thoar (Australian Aboriginal) sunrise.

Thomar (Australian Aboriginal) little river.
Tomar

Thomas (Hebrew) twin.
Didymus, Dummas, Foma, Tam, Tamas, Tamaso, Tamassa, Tamasso, Tamasz, Tamati, Tammeas, Tammen, Tammeos, Tammy, Tavish, Taviss, Teo, Thom, Thoma, Thomasin, Thomasino, Thomaso, Thomaz, Thomos, Thumas, Tom, Toma, Tomas, Tomasino, Tomaso, Tomasz, Tomaz, Tomhas, Tomi, Tomie, Tommi, Tommie, Tommy, Tomy, Tuomas

Thompson (English) son of Thomas.
Thomason, Thomison, Thomsen, Thomson, Tompson, Tomson

Thor (Norse) god of thunder.
Tor, Thorin, Tyrus

Thorbert (Norse) the brilliance of Thor.
Thorbertt, Thorbirt, Thorbirtt, Thorburt, Thorburtt

Thorbjorn (Scandinavian) Thor's bear.
Thorborn, Thorburn, Thurbjorn, Thurborn, Thurburn

Thorburn (Norse) Thor's bear.
Thorborn, Thurborn, Thurburn

Thorleif (Scandinavian) Thor's beloved.
Thorlief

Thorley (English) Thor's meadow, thorny meadow.
Thorlea, Thorlee, Thorleigh, Thorli, Thorlie, Thorly

Thormond (Scandinavian) defended by Thor.

Thormon, Thormonde, Thormun, Thormund, Thormunde, Thurmon, Thurmond, Thurmund

Thorne (English) thorn.
Thorn, Thornie, Thorny

Thornton (English) town of thorn bushes.
Thorne, Thorntan, Thornten, Thorntin, Thorntyn, Thortan, Thorten, Thortin, Thorton, Thortyn

Thorpe (English) village.
Thorp

Thuc (Vietnamese) aware.
Thuk

Thurlow (English) Thor's hill.
Thurlo, Thurlowe

Thurston (English) Thor's stone.
Thorstain, Thorstan, Thorstein, Thorsten, Thorstien, Thorston, Thurstan, Thurstain, Thursten, Torsten, Torston

Tiago (Spanish) supplanter, a form of Jacob.
Tiaga

Tiba (Native American) grey.
Tyba

Tibbot (Irish) bold.
Tibbott, Tibot, Tibott, Tybbot, Tybot

Tiberio (Italian) the River Tiber in Italy.
Tiberia, Tiberias, Tiberios, Tiberiouis, Tiberius, Tibus, Tyberio, Tyberius, Tyberrius

Tibor (Hungarian) holy place.
Tybor

Ticho (Spanish) noble, a form of Patrick.
Tiko

Tieler (English) tile layer, a form of Tyler.
Tielar, Tielor, Tielyr

Tien (Chinese) heaven.
Tienn

Tiennan (French) crowned, a form of Stephen.
Tienan

Tiernan (Irish) lord.
Tiarnach, Tiernan, Tierney, Tiernnan

Tierney (Irish) lordly.
Tiernan, Tiernie, Tierny, Tyrney

Tiger (American) tiger.
Ti, Tig, Tige, Tigger, Tighe, Tigher, Ty, Tyg, Tyge, Tyger, Tygger, Tygh, Tyghe

Tiimu (African) caterpillar living in the ground.
Timu, Tymu

Tiktu (African) bird digging for potatoes.

Tilden (English) valley under cultivation.
Tildan, Tildin, Tildon, Tillde

Tim (Greek) honours God.
Timm, Timmie, Timmy

Timeus (Greek) honour.
Timius

Timin (Arabic) born near the sea.
Timyn, Tymin, Tymyn

Timon (Greek) honourable.
Timmon

Timoteo (Spanish) honours God, a form of Timothy.
Timotio

Timothy (Greek) honours God.
Tadhg, Taidgh, Tiege, Tim, Tima, Timathee, Timathey, Timathie, Timathy, Timka, Timkin, Timmie, Timmothee, Timmothey, Timmothie, Timmothy, Timmy, Timofee, Timofei, Timofey, Timofie, Timok, Timon, Timotao, Timotei, Timotejs, Timoteo, Timothe, Timothee, Timothey, Timthe, Tiomoid, Tisha, Tymmothee, Tymmothey, Tymmothie, Tymothey, Tymothi, Tymothie, Tymothy

Timur (Russian) conqueror.
Tymur

Tino (Greek) a form of Augustine, Antonio, Valentino.
Tinno

Tipene (Maori) crowned, a form of Stephen.
Tipen

Tiquan (American) combination of the prefix Ti and Quan.
Tiquann, Tiquawn, Tiquine, Tiquon, Tiqwan

Tisha (Russian) honours God, a form of Timothy.
Tysha

Tishawn (American) combination of the prefix Ti and Shawn.
Tishaun, Tishean, Tishon, Tishun, Tisshan

Tito (Italian) lord, honourable title, a form of Titus.
Titas, Titis, Titos, Titto, Tittos, Tittus, Titus

Titus (Greek) lord, honourable title.
Titan, Tite, Titek, Titis, Tito, Tittan, Tittek, Tittis, Tittos, Tyttus, Tytus

Tivon (Hebrew) nature lover.
Tibon, Tybon, Tyvon

BOYS

TJ (American) combination of the initials T and J.
TeeJae, Teejae, Teejay, Tj, T-J, T-jay, Tjayda

Tobar (Gypsy) road; (Irish) fountain.
Tobbar

Tobi (African) great; (Hebrew) God is good, a unisex name.
Tobbee, Tobbey, Tobbi, Tobbie, Tobby, Tobee, Tobey, Tobie, Toby

Tobias (Hebrew) God is good.
Tobbia, Tobbiah, Tobbin, Tobbye, Tobbyn, Tobia, Tobiah, Tobies, Tobin, Tobit, Tobye, Tobyn

Tobin (Hebrew) God is good, a form of Tobias.
Tobben, Tobbin, Tobbyn, Toben, Tobian, Tobyn, Tovin

Tobit (Hebrew) son of Tobias.
Tobin, Tobitt, Tobyn, Tobyt, Tobytt

Toby (Hebrew) God is good, a form of Tobias.
Tobbee, Tobbey, Tobbie, Tobby, Tobe, Tobee, Tobey, Tobie

Todd (Latin) fox.
Tad, Tod, Todde, Toddie, Toddy

Todor (Hungarian) gift from God, a form of Theodore.
Teodor, Teodore, Theodor, Theodore, Todar, Todas, Todos

Togar (Australian Aboriginal) smoke.
Togir, Togor, Togyr

Tohon (Native American) cougar.

Tokala (Native American) fox.
Tokelua

Tokoni (African) helper.
Tokonie, Tokony

Tolman (English) tax collector.
Toland, Tolbert, Toller, Tollman

Tom (Hebrew) twin, a form of Thomas.
Thom, Thomee, Thomey, Thomi, Thomie, Thomm, Thommee, Thommey, Thommi, Thommie, Thommy, Thomy, Tomee, Tomey, Tomi, Tomie, Tomm, Tommee, Tommey, Tommi, Tommie, Tommy, Tomy

Toma (Illyrian) twin, a form of Thomas.
Thoma, Thomah

Tomas (German) twin, a form of Thomas.
Tomaisin, Tomas, Tomasin, Tomaso, Tomasz, Tomaz, Tome, Tomek, Tomelis, Tomes, Tomico, Tomik, Tomis, Tommas, Tommaso, Tomo, Tomson

Tombe (African) northerner.

Tomer (Hebrew) tall.
Tomar, Tomir, Tomyr

Tomey (Irish) twin, a form of Thomas.
Tome, Tomee, Tomi, Tomie, Tomy

Tomi (Japanese) wealthy, rich.
Tomie, Tomy

Tomkin (English) little Thomas.
Thomkin, Thomkyn, Tomkyn

Tommy (Hebrew) twin, a form of Thomas.
Thomee, Thomey, Thomi, Thomie, Thommee, Thommey, Thommi, Tommie, Thommy, Tomy, Tom, Tomee, Tomey, Tomi, Tomie, Tommee, Tommey, Tommi, Tommie, Tomy

Tomos (Welsh) twin, a form of Thomas.
Thomos

Tonda (Slavic) priceless, a form of Tony.
Toek

Tong (Vietnamese) fragrant.

Tonio (Italian) priceless, a form of Antonio.
Tonek, Toney, Toni, Tony, Tonyo

Tony (Italian) priceless, a form of Antonio.
Tonee, Toney, Toni, Tonie, Tonio, Tonis, Tonnee, Tonney, Tonni, Tonnie, Tonny

Toolan (Australian Aboriginal) wattle.

Topper (English) hill top.
Toper

Tor (Norwegian) thunder; (African) royalty.
Thor, Thorr, Torr

Torian (Irish) chief, a form of Torin.
Toran, Torean, Toriano, Torien, Torrian, Torrien, Torryn

Torin (Irish) chief.
Toran, Torien, Torran, Torrien, Torrin, Torryn, Toryn

Torio (Japanese) bird's tail.
Torrio

Tormey (Irish) thunder spirit.
Torme, Tormee, Tormi, Tormie

Tormod (Scottish) north.
Tormed, Tory

Torquil (Scottish) Thor's kettle, pot.
Torkel, Torquill

Torr (English) tower.
Tor, Tory

Torrance/Torrence (Latin) smooth, earthly, tender; (Irish) small, rocky hills.
Torance, Toreence, Toren, Torence, Torey, Torin, Torince, Torn, Torne, Torr, Torrance, Torren, Torrence, Torreon, Torrin, Torry, Turance

Torrey (Latin) smooth, earthly, tender; (Irish) small, rocky hills, a form of Torrence.
Toreey, Torie, Torre, Torri, Torrie, Torry

Toru (Japanese) sea.

Tory (Norse) Thor, god of thunder.
Torey, Tori, Torie, Torrey

Toshi (Japanese) mirror reflection.
Toshee, Toshey, Toshie, Toshy

Tovi (Hebrew) good.
Tovee, Tovey, Tovie, Tovy

Townley (English) meadow town.
Townlea, Townlee, Townleigh, Townli, Townlie, Townly

Townsend (English) end of town.
Tawny, Townes, Townie, Townsen, Townsende, Townshend

Tracey (Irish) warrior, a unisex name.
Trace, Tracee, Traci, Tracie, Tracy, Trayce, Traycee, Traycey, Traycie, Traycy, Tre, Trea

Trader (English) skilled worker.
Trade

Trahern (Welsh) strong as iron.
Trahearn, Trahearne, Traherne

Tramaine (English) house at the rock, a form of Tremayne.
Tramain, Traman, Tramane,

*Traymon, Tremain, Tremaine,
Tremayn, Tremayne*

Trant (English) clever, cunning.

Tranter (English) wagon driver,
wagon maker.
Trantor

Traquan (American) combination
of Travis and Quan.
*Traequan, Traqon, Traquawn, Traquon,
Trayquan, Trayquane, Trayquon*

Trashawn (American)
combination of Travis and Shawn.
*Trasean, Trasen, Trashon, Trashone,
Trashun, Trayshaun*

Traugott (German) trust in God.
Traugot

Travell (English) traveller.
*Travail, Traval, Travale, Travall,
Travel, Travele, Travelle, Travellis,
Trevel, Trevele, Trevell, Trevelle*

Travers (French) crossroads.
*Trav, Travares, Travaress, Travarus,
Traverez, Traverse, Traverus, Travoris*

Travis (French) crossroads.
*Travais, Travees, Travers, Traves,
Traveus, Travious, Travise, Traviss,
Travisse, Travius, Travous, Travus,
Travys, Travyse, Travyss, Travysse,
Trayvis, Trevais, Trevis, Treviss*

Trayton (English) town of many trees.
Treyton

Trayvon (American) combination
of Tray and Von.
*Trayvean, Trayvin, Trayvion,
Trayvond, Trayvone, Trayvonne,
Treavan, Treavin, Treavion, Treavon,
Trevian, Trevien, Trevine, Trevinne,
Trevion, Trevione, Trevionne,
Trevyeon, Trevyn*

Trefor (Welsh) (Irish) prudent,
cautious; (Welsh) village home, a
form of Trevor.
Treffor

Tremayne (English) house at the
rock.
*Tramain, Tramaine, Tremain,
Tremaine, Tremane, Tremayn,
Treymain, Treymaine, Trimaine*

Trent (Latin) torrent, rapid stream;
(French) thirty.
Trente, Trentino, Trento, Trentonio

Trenton (English) town by the
rapid stream.
*Trendon, Trendun, Trenten, Trentin,
Trentton, Trentyn, Trinten, Trintin,
Trinton*

Trequan (American) combination
of Trey and Quan.
*Trequane, Trequanne, Trequaun,
Trequian, Trequon*

Treshawn (American)
combination of Trey and Shawn.
*Tresean, Treshaun, Treshon, Treshun,
Treysean, Treyshaun, Treyshawn,
Treyshon*

Trevaughn (American)
combination of Trey and Vaughn.
*Trevaughan, Trevaughin, Trevaugn,
Trevaun, Trevaune, Trevaunn,
Trevaunne*

Trevelyan (English) mill place,
Elian's home.

Trevis (English) crossroads, a form
of Travis.
*Treves, Trevez, Treveze, Treviss,
Trevius*

Trevon (American) combination
of Trey and Von.
Travion, Travon, Tre, Treavon,

Trevan, Treven, Treveyon, Trevin, Trevion, Trevohn, Trevoine, Trevone, Trevonn, Treyvon

Trevor (Celtic) prudent, cautious; (Welsh) village home.
Travor, Treavor, Trebor, Trefor, Trev, Trevar, Trevares, Trevarious, Trevarius, Trevaro, Trevaros, Trevarus, Trever, Trevore, Trevores, Trevoris, Trevoro, Trevoros, Trevorus, Trevyr, Treyvor

Trey (English) third-born child.
Trae, Trai, Tray, Treye, Tri, Trie

Trigg (Scandinavian) trustworthy.
Trig, Triggie, Triggy

Trilby (Italian) singer; (English) soft hat, a unisex name.
Trilbee, Trilbey, Trilbie, Trillby

Trini (Latin) third, three.
Trinie, Trinity, Trinnie, Trinny, Triny

Trinity (Latin) blessed threefold, holy trinity, the Father, Son and Holy Spirit, a unisex name.
Trenedy, Trini, Trinidy, Trinitey, Trinitie

Trip (English) traveller.
Tripp, Trippe

Tristam (Latin) sorrowful, a form of Tristan.
Tristan, Tristiam, Tristian, Tristram, Tristran, Trystam, Trystan, Trystram, Trystran

Tristan (Welsh) riot; (Latin) sad, sorrowful, the melancholy one, the name of an Arthurian knight who features in *Tristan and Isolde*.
Treston, Tris, Trisam, Trisan, Tristam, Tristen, Tristiam, Tristian, Tristim, Tristin, Triston, Tristrim, Tristrin, Tristyn, Trystan

Tristram (Latin) sorrowful, a form of Tristan.
Tristam, Tristem, Tristiam, Tristrym, Trystim

Tristran (Welsh) riot; (Latin) sad, sorrowful, the melancholy one, a form of Tristan.
Treston, Tris, Trisan, Tristam, Tristan, Tristano, Tristen, Tristian, Tristin, Triston, Tristyn, Trystan

Trot (English) trickling stream.
Trott

Troy (Irish) soldier; (French) curly-haired; (English) water.
Troi, Troye, Troyton

True (English) faithful, loyal.
Tru, Truett, Truit, Truth, Truthe

Truitt (English) honest, little.
Truet, Truett, Truit, Truyt, Truytt

Truman (English) faithful, true, trusted man.
Trueman, Truemen, Trumain, Trumaine, Trumann, Trumen

Trumble (English) strong, bold.
Trumbal, Trumball, Trumbel, Trumbell, Trumbull

Trung (Vietnamese) loyal, faithful.

Trustin (English) able to be trusted.
Trustan, Trusten, Truston, Trustyn

Tryphon (Greek) small, dainty, delicate.
Trifen, Trifon, Triphen, Triphon, Tryfen, Tryfon, Tryphen

Trystan (Welsh) riot; (Latin) sad, sorrowful, a form of Tristan.
Tryistan, Trysten, Trystian, Trystin, Trystn, Tryston, Trystyn

Tse (African) younger twin.

Tu (Vietnamese) twin.

Tuaco (African) eleventh-born child.

Tuari (African) young eagle.
Tuarie, Tuary

Tucker (English) tucker of cloth.
Tucka, Tuckar

Tudor (Welsh) gift from God, a form of Theodore, ruler of the people.
Todor, Tudour

Tudur (Welsh) gift from God, a form of Theodore, ruler of the people, a form of Tudor.

Tuki (Australian Aboriginal) bullfrog.

Tullis (Latin) title.
Tulis, Tulli, Tullie, Tullius, Tullos, Tully

Tully (Irish) has the peace of God, mighty people, a unisex name.
Tulee, Tuleigh, Tuley, Tulie, Tulio, Tull, Tullee, Tulleigh, Tulley, Tullie, Tullio, Tullis, Tullius, Tullos, Tuly

Tumaini (African) one who brings hope.

Tumu (African) deer thinking about his food.

Tung (Chinese) everyone; (Vietnamese) dignified person.
Tunge

Tupi (Native American) pull up.
Tupe, Tupee, Tupie, Tupy

Turner (English) maker of wooden objects with a lathe.

Turnor

Turpin (Scandinavian) Thor, thunder god.
Thorpin, Thurpin, Torpin

Tut (Arabic) strong, courageous.
Tutt

Tuyen (Vietnamese) angelic, a unisex name.

Twain (English) divided in two.
Tawine, Twaine, Twan, Twane, Tway, Twayn, Twayne

Twia (African) born after twins.

Twitchell (English) narrow passage.
Twitchel

Tye (Anglo-Saxon) enclosure.
Ti, Tie, Ty

Tyee (Native American) chief.
Tyke

Tyger (English) tiger, a form of Tiger.
Tige, Tiger, Tyg, Tygar, Tyge

Tyler (English) tiler or tile maker, a unisex name.
Tieler, Tila, Tilar, Tiler, Tiller, Tilor, Ty, Tyel, Tyla, Tylar, Tyle, Tylee, Tyller, Tylor

Tymon (Slavic) honours God, a form of Timothy.
Timon, Tymain, Tymaine, Tymane, Tymeik, Tymek, Tymen

Tynan (Irish) dark.
Ty, Tynen, Tynnan

Tyquan (American) combination of Ty and Quan.
Tykwan, Tykwane, Tykwon, Tyquane, Tyquann, Tyquin, Tyquine, Tyquon, Tyquone, Tyqwan

Tyree (Scottish) island dweller.

Tyra, Tyrae, Tyrai, Tyray, Tyre, Tyreav, Tyrece, Tyreece, Tyrees, Tryreese, Tyres, Tyresse, Tyrey, Tyrez, Tyreze, Tyrice, Tryrie, Tyriece, Tyry

Tyrick (American) combination of Ty and Rick.

Tryik, Tryiq, Tryque, Tyreck, Tyreek, Tyreik, Tyrek, Tyreke, Tyric, Tyrick, Tyrrick

Tyrone (Greek) ruler, monarch; (Irish) Owen's land.

Tayron, Tayrone, Teiron, Terron, Ty, Tyerone, Tyhrone, Tyrain, Tyraine, Tyran, Tyrane, Tyrin, Tyrohn, Tyron, Tyroney, Tyronn, Tyronne, Tyroon, Tyroun

Tyshawn (American) combination of Ty and Shawn.

Tysean, Tyshan, Tyshane, Tyshaun, Tyshinn, Tyshion, Tyshon, Tyshone, Tyshonne, Tyshun, Tyshunn

Tyson (French) firebrand.

Tison, Tiszon, Tycen, Tycon, Tyesn, Tyeson, Tysen, Tysie, Tysin, Tysne, Tysone

Tyvon (American) combination of Ty and Von.

Tyvan, Tyvin, Tyvinn, Tyvonn, Tyvonne

Tzadok (Hebrew) righteous.

Tzadik, Zadok

U

Ualter (Irish) army ruler, a form of Walter.
Uailtar, Ualtar, Ualteir, Ualter, Ualtor

Ualsi (African) walrus.
Ualsee, Ualsey, Ualsie, Ualsy, Ualusee, Ualusey, Ualusi, Ualusie, Ualusy

Uba (African) wealthy.

Ubadah (Arabic) servant of God, one who serves God.
Ubada, Ubaida, Ubaidah, Ubayda, Ubaydah

Ubaid (Arabic) faithful.

Ubaldus (German) peace of mind.
Ubald, Ubaldas, Ubalt, Ubaltas, Ubalus

Uberto (Italian) bright mind, bright spirit, a form of Hubert.
Huberto, Ubert, Ubirt, Ubirto, Uburt, Uburto

Ucello (Italian) bird.
Uccelo, Uccello, Ucelo

Uche (African) thoughtful.

Uday (Hindu) to rise.
Udae, Udai

Udell (English) valley of the yew trees.
Dell, Eudel, Eudell, Udal, Udale, Udall, Udel, Udele, Udelle, Yudel, Yudell

Udit (Hindu) shining.

Udo (Japanese) ginseng plant.

Udolf (English) prosperous wolf.
Udo, Udolfe, Udolfo, Udolph, Udolphe, Udolpho, Udulf, Udulfe, Udulfo, Udulph, Udulphe, Udulpho

Ueli (Swiss) noble ruler.
Uelie

Uffo (German) wild bear.
Ufo

Ugo (Italian) bright mind and spirit, intelligent, a form of Hugh, Hugo.
Hugh, Hugo, Ugon

Ugutz (Slavic) God is gracious, a form of John.

Uhila (African) lightning.
Uhilah, Uhilla, Uhyla, Uhylah

Uilliam (Irish) determined protector, a form of William.
Uileog, Ulick, Uilleam, Uilliem

Uistean (Irish) intelligent.
Uisdean

Uja (Hindu) to grow.

Ujala (Hindu) bright, shining.
Ujalah

Uku (Hawaiian) flea.

Ulan (African) first-born twin, a unisex name.
Ulen, Ulin

Uland (German) noble country.
Ulan, Ulland

Ulbrecht (German) noble, bright, a form of Albert.
Ulbrech, Ulbret, Ulbrett, Ulbryght

Ulf (German, Norse) wolf.
Ulfe, Ulfer, Ulph

Ulfred (German, Norse) peaceful wolf.
Ulfreid, Ulfrid, Ulfried

Ulger (German, Norse) warring wolf.
Ulgar

Ulick (Norse) rewarding mind.
Ulic, Ulik, Ullic, Ullick, Ullik, Ullyc, Ullyck, Ullyk, Ulyc, Ulyck, Ulyk

Ulisse (Latin) the angry one, wrathful, a form of Ulysses.
Ulishes, Ulisses, Ulysses

Ullivieri (Italian) olive tree.
Ulivieri, Uliviero, Ulliviero

Ullock (German, Norse) sporting wolf.
Ulloc, Ulloch, Ullok, Uloc, Uloch, Ulock, Ulok

Ulmer (German, Norse) famous wolf.
Ullmar, Ullmer, Ulmar, Ulmor, Ulmore

Ulmo (German) from Ulm, Germany.

Ulrick (German, Norse) ruling wolf.
Uli, Ull, Ullric, Ullrich, Ullrick, Ullrik, Ullryc, Ullrych, Ullryck, Ullryk, Ulric, Ulrich, Ulrick, Ulrico, Ulrik, Ulrike, Ulu, Ulwe, Ulz

Ultan (German) noble stone.
Ulten, Ultin, Ulton

Ultman (Hindu) a god.

Ulysses (Latin, Greek) the angry one, wrathful, a form of Odysseus.
Eulises, Oulixes, Oulixeus, Ulick, Ulik, Ulises, Ulixes, Ulixeus, Ulussius, Ulyses, Ulysees, Ulysse, Ulyssees, Ulysses, Ulysus

Umang (Hindu) enthusiastic.
Umanga

Umar (Arabic) blooming, flourishing, long-lived.
Umair, Umayr, Umer

Umberto (Italian) famous warrior, dark yellow colour of earth, a form of Humbert.
Humbet, Humberto, Ubero, Umbert, Umbirt, Umbirto, Umburt, Umburto

Umi (African) new life.
Umee, Umie, Umy

Umit (Turkish) hope.
Umitt

Unai (Basque) shepherd.
Unay

Uner (Turkish) famous.
Unar

Unika (African) shining, bright.
Unikah

Unique (Latin) one of a kind, the only one, unique, a unisex name.
Uneek, Unek, Unikque, Unyque

Unity (Latin) together in a commom cause, oneness, unity, a unisex name.
Unite, Unitee, Unitey, Uniti, Unitie

Unkas (Native American) fox.

Uno (Latin) one.
Unno

Unwin (Anglo-Saxon) not friendly.
Unwen, Unwenn, Unwinn, Unwyn, Unwynn

Upshaw (English) upper wooded area.
Upshawe

Upton (English) upper town.
Uptown

Upwood (English) upper forest.

Urban (Latin) belonging to the city, city dweller, name of several early saints and popes.
Ueban, Uerburn, Urbain, Urbanus, Urben, Urbern, Urberne

Urbano (Italian) city dweller, a form of Urban.
Urban, Urbanius, Urbanus

Uri (Hebrew) my light, God's light, a form of Uriah, a unisex name
Urie, Ury

Uriah (Hebrew) my light.
Uri, Uria, Urias, Urijah, Urya, Uryah

Urian (Greek) from heaven.
Urihaan, Uryan

Uriel (Hebrew) God is my light, an angel name.
Urel, Urial, Uriale, Uriall, Urialle, Urie, Uriele, Uriell, Urielle

Urien (Welsh) born in town.
Urian

Ursel (German) little bear.
Ursal, Ursall, Ursan, Ursell, Ursus

Ursus (Latin, Greek) bear.
Ursa, Ursah, Ursal, Ursall, Ursel, Ursell, Ursen, Ursin, Ursyn, Ursus

Urtzi (Basque) sky.

Urvil (Hindu) sea.
Ervil, Ervill, Ervyl, Ervyll, Urvill, Urvyl, Urvyll

Usama (Arabic) lion.
Usamah

Useni (African) tell me what you know.
Jusene, Juseni, Usene, Usenet, Usenie, Useny

Usi (African) smoke.

Ustin (Russian) just, righteous, a form of Justin.
Ustan, Usten, Ustyn

Utachi (Native American) bear with strong claws.
Utach, Utatci

Uthman (Arabic) companion of the prophet.
Usman, Uthmaan

Uttam (Hindu) the best.
Utam

Utu (Polynesian) return.

Uyeda (Japanese) rice field.
Uyedah

Uzair (Arabic) helpful.
Uzaire, Uzayr, Uzayre

Uzi (Hebrew) my strength.
Uzee, Uzey, Uzie, Uzy

Uziel (Hebrew) God is my strength.
Uzial, Uziall, Uziell, Uzyal, Uzyall, Uzyel, Uzyell, Uzzel

Vachel (French) one who tends cows, little cow.
Vache, Vachell

Vaclav (Czech) wreath of glory.
Vaklav, Vasek

Vadin (Hindu) skilled speaker.
Vaden

Vail (Anglo-Saxon) valley, a unisex name.
Vaile, Vaill, Vaille, Vale, Valle, Vayl, Vayle, Vayll, Vaylle

Vaina (Finnish) river's mouth.
Vain, Vaino, Vayna, Vayno

Val (Latin) strength, a form of Valentine, a unisex name.

Valborg (Swedish) protection from the slaughter.
Valbourg, Valburg

Valdemar (German) famous ruler.
Valdimar, Valdymar, Vlademar, Vladimar, Vladymar

Valdus (German) powerful, a battle hero, famous ruler.
Valdis, Valdys

Valentine (Latin) strong, powerful, brave.
Val, Valence, Valencio, Valente, Valentijn, Valentin, Valentino, Valentio, Valentyn, Valentyne, Valentyno

Valentino (Italian) strong, powerful, brave, a form of Valentine.
Tino, Val, Valentine, Valento, Valentyn, Valentyno

Valerian (Latin) strong, healthy.
Val, Valarian, Valarien, Valerien, Vallarian, Vallarien, Vellerian, Vellerien

Valerii (Russian) strong, healthy, a form of Valerian.
Valera, Valeri, Valerie, Vaalerij, Valerik, Valeriy, Valery

Valfrid (Swedish) strong peace.
Valfred

Valgard (Norse) foreign spear.
Valgarde

Valiant (Latin) strong protector, brave, valiant.
Valient, Valliant, Vallient

Valin (Hindu) mighty warrior, a form of Balin.
Balin, Valan, Valen, Vallin, Valon, Valyn

Vallis (French) from Wales.
Valis

Vamana (Hindu) worthy of praise.
Vamanah

Van (Dutch) of, from.
Vander, Vann, Vanno

Vance (Anglo-Saxon) thresher.
Vanse

Vandan (Hindu) saved.
Vanden, Vandin, Vandon, Vandyn

Vander (Dutch) belonging.
Vanda, Vandar, Vandir, Vandor, Vandyr

Vanya (Russian) God is gracious.
Vanechka, Vanek, Vanja, Vanka, Vanusha

Varad (Hungarian) fortress.
Vared, Varid, Varod, Varyd

Varden (French) green hill.
Vardan, Vardin, Vardon, Vardyn

Varen (Hindu) better.
Varan, Varin, Varon, Varyn

Varian (Latin) variable, the changeable one, a unisex name.
Vari, Varien, Variun, Varyan

Varick (Icelandic) sea drifter.
Varak, Varek, Varic, Varik, Varric, Varrick, Varrik, Warick, Warrick

Varil (Hindu) water.
Varal, Varel, Varril, Varol, Varyl

Vartan (Armenian) rose grower.
Varten, Vartin, Varton, Vartyn

Varun (Hindu) rain god.
Voron, Varron, Varrun

Vasant (Hindu) spring.
Vasan, Vasante, Vasanth

Vashawn (American) combination of the prefix Va and Shawn.
Vasean, Vashae, Vashan, Vashann, Vashaun, Vashawnn, Vashon, Vashun, Vishon

Vasilis (Greek) royal, like a king, a form of Basil.
Vas, Vasaya, Vaseleior, Vaselis, Vaselios, Vashon, Vasil, Vasile, Vasileios, Vasili, Vasillis, Vasillos, Vasillus, Vasilos, Vasilus, Vasily, Vassilios, Vasylis, Vasylko, Vasyltso

Vasily (Russian) royal, like a king, a form of Basil.

Vasilek, Vasili, Vasilie, Vasilii, Vasilije, Vasilik, Vasiliy, Vassili, Vassilii, Vassilij, Vassily, Vasya, Vasyenka

Vasin (Hindu) ruler, lord.
Vasan, Vasen, Vason, Vasun, Vasyn

Vasu (Hindu) wealthy, prosperous.

Vaughan (Welsh) small.
Van, Vaughen, Vaughn, Vauhn, Vaun, Vaune, Voughan

Veasna (Cambodian) lucky.

Ved (Hindu) sacred knowledge, sacred writings.

Vedie (Latin) sight.
Vedi, Vedy

Veer (Hindu) brave.
Vear, Veare, Veere, Vere

Vegard (Scandinavian) protected place.

Veiko (Finnish) brother.
Veyko

Veit (Swedish) wide.
Veyt

Velvel (Hebrew) wolf.
Velvell

Venedict (Russian) blessed, a form of Benedict.
Venedicto, Venedictos, Venka, Venya

Venkat (Hindu) sacred hill.

Venn (Irish) fair-haired; (English) marsh.
Ven

Ventura (Latin) venture, a unisex name.

Verdun (French) fort on the hill.
Virdun

Vere (Latin) truth; (French) alder tree.
Verre

Vered (Hebrew) rose.
Verad, Verid, Verod, Veryd

Verge (Latin) stick, edge.

Vergil (Latin) flourishing, staff bearer, a form of Virgil.
Verge, Vergel, Vergell, Virgil, Virgill

Verlin (Latin) flourishing, blooming.
Verlan, Verlain, Verline, Verlinn, Verlion, Verlon, Verlyn, Verlyne, Verlynn

Vermundo (Spanish) bear protection, protective bear.
Vermond, Vermonde, Vermondo, Vermund, Vermunde

Vern (French) alder tree grove; (Latin) youthful, spring time, a form of Vernon.
Vernal, Verne, Verneal, Vernel, Vernell, Vernelle, Vernen, Vernial, Vernin, Vernine, Vernis, Vernol, Vernon, Vernyn

Vernados (German) courage of a bear.
Vern, Vernard, Vernarde, Vernardo

Verner (German) defending army.
Varner, Werner

Verney (French) alder tree grove.
Vernee, Verni, Vernie, Verny, Virnee, Virnet, Virni, Virnie, Virny

Vernon (French) alder tree grove; (Latin) youthful, spring time.
Vern, Vernal, Vernan, Verne, Verneal, Vernel, Vernen, Verney, Vernin, Veryn

Verrill (German) masculine; (French) loyal.
Veril, Verill, Verril, Verrall, Verrell, Verroll, Verryl, Verryll, Veryl, Veryll

Veston (English) church town.
Vestan, Vesten, Vestin, Vestyn

Vian (English) gracious in life or lively, full of life, a form of Vivien.
Vien

Vicar (English) priest, clergy member.
Vickar, Vicker, Vickor, Vikar

Victor (Latin) victorious conqueror.
Vic, Victa, Victar, Victer, Victoir, Victoire, Victorien, Victorio, Victoriano, Viitrin, Vittorio, Vittorios, Vitya, Wikoli, Wiktor, Witek

Victorio (Spanish) victorious conqueror, a form of Victor.
Victoriano, Vittorio

Vidal (Latin) vital, lively, life, a unisex name.
Vidali, Vidaly, Vital, Vitali, Vitaly, Vydal, Vydali, Vydaly, Vytal, Vytali, Vytaly

Vidya (Hindu) wise.
Vidyah

Vijay (Hindu) victorious.
Veejay, Vijai

Viking (Scandinavian) Viking.
Vicking, Vikin

Vilfred (German) peaceful king, a form of Wilfred.
Vilfreid, Vilfrid, Vilfried

Vilhelm (German) determined guardian, a form of William.
Vilhelms, Villem, Villhelm

Vimal (Hindu) pure.

Vinay (Hindu) polite.

Vince/Vincent (Latin) conqueror, victor.
Vencent, Vencient, Vicenzo, Vikent, Vikenti, Vikesha, Vin, Vince, Vincente, Vincento, Vincentos, Vincenty, Vincenzo, Vinci, Vincien, Vincient, Vinciente, Vinciento, Vincint, Vincinto, Vincintos, Vinkento, Vinnie, Vinny, Vinsent, Vinsint, Vinsinte, Vyncent, Winsent

Vincente (Spanish) conqueror, victor, a form of Vincent.
Vencente

Vincenzo (Italian) conqueror, victor, a form of Vincent.
Vincentia, Vincentio, Vincenzius, Vinny, Vinsenz, Vinsenzo

Vinci (Italian, Hungarian) conqueror, victor, a form of Vincent.
Vinco, Vincze

Vine (French) vineyard worker.
Viner, Vyne, Vyner, Vynne, Vynner

Vinny (English) a form of Calvin, Melvin, Vincent.
Vinn, Vinnee, Vinney, Vinni, Vinnie

Vinod (Hindu) happy, joyful.
Vinodh, Vinood

Vinson (English) son of Vincent.
Vinnis, Vinnson, Vinsan, Vinsen, Vinsin, Vinsun, Vinsyn

Vipul (Hindu) plentiful.
Veepil, Veepul, Vipuel

Viraj (Hindu) resplendent.
Veeratj, Veeritj, Viratj, Viratjs, Virraj

Virat (Hindu) large.
Veerat, Viraat, Viraet, Virrat

Virgil (Latin) staff bearer
Vergil, Virge, Virgel, Virgial, Virgie, Virgile, Virgilio

Virgilio (Spanish) flourishing, staff bearer, a form of Virgil.

Virote (Thai) strong and powerful.

Vishal (Hindu) large.
Vishaal, Vishall

Vishnu (Hindu) protector.
Visnu

Vitale (French, Italian) alive, lively, full of life, a form of Vitalis.
Vital, Vitalis, Vitality, Vitall, Vitalle, Vitel, Vitele, Vitell, Vitelle, Vitellius, Vito, Vitus

Vitalis (Latin) alive, lively, full of life.
Vitali, Vitalie, Vitalli, Vitallie, Vitallis, Vitally, Vitaly, Vitel, Vitelis, Vitle, Vytali, Vytalie, Vytalis, Vytalli, Vytallie, Vytallis, Vytally, Vytell, Vytelli, Vytellis, Vytle, Vytlell

Vitas (Latin) alive, lively, full of life.
Vidal, Vietas, Vietes, Vietis, Vitus

Vito (Italian, Spanish) victorious conqueror, a form of Vittore, Vittorio.
Veit, Vidal, Vidale, Vital, Vitale, Vitali, Vitalis, Vitas, Vitin, Vitis, Vitus, Vitya, Vytal, Vytali, Vytas, Vyto

Vittore (Italian) victorious conqueror, a form of Victor.
Vito, Vitor, Vitore, Vitori, Vitorio, Vitt, Vittor, Vittori, Vittorias, Vittorio

Vittorio (Spanish) victorious conqueror, a form of Victor.
Vitt, Vittore, Vittori, Vittorie

Vitya (Russian) victorious conqueror, a form of Victor.
Vitenka, Vitia, Vitka

Vivek (Hindu) wisdom.

Vivian (Latin) gracious in life or lively, full of life, a unisex name.
Vivien, Vivyan, Vivyen, Vyvian, Vyvien, Vyvyan, Vyvyen

Vlad (Russian) ruling prince.
Vladd, Vladimir

Vladimir (Russian) ruling prince.
Bladimir, Vimka, Vlad, Vladamar, Vladameer, Vladamer, Vladamere, Vladamir, Vladamyr, Vladik, Vladimar, Vladimeer, Vladimer, Vladimere, Vladimyr, Volodimir, Volodya, Volya, Vovo, Wladimir

Vladislav (Russian) ruling prince.
Vladik, Vladya, Vladyslav, Vlas, Vlasislava, Vyacheslav, Wlasislav

Vogel (German) bird.
Voegel, Vogal, Vogil, Vogol, Vogyl

Volker (German) folk person.
Folke, Volk, Volke

Volney (German) the people's spirit, nation's spirit.
Volnee, Volni, Volnie, Volny

Vuai (African) savior.
Vuay

Waban (Native American) east wind.
Waben, Wabin, Wabon, Wabyn

Wade (Anglo-Saxon) one who wades in the water.
Wad, Wades, Wadesworth, Wadi, Wadie, Waed, Waede, Waid, Waide, Wayd, Wayde, Waydell, Whaid

Wadi (Arabic) calm, peaceful.

Wadley (English) meadow river ford.
Wadlea, Wadlee, Wadleigh, Wadli, Wadlie, Wadly

Wafiq (Arabic) successful.
Wafeeq

Waggoner (German) wagon maker.
Wagnor

Wagner (German) wagon maker.
Waggoner, Wagnar, Wagnor, Wagoner

Wahid (Arabic) unique person.
Waheed

Wahkan (Native American) sacred.
Waekan, Wahkaan

Wainwright (English) wagon-maker.
Wain, Waine, Wainewright, Wainright, Wayne, Wayneright, Waynright, Waynwright, Wright

Waite (Anglo-Saxon) guardian, watchman.
Wait, Waitt, Waitte, Wayt, Wayte

Wajid (Arabic) finder.

Wakeley (English) wet meadow.
Wakelea, Wakelee, Wakelei, Wakeleigh, Wakeli, Wakeli, Wakely, Waklea, Waklee, Waklei, Wakleigh, Wakley, Wakli, Waklie, Wakly

Wakeman (English) watchman.
Wake

Wakil (Arabic) lawyer, advocate.

Wakiza (Native American) determined warrior.
Wakyza

Walby (English) house by a wall.
Walbee, Walbey, Walbi, Walbie, Wallbee, Wallbey, Wallbi, Wallbie, Wallby

Walcott (English) cottage by the wall.
Walcot, Wallcot, Wallcott, Wolcot

Waldemar (German) well-known, powerful.
Waldimar

Walden (English) wooded valley.
Waldin, Waldi, Waldo, Waldon, Welti, Weltin

Waldo (German) to wield power and reign, famous, powerful warrior.
Oswald, Oswaldo, Wal, Wald, Walde, Waldemar, Walden, Waldy, Walldo, Wally, Walter

Waleed (Arabic) newborn child.
Waled, Walid

Walerian (Polish) strong, brave.
Waleryan

Wales (English) from Wales, England.
Wael, Waels, Wail, Wali, Walie, Walles, Waly

Walford (English) ford of the Welshman.
Walforde, Wallford, Wallforde

Walfred (German) peaceful ruler.
Walfredo, Walfreid, Walfrid, Walfried

Wali (Arabic) servant of Allah.

Walker (English) cloth walker, cloth cleaner, a unisex name.
Wallie, Wallker, Wally

Wallace (English) stranger, Welsh.
Walace, Wallach, Wallas, Wallase, Wallass, Wallie, Wallis, Wallise, Walliss, Wally, Wallyce, Wallyse, Walsh, Welsh

Waller (English) builder of walls.
Waler

Wallis (English) foreigner from Wales, a form of Wallace, a unisex name.
Walice, Walis, Walise, Wallice, Wallise, Walliss, Wallisse

Walsh (English) stranger, Welsh, a form of Wallace.
Walshe

Walter (German) army ruler.
Gautier, Guatlero, Gutierre, Ladislav, Valtar, Valter, Vander, Vladimir, Walder, Waldo, Walli, Wallie, Wally, Walt, Waltar, Walte, Walther, Waltil, Waltr, Wat, Waterio, Watkins, Watson, Waulter

Walton (English) fortified town with walls.
Walt, Walte, Waltan, Walten, Waltin, Waltyn

Walwyn (English) Welsh friend.
Walwen, Walwenn, Walwin, Walwinn, Walwynn, Walwynne, Welwyn

Wamblee (Native American) eagle.
Wamblea, Wambleigh, Wambley, Wambli, Wamblie, Wambly

Waneta (Native American) charger.

Wang (Chinese) like a king.

Wanikiya (Native American) saviour.
Wannikiya

Wapi (Native American) lucky.
Wapie, Wapy

Warburton (English) fortified town.
Warberton

Ward (English) guardian, watchman.
Warde, Warden, Wardon

Wardell (English) guardian's hill.
Wardel, Wardele, Wardelle

Warden (English) valley guardian.
Wardan, Wardin, Wardon, Wardun, Wardyn

Wardley (English) guardian's meadow.
Wardlea, Wardlee, Wardleigh, Wardli, Wardlie, Wardly

Ware (English) wary.
Waire

Warford (English) ford by the weir.
Warforde

Warick (English) village hero.
Waric, Warik, Warric, Warrick, Warrik, Warryk, Waryk

Waring (German) shelter.
Warin, Waryn

Warmond (Anglo-Saxon) true guardian, protector.
Warmon, Warmonde, Warmondo, Warmun, Warmund, Warmunde, Warmundo

Warner (German) protecting warrior.
Werner

Warrack (Australian Aboriginal) banksia.
Warrac, Warrak

Warren (German) defender, protector, enclosure, rabbit burrow.
Ware, Waren, Waring, Warrener, Warrenson, Warrin, Warriner, Worrin

Warrick (English) leader.
Waric, Warick, Warik, Warric, Warrik, Warryck, Warryk, Warrwic, Warrwick, Warrwik, Warwic, Warwick, Warwik

Warwick (English) farm with a dam, weir, fish trap.
Waric, Warick, Warik, Warric, Warrick, Warrik, Warryck, Waryck, Warrwic, Warrwick, Warrwik, Warwic, Warwik, Warwyk

Washington (English) town near water.

Wasim (Arabic) graceful, good-looking.
Waseem, Wasseem, Wassim

Watende (African) there will be revenge.
Watend

Watkins (English) son of Walter.
Watken, Watkens, Watkin, Watty, Whatie

Watson (English) son of Walter.
Watsen, Wathson, Whatson

Waverly (English) from the windy meadow of aspens.
Waverlee, Waverley, Waverlie

Wayne (English) wagon maker.
Waine, Wanye, Wayn, Waynell, Waynn, Waynne, Wene, Whayne

Wazire (Arabic) minister.
Wazeer

Webb (English) weaver.
Web, Weber, Webster

Weber (German) weaver.
Webber

Webster (English) weaver.
Web, Webbster, Webstar

Weeronga (Australian Aboriginal) quiet.

Wei (Chinese) valuable, great, a unisex name.

Wei-Quo (Chinese) precious and ruler of the country.

Weiss (German) white.
Weis, Weise, Weisee, Weisse, Weys, Weyse, Weyss, Weysse

Welborne (English) spring-fed stream.
Welbirn, Welbirne, Welborn, Welbourn, Welbourne, Welburn, Welburne, Welbyrn, Welbyrne, Wellbirn, Wellbirne, Wellborn, Wellborne, Wellbourn, Wellbourne, Wellburn, Wellburne, Wellbyrn, Wellbyrne

Welford (English) ford near the well.
Welforde, Wellford

Wellington (English) wealthy one's town.

Wells (English) well, stream.
Welles

Welsh (English) stranger, Welsh, a form of Walsh, Wallace.
Waalsh, Walsh, Wallace, Welsch

Welton (English) town near the well, stream.
Weldan, Weldon, Wellton, Weltan

Wemilo (Native American) everyone speaks to him.

Wen (Chinese) cultured, ornamental, refined, a unisex name.

Wenceslaus (Slavic) wreath of glory.
Vencel, Venceslaus, Venzel, Wenceslao, Wenceslas, Wenzel, Wenzelas, Wenzell

Wendel (German) wanderer.
Wendal, Wendale, Wendall, Wendalle, Wendele, Wendell, Wendelle, Wendil, Wendile, Wendill, Wendille, Wendle, Wendie, Wendyl, Wendyll

Wene (Native American) wagon maker, a form of Wayne.
Weane

Wenford (English) white ford.
Wenforde, Wynford

Wenlock (Welsh) lake at the holy monastery.
Wenlocke

Wentworth (English) white one's estate.
Wentworthe

Wenutu (Native American) clear sky.

Wenzel (Slavic) to know.
Wensel, Wensell, Wenzell, Wenzil, Wenzill, Wenzyl, Wenzyll

Wes (English) weat meadow, a form of Wesley.
Wess

Wesh (Gypsy) woods.

Wesley (English) west meadow.
Wellesley, Wes, Weseley, Wesely, Weslan, Wesle, Weslee, Wesleigh, Weslie, Wesly, Wessley, Westleigh, Westley, Wezley

Westbrook (English) west brook.
Brook, West, Westbrooke

Westby (English) west farmland.
Wesbee, Wesbey, Wesbi, Wesbie, Wesby, Westbee, Westbey, Westbi, Westbie

Westcott (English) west cottage.
Wescot, Wescott, Westcot

Westley (English) west meadow, a form of Wesley.
Wellesley, Wesley, Westlee, Westlie, Westly

Weston (English) west town.
West, Westen, Westin

Wetherby (English) wether sheep farm.
Wetheral, Weatherbey, Weatherbie, Weatherby, Wetherbey, Wetherbie, Wetherell, Wetherly

Wharton (English) town by a lake.
Warton

Wheatley (English) wheat meadow.
Whatley, Wheatlea, Wheatleigh,

Wheatli, Wheatlie, Wheatly, Wheetly

Wheeler (English) wagon driver, wheel maker.
Wheelar

Whistler (English) piper, one who whistles a tune.

Whitaker (English) white field.
Whitacker, Whittacker, Whittaker, Whiymaker

Whitby (English) white house.
Whitbea, Whitbee, Whitbey, Whitbi, Whitbie

Whitcomb (English) white valley.
Whitcom, Whitcombe, Whitcumb

Whitelaw (English) white, small hill.
Whitlaw

Whitey (English) white-skinned, fair-haired.
Whity

Whitley (English) white meadow, a unisex name.
Whitlea, Whitlee, Whitleigh, Whitli, Whitlie, Whitly, Witly

Whitmore (English) white moor, marsh.
Whitmoor, Whitmor, Whittmor, Whittmore, Whittemor, Whittemore, Witmor, Wittmor, Wittmore, Wittemor, Wittemore

Whitney (English) white island, a unisex name.
Whitnee, Whitnie, Whitny, Whittnee, Whittney, Whittnie, Whittny, Widney, Widny, Witnee, Witney, Witnie, Witny, Wittnee, Wittney, Wittnie, Wittny

Wicasa (Native American) man.

Wicent (Polish) conqueror, victor, a form of Vincent.
Wiccent, Wicente, Wicek, Wicient, Wicus

Wichado (Native American) willing, eager.

Wickham (English) village enclosure.
Wick, Wicks, Wikham, Wyckham, Wykham

Wickley (English) village meadow.
Wickes, Wicklea, Wickleigh, Wicklie, Wickly, Wicks

Wid (English) wide.

Wies (German) famous warrior.
Weis, Weiss, Wiess, Wyes, Wyess

Wikoli (Hawaiian) victorious conqueror, a form of Victor.

Wiktor (Polish) victorious conqueror, a form of Victor.
Wittor

Wilanu (Native American) to pour water onto flour.

Wilbert (German) brilliant.
Wilber, Wilberto, Wilbirt, Wilbirto, Wilburt, Wilburto, Wilbyrt

Wilbur (English) fortification of a wall; (German) bright.
Wilber, Wilbor, Wilburn, Wilburt, Willbur, Wilver, Wylbur

Wilder (English) wilderness.
Wild, Wilde, Wyld, Wylde, Wylder

Wildon (English) wooded hill.
Wildan, Wilden, Wildin, Wildyn, Willdan, Willden, Willdin, Willdon, Willdyn

Wiley (English) willow meadow.
Whileigh, Whiley, Whily, Wildy, Wile, Wilee, Wileigh, Wili, Wilie, Willey, Wily, Wyley, Wylie, Wyly

Wilford (English) willow tree ford.
Wilferd, Wilforde

Wilfred (Anglo-Saxon) peacemaker, desiring peace.
Fredo, Wilferd, Wilfredo, Wilfreid, Wilfrid, Wilfride, Wilfried, Wilfryd, Will, Willferd, Willfred, Willfredo, Willfreid, Willfrid, Willfride, Willfried, Willie, Willy

Wilfredo (Spanish) peacemaker, desiring peace, a form of Wilfred.
Fredo, Wilfred, Wilfrido, Willfredo

Wilhelm (German) the resolute protector, determined guardian, a form of William.
Wilhelmus, Willem, Willhelm

Wiliama (Hawaiian) determined guardian, a form of William.

Wilkie (English) son of William, a form of Wilkins.
Wilke, Wilkey, Wikie, Wilky

Wilkins (English) son of William.
Wilken, Wilkens, Wilkes, Wilkie, Wilkin, Wilks, Wilkyns

Will (English) determined guardian, a form of William.
Whil, Whill, Wil, Wille, Wilm, Wim

Willard (Teutonic) resolute, brave, strong-willed.
Wilard, Wiliard, Williard, Willyard, Wilyard

Willem (German) determined guardian, a form of William.
Willim

William (English) determined guardian.
Bill, Billie, Billy, Vasyl, Vilheim, Vili, Viliam, Viljo, Ville, Villiam, Welfel, Wilek, Wil, Wilhelm, Will, Willaim, Willam, Willeam, Willem, Williams, Willie, Williem, Willil, Willis, Willium, Williw, Willum, Willy, Willyam, Wim

Willis (English) son of William.
Williss, Will, Wills, Willys, Wyllis

Willoughby (English) farm by the willows.
Wilobee, Wilobey, Wilobie, Wiloby, Willobee, Willobey, Willobie, Willoughbee, Willoughbey, Willoughbie, Willowbee, Willowbey, Willowbie, Willowby

Willy (German) determined guardian, a form of William.
Wile, Wille, Willey, Willi, Willia, Willie

Wilmer (German) determined, famous.
Willmar, Willmer, Wilm, Wilmar, Wyllmar, Wyllmer, Wylmar, Wylmer

Wilmot (German) determined guardian, a form of William.
Willmont, Willmot, Wilm, Wilmont

Wilny (Native American) eagle singing while flying.
Wilni, Wilnie

Wilson (English) son of William.
Wilkinson, Willsen, Willson, Wils, Wilsen, Wolson

Wilstan (German) wolf stone.
Wilsten, Wilstin, Wilstyn

Win (Cambodian) bright.
Winn, Winne, Wyn, Wynn, Wynne

Wincent (Polish) conquerer, victor, a form of Vincent.
Wicek, Wicenty, Wicient, Wicus,

Wince, Wincento, Wincenty,
Wincient

Winchell (English) bend in the road.
Winchel, Wynchel, Wynchell

Windsor (English) riverbank with a winch.
Wincer, Winsor, Wyndsor

Winfield (English) friendly field.
Field, Winfeld, Winfred, Winfreid,
Winfrey, Winifield, Winnifield,
Winnfeld, Winnfield, Wynfield,
Wynnfield

Winfred (English) friend of peace.
Win, Winfreid, Winfrid, Winfried,
Winn, Winnie, Winny, Wyn, Wynfred

Winfried (German) friend of peace.
Winfred, Winfreid, Winfrid, Winfryd,
Wynfrid, Wynfryd

Wing (Chinese) glory.

Wingi (Native American) willing.
Wing, Wingie, Wingy

Winslow (English) friendly hill.
Winsloe, Winslowe, Wynsloe,
Wynslow, Wynslowe

Winston (English) friendly town.
Winstan, Winsten, Winstin,
Winstone, Wynstan, Wynsten,
Wynstin, Wynston, Wynstone

Winter (English) born in winter, a unisex name.
Winterford, Wintir, Wynter

Winthrop (English) victory at the crossroads.
Winthropp, Wynthrop, Wynthropp

Winton (English) friendly town, a form of Winston.
Winten, Wynten, Wynton

Wirrin (Australian Aboriginal) tea-tree.
Wirin, Wirryn, Wiryn

Wirt (English) worthy.
Weerte, Wert, Werte, Wirte, Wurt,
Wurte

Wit (Polish) life.
Witt, Witte, Wyt, Wyter, Wytt, Wytte

Witek (Polish) victorious conqueror, a form of Victor.
Victor, Vitek, Witec, Witeck

Witha (Arabic) handsome.
Wytha

Witter (Anglo-Saxon) wise warrior.
Wit, Witer, Witt, Wyt, Wyter, Wytt,
Wytter

Witton (English) wise man's town.
Whiton, Whitton, Whyton, Whytton,
Witon, Wyton, Wytton

Wolcott (English) cottage in the woods.
Wolcot

Wolf (English, German) wolf.
Wolfe, Wolff, Wolffe, Wolph, Wolphe,
Woolf, Woolfe

Wolfgang (German) path of the wolf.
Wolfe, Wolfegang, Wolff,
Wolffgang, Wolfy, Woolfgang

Wood (English) a form of Edward, Elwood, Woodrow.
Woode, Woody

Woodford (English) ford in the forest.
Woodforde

Woodley (English) forest meadow.
Woodlea, Woodlee, Woodleigh,
Woodli, Woodlie, Woodly

Woodrow (English) forest passage.
Woodman, Woodroe, Woodrowe, Woody

Woodruff (English) forest ranger.
Woodruf

Woodward (English) forest guardian.
Woodard, Woodwarde

Woody (English) a form of Edward, Elwood, Woodrow.
Woodey, Woodie

Worcester (English) forest army camp.
Worchester

Wordsworth (English) wolf guardian's farm.
Wordie, Wordswirth, Wordswirthe, Wordsworthe, Wordy, Worth

Worie (African) born on market day.

Worth (English) wolf guardian's farm, a form of Wordsworth.
Wirth, Wirthe, Worthe, Worthey, Worthington, Worthy

Wouter (German) powerful warrior.

Wray (Scandinavian) corner house; (English) crooked.
Rae, Ray, Wrae, Wrai, Wraie

Wren (Welsh) ruler, chief, a unisex name.
Ren, Renn, Wrenn

Wright (English) wagon maker, a form of Wainwright.

Wuliton (Native American) to do well.
Wulitan, Wuliten, Wulitin, Wulityn

Wunand (Native American) God is good.
Wunande

Wuyi (African) flying vulture.

Wyatt (French) little warrior.
Wiat, Wiath, Wiatt, Wiatte, Wiatth, Wyat, Wyatte, Wye, Wyeth, Wyett, Wyetth, Wyitt, Wyith, Wytt

Wyborn (Scandinavian) war bear.
Wiborn, Wiborne, Wieborn, Wieborne, Wyborne, Wybourn, Wybourne

Wyck (Scaninavian) village.
Wic, Wick, Wicke, Wik, Wyc, Wycke, Wyk

Wylie (English) charming.
Wilee, Wiley, Wilie, Wily, Wye, Wylee, Wyley, Wyllie, Wylly, Wyly

Wyman (English) warrior.
Wiman, Wimen, Wymen

Wymer (English) famous in battle.
Wimer

Wyn/Wynn (Celtic) fair, light-skinned; (English) friend.
Win, Wine, Winn, Winne, Wyne, Wynne

Wyndham (Scottish) village near the winding road.
Windam, Windham, Wyndam, Wynndam

Wynford (Welsh) white ford.
Winford, Winforde, Wynforde

Wynono (Native American) first-born son.
Winono

Wyome (Native American) plain.
Wiome

Wythe (English) willow tree.
With, Withe, Wyth

Xan (Greek) helper or defender of humankind, a form of Alexander.

Xander, Xandra, Xane, Xann, Zan, Zander, Zane, Zandra

Xander (Greek) helper or defender of humankind, a form of Alexander.

Xan, Xand, Xanda, Xande, Xane, Xann, Zan, Zand, Zanda, Zande, Zander, Zane, Zann

Xanthippus (Greek) light-coloured horse.

Xanthipus, Xanthyppus, Xanthypus, Zanthippus, Zanthipus, Zanthypus, Zanthyppus

Xanthus (Latin) golden-haired, blond.

Xanthios, Xanthius, Xanthos, Zanthios, Zanthius, Zanthos, Zanthus

Xanto (Greek) blond.

Xandy, Zandy, Zanto

Xavier (Spanish) of the bright new house; (Arabic) bright, brilliant.

Exavier, Javier, Saverio, Xaivier, Xavaeir, Xaver, Xavian, Xaviar, Xaviere, Xavior, Xavon, Xavyer, Xerer, Xizavier, Xxavier, Zavier

Xenophon (Greek) strange voice.

Xeno, Xenofon, Zeno, Zenofon, Zenophon

Xenos (Greek) stranger.

Xenno, Xennos, Xeno, Xenoss, Zenno, Zennos, Zeno, Zenos, Zenoss

Xerxes (Persian) king.

Xerus, Xerxe, Xerxis, Xrus, Zerus, Zerxes, Zerxis, Zrus

Xeven (Slavic) lively.

Xyven, Zeven, Zyven

Ximen/Ximenes (Spanish) he heard, listener, a form of Simon.

Ximene, Xymen, Xymene, Xymenes, Xymon, Zimen, Zimene, Zimenes, Zymen, Zymene, Zymenes, Zymon

Xylon (Greek) of the woods, forest.

Xilon, Zilon, Zylon

Yabarak (Australian Aboriginal) sea.
Yabarac, Yabarack

Yadid (Hebrew) friend, beloved.
Yaddid, Yaded, Yadyd

Yadon (Hebrew) he will judge.
Yadean, Yadin, Yadun, Yaedean Yaeden, Yaedin, Yaedon, Yaedun

Yael (Hebrew) mountain goat, a form of Jael, a unisex name.
Jael, Jaele, Jaell, Jaelle, Yaele, Yaell, Yaelle

Yafeu (African) bold.

Yago (Spanish) supplanter, a form of James.
Iago, Jago, Yaego

Yahto (Native American) blue.

Yahyah (Arabic) God is gracious, a form of John.
Yahya, Yaya

Yair (Hebrew) he will enlighten.
Yaire, Yahir

Yakecen (Native American) song from the sky.

Yakez (Native American) heaven.

Yakir (Hebrew) precious, honoured.
Yakire, Yakry, Yakyre

Yakov (Russian) supplanter, a form of Jacob.
Yacob, Yacov, Yakob

Yale (Welsh) fertile; (English) old, elder.
Yael, Yaele, Yaell, Yaelle, Yail, Yaile, Yaill, Yaille, Yayl, Yayle, Yayll, Yaylle

Yama (Hindu) god of the setting sun.

Yamin (Hebrew) right hand.

Yan (Russian) God is gracious, a form of John.
Yanichek, Yanik, Yanka, Yann, Yannick

Yancy (Native American) Englishman, a unisex name.
Yance, Yancee, Yancie, Yank, Yankee

Yanni (Greek) God is gracious, a form of John.
Ioannais, Ioannis, Yani, Yannis, Yanny, Yiannis, Yoannais, Yoannes, Yoannis, Yoni

Yannick (French) the Lord is gracious, a form of John, a unisex name.
Yanic, Yanick, Yanik, Yann, Yannic, Yanig, Yannik

Yao (African) born on a Thursday.

Yaphet (Hebrew) handsome, attractive.
Yafet, Yafeth, Yapheth, Yarafeth, Yarapheth, Yefat, Yephat

Yarb (Gypsy) herb.

Yardan (Arabic) king.

Yarden (Hebrew) flowing down, descending, a form of Jordan.
Yardan, Yardin

Yardley (English) enclosed meadow.
Lee, Yard, Yardlea, Yardlee,
Yardleigh, Yardli, Yardlie, Yardly

Yarin (Hebrew) to understand.
Yareen

Yarran (Australian Aboriginal)
acacia.
Yaran

Yasar (Arabic) wealthy.
Yaser, Yassar, Yasser

Yasashiku (Japanese) polite,
gentle.
Yasa, Yasash, Yasashik

Yash (Hindu) glorious, famous.
Jash, Jashe, Yashe

Yasin (Arabic) prophet.
Yaseen, Yasine, Yasseen, Yassin,
Yassine, Yazen

Yasir (Arabic) wealthy.
Yaasir, Yaesir, Yasser, Yassir

Yasuo (Japanese) peaceful, calm
one.
Yaesua, Yaesuo

Yates (English) gate keeper, guard
of the gate, a unisex name.
Yaetes, Yaites

Yavin (Hebrew) God understands.
Javin, Yavine

Yazid (Arabic) increasing.
Yazeed

Yechiel (Hebrew) God lives.
Yechel

Yefrem (Russian) fruitful, a form of
Ephraim.
Yefraim, Yephraim, Yephrem

Yegor (Slavic) farmer, a form of
George.
Igor, Ygor

Yehuda (Hebrew) praised, a form
of Yehudi.
Huda, Hudea, Yeehuda, Yehudea,
Yehueda

Yehudi (Hebrew) praised, a form
of Judah.
Yechuda, Yechudi, Yechudit,
Yehuda, Yehudah, Yehudit

Yelutci (Native American) bear
moving quietly.
Yelutki

Yeoman (English) servant,
attendant.
Yeomann, Yeomen, Yeomenn,
Yoeman, Youman

Yeremy (Slavic) God has uplifted,
a form of Jeramiah.
Yarema, Yarmeka, Yeremia,
Yeremiah, Yerik

Yervant (Armenian) ruler, king.

Yestin (Welsh) just, a form of Justin.
Yestan, Yesten, Yeston, Yestyn,
Yustan, Yusten, Yustin, Yuston,
Yustyn

Yevgeni (Russian) noble, well-born,
a form of Eugene.
Eugene, Gena, Yegeni, Yevgenie,
Yevgenij, Yevgeniy, Yevgeny

Yigael (Hebrew) God will redeem.
Yagael, Yagel, Yigaele, Yigaell,
Yigaelle, Yigal, Yigel

Yileen (Australian Aboriginal) dream.

Yirmaya (Hebrew) God has
uplifted, a form of Jeremiah.
Yirmayahu

Yisrael (Hebrew) prince of God, a form of Israel.
Yesarel, Yisroel

Yitro (Hebrew) abundant, a form of Jethro.
Yithro

Yitzhak (Hebrew) laughing, happy one.
Yitzaak, Yitzac, Yitzack, Yitzak, Yitzchok, Yitzhac, Yitzhhack

Yochanan (Hebrew) God is gracious, a form of John.
Yochan, Yohanan

Yoel (Hebrew) God is willing, a form of Joel.
Joel, Joell, Joelle, Yoell, Yoelle

Yogi (Hindu) one who practises yoga.
Yogee, Yogey, Yogie, Yogy

Yohance (African) God is gracious, a form of John.
Yohanse

Yona (Native American) bear.

Yonatan (Hebrew) gift of the Lord, a form of Jonathon.
Yonathan, Yonathon, Yonaton, Yonattan, Yonatton

Yong (Chinese) brave one.
Yonge

Yoni (Greek) God is gracious, a form of John.
Yani, Yanni, Yonie, Yonis, Yonnas, Yonni, Yonnie, Yonny, Yony

Yonus (Hebrew) dove.
Yonna, Yonnas, Yonnos, Yonnus, Yona, Yonas, Yonos

Yoofi (African) born on a Friday.

Yooku (African) born on a Wednesday.

Yoram (Hebrew) God is praised, exalted, a form of Joram.
Joram, Jorem, Jorram, Jorrem, Yorem, Yorram, Yorrem

Yorick (Greek, English) farmer, a form of George.
Yiorge, Yiorgis, Yorgo, Yorgos, Yoric, Yorik, Yorric, Yorrick, Yorrik

York (English) farm with yew trees.
Yorik, Yorke, Yorker, Yorkie, Yorrick

Yorkoo (African) born on a Thursday.

Yosef (Hebrew) God will increase, a form of Joseph.
Josef, Joseph, Toceph, Yoosuf, Yoseff, Yoseph, Yosief, Yosieph, Yosif, Yosiph, Yosuf, Yosuph, Yosyf, Yosyph, Yousef, Youseph, Yusif, Yusiph

Yoshi (Japanese) quiet, respected, a unisex name.
Yoshiki, Yoshiuki

Yotimo (Native American) bee flying into hive.

Yottoko (Native American) mud.
Yotoko

Young (English) young, youthful.
Younge, Yung, Yunge

Youssef (Arabic) God will increase, a form of Joseph.
Yoousef, Yousaf, Yousaff, Youseef, Youseeff, Yousef, Youseff, Youseph, Yousiph, Yousseff, Yousseph, Yousif, Yousiph, Yousuf, Yousuph, Yusef, Yuseph, Yov, Yussel, Yussell

Yovani (Slavic) God is gracious, a form of Jovan.
Yovan, Yovann, Yovanni, Yovanny, Yovany, Yovni

Yoyi (Hebrew) farmer, a form of George.
Yrji, Yrjo

Yu (Chinese) universe.

Yuan (Chinese) one copy only, original.

Yudan (Hebrew) judgement.
Yuddan, Yuden, Yudin, Yudon, Yudyn

Yuki (Japanese) snow, lucky, a unisex name.
Yukee, Yukey, Yukie, Yukiko, Yukio, Yuky, Yuuki

Yul (Chinese) beyond the horizon.

Yule (Anglo-Saxon) born at Christmas.
Yul, Yulle

Yuli (Basque) youthful.
Yulli

Yuma (Native American) son of the chief.

Yunus (Arabic) dove, a form of Jonah.
Yonah, Yoonus, Younis, Yunis

Yuri (Russian) farmer, a form of George; (Australian Aboriginal) I hear.
Yuree, Yurey, Yurie

Yushua (Arabic) God is my salvation, a form of Joshua.
Yoshua

Yusif (Slavic) God will increase, a form of Joseph.
Yusiff, Yusiph, Yusef, Yuseff, Yuseph, Yussof, Yusef, Yussoff, Yussoph, Yusuf, Yusuff, Yusup, Yusuph, Yuzef, Yuzep, Yuzeph

Yusuf (Arabic) God will increase, a form of Joseph.
Yussef, Yusseph, Yusuph

Yutu (Native American) coyote out hunting.

Yves (French) little archer.
Ives, Yives, Yven, Yvens, Yvon, Yvons, Yyves

Yvon (French) little archer, a form of Ivar, Yves.
Yuvon, Yvan, Yvar, Yvonn

Ywain (Celtic) well born, noble, a form of Owen.
Ywen

Z

Zabdi (Hebrew) gift, a form of Zabdiel.
Zabad, Zabadi, Zabdy, Zabi

Zabdiel (Hebrew) gift.
Zabdi, Zabdial, Zabdil, Zabdyl, Zebdial, Zebdiel

Zac (Hebrew) God remembers, a form of Zachariah.
Zaac, Zacc, Zach, Zache, Zack, Zacs, Zacz, Zak, Zakk, Zeke

Zacarias (Italian) God remembers, a form of Zachariah.
Zacari, Zacarie, Zacarious, Zacarius, Zacary, Zaccari, Zaccarias, Zaccarie, Zaccary, Zacerias, Zacery, Zachariah, Zacharias, Zacharus, Zachary, Zackarias, Zackary, Zacory, Zacyre

Zaccheus (Hebrew) God remembers, a form of Zachariah.
Zaccaeus, Zacceus, Zacchaeus, Zacchious, Zaccious, Zacchius, Zaccius

Zachariah (Hebrew) God remembers.
Zac, Zacari, Zacariah, Zacarius, Zaccaria, Zaccariah, Zaccarius, Zach, Zacharia, Zacharius, Zacharria, Zacharriah, Zacharrius, Zachary, Zacharya, Zacharyah, Zachory, Zachorya, Zachoryah, Zachury, Zachurya, Zachuryah, Zack, Zackaria, Zackariah, Zackary, Zackarya, Zackaryah, Zako, Zaquero, Zecharia, Zechariah, Zeggery, Zeke, Zhachory, Zhachorya, Zhachoryah

Zacharias (Hebrew) God remembers, a form of Zachariah.
Zac, Zacchari, Zachary, Zacheri, Zacheriah, Zack, Zackariah

Zachary (Hebrew) God remembers.
Xachary, Zac, Zacari, Zacarie, Zacary, Zaccari, Zaccarie, Zaccary, Zach, Zacha, Zachaery, Zachari, Zacharie, Zacharios, Zackarri, Zachkarrie, Zacharry, Zachaury, Zacheri, Zacherie, Zachery, Zachory, Zachrey, Zachry, Zachuery, Zachury, Zack, Zackaray, Zackari, Zackaria, Zackariah, Zackarie, Zackary, Zackery, Zackory, Zackury, Zakery, Zakkary, Zechery, Zeke

Zadock (Hebrew) just, righteous.
Zaddric, Zaddick, Zaddik, Zaddoc, Zaddok, Zadic, Zadik, Zadoc, Zadok, Zaydok

Zafar (Arabic) triumphant, winner.

Zafir (Arabic) victorious, victory.
Zafar, Zafeer, Zafer, Zaffer, Zaffir

Zahid (Arabic) self-denying.
Zaheed, Zahied, Zahyd, Zaid

Zahir (Arabic) bright, radiant, shining.
Zahair, Zahah, Zaheer, Zahi, Zair, Zaire, Zayyir

Zahur (African) flower.
Zaher, Zahir, Zahyr

Zaid (Arabic) increase, growth.
Zaied, Zaiid, Zayd, Zayde

Zaide (Hebrew) elder.
Zade, Zaid, Zayde, Zayedd

Zaim (Arabic) general.
Zaime, Zaym, Zayme

Zakariya (Hebrew) God remembers, a form of Zachariah.
Zakariyah

Zakary (Hebrew) God remembers, a form of Zachariah.
Zac, Zack, Zak, Zakai, Zakarai, Zakare, Zakaree, Zakari, Zakarie, Zakariye, Zake, Zakhar, Zaki, Zakir, Zakiry, Zakk, Zakkai, Zakkare, Zakkaree, Zakkari, Zakkarie, Zakkary, Zako, Zakquary, Zakree, Zakri, Zakris, Zakry

Zaki (Arabic) intelligent, pure, bright.
Zakee, Zakia, Zakie, Zakiy, Zakki

Zakkai (Hebrew) innocent, pure.
Zakai

Zako (Hebrew) God remembers, a form of Zachary.
Zacko, Zaco, Zak

Zale (Greek) strength of the sea.
Zail, Zaile, Zaill, Zaille, Zalle, Zayl, Zayle, Zayll, Zaylle

Zalman (Hebrew) man of peace, a form of Solomon.
Salman, Salmen, Salmin, Salmon, Salmyn, Zalmen, Zalmin, Zalmon, Zalmyn, Zeloman, Zelomon

Zamiel (German) asked of God, God has heard, a form of Samuel.
Zamal, Zamual, Zamuel

Zamir (Hebrew) song.
Zameer

Zander (Greek) helper or defender of humankind, a form of Alexander.
Xander, Zanda, Zandar, Zandor, Zandore, Zandra, Zandrae, Zandy

Zane (English) God is gracious, a form of John.

Zain, Zaine, Zayn, Zayne, Zhain, Zhaine, Zhane, Zhayn, Zhayne

Zaquan (American) combination of the prefix Za and Quan.
Zaquain, Zaquon

Zareb (African) protector.

Zared (Hebrew) ambush.
Zarred, Zarryd, Zaryd

Zarek (Slavic) may God protect the king.
Zareck, Zarick, Zarik, Zarreck, Zarrick, Zereck, Zerek, Zeric, Zerick, Zerreck, Zerrek, Zerric, Zerrick

Zavier (Spanish) of the bright new house; (Arabic) bright, brilliant, a form of Xavier.
Zavair, Zaverie, Zaverrie, Zavery, Zaviair, Zaviaire, Zaviar, Zaviare, Zaviere, Zavior, Zaviore, Zavyr, Zavyrius, Zxavian, Zxavien

Zayne (English) God is gracious, a form of Zane.
Zane, Zayan, Zayin, Zayn

Zeb (Hebrew) a form of Zebadiah, Zebedee, Zebulun.
Zebb, Zev, Zevv

Zebadiah (Hebrew) God's gift.
Zeb, Zebadia, Zebedee, Zebedia, Zebediah, Zebidia, Zebidiah

Zebedee (Hebrew) God's gift, a form of Zebadiah.
Zebadee, Zebadi, Zebadie, Zebady, Zebedi, Zebedie, Zebedy, Zebidee, Zebidi, Zebidie, Zebidy

Zebulun (Hebrew) to exalt.
Zeb, Zebilan, Zebulan, Zebulin, Zebulon, Zebulyn, Zev, Zevulun, Zhebulen, Zhebulun, Zubin

Zed (Hebrew) God is mighty and right, a form of Zedekiah.
Zedd

Zedekiah (Hebrew) God is mighty and right.
Zadaios, Zadaikos, Zadaray, Zaddarry, Zaddaury, Zaddekia, Zaddekiah, Zaddery, Zadekia, Zadekiah, Zadery, Zadory, Zed, Zeda, Zedaery, Zedakia, Zedakiah, Zedary, Zedcary, Zedd, Zedekia, Zedidiah, Zedikia, Zedikiah, Zedikias, Zeke

Zeeman (Dutch) sailor, seaman.
Zeaman, Zeman, Zemen, Ziman, Zimen, Zymen, Zymin, Zymyn

Zeev (Hebrew) wolf.
Zeevi, Zeff, Zif, Ziv

Zeferino (Greek) west wind, a form of Zephyr.
Zepherino

Zeheb (Turkish) gold.

Zeke (Hebrew) strength of God, a form of Ezekiel.
Zeak, Zeake, Zeek, Zeeke, Zeki, Zeyk, Zeyke

Zeki (Turkish) intelligent.
Zeeki, Zeke, Zekie, Zeky

Zelgai (Afghan) heart.

Zelig (Yiddish) blessed.
Zeleg, Zeligman, Zelik, Zelleg, Zellig

Zelimir (Slavic) peace wish.
Zelimeer, Zelimyr

Zelman (Hebrew) man of peace, a form of Solomon.
Zelima, Zelimer, Zellman, Zellmen, Zelmen

Zemar (Afghan) lion.

Zenas (Greek) living.
Zennas

Zenda (Czech) well born, noble, a form of Euguene.
Zendah

Zeno (Greek) living, bright sky, a form of Zeus.
Xeno, Zeeno, Zino

Zenobias (Greek) bright sky, given life by Zeus.
Zenobi, Zenobia, Zenobiah, Zenobio, Zenobius

Zenon (Greek) living, bright sky, a form of Zeno.
Xennon, Xenon, Xenos, Zenos, Zennon, Zeus

Zephan (Hebrew) protected treasure of God, the Lord has hidden.
Zefan, Zefon, Zephon

Zephaniah (Hebrew) protected treasure of God, a form of Zephan.
Zaf, Zafania, Zaph, Zaphania, Zaphaniah, Zeph, Zephan, Zephania

Zephyr (Greek) west wind, a unisex name.
Zefer, Zeferno, Zeffer, Zeffrey, Zepher, Zephery, Zephir, Zephire, Zephram, Zephran, Zephrin, Zephyrr

Zerach (Hebrew) light.
Zerac, Zerack, Zerak, Zerrac, Zerrach, Zerrack, Zerrak

Zero (Greek) empty, nothing.
Zeero, Ziro

Zeroun (Armenian) wise, respected.

Zeshawn (American) combination of Zeke and Shawn.
Zesean, Zeshan, Zeshain, Zeshaun, Zeshon, Zishan, Zshawn

Zesiro (African) older of twins.
Zesyro

Zethan (Hebrew) shining.
Zethen, Zethin, Zethon, Zethyn

Zeus (Greek) living, bright sky.
Zeuss, Zoeus

Zeusef (Portuguese) God will increase, a form of Joseph.
Zeuseph

Zev (Hebrew) wolf.
Zevi, Zevie, Zevv, Zevy, Zhev, Zhvie, Zhvy, Zvi

Zhixin (Chinese) ambitious.
Zhi, Zhipeng, Zhiuan, Zhi-yang

Zhuang (Chinese) strong.
Zhang, Zhuen, Zhueng

Zia (Arabic) light, a unisex name.
Ziah, Zieh

Ziggy (Teutonic) victorious protector, a form of Sigmund.
Zig, Zigg, Ziggi, Ziggie, Zigy

Zikomao (African) thank you.

Zimon (Hebrew) he heard, listener, a form of Simon.
Ziman, Zimen, Zimin, Zimyn, Zyman, Zymen, Zymin, Zymon, Zymyn

Zimra (Hebrew) song of joy, praise, a unisex name.
Zemora, Zimraan, Zimran, Zimrat, Zimri, Zimria, Zimriah, Zimriya, Zymra, Zymri, Zymriah

Zimri (Hebrew) valuable.
Zimry, Zymri

Zinan (Japanese) second-born son.
Zynan

Zindel (Hebrew) helper or defender of humankind, a form of Alexander.
Zindele, Zindell, Zindelle, Zindil, Zunde, Zundel, Zundele, Zundell, Zundelle

Zion (Hebrew) sign, symbol.
Tzion, Zyon

Ziskind (Hebrew) sweet child.

Zitomer (Czech) famous living person.
Zitomar, Zitomor, Zittomar, Zittomer, Zittomor

Ziv (Hebrew) shining bright with life.
Zevan, Zevin, Zevon, Zevyn, Ziay, Zivan, Ziven, Zivin, Zivon, Zivyn, Zyv

Zivan (Hebrew) shining bright with life.
Zevan, Zeven, Zevin, Zevon, Zevyn, Ziv, Ziven, Zivin, Zivon, Zivu, Zivyn, Ziven, Zivin, Zivon, Ziya, Zyvan, Zyven, Zyvin, Zyvon

Ziyad (Arabic) to grow and increase.
Zayad, Zeeyad, Ziyaad

Zlatan (Czech) gold.
Zlatka, Zlaton, Zletic

Zohar (Hebrew) radiant light.

Zola (Latin) mound of earth; (German) prince, a unisex name.
Zoilo, Zolah, Zollo, Zollah, Zollie

Zoltan (Arabic) ruler, sultan.
Soltan, Sultan, Zoltann, Zolten, Zoltin, Zoltyn, Zolton, Zsoltan

Zoltin (Hungarian) life.
Zoltan, Zolten, Zolton, Zoltyn

Zomeir (Hebrew) one who prunes trees.
Zomeer, Zomer, Zomir, Zomyr

Zomelis (Hebrew) God has asked me.
Zomellis

Zonar (Latin) sound.

Zoran (Slavic) of the dawn.
Zoren, Zorin, Zoron, Zorran, Zorren, Zorrin, Zorron

Zoro (Persian) star.
Zoran, Zoren, Zorian, Zoron, Zorro, Zorya

Zorya (Slavic) star.
Zoria

Zosime (French) full of life, lively, a form of Zosimus.
Zosyme

Zosimus (Greek) full of life, lively.
Zosimas, Zosime, Zosimos, Zowie

Zotikos (Greek) saintly.
Zotikas

Zotom (African) bitter.

Zowie (Greek) full of life, lively.
Zoi, Zosime, Zosimus, Zowe, Zowee, Zowey, Zowi, Zowy

Zsigmond (Teutonic) victorious protector, a form of Sigmund.
Zigmond, Zigmonde, Zigmondo, Zigmund, Zigmunde, Zigmundo, Zsigmonde, Zsigmondo, Zsigmund, Zsigmunde, Zsigmundo

Zsolt (Polish) ruler, sultan.
Zsolto, Zsoltt

Zuberi (African) strong.
Zuber, Zuberee

Zubin (Hebrew) exalted, praised one.
Zeban, Zeben, Zebin, Zebun, Zebyn, Zuban, Zebulon, Zuben, Zubon, Zubeen, Zubyn

Zuhayr (Arabic) bright, shining.
Zuhayrr

Zuka (African) silver coin.
Zucca, Zucka, Zukka

Zuriel (Hebrew) God is my foundation.
Zuri, Zurial, Zuriall, Zuriele, Zuriell, Zurielle, Zurl